VOLUME TWO

FOURTH EDITION

Intermediate Accounting

Thomas H. Beechy

Schulich School of Business
York University

Joan E. D. Conrod

Faculty of Management
Dalhousie University

McGraw-Hill Ryerson

Toronto   Montréal   Boston   Burr Ridge, IL   Dubuque, IA   Madison, WI   New York
San Francisco   St. Louis   Bangkok   Bogotá   Caracas   Kuala Lumpur   Lisbon   London
Madrid   Mexico City   Milan   New Delhi   Santiago   Seoul   Singapore   Sydney   Taipei

McGraw-Hill Ryerson

Intermediate Accounting
Volume 2
Fourth Edition

ISBN-13: 978-0-07-097886-7
ISBN-10: 0-07-097886-7

3 4 5 6 7 8 9 10   DOW   0 9

Printed and bound in the United States

Editorial Director: Joanna Cotton
Senior Marketing Manager: Joy Armitage Taylor
Senior Sponsoring Editor: Rhondda McNabb
Developmental Editor: Marcia Luke
Senior Editorial Associate: Christine Lomas
Senior Production Coordinator: Paula Brown
Senior Supervising Editor: Anne Nellis
Copy Editor: Karen Rolfe
Cover Design: ArtPlus Design & Communications
Interior Design: Bookman Typesetting company/ArtPlus Design & Communications
Cover Image Credits: Canadian Flag © Artplus Ltd.; Handshake © Artplus Ltd,; Canadian Money © Punchstock/Superstock; Handheld © David Chasey/GettyImages; World Map © Cartesia/GettyImages; TSX Sculture © Ingram Publishing/Superstock
Composition: Bookman Typesetting Company
Printer: R. R. Donnelley

Library and Archives Canada Cataloguing in Publication
Beechy, Thomas H., 1937–
    Intermediate accounting / Thomas H. Beechy, Joan E.D. Conrod. —4th ed.

Includes bibliographical references and index.
ISBN 978-0-07-097885-0 (v. 1). —ISBN 978-0-07-097886-7 (v. 2)

    1. Accounting—Textbooks.   I. Conrod, Joan E. D. (Joan Elizabeth Davison), 1956–
II. Title.

HF5635.B466 2008   657'.044   C2007-903274-5

About the Authors

Thomas H. Beechy, York University

Thomas H. Beechy is a Professor of Accounting at the Schulich School of Business, York University. For many years, he was also the Associate Dean of the school. He currently holds the additional titles of Executive Director of International Relations and of Assistant Dean—Special Projects. Professor Beechy holds degrees from George Washington University (BA), Northwestern University (MBA), and Washington University (DBA). He has been active in research and publication for almost 40 years, having published six books, including *Canadian Advanced Financial Accounting*, and numerous articles in major accounting journals. Professor Beechy has been a leader in Canadian accounting education, emphasizing the importance of case analysis in developing students' professional judgement and accounting skills. He has been an active researcher and advocate in both business and non-profit financial reporting. He has been particularly active in international accounting circles.

Joan E. D. Conrod, Dalhousie University

Joan E. D. Conrod is a Professor of Accounting in the Faculty of Management at Dalhousie University. Her teaching excellence has been recognized through awards such as the PWC Leaders in Management Education Award, the Dalhousie University Alumni Award for Teaching Excellence, and the AAU Distinguished Teacher award. She was awarded her FCA from the Nova Scotia Institute of Chartered Accountants in 1999. Joan is an active member of the University community, and has served on the Dalhousie University Senate and the Board of Governors. She is a past president of the Canadian Academic Accounting Association. Joan has a lengthy history of involvement in professional accounting education. She has taught financial and managerial accounting courses to CA students across Canada, but particularly in Atlantic Canada, for 20 years. She has served on CA education committees at the local, regional, and national levels. Her publications include the text *Intermediate Accounting*, with Tom Beechy, *Financial Accounting 3* for CGA-Canada, and a variety of case material and other publications.

Brief Table of Contents—Volume 2

Table of Contents—Volume 2

CHAPTER 14

COMPLEX DEBT AND EQUITY INSTRUMENTS — 834

CHAPTER 15

ACCOUNTING FOR CORPORATE INCOME TAX — 899

ACCOUNTING FOR TAX LOSSES   954

CHAPTER 16

ACCOUNTING FOR LEASES   1006

CHAPTER 17

CHAPTER 18 — PENSIONS AND OTHER POST-RETIREMENT BENEFITS — 1072

CHAPTER 19 — EARNINGS PER SHARE — 1135

RESTATEMENTS 1192

CHAPTER 20

FINANCIAL STATEMENT ANALYSIS 1242

CHAPTER 21

APPENDIX

COMPLEX CASH FLOW STATEMENT ILLUSTRATION   1304

Preface

There is a vast body of knowledge that must be mastered before you can account for the activities of an enterprise. Intermediate accounting is the essential course for gaining the technical skills and judgement you need to succeed. These skills are crucial for anyone who hopes to either use or prepare accounting information.

Accounting in general involves a blend of technical know-how and professional judgement. So that's what *Intermediate Accounting* appropriately dwells on: technical knowledge and professional judgement, covering the range of corporate reporting topics.

In selecting material to include in this book, we have assessed the realities of Canadian business practice. Accounting practices and policies remain in the public eye, with both fraud and judgement issues causing material restatements. This text reviews many critical issues that have been problematic in the past. Our accounting standards will be migrating to international standards in 2011. Many international standards are similar to Canadian standards, but there are important differences. This text describes and explores the alternatives.

Intermediate Accounting covers the technical elements of financial reporting, but keeps an eye on the critical judgement issues. After you master the contents of *Intermediate Accounting*, you will be able to account for the wide range of events and transactions found in this unique and challenging business environment.

TECHNICAL KNOWLEDGE

Accountants have to be able to account for things! There is a base level of expertise that must become part of every accountant's body of knowledge: how to record a receivable, capitalize a lease, account for a pension, or prepare a cash flow statement. Some of the transactions that we must account for are very complex, and their accounting treatment is equally complex. An affinity for numbers is important.

PROFESSIONAL JUDGEMENT

Judgement, it is often said, is the hallmark of a profession. There are often different ways to account for the same transaction. Professional accountants have to become expert at sizing up the circumstances and establishing the appropriate accounting policy for those circumstances. Once an accounting policy has been established, there are usually estimates that must be made before the numbers can be recorded. Accounting estimates also require the exercise of professional judgement. Professional judgement is not acquired overnight. It is nurtured and slowly grows over a lifetime. In this book, we begin the development process by explicitly examining the variables that companies consider when evaluating their options, and the criteria that accountants use to make choices. Opportunities to practise judgement are provided in the case material.

A CANADIAN AGENDA

Issues that receive the most attention in this book are those that are relevant in a Canadian context. Many times, the topics covered in other intermediate texts are determined by U.S. standards and priorities because those books are adaptations of U.S. texts. However, there are some significant differences between Canadian and U.S. businesses and business environments that dictate a different emphasis and coverage. In addition, Canadian standards are swiftly being harmonized with international accounting standards. While some U.S. standards are also moving to international accounting standards, their strategic direction remains U.S.–based. We hope you appreciate the Canadian emphasis!

AN INTERNATIONAL PERSPECTIVE

Following a Canadian agenda means that we all must come up to speed on international standards. Every chapter will explain the differences between current Canadian practice and the policies recommended by the International Accounting Standards Board. If there are differences, the alternatives are reviewed and explained in the chapter material.

OTHER KEY FEATURES

Integration of Cash Flow Material throughout the Text

The cash flow statement is covered in Chapter 5, following reviews of the income statement and balance sheet. Students can thus learn how to do the cash flow statement early in the course. Following this chapter, though, the cash flow implications of various complex transactions are reviewed in each relevant chapter. There is cash flow assignment material in most chapters of the book. For those instructors who like to emphasize cash flow material at the end of the course, an appendix has been added to the final chapter that summarizes cash flow statement issues and provides a comprehensive example. This is reinforced with assignment material in the last chapter.

The Accounting Cycle

The basic debit and credit of the accounting world is not really a topic for an intermediate accounting course. It represents the baby steps; we're trying to learn how to run, or at least jog. For many students, this material was covered in a high school course or an introductory accounting course. Others, who avoided the course in high school and/or who took a conceptually oriented introductory course in college or university, may need a refresher or further grounding in this area. To answer this need, we have included the accounting cycle as an appendix to Volume I. This provides maximum flexibility to instructors. Some courses may formally devote time to this appendix; others may use it as a reference only.

Accuracy

The text has been extensively reviewed and proofread prior to publication. Chapter material has been reviewed by professional accountants. All assignment materials have been solved independently by multiple individual "assignment checkers" in addition to the authors. Nevertheless, errors may remain, for which we accept full responsibility. If you find errors, please e-mail the authors at **j.conrod@dal.ca** or **tbeechy@schulich.yorku.ca**. There are thousands of calculations in this text—it's a daunting task to bring them to the degree of accuracy we'd like to be famous for. Your help will be greatly appreciated.

PEDAGOGICAL WALKTHROUGH

INTRODUCTION

Bombardier Inc., a major transportation manufacturing company, has operations in Canada, Germany, the United Kingdom, Switzerland, France, Australia, China, and other countries. Bombardier is listed on the Toronto Stock Exchange. As a Canadian public company, the company prepares its financial statements using Canadian generally accepted accounting principles (GAAP).

Many international companies list their securities on the stock exchanges in the foreign countries in which they operate. For example, the giant international automobile company Daimler-Chrysler is listed on all of the world's major stock exchanges including New York, Frankfurt, Tokyo, and London.

In the future, Bombardier may choose to list internationally. However, Canadian GAAP is accepted only in Canada, and Canada is a very small player in the international financial market. Will the company

Fortunately the answer to that question is "no," because almost all other countries permit foreign companies to report their financial results on the basis of *International Financial Reporting Standards* (IFRS).

The CICA's Accounting Standards Board (AcSB) has decided that it is time for Canada's public-company accounting standards to become international also. Canadian standard setting is changing with the international tide.

But even after Canada adopts IFRS for public companies, a company like Bombardier will need to make many accounting choices. Those choices will be affected by a variety of competing objectives. The company could make choices with an objective of reducing its income taxes, maximizing its reported earnings, or helping investors and creditors to estimate the future cash flows of the company.

Introduction

Each chapter has an introduction that explains the objectives of the chapter in narrative form.

In financial reporting, however, there often are multiple users. The various users often have conflicting objectives, and the financial statements must be prepared on a basis that optimizes the trade-offs between the various users' needs. The various (and potentially conflicting) objectives of financial reporting will be discussed later in this chapter.

CONCEPT REVIEW

1. What is the essential difference between a bookkeeper and an accountant?
2. What is the general realm of financial reporting? How does financial reporting differ from management accounting?
3. Describe the difference between point statements and flow statements. Give examples of each.

Concept Review

Throughout each chapter, there are periodic questions. Students can stop and think through the answers to these basic questions, covering the previously explained material. This helps comprehension and focus! Answers to these questions can be found on the Online Learning Centre.

---

the parent's statements, the subsidiary may use the parent's home country GAAP instead of Canadian GAAP.

Exhibit 1-1 summarizes the reporting requirements for public and private companies.

EXHIBIT 1-1

REPORTING REQUIREMENTS FOR PUBLIC AND PRIVATE COMPANIES

Reporting Basis	Rationale
Canadian Public Corporations	
Canadian GAAP	Shares traded primarily in Canada
U.S. GAAP	Shares traded primarily in U.S.
Canadian Private Corporations	
Canadian GAAP	General purpose statements
Canadian GAAP	Subsidiary of Canadian public corporation
Canadian GAAP, Differential Reporting	Limited users; shareholders agree
DBA	Specialized reporting for specific users
Foreign or International GAAP	Subsidiary of non-Canadian parent

Figures and Tables

Where appropriate, chapter material is summarized in figures and tables to establish the patterns and help reinforce material.

THE EXERCISE OF ETHICAL PROFESSIONAL JUDGEMENT

Chapter 1 gave examples of the many accounting choices that are affected by the financial reporting objectives *in any particular situation*. Reporting objectives (and motivations) do vary, and choices of accounting policies and accounting estimates are significantly affected by whether the primary reporting objective is, for example, income tax minimization, cash flow prediction, or net income maximization.

ETHICAL ISSUES

The ability to make appropriate choices in accounting is ethical professional judgement. Professional judgement permeates the work of a professional accountant, and it involves an ability to build accounting measurements that take into account:

- The objectives of financial reporting in each particular situation;
- The facts of the business environment and operations; and
- The organization's reporting constraints (if any).

Ethical Issues

Many chapters discuss accounting issues that raise ethical concerns. These concerns are highlighted in the chapter. Where ethics is particularly problematic, we have included a separate "ethical issues" section to help students focus on the ethical aspects of policy choice.

Ethics assignment material has also been incorporated into the case material. Essentially, when an accountant makes a recommendation on a contentious choice of accounting policy, ethics are tested. Students exercise true-to-life ethical judgement when they have to make a tough judgement call and recommend an accounting policy that is "good" for one group but "bad" for another. These ethical overtones are highlighted in the case solutions to help instructors draw them out in discussion and evaluation.

INTERNATIONAL PERSPECTIVE

The IASC accounting principles, or concepts, are set out in a section called a "Framework," which appears essentially as a preface to the IFRS. The Framework is not an IFRS. The Framework has roughly the same structure and content/conclusions as Section 1000 of the *CICA Handbook*, "Financial Statement Concepts," although the terminology is not identical. The Framework has the following (familiar) sections:

- Users of financial statements and their information needs;
- The objective of financial reporting;
- Underlying assumptions;
- Qualitative characteristics of financial statements;
- Elements of financial statements;
- Recognition criteria;
- Measurement of the elements of financial statements; and
- Concepts of capital and capital maintenance.

Refer to Exhibit 2-5 for a listing of the accounting principles identified.

International Perspective

New to the fourth edition, every chapter includes a review of international accounting policies, highlighting similarities and differences between current Canadian practice and the policies recommended by the International Accounting Standards Board.

RELEVANT STANDARDS

CICA Handbook:
- Section 1000, Financial Statement Concepts

IASB:
- Framework for the Preparation and Presentation of Financial Statements

Relevant Standards

At the end of each chapter, there is a comprehensive list of the Canadian and international standards that are relevant to the material in the chapter. We have not quoted the standards directly in chapter material and we have not provided paragraph references to either the *CICA Handbook* or to international standards. This omission is intentional—the two sources are harmonized but may use different words. The focus is on the application of standards, not the technicalities.

SUMMARY OF KEY POINTS

1. Accounting principles consist of three different sets of concepts: (1) underlying assumptions, (2) measurement methods, and (3) qualitative criteria.

2. *Underlying assumptions* include the basic postulates that make accounting measurements possible (such as *separate entity*, *unit of measure*, and *time period*), as well as underlying measurement assumptions that usually, but not always, are true in a given reporting situation. These measurement assumptions include *continuity*, *proprietary approach*, and *nominal dollar financial capital maintenance*.

3. *Qualitative criteria* are the criteria used in conjunction with an enterprise's financial reporting objectives to determine the most appropriate measurement methods to use in that particular reporting situation. Qualitative criteria include relevance, reliability, comparability, objectivity, understandability, materiality, conservatism, and the cost/benefit trade-off.

4. A critical qualitative criterion is that of *relevance*; relevance should be determined with reference to the users of the financial statements and the resulting financial reporting objectives. Relevance is enhanced if information is timely, and has predictive and feedback value.

Summary of Key Points

A summary of key points concludes each chapter. This provides a list of the key ideas and reinforces the chapter material.

KEY TERMS

accrual-basis accounting, 44
accruals, 44
commitment, 56
comparability, 51
conservatism, 51
consideration, 59
consistency, 51
constant dollar (capital maintenance), 47
constant dollars, 47
continuity assumption, 45
cost/benefit effectiveness, 52
deferrals, 44
differential reporting, 52
elements, 53
entity concept (assumption), 46
executory contract, 57
freedom from bias, 51
full disclosure, 61
going-concern assumption, 45

nominal dollars, 47
non-arbitrariness, 51
period costs, 60
physical capital maintenance, 47
professional judgement, 42
proprietary assumption, 45
purchasing power parity, 47
qualitative criteria (characteristics), 40
quantifiability, 51
realization, 57
recognition, 55
relevance, 48
reliability, 49
separate-entity assumption, 44
substance over form, 49
time-period assumption, 43
underlying assumptions
   (postulates), 40
uniformity, 51

Key Terms and the Glossary

Every chapter concludes with a list of key terms used in the chapter. These terms are explained in the chapter, and are also defined in the glossary, which is available on the Online Learning Centre (**www.mcgrawhill.ca/olc/beechy**).

REVIEW PROBLEM

The following pre-tax amounts are taken from the adjusted trial balance of Killian Corporation at 31 December 20X5, the end of Killian's fiscal year:

Account	Amount
Sales revenue	$1,000,000
Service revenue	200,000
Interest revenue	30,000
Gain on sale of capital asset	100,000
Cost of goods sold	600,000
Selling, general, and administrative expense	150,000
Depreciation expense	50,000
Interest expense	20,000
Loss on sale of long-term investment	10,000
Extraordinary item, loss from earthquake damage	200,000
Cumulative effect of change in accounting policy (gain)	50,000
Impairment loss on business segment assets	60,000
Loss on operation of discontinued business segment	10,000

Review Problem

There is a review problem with a solution in each chapter beginning in Chapter 3. This provides additional reinforcement of chapter content.

CASE 3-3

CASHGO LIMITED

CashGo Ltd. is a food distributor and retailer in eastern Canada. The company also owns both a bakery and a dairy, each of which has significant sales through other market channels in addition to CashGo's stores. CashGo is a private company; all of the shares are owned by the founder's family. The company has not needed external share capital as the company is quite profitable and the banks are eager to provide debt financing as needed. The banks require CashGo to give them annual audited financial statements, prepared in accordance with Canadian GAAP.

The CashGo CFO currently is overseeing the preparation of the company's consolidated financial statements for 20X7. There have been many changes to the recommendations of the *CICA Handbook*, not all of which the CFO is sure that she understands. She has come to you for advice on how to report the results of some of the company's 20X7 transactions and events. She also would appreciate receiving draft statements of income, comprehensive income, and retained earnings. CashGo does not wish to provide any more detail in the statements than is necessary to comply with current reporting requirements.

Specific concerns:

1. In the final quarter of 20X7, the Halifax region suffered a major hurricane, which knocked out the electricity in the Halifax region for several days. Hurricanes are extremely uncommon in Nova Scotia. A great quantity of frozen and other perishable foods was spoiled and had to be discarded. The loss amounted to $11 million. The inventory was not insured against this type of loss.

2. CashGo is a private company. In 20X7, the company elected to use the differential reporting option on income taxes, applied retrospectively. The cumulative adjustment for prior years was to eliminate the $46 million credit balance of future income taxes. CashGo has tentatively classified this amount as "Gain on income tax reversals."

Cases

More than 60 cases are included in *Intermediate Accounting*, and there is at least one new case in every chapter in the fourth edition. The cases are meant to portray circumstances reflective of real life. Students have to put themselves into the situation and grapple with the facts to arrive at appropriate accounting policies for the circumstances. A blend of professional judgement and technical skills is needed to respond to a case. Case coverage is not limited to "one chapter" bites, but often integrates material learned to date. For those trying to build a base of professionalism, the use of cases consistently over the term is highly recommended. Cases can be assigned for class debriefing, class presentations, or written assignments.

Assignment Material

There is an extensive range of assignment material at the end of each chapter. The assignments give students the opportunity to learn by doing.

 Stars accompanying each assignment indicate length, with one star being the shortest assignment and three stars being the longest assignment.

 Helping students practise on their own, we have selected a few assignments from each chapter and put their solutions on the Online Learning Centre. These selected assignments are highlighted by the icon in the margin.

 Excel® templates for selected assignments provide an introduction to basic spreadsheet applications. These assignments are identified with the icon in the margin and are available on the Online Learning Centre.

Integrative Problems

From time to time, we include integrative problems that formally deal with accounting topics covered in five or six chapters. These problems are a great pre-test review!

TOPICAL REVIEW IDENTIFYING KEY CHANGES

Chapters 1 and 2

The book starts with a review of the GAAP (and non-GAAP) world and establishes the common reporting motivations of companies and financial statement users, as well as the basic concepts of accounting. This is fundamental material that supports professional judgement. Chapter 1 has been extensively revised and rewritten for this edition, with the addition of two new exhibits (Exhibits 1.1 and 1.3) to further clarify the material. Chapter 2 includes a summary of the IASB framework of underlying assumptions, qualitative characteristics, constraints, and concepts of capital.

Chapters 3 and 4

These chapters review the income statement, retained earnings statement, balance sheet, and disclosure notes. There is a complete explanation of the statement of comprehensive income. Real-life examples show the degree of diversity that exists and how little information some companies provide in their financial statements. The chapters highlight the judgemental issues inherent in the statements and disclosures.

Chapter 5

The cash flow statement (CFS) is dealt with in sequence, as a primary financial statement. Again, coverage begins with a real-life example, to analyze the nature of information presented and the judgemental issues involved. The chapter deals with the mechanics of statement preparation, using both a format-free approach and the T-account method. T-accounts have been re-emphasized, because they are widely used in the classroom. The journal-entry-based worksheet is included in an appendix. CFS issues are reviewed in every subsequent chapter of the text and include CFS assignment material. We summarize text topics that impact on the CFS in an appendix to Chapter 21, for those who wish to reinforce this topic as a stand-alone topic later in the course.

Chapter 6

Revenue and expense recognition are surely the most judgemental areas of accounting policy choice in the GAAP world. For the fourth edition of the book, we have extensively revised and reorganized the material for greater clarity and better flow. The increasingly important area of multiple deliverables has been expanded and given more prominence. The emphasis of the text material is on the financial statement impact of these policies on net assets. There is extensive discussion of the criteria to be applied to determine appropriate revenue recognition policy and the numeric implications. Expense recognition is critically reviewed, both from a theoretical and practical perspective.

Chapter 7

Issues related to monetary balances—cash, receivables, and payables—are gathered and reviewed together. Important topics such as foreign currency translation (a must, in this age of globalization) and the rules governing the transfer of receivables are incorporated. The material on bank reconciliations has been moved to an appendix. Material covering the mathematical basics of present and future value is available on the Online Learning Centre (**www.mcgrawhill.ca/olc/beechy**), as is a more extensive set of compound interest tables.

Chapter 8

This chapter has been completely revised and reorganized. Introductory accounting texts always cover inventory systems and the cost flow assumptions and so we've moved that basic material into an appendix, available for review if needed. This fourth edition is based on the new Canadian inventory standard, which is harmonized with international standards. The chapter includes a review of policy decisions in this critical area, as well as the mechanics of inventory costing methods, lower of cost or market writedowns, and inventory estimation techniques.

Chapters 9 and 10

Accounting for capital assets, both tangible and intangible, follows a common pattern. These chapters systematically look at acquisition, amortization, impairment, and disposal. New accounting standards on the international scene will eliminate most instances of costs being reported as long-term deferred assets, such as startup costs, and coverage has been adjusted to reflect this reality. We have also clarified the material on non-monetary exchanges. We explain and illustrate the accounting standards relating to asset retirement obligations, held-for-sale assets, and asset impairments.

Chapter 11

This chapter reflects the financial instrument rules, a joint project of the AcSB, IASB, and FASB, implemented for publicly accountable enterprises in 2007. Accounting for held-to-maturity, held-for-trading, available-for-sale, significant influence, and control investments is covered. In particular, the fourth edition reflects the new standards for consolidation, to be implemented in 2009. Both policy and numeric issues are thoroughly explored. The chapter includes a number of helpful diagrams and figures, including a comparison of the cost and equity method, to clarify the roadmap through this territory.

Chapters 12 and 13

These chapters deal with straightforward debt and shareholders' equity issues. The debt chapter looks at the always-challenging long-term debt issues, emphasizing the effective interest method of calculating interest expense. The new approach for accounting for guarantees has been incorporated. The requirement for reporting other comprehensive income, including certain types of unrealized foreign currency gains/losses, is fully explained and assignment material on this topic is included. Summary charts have been incorporated where appropriate.

Chapter 14

One major topic in this chapter is classification of debt versus equity and appropriate treatment of hybrid financial instruments. Students learn how to determine the substance of a financial instrument, rather than its legal form, and account for it accordingly. Basic patterns for option accounting are established. A major new section on the various forms of incentive contracts (traditional options, SARs, and various kinds of deferred compensation agreements) has been added, with examples and summary charts to help establish the patterns. The material on derivative instruments has been gathered in this chapter and has been clarified with the addition of an example, which traces the impact of derivatives on accumulated other comprehensive income. We think that the revised material is clear and understandable; this is an important topic in financial reporting!

Chapters 15 and 16

Accounting for income tax remains two separate chapters, to acknowledge that many instructors prefer to spend two blocks of time on this most challenging area. The Chapter 15 material establishes a three-step process for typical situations. The focus of Chapter 16 remains accounting for the tax effect of losses—carrybacks and carryforwards. This is difficult material for students, but the Chapter 16 problems incorporate the prior chapter material and allow solid reinforcement of the steps associated with tax accounting.

Chapter 17

The main body of this chapter focuses on the lessee. Most companies lease something as a lessee, and thus lessee accounting is very commonly encountered in practice. Both the judgemental issues of lease classification and the complex calculations are extensively reviewed in this chapter, with examples.

Lessors, on the other hand, are rare. They tend to be quite specialized entities—financial intermediaries. Since lessors comprise a specialized industry, accounting by lessors is presented in a chapter appendix. The appendix includes an overview of the major aspects of lessor accounting and how it contrasts with lessee accounting. The appendix may be omitted if the instructor does not wish to address this specialized industry.

Chapter 18

Pensions and other post-retirement benefits are complex, long-term arrangements with employees. Accounting issues are also complex and have been structured in a worksheet format to improve clarity and comprehension. In addition, this chapter now contains an example of accounting for other post-retirement benefits and enhanced coverage of defined contribution plans, since the latter are gaining in popularity.

Chapter 19

Earnings per share material includes an explanation of basic and diluted EPS. The procedural steps associated with organizing a complex EPS question are emphasized to provide more comfort and support in this complicated area. Differences between Canadian and international approaches are explained and there are a variety of useful summary figures and tables.

Chapter 20

Accounting policy changes and error corrections require restatement of one or more prior years' financial statements. Restatement is surely an important topic, given the number of fraud-based restatements reported in the public press in recent years. Also, the ongoing changes in accounting standards means that companies must often restate their accounts. This chapter deals with the theory and mechanics related to such restatement, reflecting current standards.

Chapter 21

The text concludes with a review of financial statement analysis and emphasizes the importance of accounting policy choice and disclosure in the analysis of published financial statements. There is an extensive case illustration, based on a real Canadian company, which demonstrates the importance of accounting policy choice.

Appendix

An appendix on the cash flow statement follows as a stand-alone review of Chapter 5. The appendix summarizes the impact on the CFS of many types of transactions that the text has covered since the CFS was first discussed. A comprehensive example is provided. This appendix is meant to reinforce the CFS for instructors who like to deal with the statement as a stand-alone topic that reviews many topics within *Intermediate Accounting*.

ACKNOWLEDGEMENTS

The text would not have been possible without the contributions of a great many people. We recognize and appreciate all of their efforts.

Our thanks and gratitude are extended to the outstanding faculty reviewers who provided criticism and constructive suggestions on the text material. It hasn't been possible to incorporate all of the (sometimes conflicting!) suggestions, but the quality of this book has improved thanks to the people who reviewed it: Mark Binder, Red River College; Esther Deutsch, Ryerson University; George Fisher, CGA-Canada; Stuart H. Jones, University of Calgary; Michelle Loveland, University of Western Ontario; Marie Madill-Payne, George Brown College; Ron Naraine, Fanshawe College; Joe Nemi, University of Guelph/Humber; Joe Pidutti, Durham College; Carmel Robbins, SAIT Polytechnic; and Douglas Yee, British Columbia Institute of Technology. To numerous other colleagues and users whose constructive comments and suggestions have led to improvements, our thanks.

In this edition, we were also fortunate in having a team of experienced reviewers who were at the cutting edge in technical and judgemental issues. These individuals carefully reviewed our manuscript to ensure that our interpretations and presentations were balanced, correct, and thorough. The quality of this edition owes much to the efforts of Judy Cumby, FCA; Tashia Batstone, FCA; and Tammy Crowell, CA.

We are grateful to our dedicated team of assignment checkers, Jeff Christian, CA; Kimberly Morse; Cheryl Nachtigal, CGA; Duncan Ferguson, CA; and Douglas Cashin, CA, who have exhaustively checked the accuracy of the assignment material.

We also appreciate the permissions granted by the following organizations to use their problem and case material:

- The Canadian Institute of Chartered Accountants
- The Certified General Accountants' Association of Canada
- The Society of Management Accountants
- The Ontario Institute of Chartered Accountants
- The Atlantic School of Chartered Accountancy
- The American Institute of Certified Public Accountants

We are grateful to the people at McGraw-Hill Ryerson who guided this manuscript through its development process. We appreciate the strong support of Rhondda McNabb, our Senior Sponsoring Editor; Marcia Luke, our Developmental Editor; and the production team, led by Kelly Dickson and including Anne Nellis and Erin Moore, who have all contributed in significant ways to this final product. And, of course, Karen Rolfe has been a welcome and active partner in this enterprise, as our copy editor. She has greatly improved the quality of the final manuscript!

On a personal level, we would like to thank our friends and family members for their support and encouragement throughout the lengthy process of bringing this book to fruition, especially, in Halifax—Peter Conrod and Warren and Carmita Fetterly; and in Toronto—Calvin Luong and Brian McBurney.

Thomas H. Beechy
Schulich School of Business
York University
Toronto, ON

Joan E. D. Conrod
Faculty of Management
Dalhousie University
Halifax, NS

TECHNOLOGY SOLUTIONS

LYRYX LEARNING INC
Online Learning and Assessment
lyryx.com

Lyryx Assessment for Intermediate Accounting

Lyryx Assessment is a Web-based teaching and learning tool that has captured the attention of post-secondary institutions across the country.

Developed specifically for *Intermediate Accounting*, Fourth Edition by Beechy and Conrod, Lyryx Assessment is a leading-edge online assessment system that delivers significant benefits to both students and instructors.

After registering their course with McGraw-Hill Ryerson, instructors can create labs of their choice by selecting problems from our test bank and setting deadlines. Instructors have access to all the students' marks and can view their best labs. At any time, instructors can download the class grades for their own programs to analyze individual and class performance.

The assessment takes the form of a homework assignment called a "lab," which corresponds to the chapters in the *Intermediate Accounting* text. The labs are algorithmically generated and automatically graded, so students get instant scores and feedback—no need to wait until the next class to get results!

With new labs randomly generated each time, students have unlimited opportunities to try a type of question. Student motivation is high with these labs, because they can be tied to assessment and because students can try as many times as they want prior to the due date, with only their best grade being recorded.

If students are doing their intermediate accounting practice and homework, they will improve their performance in the course. Recent research regarding the use of Lyryx has shown when labs are tied to assessment, even if worth only a small percentage of the total grade for the course, students will do their homework—and more than once. The result is improved student success in intermediate accounting!

Instructors: Please contact your *i*Learning Sales Specialist for additional information on the Lyryx Assessment for *Intermediate Accounting*.

Lyryx Quick Start

Developed to address the need to quickly "refresh" student learning from their introductory financial accounting course, Lyryx Quick Start is the perfect solution. This product contains the essential material needed to prepare students for *Intermediate Accounting*. There are explorations and labs reviewing:

- The accounting cycle
- Financial statements
- Cash flows.

Like Lyryx for Intermediate Accounting, new labs are generated each time, providing students with unlimited opportunity to practise. The result is students who are well prepared to begin the intermediate accounting course.

Instructors: Please contact your *i*Learning Sales Specialist for additional information on Lyryx Quick Start.

FOR THE STUDENTS

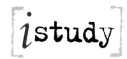

iInteract iLearn iSucceed

iStudy Intermediate Accounting

Available 24/7: providing instant feedback when you want, how you want, and where you want. This online *i*Study space was developed to help you master concepts and achieve better grades with all the learning tools you've come to expect, including chapter summaries, quiz questions, and additional problems. *i*Study offers the best, most convenient way to learn, interact, and succeed.

*i*Study can be purchased through the Online Learning Centre or by purchasing a PIN code card through the campus bookstore.

Instructors: Please contact your *i*Learning Sales Specialist for more information on how to make *i*Study part of your students' success.

Online Learning Centre (OLC) www.mcgrawhill.ca/olc/beechy

Updated for the fourth edition, the Beechy/Conrod *Intermediate Accounting* OLC provides a wealth of additional content and exercises, including:

- Solutions to Concept Review exercises;
- Solutions to selected text assignments;
- Self-study quizzes;
- A glossary of all key terms in the text;
- Excel assignment downloads to help solve selected in-text assignments;
- Compound interest tables;
- Appendix: Interest—Concepts of Future and Present Value
- Chapter 14 Appendix: Financial Restructuring; and
- Chapter 18 Appendix: Actuarial Cost Methods.

INSTRUCTOR SUPPLEMENTS

For the Instructor

- **Instructor's Resource CD-ROM.** A one-stop convenient source of supplemental material.
  - **Instructor's Manual.** There is a brief topical outline for each chapter that indicates the topics to discuss in class and an assignment guide that provides, at a glance, the topical content of each exercise, problem, and case.
  - **Solutions Manual.** This comprehensive manual provides solutions to all cases, questions, assignments, and comprehensive problems.
  - **Computerized Test Bank.** With an abundance of objective questions, multiple-choice questions, and short exercises, this supplement is a valuable resource for instructors when preparing quizzes and examinations.
  - **Microsoft® PowerPoint® Slides.** This PowerPoint® presentation can be used to review chapter concepts.
  - **Excel Template Solutions.** Solutions are provided to all Excel Template assignments.

Many of these Instructor resources are also available for download from the Instructor Area of the Online Learning Centre.

SUPERIOR SERVICE

Service takes on a whole new meaning with McGraw-Hill Ryerson (MHR). More than just bringing you the textbook, MHR has consistently raised the bar in terms of innovation and educational research—both in accounting and in education in general. These investments in learning and the education community have helped MHR understand the needs of students and educators across the country, and allowed MHR to foster the growth of truly innovative, integrated learning.

Integrated Learning Sales Specialists

i-Learning
ADVANTAGE
McGraw-Hill Ryerson

- The Integrated Learning Sales Specialists are the McGraw-Hill Ryerson representatives who have the experience, product knowledge, training, and support to help instructors assess and integrate any MHR products, technology, and services into courses for optimum teaching and learning performance. Whether it's using the test bank software, helping students improve their grades, or putting an entire course online, the *i*Learning Sales Specialist is there to help.

Instructors: Contact your local *i*Learning Sales Specialist today to learn how to maximize all of McGraw-Hill Ryerson's resources!

*i*Services

- McGraw-Hill Ryerson takes pride in developing the tools necessary to ensure a rich teaching and learning experience. MHR can assist in integrating technology, events, conferences, training, and more, into the services surrounding the textbook. MHR calls it *i*Services; for additional information, visit http://www.mcgrawhill.ca/higher education/iservices.

Teaching, Learning & Technology Conference Series The educational environment has changed tremendously in recent years, and McGraw-Hill Ryerson continues to be committed to helping you acquire the skills you need to succeed in this new milieu. Our innovative Teaching, Learning & Technology Conference Series brings faculty together from across Canada with 3M Teaching Excellence award winners to share teaching and learning best practices in a collaborative and stimulating environment.

Pageout Create an individualized course page for free—quickly and easily. The professionally designed website links directly to OLC material, allows instructors to post a class syllabus, offers an online gradebook, and much more! No knowledge of HTML is required. Visit www.pageout.net.

Course Management The *Intermediate Accounting* Online Learning Centre content is available for course management systems, such as Blackboard. Ask your *i*Learning Sales Specialist for details.

CHAPTER 12

Liabilities

INTRODUCTION

What is a liability? The answer might seem rather obvious: an amount owed from one entity to another. How do you measure interest expense? The simple answer is that interest expense is equal to interest paid. However, life can get a lot more complicated, as explored in this chapter:

- Does a liability exist if one entity has promised services, not money, to another? How would the obligation be valued?
- Does a liability exist if money has to be paid only if another event happens?
- How can a liability be recorded if the amount is uncertain?
- Is disclosure needed when a liability fails the recognition criteria?
- How should a long-term liability be valued if the interest rate does not reflect the market rate?
- How is interest expense measured when the face value of a debt is different than the proceeds received on issuance?
- How is interest expense measured when no interest is paid?

Liability financing is an integral part, perhaps even a dominant part, of many companies' capital structure. For example, Shaw Communications Inc. reported total assets of $7.5 billion in 2006. Of this amount, only $1.8 billion is financed through shareholders' equity, with the balance, $5.7 billion, provided by debt in various forms. A sizeable portion of the debt is unearned revenue and deposits ($1.1 billion, or 15% of total assets) but long-term debt is 40% of total assets. On the income statement, interest is reported at $254 million, eating up a significant portion of the reported $580 million in operating income. Appropriate measurement of these amounts is critical.

This chapter reviews the common forms of debt. This is very technical material, and many calculations are complex. Chapter 13 will discuss accounting for share equity. Then, in Chapter 14, coverage returns to debt arrangements, those that have some attributes of debt and some attributes of equity. Innovative financial markets have introduced significant complexities into the accounting world!

WHAT IS A LIABILITY?

According to our accounting standards, a liability has three essential characteristics:

1. A duty or responsibility to others, requiring some sacrifice. This sacrifice could be settlement by future transfer or use of assets, provision of services, or other yielding of economic benefits. The sacrifice must happen at a specified or determinable date, on occurrence of a specified event, or on demand;

2. The duty or responsibility is a binding obligation, with little or no discretion to avoid the duty; and

3. The transaction or event that created the obligation has already occurred.

These characteristics can be simplified for practical purposes by remembering that a liability:

- Is a highly probable *future* sacrifice of assets or services;
- Constitutes a *present* obligation; and
- Is the result of a *past* transaction or event.

Notice that there are three time elements in the definition: a *future* sacrifice, a *present* obligation, and a *past* event. All three elements are necessary for a liability to be recognized.

Accruals   A liability need not be the result of an explicit contract. Companies often report accrued liabilities as a result of net income measurement. Recognition of revenue, *followed by matching the related expenses,* leads to the recognition of liabilities. These liabilities are the offset to expenses that are matched to revenue in a period, even though there is no obligation to any specific individual or organization at the time. Examples include:

- Accrual of the estimated costs of fulfilling warranties in the future for goods sold in the current period;
- An estimate of the liability under special coupon or other promotional activities carried out in the current period (e.g., frequent-flier points for an airline);
- An annual provision for major maintenance costs that are incurred regularly, but not every year (e.g., the cost of relining furnaces in a steel mill, which is done every few years); or
- A liability for environmental cleanup costs by a resource company, even if it is under no legal requirement (at the time of reporting) to incur such costs.

In these examples, there is no *present obligation* in the sense that a specific identifiable person or organization recognizes the existence of an offsetting receivable. Therefore, the second requirement of the liability definition provides only that *the entity is obligated* in a general sense, and not that it be obligated to any particular identifiable party.

TYPES OF LIABILITIES

There are two basic types of liability:

- Financial liabilities and
- Non-financial liabilities.

We will briefly discuss the nature of each then move to a general discussion of liability measurement.

Financial Liabilities

A financial liability is a *financial instrument,* which is a contract that gives rise to a financial asset of one party and a financial liability or equity instrument of another party. That is, one party has an account payable and the other party has an account receivable. Another example is a loan payable and a loan receivable. The two elements are mirror images of each other.

A liability does not arise from a *commitment*, such as a purchase order for inventory.[1] A liability arises only when the inventory items have been delivered, thereby creating a receivable on the books of the other party.

Measurement of Financial Liabilities Financial liabilities are measured as the fair value of the consideration received. Normally, this is the stated amount of the transaction. Technically, the fair value is determined by the market value that is reflected in the transaction price. A company receives an invoice for the fair value of goods shipped by a supplier; the goods are the consideration, and their invoice value is both the fair value and the transaction price.

When market prices are not readily available, or if payments are to be received far in the future, fair value is estimated as the present value of all future cash payments discounted using the market interest rate as the discount rate. The discount rate is *the borrower's interest rate for additional debt of similar term and risk, also called the* **incremental borrowing rate (IBR).** However, current liabilities normally are not discounted because the short time span means that the difference between the nominal amount and the discounted amount will be immaterial.

Assume that Radial Information Limited bought a capital asset. The company paid no money upfront, but agreed to pay $18,000 in three years' time, with no additional interest. Radial could borrow a similar amount over three years from the bank at 9%. Assuming annual compounding, the present value of the liability is $13,900 ($18,000 $\times$ ((P/F, 9%, 3); $18,000 $\times$ .77218)). This is the value at which the capital asset and the liability will be recorded. As illustrated later in the chapter, the liability will increase by 9% interest on the balance each year, and be equal to $18,000 at maturity. If, on the other hand, Radial bought a capital asset and agreed to pay $18,000 for it in six months' time, again with no additional interest, the liability and the capital asset would be recorded at $18,000, with no interest, because the interest-free period is short.

Non-Financial Liabilities

A non-financial liability can be defined by what it is *not*—any liability that is not a financial liability is a non-financial liability. A non-financial liability has no offsetting financial asset on the books of another party. Most non-financial liabilities arise from two sources:

- Revenue received in the current period but not yet earned (that is, unearned or deferred revenue); or
- Costs that are expected to arise in the future but that are related to transactions, decisions, or events that took place in the current period (i.e., estimated liabilities, such as a warranty liability).

In addition, accounting standards sometimes identify specific future non-financial liabilities that are to be recognized. An example is the requirement that legislative or contractual **asset retirement obligations** must be recognized when an asset is acquired. For example, if a mine site is acquired that will have to be restored at the end of ten years at a cost of $1,000,000, the present value of the $1,000,000 obligation is recorded as a liability. There is a corresponding increase to the asset account, which is amortized over the life of the mine. (See Chapter 9 for a complete discussion and example.)

contractual obligation

a commitment or agreement to enter into a transaction; there will be a liability once an event contemplated in the agreement has occurred

Contractual Obligations

Companies often have contracts that require them to pay another party in the future, after the other party has performed some service or obligation. These contracts are known as **contractual obligations**. The contracts commit the enterprise to a future expenditure.

---

[1] An exception applies to governments and non-profit organizations, which often recognize a purchase order as a liability when it is issued. This is done in order to keep expenditures within budget and to control costs.

However, they do not become *liabilities* until the other party has performed the service specified in the contract. The other party to the contract is most often another business enterprise, such as a supplier, but the contract may also be with an individual. Employment contracts are a good example; the company agrees to pay the employee, but only after the employee provides her services.

Usually, contractual obligations are not disclosed, because their presence is ordinary and assumed. Under certain circumstances, contractual obligations will be included in the disclosure notes. The following circumstances would call for note disclosure:

- Commitments that involve a high degree of speculative risk;
- Commitments for expenditures that are much larger than usual, such as for substantial capital asset purchases;
- Commitments to issue shares; or
- Commitments that will require a certain level of significant expenditure for a considerable time into the future, such as "take or pay" agreements for fuel or other resources.[2]

Contractual obligations are also called *executory contracts*, because they do not become liabilities until they have been *executed* by one party or the other. For example, suppose that a company issues a purchase order to buy new equipment. The contract is an executory contract and is not recorded. Recording occurs only when and if one of two things happens:

1. The buyer pays a deposit to the seller, at which point the buyer and the seller record the deposit only.

2. The equipment is delivered by the seller, at which point the *buyer* records a liability and the seller records the sale.

In both situations, an obligation (liability) is created when an amount is recorded, although each is on the books of a different party—on the seller's books in the first situation, and on the buyer's books in the second situation. Each liability is a financial instrument because each is offset by a corresponding financial asset (that is, a receivable) on the other party's books.

In the first situation, in which the seller pays a deposit, only the deposit is recorded. The remainder of the contract price is not recorded until the contract is fully executed—when the seller actually delivers the equipment.

Estimated Liabilities

Estimated liabilities pose valuation problems. The liability exists, but the amount is not known with certainty. This situation usually arises for non-monetary liabilities, or obligations to provide services rather than money. Examples include warranty liabilities, where the obligation is to provide repairs, and environmental liabilities, where the obligation is to provide environmental cleanup, which may cost a little or a lot.

When no estimate is possible, the item cannot be recorded, as it does not meet the recognition criteria discussed in Chapter 2. However, most of the time, a reasonable estimate can be made. Measurement uncertainty is disclosed when estimates are used. In later periods, when estimates change, they are adjusted in that year. For example, if a $2,000,000 warranty liability was in place at the beginning of 20X7, based on 1% of past sales, and it was determined that the cumulative balance should be $2,700,000, based on 1.7% of past sales, the additional $700,000 liability would be recorded and expensed in 20X7. There would be no retrospective restatement, because this was a change in estimate.

Warranty Liabilities Warranty liabilities are estimated liabilities. To illustrate accounting for warranties, assume that Rollex Limited sells merchandise for $200,000 during 20X2. Rollex's merchandise carries a one-year unconditional warranty for parts and labour. The recognition criteria indicate that when a liability exists and is probable and measurable, it

---

[2] A "take or pay" contract requires a company to *take* a certain quantity of goods, at a certain price, in a certain period of time, or *pay* for the goods whether they are taken or not.

must be recorded. Alternatively, one can reason that the future warranty costs are the result of current year's sales, and *matching* requires that the estimated costs of fulfilling the warranty be recognized in the period of the sale. Rollex's past experience has indicated that warranty costs will approximate 0.6% of sales. The entry to record the sales and the warranty obligation in 20X2 will be as follows:

Accounts receivable	200,000	
Sales revenue		200,000
Warranty expense	1,200	
Warranty liability (current)		1,200

If, in 20X3, Rollex incurs costs of $850 to repair or replace defective merchandise, the cost is charged to the liability account:

Warranty liability	850	
Cash (and other resources used)		850

The balance in the warranty liability account will be $350, credit.

In 20X3, Rollex sells another $240,000 worth of merchandise. The entries to record the sales and the warranty expense are as follows, assuming that Rollex now plans to use an estimate of 0.4% of sales:

Accounts receivable	240,000	
Sales revenue		240,000
Warranty expense	960	
Warranty liability (current)		960

After these entries, the warranty liability will have a credit balance of $1,310.

The warranty liability will be carried forward from year to year, adjusted each year for management's estimate of the future warranty costs. As is the case for all accounting estimates, the estimate of annual warranty cost may be changed in the light of new experience or as the result of improved (or worsened) product designs.

If, in any year, the charges to the warranty liability for warranty work done are higher than the balance in the liability account, the liability account will *temporarily* go into a debit balance until the year-end adjustment is made. However, this is not a problem. The temporary existence of a debit balance simply indicates that the cost has not been accrued yet. The ending warranty liability has to be reviewed for reasonableness, though. If costs are creeping up, the liability will end up at a low amount and the estimate that is accrued each year may need upward revision. On the other hand, if the warranty credit balance builds up over time, the rate should be revised downward. Sometimes, the "excess" in a particular year may not call for an increase in the regular estimate if it is a one-time occurrence.

The warranty liability is current if the warranty is for one year or less. If the warranty is for a longer period, the liability should be split between current and long-term portions.

Contingent Liabilities

A contingent liability will arise only if some future event occurs. That is, a **contingent liability** is one that will become a real liability only *if and when* another event happens. Examples of contingent liabilities are as follows:

- A company has received a government loan that will be forgiven, *if* the company maintains certain employment levels and/or makes specified investments; if the conditions are not met, the loan must be repaid.

- A company is being sued for patent infringement; if the company loses the case, a substantial penalty may be assessed by the court.

Contingent liabilities should be distinguished from **estimated liabilities**. Estimated liabilities are those that are known to exist, but for which the exact amount is unknown. Uncertainty about the amount involved does not of itself mean that the liability is a contingent liability.

Reporting Contingent Liabilities An enterprise has the following three possibilities for reporting contingent liabilities:

1. *Accrue* the estimated cost as a liability in the balance sheet and as a loss on the income statement.

2. *Disclose* the contingency and the possible liability in the notes to the financial statements.

3. *Neither* accrue the contingency in the financial statements nor disclose it in the notes.

The accounting treatment depends on two characteristics of the contingency:

1. The likelihood of the contingency occurring, and

2. The measurability of the resulting liability or loss.

A contingent loss is *accrued* when the occurrence of the loss is likely, and the amount can be measured. A contingent loss is neither recorded nor disclosed when it is not likely and not material. A contingent loss is *disclosed* when:

- The occurrence of the loss is likely, but the amount cannot be measured, or
- The occurrence of the loss is likely, and the amount can be measured and has been recorded, but there is some chance that the amount recorded is not high enough (this is an example of disclosure of measurement uncertainty) or,
- The likelihood of the loss event can't be determined, regardless of whether or not the amount can be measured, or
- The occurrence of the loss is unlikely, but the amounts involved are material (in other words, the event would have a significant adverse effect on the company).

The reporting consequences of the relationship between *likelihood and measurability* are shown in the following table:

	Measurable	Not Measurable
Likely	Record (plus disclose if amount recorded is uncertain)	Disclose in the notes
Undeterminable	Disclose in the notes	Disclose in the notes
Not Likely	Do not record or disclose unless material	Do not record or disclose unless material

A **recurring operating contingent loss exposure** need not be disclosed in the financial statements. This is a loss exposure that normally exists in the business's operations and merits no special reporting treatment.

For example, there always is a risk of loss through theft or fire. Many large companies self-insure such losses, meaning that they carry no external fire or theft insurance. Known (likely) losses are, of course, recorded. However, the ongoing risk of uninsured losses is not reported in the disclosure notes because it is a normal risk. The informed financial statement reader should be aware of the risk and need no special cue to realize its presence.

Evidence from Practice *Financial Reporting in Canada 2006* reported that 77% of the 200 surveyed public companies disclosed the existence of one or more contingent losses. The most common disclosure was for lawsuits and claims, reported by 86% of the companies that disclosed contingent losses. Other common contingencies related to environmental matters (29%), and possible tax reassessments (8%).

Reporting Ongoing Lawsuits Lawsuits pose an interesting problem. Company lawyers are seldom willing to admit that their clients are likely to lose a lawsuit, although obviously there is a loser and a winner in every case. Even if the company and its lawyers believe privately that they are likely to lose a case (and thus incur a significant liability), they will be reluctant to admit this prior to the court judgement. Therefore, disclosure of contingent liabilities relating to lawsuits (and, for similar reasons, to other claims and tax assessments) is almost always by note, regardless of the guidelines regarding likelihood and measurability.

ETHICAL ISSUES

Assume that a company is being sued by an ex-employee for $500,000 for wrongful dismissal. The company is defending itself actively, but might be willing to settle the lawsuit for $200,000. Should the $200,000 be recorded? Recording this amount, which would make it known, would be of significant interest to the plaintiff and hurt the company's bargaining position in discussions to end the lawsuit. On the other hand, leaving the $200,000 out of the financial statements understates probable liabilities and overstates profits.

The company is ethically required to follow appropriate reporting, but is equally ethically bound to serve its shareholders' best interests. What might be done is to accrue the $200,000 amount, but include it with various other liabilities in the balance sheet presentation (e.g., accounts payable and accrued liabilities), so its presence is indistinct. The disclosure notes could indicate that "appropriate recognition" has been given to pending lawsuit amounts. This could be taken to mean that an accrual has been made, or no accrual has been made. In this way, the plaintiff is not given any inappropriate information, but the financial statements are fairly presented.

Contingent Gains While on the subject of contingencies, a reminder that contingent gains are not recorded until realized. If a company is suing a supplier, for instance, no amount is recorded even if it is likely that the company will win and the amount can be estimated. In fact, a winning court judgement may not even be recorded until it seems likely that the judgement will be paid. Disclosure is the appropriate route.

Guarantees

Guarantees are a type of contingent liability. A loan guarantee requires the guarantor to pay loan principal and interest if the borrower defaults. The financial instruments rules require that loan guarantees be recorded at their fair value. This is a somewhat different approach than the contingencies framework, and has a different result. Assume that a loan guarantee is issued for a related company, and there is only a 10% chance that it will have to be honoured. Under the contingencies rules, no amount is recorded. Under the financial instruments rules, the 10% probability has a positive fair value. Therefore, implementation of the financial instruments rules means that a liability will be recorded at fair value for many guarantees. Extensive disclosure of guarantees is also required, including the maximum potential future payment, the identity of the other party, and collateral, if any.

Summary Refer to the following chart as a summary:

Possible Financial Statement Element	Record?	Disclose?
Contractual obligations (also known as executory contracts)	No—wait and record only on delivery (record advance payment if made)	Not usually, but disclose if unusual or if in a sensitive area
Estimated liabilities	Yes—best estimate recorded	Measurement uncertainty disclosed if appropriate
Contingent liabilities	Record if likely and measurable	Disclose measurement uncertainty if appropriate Disclose if likely and not measurable Disclose if not likely but material
Recurring operating contingent loss exposure	Known/estimable losses are recorded	No disclosure of normal risk
Guarantees	Fair value is recorded	All guarantees are disclosed

CONCEPT REVIEW

1. What are the three essential characteristics of a liability?
2. What is the definition of a financial liability?
3. Why are contractual obligations not recorded as liabilities?
4. Under what circumstances are contingent liabilities recognized in the balance sheet?

CURRENT LIABILITIES

Most companies segregate their liabilities between current and long term. A current liability is one that is due or payable *within the next operating cycle or the next fiscal year, whichever period is longer.* For many companies, the effective guiding time period is one year.

For some types of enterprise, the operating cycle is longer than one year. In such cases, the longer period is used for classifying current liabilities (and current assets). For example, a producer of fine wine must age the inventory for more than one year before releasing it for sale. The current asset of inventory will include all wine held in storage, most of which will not be ready for sale until long after the current year-end. *Current* accounts payable may have a duration of longer than a year, if suppliers offer such payment terms.

Remember that not all companies segregate their liabilities between current and long term. For example, financial institutions normally do not segregate on the basis of maturity date.

Reporting

In North America, current liabilities normally are listed by descending order to the strength of the creditors' claims. In other countries, this may be reversed. There are no reporting requirements in this area in Canada. A common sequence is:

- Bank loans;
- Other notes payable;
- Current portion of long-term liabilities;
- Trade accounts payable;
- Other payables;
- Accrued liabilities;
- Unearned revenues; and
- Miscellaneous deferred credits.

Most current liabilities are monetary and were described in Chapter 7. Others are non-monetary estimated liabilities, like warranties and unearned revenues.

SOURCES OF SHORT-TERM FINANCING

The discussion that follows is a review of the common forms of financing, which are summarized in Exhibit 12-1.

Trade Credit The most obvious source of short-term financing is through the trade credit extended by suppliers. Some corporations use trade creditor financing to its fullest extent as a source of "interest-free" financing, sometimes stretching the ethical boundaries of business practice. For example, large corporations may rely on their purchasing power and their "clout" as big customers of smaller suppliers to put off paying their trade accounts payable.

Some purchases are made by signing **promissory notes** that obligate the company to pay the supplier (or an intermediary, such as a bank) at or before a given date. The notes may bear interest, or they may be non–interest bearing. The use of notes for trade purchases is particularly common in international trade, since the banks that act as intermediaries are better placed to enforce payment. Promissory notes are legally enforceable negotiable instruments, so corporations cannot "play games" by delaying payment past the due date without risk of serious repercussions.

EXHIBIT 12-1

SOURCES OF FINANCING

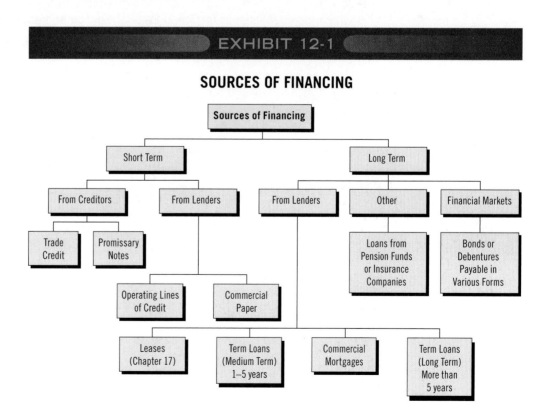

lien/charge

a claim by a creditor on the assets of a company as security on a loan or debt; the party placing the lien has first claim on assets in the event of default

Short-Term Bank Loans Like individuals, Canadian business entities borrow from chartered banks. Lending arrangements can be classified according to term and security.

Short-term bank loans to business entities usually take the form of **operating lines of credit**. These loans are granted to help finance working capital, and typically are secured by a **lien** or **charge** on accounts receivable and/or inventory. There normally is a gap between the time that cash is paid to suppliers for inventory and the time that money is received from customers who, in the end, buy the inventory. Businesses can use equity funds to finance this cash flow, but receivables and inventories are reasonable collateral for loans, and it is cheaper to borrow for this purpose. The interest rate on bank lines of credit is usually flexible and is based on the bank's prime rate (e.g., prime, or prime plus 1%).

There is typically a limit on working capital loans, expressed as a percentage of the collateral base. For example, a business may have a line of credit (also called a *credit facility*) that allows the company to borrow up to 75% of the net realizable value of accounts receivable and 50% of the book value of inventory. These loans often increase and decrease in seasonal businesses, following the ebb and flow of cash.

Operating lines of credit are due on *demand*, which means that if the bank gives the customer appropriate notice, usually a few business days, the loans have to be repaid immediately. In practice, repayment is not normally demanded unless the amount of collateral declines or the company otherwise violates some aspect of the loan agreement.

Despite their "due on demand" status, lines of credit often are a permanent fixture on the balance sheet. The credit facility may be attached to the business's current account (i.e., the business chequing account) and drawn on as an overdraft. This is why the definition of *cash* on the cash flow statement includes overdrafts. Companies use such loans as part of their cash management strategies.

Reporting Example Andrew Peller Ltd. (formerly Andres Wines Ltd.) included the following information in the company's 2006 annual report:

The Company has established the following credit facilities:

A demand loan facility with a borrowing limit of $43 million (2005—$43 million) which incurs interest at the Royal Bank of Canada prime rate. As at March 31, 2006, the unused portion of the demand loan facility was $5.7 million. ...

[Three other credit arrangements are listed]

The Company and its subsidiary companies have provided accounts receivable, inventory and property plant and equipment as security for these loan facilities.

Large corporations that have good credit ratings can issue **commercial paper,** which is a type of short-term promissory note that is sold (through a financial intermediary, again usually a bank) in open markets. The issuer of commercial paper does not know who the purchaser is, and settlement at the due date is through the financial intermediary.

A final type of short-term financing that merits mention is the sale or assignment of a company's receivables to a finance company. It represents another way current assets can be used as a source of short-term financing.

LONG-TERM LIABILITIES

A **long-term liability** is a liability with repayment terms extending beyond one year from the current balance sheet date or the operating cycle of the borrower, whichever is longer. A long-term liability is a liability that is not current, so long-term liabilities are often known as **non-current liabilities.**

Long-term debt is often an attractive means of financing for the debtor. Creditors do not acquire voting privileges in the debtor company, and issuance of debt causes no ownership dilution. Debt capital is obtained more easily than equity capital for many companies, especially private companies. Interest expense, unlike dividends, is tax deductible. Furthermore, a firm that earns a return on borrowed funds that exceeds the rate it must pay in interest is using debt to its advantage and is said to be successfully levered (or leveraged).

Leverage is risky. If sales or earnings decline, interest expense becomes an increasing percentage of earnings. Business failures frequently are caused by carrying too much debt in expectation of high sales and profits. If sales and profits (and operating cash flows) do not materialize, overlevered companies soon find themselves in financial difficulty. Firms often attempt to restructure their debt by extending maturity dates or requesting a reduction in principal or interest.

Debt is an attractive investment for *investors (lenders)* because it provides legally enforceable debt payments, eventual return of principal, and a priority claim to assets if the corporation restructures its debt or if it goes into receivership or bankruptcy. Creditors can further reduce their risk by extending secured debt, in which the obligation is contractually tied to specific assets that the creditor can seize in the event of the debtor's default. Debt investments generally are less risky than equity investments and consequently provide a lower return.

Long-term debt can take a wide variety of forms, including:

- Bank loans;
- Notes payable;
- Mortgages;
- Other asset-based loans;
- Publicly issued bonds, secured or unsecured; and
- Long-term leases.

Long-term leases are the subject of Chapter 17. The other forms of financing are discussed in the rest of this chapter. More inventive forms of financing that have at least some of the characteristics of long-term debt are discussed in Chapter 14.

Long-Term Bank Financing

For accounting purposes, any loan that is not current is long term. From a financial institution's point of view, however, non-current loans can be identified as **term loans** and **commercial mortgages**. *Term loans* might better be characterized as *medium-term* loans because they are usually for periods of 1.5 to 5 years. Banks will lend on this term if there is appropriate collateral, such as tangible capital assets including equipment, land, or buildings. Land and buildings would also qualify for longer-term loans. Security is lodged in the form of a claim on the capital asset. At the end of the loan term, after all the payments have been made, the security is released. The repayment terms of medium-term loans can be structured in either of two ways:

1. *Blended payments.* The interest rate is fixed at the beginning of the loan term, and regular equal annuity payments are made, which include both principal and interest. For example, a $1,000,000, five-year loan at an interest rate of 7% could be repaid in five annual instalments of $243,891 ($1,000,000 ÷ (P/A, 7%, 5)(4.10020)). Each payment includes some interest and some principal.

2. *Designated monthly principal payments, plus accrued interest on the outstanding balance.* The interest rate may be *fixed* at the beginning of the loan term, or may *float* with prime interest rates. The borrower makes an interest payment at the end of every month, based on the loan balance for that month and the interest rate in effect. In addition, the borrower and lender work out a repayment scheme for the principal that will fully repay the loan by the end of its term. The payment terms may require equal monthly, quarterly, or semi-annual principal payments (plus interest), or lump-sum payments following a busy season. Sometimes there is a large final lump-sum payment required; this is known as a *balloon payment.*

For accounting purposes, interest is accrued as time passes, and is paid when due. If principal and interest payments are *blended,* the portion of each payment that represents

leverage

associated with debt financing; the ability of a company to earn a rate of return on equity that is higher than its return on assets because debt, with a cost less than the return generated on assets, is used to partially finance those assets

commercial mortgage

term loan secured by tangible property; generally has interest rate and payment terms set for a period of up to five years principal is recorded as a reduction of the loan. Alternatively, if designated lump-sum principal payments are made, these are recorded as a direct reduction of the loan. Medium-term loans are classified as long term on the borrower's balance sheet, although the principal portion due within one year or operating cycle is classified as a current liability.

Long-Term Loans **Long-term loans,** in the eyes of the lenders, are loans with repayment terms extending beyond five years. Banks typically grant such loans as asset-based financing or as commercial mortgages. Commercial mortgages are secured against land and buildings, and involve regular blended payments (e.g., monthly or semi-monthly). The **amortization period** of such loans could be for as long as 25 years, but the **term,** or the lender's commitment to extending the loan, is usually a shorter period. The term normally will not exceed five years, and may be shorter. The lender is under no obligation to renew the loan at the end of the term if it is not satisfied with the creditworthiness of the borrower.

When a long-term loan is extended at a fixed interest rate, the interest rate is fixed only for the term of the loan, not for the entire amortization period. The interest rate is reset at the end of each term (or, more precisely, at the beginning of the next term, if the bank agrees to offer another term). For example, a business could arrange a 25-year (amortization period) mortgage with a five-year term. Blended payments would be devised to repay all principal after 25 years, but the interest rate would be reset after every five years. The blended payments would be recalculated, and could go up, if interest rates increased, or down, if rates decreased.

For example, assume that Medical Arts Building Limited reported a mortgage in its 30 September 20X9 disclosure notes as follows:

6.75% mortgage loan, repayable at $18,880 per month including principal and interest, due 1 April, 20X11	$2,213,335
Security for the mortgage consists of land and buildings, an assignment of insurance proceeds, and a general assignment of rents and leases.	

1 April 20X11 is the end of the *term,* but the mortgage would not be fully repaid at that time, since the $18,880 blended monthly payments are not high enough to achieve this. Instead, repayment amounts and interest rates would be renegotiated at that time.

Long-term loans with a floating interest rate can also be arranged. Floating-rate loans normally provide for an adjustment of the interest rate (and the monthly payment) at six-month intervals. The blended payments for the next six months are recalculated at that time. Like fixed-rate loans, the term of a floating-rate loan is limited so that the lender can periodically reassess the risk of the loan.

Other Sources of Long-Term Debt

For small and most medium-sized private companies, chartered banks are the major source of financing. However, large companies (both public and private) have other sources of financing available. Larger corporations can arrange loans with life insurance companies or pension funds, which have money to invest for long periods of time. Leasing companies are another source of asset-backed lending.

Bonds or Debentures Payable

A bond (or *debenture*) is a debt security issued by corporations and governments to secure large amounts of capital on a long-term basis. A bond represents a formal promise by the issuing organization to pay principal and interest in return for the capital invested.

A formal bond agreement, known as a **bond indenture,** specifies the terms of the bonds and the rights and duties of both the issuer and the bondholder. The indenture specifies any restrictions on the issuing company, the dollar amount authorized for issuance, the interest

---

long-term loans

as defined by lenders, loans with repayment terms extending beyond five years; accounting definition of long-term loans includes those due beyond the next operating cycle or fiscal year

amortization period

for debt, hypothetical period over which loan is to be repaid; used as basis for calculating periodic repayments; note that the amortization period may be longer than the actual term of the existing loan agreement, assuming renewal rate and payment dates, the maturity date, and any conversion and call privileges. An independent trustee is appointed to protect the interests of both the issuer and the investors. The trustee (usually a financial institution) maintains the necessary records and disburses interest and principal. The investors receive bond certificates, which represent the contractual obligations of the issuer to the investors.

Debt Covenants

Debt agreements often restrict the operations and financial structure of the borrower to reduce the risk of default. **Covenants** are restrictions placed on a corporation's activities as a condition of maintaining the loan. If the covenants are broken, the lender has the right to call the loan: the lender can demand immediate repayment of the principal. Bankers also refer to covenants as **maintenance tests**. Restrictions can be either accounting based or behavioural (restricted actions). Examples of each type are as follows:[3]

Accounting-Based Covenants

- Maximum debt-to-equity ratio;
- Minimum interest coverage ratio;
- Minimum inventory turnover (i.e., the relationship between cost of goods sold and inventory); and
- Restrictions on dividend payout.

Restricted Actions

- Limitations on the issuance of additional debt without the permission of the lender;
- Restrictions on dividend payments;
- Prohibition or restriction on the redemption or retirement of shares;
- Limitations on the ability of the company to pledge assets as security for other purposes;
- Requirement that current management or key employees remain in place; and
- Limitations on a transfer of control.

Reporting Example CHC Helicopter Corporation reported the following in its 2006 disclosure notes:

> The terms of certain of the Company's debt arrangements and helicopter lease arrangements impose operating and financial limitations on the Company. Such agreements limit the extent to which the Company may, among other things, incur additional indebtedness, create liens, make capital expenditures, sell or sublease assets, engage in mergers or acquisitions and make dividend and other payments. During the year ended April 30, 2006 and 2005 the Company was in compliance with all material covenants and other conditions imposed by its debt and helicopter lease agreements.

Sinking Funds

A debt agreement may require that the company establish a **sinking fund.** A sinking fund is a cash fund restricted for retiring the debt. Each year, the company pays into the sinking fund. The sinking fund may be *trusteed*, in which case the fund is handled by the trustee and the company has no access to the funds. The trustee is responsible for investing the fund in

---

[3] These examples are the most common ones cited by Bilodeau and Lanfranconi, "The Contractual Use of Accounting Numbers," *CGA Magazine*, August 1993, pp. 36–40 .

appropriate investments, which often includes the purchase of the company's bonds in the open market. Repurchase of the bonds to which the sinking fund is linked has the effect of reducing the outstanding debt.

If a fund is not trusteed, the company must maintain the cash as a separate amount and not co-mingle the sinking fund with other cash reserves. However, the investments in the fund may be invested as a part of a larger investment pool, as long as the fiduciary requirements of the debt agreement are followed.

Whether trusteed or not, the balance of the cash and investments in the sinking fund is reported as an investment on the balance sheet, usually under *investments and other assets*. The investments are accounted for as are other investments, as described in Chapter 11. The amount in the sinking fund is not offset against the company's liability unless the company is relieved of the risk of investment losses in the sinking fund once it makes the required payments into the fund.

CONCEPT REVIEW

1. How can leverage increase risk and return for common shareholders?

2. What is a blended payment?

3. What is a debt covenant?

4. If a company has a sinking fund for its long-term debt, can the company subtract the sinking fund from the debt on the balance sheet? Explain.

ACCOUNTING FOR LONG-TERM DEBT

Effective versus Nominal Interest Rates

The nominal interest rate is the interest rate stated in the loan agreement. The **effective interest rate**, or **yield**, is the true cost of borrowing. The effective interest rate is the market interest rate, for debt of similar term, security, and risk. Using the effective interest rate as the discount rate, the proceeds on issuing a liability can be calculated as:

$P = [I \times (P/A, i, n)] + [F \times (P/F, i, n)]$, where

P = current market price of the loan
I = dollar amount of each period's interest payment, or
  = nominal rate times the loan face value
F = maturity value of the loan
n = the number of periods to maturity
i = the interest rate that makes the equation work

When a liability pays the effective market interest rate, the liability will be issued for its par value, or maturity amount. When the nominal and market interest rates are different, issue proceeds will be greater or less than the maturity amount.

Example Suppose that a company issues a five-year bond with a face value of $100,000, at a nominal interest rate of 7%, to be paid annually. The company is required to pay $7,000 interest at the end of each year. If the market rate of interest is 6%, then the bond will raise $104,213 on issuance ([$7,000 × (P/A, 6%, 5)] + [$100,000 × (P/F, 6%, 5)]). (Alternatively, if one knew the issuance price, maturity amount, interest and term, one could solve for the effective interest rate using the above equation.)

Annual versus Semi-Annual Effective Rates What if interest payments are semi-annual instead of annual? If the bond sells at its face value of $100,000, the nominal rate is 3.5% per six-month period, or $3,500 per period. Is the return rate still 7%? No. Because of compounding, the effective return is slightly higher, at 7.12%. Despite the difference between the nominal rate of 7% and the real return of 7.12% for semi-annual compounding, financial markets still refer to the rate as 7% per annum. *Financial markets express interest rates in annual rates.*

That is, the lender will quote the nominal interest rate and the compounding period, and expect the borrower to understand that the real return is higher. In this case, the rate would be described as 7% per annum, compounded semi-annually. We will also, in this text, quote per annum rates and compounding periods. Just remember that if compounding is more than once per year, *the per annum interest rate understates the real return.*

Measurement of Interest Expense

Accounting for long-term debt is simple if the effective interest rate and the nominal interest rate are the same. If these two rates are the same, then the liability is issued at its maturity value. Interest is accrued as time passes, and interest payments are accounted for as cash is disbursed. Cash amounts correctly state the liability amount and interest expense.

Premium or Discount Amortization If the nominal interest rate is different from the market interest rate at the time the note is issued, the loan is issued above or below par, or at a premium or a discount. Present value techniques are used to initially value the loan, and then the initial discount or premium has to be amortized over the life of the liability. The net liability is carried on the balance sheet at amortized cost. *Amortized cost* simply means that the net liability is valued at its par value, netted with the premium or discount still on the books.

There are two methods used to amortize the premium or discount over the life of the bond: (1) the straight-line method and (2) the effective-interest method. Accounting standards clearly require the effective-interest rate method. This is the preferable method because it measures the interest cost more accurately; that is, interest expense will be a contract percentage of the liability carrying value and the cost of capital is correctly stated. Accordingly, the examples in this text will emphasize the effective-interest method. Remember, however, that when the difference between the required method and a simpler alternative method is immaterial, either can be used, and thus the straight-line method will be encountered in practice.

Example Assume that Fema Company purchased equipment on 1 January 20X5, and issued a two-year, $10,000 note with a 3% stated or nominal interest rate at a time when the market rate of interest for debt of similar term and risk is about 8%. Interest is payable each 31 December and the entire principal is payable 31 December 20X6. The $10,000 principal amount is called the *face value, maturity value* or *par value.* The 8% market rate is known as the borrower's incremental borrowing rate (IBR) and is the rate for a loan with similar term and similar security.

Since the nominal interest rate is less than the market rate, the principal amount of the note will not be used to value the transaction. Recording the asset and the liability at the face value of $10,000 will not only overstate both the asset and the liability, but also understate the interest expense in each year because interest would be recorded at 3% instead of the "true" rate of 8%. Instead, the transaction is valued at the loan's present value. At 8%, the present value of the note is computed as follows:

Present value of maturity amount:
$10,000 × (P/F, 8%, 2) = $10,000 × (.85734) = $8,573

Present value of the nominal interest payments:
$10,000 × 3% × (P/A, 8%, 2) = $300 × (1.78326) =   535

Present value of the note at 8% $9,108

Initially, the note and the capital asset should be recorded on the books at its present value. The difference between face value and present value ($10,000 − $9,108 = $892) represents the *discount* on the note, or implicit interest in addition to the 3% cash payments. This is amortized to interest expense over the life of the liability.

Effective-Interest Method Under the effective-interest method, the interest expense for each period is calculated as the outstanding net liability balance times the effective interest rate. The outstanding liability balance is calculated as the face value less any discount or plus any premium. The amount of cash outflow is governed by the nominal rate. Amortization is the difference between the effective-interest calculation and the cash outflow. In the example for Fema Company, the entries are:

1 January 20X5—issue note		
Equipment	9,108	
Discount on long-term notes payable		
(contra notes payable)	892	
Long-term notes payable		10,000
The outstanding liability is $9,108 ($10,000 − $892)		
31 December 20X5—interest, effective-interest method		
Interest expense ($9,108 × 8%)	729	
Discount on long-term notes payable ($729 − $300)		429
Cash		300
The outstanding liability is $9,537: [$10,000 − ($892 − $429)]		
31 December 20X6—interest		
Interest expense ($9,537 × 8%)	763	
Discount on long-term notes payable ($763 − $300)		463
Cash		300
The outstanding liability is $10,000: [($10,000 − ($463 − $463)]		
31 December 20X6—note maturity		
Long-term notes payable	10,000	
Cash		10,000

In this example, there is a significant difference between the nominal interest rate of 3% and the market rate of 8%. The effect of simply accepting the 3% nominal rate as the basis for accounting is that the cost of the equipment would be overstated, at $10,000 instead of $9,108, and the interest expense would be understated, as $600 over the two years instead of $1,492 (that is, $600 plus the discount of $892). Note that a financial statement reader can easily determine the effective cost of borrowing by dividing interest expense by the carrying value of the loan (e.g., in 20X5, $729 ÷ (carrying value during the year, $9,108) = 8%).

Straight-Line Method The straight-line method of discount amortization is acceptable *only* if it yields results not materially different from the effective-interest method. Under the straight-line method, Fema amortizes $446 ($892 ÷ 2) of the discount and recognizes $746 of interest expense ($300 + $446) each period. Interest expense for any period is the amount of cash paid out (based on the nominal interest rate) plus discount amortization or minus premium amortization. While simple, the cost of capital may be inaccurately conveyed. For example, in 20X5, interest expense would be $746; divide this by the carrying value during the year of $9,108, and the cost of capital appears to be 8.2%. While that doesn't look like much, cost of capital is highly sensitive and a difference of 0.2% is material.

Bond Price Quotations Liabilities are traded in financial markets, priced at present value. Bond prices are based on discounted present values. They are stated as a percentage of face, or par, value. A $100,000 bond with a price of 92 would sell for $92,000. If the price were 103, it would sell for $103,000.

Subsequent Changes in Fair Value After issuance, the fair value of the liability will change due to changes in the market rate of interest. The price may also change in response to changes in the creditworthiness of the issuing company, for which the market will demand a higher (or lower) rate of interest.

Impact of Changing Fair Value Changes in fair market value of a liability subsequent to the liability's initial issuance *are not recorded* in the issuing company's financial reports. The only market price differential that has an impact on the financial statements of the issuing company is the difference between face value and market value *at the date of issuance.* Fair market values are disclosed, however.

Balance Sheet Classification On a classified balance sheet, long-term loans are obviously classified as long-term liabilities. However, the portion of *principal* that is due within the next year (or operating cycle) is classified as a current liability. Any accrued interest at the balance sheet date is also classified as a current liability. The usual practice is to disclose the total amount of any outstanding long-term bonds or loan, and then to adjust for the reclassification of the amount due within the next year as a current liability. This disclosure can be shown either in the notes to the financial statements or on the face of the balance sheet. An example is given later, in Exhibit 12-7.

Sometimes a company will make an arrangement to refinance a maturing long-term liability. For example, say that a long-term loan will come due in 20X8. By the end of 20X7, plans are underway to replace this long-term loan with a new long-term loan. Does the maturing loan have to be classified as a current liability at the end of 20X7? The answer to that is *if* the plans are far enough along that there is a contractual commitment for the replacement financing, the amount may be left as long term. If the plans have *not been firmed up* through a legally enforceable arrangement, then the maturing loan is a current liability at the end of 20X7.

Bonds Payable

Example To illustrate accounting for bonds payable, assume that on 1 January 20X5, Gresham Limited, a calendar-year firm, issues $100,000 of 7% debentures dated 1 January 20X5, which pay interest each 31 December. The bonds mature on 31 December 20X9. Notice the simplifying assumptions: this bond is for only a five-year term, and pays interest annually at the end of Gresham's fiscal year. (Always assume that the effective interest rate is quoted for compounding periods identical to those offered by the bond unless told otherwise.)

1. The **face value** or *par value* (also called *maturity*, or *principal value*) of a bond is the amount payable when the bond is due ($100,000 for Gresham).

2. The **maturity date** is the end of the bond term and the due date for the face value (31 December 20X9, for Gresham).

3. The **nominal interest rate** (also called *the coupon, stated,* or *contractual rate*) is the rate that determines periodic interest payments. For Gresham, the nominal rate is 7%, paid annually.

4. The **interest payment dates** are the dates the periodic interest payments are due (31 December for Gresham). Gresham pays $7,000 interest on the $100,000 bond on each 31 December regardless of the issue price or market rate of interest at date of issue.

5. The **bond date** (authorization date) is the earliest date the bond can be issued land represents the planned issuance date of the bond issue (1 January 20X5 for Gresham).

Three situations will illustrate accounting for bonds, under different effective interest rate assumptions:

Situation A: Effective interest rate = 7%
Situation B: Effective interest rate = 6%
Situation C: Effective interest rate = 8%

Situation A The bond will sell at face value because the market and stated interest rates are both 7%. The price of the bonds will be equal to the present value of the future cash flows at the market rate of 7%:

Issue price = [$100,000 × (P/F, 7%, 5)] + [($100,000 × 7%) × (P/A, 7%, 5)]
            = $100,000

When the bonds are issued, the issuer records a long-term liability, and interest is recorded as time passes. The bond is repaid at maturity.

1 January 20X5—issue bonds		
Cash	100,000	
Bonds payable		100,000
31 December each year, 20X5 through		
* 20X9—interest payment*		
Interest expense	7,000	
Cash ($100,000 × 7%)		7,000
31 December 20X9—bond maturity		
Bonds payable	100,000	
Cash		100,000

Interest expense for bonds issued at face value equals the amount of the interest payment. The book value of the bonds remains $100,000 to maturity. Changes in the fair market value of the bond, caused by changes in the market rate of interest subsequent to the issuance date, are not recognized in the financial statements.

Situation B The market rate of interest is 6%; the bonds sell at a premium.

Issue price = [$100,000 × (P/F, 6%, 5)] + [($100,000 × 7%) × (P/A, 6%, 5)]
            = $104,213

The bonds sell at a *premium* because they pay a stated rate that exceeds the market rate on similar bonds. The initial $4,213 premium is recorded in an account titled *premium on bonds payable*, which is shown with the bonds payable account on the balance sheet. The following entry is made to record the issue:

1 January 20X5—issue bonds		
Cash	104,213	
Bonds payable		100,000
Premium on bonds payable		4,213

Total interest expense over the term of a bond is *not* equal to total cash interest when a bond is sold at a premium or discount. Instead, interest expense must equal the total cash payments required by the bond (face value and interest) less the aggregate issue price. Total interest expense is as is shown by this calculation:

Face value	$100,000
Total cash interest: 7% × $100,000 × 5 years	35,000
Total cash payments required by bond	135,000
Issue price	104,213
Total interest expense for bond term ($35,000 − $4,213)	$ 30,787

Gresham received $4,213 more than face value at issuance but will pay only face value at maturity. Therefore, the effective rate is less than the stated rate, and total interest expense for Gresham over the bond term is *less* than total interest paid.

Amortization The premium or discount must be completely amortized over the bond term, using the effective-interest method, so that net book value equals face value at maturity. Amortized premium reduces periodic interest expense relative to interest paid, and amortized discount increases interest expense. The net bond liability equals face value plus the remaining unamortized bond premium or less the remaining unamortized bond discount. The following entries illustrate this amortization:

31 December 20X5		
Interest expense ($104,213 × 6%)	6,253	
Premium on bonds payable	747	
Cash ($100,000 × 7%)		7,000
The carrying value of the bond is now $103,466		
($104,213 − $747)		
31 December 20X6		
Interest expense ($103,466 × 6%)	6,208	
Premium on bonds payable	792	
Cash		7,000
The carrying value of the bond is now $102,674		
($103,466 − $792)		

The bonds are disclosed in the long-term liability section of Gresham's 31 December 20X6, balance sheet as follows:

Bonds payable	$100,000
Premium on bonds payable ($4,213 − $747 − $792)	2,674
Net book value of bonds payable	$102,674

Interest expense under the effective-interest method is the product of the effective interest rate (6%) and net liability balance at the beginning of the period. In effect, the company returns part of the original "excess" proceeds with each interest payment. In 20X5, this amount is $747, which reduces the net bond liability at the beginning of 20X6. Consequently, 20X6 interest expense is less than that for 20X5.

Proof of Book Value The book value of the bonds at 31 December 20X6 is the present value of remaining cash flows *using the effective interest rate at the date of issuance:*

$$PV_{31/12/20X6} = [\$100,000 \times (P/F, 6\%, 3)] + [(\$100,000 \times 7\%) \times (P/A, 6\%, 3)]$$
$$= \$102,674$$

An amortization table is often prepared to support bond journal entries. The table gives all the data necessary for journal entries over the term of the bond and each year's ending net liability balance. An amortization table is shown in Exhibit 12-2.

Straight-Line Amortization If straight-line amortization were to be used, then the $4,213 premium would be amortized over the five-year term of the bond, at the rate of $843 ($4,213 ÷ 5) per year. This produces interest expense of $6,157 ($7,000 − $843) annually. The premium is reduced to zero at the maturity date of the bond, and interest expense is less than interest paid. As compared to the effective-interest method, interest expense is not as accurately measured.

Situation C The market rate of interest is 8%; the bonds sell at a discount.

$$\text{Issue price} = [\$100,000 \times (P/F, 8\%, 5)] + [(\$100,000 \times 7\%) \times (P/A, 8\%, 5)]$$
$$= \$96,007$$

The Gresham bonds sell at a discount in this case because the stated rate is less than the yield rate on similar bonds. The discount is recorded in the discount on bonds payable account, a contra-liability valuation account, which is subtracted from bonds payable to yield the net liability. The entries for the first two years after the bond issuance follow, along with an amortization table (Exhibit 12-3) and the relevant portion of the balance sheet after two years.

EXHIBIT 12-2

AMORTIZATION TABLE FOR GRESHAM LIMITED BONDS

Situation B—Bonds Sold at Premium; Effective interest amortization

Date	Interest Payment @ 7%	Interest Expense @ 6%	Premium Amortization[1]	Unamortized Premium[2]	Net bond Liability[3]
1 Jan. 20X5				$4,213	$104,213
31 Dec. 20X5	$ 7,000	$ 6,253	$ 747	3,466	103,466
31 Dec. 20X6	7,000	6,208	792	2,674	102,674
31 Dec. 20X7	7,000	6,160	840	1,834	101,834
31 Dec. 20X8	7,000	6,110	890	944	100,944
31 Dec. 20X9	7,000	6,056	944	0	100,000
	$35,000	$30,787	$4,213		

[1] Interest payment − Interest expense
[2] Previous unamortized premium − Current period's amortization
[3] $100,000 face value + Current unamortized premium

EXHIBIT 12-3

AMORTIZATION TABLE FOR GRESHAM LIMITED BONDS

Situation C—Bonds Sold at Discount

Date	Interest Payment @ 7%	Interest Expense @ 8%	Discount Amortization[1]	Unamortized Discount[2]	Net Bond Liability[3]
1 Jan. 20X5				$3,993	$ 96,007
31 Dec. 20X5	$ 7,000	$ 7,681	$ 681	3,312	96,688
31 Dec. 20X6	7,000	7,735	735	2,577	97,423
31 Dec. 20X7	7,000	7,794	794	1,783	98,217
31 Dec. 20X8	7,000	7,857	857	926	99,074
31 Dec. 20X9	7,000	7,926	926	0	100,000
	$35,000	$38,993	$3,993		

[1] Interest expense − Interest payment
[2] Previous unamortized discount − Current period's amortization
[3] $100,000 face value − Current unamortized discount

Portion of Long-Term Liability Section of Balance Sheet

31 December 20X6

Bonds payable	$100,000
Discount on bonds payable	(2,577)
Net book value of bonds payable	$ 97,423

Journal entries

1 January 20X5—issue bonds		
Cash	96,007	
Discount on bonds payable	3,993	
Bonds payable		100,000
31 December 20X5—interest expense		
Interest expense	7,681*	
Discount on bonds payable		681
Cash ($100,000 × 7%)		7,000
*$7,681 = $96,007 × 8%		
31 December 20X6—interest expense		
Interest expense	7,735*	
Discount on bonds payable		735
Cash ($100,000 × 7%)		7,000
*$7,735 = ($96,007 + $681) × 8%		

Exhibit 12-4 summarizes several aspects of bond accounting. The exhibit relates to bonds with semi-annual interest payments, which is the usual situation.

EXHIBIT 12-4

SUMMARY TABLE: ACCOUNTING FOR BONDS
(assuming semi-annual interest payments)

Price of bond issue = Present value of the cash flow to the investor
= Discounted principal payments + Discounted interest payment annuity
= [(Face value) × (P/F, i, n)] +
   [(Face value × s) × (P/A, i, n)]

Where: i = effective interest rate *per six-month period*
n = number of semi-annual periods in bond term
s = stated (nominal) interest rate per six-month period

Discount or premium =
When effective rate (i) exceeds stated rate (s):
   Initial discount = Face value − Price of bond issue

When stated rate (s) exceeds effective rate (i):
   Initial premium = Price of bond issue − Face value

Net book value of bonds = Face value *plus* unamortized premium or *minus* unamortized discount

As Maturity Approaches:	Premium	Discount
The unamortized amount	Declines	Declines
The net book value	Declines	Increases
Annual interest expense	Declines*	Increases*

*Under effective-interest method; constant under straight-line method.

Two Methods of Amortizing Premium and Discount:

	Effective Interest	Straight Line
Calculations:		
Calculation of interest expense	Discount rate × Net carrying value of bond	Cash paid + Discount amortization or − Premium amortization
Calculation of discount or premium amortization	Difference between cash paid and expense	Discount or premium ÷ Period that bond is outstanding
Patterns:		
Annual interest expense	Changes each year	Constant over term
Annual interest expense as a percentage of beginning book value	Constant over term	Changes each year

Interest Dates Different from Statement Dates

The preceding situations all specified interest dates that coincided with the fiscal year-end. However, this coincidence is not frequent in practice. When the end of a fiscal period falls between interest dates, it is necessary to accrue interest from the last (previous) interest date, and to bring the bond discount/premium amortization up to date.

For example, assume the facts for Situation C for Gresham Limited bonds, except that the fiscal year-end is 30 September. The bonds are issued on the bond date, 1 January 20X5, and interest is payable annually on 31 December. On 30 September 20X5, interest must be accrued and discount amortized: *Issued @ Jan 1   YIE @ Sept 30   Int. Dec 31*

30 September 20X5—interest accrued		
Interest expense[1]	5,761	
Accrued interest payable[2]		5,250
Discount on bonds payable[3]		511

[1] $7,681 (first full year's expense) × 9/12
[2] $100,000 × 7% × 9/12
[3] $681 (first full year's amortization) × 9/12

The amortization is derived from the amortization table in Exhibit 12-3 and is allocated evenly over the period between interest dates. The loan balance is not recalculated and included in the table, because compounding is tied to interest dates and not to reporting periods. That is, an amortization table is always based on the *bond's* dates and terms. Then it is possible to adjust calculations to fit the fiscal year.

When the interest is paid on 31 December, the following entry is made, assuming that the interest accrual has not been reversed:

31 December 20X5—interest payment		
Interest expense[1]	1,920	
Accrued interest payable	5,250	
Discount on bonds payable[2]		170
Cash		7,000

[1] $7,681 × 3/12
[2] $681 × 3/12

Bonds Issued between Interest Dates

In the previous examples, bonds were sold on their issue date, an assumption chosen in order to emphasize the accounting principles regarding effective interest rates and bond amortization. However, bonds may not necessarily be sold on their initial issue date. Bonds that are sold at some time later than their initial issue date are sold at a price that reflects the future cash flows discounted to the actual date of sale.

For example, suppose that the Gresham Limited bonds are sold on 1 January 20X6 instead of on their bond date of 1 January 20X5. The price of the bonds will be the present value of the future cash flows from interest ($7,000 per year for *four* years) and principal ($100,000 received *four* years hence). If the market rate of interest is 8% (Situation C), the price of the bonds will be:

Issue price = [$100,000 × (P/F, 8%, 4)] + [($100,000 × 7%) × (P/A, 8%, 4)]
          = $96,688

This price can be verified by referring to the net bond liability shown in Exhibit 12-3 for 31 December 20X5. The discount will be amortized over the four years remaining until maturity.

More often, the delayed issuance of the bonds does not coincide with an interest date but is *between interest dates*. In this case, the bond issue price cannot be directly calculated as a present value figure, since the present value figure must be at a particular interest date. Instead, the present value of the bond must be calculated as of the two interest dates (one before, one after) the issuance date. The difference between these two values is then pro-rated to the issuance date.

For example, if the Gresham bonds in Exhibit 12-3 were issued on 1 March 20X5 when the effective interest rate was 8%, the proceeds would be $96,121. This is $96,007 present value on 1 January 20X5 plus 2/12 of the $681 difference between the present value of the bond on 1 January 20X5 and the $96,688 present value on 31 December 20X5. The present value has to be calculated twice and the difference pro-rated.

Accrued Interest When bonds are sold between interest dates, the cash collected also includes interest accrued since the last interest date. Accrued interest is added to the price because the holder of the bonds on any interest date receives the full amount of interest since the last interest date, even if he or she bought the bonds only the week before.

Example Assume that the Gresham Limited bonds are sold on 1 June 20X5, five months after the bond date but seven months before the next interest date. The holders of the bonds on 31 December 20X5 will receive the full 12-month interest payment of $7,000, despite the fact that they held the bonds for only seven months. To compensate for the fact that they have earned only seven months' interest but will receive 12 months' interest, they pay the issuing company for the interest for the period that they did not hold the bonds.

Assume that Gresham received net proceeds of $96,291 for the bond, plus accrued interest of $2,917. Note that:

- The $96,291 proceeds is $96,007 plus 5/12 of the $681 difference between the two surrounding present values.
- Interest of $2,917 is five months' accrued interest ($100,000 $\times$ 7% $\times$ 5/12).

The bond issuance will be recorded by Gresham Limited as follows:

1 June 20X5—initial issuance of bonds		
Cash ($96,291 + $2,917)	99,208	
Discount on bonds payable[1]	3,709	
Interest expense[2]		2,917
Bonds payable		100,000
[1] $100,000 − $96,291		
[2] $100,000 $\times$ 7% $\times$ 5/12		

Initial Discount Amortization After a bond is issued between interest dates, the discount amortization will be the amount needed to get the bond to the "end point" in the amortization schedule at the end of the relevant period. For this bond, the issuance proceeds were $96,291 and the 20X5 period ends with an amortized value of $96,688 in the table. Therefore, amortization of $397 is needed ($96,688 − $96,291).

When the company pays the $7,000 interest on 31 December 20X5, the entry to record the interest payment and the discount amortization will be as follows:

31 December 20X5—payment of interest and amortization of discount		
Interest expense	7,397	
Cash		7,000
Discount on bonds payable ($96,291 − $96,688)		397

The initial credit of $2,917 to interest expense when the bonds were issued offsets the actual interest payment of $7,000 plus discount amortization of $397 on 31 December 20X5, leaving a debit balance of $4,480 to flow through to the income statement. This represents seven months' expense.

When the bonds were issued, the accrued interest portion of the proceeds could have been credited to *interest payable* instead of interest expense; the debit for the payment of interest on 31 December would then have to be split between interest expense and interest payable. The entries would appear as follows. They are identical to those shown above, except where shown in bold type:

1 June 20X5		
Cash	99,208	
Discount on bonds payable	3,709	
Interest payable		**2,917**
Bonds payable		100,000
31 December 20X5		
Interest expense	**4,480**	
Interest payable ($7,000 × 5/12)	**2,917**	
Cash		7,000
Discount on bonds payable		397

Observations on Bond Amortization

Bond discount or premium is amortized in order to measure the "true" cost of debt. Remember that the cost of capital is a sensitive issue for many companies. However, bond amortization is a form of interperiod allocation, departing (as all interperiod allocations do) from the underlying cash flow as the basis of financial reporting. The effective-interest method of amortization achieves a constant *rate* of interest expense over the life of the bond, while the straight-line method achieves a constant *amount* of interest expense each year.

This chapter has emphasized the use of the effective-interest method of amortization. The effective-interest method is the method prescribed by accounting standards, because it best reflects the underlying basis of valuation for long-term debt. It also is the method used in other major areas of long-term liability accounting, such as lease accounting (Chapter 17) and pension accounting (Chapter 18).

Accounting measurement is based on the *historical* interest rate and market value as of the date of issuance. Amortization does not reflect *current* market interest rates or market values. Therefore, the only inherent advantage of the effective-interest method is that it provides a measure of interest expense (and liability valuation) that reflects the present value process by which the liability was originally valued and recorded.

Debt Issue Cost

Debt issue cost includes legal, accounting, underwriting, commission, engraving, printing, registration, and promotion costs. These costs are paid by the issuer and reduce the *net proceeds* from the debt issue, thus increasing the overall cost for the issuer.

Accounting standards require that debt issue cost be recorded and amortized independently, reducing the net proceeds of the bond issue. In theory, there are two ways of amortizing debt issue costs:

1. On a straight-line basis over the life of the bond; or

2. On an effective-interest basis, proportionate to the amortization of the debt discount or premium.

Often, the straight-line method is used in practice, due to the relatively small amounts involved.

Alternatively, dept issue costs may be expensed immediately but this will misrepresent the cost of capital if the amounts are material.

When debt issue costs are amortized, the additional expense is usually added to interest expense on the income statement. Alternatively, it can be included in "other financing expense." When the amortization expense is included in interest expense, it does not need to be disclosed separately.

On the balance sheet, companies must deduct the debt issue cost from the total long-term liabilities. The amount acts as an additional discount. In the past, companies have reported these issuance costs as deferred charges, but they do not meet the test for an internally developed intangible asset, and thus do not meet the requirements for asset recognition. If the issue costs are material, they must be disclosed in the detailed note disclosure of long-term debt.

Upfront Fees

Banks often charge upfront administrative fees to process a loan application. If the bank decides *not* to extend the loan, the bank will report the fee as revenue immediately, and the prospective borrower will charge the fee to expense. If the loan *is* extended, the borrower will treat the fee as part of the loan. In effect, the fee increases the loan's effective interest rate. For example, assume that a firm borrows $100,000 for two years, and agrees to pay 7%, with interest paid annually. In addition, the bank charges the firm an administrative fee of $3,520 on the day the loan is granted. The lender will advance the borrower the net proceeds, or $96,480 ($100,000 − $3,520), at the inception of the loan.

The effective interest rate inherent in the cash flow pattern, including the fee, has to be calculated, in order to determine the effective interest rate charged. The payments to the lender are $3,520 at the beginning of the loan, $7,000 at the end of years 1 and 2, and then the principal after two years. That is,

$$\$100,000 = \$3,520 + [\$7,000 \times (P/A, i, 2)] + [\$100,000 \times (P/F, i, 2)] \text{, or}$$
$$\$\ 96,480 = [\$7,000 \times (P/A, i, 2)] + [\$100,000 \times (P/F, i, 2)]$$

Since the cash flow streams are uneven, this calculation must be done with a financial calculator or computer spreadsheet with the IRR function. The discount rate that will equate the cash flow streams to the principal amount of $100,000 is 9%.

Accounting for the transaction is as follows:

At the inception of the loan		
Cash	96,480	
Deferred financing cost	3,520	
Bank loan payable		100,000
At the end of the first year, to record interest expense		
Interest expense[1]	8,683	
Deferred financing cost		1,683
Cash[2]		7,000

[1] $96,480 × 9%
[2] $100,000 × 7%

At the end of the second year, to record interest expense		
Interest expense[1]	8,837	
Deferred financing cost		1,837
Cash		7,000

[1] ($96,480 + $1,683) × 9%, rounded by $2

Note that interest expense is measured using the effective-interest method. After the second entry, the balance in the deferred financing cost account is zero.

Liabilities Held for Trading

Throughout the foregoing discussion, we have said that a financial liability should be recorded at amortized cost. There is one exception to this rule. The financial instruments rules require that an entity should measure financial liabilities that are classified as held for trading at *fair value*. A financial liability held for trading is one that is incurred mostly for the purpose of selling or repurchasing in the short term, or is part of a portfolio of financial instruments that are managed together and for which there is evidence of a recent actual pattern of short-term profit taking.

Financial institutions are the major example of organizations that have financial liabilities held for trading. This provision is not relevant for other enterprises in the normal course of business.

CONCEPT REVIEW

1. How does a premium on bond payable arise? What does it represent?

2. For a bond to sell at par, what must be the relationship between the nominal rate and the effective rate of interest? At a discount? At a premium?

3. What are the two methods of amortizing premium or discount? Which method is recommended by accounting standards?

4. How should unamortized debt issue costs be reported in the financial statements?

DEBT RETIREMENT

Derecognition

When debt is put on the balance sheet, it is *recognized*. When it is removed from the balance sheet, it is **derecognized** or *extinguished*. The vast majority of financial liabilities, both current and long term, are derecognized through the normal course of events by paying the amount of the liability to the creditor or bond holder at maturity. Sometimes, however, debt is repaid before its maturity, either by arrangement with the debt holder or through open-market transactions. In this section, we will illustrate both "normal" debt retirement and early extinguishment of debt.

Derecognition at Maturity

Debt retirement at maturity is straightforward. By the time the debt reaches full maturity, all of the discount or premium is fully amortized, thereby making the carrying value of the debt equal to its face value. As well, any debt issue cost will be fully amortized.

For example, assume that a company pays the full amount of an outstanding $1,000,000 bond at maturity. The entry to record extinguishment of the debt is:

Bonds payable	1,000,000	
Cash		1,000,000

There are no gains or losses to be recorded. Any costs incurred to retire the bond (such as trustee management fees, clerical costs, or payment fees) will be charged immediately to expense.

Early Extinguishment

Borrowers will sometimes retire debt before maturity. Retirement of debt improves the debt-to-equity ratio and can facilitate future debt issuances. Bonds may be purchased on the open market. In an open-market purchase of bonds, the issuer pays the market price, as would any investor buying the bonds.

Alternatively, the terms for early retirement might set out in the original bond indenture. Bonds may be **redeemable**, which means that the *borrower* may pay back the loan using a **call option** that sets a specific price at a specific time prior to maturity. *Investors can force repayment* of a bond if the bond is **retractable**.

If bonds carry a call privilege, the issuer may retire the debt by paying the call price during a specified period. Typically, the **call price** exceeds face value by a modest premium (e.g., 5%), which may decline each year of the bond term.

call price

price set by the company at which investors can be required/allowed to submit bonds for redemption

Fair Value and the Gain or Loss A major incentive for retiring bonds before maturity is the change in fair value that is caused if interest rates increase. When interest rates increase, the fair market value of an existing liability will decline, because the discount rate has increased. The fair value will then rest below book value. If the liability is retired at its fair value, the company will record a gain on retirement.

If interest rates *drop* (causing bond prices to *rise*), firms can retire existing, more expensive bonds by buying them on the open market at a loss, and then issuing new bonds with lower interest rates. A *loss* occurs in this case because bond prices have increased above book value. However, the new, lower-rate bonds will reduce the cash flow for interest as well as the reported interest expense in each future year. If the bonds are callable and market interest rates decline, the bonds can be called at their stated call price, which will reduce the loss incurred by the retirement.

Recording Early Debt Retirement Accounting for debt retirement prior to maturity involves:

- Updating interest expense to the retirement date, through recording interest payable, discount or premium amortization, and related debt issue costs;
- Removing the liability accounts, including the appropriate portion of the premium or discount and bond issue costs;
- Recording the transfer of cash, other resources, or the issuance of new debt securities; and
- Recording a gain or loss.

Gains or losses on bond retirements may be classified either as *ordinary* gains and losses or as *unusual* items, depending on their frequency and the circumstances surrounding the transaction. They may not be classified as extraordinary, because such transactions are carried out in the normal course of operations and are a management decision.

As a basis for an example, Exhibit 12-5 repeats a portion of the amortization table for the Gresham bonds from Exhibit 12-2. Assume that interest rates have increased since the bonds were issued, and assume that on 1 March 20X6, Gresham purchases 20% ($20,000 face value) of the bonds on the open market at 90. The price decline reflects increased market interest rates. Gresham has undertaken this transaction because the company has idle funds and wishes to reduce its debt-to-equity ratio.

The $2,667 gain on bond retirement is the difference between the net book value of the bond and the cash paid on retirement. Brokerage fees and other costs of retiring the bonds also decrease the gain or increase the loss.

Extinguishment does not affect the accounting for the remaining 80% of the bond issue; 80% of the values in the amortization table would be used for the remaining bond term.

EXHIBIT 12-5

OPEN-MARKET EXTINGUISHMENT
Gresham Limited Bonds

Data:

Issue date: 1 January 20X5
Stated (nominal) interest rate: 7% per annum
Interest payment date: 31 December

Maturity date: 31 December 20X9
Bond repurchase date: 1 March 20X6
Bond face value extinguished: $20,000

Total face value: $100,000
Bond date: 1 January 20X5
Yield rate at issuance: 6% per annum

Bond repurchase price: 90

Partial Amortization Table

Date	Interest payment @ 7%	Interest expense @ 6%	Premium amortization	Unamortized Premium	Net bond liability
1 Jan. 20X5				$4,213	$104,213
31 Dec. 20X5	$7,000	$6,253	$747	3,466	103,466
31 Dec. 20X6	7,000	6,208	792	2,674	102,674

Entries:

1 March 20X6—update interest and premium amortization on portion retired

Interest expense	207[1]	
Premium on bonds payable	26	
Interest payable		233[2]

1 March 20X6—record purchase of bonds; eliminate relevant accounts and recognize gain

Bonds payable	20,000	
Premium on bonds payable	667[3]	
Interest payable	233	
Cash		18,233[4]
Gain on bond redemption		2,667

Calculations

[1] 6% × $103,466 × 2/12 × 20% of the bond issue being redeemed
[2] $20,000 bonds being redeemed × 7% × 2/12
[3] ($3,466 unamortized bond premium × 20% being redeemed)
  − $26 amortized in previous entry
[4] $20,000 being redeemed × 90% purchase price + $233 interest payable

Extinguishment of Bonds by Refunding

When a **refunding** takes place, one bond issue is replaced with another bond issue. The two basic reasons for refunding are:

1. To give management greater flexibility by retiring a bond that has restrictive covenants; and

2. To take advantage of lower market interest rates.

One way of refunding is to issue new bonds in direct exchange for the old bonds. Obviously, the lender has to be agreeable to this scheme. A residual amount of cash is involved if the two bond issues have different fair market values (present values). More frequently, however, the proceeds from a new bond issue are used to retire the old issue because the holders of the old issue do not necessarily wish to become the new creditors. In both cases, the accounting for refunding is similar to all other forms of debt retirement.

Example Assume that on 1 January 20X5, WestCal Corporation issued $100,000 of 10-year, 6% bonds at face value with interest payable each 30 June and 31 December. On 1 January 20X9, WestCal issues at face value $105,000 of 20-year, 5% bonds with the same interest dates as the 6% bonds. The market price of the old bonds is 105. The old bonds are retired.

1 January 20X9—issue 5% bonds		
Cash	105,000	
Bonds payable		105,000
1 January 20X9—retire 6% bonds		
Bonds payable	100,000	
Loss on bond extinguishment	5,000	
Cash		105,000

The accounting loss of $5,000 is caused by the decrease in interest rates between the time the 6% bonds were issued and the time they were retired.

Defeasance

A transaction called a **defeasance** may be used to engineer derecognition of a bond liability without formally repaying it; repayment is often not appealing to the investor. To set the stage for a defeasance, the bond indenture will contain a provision that permits the corporation that issued the bonds to transfer investments into an irrevocable, trusteed fund. The trustee is then responsible for interest and principal payments on the debt, using money generated by the investments. If and when such a trust is set up and fully funded, accounting standards allow the liability to be derecognized. The bonds still exist, but the trust assumes all responsibility for them, and the issuer has no further liability. Furthermore, the *investor has consented* to the transaction as part of the original bond indenture. The entry to record a defeasance is a debit to the liability account and credit to cash or investments, with a gain or loss recorded for any difference in amounts.

Example Assume that a bond with a par value of $100,000 and remaining unamortized premium is *defeased* according to the terms of the bond indenture for $92,600. The $92,600 is the present value of the bond payments, discounted at market rates, or the investment required in interest-bearing securities that will yield interest and principal amounts to cover the required cash flows for the bond. The following entry would be made:

Bonds payable (par value)	100,000	
Premium on bonds payable (remaining balance)	6,000	
Cash		92,600
Gain on bond defeasance		13,400

Taking the liability off the books in essence nets the liability with the investments segregated for liability repayment. Netting is not allowed unless very stringent criteria are met, and an important criterion for netting is that the *borrower has a legal release from the creditor.* The agreement in the bond indenture establishes this release.

In-Substance Defeasance In-substance defeasance established a trust for bond interest and principal repayment *even though the original bond indenture was silent on the possibility.* In essence, it established the trust without creditor permission or perhaps even creditor knowledge of the arrangement. In the past, an in-substance extinguishment was recorded, derecognizing the bonds and setting up a gain or loss, if certain criteria were met. Under new accounting standards, this is no longer allowed because there is no legal release provided by the creditor. Using current standards, the company would record a separate investment account if funds were transferred to the trustee, and then would continue to report an investment and a liability.

The Concern with In-Substance Defeasance Standard setters had many reasons to be concerned about in-substance defeasance transactions recorded as extinguishments.

Companies had a tendency to set up an in-substance defeasance if interest rates increased. The increase in interest rates would reduce the amount of investments needed to fully service the related debt, and reduce the market value of the debt. The defeasance transaction would then result in a gain for the company. This might allow management an avenue to manipulate net income. In-substance defeasance rarely was undertaken when interest rates fell and a loss ensued.

Another concern of standard setters was that the borrowing company would have debt legally outstanding that was not reported on the balance sheet. This situation did not appeal to the basic representational faithfulness of balance sheet reporting. Finally, standard setters were concerned that something might go awry with the trust or the debt to make the in-substance defeasance economically or legally unsuccessful. For example, if the debt were subject to financial statement covenants, and the covenants were breached, then the debt might become due immediately. If this happened, the investments in the trusteed fund would not be sufficient to repay principal, because they needed time to mature to reach maturity value. For all these reasons, debt may not be extinguished through an in-substance defeasance.

CONCEPT REVIEW

1. If gains and losses on debt retirement seldom occur, why are they not classified as extraordinary items?

2. What is a retractable bond?

3. Under current accounting standards, what are the accounting implications of a defeasance transaction? An in-substance defeasance?

FOREIGN EXCHANGE ISSUES

Many Canadian companies borrow from foreign lenders. The most common source of non-Canadian financing is the United States, both through U.S. banks and other financial institutions and, for a few large public companies, through the bond markets. Corporations also borrow in other currencies, such as euros, Japanese yen, etc. Of the 200 Canadian public companies included in *Financial Reporting in Canada 2006*, 111 had long-term debt denominated in a foreign currency.[4]

The most obvious point about these loans is that they may subject the borrowing company to an additional form of risk, that of exchange fluctuations. For example, if a company borrows US$100,000 when the exchange rate for US$1.00 is Cdn$1.05, the company will receive Cdn$105,000. If the exchange rate changes to US$1.00 = Cdn$1.12 by the time that the debt must be repaid, the company will have to pay Cdn$112,000 to buy US$100,000 dollars for debt principal repayment, and thus have to repay more than it borrowed. This $7,000 difference ($105,000 less $112,000) is called an *exchange loss*, and it is equal to the change in the exchange rates multiplied by the principal: ($1.05 − $1.12) × US$100,000.

Note that exchange rates can be expressed in U.S. dollar equivalencies, as shown above, where US$1.00 = Cdn$1.05, or can be described as Canadian dollar equivalencies, Cdn$1.00 = US$0.9524 (that is, $1.00 ÷ $1.05). There are also differences between buying and selling exchange rates, as quoted by exchange brokers or banks; the brokers make their profit on the spread between the buying and selling rates.

Hedging Companies may take a number of actions to reduce their risk of losses (and gains) from changes in exchange rates. These actions are called **hedges**, and often involve arranging equal and offsetting cash flows in the desired currency. Hedging will be explored in Chapter 14.

hedge

a protective measure; to enter into a transaction intended to offset the risk assumed in another transaction; to arrange for the matching of amounts and timing of sources and uses of cash, interest rates, foreign currency transactions, etc.

ACCOUNTING FOR FOREIGN CURRENCY–DENOMINATED DEBT

The basic principle underlying balance sheet reporting of foreign currency monetary liabilities is that they should be reported on the balance sheet in the equivalent amount of reporting currency (normally, Canadian dollars for Canadian companies) at the **spot rate** on the *balance sheet date*. The loan principal is translated into Canadian dollars on the day it is borrowed at the current, or *spot*, exchange rate. At every subsequent reporting date, the loan is remeasured at the spot rate. If exchange rates have changed, an exchange gain or loss will result. This gain or loss is *unrealized. The exchange gain or loss is included in net income in the year in which it arises.*

Exhibit 12-6 illustrates accounting for a long-term loan, whose Canadian dollar equivalent is $545,000 when borrowed and $565,000 when retired. When the Canadian dollar equivalent goes up during the life of the bond, a loss is recorded. When the Canadian dollar equivalent goes down, a gain is recorded.

The effect of an exchange fluctuation appears on the income statement in the year of the change in rates. This makes it easier for financial statement users to determine the impact of an exchange rate fluctuation on the company's financial position. Of course, it also makes income fluctuate if exchange rates are volatile.

Interest Expense Annual interest, also denominated in the foreign currency, is accrued using the exchange rate in effect during the period—the *average exchange rate*. When it is paid, cash outflows are measured at the exchange rate in effect on that day. The difference between the expense and the cash paid is also an exchange gain or loss.

---

[4] Some of these companies report in U.S. dollars, though, and to them debt that is denominated in Canadian dollars is "foreign currency" debt!

> EXHIBIT 12-6

EXCHANGE GAINS AND LOSSES ON LONG-TERM DEBT

Data:

Four-year term loan, US$500,000
Funds borrowed 1 January 20X6; due 31 December 20X9
Exchange rates:

1 January 20X6	US$1 = Cdn$1.09
31 December 20X6	US$1 = Cdn$1.10
31 December 20X7	US$1 = Cdn$1.12
31 December 20X8	US$1 = Cdn$1.08
31 December 20X9	US$1 = Cdn$1.13

Entries:

Note: entries are for principal only

1 January 20X6—to record receipt of loan proceeds		
Cash ($500,000 × $1.09)	545,000	
Long-term debt		545,000
31 December 20X6—to record adjustment to spot rate		
Exchange loss	5,000	
Long-term debt [$500,000 × ($1.09 − $1.10)]		5,000
31 December 20X7—to record adjustment to spot rate		
Exchange loss	10,000	
Long-term debt [$500,000 × ($1.10 − $1.12)]		10,000
31 December 20X8—to record adjustment to spot rate		
Long-term debt [$500,000 × ($1.12 − $1.08)]	20,000	
Exchange gain		20,000
31 December 20X9—to record adjustment to spot rate		
Exchange loss	25,000	
Long-term debt [$500,000 × ($1.08 − $1.13)]		25,000
31 December 20X9—to repay loan		
Long-term debt ($500,000 × $1.13)	565,000	
Cash		565,000

Summary:

Canadian dollar cash borrowed	$545,000
Canadian dollar cash repaid	565,000
Exchange loss over the life of the loan	$ 20,000

Accounting recognition of loss:

20X6	$ 5,000 dr.
20X7	10,000 dr.
20X8	20,000 cr.
20X9	25,000 dr.
Total	$20,000 dr.

For example, if the US$500,000 loan had an interest rate of 7%, and exchange rates were US$1.00 = Cdn$1.08 on average over the first year, the interest expense accrual would be recorded as follows:

Interest expense	37,800*	
Interest payable		37,800
*$500,000 × 7% × $1.08		

At year-end, the exchange rate is $1.10, and the interest is paid:

Interest payable	37,800	
Exchange loss	700	
Cash		38,500*
*$500,000 × 7% × $1.10		

This exchange loss is recognized on the income statement in the year in which it arises. If the interest is not due at year-end, the interest payable account is adjusted to the year-end spot rate, and again an exchange gain or loss is recognized.

CONCEPT REVIEW

1. What is the purpose of hedging?

2. A Canadian company borrows US$1,000,000 when the exchange rate is Cdn$1.10. The exchange rate is $1.08 at the end of the fiscal year. How much long-term debt is reported on the balance sheet? How much is the exchange gain or loss?

3. A loan requires that US$10,000 be paid in interest annually, at the end of each fiscal year. The average exchange rate is US$1 = Cdn$1.15, and the year end rate is US$1 = Cdn$1.10. How much expense and exchange gain is recorded?

CASH FLOW STATEMENT

The cash flow statement will reflect cash paid and cash received. The presence of multiple accounts related to a particular liability can complicate analysis in the area. For example, consider the accounts of Hilmon Limited:

During the year, the 8% bonds were issued for $4,750,000. The 7 1/2% bonds were retired for 102. Interest expense was $252,000, and a loss was reported on retiring the 7 1/2% bond.

	20X5	20X4
Bonds payable, 8%	$5,000,000	0
Discount on bonds payable	246,000	0
Interest payable	125,000	$ 25,000
Bonds payable, 7 1/2%	0	2,000,000
Premium on bonds payable	0	18,000

Both discount and premium amortization were recorded during the period—$4,000 on the discount and $2,000 on the premium.

These transactions would appear in the cash flow statement as follows:

1. In the financing section, an inflow of cash from issuing the 8% bond, $4,750,000, is reported. The proceeds are reported at their actual cash amount, and par value is not separately reported.

2. In the financing section, an outflow of cash from retiring the 7 1/2% bond, $2,040,000 ($2,000,000 × 102%), is reported. Again, the par value of the bond is irrelevant, as is the carrying value. It is the cash flow that is important. It is *not acceptable* to net an issuance with a disposal, or lump several issuances and disposals together. Transactions are to be shown separately.

3. In the operating activities section, reported using the indirect method, the loss on the bond retirement must be added back to net income. This loss is $24,000. (The carrying value of the bond on the day of retirement was $2,016,000, including the premium but after this year's $2,000 premium amortization. The cost of bond retirement was $2,040,000; the difference is the $24,000 loss.)

4. In the operating activities section, the discount amortization of $4,000 will be added back as a non-cash charge, and $2,000 premium amortization subtracted. These items were included in interest expense but do not reflect cash paid. The $100,000 increase in interest payable will also be subtracted as part of the non-cash working capital changes. In the supplementary disclosure of interest paid, these adjustments would be made to the interest expense line. The cash paid for interest for the year will be $150,000 (the expense, $252,000, adjusted for discount and premium amortization, net subtraction of $2,000, and also reduced for the increase in interest payable of $100,000).

Premium/discount amortization Discount amortization is an add-back in the operating activities section of the CFS, and decreases interest expense from the expense to the cash paid. Premium amortization, on the other hand, is a deduction in the financing section of the CFS. Standard setters have made this determination on the basis that a premium is part of the original borrowed amount and part of the interest paid each year is a repayment of principal.

DISCLOSURES FOR LONG-TERM LIABILITIES

Most liabilities are financial instruments, and accordingly the following information must be disclosed:

1. The *accounting policies* used for reporting;

2. The *fair value* of each class of liability, and the method used (discounted cash flow, most likely) to establish fair value; and

3. The *nature and extent of risks* arising from financial instruments, including, as appropriate, interest rate risk, liquidity risk, and market risk.

Additional disclosure is required for long-term debt, primarily related to the terms of the debt contract, security, and future cash flows:

- The title of the issue, interest rate, interest expense on long-term debt in total, maturity date, amount outstanding, assets pledged as collateral, sinking fund, if any, and redemption or conversion privileges;

- The aggregate amount of payments required in the next five years to meet sinking fund or retirement provisions;

- If the debt is denominated in a foreign currency, then the currency in which the debt is to be repaid;

- Secured liabilities must be shown separately, and the fact that they are secured must be disclosed; and

- Details of any defaults of the company in principal, interest, sinking fund, or redemption provisions, carrying value of loans payable in default, and any remedy of the default that was undertaken by the financial statement completion date.

EXHIBIT 12-7

ENBRIDGE GAS DISTRIBUTION INC. SELECTED LONG-TERM DEBT DISCLOSURE

5. LONG-TERM DEBT [excerpts]

($ millions) December 31,	Weighted Average Interest Rate	Maturity	2006	2005
Debentures	11.1%	2009–2024	$ 585.0	$ 585.0
Medium-Term Notes	6.0%	2008–2036	1,665.0	1,190.0
Other			8.2	8.2
			$2,258.2	$1,783.2

For the year ended December 31, 2006, the effective interest rate of long-term debt, after giving effect to the interest rate swap agreements and all related issue costs, was 7.4% (2005 − 7.7%). The Company issued $475.0 million of new medium-term notes during the year.

Long-term debt maturities are as follows:

($ millions)	2007	2008	2009	2010	2011	Thereafter
Maturities	—	270.0	100.0	150.0	150.0	1,588.2

The Company's borrowings, whether debentures or medium term notes, are unsecured. When issuing any new indebtedness with a maturity of over 18 months, covenants contained in the Company's trust indentures require that the pro-forma long-term debt interest coverage ratio be at least 2.0 times for twelve consecutive months out of the previous 23 months. At December 31, 2006, this ratio stood at 1.87, effectively temporarily precluding the Company from issuing any further new long term debt until the ratio is restored to the threshold level of 2.0 times. The Company is permitted to refinance maturing long term debt with a matching long term debt issue without the requirement to meet the 2.0 times interest coverage test.

Credit Facilities

At December 31, 2006, the Company had committed lines of credit of $1.0 billion (December 31, 2005 − $800.0 million) and uncommitted lines of credit of $5.8 million (December 31, 2005 − $305.8 million). Of this, $1,003.1 million was unused at December 31, 2006 (December 31, 2005 − $802.3 million).

Under its $1.0 billion commercial paper program (December 31, 2005 − $800.0 million), the Company borrowed $805.2 million, net of unamortized discount of $2.8 million at December 31, 2006 (December 31, 2005 − $774.8 million, net of unamortized discount of $2.2 million), with interest cost ranging between 4.2% to 4.3% and the latest maturity in March 2007. This leaves $192.0 million unused at December 31, 2006 (December 31, 2005 − $23.0 million unused).

Interest Expense

($ millions) Year ended December 31,	2006	2005
Long-term debt	$151.9	$141.0
Interest on loans and notes payable to affiliate	27.3	29.9
Other interest and finance costs	27.6	19.3
Capitalized	(3.9)	(2.7)
	$202.9	$187.5

8. FINANCIAL INSTRUMENTS [excerpts]

Fair Values

The fair value of the long-term debt, excluding the loans from affiliate companies, is $2,602.9 million (December 31, 2005 − $2,172.6 million) as compared to the book value of $2,258.2 million (December 31, 2005 − $1,783.2 million). The Company recovers, through regulated distribution rates, interest at existing rates.

Source: www.sedar.com, Enbridge Gas Distribution Inc., Audited Annual Financial Statements, February 23, 2007.

Reporting Example Exhibit 12-7 shows the 2006 long-term debt disclosure for Enbridge Gas Distribution Inc., a pipeline company. The company lists two significant types of outstanding debt: (1) debentures and (2) medium-term notes. Some of the points that you should observe about Enbridge's disclosure are:

- The maturity dates of the *medium-term* notes extend 30 years after the balance sheet date, which actually is longer than the maturities for the nominally long-term debentures.
- The interest rates in the debt table are nominal rates. The company explains that its effective rate for 2006 was 7.4%.
- The company's debt is unsecured.
- The company discloses its *restrictive covenant*—the company must maintain earnings of at least twice the level of its annual interest payment obligation—a two-times-debt-interest coverage requirement.
- The company has extensive unused lines of credit.
- The company capitalizes some of its interest. This is normal for a company of this type that constructs a lot of its pipeline facilities itself.
- The company discloses that the fair value of its debt ($2,602.9 million) is higher than its book value ($2,258.2 million). This means that Enbridge's nominal interest rates are higher than the year-end 2006 market interest rates.

Enbridge's debt disclosure is relatively brief because the company does not have many different types of debt. Some large public companies have debt disclosures that go on for several pages.

INTERNATIONAL PERSPECTIVE

The Canadian and international standards for liability accounting are similar. There are some differences in terminology and approach, but impact of these differences is slight. Much of the similarity stems from the common financial instruments rules, which were developed as a joint project between the IASB, Canada, and the U.S. Since these standards govern the accounting model for a significant section of the financial statement, the similarity of standards between these major jurisdictions provides a fair bit of common ground.

RELEVANT STANDARDS

CICA Handbook:
- Section 1651, Foreign Currency Translation
- Section 3210, Long-Term Debt
- Section 3280, Contractual Obligations
- Section 3290, Contingencies
- Section 3855, Financial Instruments—Recognition and Measurement
- Section 3861, Financial Instruments—Disclosure and Presentation
- Section 3862, Financial Instruments—Disclosures
- Section 3863, Financial Instruments—Presentation
- Acg-14, Disclosure of Guarantees

IASB:
- *IAS* 1, Presentation of Financial Statements
- *IAS* 21, The Effects of Changes in Foreign Exchange Rates
- *IAS* 37, Provisions, Contingent Liabilities and Contingent Assets
- *IAS* 32, Financial Instruments: Disclosure and Presentation
- *IAS* 39, Financial Instruments: Recognition and Measurement

SUMMARY OF KEY POINTS

1. Liabilities are highly probable future sacrifices of assets or services, constituting a present obligation as the result of past transactions or events.

2. Contingent losses are recorded when likely and measurable; otherwise, note disclosure is used.

3. Liabilities are initially recognized at the transaction amount. If the liabilities are long term, and the stated rate is different than the effective market interest rate, then present values, with the discount rate based on market interest rates, are used.

4. Estimated liabilities must be recorded if measurable, with estimates corrected as information is available. Corrections change current and future years but not past years.

5. Long-term liabilities are those liabilities with a term extending more than one year from the balance sheet date or the operating cycle, whichever is longer.

6. A common source of borrowed money is bank debt, which can be short, medium, or long term, depending on the needs of the borrower and the collateral available. Repayment can involve monthly interest and lump-sum principal, or monthly blended payments that include both principal and interest.

7. The recorded value at date of issuance for long-term debt is the present value of all future cash flows discounted at the current market rate for debt securities of equivalent risk. Using the effective-interest method, interest expense is the product of the market rate at issuance and the balance in the liability at the beginning of the period. The net book value of long-term debt at a balance sheet date is the present value of all remaining cash payments required, discounted at the market rate at issuance.

8. Straight-line amortization of a discount or premium is permitted when the difference between straight-line and effective-interest methods is immaterial. When straight-line amortization is used, interest expense is cash paid plus discount amortization or less premium amortization, and the bond carrying value is par value, increased (premium) or decreased (discount) by the unamortized balance.

9. Bonds are long-term debt instruments that specify the face value paid at maturity and the stated interest rate payable according to a fixed schedule. Bonds are a significant source of capital for many firms; different forms of bonds appeal to different investors' preferences.

10. The price of a bond at issuance is the present value of all future cash flows discounted at the current market rate of interest for bonds of similar risk.

11. Bonds are sold at a premium if the stated rate exceeds the market rate and at a discount if the stated rate is less than the market rate.

12. Accrued interest is paid by the investor when a bond is issued between interest dates; the investor is then entitled to a full interest payment on the next interest payment date. The issuer records accrued interest received as a credit to interest expense or payable; the choice affects appropriate recognition on the interest payment date.

13. Upfront fees are sometimes charged by financial institutions when arranging a loan. Such fees are a cost of borrowing, and are charged to interest expense over the life of the loan. Such fees increase the effective interest cost of the loan.

14. Bonds retired at maturity are recorded by reducing the liability and the asset given in repayment. No gain or loss arises. Bonds retired before maturity, through call, redemption, or open market purchase, typically involve recognition of a gain or loss as the difference between the book value of the debt (including all related accounts, such as unamortized premium or discount, and upfront fees) and the consideration paid.

15. If a bond is retired though a refunding, a new bond is issued as its replacement. This is usually done to secure lower-cost debt financing.

16. A defeasance is an arrangement whereby the debtor irrevocably places investments in a trust fund for the sole purpose of using those resources to pay interest and principal on specified debt. The creditor agrees to this and legal release is given. In an in-substance defeasance, the transaction is the same except there is no legal release by the creditor. Debt subject to a defeasance arrangement is derecognized, but debt subject to an in-substance defeasance is left on the books.

17. Many long-term loans are denominated in a foreign currency, which causes exchange gains or losses when exchange rates fluctuate. Exchange gains and losses are reported on the income statement.

18. Disclosures for long-term debt include the major terms and cash flows agreed to in the loan contract. Disclosure is also required for accounting policy, fair value, and nature and extent of risks.

KEY TERMS

amortization period, 722
asset retirement obligation, 713
bond date, 727
bond indenture, 722
call option, 738
call price, 738
commercial mortgages, 721
commercial paper, 720
contingent liability, 715
contractual obligations, 713
covenants, 723
defeasance, 740
derecognition, 737
effective interest rate, 724
estimated liabilities, 716
face value, 727
hedges, 742
incremental borrowing rate (IBR), 713
interest payment dates, 727
leverage, 721

lien/charge, 720
long-term liability, 720
long-term loans, 722
maintenance tests, 723
maturity date, 727
nominal interest rate, 727
non-current liabilities, 720
operating lines of credit, 720
promissory notes, 719
recurring operating contingent loss
    exposure, 716
redeemable, 738
refunding, 739
retractable, 738
sinking fund, 723
spot rate, 742
term, 722
term loans, 721
yield, 724

REVIEW PROBLEM

On 1 August 20X6, Pismo Corporation, a calendar-year corporation that records adjusting entries only once per year, issued bonds with the following characteristics:

a. $50,000 total face value

b. 12% nominal rate

c. 16% yield rate

d. Interest dates are 1 February, 1 May, 1 August, and 1 November

e. Bond date is 31 October 20X5

f. Maturity date is 1 November 20X10

Required:

1. Provide all entries required for the bond issue through 1 February 20X7 using the effective-interest method.

2. On 1 June 20X8, Pismo retired $20,000 of bonds at 98 through an open market purchase. Provide the entries to update the bond accounts in 20X8 (entries have been completed through 1 May 20X8) for this portion of the bond and to retire the bonds.

3. Provide the entries required on 1 August 20X8.

REVIEW PROBLEM—SOLUTION

1. *1 August 20X6—issue bonds and incur issue costs*

Cash	43,917[1]	
Discount on bonds payable ($50,000 − $43,917)	6,083	
Bonds payable		50,000

[1] Four and one-quarter years, or 17 quarters, remain in the bond term: $43,917 = [$50,000 × (P/F, 4%, 17)] + [($50,000 × 3%) × (P/A, 4%,17)]

1 November 20X6—interest payment date

Interest expense	1,757[1]	
Discount on bonds payable		257
Cash		1,500[2]

[1] $1,757 = $43,917 × 4%
[2] $1,500 = $50,000 × 3%

31 December 20X6—adjusting entry

Interest expense	1,178[1]	
Discount on bonds payable		178
Interest payable		1,000[2]

[1] $1,178 = ($43,917 + $257) × 4% × (2/3 of quarter)
[2] $1,000 = $1,500 × 2/3

1 February 20X7—interest payment date

Interest expense	589[1]	
Interest payable	1,000	
Discount on bonds payable		89
Cash		1,500

[1] $589 = ($43,917 + $257) × 4% × (1/3 of quarter)

2. On 1 May 20X8, the remaining term of the bonds is 2 1/2 years, or 10 quarters, and the $20,000 of bonds to be retired have the following book value:

$18,378 = [$20,000 × (P/F, 4%,10)] + [($20,000 × 3%) × (P/A, 4%,10)]

On 1 May 20X8, the remaining discount on the portion of bonds to be retired is therefore $1,622 ($20,000 − $18,378).

1 May 20X8—update relevant bond accounts before retirement

Interest expense	245[1]	
Discount on bonds payable		45
Cash		200[2]

1 June 20X8—remove relevant bond accounts

Bonds payable	20,000	
Loss, bond extinguishment	1,177	
Discount on bonds payable		1,577[3]
Cash (.98 × $20,000)		19,600

[1] $245 = $18,378 × 16% × 1/12
[2] $200 = $20,000 × 12% × 1/12
[3] $1,577 = $1,622 − $45

3. On 1 May 20X8, the remaining term of the bonds is 2 1/2 years, or 10 quarters, and the remaining $30,000 of bonds have the following book value:

$$\$27,567 = \$30,000 \, (P/F, 4\%, 10) + [(\$30,000 \times 3\%) \times (P/A, 4\%, 10)]$$

On 1 May 20X8, the remaining discount is therefore $2,433 (i.e., $30,000 − $27,567).

1 August 20X8—interest payment date

Interest expense	1,103[1]	
Discount on bonds payable		203
Cash		900[2]

[1] $1,103 = $27,567 × 4%
[2] $900 = $30,000 × 3%

QUESTIONS

Q12-1 What three time elements are embedded in the definition of a liability?

Q12-2 What is the correct accounting recognition given to a purchase order for inventory issued in the normal course of business? Is the purchase order a liability?

Q12-3 When is a contingent liability recognized? Disclosed? Neither recognized nor disclosed?

Q12-4 A firm is being sued for $550,000 by an unhappy customer; the lawsuit is in its early stages, and the firm feels that it has a good case and is willing to defend itself. However, legal costs will be high, and the company, in all likelihood, will be prepared to settle with the ex-customer for $150,000. Why is accounting for this lawsuit complicated at this stage?

Q12-5 A company borrows $10,000 for two years, interest free, when the market interest rate is 10%, compounded annually. At what amount should the liability be valued? How would your answer change if the liability were a current liability, with a term of six months?

Q12-6 If a mid-size company with substantial investments in inventory and a fairly new manufacturing facility were a potential borrower, for what kinds of bank financing would the company likely be eligible?

Q12-7 What is commercial paper?

Q12-8 Describe two payment schemes typically associated with medium-term bank loans.

Q12-9 A commercial mortgage has a term of 5 years and an amortization period of 25 years. Explain the meaning of these two periods.

Q12-10 What is a debt covenant? Give two examples of an accounting-based covenant, and two restricted actions.

Q12-11 Distinguish between the par amount and the issue price of a bond. When are they the same? When different? Explain. If a $5,000 bond is sold for 101, how much cash is paid/received?

Q12-12 What is the primary conceptual difference between the straight-line and effective-interest methods of amortizing a discount or premium on a bond or note payable? Why is the effective-interest method required?

Q12-13 Assume that a $1,000, 8% (payable semi-annually), 10-year bond is sold at an effective rate of 6%. Compute the price of this bond.

Q12-14 Explain why and how a bond discount and bond premium affect (a) the balance sheet and (b) the income statement of the issuer of the bond.

Q12-15 When the end of the accounting period of the issuer is not on a bond interest date, adjusting entries must be made for (a) accrued interest and (b) discount or premium amortization. Explain in general terms what each adjustment amount represents.

Q12-16 When bonds are sold (or purchased) between interest dates, accrued interest must be recognized. Explain why.

Q12-17 How would the payment of a $5,000 upfront administration fee on a $50,000, 6%, five-year loan affect subsequent recognition of interest expense?

Q12-18 Under what circumstances will a gain or loss occur on the repayment of a bond payable?

Q12-19 When will a bond discount or premium be included in an entry to retire bonds? How is the amount calculated?

Q12-20 What is a bond refunding and why does it take place?

Q12-21 What is meant by defeasance? Can debt that is subject to a defeasance arrangement be derecognized? Contrast this with an in-substance defeasance.

Q12-22 Assume that a Canadian company borrowed US$325,000, for five years, when US$1 = Cdn$1.10. If the exchange rate at the end of the first year is US$1 = Cdn$1.08, and at the end of the second year is US$1 = Cdn$1.16, how much exchange gain or loss would be shown on the income statement in the second year?

Q12-23 What exchange rate is used to measure interest expense that is denominated in a foreign currency?

Q12-24 How can an exchange loss occur on annual interest paid in foreign currency on foreign currency–denominated debt? Use, as an example, a loan denominated in euros, with an annual interest payment of €40,000, and an exchange rate during the year of €1 = Cdn$1.65.

Q12-25 Interest expense of $45,500 is recorded, after discount amortization of $4,500. Interest payable has increased by $2,000 during the year. How much cash was paid for interest?

CASE 12-1

DARCY LIMITED

You are a professional accountant in public practice. You have just left a meeting with Michel Lessard, a local entrepreneur, who is considering a potential acquisition. Mr. Lessard, with four others, is considering buying Darcy Ltd (DL), a company that is now the subsidiary of Micah Holdings Limited (MHL), a private investment holding company.

The group of potential investors is scheduled to meet later in the week to finalize an offer for DL. You have the financial statements prepared by the company (Exhibit 1) and a page of notes from your discussion with Mr. Lessard (Exhibit 2). While the group has hired a lawyer to investigate various issues and appropriate conditions for the purchase, they would like advice on the price to be offered in the first round of negotiations.

You generally understand that the potential investors would be willing to pay six times earnings, a common valuation rule of thumb in this industry. Another valuation norm in this industry is 1.2 times net tangible assets less liabilities. Mr. Lessard has asked that both valuation rules be applied, and he is hoping the two results will be in the same ballpark.

When earnings are used for valuation purposes, earnings must be "sustainable" or "continuing" earnings, excluding unusual and infrequent items, and, in valuation, elements must be measured at fair values, neither high nor low. Appropriate accounting polices must be used for this measurement of earnings and net assets, recognizing the purpose of the accounting measurements.

Required:

Evaluate the investment based on the information given, and provide a report that provides a range of valuation for the potential investors to discuss next week and any other issues you think are important. Your report must include an explanation of adjustments made.

EXHIBIT 1

DARCY LIMITED

Balance Sheet

As of 31 December
(in thousands)

Assets	20X7	20X6
Current assets		
Cash	$ —	$ 1,400
Accounts receivable (less allowance of $270 in 20X7 and $420 in 20X6)	18,720	8,583
Inventory	2,680	3,200
Prepaid expenses and deposits	45	100
	21,445	13,283
Property plant and equipment (net)	19,800	16,600
Goodwill	400	350
	$41,645	$30,233
Liabilities		
Current liabilities		
Operating loan	$ 8,045	$ —
Accounts payable and accrued liabilities	3,750	3,188
Deferred revenue	850	790
Warranty liability	75	545
	12,720	4,523
Long-term liabilities		
Note payable, 2%, due 1 October 20X12	2,600	—
Future income tax	1,835	2,210
Shareholders' equity		
Share capital	20,700	20,700
Retained earnings	3,790	2,800
	24,490	23,500
	$41,645	$30,233

EXHIBIT 1 *(cont'd)*

DARCY LIMITED
Income Statement

For the year ended 31 December
(in thousands)

	20X7	20X6
Revenue	$32,670	$44,960
Operating costs	24,180	32,970
	8,490	11,990
Other operating costs		
Selling general and administrative	3,580	3,980
Amortization	2,130	1,650
Research	120	350
Bad debts	60	120
Warranty	650	900
Gain on disposal of property	(80)	—
Gain on appreciation of goodwill	(50)	(50)
	6,410	6,950
Operating income	2,080	5,040
Financing		
Interest expense	430	410
Income before tax	1,650	4,630
Income tax	660	1,850
Net income	990	2,780
Retained earnings, opening	2,800	20
Dividends	—	—
Retained earnings. closing	$ 3,790	$ 2,800

EXHIBIT 2

NOTES FROM MEETING WITH MICHEL LESSARD

(amounts in thousands)

1. The principal business activity of DL is the manufacturing of equipment for the oil and gas industry.
2. The note payable is a 2% loan offered as 100% financing by the equipment manufacturer, issued for new equipment bought on 1 October 20X7. The equipment has an eight-year life. Annual interest is paid on the anniversary date, and 2% interest for three months has been accrued in the financial statements as presented.
3. Goodwill has been written up by $50 each year based on management estimates of improved operations.
4. The pre-20X7 base of property, plant, and equipment includes land that is likely worth approximately 150% of its $7,000 cost. Other pre-20X7 property, plant, and equipment would likely have a replacement cost of 120% of net book value at the beginning of 20X7. Values have risen only slightly through 20X6 and 20X7.
5. For capital assets, straight-line amortization over periods ranging from four to eight years has been used. Amortization periods seem reasonable.

> ### EXHIBIT 2 *(cont'd)*

6. The research program was curtailed in 20X7 to save operating cash flow but Mr. Lessard believes that the ongoing research activity is needed to keep the company competitive.

7. DL provides a three-year limited warranty on equipment sold. The warranty expense has been recorded based on 2% of sales revenue. Warranty claims history is as follows:

Year	Sales	Claims Paid re: Current-Year Sales	Claims Paid re: Sales of One Year Prior	Claims Paid re: Sales of Two Years Prior
20X4	$31,020	$260	$160	$500
20X5	37,810	190	320	420
20X6	44,960	230	325	460
20X7	32,670	190	300	630

8. Revenue is recognized on delivery. Unearned revenue arises because of pre-paid orders.

9. During 20X7, DL provided inventory, with a cost of $23 and list price of $31, to a customer. In return, the customer will do machining work for DL during 20X8. This machining work is for a second customer's special order, which DL does not have the expertise to complete. DL expensed the cost of inventory provided, $23, as part of operating costs and made no other entries. The machining work would be worth something in the range of $28–$30 if DL had to have it done by another party.

10. The allowance for doubtful accounts has historically been approximately 5% of outstanding accounts receivable. The year-end balance of accounts receivable is extremely high this year because of a single, $7,620 account receivable ($7,000 U.S. dollars) with a foreign government. DL has stated, and Mr. Lessard agrees, that collection risk is minimal for this account.

11. The tax rate is 40% and market interest rates are in the range of 6%. The year-end exchange rate is US$1 = Cdn$1.12.

CASE 12-2

SIRSI ENTERPRISES LIMITED

The accountant for Sirsi Enterprises Limited (SEL) has asked for your advice regarding if and how she should report the following items in SEL's financial statements for 20X1:

1. *A loan guarantee given to the Royal Bank.* The guarantee is of a $1.5 million loan taken out by SEL's CEO for major renovations to his house. The CEO is not in any financial difficulty, and therefore there is no expectation that SEL will have to fulfill its guarantee obligation.

2. *A bonus to the CFO for exceeding analysts' profit expectations for the third quarter of 20X1.* The bonus is $250,000. If the CFO also manages to increase profits for the fourth quarter, his bonus for the third quarter will be increased by an additional $100,000. As well, he will receive a $350,000 bonus for the higher fourth-quarter performance.

3. *Contingent rents for retail space.* SEL must pay rents on its leased retail space. The company pays a base rate of $100 per square foot per month, plus 4% of gross sales. The base rent is paid at the beginning of each month. The contingent rent is payable only after SEL's financial statements have been audited and the lessor has reviewed the statements. The general ledger shows that retail sales for 20X1 were $20 million.

4. *Damage to a customer's facilities.* A customer is suing SEL for faulty work done by SEL's contract division. The customer alleges that due to SEL employees' negligence, the customer's entire computer system crashed and was inoperable for four days. The lawsuit is for $4.5 million. SEL has suspended the employees involved in the work pending an internal investigation.
5. *An interest-free long-term note payable.* SEL borrowed $5.5 million from a venture capitalist at the end of 20X1. SEL signed a promissory note for $8.0 million. The note is due in 20X6 and bears no interest.

Required:
Write a report to the SEL accountant explaining how each of the above items should be presented in SEL's 20X1 financial statements.

CASE 12-3

HOMEBAKE INCORPORATED

Homebake Inc. is a growing company in the consumer small appliance industry. After months of research and testing, Homebake introduced its new home breadmaker in retail stores in September 20X5, just in time for the Christmas season. The breadmaker had many more features than other similar models on the market, but it sold for the same price as the unit offered by the company's main competitor. Consumers were demanding products that would allow them to make preservative-free, fresh bread in their homes, and Homebake was anticipating that sales of its breadmaker would be high. The breadmaker came with a two-year warranty on all parts and labour and an unconditional guarantee that allowed consumers to return the product for a full refund if not completely satisfied.

In October 20X5, the company began to receive returns and complaints from some of the consumers who had purchased the product. Although the breadmaker had been tested thoroughly and all mechanical parts were performing satisfactorily, some consumers were having trouble removing the freshly baked bread from the breadpan. It seemed that the non-stick coating would allow for easy removal of the bread for a week or two, depending on the frequency of use, and then would suddenly stop working. Consumers were having to use spatulas and knives to remove the fresh, soft bread from the pan, often scarring the coating and making it even less effective, and ruining the bread in the process.

Research into the problem showed that although the breadpans themselves were manufactured by Homebake, the non-stick coating was applied by three independent suppliers. One of the suppliers had used a substandard coating mixture on the breadpans that it finished for Homebake. Homebake knew it would have to immediately remedy the problem and provide those consumers who complained with a new breadpan made by one of the other suppliers; otherwise, the consumers would return their breadmaker for a full refund.

Unfortunately, the breadpans could not be identified by supplier, and Homebake had no way of knowing how many of the substandard pans had been sold or were sitting on shelves in retailers' stores waiting for the Christmas rush.

The company set up a toll-free line that consumers or retailers could call for a replacement pan. When consumers or retailers called, highly trained customer service representatives explained the problem and reassured the callers that a replacement pan would be sent out immediately by courier. They reminded callers of the Homebake breadmaker's unique features and urged them not to return the product. They also told consumers about how much good feedback the company had received from other Homebake breadmaker owners who were using the good breadpans. Finally, they promised to send out free bread mixes and coupons with the breadpans and reminded callers that the pan would be delivered in fewer than three days. The company felt that there would be few breadmakers returned when consumers and retailers were treated with this kind of respect and courtesy.

It is now 6 January 20X6. You are employed as controller for Homebake. You are in the process of preparing year-end financial statements when the president of the company calls you into her office. You are glad for the meeting, for you were just considering what should be done about the potential warranty liability from the sale of breadmakers. A reasonable estimate and accrual of normal returns and warranty costs has been made from past experience with other similar products and from the experience of other manufacturers with this product. However, the breadpan failure is unique, and you have not yet determined how to account for the expenses relating to it.

From your data, you have learned that the breadmakers, which sell for $199.99 in retail stores, cost Homebake $75 to manufacture and are sold to retailers for $125. The cost of sending out a second breadpan, including shipping and the free mixes and coupons, is $20. Over 3,600,000 original breadpans have been shipped, and approximately one-third are estimated to be faulty. By 31 December 20X5, only 100,000 replacement breadpans had been shipped, since many of the breadmakers were purchased as Christmas gifts and had not yet been used.

When you arrive at the president's office, you learn that the breadpan liability is the focus of the meeting. The president is wondering how the returns will be accounted for in the year-end statements. Her comments to you are:

"I was thinking about the problem with the breadpans. I think the best way to deal with this is to expense all the costs of shipping new pans as we incur them. I know this is not our normal accrual accounting procedure, but this is not a normal situation. We will be suing the supplier of the faulty pans, and more than likely we will recover all of the costs we have incurred. But there is no way this case will make it through the courts until sometime next year. If we recognize only the costs incurred to the year-end, then next year when we have the settlement from the lawsuit, we can match the settlement against the costs of shipping the new breadpans and there will be no impact on our profitability picture. You know that we are a small company, and this project is going to allow us to grow and expand to be a much bigger company. But we can't do that if we don't have the confidence of our banker and the general public. We need to show a good bottom line this year, so we can survive next year."

You leave the president's office feeling as if she used the meeting more to convince you of her ideas than to listen to your expertise. You are not convinced that the cash basis will provide the proper matching of revenues and expenses, since the revenue from the sale of the 3,600,000 breadmakers would be recognized in the 20X5 financial statements. However, the president did not seem very open to any other way of accounting for the costs of the faulty breadpans.

The president has asked you to jot down some rough figures for the next meeting, which is in two days. Your plan is to present both her approach and what you think would be more acceptable under GAAP, since Homebake requires audited statements for shareholders and bankers.

Required:

Respond to the president's request.

CGA-Canada, adapted. Extracts from *Financial Accounting* 1 and 2, published by the Certified General Accountants Association of Canada, © CGA-Canada, reproduced with permission. Because of *Tax Act* updates and/or changes to the *CICA Handbook*, the contents of examinations published before 2005 may be out of date; therefore the currency of the contents is the sole responsibility of the user.

ASSIGNMENTS

★ **A12-1 Types of Liabilities:** The following items pertain to the 20X9 operations of Damon Auto Corporation

a. A guarantee of an $850,000 bank loan taken out by another company.

b. A purchase order for manufacturing equipment with an invoice price of $850,000, to be installed next year.

c. An invoice received from a supplier, for manufacturing equipment with an invoice price of $785,000, where the equipment has been installed and accepted by Damon.

d. An employment contract for the Chief Information Officer (CIO) that requires Damon to pay the CIO $180,000 per year for the next three years.

e. A lawsuit for $2 million brought against Damon by a suppler for damages caused by faulty merchandise. The outcome of the lawsuit is not determinable.

f. A purchase order that required Damon to pay for at least 17,000 inventory units from a major supplier within the next year whether the units are needed or not.

g. A lawsuit for $1.7 million in damages filed by Damon against a former employee, who joined a competitor and is alleged to have used confidential information to solicit current Damon customers on behalf of the new employer.

Required:
Explain how each of these items will affect the financial statements of Damon at year-end 20X9.

★ **A12-2 Contingencies:** For each of the following items, indicate whether the appropriate accounting treatment is to:

A—Record the estimated liability in the balance sheet and report a loss on the income statement.

B—Disclose the possible liability in the notes to the financial statements.

C—Neither record nor disclose.

1. A prior employee has sued the company for $1 million for health-related issues that the employee claims were caused by working conditions. The company will likely successfully defend itself. However, the amount is material and if the lawsuit is successful, other employees will likely also sue.

2. The company has guaranteed the $10 million loan of another company. This amount is material. The other company has a poor credit rating and there is a 40% chance of having to make a payment under the guarantee.

3. The company is in the process of being audited by CRA for two prior years; there is no indication at present that anything is amiss.

4. The company has been audited by CRA, resulting in a tax assessment for $1.5 million, an amount that would have a significant impact on the company's financial position. The company has appealed the decision, and feels it has a good case.

5. The company has guaranteed the $8 million loan of another company. This amount is material. There is no real possibility of any payment ever having to be made.

6. A customer has sued the company for $1.2 million. The company may lose but may well offer to settle the suit for $700,000 in the next six months. The customer may or may not accept the settlement. The amount would have a significant impact on the company's financial position.

7. A customer has sued the company for $4 million, and it is likely that the company will come to a negotiated settlement in an amount that is less than $4 million. The amount cannot be estimated reliably. The amount would have a significant impact on the company's financial position.

★ **A12-3 Warranty:** Helpi Auto Parts Ltd. offers a six-month warranty that covers the cost of parts and labour for repairs. Warranty costs are estimated to be 1.5% of sales for parts plus 3% of sales for labour. On 1 April, the warranty liability had a $16,400 credit balance. Warranty work in April consumed $8,700 of parts and $14,000 of labour. Sales amounted to $550,000 in April.

Required:

1. What amount of warranty expense should be recorded in April?
2. What is the balance in the warranty liability at the end of April?

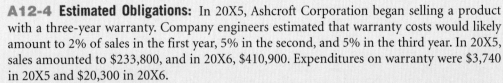

A12-4 Estimated Obligations: In 20X5, Ashcroft Corporation began selling a product with a three-year warranty. Company engineers estimated that warranty costs would likely amount to 2% of sales in the first year, 5% in the second, and 5% in the third year. In 20X5, sales amounted to $233,800, and in 20X6, $410,900. Expenditures on warranty were $3,740 in 20X5 and $20,300 in 20X6.

This product was sold with a coupon offer. For every dollar of sales, the customer receives a coupon. When enough coupons are collected, the customer can cash them in for a free T-shirt. It takes 1,000 coupons to receive a free T-shirt. The company estimated that 32% of coupons issued would be redeemed. In 20X5, 52 T-shirts, costing $8 each, were distributed. In 20X6, 82 T-shirts were distributed.

Required:

1. For 20X5 and 20X6, calculate warranty expense for the product warranty and promotion expense with relation to the coupon offer.
2. For each year, calculate the ending balance in the related liability account.
3. Have the cost estimates been accurate? Comment.

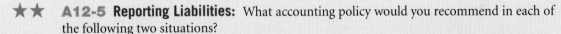

A12-5 Reporting Liabilities: What accounting policy would you recommend in each of the following two situations?

Case A Canuck Airlines has accumulated a liability of 4 billion kilometres due to its frequent-flier program. Industry analysts claim that this estimated liability for free flights amounts to $270 million of lost revenue but could be $40 million higher depending on the assumption about the price of fares forgone.

The airlines argue that the actual cost of each free flight is approximately $8 per flight—for food, insurance, and other miscellaneous costs. That is the cost of filling an otherwise empty seat. Furthermore, flyers with free tickets often bring along a paying customer, which more than offsets the negligible cost. Consequently, the average liability recorded is only a fraction of the amount industry analysts insist exists.

Case B In December, Ben Wilson, the controller of Fargo Company, a calendar-fiscal-year company, is faced with a tough situation. The bond indenture of a major issue of Fargo bonds requires maintaining a 3-to-1 current ratio as measured at each balance sheet date. Fargo has recently experienced cash shortages caused by a downturn in the general economy and in the demand for Fargo's products. However, leading economic indicators suggest that an upturn is expected.

A substantial account payable is due in January. Fargo does not have the cash to pay the debt before the end of the current year. Furthermore, the January cash budget based on a realistic estimate of sales and collections from accounts receivable indicates a cash shortage requiring short-term financing. The large payable is enough to cause the current ratio at 31 December to fall below 3.0. The controller initiated a search for a financial institution willing to refinance the payable on a long-term basis. If successful, the payable would be reclassified as long term, enabling Fargo to comply with the bond indenture. Several financial institutions are willing to refinance the payable, but none agree to do so on a non-cancellable basis. The basis must be non-cancellable to qualify for reclassification. However, at the end of the day, Wilson accepted the best (cheapest) of these offers.

The controller is quite stressed by the situation. Non-compliance with the bond indenture may lead to technical default. If the bondholders exercise their right and call the bonds, Fargo may be forced into bankruptcy. The controller is confident that Fargo will rebound in the coming year and reasons that more harm will come to the company, its employees, and its shareholders if he does not take action that will result in compliance with the bond indenture. Mr. Wilson therefore decides to reclassify the payable despite the fact that the financing arrangement is cancellable.

A12-6 Estimated Obligations: At the end of 20X5, Fulton Limited has a balance of $74,900 in the warranty liability account, and $70,000 in unearned revenue. These balances were both correctly calculated. Transactions in 20X6 are summarized as follows:

a. Warranty claims were made during the year. Fulton spent $24,800 on parts and $66,000 in labour on warranty work.
b. Work was completed and delivered to the customer who had paid in full in advance. There was no warranty associated with this job.
c. Sales of $4,768,200 were recorded for goods that carried a warranty. Warranty work is estimated to cost 1.5% of sales.
d. Customers made deposits of $65,400 on work that will be carried out in the next fiscal period.

Required:

1. List the items that would appear on the 20X6 income statement as a result of the 20X6 transactions.
2. List the balances of the warranty liability and unearned revenue accounts that would appear on the 20X6 balance sheet.

 A12-7 Estimated Warranty Costs: Habek Hardware Incorporated provides a product warranty for defects on two major lines of items sold since the beginning of 20X5. Line A carries a two-year warranty for all labour and service (but not parts). The company contracts with a local service establishment to service the warranty (both parts and labour). The local service establishment charges a flat fee of $60 per unit payable at date of sale regardless of whether the unit ever requires servicing.

Line B carries a three-year warranty for parts and labour on service. Habek purchases the parts needed under the warranty and has service personnel who perform the work and are paid by the job. On the basis of experience, it is estimated that for Line B, the three-year warranty costs are 3% of dollar sales for parts and 7% for labour and overhead. Additional data available are as follows:

	Year		
	20X5	**20X6**	**20X7**
Sales in units, Line A	1,000	1,300	n/a
Sales price per unit, Line A	$ 610	$ 660	n/a
Sales in units, Line B	600	800	n/a
Sales price per unit, Line B	$ 700	$ 750	n/a
Actual warranty outlays, Line B:			
Parts	$3,000	$ 9,600	$12,000
Labour and overhead	$7,000	$22,000	$30,000

There were no sales of either product in 20X7.

Required:

1. Give entries for annual sales and expenses for 20X5 and 20X6 separately by product line. All sales were for cash.
2. Complete the tabulation below:

	Year-End Amounts		
Accounts	**20X5**	**20X6**	**20X7**
Warranty expense (on income statement)	$	$	n/a
Estimated warranty liability (on balance sheet)	$	$	$

★ **A12-8 Terminology:** Briefly define each of the following:

1. bond indenture
2. lien
3. maintenance test
4. executory contract
5. commercial paper
6. demand loan
7. operating line of credit
8. leverage
9. contractual obligation
10. covenant
11. commercial mortgage
12. term loan

★★ **A12-9 Long-Term Note—Borrower and Lender:** On 1 January 20X9, a borrower signed a long-term note, face amount, $700,000; time to maturity, four years; stated rate of interest, 6%. The effective rate of interest of 7% determined the cash received by the borrower. The principal of the note will be paid at maturity; stated interest is due at the end of each year.

Required:

1. Compute the cash received by the borrower.
2. Give the required entries for the borrower for each of the four years. Use the effective-interest method.

★★★ **A12-10 Note with Below–Market Interest Rate:** Sable Company purchased merchandise for resale on 1 January 20X5, for $5,000 cash plus a $20,000, two-year note payable. The principal is due on 31 December 20X6; the note specified 3% interest payable each 31 December. Assume that Sable's going rate of interest for this type of debt was 8%. The accounting period ends 31 December.

Required:

1. Give the entry to record the purchase on 1 January 20X5. Show computations (round to the nearest dollar).
2. Complete the following tabulation:

Amount of cash interest payable each 31 December	$_____
Total interest expense for the two-year period	$_____
Amount of interest reported on income statement for 20X5	$_____
Amount of net liability reported on the balance sheet at 31 December 20X5	$_____

3. Give the entries at each year-end for Sable.

★★ **A12-11 Bonds—Compute Four Bond Prices:** Compute the bond price for each of the following situations (show computations and round to nearest dollar):

a. A 10-year, $1,000 bond with annual interest at 6% (payable semi-annually) purchased to yield 8% interest.
b. An eight-year, $1,000 bond with annual interest at 6% (payable annually) purchased to yield 6% interest.
c. A 10-year, $1,000 bond with annual interest at 7% (payable 3.5% semi-annually) purchased to yield 6% interest.
d. An eight-year, $1,000 bond with annual interest at 6% (payable annually) purchased to yield 7% interest.

★ ★ ★

A12-12 Bonds—Compare Effective Interest, Straight Line: ABC Company issues a $5,000,000, 8 1/2% bond on 1 October 20X4. At this time, market interest rates are in the range of 8%. The bond had a 20-year life from 1 October 20X4, and paid interest semi-annually on 31 March and 30 September.

Required:

1. Calculate the proceeds that would be raised on bond issuance.
2. Prepare an amortization table using the straight-line method. Complete the first four payments *only*.
3. Prepare journal entries for 20X4 and 20X5, using straight-line amortization. ABC has a 31 December fiscal year-end.
4. Repeat requirement 2 using the effective-interest method.
5. Prepare journal entries for 20X4 and 20X5, using the effective-interest method of amortization.
6. Which method of amortization is required by Canadian GAAP? Why?

★ ★ ★

A12-13 Bonds—Effective Interest, Straight Line: On 30 September 20X1, Golf Mania Company issued $3 million face-value debentures. The bonds have a nominal interest rate of 10% per annum, payable semi-annually on 31 March and 30 September, and mature in 10 years, on 30 September 20X11. The bonds were issued at a price to yield 8%. Golf Mania Company's fiscal year ends on 30 September.

Required:

1. Determine the price at which the bonds were issued.
2. Prepare journal entries to record the issuance of the bonds, payment of interest, and all necessary adjustments for the first two years (that is, through 30 September 20X3), using straight-line amortization.
3. Prepare the journal entries relating to the bonds through 30 September 20X3, as above, but using the effective-interest method of amortization.
4. Compute the amount of unamortized bond premium remaining on 1 October 20X7 under the effective-interest method, without preparing an amortization schedule. (Note: At any point in time, the book value of the bonds is equal to the present value of the remaining cash flows.)
5. Calculate the amount of premium amortization, using the effective-interest method, for the six months ending 31 March 20X8.

★ ★

A12-14 Bonds—Effective Interest, Recording and Reporting: On 1 May 20X5, Ginko Corp. issues $10,000,000 of 7% bonds, with interest paid semi-annually on 30 April and 31 October. The bonds were originally dated 1 November 20X0, and were 20-year bonds. The effective interest rate on the day of issuance was 8%. The company uses the effective-interest method to measure interest expense.

1. Calculate the issue proceeds at 1 May 20X5
2. Provide the journal entry for:
   a. 1 May 20X5
   b. 30 June 20X5 (the fiscal year-end)
   c. 31 October 20X5
   d. 30 April 20X6
3. Show how the bond would be presented on the 30 June 20X5 balance sheet

★★ **A12-15 Bonds Issued between Interest Dates:** Ralson Smita Ltd. (RSL) issued $950,000 of three-year, 7% (payable semi-annually) bonds payable for $934,788 plus accrued interest. Interest is payable each 28 February and 31 August. The bonds were dated 1 March 20X8, and were issued on 1 June 20X9. The accounting period ends on 28 February.

Required:

1. How much accrued interest should be recognized at date of sale?
2. Explain how the $934,788 would be calculated.
3. Assume that the present value of the bond would have been $936,818 if it had been issued on 31 August 20X9. This reflected a market interest rate of 8%. Give entries from 1 June 20X9 through 28 February 20X10.

★★★ **A12-16 Bonds Issued between Interest Dates:** Randy Corporation issued $200,000 of 7.6% (payable each 28 February and 31 August), four-year bonds. The bonds were dated 1 March 20X4, and mature on 28 February 20X8. The bonds were issued (to yield 8%) on 30 September 20X4, for appropriate proceeds plus accrued interest. The accounting period ends on 31 December.

eXcel

Required:

1. Calculate the present value of the bond assuming that it was issued on 1 March 20X4.
2. Prepare an amortization schedule using the effective-interest method of amortization.
3. Calculate the proceeds of the bond reflecting the fact that it was issued on 30 September 20X4. Also calculate the accrued interest.
4. Give entries from date of sale through 28 February 20X5. Base amortization on (2) above. Credit the accrued interest collected on 30 September 20X4 to accrued interest payable in the initial journal entry.

★★★ **A12-17 Bonds Issued between Interest Dates:** Radian Company issued to Seivers Company $30,000 of three-year, 6% bonds dated 1 December 20X5. Interest is payable semi-annually on 31 May and 30 November. The bonds were issued on 28 February 20X6. The effective interest rate was 8%.

eXcel

Required:

1. Calculate the present value of the bond assuming that it had been issued on 1 December 20X5.
2. Prepare a bond amortization schedule. Use the effective-interest method of amortization.
3. Calculate the proceeds of the bond reflecting the fact that it was issued on 28 February 20X6. Also calculate the accrued interest.
4. How much amortization is included in interest expense for the period ended 31 May 20X6?

★★★ **A12-18 Bonds—between Interest Dates; Effective Interest:** On 1 January 20X1, THB Corporation issued $100,000 of five-year, 12% unsecured debentures at a net price of $89,944. Interest is payable annually, on the anniversary date of the bonds.

Required:

1. Determine the effective interest rate or effective yield on the bonds.
2. Prepare an amortization schedule for the life of the bond, under the effective-interest method.
3. Assume instead that the bond was issued on 1 March 20X1. Calculate the proceeds on issuance of the bond and the accrued interest.
4. Assume instead that the bond was issued on 31 August 20X2. Calculate the proceeds on issuance of the bond and the accrued interest.

★★ **A12-19 Upfront Fees and Notes Payable:** On 30 June 20X4, a borrower arranged a $900,000 four-year note payable that required 10% interest, paid annually at the end of each loan year, and principal repayment at the end of the fourth year. On signing the note payable contract, the borrower agreed to a $54,600 upfront fee, which was deducted from the cash proceeds of the note.

Required:

1. Calculate the effective interest rate associated with the loan.
2. Give the required entries for the borrower over the life of the loan.

★★ **A12-20 Upfront Fees and Notes Payable:** On 1 January 20X8, a borrower arranged a $500,000 three-year 2% note payable, with interest paid at the end of each loan year. There was an upfront fee of $53,460, which was deducted from the cash proceeds of the note on 1 January, 20X8.

Required:

1. Calculate the effective interest rate associated with the loan. What net amount is received on 1 January 20X8?
2. Calculate the interest expense reported by the borrower for each year of the loan.

★★ **A12-21 Upfront Fees and Notes Payable:** Marius Corp. borrowed $600,000 from a lender with a three-year term. The loan required payments for interest of $18,000 at the end of each loan year. In addition, Marius paid an upfront fee of $32,677, which it will expense as a miscellaneous bank charge. Management was delighted to get a 3% loan, because other financial institutions had indicated that the interest rate would be in the range of 4%.

Required:

1. Did Marius get a 3% loan? Explain, and calculate the effective interest rate associated with the loan.
2. What is the appropriate accounting treatment of the upfront fee? When is it expensed?
3. Give the required entries for Marius over the life of the loan.

★★ **A12-22 Bond Issuance, Retirement:** On 1 May 20X8, Wharf Minco (WM) issued bonds with a face value of $5,000,000 and a stated annual interest rate of 5% for a price that would yield a market rate of interest of 6%. The bonds pay interest each 1 May and 1 November and mature on 1 November 20X16.

On 1 May 20X9, after interest is paid, WM buys back (redeems) bonds with a face value of $2,300,000 for $2,050,000. The company uses the effective-interest method of amortization.

Required:

Prepare all necessary journal entries from 1 May 20X8 to 1 November 20X9 inclusive. Include adjusting journal entries as of 31 December, the company's year-end.

★★ **A12-23 Debt Issuance and Early Retirement:** On 1 January 20X4, Quaid Company issued $100,000 of 10% debentures. The following information relates to these bonds:

Bond date	1 January 20X4
Yield rate	8%
Maturity date	1 January 20X9
Interest payment date	31 December

On 1 March 20X5, Quaid retires $10,000 (face value) of the bonds when the market price is 110. Accrued interest on these bonds was paid to the date of retirement.

Required:
Provide entries for Quaid on the following dates under both the effective interest and straight-line methods of amortization.

1. 1 January 20X4, bond issuance.
2. 31 December 20X4, first interest payment.
3. 1 March 20X5, entries to record appropriate interest on the portion of the bond retired and to extinguish the bonds.

★★ **A12-24 Bond Retirement:** The following cases are independent:

Case A On 1 January 20X5, Radar Company issued $200,000 of bonds payable with a stated interest rate of 12%, payable annually each 31 December. The bonds matured in 20 years and had a call price of 103, exercisable by Radar Company at any time after the fifth year. The bonds originally sold to yield 10%.

On 31 December 20X16, after interest was paid, the company called the bonds. Radar Company uses effective interest amortization; its accounting period ends 31 December.

Required:
Give the entry for retirement of the debt.

Case B On 1 January 20X2, Nue Corporation issued $200,000 of 10%, 10-year bonds to yield 11%. Interest is paid each 31 December, which also is the end of the accounting period. The company uses effective interest amortization. On 1 July 20X5, the company purchased all of the bonds at 101 plus accrued interest.

Required:
1. Give the issuance entry.
2. Give all entries on 1 July 20X5.

★★★ **A12-25 Bond Retirement:** The following three cases are independent.

Case A At 31 December 20X3, Happy Ltd reports the following on its balance sheet:

Bonds payable, due 30 June 20X16, 6%, interest payable annually on 30 June	$10,000,000
Discount on bonds payable	124,500
Upfront fees	35,700

On 1 March 20X4, 80% of the bond issue was bought back in the open market and retired at 99 plus accrued interest.

Required:
Provide the entries to record the interest and the retirement. Record interest and amortization only on the portion of the bond that is retired; amortization of $381 must be recorded for the upfront costs and $1,328 on the discount.

Case B On 31 December 20X7, Devon Company has the following bond on the balance sheet:

Bond payable, 8%, interest due semi-annually on 31 March and 30 September; maturity date, 30 September 20X10	$18,000,000
Discount on bonds payable	132,000
	$17,868,000

Appropriate interest was accrued, as accrued interest payable, to 31 December 20X7 and the bond discount was amortized to 31 December 20X7. On 31 March 20X8, semi-annual interest was paid and the bond discount was amortized by $12,000. Then, 40% of the bond was retired at a cost of $7,030,000 (exclusive of interest).

Required:
Provide the entries to record the bond interest and retirement on 31 March 20X8.

Case C On 31 December 20X7, a company has the following bond on the balance sheet:

Bond payable, 7%, interest due semi-annually on
    31 Dec. and 30 June; maturity date, 30 June 20X11 $10,000,000
Premium on bonds payable   84,000
     $10,084,000

On 28 February 20X8, 20% of the bond was retired for $2,200,000 plus accrued interest to 28 February. Interest was paid on this date only for the portion of the bonds that were retired. Premium amortization was recorded on this date in the amount of $800, representing amortization on the retired debt only.

Required:
Provide the entries to record the bond interest on 28 February and the bond retirement.

 A12-26 Bond Issuance and Retirement, Accrued Interest: On 1 June 20X5, Bridle Corp. issued $40,000,000 of 7.5% bonds, with interest paid semi-annually on 30 April and 31 October. The bonds were originally dated 1 November 20X4, and were 15-year bonds. The bonds were issued to yield 8%; accrued interest was received on issuance. The company uses the effective-interest method to amortize the discount. On 31 December 20X5, 10% of the bond issue was retired for 99 plus accrued interest.

Required:
1. Calculate the issue proceeds and the accrued interest. Note: Begin by calculating the present value of the bond at 30 May and 31 October 20X5
2. Provide the journal entry for 1 June 20X5.
3. Provide the journal entry at 31 October 20X5.
4. Provide the journal entry at 31 December 20X5.

 A12-27 Bonds Payable: Issuance and Defeasance; Entries: On 1 April 20X5, Raptor Company sold 10,000 of its 11%, 15-year, $1,000 face value bonds, to yield 12%. Interest payment dates are 1 April and 1 October, and the company uses the effective-interest method of amortization. The bond indenture allows for defeasance.

Required:
1. Give the entry that would be made on 1 April 20X5.
2. Assume instead that the bonds were issued on 30 April 20X5 at 101 plus accrued interest. Give the entry that would be made on April 30.
3. Assume instead that the bonds were issued on 1 June 20X5 for 99 plus accrued interest. Give the entry that would be made on 1 June.
4. Return to the original facts. On 1 April 20X6, Raptor exercised its defeasance option. The cash transferred to the trustee was $9,200,000. Prepare journal entries on the interest dates, 1 October 20X5, 31 December 20X5, and 1 April, 20X6. Then, prepare the journal entry that would be recorded for the defeasance on 1 April 20X6.
5. Explain the difference between a defeasance and an in-substance defeasance, and describe how your entry in requirement 4 would be different if Raptor had undertaken an in-substance defeasance.

A12-28 Retirement—Open Market Purchase: On 1 July 20X2, Coputer Corporation issued $600,000 of 5% (payable each 30 June and 31 December), 10-year bonds payable. The bonds were issued to yield 6%. Use effective interest amortization for the discount.

Due to an increase in interest rates, these bonds were selling in the market at the end of June 20X5 at an effective rate of 8%. Because the company had available cash, $200,000 (face amount) of the bonds were purchased in the market and retired on 1 July 20X5.

Required:

1. Give the entry by Coputer Corporation to record issuance of the bonds on 1 July 20X2.
2. Give the entry by Coputer Corporation to record the retirement of part of the debt on 1 July 20X5. How should the gain or loss be reported on the 20X5 financial statements of Coputer Corporation?
3. Was the retirement economically favourable to the issuer, investor, or neither?

 A12-29 Debt Issuance, Early Retirement: Calcified Limited issued long-term promissory notes of $1,000,000 on 1 April 20X0. The notes mature on 31 March 20X8. Interest is payable annually at a nominal rate of 5%. At the date of issue, the market rate of interest for debt of equivalent risk and maturity was 7%. The notes contain an option for Calcified to retire the debt on any anniversary date on or after 31 March 20X6. The amount required for retirement will be based on the market interest rate on the retirement date.

Required:

1. How much did Calcified receive when the notes were issued?
2. What amounts relating to the notes will appear on Calcified's balance sheet at 31 March 20X2?
3. Suppose that Calcified exercises its retirement option on 1 April 20X7 when the market interest rate is 8%. In general journal form, make the entry to record retirement of the notes.

 A12-30 Bond Issuance, Defeasance: Computer Medic Limited issues $800,000 of 9.5% bonds on 1 July 20X1. Additional information on the bond issue is as follows:

Bond date	1 January 20X1
Maturity date	1 January 20X11
Yield rate	12%
Interest payment dates	30 June, 31 December

Required:

1. Record the bond issue and the first interest payment under the effective-interest method.
2. On 1 August 20X6, the company defeased 30% of the bonds for the market price of 103 plus accrued interest. Record the entries necessary to update the portion of the bond issue defeased (interest from 30 June 20X6) and to record the defeasance.
3. What critical element of a defeasance allows it to be recorded with derecognition of the bond? Contrast this to in-substance defeasance.
4. Have interest rates risen or fallen between the issuance of the bonds and the early retirement? (Assume no significant change in the company's risk.)
5. Discuss the nature of the gain or loss on retirement you recorded in (2). In explaining this item to a financial statement user, what cautions would you include in your discussion?
6. Record the entry to accrue interest expense on 31 December 20X6, on the remaining bonds.

A12-31 Bonds, Comprehensive: Batra Company sold $1,500,000 of five-year, 12% bonds on 1 August 20X2. Additional information on the bond issue is as follows:

Bond date	1 February 20X2
Maturity date	31 January 20X7
Yield rate	10%
Interest payment dates	31 July and 31 January
Bond discount/premium amortization	Effective-interest method
Proceeds on issuance	$1,606,617

Required:

1. Record the bond issuance on 1 August 20X2.
2. Prepare the adjusting journal entries on 31 December 20X2.
3. Give the entry to record the interest payment on 31 January 20X3.
4. On 31 July 20X5, after interest is paid, Batra purchases and retires 40% of the bond issue at 98. Record the bond retirement.
5. What item(s) will appear on the cash flow statement with respect to the retirement? Also indicate the appropriate section.
6. How will the remaining bond appear on the balance sheet directly after the retirement?
7. Assume that bonds of similar risk and maturity are yielding 14%. What fair value disclosure will the company make?
8. If the market low-risk interest rate was 8% on 31 July immediately after the retirement in requirement 5, how much money would have to be invested in securities to defease the remaining bond?

 A12-32 Foreign Exchange: On 1 January 20X4, Traker Limited borrowed US$450,000, a five-year loan. Traker Limited has a 31 December year-end. Exchange rates were as follows:

	US$1 =
1 January 20X4	Cdn$1.10
31 December 20X4	1.05
31 December 20X5	1.12
31 December 20X6	1.11
31 December 20X7	1.05
31 December 20X8	1.09

Required:

Prepare journal entries to reflect the exchange gains and losses on the loan principal over the five-year loan term. Deal only with gains and losses caused by the loan principal. Ignore any gains and losses caused by interest accruals during the year.

 A12-33 Foreign Exchange: In order to take advantage of lower U.S. interest rates, Zhang Limited borrowed $8 million from a U.S. bank on 1 May 20X2. Annual interest, at 7 1/4%, was due each subsequent 1 May, with lump-sum principal due on 1 May 20X5. Zhang Limited has a 31 December year-end. Exchange rates were as follows:

	US$1 =
1 May 20X2	Cdn$1.09
31 December 20X2	1.12
1 May 20X3	1.14
31 December 20X3	1.10
Average, 1 May 20X2 − 31 December 20X2	1.11
Average, 1 January 20X3 − 31 December 20X3	1.09

Required:

1. Calculate the loan principal that would appear on the 31 December 20X2 and 20X3 balance sheet and the related exchange gain or loss on the 20X2 and 20X3 income statement.

2. Calculate interest expense for the years ended 31 December 20X2 and 20X3. Why would there be an exchange gain or loss related to interest expense? Calculate this gain or loss for the year ended 31 December 20X2.

★ **A12-34 Foreign Exchange:** On 1 February 20X9, Development Action Limited (DAL) obtained a five-year loan from a major New York bank. The loan is for US$2,000,000, bears interest at 5% per annum (paid annually), and matures on 31 December 20X14. The promissory note was issued at par. DAL reports in Canadian dollars. At the date the note was issued, the exchange rate was US$1.00 = Cdn$1.15. On 31 December 20X9, the exchange rate was US$1.00 = Cdn$1.12, and the average exchange rate for the last 11 months of the year was $1.13.

Required:

1. Prepare the journal entry to record the loan on 1 February 20X9.

2. What amounts relating to the loan will appear on DAL's balance sheet and income statement on 31 December 20X9?

★★ **A12-35 Debt Issuance, Subsequent Reported Values:** Pinnacle Limited issued $1,000,000 in promissory notes on 30 June 20X0. The notes mature on 30 June 20X6, and bear interest at 8% per annum, payable every six months after issuance. The notes were issued to yield 12% per annum. Pinnacle's fiscal year ends on 31 December. Pinnacle uses the effective-interest method of amortization.

Required:

1. What were the proceeds from issuance?

2. What amounts will be shown on Pinnacle's financial statements for the year ended 31 December 20X0?

3. Assume that on 31 December 20X3 the market rate of interest is 10% for notes of similar risk and maturity. Determine:
   a. The book value (including unamortized discount/premium) that will be shown on the balance sheet at that date; and
   b. The fair value that will be disclosed in the notes.

★★ **A12-36 Partial Cash Flow Statement:** The following balances are from the balance sheet of Merit Ltd.

Account	20X9	20X8
Bonds payable, 7%	$17,000,000	$20,000,000
Premium on bonds payable	116,800	152,500
Bonds payable, 6.5%	4,000,000	10,000,000
Discount on bonds payable	21,300	61,500
Bonds payable, 7.25%	5,000,000	0
Premium on bonds payable	132,000	0

OTHER INFORMATION:

a. A portion of the 7% bond payable was retired at 101. Premium amortization of $14,700 was recorded during the year.

b. A portion of the 6.5% bond payable was retired at 97.5. Discount amortization of $5,200 was recorded during the year.

c. The 7.25% bond was issued in 20X9 in exchange for land. Premium amortization of $17,200 has been recorded during the year.

Required:

Prepare cash flow statement disclosures related to the above transactions. Indicate the section of the cash flow statement, the caption for the item, the amount, and whether the item is an increase (or add back), or a decrease (or deduction.)

★★★ **A12-37 Comprehensive Cash Flow Statement:** The 20X6 comparative balance sheets and the 20X6 income statement for Gamme Company follow.

	December 31	
Comparative Balance Sheets	**20X6**	**20X5**
Cash	$ 49,582	$ 35,000
Cash equivalent short-term investments	14,000	28,000
Accounts receivable	75,000	50,000
Allowance for doubtful accounts	(3,000)	(2,000)
Inventory	40,000	120,000
Prepaid insurance	30,000	20,000
Long-term investment, equity method	45,000	40,000
Land	350,000	250,000
Building and equipment	205,816	100,000
Accumulated depreciation	(80,000)	(50,000)
Intangible assets, net	35,000	45,000
Total assets	$761,398	$636,000
Accounts payable	$ 70,000	$ 40,000
Income tax payable	8,000	5,000
Dividends payable	12,000	6,000
Note payable, building	63,398	—
Future income tax	25,000	20,000
Mortgage payable	80,000	—
Note payable	100,000	—
Bonds payable	—	180,000
Unamortized bond discount	—	(12,000)
Common shares	300,000	300,000
Retained earnings	103,000	97,000
Total liabilities and owners' equity	$761,398	$636,000

Income Statement, 20X6		
Sales		$620,000
Cost of goods sold		(400,000)
Gross margin		$220,000
Bad debt expense	$ (18,000)	
Interest expense	(23,000)	
Depreciation	(42,000)	
Amortization of intangibles	(10,000)	
Other expenses	(86,000)	
Gain on sale of short-term investments	3,000	
Gain on bond retirement	20,000	
Gain on sale of equipment	5,250	
Investment revenue	30,000	
Income tax expense	(23,250)	(144,000)
Net income		$ 76,000

ADDITIONAL INFORMATION ABOUT EVENTS IN 20X6:

a. The long-term equity investment represents a 25% interest in Wickens Company. During 20X6, Wickens paid $100,000 of dividends and earned $120,000.

b. At the end of 20X6, Gamme acquired land for $100,000 by assuming an $80,000 mortgage and paying the balance in cash.

c. Equipment (cost, $20,000; book value, $8,000) was sold at a gain.

d. Gamme constructed equipment for its own use in 20X6. The cost of the finished equipment, $50,000, includes $5,000 of capitalized interest.

e. Gamme bought a building for $75,816 during the year, borrowing all the purchase price. By year-end, the loan had been reduced to $63,398.

f. The bonds were retired before maturity at a $20,000 gain. Discount amortized in 20X6: $4,000.

g. Gamme declared $70,000 of dividends in 20X6.

Required:

Prepare the 20X6 cash flow statement for Gamme Company, using the indirect method to present the operating section.

CHAPTER 13

Shareholders' Equity

INTRODUCTION

Shareholders' equity is the difference between the assets and liabilities of an entity. Equity is the *residual interest* in net assets because it is what is left when liabilities are subtracted from assets—the residual. Equity is therefore sometimes referred to as **net assets**. Equity has various components, or sources, however.

Generally, shareholders' equity includes the *net contribution to the firm by the owners*, called contributed capital, plus the firm's *cumulative earnings retained* in the business.

Manitoba Telcom Services Inc. reports total assets of $2,984.2 million, which are financed through $1,554.4 in debt (52% of assets) and $1,429.8 in equity (48% of assets). Equity is subdi-

vided into $1,115 of share capital, contributed surplus of $18.2, and $96.6 of retained earnings. The notes disclose that the share capital is all from common shares, although the company is authorized to issue preferred shares if it wishes. Contributed capital has arisen from stock options, and retained earnings is cumulative net income less dividends.

This chapter examines accounting issues related to contributed capital, particularly issuance and retirement of share capital. Accounting and disclosure for retained earnings is also covered, including accounting for dividends. Other components of shareholders' equity are also discussed, with special attention given to accumulated other comprehensive income.

THE CORPORATE FORM OF ORGANIZATION

The whole topic of accounting for shareholders' equity applies only to corporations; only corporations can have shareholders and shareholder's equity. Partnerships and sole proprietorships have ownership interests, but not share capital. A corporation may be formed either provincially or federally, and there is legislation governing the rights and responsibilities associated with incorporation. The discussion in this text is based on the federal *Canada Business Corporations Act (CBCA)*, with occasional references to provincial legislation.

Private versus Public Corporations

Private Companies Corporate entities may be either private or public. The vast majority of corporations in Canada are private, many of which are quite small. However, approximately half of the corporations on the *Financial Post*'s list of the 500 largest Canadian corporations are private. **Private companies** have a limited number of shareholders (generally limited to a maximum of 50 by the provincial securities acts.) Shares cannot be publicly traded. Private companies generally have a **shareholders' agreement** that describes the ways in which shareholders can transfer their shares, as well as other rights and responsibilities of the shareholders.

Private companies may adopt *differential disclosure*, with unanimous shareholder consent. Using this reporting alternative, companies may choose not to follow certain complex *CICA Handbook* accounting recommendations if they do not meet user needs.

Public Companies **Public companies** are those whose securities, either debt or equity, are traded on stock exchanges. Public companies must, in addition to the reporting requirements required by GAAP, comply with the extensive reporting requirements that govern the particular stock exchange or exchanges on which the companies' securities trade.

Share Capital

Share capital, represented by share certificates, represents ownership in a corporation. Shares may be bought, sold, or otherwise transferred by the shareholders without the consent of the corporation unless there is an enforceable agreement to the contrary.

classes of shares

within each group of share capital (common or preference), different types of shares may be created, each with differing rights and privileges; dividend entitlements and voting rights are characteristics that might be altered among classes

Common Shares A corporation may be authorized to issue several different **classes of shares**, each with distinctive rights. At least one class of shares is the **common shares**, which provides the right to vote and receive the residual interest in the net assets of the company on dissolution. Voting rights include the power to vote for the members of the Board of Directors. Common shareholders are entitled to dividends only as *declared*, and they are at risk if the Board of Directors chooses to reduce or eliminate a dividend.

Preferred Shares **Preferred shares** are so designated because they confer certain preferences over common shares. Preferred shares are not always titled "preferred," and may have a variety of names (for example, Class A shares). The most common feature of preferred shares is a priority claim on dividends declared, usually at a stated rate or amount. Characteristics of preferred shares often involve the following:

- *Limited or non-existent voting rights.* Typically, preferred shares are non-voting. They may be given voting rights in certain circumstances, such as when preferred dividends have not been paid or during a vote on a takeover bid.
- *Dividend priority.* A corporation generally has no obligation to declare dividends. When the Board of Directors does declare a dividend, preferred shareholders have preference, which means that they get their preferred dividend before any common dividend. The dividend rate on preferred shares must be specified, usually as a dollar amount per share, such as $1.20 per share. Alternatively, the dividend may be described as a percentage or rate, such as 8 1/4%, 6%, or floating rate (i.e., tied to prime interest rates). When the dividend rate is a percentage, it must refer to some sort of stated

principal value for the share, which is a reference price, such as $100 or $10. This value has no special legal significance.

- *Cumulative dividends.* Preferred shares may have the right to receive cumulative unpaid past dividends (called **dividends in arrears**) in the current year before any common dividends can be paid. Preferred shares are normally cumulative, to reduce the risk of non-payment.

- *Participating dividends.* Preferred shares may have the right to share additional dividends with common shares, once the annual dividend has been paid to the preferred shareholders and the common shareholders receive some kind of base return.

- *Assets upon liquidation.* In case of corporate dissolution, preferred shares may have a priority over the common shareholders on the assets of the corporation up to a stated amount per share.

- *Conversion.* Preferred shareholders may have the right to convert to common shares, or to another class of preferred shares with different entitlements.

- *Guarantee.* Preferred shareholders may have a guaranteed return of their invested principal at some point in time through redemption or retraction provisions.

The accounting implications of these terms will be explored in later sections of this chapter and the next.

Special Terms and Conditions While "classic" common and preferred shares abound, so do more exotic examples. In Canada, preferred issues are often structured to look a lot like debt—they pay a dividend related to interest rates, and provide for repayment at a specific point in time. These preferred share issues are designed to be sold to investors who want preferential dividend income, along with some of the security provided by debt. The result is not permanent equity investment. We'll take a closer look at these types of preferred shares in the next chapter.

Some companies issue a class of common shares that has no voting rights or limited voting rights. These shares are called **restricted shares** or **special shares**. For example, Four Seasons Hotels has two types of common shares, variable voting and limited voting. The limited voting shares have one vote each, while the variable voting shares had, in 2005, 16.09 votes each. However, if an additional quantity of *limited* voting shares is issued, the number of votes carried by each *variable* voting share increases proportionately. In the case of Four Seasons, the variable voting shares are held exclusively by the company's founder and his family. This example shows that the objective in establishing the voting rights is to keep control in certain hands.

Par Value versus No–Par Value Shares

While the *CBCA* and most provincial business corporation acts prohibit the use of par value shares, one or two provincial jurisdictions do allow their issuance. **Par value shares** have a designated dollar amount per share, as stated in the articles of incorporation and as printed on the face of the share certificates. Par value shares may be either common or preferred.

Par value shares sold initially at less than par are said to have been issued at a **discount**. Par value shares sold initially above par are said to have been issued at a **premium**. When par value shares are issued at a premium, the par value is assigned to the share account, and any excess to the premium on share capital account, a component of contributed capital. Par values are usually set very low, and thus a major portion of the proceeds on issuance is classified as the premium. The difference in classification has no economic significance.

No-par shares do not carry a designated or assigned value per share. This allows for all consideration received on sale of the securities to be classified in the share capital account, and it avoids the need to divide the consideration into two essentially artificial components, par value and excess over par.

Only 4 of 200 of Canadian public companies surveyed by *Financial Reporting in Canada 2006* reported a par (or stated) value for any of their share classes. Such shares are quite common in other parts of the world.

TERMS RELATED TO SHARE CAPITAL

The following terms are used to describe important aspects of share capital:

- *Authorized share capital.* The maximum number of shares that can be legally issued. Under the *CBCA*, a corporation is entitled to issue an unlimited number of shares. The corporation may choose to place a limit on authorized shares. Such a limit must be stated in the articles of incorporation and can be changed at a later date by application to the appropriate ministry for an amendment to the corporation's articles of incorporation.

- *Issued share capital.* The number of shares that have been issued to shareholders to date.

- *Outstanding share capital.* The number of shares that have been issued and are currently owned by shareholders. Issued shares will be lower than outstanding shares if there are treasury shares outstanding. Shares that have been repurchased from shareholders and retired are considered to be neither issued nor outstanding.

- *Treasury shares.* Shares that are reacquired by the corporation, and held pending resale. Treasury shares are *issued* but not *outstanding*.

- *Subscribed shares.* Unissued shares set aside to meet subscription contracts (i.e., shares "sold" on credit and not yet paid for). Subscribed shares are usually not issued until the subscription price is paid in full.

CONCEPT REVIEW

1. What is the essential difference between a public and a private corporation?
2. What is the most common preference right of preferred shares over common shares?
3. What are restricted shares?
4. What are treasury shares?

ACCOUNTING FOR SHARE CAPITAL AT ISSUANCE

Accounting for shareholders' equity emphasizes source; therefore, if a corporation has more than one share class, separate accounts must be maintained for each. If there is only one share class, an account entitled *share capital* may be used. In cases where there are two or more classes, account titles associated with the shares are used, such as *common shares; class A shares; preferred shares, $5;* or *preferred shares, $1.25.* The dollar amounts listed with no-par preferred shares indicate the dividend entitlement.

Authorization The articles of incorporation will authorize an unlimited (or, less frequently, a limited) number of shares. This authorization may be recorded as a memo entry in the general journal and in the ledger account by the following notation:

Common shares—No-par value (authorized: unlimited shares)

No-Par Value Shares Issued for Cash When shares are issued, a share certificate, specifying the number of shares represented, is prepared for each shareholder. Companies keep track of the number of shares held by each shareholder in a shareholder ledger, a subsidiary ledger to the share capital account.

In most cases, shares are sold and issued for cash rather than on a subscription (i.e., credit) basis. The issuance of 10,000 common shares, no-par, for cash of $10.20 per share would be recorded as follows:

Cash	102,000	
Common shares, no-par (10,000 shares)		102,000

Notice that the common share account is credited for the total proceeds received.

Shares Issued on a Subscription Basis Prospective shareholders may sign a contract to purchase a specified number of shares on credit, with payment due at one or more specified future dates. Such contractual agreements are known as **stock subscriptions**, and the shares involved are called subscribed share capital. Shares may not be issued until fully paid, according to the terms of incorporation legislation. Because financial statement elements have been created by a legal contract, accounting recognition is necessary. The purchase price is debited to stock subscriptions receivable, and share capital subscribed is credited.

To illustrate, assume that 120 no-par common shares of BT Corporation are subscribed for at $12 by J. Doe. The entry by BT Corporation would be as follows:

Stock subscriptions receivable—common shares (Doe)	1,440	
Common shares subscribed, no-par (120 shares)		1,440

The receivable will be paid in three $480 instalments. Assume the third and last collection on the above subscription is received. The entries would be as follows:

To record the collection		
Cash	480	
Stock subscriptions receivable—common shares (Doe)		480
To record issuance of shares		
Common shares subscribed, no-par (120 shares)	1,440	
Common shares, no-par (120 shares)		1,440

A credit balance in common shares subscribed reflects the corporation's obligation to issue the 120 shares on fulfilment of the terms of the agreement by the subscriber. This account is reported in shareholders' equity on the balance sheet along with the related share capital account.

There are two alternative ways to present stock subscriptions receivable. Some argue it should be classified as an asset: a current asset if the corporation expects current collection; otherwise, a non-current asset under the category other assets. Others argue it should be offset against the common shares subscribed account in the shareholders' equity section of the balance sheet. This presentation ensures that the equity accounts include only paid-in amounts as capital; promises of future payment are recorded but netted out. Offset is the preferred approach, as it maintains the integrity of the equity elements of financial statements.

Default on Subscriptions When a subscriber defaults after partial fulfillment of the subscription contract, certain complexities arise. In case of default, the corporation may decide to (1) return all payments received to the subscriber; (2) issue shares equivalent to the number paid for in full, rather than the total number subscribed; or (3) keep the money received. The first two options involve no disadvantage to the subscriber, although the corporation may incur an economic loss if share prices have dropped. The third option is not common, although legislation generally does not prevent it.

Non-Cash Issuance of Share Capital Corporations sometimes issue share capital for non-cash consideration. In one example, Butterfield Equities Corporation privately placed 1.8 million preferred shares and 100,000 common shares, primarily in exchange for real estate.

When a corporation issues its shares for non-cash assets or services or to settle debt, the transaction should be recorded at fair value—but there are two fair values present, the fair value of the asset received, and the fair value of the shares issued. In general, the transaction is valued at the fair value of the shares given up, unless the valuation of the shares is problematic. If the fair value of the assets is more clearly determinable, then this value should be used.

To value the shares given up, it is necessary for the shares to be actively traded. Many Canadian corporations do not have actively traded shares. Therefore, it is often far easier to assess the value of the assets received. Even this can be complicated, since appraisals may not be accurate. Finally, the lower-of-cost-or-market rule always applies. No asset may be recorded at a value higher than its market value.

To illustrate, assume that Bronex Corporation issued 136,000 Class A shares in exchange for land. The land was appraised at $420,000, while the shares, based on the only prior transaction in the shares, were valued at $450,000. The Board of Directors passed a motion approving the issuance of shares to be valued at the average of these two prices, $435,000. The valuation could have been based on the value of the shares, but perhaps the fact that there was only one prior transaction meant that the valuation was suspect. The quality of the appraisal on the land value would be critically examined. The choice of average values is justifiable on materiality grounds. The two values were reasonably close to each other, but the Board must be convinced that the value of $435,000 does not overstate the fair value of the land. The following entry would be recorded:

Land	435,000	
Share capital, Class A (136,000 shares)		435,000

The issuance of share capital for non-cash consideration can involve questionable valuations. Some companies have rejected market values or independent appraisals and permitted directors to set arbitrary values. In some cases, the overvaluation of assets received results in overvaluation of shareholders' equity. This is referred to as **watered stock**.[1] Here, the value of the resources received for shares is less than (i.e., it waters down) the recorded value of the shares issued. In contrast, some companies that undervalue assets understate shareholders' equity—resulting in a condition often called **secret reserves**.

Basket Sale of Share Capital A corporation usually sells each class of its share capital separately. However, a corporation may sell two or more classes for one lump-sum amount (often referred to as a *basket sale*).

When two or more classes of securities are sold and issued for a single lump sum, the total proceeds must be allocated logically among the several classes of securities. Two methods used in such situations are (1) the *proportional method*, in which the lump sum received is allocated proportionately among the classes of shares on the basis of the relative market value of each security, and (2) the *incremental method*, in which the market value of one security is used as a basis for that security and the remainder of the lump sum is allocated

---

[1] This term originated from an old cattle-raising practice. Cattle farmers would drive their cattle (i.e., their stock) to market. The day before market day, the farmers would give their stock lots of salt, followed by copious quantities of water. The cattle would drink a lot of water, which would increase their weight and therefore their market value. Only later would the buyer realize that he had bought not only cattle, but also a lot of water: watered stock.

to the other class of security. When there is no market value for any of the issued securities, proceeds may be allocated arbitrarily.

To illustrate, assume Vax Corporation issued 1,000 no-par common shares, and 500 no-par preferred shares, in three different situations:

Situation 1—Proportional method. The common shares were selling at $40 per share and the preferred at $20. Assume the total cash received is $48,000, which is acceptable to the Board of Directors. Because reliable market values are available for both share classes, the proportional method is preferable as a basis for allocating the lump-sum amount, as follows:

Proportional allocation	
Market value of common (1,000 shares × $40)	$40,000 = 4/5 of total
Market value of preferred (500 shares × $20)	10,000 = 1/5
Total market value	$50,000 = 5/5

Allocation of the lump-sum sale price of $48,000	
Common ($48,000 × 4/5)	$38,400
Preferred ($48,000 × 1/5)	9,600
Total	$48,000

The journal entry to record the issuance

Cash	48,000	
Common shares, no-par (1,000 shares)		38,400
Preferred shares, no-par (500 shares)		9,600

Situation 2—Incremental method. The common shares were selling at $40; a market for the preferred has not been established. Because there is no market for the preferred shares, the market value of the common ($40,000) must be used as a basis for the entry:

Cash	48,000	
Common shares, no-par (1,000 shares)		40,000
Preferred shares, no-par (500 shares)		8,000

Situation 3—Arbitrary allocation. When there is no established market for either class of shares, an arbitrary allocation is used. In the absence of any other logical basis, a temporary allocation may be made by the Board of Directors. If a market value is established for one of the securities in the near future, a correcting entry based on such value would be made.

Share Issue Costs Corporations often incur substantial expenditures when they issue shares in a public offering. These expenditures include registration fees, underwriter commissions, legal and accounting fees, printing costs, clerical costs, and promotional costs. These expenditures are called **share issue costs**. While share issue costs are usually not large compared with the total capital raised, they are large enough to require careful accounting. Two methods of accounting for share issue costs are found in practice:

1. *Offset method.* Under this method, share issue costs are treated as a reduction of the amount received from the sale of the related share capital. The rationale to support this method is that these are one-time costs that cannot be reasonably assigned to future periodic revenues and that the net cash received is the actual appropriate measure of capital raised. Therefore, under this method, share issue costs are debited to the share capital account.

2. *Retained earnings method.* Companies will charge share issue costs directly to retained earnings. This reduces common equity, but records the gross proceeds received from the sale of shares to the share capital account. Retained earnings are reduced as a result.

Both methods are found in practice.

RETIREMENT OF SHARES

A company can buy back any of its shares, preferred or common, at any time, if they are offered for sale. Such a sale can be a private transaction, or a public (stock market) transaction. Legislation provides conditions (typically solvency tests that must be met subsequent to the purchase) for the purchase and cancellation of outstanding shares. Corporations that intend to buy back their own shares must file their plans with the relevant securities commissions; the plan is known as a *normal course issuer bid.*

Shares may also be bought back according to the terms of the shares themselves. Some preferred shares are *retractable*, which means that, at the option of the shareholder, and at a contractually arranged price, a company is required to buy back its shares. Other preferred shares are **callable**, or *redeemable*, which means that there are specific buy-back provisions, at the option of the company. In either of these transactions, the company deals directly with the shareholder.

Reasons for Share Retirement   Why is repurchase of shares a good strategy for the company? The company may want to:

- *Increase earnings per share* (EPS). EPS is the ratio obtained by dividing net income by outstanding shares.[2] Idle cash does not earn high rates of return. If idle cash can be used to reduce the denominator (number of shares outstanding) of the EPS ratio without hurting the numerator (income) in a proportional fashion, EPS will rise. EPS is considered a critical indication of a company's earning performance and future prospects. Changes in EPS that reflect economic conditions (not just accounting allocations) should affect share price. So, if EPS increases, market price should rise as well.

- *Provide cash flow to shareholders in lieu of dividends.* A repurchase offer enables those shareholders who want to receive cash to do so through offering all or part of their holdings for redemption (and to pay taxes on capital gains on the shares rather than as ordinary dividend income). Those shareholders who do not wish to receive cash at the time can continue to hold their shares.

- *Acquire shares when they appear to be undervalued.* A corporation with excess cash may feel that buying undervalued shares for cancellation will benefit the remaining shareholders. These transactions also help make a market (i.e., provide a buyer) for the shares.

- *Buy out one or more particular shareholders, and thwart takeover bids.*

- *Reduce future dividend payments by reducing the shares outstanding.*

---

[2] The calculation of earnings per share is examined in depth in Chapter 19.

ETHICAL ISSUES

Companies must exercise extreme care in transactions involving their own shares because of the opportunity that the corporation has to use insider information to the detriment of a selling shareholder. For example, an oil company with inside knowledge of a profitable oil discovery could withhold the good news and acquire shares at an artificially low market price. This would unfairly deprive the selling shareholder of true market value. For these reasons, security laws prohibit corporations from engaging in deceptive conduct, including acts related to transactions involving their own shares.

Accounting for Retirement When shares are purchased and immediately retired, contributed capital allocated to the shares is removed from the accounts. Where the reacquisition cost of the acquired shares is different from the average original issuance price, (i.e., the *paid-in* capital) accounting standards require that the cost be allocated as follows for no-par shares:

Condition	First, DEBIT	Then, Either/Or	
		CREDIT	DEBIT
When the reacquisition cost is *lower* than the average price per share issued to date	Share capital, at the average paid-in value per issued share	Other contributed capital from share retirement	n/a
When the reacquisition cost is *higher* than the average price per share issued to date	Share capital, at the average paid-in value per issued share	n/a	1. Other contributed capital that was created by earlier cancellation or resale transactions in the same class of shares, if any, then 2. Retained earnings

The effect of these standards is to ensure that a corporation records no income effect (i.e., no gain or loss on the income statement) from buying back its own shares. If a company could record gains and losses from transactions in its own shares, the potential for income manipulation is obvious.

Illustration: Case 1. Assume that Sicon Corporation has 200,000 no-par common shares outstanding. There is $1 million in the common share account, the result of an average issuance price per share of $5. The contributed capital account from previous retirement transactions of common shares has a $7,200 credit balance. The corporation acquired and retired 10,000 shares at a price of $6.25 per share. The specific shareholder who sold these shares back to Sicon Corporation had originally paid $4 per share. The transaction would be recorded as follows:

Common shares (10,000 shares) [($1,000,000 ÷ 200,000) × 10,000]	50,000	
Contributed capital, common share retirement	7,200	
Retained earnings ($62,500 − $50,000 − $7,200)	5,300	
Cash (10,000 × $6.25)		62,500

The first step in constructing this journal entry is to compare the cost to retire the shares ($62,500) with the *average* initial issuance price to date ($50,000). The specific issue price of these shares ($4) is irrelevant. The corporation paid $12,500 more to retire these shares than the average original proceeds. The $12,500 is debited first to contributed capital from prior common share retirements until that account is exhausted. This contributed capital account may never have a debit balance. Retained earnings is debited for the remainder. The effect of this transaction is to reduce paid-in capital by $57,200, retained earnings by $5,300 and total shareholders' equity by $62,500. No loss is recorded on the income statement. Assets are reduced by $62,500.

Illustration: Case 2. If the shares were reacquired for $4.25 per share, the entry to record the transaction would be:

Common shares (10,000 shares)		
[($1,000,000 ÷ 200,000) × 10,000]	50,000	
Contributed capital, common share retirement		
($50,000 − $42,500)		7,500
Cash (10,000 × $4.25)		42,500

Total shareholders' equity and paid-in capital go down by $42,500 ($50,000 less $7,500), reflecting the fact that the corporation paid less to repurchase the shares than the average issuance price to date. No gain is recorded on the income statement. Assets are reduced by $42,500.

The price paid for the shares may be the current market price, or a price agreed on when the shares were originally issued, as is the case for redeemable or retractable shares. In all cases, the entries follow the same pattern: retirement price is compared to the original issuance price to date, and the difference is a capital amount.

Note that the contributed capital account involved in the above example was identified as contributed capital, common share retirement. Subsequent common share retirements will increase or decrease this account. However, if there are retirements of any other class of shares (e.g., preferred shares) then a separate contributed capital account would have to be set up. These contributed capital accounts are used only for transactions involving the *same class of shares.*

Conversion of Shares

Shares of any class may include the provision that they may be converted, at particular times and/or in particular quantities, into shares of another class. For example, preferred shares may be convertible into common shares. Conversions are accounted for at *book value,* with an equal decrease to one share class and increase to another. For example, if 20,000 preferred shares, issued for an average of $36.70 per share, were to convert according to pre-established terms to 60,000 common shares (that is, 3-for-1):

Preferred shares (20,000 × $36.70)	734,000	
Common shares		734,000

TREASURY STOCK

A firm may also buy its own shares and hold them for eventual resale. This is called **treasury stock.** Such shares may not vote at shareholder meetings or receive dividends. The *CBCA* (and provincial legislation modelled after the Act) provides that corporations that reacquire their own shares must immediately retire those shares. Thus, corporations may not engage in treasury stock transactions in most Canadian jurisdictions. Some provincial corporations' acts do allow treasury stock transactions, but such transactions are increasingly rare in

Canada. However, 12 out of 200 companies in *Financial Reporting in Canada 2006* disclose treasury shares. Treasury shares are far more common in other countries, where corporations regularly engage in treasury stock transactions, subject to the insider trading rules of the various stock exchanges.

The key to a treasury stock acquisition is that reacquired shares may be reissued. The company may eventually reissue the shares to raise additional capital—a process far faster through the issuance of treasury stock than a new share issue. The shares may also be used for stock dividends, employee stock option plans, and so on. A corporation that is allowed to engage in treasury stock transactions may have additional flexibility over one not so permitted. However, the importance of this aspect of treasury shares has decreased in recent years due to the prevalence of **shelf registration**, which is a standing approval (from the securities commissions) to issue more shares as needed.

Accounting for Treasury Stock When a company buys treasury stock, the cost of the shares acquired is debited to a treasury stock account, which appears as a *deduction* at the end of the shareholders' equity section. When the shares are resold, the treasury stock account is credited for the cost, and the difference, which is the "gain or loss," affects various equity accounts. The "gain or loss" is not reported on the income statement; a firm cannot improve reported earnings by engaging in capital transactions with its own shareholders. The balance in the treasury stock account is shown as a deduction from the total of shareholders' equity.

When treasury stock is resold at a price in excess of its cost, the excess should be recorded as contributed capital in a separate contributed capital account. Where the shares are sold at less than their cost, the deficiency should be charged as follows:

Condition	First, CREDIT	Then, Either/Or	
		CREDIT	DEBIT
When the resale price is *higher* than the average price per share	Treasury stock, at the average price per share	Other contributed capital from treasury stock transactions	n/a
When the resale price is *lower* than the average price per share	Treasury stock, at the average price per share	n/a	1. Other contributed capital from treasury stock transactions, if any, then 2. Retained earnings.

This method of accounting for treasury stock is called the **single-transaction method**. The treatment is the same as that used for share retirement. An example will illustrate the sequence of entries.

1. *To record the initial sale and issuance of 10,000 common shares at $26 per share*		
Cash (10,000 shares × $26)	260,000	
Common shares (10,000 shares)		260,000
2. *To record the acquisition of 2,000 common treasury shares at $28 per share*		
Treasury stock, common (2,000 shares × $28)	56,000	
Cash		56,000

Note: The cash price paid is always the amount debited to the treasury stock account.

3. *To record sale of 500 treasury shares at $30 per*
   share (above cost)

Cash (500 shares × $30)	15,000	
Treasury stock, common (500 shares at cost, $28)		14,000
Contributed capital from treasury stock transactions		1,000

Note: Had this sale been at cost ($28 per share), no
amount would have been entered in the contributed
capital account. If treasury shares are bought in a
series of acquisitions at different prices, weighted
average cost is used on disposition.

4. *To record the sale of another 500 treasury shares*
   at $19 per share (below cost)

Cash (500 shares × $19)	9,500	
Contributed capital from treasury stock transactions*	1,000	
Retained earnings	3,500	
Treasury stock, common (500 shares at cost, $28)		14,000

*The debit is limited to the current balance in this
account (see entry (3)); any remainder is allocated to
retained earnings.

Assuming entries (1) through (4), and a beginning balance in retained earnings of $40,000, the balance sheet will reflect the following:

Shareholders' Equity

Contributed capital	
Common shares, 10,000 shares issued, of which 1,000 are held as treasury stock	$260,000
Retained earnings ($40,000 − $3,500)	36,500
Total contributed capital and retained earnings	$296,500
Less: Treasury stock, 1,000 shares at cost	28,000
Total shareholders' equity	$268,500

CONCEPT REVIEW

1. What value is given to shares when they are issued in exchange for non-cash assets?

2. How can the separate classes of shares be valued when shares are issued as a basket?

3. When shares are redeemed and retired, how should the cost of the redemption be charged to the shareholders' equity accounts?

RETAINED EARNINGS

Retained earnings represents accumulated net income or net loss (including all gains and losses), error corrections, and retroactive changes in accounting policy, if any, less accumulated cash dividends, property dividends, stock dividends, and other amounts transferred to contributed capital accounts. If the accumulated losses and distributions of retained earnings exceed the accumulated gains, a **deficit** will exist (i.e., a debit in retained earnings). The following items affect retained earnings:

Decreases (debits)

- Cash and other dividends;
- Spinoff of investment to shareholders;
- Stock dividends;
- Share retirement and treasury stock transactions;
- Share issue costs;
- Error correction (may also be a credit) (see Chapter 20); and
- Effect of a change in accounting policy applied retrospectively (may also be a credit) (see Chapter 20).

Increases (credits)

- Net income (including discontinued operations and/or extraordinary items) (will be a debit if a net loss); and
- Removal of deficit in a financial reorganization.

Appropriations and Restrictions of Retained Earnings

Appropriated retained earnings and restricted retained earnings constrain a specified portion of accumulated earnings for a specified reason. **Appropriated retained earnings** are the result of discretionary management action. **Restricted retained earnings** are the result of a legal contract or corporate law. Retained earnings are appropriated and restricted primarily to reduce the amount of retained earnings that financial statement readers might otherwise consider available to support a dividend declaration.

The following are examples of some of the ways in which appropriations and restrictions of retained earnings may arise:

- To fulfill a contractual agreement, as in the case of a debt covenant restricting the use of retained earnings for dividends that would result in the disbursement of assets;
- To report a discretionary appropriation of a specified portion of retained earnings in anticipation of possible future losses; or
- To fulfill a legal requirement, as in the case of a provincial corporate law requiring a restriction on retained earnings equivalent to the cost of treasury stock held.

It is essential to understand that an appropriation of retained earnings *does not involve any segregation of assets*. Retained earnings appropriations are just accounting entries that divide existing retained earnings into multiple accounts. If management actually sets aside funds for a specific purpose, restricted cash investments will be reported as an asset on the balance sheet.

Appropriation or restriction of retained earnings is made by transferring (debiting) an amount from retained earnings to (crediting) an appropriated retained earnings account. The entry has no effect on assets, liabilities, or total shareholders' equity. When the need for an appropriation or restriction no longer exists, the appropriated balance is returned to the unappropriated retained earnings account.

The authors of *Financial Reporting in Canada 2006* did not find a single example of a retained earnings reserve or appropriation in their sample of 200 companies. The authors observe that "this is similar to the findings of previous editions of *Financial Reporting in Canada* and indicates that the use of retained earnings reserves is not a significant financial reporting practice."

DIVIDENDS

Nature of Dividends

A dividend is a distribution of earnings to shareholders in the form of assets or shares. A dividend typically results in a credit to the account that represents the item distributed (cash, non-cash asset, or share capital) and a debit to retained earnings.

Some corporate legislation and bond covenants place restrictions on the amount of assets and/or retained earnings that may be used for dividends. These constraints recognize the effects of dividends; that is, dividends require (1) a disbursement of assets and (2) a reduction in retained earnings by the same amount. The company must have both assets and retained earnings to be eligible to declare/distribute dividends.

Relevant Dividend Dates

Four dates have legal significance for dividends:

declaration date

the date that the Board of Directors formally approves a dividend

Declaration Date On the **declaration date**, the corporation's Board of Directors formally announces the dividend declaration. The courts have held that formal declaration of a cash or property dividend constitutes an enforceable contract between the corporation and its shareholders. Therefore, on the dividend declaration date, such dividends are recorded and a liability (i.e., dividends payable) is recognized.

Record Date The **record date** is the date on which the list of *shareholders of record,* who will receive the dividend, is prepared. Usually, the record date follows the declaration date by two to three weeks, to allow for changes in share ownership to be recorded. No entry is made in the accounts on the record date, but the list will determine the names on the eventual dividend cheques.

Ex-Dividend Date An investor who holds (buys) shares on or after the **ex-dividend date** *does not* receive the dividend. Technically, the ex-dividend date is the day following the record date, but, to provide time to record the transfer of shares, the effective ex-dividend date is usually three or four days prior to the date of record. Thus, the investor who holds shares on the day prior to the stipulated ex-dividend date receives the dividend.

payment date

the date on which dividends are paid or distributed to the shareholders of record

Payment Date This date is also determined by the Board of Directors and is usually stated in the declaration. The **payment date** typically follows the declaration date by four to six weeks. At the date of payment, the liability recorded at date of declaration is debited and the appropriate asset account is credited.

Note that, of these four dates, the only ones that affect the accounting records of the company that declares the dividend are (1) the declaration date and (2) the payment date. The other two dates are significant for investors, but not for accounting. The entries for dividend declaration and payment will be illustrated shortly.

Legality of Dividends

The requirement that there be retained earnings or certain elements of contributed capital before dividends can be declared has already been mentioned. Precise identification of the elements of shareholders' equity that are available for cash, property, and stock dividends, respectively, would require study of the provisions of the particular incorporating legislation. However, at least two provisions appear to be uniform: (1) dividends may not be paid from **legal capital** (legal capital is usually the amount in the share capital accounts) without permission from creditors and (2) retained earnings are available for dividends unless there is a contractual or statutory restriction.

Under the *CBCA*, a liquidity test must also be met: Dividends may not be declared or paid if the result would be that the corporation became unable to meet its liabilities as they came due, or if the dividend resulted in the realizable value of assets being less than liabilities plus stated capital.

Cash Dividends

Assume the Board of Directors of Bass Company, at its meeting on 20 January 20X2, declares a dividend of $0.50 per common share, payable 20 March 20X2, to shareholders of record on 1 March 20X2. Assume that 10,000 no-par common shares are outstanding.

At declaration date—20 January 20X2		
Common dividends declared*—10,000 shares × $0.50	5,000	
Cash dividends payable		5,000
Later closed to retained earnings; or retained earnings may be debited directly		
At payment date—20 March 20X2		
Cash dividends payable	5,000	
Cash		5,000

Cash dividends payable is reported on the balance sheet as a current liability.

Preferred shares typically have first preference on amounts declared as dividends. Assume that Bass Company, in addition to the 10,000 common shares mentioned above, also has 5,000 $1.20 preferred shares outstanding. The Board of Directors declared dividends totalling $10,000, with the same declaration and payment dates as in the previous example. The first $6,000 will go to the preferred shareholders (5,000 shares × $1.20 per share); the remaining $4,000 will be distributed to the common shareholders at the rate of $0.40 per share ($4,000 ÷ 10,000 shares). Entries will be as follows:

At declaration date—20 January 20X2		
Preferred dividends declared*	6,000	
Common dividends declared*	4,000	
Cash dividends payable, preferred (5,000 × $1.20)		6,000
Cash dividends payable, common (10,000 × $0.40)		4,000
Later closed to retained earnings; or retained earnings may be debited directly		
At payment date—20 March 20X2		
Cash dividends payable, preferred	6,000	
Cash dividends payable, common	4,000	
Cash		10,000

In corporate reporting, it is important to distinguish the portion of the dividend attributable to the preferred shares versus the common.

If Bass Company were to have declared $5,000 of dividends, the preferred shareholders would have received it all. They have preference for the first $6,000 each year.

Cumulative Dividends on Preferred Shares

Cumulative preferred shares provide that dividends not declared in a given year accumulate at the specified rate on such shares. This accumulated amount must be paid in full if and when dividends are declared in a later year *before any dividends can be paid on the common shares*. If cumulative preference dividends are not declared in a given year, they are said to have been *passed* and are called *dividends in arrears* on the cumulative preferred shares.

If only a part of the preferred dividend is met for any year, the remainder of the cumulative dividend is in arrears. Cumulative preferred shares carry the right, on dissolution of the corporation, to dividends in arrears to the extent the corporation has retained earnings.

However, different provisions for dividends in arrears may be stipulated in the articles of incorporation and bylaws.

Dividends in arrears are not liabilities. Since preferred shareholders cannot force the Board of Directors to declare dividends, dividends in arrears do not meet the definition of a liability. Accounting standards require that dividends in arrears for cumulative preference shares be disclosed, usually in the notes to the financial statements.

Participating Dividends on Preferred Shares

Participating preferred shares provide that the preferred shareholders participate above the stated preferential rate on a pro rata basis in dividend declarations with the common shareholders.

- First, preferred shareholders receive their preference rate.
- Second, the common shareholders receive a specified matching dividend if the amount declared is high enough.
- If the total declared dividend is larger than these two amounts, the excess is divided on a pro rata basis between the two share classes.

The pro rata distribution is not based on the number of shares outstanding, for they may be of different size. Rather, the two classes' total base level dividends are used for the pro rata allocation, or their respective capital balances. Participation terms must be specified in the articles of incorporation and stated on the share certificates.

Reporting Example An example of a company that has participating shares is Tembec Inc., a Quebec-based integrated forest products company. In its capital structure, Tembec Inc. has:

- An unlimited number of Series 2 Class B shares entitled to a preferential and non-cumulative dividend *equal to the dividend yield percentage of the common shares*; and
- 250,000 Class C shares, with a par value of $1 each, non-voting and *participating*.

The Class C shares are clearly participating. Notice that the dividend for the Class B shares is defined by the dividends on the common shares; this makes them equally participating with common shares. The Class B shares are non-cumulative, which is common for participating shares.

Partially versus Fully Participating Shares may be *partially participating* or *fully participating*. If partially participating, preferred shares may participate in dividend declarations in excess of their preference rate, but the participation is capped at a certain level. Dividends above this level accrue solely to the common shareholders. Fully participating shares, on the other hand, share in the full extent of dividend declarations.

For example, a corporation may issue preferred shares entitled to a dividend of $0.50, with participation up to $0.70 after common shareholders receive $0.25 per share. In this case, participation with the common shareholders would be limited to the additional $0.20 above the regular $0.50 rate. The $0.25 dividend to the common shareholder is the matching dividend, and it is specified in the articles of incorporation. It is meant to provide the same rate of return on the common shares in the initial allocation and acknowledges that the share classes are of different relative size and value.

Example The following three cases, A, B, and C, illustrate various combinations of cumulative versus non-cumulative rights and of participating versus non-participating rights. Assume that Mann Corporation has the following share capital outstanding:

Preferred shares, no-par, dividend entitlement, $0.50 per share; 10,000 shares outstanding	$100,000
Common shares, no-par, 40,000 shares outstanding	200,000

Case A Preferred shares are non-cumulative and non-participating; dividends have not been paid for two years; dividends declared, $28,000.

	Preferred	Common	Total
Step 1—Preferred, current ($0.50 × 10,000)	$5,000		$ 5,000
Step 2—Common (balance)		$23,000	23,000
Total	$5,000	$23,000	$28,000

Because the preferred shares are non-cumulative, preferred shares may receive dividends only for the current year regardless of the fact that dividends were missed in two previous years.

Case B Preferred shares are *cumulative* and *non-participating;* dividends are two years in arrears; total dividends declared, $28,000.

	Preferred	Common	Total
Step 1—Preferred in arrears ($0.50 × 10,000 × 2)	$10,000		$10,000
Step 2—Preferred, current ($0.50 × 10,000)	5,000		5,000
Step 3—Common (balance)		$13,000	13,000
Total	$15,000	$13,000	$28,000

Preferred shares receive their dividends in arrears and the current dividend before the common shares receive any dividend.

Case C Preferred shares are cumulative, two years in arrears and fully participating after common shares have received $0.25 per share. That is, preferred will receive its basic $0.50 per share dividend, then common will receive $0.25 per share ($10,000 total). The base dividend is $15,000 (that is, $5,000 + $10,000). Payment of dividends in arrears does not affect this calculation, which is based on *one* year's base dividend. Participation is in the same ratio as the base dividend, that is, 1/3 ($5,000/$15,000) for the preferred and 2/3 ($10,000/$15,000) for the common. Total dividends declared are $37,000.

	Preferred	Common	Total
Step 1—Preferred, in arrears ($5,000 × 2)	$10,000		$10,000
Step 2a—Preferred, current (10,000 × $0.50)	5,000		5,000
b—Common, matching (40,000 × $0.25)		$10,000	10,000
c—Extra dividend, participating 1/3 : 2/3	4,000	8,000	12,000*
Totals	$19,000	$18,000	$37,000

*Extra dividend available: $37,000 − $10,000 − $5,000 − $10,000 = $12,000.

Had the preferred shares been *partially* participating, say, to a total of $0.75 per share, then the current year (excluding arrears) preferred dividend would have been limited to

$7,500, and participation would have been a maximum of $2,500 ($7,500 − $5,000). The common shares would then have received more of the final $12,000 layer of dividends ($9,500, or $12,000 − $2,500).

In the absence of an explicit stipulation in the articles of incorporation or bylaws, preferred shareholders have no right to participate in dividends with common shares beyond their stated dividend rate.

Property Dividends and Spinoffs

Corporations occasionally pay dividends with non-cash assets. Such dividends are called **property dividends** or *dividends in kind.* The property may be investments in the securities of other companies held by the corporation, real estate, merchandise, or any other non-cash asset designated by the Board of Directors. A property dividend is recorded at the current market value of the assets transferred on the declaration date.

When the book value of the property to be distributed as the dividend is different from its market value on the declaration date, the corporation should recognize a gain or loss of the asset as of the declaration date. Most property dividends are paid with the securities of other companies that the dividend-issuing corporation has held as an investment. This kind of property dividend avoids the problem of indivisibility of units that would occur with most non-cash assets.

Spinoffs An alternative transaction to a property dividend is a **spinoff,** in which the shares of a wholly or substantially owned subsidiary are distributed to the parent company's shareholders. The parent company's shareholders now directly own the subsidiary rather than exercise control indirectly through the corporation. For example, BCE Inc. created an income trust with land-based telephone assets of Aliant and other Ontario and Quebec operations in mid-2006. Each existing share of BCE was converted into .915 of a new BCE share plus 0.0725 of one share in the Bell Aliant income trust operation. If a shareholder owned 10,000 BCE shares prior to the spinoff, that shareholder owned 9,150 BCE shares and 725 Bell Aliant income trust shares after the spinoff.

A spinoff is different from a property dividend. A property dividend represents a distribution of an asset of the company, while a spinoff represents a division of the consolidated reporting entity itself. A spinoff is valued at the *book value* of the spun-off shares, whereas a property dividend is recorded at market value. If market value were used to value the subsidiary's shares in a spinoff, the parent company would be able to recognize a gain (or loss) on the spun-off shares. But a spinoff is not a part of the business of the enterprise; it is, in effect, a capital transaction, and companies may not recognize gains and losses from capital transactions.

Example Assume that Sun Corporation announced a spinoff of a subsidiary called E&P Limited, the shares of which are carried on Sun's non-consolidated balance sheet at a book value of $899,600, and had a market value in the range of $2 million. The spinoff will require the following entries:

At declaration date		
Spinoff of investment in E&P Ltd. common shares		
(or, retained earnings debited directly)	899,600	
Spinoff obligation		899,600
At date of distribution (payment)		
Spinoff obligation	899,600	
Investment in E&P Ltd common shares		899,600

The distinction between a property dividend and a spinoff is not always clear. A corporation may hold shares of another corporation that is *not* a subsidiary, and may decide to transfer these shares to its own shareholders. If the distribution is viewed as a spinoff, the transaction will be accounted for at the book value of the shares held. On the other hand, if the distribution is viewed as a property dividend, the transaction will be recorded at market value and a gain or loss will be reported.

Property Dividend Accounting Assume that E&P Limited is *not* a subsidiary of Sun Corporation and that Sun Corporation's Board of Directors resolved that the transaction was a property dividend. The transaction is now accounted for at its fair value of $2 million. This latter amount could be determined easily if the shares of E&P were publicly traded. Sun will recognize the gain in market value over book value ($2,000,000 less $899,600, or $1,100,400) before recording the distribution:

At declaration date		
Investment in E&P Ltd. common shares	1,100,400	
Gain on disposition of investment		1,100,400
Property dividend declared (or, retained earnings)	2,000,000	
Property dividend payable		2,000,000
At date of distribution (payment)		
Property dividend payable	2,000,000	
Investment in E&P Ltd. common shares		2,000,000

The balance sheet of the parent company (Sun Corporation, in this example) is unaffected by whether the transaction is treated as a spinoff or as a property dividend. If the transaction is recorded as a spinoff, retained earnings is decreased by $899,600. If it is a property dividend, retained earnings is increased by the gain of $1,100,400 and decreased by the dividend for $2,000,000, which nets out to $899,600. The increase in retained earnings caused by recording a gain is exactly offset by the higher value assigned to the property dividend. The income statement for the year of the transaction, however, will reflect the amount of the gain if the transaction is treated as a property dividend. To summarize:

Type of Distribution	Recorded At	Effect on Net Income	Effect on Retained Earnings
Property dividend	Market value	Changed by gain or loss on shares	Changed by gain or loss included in net income Reduced by dividend recorded at market value Net: reduced by book value
Spinoff	Book value	None	Reduced by distribution recorded at book value

Liquidating Dividends

Liquidating dividends are distributions that are a return of the amount received when shares were issued, rather than assets acquired through earnings. Owners' equity accounts other than retained earnings are debited. Since such dividends reduce contributed capital, they typically require creditor approval.

Liquidating dividends are appropriate when there is no intention or opportunity to conserve resources for asset replacement. A mining company might pay such a liquidating dividend when it is exploiting a non-replaceable asset. Mining companies sometimes pay dividends on the basis of earnings plus the amount of the deduction for depletion. Shareholders must be informed of the portion of any dividend that represents a return of capital, since the liquidation portion of the dividend is not income to the investor and is usually not taxable as income; it reduces the cost basis of the shares.

When accounting for a liquidating dividend, a different contributed capital account, rather than retained earnings, is debited. That is, share capital, not retained earnings, is often debited. Before debiting the share capital accounts, any other contributed capital accounts would be debited and eliminated.

Scrip Dividends

A corporation that has a temporary cash shortage might declare a dividend to maintain a continuing dividend policy by issuing a **scrip dividend**. A scrip dividend (also called a *liability dividend*) occurs when the Board of Directors declares a dividend and issues promissory notes, called scrip, to the shareholders. This declaration means that a relatively long time (e.g., six months or one year) will elapse between the declaration and payment dates. In most cases, scrip dividends are declared when a corporation has sufficient retained earnings as a basis for dividends but is short of cash.

Stock Dividends

A stock dividend is a proportional distribution to shareholders of additional common or preferred shares of the corporation. A stock dividend does not change the assets, liabilities, or total shareholders' equity of the issuing corporation. It does not change the proportionate ownership of any shareholder. It simply increases the number of shares outstanding.

For instance, assume Early Broadcasting Limited has 120,000 common shares outstanding. One shareholder, J.S. Brown, owns 12,000 shares, or one-tenth of the shares. The corporation declares and issues a 10% stock dividend. This has the following effect on share capital:

	Before Dividend		After Dividend*	
Total shares outstanding	120,000	*100%*	132,000	*100%*
Brown's shareholding	12,000	*10%*	13,200	*10%*
Previous outstanding total × 110%.				

Brown's relative ownership percentage has not changed. If the shares sold for $20 per share before the dividend, what will happen to that market value after the split? Logically, it should decline.

	Before	After	
A. Total market value of the company (120,000 × $20)	$2,400,000	$2,400,000	(i.e., no change)
B. Shares outstanding	120,000	132,000	
Price per share (A ÷ B)	$20	$18.18	
Brown's total market value			
12,000 × $20.00	$ 240,000		
13,200 × $18.18		$ 240,000	

What will really happen to the market price of the shares in this situation? The answer is unclear. Often, there is a smaller decrease than the size of the stock dividend would seem to dictate. Some believe that this is a market reaction to other factors (e.g., an anticipated increase in cash dividends that historically follows a stock dividend). Because of the complexity and sophistication of the stock markets, it is very difficult to determine why a share price does or does not change on a given day. However, it is generally recognized that if a company doubles its outstanding shares through a stock dividend, the market price will reduce by approximately one-half.

A stock dividend causes the transfer of an amount from retained earnings to the contributed, or paid-in, capital accounts (i.e., share capital). Therefore, it changes only the internal account balances of shareholders' equity and not the total shareholders' equity.

Reasons for a Stock Dividend   Numerous reasons exist for a company to issue a stock dividend:

- To reveal that the firm plans to permanently retain a portion of earnings in the business. The effect of a stock dividend, through a debit to retained earnings and offsetting credits to permanent capital accounts, is to raise contributed capital and thereby shelter this amount from future declaration of cash or property dividends.
- To increase the number of shares outstanding, which reduces the market price per share and, in turn, tends to increase trading of shares in the market. Theoretically, more investors can afford investments in equity securities if the unit cost is low.
- To continue dividend distributions without disbursing assets (usually cash) that may be needed for operations. The effect of a stock dividend may be purely psychological: management hopes that shareholders will feel they have received something of value.
- Stock dividends may not subject the shareholders to income tax.[3] Instead, the total purchase price of the original share investment is divided by the new number of shares, thereby reducing the per share investment cost.

Accounting Issues Related to Stock Dividends

One major issue in accounting for stock dividends is the value that should be recognized. The shares issued for the dividend could be recorded at market value, at stated (or par) value, or at some other value.

There are no accounting standards on these issues in Canada, but the *CBCA* requires shares to be issued at fair market value. In Ontario, on the other hand, legislation specifically permits the Board of Directors to capitalize any amount it desires. In the United States, small stock dividends (i.e., less than 20 to 25% of the outstanding shares) *must* be recorded at market value, while large stock dividends are recorded only as a memo entry. We will examine three alternatives: market value, stated value, and memo entry.

Market Value Method   The Board of Directors could require capitalization of the current market value of the additional shares issued. The market value of the stock dividend should be measured on the basis of the market price per share on the declaration date. This method is consistent with the view that the shareholders actually receive something of value, particularly when the price of shares does not drop proportionately. But is it encouraging a misconception?

Assume that Markholme Corporation has 464,000 common shares outstanding, originally issued for $2,320,000. The company declares and distributes a 5% common stock

---

[3] The tax status of stock dividends is a bit convoluted in Canada. In some years, stock dividends have been treated as taxable income. The rules were changed to make them tax free, but then changed back. At the moment, stock dividends are technically taxable but the corporation can make an election to have them treated as non-taxable.

dividend on 1 July 20X2, and determines that an appropriate market value is $7.25 per share. The following entry will be recorded:

Stock dividend (or, retained earnings)		
(464,000 × 5% × $7.25)	168,200	
Common shares		168,200

Stated Value Method The Board of Directors in certain jurisdictions may decide to capitalize a stated amount per share—average paid in per share to date, or par value, if applicable. This method can be rationalized based on the evidence of market value figures available. For instance, if the market price is proportionately reduced by the stock dividend, then it is clear that the shareholders have received nothing of value and should not be encouraged to believe that they have. In these circumstances, capitalization should be limited to legal requirements.

Strong arguments are made for some sort of stated value because (1) the corporation's assets, liabilities, and total shareholders' equity are not changed and (2) the shareholders' proportionate ownership is not changed.

If Markholme Corporation, explained above, declares the same 5% stock dividend, but the Board of Directors determines that the average amount paid in to date for the outstanding common shares is to be used, then $5 ($2,320,000 ÷ 464,000) will be used to determine the capitalization amount. The entry will be identical, except the amount recognized will be $116,000 (464,000 × 5% × $5).

Memo Entry Since a large stock dividend may be issued for the primary purpose of reducing market price per share, it is obvious at least in this case that the shareholder has received nothing of value. A memo entry may be recorded to identify the number of shares issued, outstanding, and subscribed. No change is made in any capital account. This parallels the treatment of a stock split, to be discussed later in this chapter. Large stock dividends are often called *stock splits effected as a stock dividend*. For example, in March 2006, The Royal Bank of Canada announced a 100% stock dividend. If a shareholder owned 100 shares before the dividend, the shareholder had 200 shares afterward. The stock dividend was accounted for with a memo entry. This treatment may also be used for small stock dividends. Markholme Corporation, above, could record a memo entry documenting the distribution of 23,200 (464,000 × 5%) shares.

Timing of Recognition

Fundamentally, a stock dividend is recorded as a debit to retained earnings and a credit to the share capital issued. However, unlike a cash dividend, a stock dividend can be revoked prior to the issuance date. As a result, many companies do not record the dividend on the declaration date, but instead record it on the issuance date. Either recording approach can be used.

Example Marvel Corporation, which has 100,000 common shares outstanding, declares a 10% common stock dividend. The Board of Directors directs that the dividend be recorded at market value. A total of 10,000 no-par common shares are issued. The market value is $5 per share. The entries are as follows:

Alternative 1: Originating Entry at Declaration		
Declaration date		
Stock dividends (or, retained earnings)	50,000	
Stock dividends distributable*		50,000
*Reported as a credit in shareholders' equity until issuance.		
Issuance date		
Stock dividends distributable	50,000	
Common shares, no-par (5,000 shares)		50,000

Alternative 2: Originating Entry at Issuance

Declaration date		
No entry		
Issuance date		
Stock dividends (or, retained earnings)	50,000	
Common shares, no-par (5,000 shares)		50,000

The differences between these two approaches are trivial. The stock dividends distributable account is not a liability, for it does not involve settlement by the future transfer of assets (cash, etc.). It is an obligation to issue equity and is properly classified in shareholders' equity. Note disclosure would accompany both alternatives.

Special Stock Dividends

When a stock dividend is of the same class as that held by the recipients, it is called an *ordinary stock dividend* (e.g., common shares issued to the owners of common). When a class of share capital other than the one already held by the recipients is issued, such a dividend is called a *special stock dividend* (e.g., preferred shares issued to the owners of common). In this case, the market value of the preferred shares issued as a dividend should be recorded.

Fractional Share Rights

When a stock dividend is issued, many shareholders will own an "odd" number of shares and be entitled to a fraction of a share. For example, when a firm issues a 5% stock dividend and a shareholder owns 30 shares, the shareholder is entitled to 1.5 shares (30 × 5%). When this happens, the firm may issue *fractional share rights* for portions of shares to which individual shareholders are entitled. The company may also write a cheque for the fractional entitlement.

To demonstrate, suppose Moon Company has 1,000,000 outstanding no-par common shares. Moon issues a 5% stock dividend. The market value of the common shares is $80 per share. The number of shares to be issued is 5% of the number of shares outstanding (1,000,000 × 5%), or 50,000 shares.

Assume the distribution of existing shares is such that 42,000 whole or complete shares can be issued. The firm will issue fractional share rights for the remaining 8,000 shares. Each fractional share right will entitle the holder to acquire 5%, or 1/20, of a share. Since there are 8,000 shares yet to be issued, there will be 8,000 × 20, or 160,000 fractional share rights issued. A market will develop for the fractional share rights, with each having a market value of approximately 1/20 of a whole share ($80 ÷ 20), or $4. Shareholders can buy or sell fractional share rights to the point where whole shares can be acquired. A holder will have to turn in 20 fractional share rights to receive one common share.

The entry for recording the issuance of the stock dividend and fractional share rights is as follows:

Stock dividends (or, retained earnings)		
(50,000 × $80)	4,000,000	
Common shares, no-par (42,000 shares × $80)		3,360,000
Common share fractional share rights		
(8,000 shares; 160,000 rights) (8,000 × $80)		640,000

When rights are turned in for redemption in common shares, the common share fractional share rights account is debited and common shares are credited. Suppose, for example, that 150,000 fractional share rights are turned in for 7,500 common shares (150,000 ÷ 20). The entry to record the transaction would be:

| Common share fractional share rights | 600,000 | |
| Common shares, no-par (7,500 shares × $80) | | 600,000 |

If the remaining rights are allowed to lapse, the corporation would record contributed capital:

| Common share fractional share rights | 40,000 | |
| Contributed capital, lapse of share rights (500 × $80) | | 40,000 |

Cash Alternative An alternative to the issuance of fractional share rights is to make a cash payment to shareholders for any fractional shares to which they are entitled. The shareholder above who owns 30 shares and is entitled to 1.5 shares will receive one share from the firm and a cash payment of $40 ($80 per share × .5 shares), representing the value of the one-half share at current market value. The entry to record the cash payment is a debit to retained earnings and a credit to cash. This procedure is simpler for the shareholder, because there is no need to buy or sell fractional shares.

If cash were offered for fractional shares, the stock dividend would be recorded, in summary form, as follows:

Stock dividends (or, retained earnings) (50,000 × $80)	4,000,000	
Common shares, no-par (42,000 shares)		3,360,000
Cash (8,000 shares × $80)		640,000

Summary Dividends and distributions are summarized as follows:

Type	Shareholder receives	Recorded at	Watch out for
Cash	Cash	Exchange amount; cash	Amount allocated to common versus preferred shares
Property	Some company asset as designated by the Board: inventory, investments, etc.	Fair value; gain or loss recorded on declaration	Distribution of shares of subsidiary could be a spinoff instead
Spinoff	Shares of subsidiary	Book value	Market value not recorded
Liquidating	Usually cash but may be other assets	Exchange amount; fair value	Debit to other contributed capital or share capital, not retained earnings
Scrip	Promissory note	Exchange amount; as stated	Shareholders get a receivable; company sets up a liability
Stock	Shares	May be recorded at fair value, book value, or an arbitrary value as decided by the Board	May be fractional shares for part shares or cash for part shares
Stock split (next section)	Shares	n/a	Disclosure only; not recorded

CONCEPT REVIEW

1. Of the four dates pertaining to cash dividends, which dates require accounting entries? What are the entries?

2. What effect does a cash dividend have on shareholders' equity? How does the effect of a stock dividend differ from that of a cash dividend?

3. What is a participating preferred dividend?

STOCK SPLITS

A **stock split** is a change in the number of shares outstanding with no change in the recorded capital accounts. A stock split usually increases the number of shares outstanding by a significant amount, such as doubling or tripling the number of outstanding shares. Stocks that sell at high market values are perceived to be less marketable, especially to smaller investors. Therefore, the primary purpose of a stock split is to increase the number of shares outstanding and decrease the market price per share. In turn, this may increase the market activity of the shares. By increasing the number of shares outstanding, a stock split also reduces earnings per share.

In contrast, a **reverse split** decreases the number of shares. It results in a proportional reduction in the number of shares issued and outstanding, and an increase in the average book value per share. Reverse splits may be used to increase the market price of shares with a low market value per share. For example, Nortel Networks effected a 10-for-1 reverse stock split in 2007; its share price was low enough to raise concerns that it would be delisted by the New York Stock Exchange, where share prices have to be at a certain per-share level to support a listing. The share price would be expected to increase tenfold after such a reverse split.

Implementation   A stock split is implemented by either:

1. Calling in all of the old shares and concurrently issuing the split shares, or, more commonly,

2. Issuing the additional split shares with notification to shareholders of the change in outstanding shares.

In Canada, it is more common simply to issue additional shares because the shares rarely have par value and there is no need to reprint or replace existing certificates.

Accounting for Stock Splits

In a stock split, *no accounting entry is needed* because there is no change in the dollar amounts in the share capital accounts, additional contributed capital, or retained earnings. No consideration has been received by the corporation for the issued shares, and since market value is directly affected by the split, shareholders clearly receive nothing of direct value.

Shares issued, outstanding, and subscribed are changed, as is par value, if any. The following dollar amounts are *not* changed:

1. Share capital account;

2. Additional contributed capital accounts,;

3. Retained earnings; and

4. Total shareholders' equity.

Consider a 200%, or 2-for-1, stock split (two new shares for each old share) and compare it with a 100% stock dividend (one additional share for each share already outstanding). For example, assume Technology Corporation has 40,000 shares outstanding, which were issued initially at $10 per share. The current balance of retained earnings is $450,000. The different effects of a 100% stock dividend capitalized at $10 per share and a 200% stock split are contrasted in Exhibit 13-1.

The stock dividend changes both contributed capital and retained earnings. The stock split, however, changes neither of these amounts. *Total* shareholders' equity is unchanged by both the stock dividend and the stock split.

Commentary Remember that the shareholder is left in the same position whether there is a 200% stock split or a 100% stock dividend—two shares will be owned for every one share previously held. Similarly, the market price of the shares should be the same whether the transaction is described as a split or a dividend.

This similarity of results makes the different accounting methods suspect, since there are alternatives available for transactions that are basically the same. This hardly seems to promote the idea of *substance over form.* Accordingly, *memo treatment* of a large stock dividend is the preferable approach because it produces the same result as the memo treatment for a stock split. This seems to be the position taken by the Toronto Stock Exchange, which views any issuance of more than 25% additional shares as a stock split, regardless of the accounting treatment.

Adjustments Required for Stock Splits When a stock is split, the per-share values all change. For example, in a 2-for-1 split, the paid-in value per share is halved. If Sincon Corporation has 40,000 outstanding shares and total contributed capital of $800,000, the average issue price is $20. After a 2-for-1 split, the company will have 80,000 shares, and the average issue price drops to $10 per share.

Similarly, other per-share amounts such as earnings per share (EPS) will change. Suppose that Sincon had EPS of $3.00 before the split and paid dividends of $2.00 per share. The equivalent EPS after the split will be $1.50. To pay dividends after the split that are equivalent to the dividend rate before the split, Sincon needs to pay only $1.00—but on twice as many shares.

EXHIBIT 13-1

TECHNOLOGY CORPORATION

Stock Dividend and Stock Split Compared

	Total Prior to Share Issue	Total After 100% Stock Dividend	Total After 2-for-1 Stock Split
Initial issue 40,000 × $10 =	$400,000		
100% stock dividend: (40,000 + 40,000) × $10 =		$800,000*	
Two-for-one stock split: 80,000 × $5			$400,000
Total contributed capital	$400,000	$800,000*	$400,000
Retained earnings	450,000	50,000*	450,000
Total shareholders' equity	$850,000	$850,000*	$850,000

*Retained earnings capitalized: 40,000 shares × $10 = $400,000 (entry: debit retained earnings, $400,000; credit share capital accounts, $400,000.) After the stock dividend, contributed capital equals $800,000, which is $400,000 + $400,000. Retained earnings is $450,000 − $400,000, or $50,000.

Because of the change in number of shares in a stock split (or a reverse split), the company must recalculate all prior years' per-share amounts so that they will be comparable to post-split per-share amounts. Earnings per share and dividends per share must be restated.

Conversion rights for senior securities must also be adjusted. If preferred shares are convertible into three common shares prior to a 2-for-1 common share split, the preferred share will be convertible into six common shares after the split.

ADDITIONAL CONTRIBUTED CAPITAL

Contributed capital is created by a number of events that involve the corporation and its shareholders. Several accounts for additional contributed (paid-in) capital were introduced in this chapter, such as contributed capital on share repurchase.

Donated Capital Sometimes a corporation will receive a donation of assets, which creates **donated capital**. An example would be a donation of land from a shareholder. In this case, the corporation records the donated asset at its fair market value, with a corresponding credit to donated capital. The donation is viewed by the accounting profession as a capital contribution rather than as an earnings item (i.e., a not a gain.) Donated capital appears in the shareholders' equity section of the balance sheet as additional contributed capital. It must be described as to source.

Other Shares may also be donated back to a company. Corporate legislation typically requires that such shares be retired, and the retirement entry is similar to the examples given earlier, except that there is no cash consideration given—the entire paid-in value of the shares (at average cost) is transferred to an additional contributed capital account. If the shares can be legally held and reissued, the shares may be accounted for as treasury shares.

Exhibit 13-2 summarizes some of the transactions that may cause increases or decreases in additional contributed capital.

EXHIBIT 13-2

TRANSACTIONS THAT MAY CHANGE ADDITIONAL CONTRIBUTED CAPITAL

Increase

1. Receipt of donated assets
2. Retirement of shares at a price less than average issue price to date
3. Issue of par-value shares at a price or assigned value higher than par
4. Treasury stock transactions, shares reissued above cost

Decrease

1. Retirement of shares at a price greater than average issue price to date, when previous contributed capital has been recorded
2. Treasury stock transactions, shares issued below cost, when previous contributed capital has been recorded
3. Financial restructuring (explained in the Appendix to Chapter 14)

OTHER COMPONENTS OF SHAREHOLDERS' EQUITY

Other Comprehensive Income

Accumulated other comprehensive income (AOCI) is a relatively new addition to the accounting vocabulary. It is a component of shareholders' equity, usually presented below retained earnings. OCI is the main repository for unrealized gains and losses. Despite the word "income" included in the title, items in this category are *not* a part of net income. In fact, they are explicitly excluded from net income by accounting standards.

The general objective of other comprehensive income is to keep companies from burying certain items in retained earnings. Standards setters in the United States originated the OCI term and its financial statement classification. Essentially, they wished to follow the **all-inclusive income concept**, which suggests that items be classified on the income statement rather than bypassing the income statement in favour of the retained earnings statement. However, constituents objected strenuously to including various *unrealized items* in net income, partially because of the potential for volatility. Therefore, standard setters set up a continuation of the income statement, which adjusted *net income* to *comprehensive income* through the inclusion of various unrealized amounts. The unrealized amounts are then accumulated in their own equity account in shareholders' equity, called *accumulated other comprehensive income*. The challenge with this classification is that there is no real conceptual basis for this new element of the financial statements, and it appears largely as a pragmatic response to concerns by users and preparers.

Component Items Companies are not permitted any leeway in assigning items to OCI; it is available only when the standard setters tell companies to use it. Currently, there are three specified items allowed in other comprehensive income, all of which are unrealized gains and losses:

- Gains and losses on available-for-sale financial instruments (Chapter 11);
- Gains and losses on certain hedging instruments (Chapters 12 and 14); and
- Translation gains and losses on self-sustaining foreign operations.

The *change* in each of these sources, and the *cumulative balances from* each of these sources must be disclosed at the end of each reporting period.

Presentation Alternatives Standard setters allow alternatives for the presentation of the *change in* other comprehensive income:

1. Changes in OCI items can be shown as an add-on to the income statement, following on from net income to arrive at a total called *comprehensive income*. This is the preferred presentation approach by the standard setters.

2. The changes in other comprehensive income can be shown as a separate statement that simply tracks the change in the equity account. This has been the common alternative chosen in practice to date. Supplementary disclosure must include the total for net income plus the changes, or comprehensive income.

3. A separate reconciliation of net income and comprehensive income can be presented; this reconciliation is *not* on the income statement.

Two presentation options (1 and 2, above) are illustrated in Exhibit 13-3. In the first option, changes in unrealized gains (net $40,000) are added to the $500,000 net income, for a $540,000 total called comprehensive income. However, net income is then folded into retained earnings, and the $40,000 change in comprehensive income is folded into the separate balance sheet equity account, accumulated other comprehensive income. The $540,000 comprehensive income amount goes nowhere on its own. One would expect a separate retained earnings statement and a statement of accumulated other comprehensive income to show the continuity during the year—opening balance, plus or minus the changes, to equal the closing balance.

In the second option, the change in other comprehensive income is directly recorded in the equity account. A separate schedule shows the change.

Companies' preference for the second alternative may reflect their disinclination to muddy the waters around net income. There has been great opposition to including unrealized amounts in net income; presenting them on the same schedule as net income, which is then totalled to comprehensive income, is not much better. Since the second alternative has been allowed, it is being adopted in practice.

In addition to the changes in OCI, the cumulative balance of OCI must be disaggregated at the end of the year into the three different possible sources. In the example in Exhibit 13-3, this is not required because there is only one source of OCI, unrealized hedging gains from available-for-sale securities. If half were from this source, and half from foreign currency amounts, this would have to be shown at the end of the year.

EXHIBIT 13-3

OTHER COMPREHENSIVE INCOME
Reporting Alternatives Illustration

Data for Pharma Corp, 20X9

Net income	$ 500,000
Opening retained earnings	1,420,000
Opening other comprehensive income, all unrealized gains on available-for-sale securities	367,000
Unrealized gains on available-for-sale securities, arising during 20X9	56,000
Realized gains on available-for-sale securities, occurring during 20X9	16,000

Presentation Alternative #1
OCI as Add-on to Income Statement

Statement of income and comprehensive income

Net income	$ 500,000
Other comprehensive income arising from available-for-sale securities	
Plus: unrealized gains occurring during the year	56,000
Less: gains realized during the year	(16,000)
	40,000
Comprehensive income	$ 540,000
Balance sheet; shareholders' equity	
Retained earnings ($1,420,000 + $500,000)	$1,920,000
Accumulated other comprehensive income ($367,000 + $40,000)	$ 407,000

Presentation Alternative #2
OCI as Separate Statement

Income statement:	
Net income	$ 500,000
Statement of accumulated other comprehensive income arising from available-for-sale securities	
Opening balance	$ 367,000
Plus: unrealized gains occurring during the year	56,000
Less: gains realized during the year	(16,000)
	40,000
Accumulated other comprehensive income, closing balance	$ 407,000
Balance sheet; shareholders' equity	
Retained earnings ($1,420,000 + $500,000)	$1,920,000
Accumulated other comprehensive income	407,000
Supplementary disclosure:	
Comprehensive income is $540,000.	

Translation Gains and Losses on Self-Sustaining Foreign Operations A common item in other comprehensive income is the **cumulative foreign currency translation account**. This item represents unrealized gains and losses that arise from a certain type of foreign currency exposure.

In Chapter 12, accounting for a liability denominated in a foreign currency was reviewed; gains and losses caused by changes in foreign exchange rates are included in net income as they arise. But many corporations have subsidiaries in one or more foreign countries. The basic operations of these foreign subsidiaries are carried out in a currency other than the Canadian dollar, and their separate-entity financial statements are reported in the host-country currency.

In order for the parent company to prepare consolidated financial statements, the foreign operation's balance sheet and income statement must be translated into the parent's reporting currency. The process of translation is a topic for advanced accounting courses, not discussed here.

However, translation of foreign operations gives rise to an overall exchange gain or loss. If the foreign operation is essentially autonomous and does not act simply as a branch of the parent, the subsidiary is called a **self-sustaining foreign operation**. The exchange gains and losses that arise from translating the financial statements of self-sustaining foreign operations do not flow through income, but instead are classified as a component of other comprehensive income. (If the foreign subsidiary is interdependent with the parent, it is not autonomous and it is classified as an **integrated foreign operation.** When these financial statements are translated to Canadian dollars, the resulting exchange gains and losses are part of net income.)

Revaluation Adjustment

One more source of amounts reported in shareholders' equity, although rare, should be mentioned. On occasion, a company will completely revalue its assets and liabilities, a process known as *comprehensive revaluation.* All of the company's assets and liabilities are restated to market value. To make the balance sheet balance, the net amount of the change in net assets must be recorded as a *revaluation adjustment* in shareholders' equity. Such a revaluation is permitted only when new costs are reasonably determinable, and there is:

1. A new controlling shareholder with all or virtually all of the voting shares; or

2. A financial reorganization involving a change in control, following receivership or bankruptcy or following a voluntary restructuring agreement with the corporation's creditors and shareholders.

SHAREHOLDERS' EQUITY DISCLOSURE

Corporations must disclose the items and conditions of all share classes. This includes all authorized share classes, whether shares are issued or not. Private companies that adopt differential disclosure may choose to disclose only issued share classes.

Companies must also disclose the changes in all equity accounts that take place during the year. In particular, companies must disclose the changes in share capital accounts in terms of the number of shares issued, repurchased, and retired, and the dollar amount assigned to the transactions. Changes in contributed capital may be summarized in a disclosure note, or a schedule or statement to demonstrate continuity from one year to the next.

Beginning in 2008, companies must disclose their objectives, policies, and processes for managing capital. This includes their definition of capital, which obviously includes equity but also may include some forms of debt. If there are externally imposed capital requirements, these requirements and compliance with the requirements must be disclosed.

Reporting Example Exhibit 13-4 shows the Royal Bank of Canada's (RBC's) statement of changes in shareholders' equity. The statement has a separate reconciliation section for each of the *seven* shareholders' equity items shown in the company's balance sheet.

The preferred share section shows the change due to issuance and redemption, as does the common share section. Contributed surplus primarily includes items related to stock options and stock appreciation rights, both forms of employee compensation that will be reviewed in Chapter 14. RBC also reports a "gain" on redemption of preferred shares in

EXHIBIT 13-4

ROYAL BANK OF CANADA STATEMENT OF CHANGES IN SHAREHOLDERS' EQUITY

For the year ended October 31 (C$ millions)	2006	2005
Preferred shares (Note 18)		
Balance at beginning of year	$ 700	$ 532
Issued	600	300
Redeemed for cancellation	(250)	(132)
Balance at end of year	1,050	700
Common shares		
Balance at beginning of year	7,170	6,988
Issued	127	214
Purchased for cancellation	(101)	(32)
Balance at end of year	7,196	7,170
Contributed surplus		
Balance at beginning of year	265	169
Renounced stock appreciation rights	(2)	(6)
Stock-based compensation awards	(18)	26
Gain on redemption of preferred shares	—	7
Initial adoption of AcG-15, *Consolidation of Variable Interest Entities*	—	54
Other	47	15
Balance at end of year	292	265
Retained earnings		
Balance at beginning of year	13,704	12,065
Net income	4,728	3,387
Preferred share dividends	(60)	(42)
Common share dividends	(1,847)	(1,512)
Premium paid on common shares purchased for cancellation	(743)	(194)
Issuance costs and other	(11)	—
Balance at end of year	15,771	13,704
Treasury shares—preferred		
Balance at beginning of year	(2)	—
Sales	51	—
Purchases	(51)	(2)
Balance at end of year	(2)	(2)
Treasury shares—common		
Balance at beginning of year	(216)	(294)
Sales	193	179
Purchases	(157)	(47)
Initial adoption of AcG-15, *Consolidation of Variable Interest Entities*	—	(54)
Balance at end of year	(180)	(216)
Net foreign currency translation adjustments		
Balance at beginning of year	(1,774)	(1,556)
Unrealized foreign currency translation gain (loss)	(499)	(619)
Foreign currency gain (loss) from hedging activities	269	401
Balance at end of year	(2,004)	(1,774)
Shareholders' equity at end of year	$22,123	$19,847

Source: www.sedar.com, Royal Bank of Canada, Audited Annual Financial Statements, November 30, 2006.

EXHIBIT 13-5

ROYAL BANK OF CANADA SHAREHOLDERS' EQUITY DISCLOSURES (EXCERPTS)

Authorized share capital

Preferred—An unlimited number of First Preferred Shares and Second Preferred Shares without nominal or par value, issuable in series; the aggregate consideration for which all the First Preferred Shares and all the Second Preferred Shares that may be issued may not exceed $20 billion and $5 billion, respectively.

Common—An unlimited number of shares without nominal or par value may be issued.

Issued and outstanding shares (1)

	2006			2005		
	Number of shares (000s)	Amount	Dividends declared per share	Number of shares (000s)	Amount	Dividends declared per share
Preferred shares						
First preferred						
Non-cumulative Series O	6,000	$ 150	$1.38	6,000	$ 150	$1.38
US$ non-cumulative Series P (2)	–	–	–	–	–	US 1.26
Non-cumulative Series S (3)	–	–	1.33	10,000	250	1.53
Non-cumulative Series W (4)	12,000	300	1.23	12,000	300	.99
Non-cumulative Series AA (5)	12,000	300	.71	–	–	–
Non-cumulative Series AB (6)	12,000	300	.41	–	–	–
		$1,050			$ 700	
Common shares						
Balance at beginning of year (1)	1,293,502	$7,170		1,289,496	$6,988	
Issued under the stock option plan (7)	5,617	127		9,917	214	
Purchased for cancellation	(18,229)	(101)		(5,911)	(32)	
Balance at end of year	1,280,890	$7,196	$1.44	1,293,502	$7,170	$1.18
Treasury shares–Preferred shares						
Balance at beginning of year	(91)	$ (2)		–	$ –	
Sales	2,082	51		–	–	
Purchases	(2,085)	(51)		(91)	(2)	
Balance at end of year	(94)	$ (2)		(91)	$ (2)	
Treasury shares–Common shares						
Balance at beginning of year	(7,053)	$ (216)		(9,726)	$ (294)	
Sales	5,097	193		5,904	179	
Purchases	(3,530)	(157)		(1,326)	(47)	
Initial adoption of AcG-15	–	–		(1,905)	(54)	
Balance at end of year	(5,486)	$ (180)		(7,053)	$ (216)	

(1) On April 6, 2006, we paid a stock dividend of one common share on each of our issued and outstanding common shares. The effect is the same as a two-for-one share split. We have retroactively adjusted the number of common shares and dividends declared per share for the stock dividend.

(2) On October 7, 2005, we redeemed non-cumulative First Preferred Shares Series P.

(3) On October 6, 2006, we redeemed non-cumulative First Preferred Shares Series S. The excess of the redemption price over the carrying value of $10 million was charged to retained earnings in preferred share dividends.

(4) On January 31, 2005, we issued 12 million non-cumulative First Preferred Shares Series W at $25 per share.

(5) On April 4, 2006, we issued 12 million non-cumulative First Preferred Shares Series AA at $25 per share.

(6) On July 20, 2006, we issued 12 million non-cumulative First Preferred Shares Series AB at $25 per share.

(7) Includes the exercise of stock options from tandem stock appreciation rights (SARs) awards, resulting in a reversal of the accrued liability, net of related income taxes, of $8 million (2005 – $10 million; 2004 – $5 million) and from renounced tandem SARs, net of related income taxes, of $2 million (2005 – $7 million; 2004 – $3 million).

Source: www.sedar.com, Royal Bank of Canada, Audited Annual Financial Statements, November 30, 2006.

contributed capital. Retained earnings shows the usual items for net income and dividends declared, and a deduction for the premium (loss) on redemption of common shares.

RBC owns treasury shares for both common and preferred shares, which are reported as a reduction, or negative number, in shareholders' equity. The last section in Exhibit 13-4 shows the accumulated amounts of items that are components of OCI. RBC calls these *net foreign currency translation adjustments*, since the two components are unrealized exchange amounts related to subsidiaries and hedging. Use of the term "other comprehensive income" is not required in the standard.

RBC provides extensive additional disclosure in addition to the information shown in Exhibit 13-4. Some of that note disclosure is included in Exhibit 13-5. In tabular format, RBC provides detail about changes in the shares outstanding, including numbers of shares of each type, the book value assigned to those shares, and the dividend rates on the various preferred shares. Explanation of share transactions is provided in clear language.

RBC provides a comprehensive example of reporting for shareholders' equity. Most companies have a much simpler capital structure and far fewer items in shareholders' equity. Often, companies have only two items—common shares and retained earnings. However, with the advent of fair-value reporting for many types of financial instruments, accumulated other comprehensive income will become standard.

CONCEPT REVIEW

1. How do a stock split and a stock dividend differ in their impact on the shareholders' equity accounts?

2. Identify at least two ways in which a corporation can obtain contributed capital other than by the issuance of new capital shares.

3. What items are included in accumulated other comprehensive income?

INTERNATIONAL PERSPECTIVE

The Canadian and international standards for share capital and comprehensive income classification and presentation are converged. Differences in these areas are slight. Of course, the entire financial instruments rules, which cause unrealized gains and losses to be recognized in other comprehensive income, are the result of a project jointly managed by Canadian and international standard setters. One would expect the resulting standards to be in line.

Internationally, differences encountered in the equity section are usually caused by the content of legislation. For example, in jurisdictions where par value shares are required, share capital accounts report par value, and contributed capital includes amounts paid in over par. In jurisdictions that permit a company to engage in treasury share transactions, treasury shares will be common elements on the balance sheet.

RELEVANT STANDARDS

CICA Handbook:
- Section 1530, Comprehensive Income
- Section 1535, Capital Disclosures
- Section 3240, Share Capital
- Section 3251, Equity
- Section 3260, Reserves

IASB:
- *IAS* 1, Presentation of Financial Statements

SUMMARY OF KEY POINTS

1. Shareholders' equity arises from two sources: contributed capital from shareholders and retained earnings, which is capital arising from earnings of the corporation not paid out to shareholders.

2. Different types of ownership claims are represented by shares with differing contractual rights; the two basic types of shares are common and preferred. Common shares generally are voting, and have the residual claim to the firm's assets. Preferred shares have one or more contractually specified preferences over common shares, including restricted or no voting rights, priority dividend rights, cumulative dividends, participating dividends, preference in liquidation rights, conversion rights, and/or guarantee of return.

3. In conformity with legislative requirements, most shares issued are no-par shares. The entire amount of consideration received on the issuance of no-par shares is recorded in the share capital account itself. In some provincial jurisdictions, par value shares may be issued. Only the par value is assigned to the share capital account as legal capital; any issue proceeds in excess of par are assigned to a premium account in the contributed capital subsection of the shareholders' equity section.

4. Authorized capital represents the total number of shares that legally can be issued. Issued shares are the number of shares that have been sold or otherwise issued to shareholders to date. Treasury stock exists when outstanding shares are reacquired by the corporation and are held pending resale. Outstanding shares are those currently held by shareholders. Subscribed shares are unissued shares that must be used to meet subscription contracts.

5. When a corporation issues shares for assets or for services rendered to the corporation, the market value of the shares issued is used to value the transaction. If this value is not readily determinable, then the market value of the goods or services received is used. If shares are issued as a basket, the proportional or incremental method could be used to value the transaction, based on information available, or the assignment could be arbitrary if information is lacking.

6. Share issue costs normally are either offset against the proceeds received, resulting in the net proceeds being recorded in share capital, or deducted from retained earnings.

7. When shares are retired, an amount of share capital relating to the shares is first removed at average cost. If the remaining balance is a credit, it is used to increase a contributed capital account on share retirement. If the remaining balance is a debit, it is debited to existing contributed capital account from prior retirements in this class of shares, if any, and any remaining balance is debited to retained earnings.

8. Treasury stock is debited to a contra shareholders' equity account titled "treasury stock," at cost. When the stock is resold, the difference between the acquisition price and the resale price is accounted for using the same rules as retirements.

9. Retained earnings represents the accumulated net income or net loss, less the dividends declared since the inception of the corporation, and certain adjustments arising from share retirement, error correction, and changes in accounting policy.

10. Dividends are distributions to shareholders and may consist of cash, non-cash assets, debt, or the corporation's own shares in proportion to the number of outstanding shares held by each shareholder.

11. Dividends are allocated to the various share classes based on their respective contractual claims. If preferred shares are cumulative, and dividends are not paid in full in a given year, dividends declared in a later year are first paid to the preferred shares for the amount in arrears plus their current dividend before any amount is allocated to common shares. If preferred shares are participating, they receive a base dividend, then the common shares receive a base dividend; any dividend declared over the base is allocated between the two share classes on a pro-rata basis.

12. Dividends may be in the form of property, rather than cash. Property dividends are accounted for at fair market value of the property distributed. In a spinoff, shares of a subsidiary are distributed to the shareholders of the company; this transaction is accounted for at book value. Scrip dividends involve distributing long-term payables to shareholders.

13. A liquidating dividend is a return of invested capital, rather than a return of earnings. Liquidating dividends reduce contributed capital rather than retained earnings.

14. Stock dividends are proportional issuances of additional shares. Stock dividends may be recorded at market value, at a stated amount, or in a memo entry. In general, small stock dividends (less than 20% to 25%) are recorded at market value, while large dividends are recorded in a memo entry.

15. Fractional shares are issued when a shareholder would receive a portion of a share as a result of a stock dividend. Fractional shares are recorded in a shareholders' equity account that may lapse and create contributed capital, or may be turned in for whole shares, creating share capital.

16. A stock split is a change in the number of shares outstanding accompanied by an offsetting change in value per share. A memo entry reflects the changed number of outstanding shares.

17. Accumulated other comprehensive income (OCI) is a shareholders' equity account. It includes unrealized gains and losses. Sources of unrealized gains and losses are available-for-sale investments, certain foreign subsidiaries, and hedging transactions. The change in OCI may be an add-on on the income statement, to arrive at comprehensive income, or the change in the balance sheet OCI account may be presented.

18. Companies are required to disclose the components of shareholders' equity, along with details of the changes in the equity accounts during the year. Complete disclosure of the terms of shares is also required.

KEY TERMS

accumulated other comprehensive
  income (AOCI), 798
all-inclusive income concept, 799
appropriated retained earnings, 784
callable, 779
classes of shares, 773
common shares, 773
cumulative foreign currency translation
  account, 801
declaration date, 785
deficit, 784
discount, 774
dividends in arrears, 774
donated capital, 798
ex-dividend date, 785
integrated foreign operation, 801
legal capital, 785
net assets, 772
no-par shares, 774
par value shares, 774
payment date, 785
preferred shares, 773

premium, 774
private companies, 773
property dividends, 789
public companies, 773
record date, 785
restricted retained earnings, 784
restricted shares, 774
reverse split, 796
scrip dividend, 791
secret reserves, 777
self-sustaining foreign operation, 801
share issue costs, 778
shareholders' agreement, 773
shelf registration, 782
single-transaction method, 782
special shares, 774
spinoff, 789
stock split, 796
stock subscriptions, 776
treasury stock, 781
watered stock, 777

REVIEW PROBLEM

On 2 January 20X1, Greene Corporation was incorporated in the province of Ontario. It was authorized to issue an unlimited number of no-par value common shares, and 10,000 shares of no-par, $8, cumulative and non-participating preferred shares. During 20X1, the firm completed the following transactions:

8 Jan.   Accepted subscriptions for 40,000 common shares at $12 per share. Down payment on the subscribed shares totalled $150,000.

30 Jan.   Issued 4,000 preferred shares in exchange for the following assets: machinery with a fair market value of $35,000, a factory with a fair market value of $110,000, and land with an appraised value of $295,000.

15 Mar.   Machinery with a fair market value of $55,000 was donated to the company.

25 Apr.   Collected the balance of the subscriptions receivable and issued common shares.

30 June   Purchased 2,200 common shares at $18 per share. The shares were retired.

31 Dec.   Closed the income summary to retained earnings. The income for the period was $198,000.

31 Dec.   Declared sufficient cash dividends to allow a $1 per share dividend for outstanding common shares. The dividend is payable on 10 January 20X2, to shareholders of record on 5 January 20X2.

Required:

1. Prepare the journal entries to record the above transactions.
2. Prepare the shareholders' equity section of the balance sheet for Greene Corporation at 31 December 20X1.

REVIEW PROBLEM—SOLUTION

Account for subscription of common shares		
Cash	150,000	
Stock subscription receivable	330,000	
Common shares subscribed (40,000 shares)		480,000
Issue preferred shares in exchange for assets; recorded at fair market value of the assets in the absence of a value for the preferred shares		
Machinery	35,000	
Factory	110,000	
Land	295,000	
Preferred shares (4,000 shares)		440,000
Record receipt of donated assets		
Machinery	55,000	
Contributed capital—donations		55,000
Record receipt of cash for subscribed shares and issuance of shares		
Cash	330,000	
Stock subscription receivable		330,000
Common shares subscribed (40,000 shares)	480,000	
Common shares (40,000 shares)		480,000

Record acquisition and retirement of common shares

Common shares ($480,000 ÷ 40,000) × 2,200	26,400	
Retained earnings	13,200	
Cash ($18 × 2,200)		39,600

Close the income summary

Income summary	198,000	
Retained earnings		198,000

Record dividends declared

Preferred dividends declared (or, retained earnings)	32,000	
Common dividends declared (or, retained earnings)	37,800	
Dividends payable, preferred shares		32,000
Dividends payable, common shares		37,800

Preferred dividend: 4,000 shares × $8
Common dividend: 37,800 shares × $1

GREENE CORPORATION

Shareholders' Equity at 31 December 20X1

Contributed capital	
Share capital	
Common shares, no-par (unlimited shares authorized,	
40,000 shares issued and 37,800 shares outstanding)	$ 453,600
Preferred shares, no-par, $8, cumulative and non-participating	
(10,000 shares authorized, 4,000 shares issued)	440,000
Other contributed capital	
Donation of machinery	55,000
Total contributed capital	$ 948,600
Retained earnings	115,000
Total shareholders' equity	$1,063,600

QUESTIONS

Q13-1 Describe the main categories of shareholders' equity.

Q13-2 If common shares and preferred shares are issued together for capital assets, how is a value placed on the transaction, and how is the value split between the two kinds of shares?

Q13-3 What is the difference, from an accounting perspective, between par and no-par shares?

Q13-4 Briefly explain the methods of accounting for share issue costs.

Q13-5 When a company has 100,000 shares issued, and 10,000 shares held as treasury shares, how many shares are outstanding? If a cash dividend of $2 per share were declared, how much total dividend would be paid?

Q13-6 How can shares that are not callable be reacquired by a company? Why must corporations exercise caution in these transactions?

Q13-7 Why will EPS increase when shares are retired?

Q13-8 Identify and explain a transaction that causes *other contributed capital* to increase but does not result in any increase in assets or decrease in the liabilities of a corporation.

Q13-9   Explain how the purchase price is allocated when shares are reacquired and retired at a cost lower than average issuance price to date. What changes if average issuance price is lower?

Q13-10 When shares are retired, is the original issue price of those individual shares relevant? Why or why not?

Q13-11 Is treasury stock an asset? Explain.

Q13-12 What is the effect on assets, liabilities, and shareholders' equity of the (a) purchase of treasury stock and (b) sale of treasury stock?

Q13-13 In recording treasury stock transactions, why are gains recorded in a contributed capital account, whereas losses may involve a debit to retained earnings?

Q13-14 What is the difference between a cash or property dividend and a stock dividend?

Q13-15 When property dividends are declared and paid, a loss or gain often must be reported. Explain this statement. How would your answer be different if the transaction were a spinoff?

Q13-16 Explain the difference between cumulative and non-cumulative preferred shares, and the difference between non-participating, partially participating, and fully participating preferred shares.

Q13-17 Explain how a stock dividend is recorded, both the timing of recognition and amount at which it should be recognized.

Q13-18 Contrast the effects of a stock dividend (declared and issued) versus a cash dividend (declared and paid) on assets, liabilities, and total shareholders' equity.

Q13-19 What are fractional share rights and why are they sometimes issued in connection with a stock dividend?

Q13-20 How is the entry to record a (cash) liquidating dividend different from the entry to record a normal cash dividend?

Q13-21 What do shareholders receive when a scrip dividend is declared?

Q13-22 Compare a stock split, both its substance and accounting recognition, to a large stock dividend. In what ways are the two the same or different?

Q13-23 If a shareholder donates a valuable piece of art to a company, to be displayed in the company boardroom, does the company record a gain on the transaction?

Q13-24 What are the components of accumulated other comprehensive income?

Q13-25 Explain the two main alternative presentations for showing the change in accumulated other comprehensive income in a corporation's financial statements. Which alternative is more popular in practice? Where is accumulated other comprehensive income shown in the financial statements?

CASE 13-1

BIRCH CORPORATION

Birch Corporation is a small, owner-managed company that manufactures and distributes wood mouldings. At 30 June 20X6, Reg Muise owned 70% of the shares of Birch while Fran Cote owned the remaining 30%. There had been a third shareholder, Harry Ma, but his shares were repurchased and retired in March 20X6. The company was established in 20X0 and has a 30 June year-end.

Reg is a talented craftsman and a natural salesman. He has taken care of production and marketing (originally assisted by Harry) while Fran has dealt with company administration, including accounting records.

It is now August 20X6. Fran has decided that she would like to become more active in the company and has approached Reg with the proposition of purchasing his 70% share of the company. After brief negotiations, Reg agreed to sell his interest in Birch to Fran at the greater of:

a. Five times 20X6 net income according to GAAP; or
b. 1.2 times the sum of present value of 20X7 through 20X9 projected cash flows from operations.

However, given that Birch Corporation has not used the services of a professional accountant in recent years, Reg has approached Smith and Toll, Chartered Accountants, LLP to provide him with recommendations as to the proposed sale of his shares. You, CA, are a staff accountant with Smith and Toll. Fran has provided the most recent internal financial statements (Exhibit I) miscellaneous information (Exhibit II) and accounting policy information (Exhibit III).

The engagement partner asked you, CA, to provide her with a detailed memo that specifically discusses the company's accounting practices. In addition, the engagement partner would be interested in any comments you may have concerning the proposed purchase price formula.

EXHIBIT I

BIRCH CORPORATION

Excerpts from the Financial Statements
Balance Sheet

As at 30 June
(unaudited, in thousands of dollars)

	20X6	20X5
CURRENT		
Cash	$ 110	$ 87
Accounts receivable	883	664
Inventory	1,208	988
Prepaids	83	57
	2,284	1,796
CAPITAL ASSETS	761	1,087
INVESTMENT IN FEINE CORPORATION	101	189
INVESTMENT IN SPENCER INCORPORATED	—	1,000
	$3,146	$4,072
CURRENT		
Accounts payable and accrued liabilities	$1,141	$1,416
Warranty payable—Rubberwood	61	10
Current portion of long-term debt	78	78
	1,280	1,504
DEFERRED GROSS PROFIT	605	390
LONG-TERM DEBT	525	563
FUTURE INCOME TAXES	14	20
	2,424	2,477
SHAREHOLDERS' EQUITY		
Common shares	169	179
Retained earnings	553	1,416
	722	1,595
	$3,146	$4,072

EXHIBIT I   (cont'd)

BIRCH CORPORATION

Excerpts from the Financial Statements
Income Statement

For the year ended 30 June
(unaudited, in thousands of dollars)

	20X6	2005
REVENUE	$1,874	$1,723
COST OF GOODS SOLD		
Beginning inventory	988	889
Purchases	976	1,003
	1,964	1,892
Ending Inventory	1,208	988
	756	904
GROSS PROFIT	1,118	819
OPERATING EXPENSES		
Amortization	326	362
Bad debts	11	9
Insurance	27	21
Interest and bank charges	23	19
Interest on long-term debt	53	66
Repairs and maintenance	25	22
Utilities	59	56
Wages and benefits	137	114
Warranty expense	55	10
	716	679
Loss from investment in Feine	(88)	(22)
Loss from share repurchase	(150)	—
Loss from share distribution	(90)	—
Net earnings before income tax	74	118
Income tax	27	36
NET INCOME	$ 47	$ 82

EXHIBIT II

MISCELLANEOUS INFORMATION

1. Birch owns 40% of the common shares of Feine Corporation (Feine), located in Fredericton, New Brunswick. Birch also holds four of ten seats on Feine's Board of Directors. Feine's year-end is 30 June. Feine has suffered losses of $88,000 in the current year and $22,000 in the previous year. To date, Feine has not paid any dividends.

2. Birch owned 100% of the common shares of Spencer Incorporated (Spencer). Spencer derives all of its revenue from providing logistical planning services to manufacturing companies—including Birch. Spencer assists companies by establishing efficient trucking routes and liaisons with third-party trucking companies to help bring products to market. Spencer's industry is intensely competitive, and Spencer has not had a good year; projections are good for 20X7, though, because pricing has improved.

EXHIBIT II   *(cont'd)*

In February 20X6, the shareholders of Birch agreed to hold the shares of Spencer directly, instead of indirectly through Birch. Accordingly, ownership of the share certificates was transferred. The investment had been recorded on Birch's books at $1,000; the investment was estimated to be worth $910. Accordingly, a loss of $90 was recorded and a dividend of $910 recorded to represent the property dividend.

3. Birch directly repurchased and retired the shares of Harry Ma, who had owned a minor stake in the company from its inception. Harry was involved in the marketing end of the business, but was going through a divorce and decided to leave the company, liquidate his investment, and pursue other interests. His shares were repurchased for $160 in cash.

4. During fiscal 20X3, Birch introduced "RubberWood®"—a rubber-like moulding that can be shaped into virtually any crevice, corner, or archway possible. Birch's new product was initially slow to be accepted in the marketplace due to the perception that such a product would not provide a wood-like appearance. Birch was so confident that its new product would look like wood and would last longer than its traditional wood mouldings that it offered its customers a life-time guarantee that if they found any manufacturer defect, or became dissatisfied with the product in any way. Birch offered to refund the purchase price 100%—no questions asked. To date, Reg has indicated that virtually everyone has been satisfied with the new product, and sales are growing. He expects growth of at least 10% a year.

5. Gross profit is expected to increase by approximately 5% over the next two years and by 6% in the third year following.

6. Operating expenses, given recent increases in oil, insurance, and wage costs, are expected to increase approximately 5% over the next two years and by 4% in the third year.

7. For purposes of calculating the present value of projected cash flows from operations, Fran feels that a 10% discount factor is appropriate. All receivables, payables, and inventory levels are expected to be stable over the projection period. Assume that changes to income do not change income tax expense.

EXHIBIT III   *(cont'd)*

ACCOUNTING POLICY INFORMATION

The engagement partner indicated, from her discussions with Fran, the following accounting policies have been consistently adhered to since the inception of Birch. Fran also indicated that all accounting policies have been reviewed with Reg.

1. Moulding revenue is recorded upon delivery of mouldings to customers.
2. RubberWood® sales have been deferred as Fran is concerned that not enough time has elapsed since the new product was introduced. She believes taking a more conservative approach to reporting RubberWood® sales has portrayed a much more realistic look at the economic substance of those transactions when reporting to Reg. She points out she also set up a warranty expense and warranty liability of roughly 10% of sales because of the generous warranty offered to RubberWood® customers.
3. Birch's investment in Feine Corporation has been accounted for using the equity method.
4. When Birch was first established in 20X0, Reg contributed cash and equipment, along with his expertise, in exchange for his common shares.

EXHIBIT III   *(cont'd)*

Reg acquired this equipment in a previous venture, which he was rolling into Birch. The capital assets included machinery and equipment, with an expected 15-year life. Because the operation was just starting up, and valuation was tricky, the shareholders agreed that the capital assets would be valued at $1, but Reg would receive common shares that gave him a substantial interest in the company. Reg estimated that the equipment was worth somewhere between $500,000 and $1,000,000, although the market for this equipment on a used basis was almost non-existent.

(ASCA, adapted)

CASE 13-2

LORENZONI WINERY

In September 20X4, Giovanni Lorenzoni purchased a 40 hectare grape vineyard in southern Ontario. Giovanni is a successful restaurateur who owns and operates a family-oriented restaurant that offers fine cuisine at reasonable prices. As a restaurateur, Giovanni had always been interested in wines and had developed a discerning palate. He had become increasingly fascinated by the prospect of developing his own wines, and when a vineyard became available, he quickly purchased it before the land became yet another suburban housing tract.

Giovanni had two sources of financing for the purchase. First, he borrowed money from the bank, using his ownership of the restaurant as collateral. Second, he convinced a retired wine master to lend him money for the land. The wine master also agreed to contribute his expertise for developing the vineyard and the wine that would be produced from the hybrid grapes.

It now is early 20X5. Giovanni wishes to establish a corporation to own and manage the vineyard and the winery. He must incorporate in order to obtain a license to produce wine; otherwise, he is considered simply a farmer. Before he establishes the corporation, he must decide on the share structure that is most appropriate for his purposes. The main factors that he must consider are as follows:

- The wine master's loan will be converted to shares. However, the wine master is not a young man any more, and he does need regular income in addition to his retirement pension from the large winery for which he used to work.

- The wine master will be responsible for developing the wine, with Giovanni's assistance and participation as a restaurateur and as a knowledgeable consumer. There is no immediate prospect of a positive cash flow, however, as it will take at least two years before any drinkable wine is produced and much longer before quality wine can be produced and sold in any reasonable volume.

- The manager of the venture capital arm of a large pension fund is interested in investing some of the fund's money in Giovanni's venture. The fund investment would repay Giovanni's bank loan for buying the vineyard, pay for wine-producing equipment, and possibly pay to acquire adjacent land for extending the vineyard. The pension fund wants to have high priority for a reasonable return on its investment, while also being able to maintain a long-term equity interest that enables the fund to participate in future success of the venture.

- Giovanni has a wife, two sons, and a daughter. He wants all members of his family to have an equity interest in the corporation, with hopes that perhaps his children will become interested in the wine business and in building it further after Giovanni retires from active participation.

- Giovanni has hopes of eventually establishing a restaurant at the vineyard, as some other wineries in the region have done. The region's summer "wine tour" has become a popular tourist attraction for visitors from both Canada and the United States, as well as from abroad. A well-known and highly reputed sous chef from another restaurant has already expressed interest in participating in such a venture. The menu for the restaurant would be based around wines of the region, but not on Giovanni's wines until they are well developed.

- An opportunity must be available for investment from other equity participants in the future, as the company's need for capital increases.

- Giovanni's income from the restaurant has placed him in a high tax bracket. He will not need dividends from the winery in the foreseeable future.

- Giovanni wishes to retain voting control of the venture.

Giovanni will consult with a lawyer who specializes in corporate start-ups. Before going to the lawyer, he would like to obtain some informal advice. For this purpose, he has asked his younger son, Paolo, to give his views on the appropriate capital structure to use. Paolo is well on his way to becoming a chartered accountant and has some experience with small business corporate structures. At the minimum Paolo should be able to advise his father on the types of shares that are appropriate for satisfying the above factors and laying the groundwork for the company's future growth and development.

Required:

Assume that you are Paolo Lorenzoni. Prepare a report for your father in which you outline and explain a corporate share structure that will satisfy Giovanni's needs.

CASE 13-3

SHARK CANADA LIMITED

It is January 20X5, and the 20X4 financial statements for Shark Canada Ltd. are being finalized. The company is a small distributor of office machinery, and has recently had severe operating losses, a symptom of industry restructuring. The small shareholder group is dominated by members of the Sharkus family; William Sharkus is the president and CEO of the operation.

You, an independent accountant, have been called in to review the financial statements (see the balance sheet below), and finalize them before the auditors arrive.

Shark Canada employs a competent bookkeeper, but usually needs help with its annual financial statements. William Sharkus has made the following comments:

"You can see that our debt/equity ratio is quite high at 1.17 ($908,819/$778,050), but it was 1.48 ($1,135,536/$769,301) last year. We really needed that improvement: we were close to our debt covenants and, with our losses, our lenders were getting nervous.

"I want you to take a look at our equity transactions to make sure they've been handled properly in these draft statements. I know you've got to do something with that share retirement—we just left it 'in limbo.' If you have any changes, make sure you quantify your recommendations—and keep an eye on that debt-to-equity ratio!

"As you know, we've had a rough couple of years, but we're confident that next year looks good."

Required:
Review the balance sheet, identify any accounting policy issues, and prepare appropriate analysis and recommendations.

(CGA-Canada, adapted)

SHARK CANADA LIMITED
Balance Sheet

As at 31 December	20X4	20X3
Assets		
Cash and short-term investments	$ 332	$ 13,453
Trade receivables	769,178	798,119
Accrued revenue receivable	34,901	35,961
Inventories	412,111	440,465
Land, buildings, and equipment (net)	460,434	598,862
Other assets	9,913	17,977
	$1,686,869	$1,904,837
Liabilities		
Notes payable (due within one year)	$ 28,466	$ 199,792
Accounts payable and accrued liabilities	103,770	89,572
Income taxes payable	48,818	17,696
Deferred revenue	16,131	19,466
Debt with original maturity exceeding one year	530,424	617,780
Future income taxes	181,210	191,230
	$ 908,819	$1,135,536
Shareholders' Equity		
Stated capital (see Notes)	$ 495,572	$ 155,572
Retained earnings	282,478	613,729
	$ 778,050	$ 769,301
	$1,686,869	$1,904,837

Notes:

Stated Capital
Share Description

$8 cumulative, non-voting, redeemable convertible preference shares, without par value. The shares are redeemable at the issue price. Authorized and issued: 1,600 shares (20X3 − 1,600 shares)	$ 16,000	$ 16,000
Class A common shares, without par value Authorized: unlimited shares		
Issued: 172,500 (20X3—115,000)	599,572	139,572
Less: shares retired	(120,000)	—
	$ 495,572	$ 155,572

OTHER INFORMATION:

- On 15 April, 57,500 shares were issued in a 50% stock dividend, which entitled every common shareholder to 0.5 shares for every share held. This dividend was capitalized at $8 per share, estimated market value.

- "Shares retired" represents a payment made to a shareholder with respect to 15,000 shares (22,500 shares, post-stock dividend) held by this dissenting shareholder entitled to remedy (redemption at market value) under the *Business Corporations Act (Ontario)*. The company offered the shareholder $8 per share ($5.33, post-stock dividend), its estimate of market value. The shareholder insisted on a higher price, and no settlement between the shareholder and the company was made. The shareholder has taken the matter to court, and final settlement will be made according to court order when a decision is reached. In the meantime, acting on legal advice, the company paid the shareholder $8 per share ($5.33, post-stock dividend) on 15 December 20X4, and this payment is reflected in the financial statements. The payment will not prevent either party from raising any issue in the legal proceedings with respect of whether any amounts are due in excess of the payment. The shares were held in escrow and were non-voting at 31 December 20X4.

ASSIGNMENTS

★ **A13-1 Classification:** Wu Operations Limited (WOL) has the following transactions:

1. Incurred costs in issuing new common shares
2. Received proceeds on issuing a new series of preferred shares
3. Issued common stock dividend
4. Purchased common shares to be held in treasury
5. Increase in unrealized gain on available-for-sale investments
6. Paid dividends on preferred shares
7. Recognized an unrealized loss on foreign subsidiary classified as self-sustaining
8. Repurchased common shares at a price in excess of the average paid in capital of those shares

Required:
What account(s) on WOL's classified balance sheet would be affected by each of the above items? Indicate if the accounts would increase or decrease.

★★ **A13-2 Effect of Transactions:** The following transactions will change the balance sheet in some way:

a. Declare a cash dividend, to be paid in three weeks' time.
b. Declare and record a stock dividend, recorded at current market value, to be distributed in two weeks time.
c. Pay a cash dividend already declared and recorded.
d. Issue common shares for land.
e. Retire common shares for cash at a price less than the average issuance price to date.
f. Record donated assets.
g. Retire preferred shares for cash at a price higher than average issuance price to date. This is the first time preferred shares have been retired.

Required:
In the table below, indicate the effect of each transaction on the accounts listed. Use I = increase, D = Decrease, and NE = No effect. The first one is done as an example.

Item	Assets	Liabilities	Share Capital	Other Contributed Capital	Retained Earnings	Total Shareholders' Equity (Combined Effect of Prior Three Columns)
a.	NE	I	NE	NE	D	D
b.						
c.						
d.						
e.						
f.						
g.						

 A13-3 Effect of Transactions: The following transactions will change an account in shareholders' equity in some way:

a. Declare and issue a 3-for-1 stock split.
b. Record donated land.
c. Acquire treasury shares.
d. Record an increase in the value (an unrealized gain) of available-for-sale investments carried at fair market value.
e. Declare dividends on preferred shares.
f. Declare a stock dividend, to be issued in four weeks' time.
g. Issue the stock dividend in (f), resulting in the issuance of common shares and fractional share rights.
h. Fractional shares issued in (g) are exchanged for common shares (75%) and the rest lapse (25%).
i. Retire common shares for cash at a price higher than the average issuance price to date. This is the first time common shares have been retired.
j. Reissue treasury shares for cash at a price higher than average acquisition cost. This is the first time treasury shares have been reissued.
k. After the transaction in (j), reissue treasury shares for cash at a price lower than average acquisition cost.
l. Record net income for the year.

Required:

In the table below, indicate the effect of each transaction on the accounts listed. Use I = increase, D = Decrease, and NE = No effect. The first one is done as an example.

Item	Share Capital	Fractional Share Rights	Other Contributed Capital	Retained Earnings	Accumulated Other Comprehensive Income	Treasury Stock
a.	NE	NE	NE	NE	NE	NE
b.						
c.						
d.						
e.						
f.						
g.						
h.						
i.						
j.						
k.						
l.						

★ **A13-4 Overview—Subclassifications of Shareholders' Equity:** Shareholders' equity has the following subclassifications:

A. Share capital
B. Additional contributed capital
C. Retained earnings unappropriated
D. Retained earnings appropriated
E. Accumulated other comprehensive income
F. Contra to shareholders' equity

For each item below, identify the letter above that corresponds to its proper classification within shareholders' equity. Use NA if the above classifications are not applicable (give explanations if needed):

1. Proceeds on share issuance.
2. Share issue costs.
3. Stock dividends declared, not issued. Dividend is not recorded until issuance.
4. Gain on translating the financial statements of a self-sustaining foreign subsidiary to Canadian dollars.
5. Treasury shares held pending resale.
6. Net loss.
7. Restriction on retained earnings.
8. Goodwill.
9. Discontinued operation.
10. Cash dividends declared, not paid.
11. Bond sinking fund.
12. Excess of retirement price over original issue proceeds, retired shares.
13. Plant site donated by shareholder.
14. Net income.
15. Correction of accounting error affecting prior year's earnings.
16. Excess of average original issue proceeds over retirement price, retired shares.

★★ **A13-5 Share Issuance:** Lake Simcoe Limited (LSL) has unlimited no-par common shares authorized. The following transactions took place in the first year:

a. To record authorization (memorandum).
b. Issued 120,000 shares at $32; collected cash in full and issued the shares. Share issue costs amounted to $71,100. Treat this amount as a reduction of the common share account.
c. Received subscriptions for 45,000 shares at $34 per share; collected 70% of the subscription price. The shares will not be issued until collection of cash in full.
d. Issued 500 shares to a lawyer in payment for legal fees related to trademark registration.
e. Issued 10,000 shares and assumed an $80,000 mortgage in total payment for a building.
f. Collected balance on subscriptions receivable in (c).

Required:
Journalize the above transactions. State and justify any assumptions you make. Assume all transactions occurred within a short time span.

★★ **A13-6 Entries and Reporting:** Gill Corporation was authorized to issue unlimited preferred shares, $0.60, no-par value, and unlimited common shares, no-par value. During the first year, the following transactions occurred:

a. 40,000 common shares were sold for cash at $12 per share.
b. 2,000 preferred shares were sold for cash at $25 per share.

c. Cash dividends of $10,000 were declared and paid. Indicate the split between common and preferred dividends.

d. 5,000 common shares, 500 preferred shares and $67,500 cash were given as payment for a small manufacturing facility that the company needed. This facility originally cost $60,000 and had a depreciated value on the books of the selling company of $40,000.

e. Share issue costs of $16,500 were paid; this amount was treated as a reduction to retained earnings.

f. 3,000 common shares were reacquired and retired for $12.50 per share.

Required:

1. Give journal entries to record the above transactions. State and justify any assumptions you made.

2. Prepare the shareholders' equity section of the balance sheet at year-end. Retained earnings at the end of the year amounted to $121,500 before any adjustments required by the above transactions.

★★ **A13-7 Non-Cash Sale of Shares—Three Cases:** Kay Manufacturing Corporation was authorized to issue unlimited no-par common shares and preferred shares. The company

issued 600 common shares and 100 preferred shares for used machinery. In the absence of other alternatives, the Board of Directors is willing to place a stated value of $10 and $50 on the common and preferred shares, respectively.

Required:

For each separate situation, give the entry to record the purchase of the machinery:

Case A   The common shares are currently selling at $70 and the preferred at $80.

Case B   The machine is felt to be worth $45,000, the common shares are selling at $70, but there have been no recent sales of the preferred.

Case C   There is no current market price for either share class; however, the machinery has been independently appraised at $44,000.

State any assumptions you make.

★★ **A13-8 Share Retirement—Entries and Account Balances:** The accounting records of Crouse Corporation showed the following:

Preferred shares, 2,000 shares outstanding, no-par	$ 72,000
Common shares, 10,000 shares outstanding, no-par	235,000
Retained earnings	75,000

The following transactions took place during the year:

15 January	Acquired and retired 1,000 common shares for $20 per share, $20,000 total
30 January	Acquired and retired 500 preferred shares at $40 per share
16 February	Acquired and retired 1,000 common shares for $26 per share
18 February	Acquired and retired 100 preferred shares at $28 per share

Required:

1. Give journal entries to record the above transactions.

2. Calculate the resulting balance in each account in shareholders' equity.

★★ **A13-9 Share Retirement—Analysis:** During 20X5, Veech Corporation had several changes in shareholders' equity. The comparative balance sheets for 20X4 and 20X5 reflected the following amounts:

Balances 31 December	20X5	20X4
Common shares	$600,000	$700,000
Preferred shares	180,000	230,000
Contributed capital, retirement of preferred shares	27,000	0
Retained earnings	135,000	120,000

In 20X5, the only transactions affecting common and preferred share accounts were the retirement of 2,000 common shares and 1,000 preferred shares, respectively. Net income was $50,000 in 20X5, and dividends declared, $20,000.

Required:

1. What was the original issue price of the common shares? The preferred?
2. What amount was paid for the common shares retired? The preferred? (*Hint:* Reconstruct the journal entries to record the retirement.)

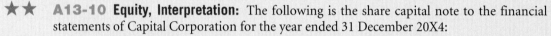 **A13-10 Equity, Interpretation:** The following is the share capital note to the financial statements of Capital Corporation for the year ended 31 December 20X4:

Note 17 Share capital
Authorized share capital consists of an unlimited number of common shares and 100,000 non-voting, cumulative preference shares with a $4 dividend.

Transactions during the period:

	Number of Shares	Share Capital
Preferred shares		
Balance as of 1 January 20X4	46,800	$ 4,567,300
Issued for cash during the period	2,450	269,500
Balance as of 31 December 20X4	49,250	$ 4,836,800
Common shares		
Balance as of 1 January 20X4	965,350	$16,584,700
Issued for cash during the period	4,200	151,200
Issued to employees under option contracts	2,000	39,000
Balance as of 31 December 20X4	971,550	$16,774,900

The company also reported $6,234,900 in retained earnings.

Required:

1. In what way are the preferred shares likely different than the common shares?
2. What does the term "cumulative" mean?
3. If the company declared a total of $350,000 of dividends on 31 December 20X4, how much would the common shareholders receive? No other dividends had yet been declared in 20X4 but dividends had been declared in all prior years.
4. What was the average issuance price for all common shares outstanding at 31 December 20X4? How does this compare to the price received for shares issued during the period?
5. Give the journal entry that would be recorded if 2,500 common shares were retired for $23 per share on 31 December 20X4.
6. Give the journal entries that would be recorded if 8,200 common treasury shares were purchased for $21 per share and then resold for $28 per share.

★★★ **A13-11 Retired Shares—Entries and Shareholders' Equity:** On 1 January 20X5, BC Ventures Corporation reported the following in shareholders' equity:

Preferred shares, no-par value, $0.70, cumulative;
    authorized, unlimited shares; issued, 80,000 shares $ 386,000
Common shares, no-par value; authorized, unlimited
    shares; issued, 80,000 shares   642,000
Contributed capital on retirement of common shares   14,000
Retained earnings   1,250,000
Accumulated other comprehensive income   38,000

During 20X5, certain shares were reacquired. In accordance with the regulations in BC Ventures' incorporating legislation, all reacquired shares were retired. Transactions were as follows:

15 January	Bought 7,000 preferred shares for $5.20 per share
12 February	Bought 2,000 common shares for $11 per share
25 February	Bought 4,000 preferred shares for $4.00 per share
26 April	Bought 5,000 preferred shares for $6.00 per share
16 July	Bought 8,000 common shares for $7.50 per share

Other transactions during the year:

30 July	Stock dividend on common shares, 5%, declared and distributed. The Board of Directors agreed to capitalize the dividend at the market value of $7.75.
30 November	The Board of Directors declared a dividend adequate to pay $1 per share to all common shareholders. This meant that they also had to declare the preferred dividend.

Required:

1. Prepare journal entries to reflect the above transactions. Show the split between common and preferred dividends in the dividend entries, as appropriate.
2. Prepare the shareholders' equity section of the balance sheet after reflecting the above transactions.

A13-12 Treasury Stock—Entries and Account Balances: On 1 January 20X1, Winnipeg Corporation issued 10,000 no-par common shares at $50 per share. On 15 January 20X5, Winnipeg purchased 100 of its own common shares at $55 per share to be held as treasury stock. On 1 March 20X5, 20 of the treasury shares were resold at $62. On 31 March 20X5, 10 of the treasury shares were sold for $59. The remaining shares were sold for $48 on 1 June 20X5. The balance in retained earnings was $25,000 prior to these transactions.

Required:

1. Provide all 20X5 entries.
2. Calculate the resulting balance in each of the shareholders' equity accounts.

A13-13 Treasury Stock—Entries and Account Balances: At 1 January 20X6, the records of Falcon Corporation provided the following:

Common shares, no-par value; 180,000 shares outstanding	$2,520,000
Retained earnings	1,980,000

During the year, the following transactions affecting shareholders' equity were recorded:

a. Purchased 1,500 shares of treasury stock at $20 per share.
b. Purchased 1,500 shares of treasury stock at $22 per share.
c. Sold 1,800 shares of treasury stock at $25.
d. Sold 600 shares of treasury stock at $18.
e. Retired 300 shares of treasury stock.

f. Split common shares 3-for-1. The remaining treasury stock is also split.

g. Declared and paid a dividend of $0.25 per common share.

Required:

1. Give entries for each of the above transactions.

2. Give the resulting balances in each capital account. Net income for 20X6 was $135,000.

★★★ **A13-14 Compute Dividends, Preferred Shares—Four Cases:** Blue Rooster Corporation has the following shares outstanding:

Common, no-par	18,000 shares
Preferred, no-par, $1.50	6,000 shares

The matching dividend, if applicable, is $2.00 per share.

Required:

Compute the amount of dividends payable in total and per share on the common and preferred shares for each separate case:

Case A Preferred is non-cumulative and non-participating; no dividends have been paid for the last two years prior to this year; dividends declared, $36,000.

Case B Preferred is cumulative and non-participating; dividends declared, $36,000. Dividends have not been paid for the last two years prior to this year.

Case C Preferred is cumulative and partially participating up to an additional $1.25; no dividends have been paid for the last three years prior to this year; dividends declared, $68,000.

Case D Preferred is cumulative and fully participating; no dividends have been paid for the last three years prior to this year; dividends declared, $90,000.

★★★ **A13-15 Compute Dividends, Preferred Shares—Four Cases:** Dunstan Limited Corporation reported net income during five successive years as follows: $50,000, $75,000, $9,000, $2,000, and $140,500. The share capital consisted of 20,000, no-par common shares, and 20,000, $0.50 no-par preferred shares.

Required:

Prepare a schedule showing the total amount each share class would receive in dividends if the entire net income amount was distributed each year.

Case A Preferred shares are cumulative and non-participating.

Case B Preferred shares are cumulative and fully participating; the matching dividend for common shares is $1.00 per share.

Case C Preferred shares are cumulative and participating up to another $0.50 per share; the matching dividend is $1.00 per share

Case D Preferred shares are non-cumulative and fully participating; the matching dividend for common shares is $1.00 per share.

★★★ **A13-16 Compute Dividends, Comprehensive—Five Cases:** Ace Corporation is authorized to issue unlimited $1.20 no-par preferred shares and unlimited no-par common shares. There are 5,000 preferred and 8,000 common shares outstanding. In a five-year period, annual dividends paid were $4,000, $40,000, $32,000, $5,000, and $42,000, respectively.

Required:

Prepare a tabulation (including computations) of the amount of dividends that would be paid to each share class for each year under the following separate cases. Where applicable, the matching dividend per common share is $3.

Case A   Preferred shares are non-cumulative and non-participating.
Case B   Preferred shares are cumulative and non-participating.
Case C   Preferred shares are non-cumulative and fully participating.
Case D   Preferred shares are cumulative and fully participating.
Case E   Preferred shares are cumulative and partially participating up to an additional $0.40 per share.

★★ **A13-17 Compute Dividends, Retire Shares:** Australia Ltd. reported the following items in shareholders' equity at 31 December 20X3:

Preferred shares, $4, 120,000 shares outstanding, cumulative, participating in dividends with common shares after the common shares have received $2.40 per share	$13,500,000
Common shares, 640,000 shares issued and 600,000 shares outstanding	28,800,000
Contributed capital on retirement of $4 preferred shares	37,200
Retained earnings	26,679,500
Treasury stock, 40,000 common shares	2,400,000

Required:

1. No dividends were declared in 20X1 or 20X2. In 20X3, $6,500,000 in cash dividends was declared. How much would be distributed to each class of shares, as described above?

2. Prepare journal entries for the following transactions, which took place after the dividend in requirement 1. The transactions occurred in chronological order:
   a. Repurchase and retirement of 30,000 common shares for $76.25 per share.
   b. Repurchase and retirement of 5,000 $4 preferred shares for $120 per share.
   c. Sale of 10,000 treasury shares at $80 per share.
   d. Declaration and distribution of a 10% stock dividend on common shares valued at $77 per share; there were fractional rights issued for 2,000 shares. The Board of Directors agreed that treasury shares would not receive the stock dividend.

★★★ **A13-18 Compute Dividends, Record Share Transactions:** Zu Corp. has the following items in shareholders' equity at 31 December 20X8:

Preferred shares, $0.60 cumulative dividend, participating with common shares after the common shares have received $0.30 per share, 15,000 shares authorized and 4,000 shares issued and outstanding	$ 360,000
Common shares, unlimited shares issued, 93,000 shares issued and 92,000 shares outstanding	1,080,000
Contributed capital on preferred share retirement	17,000
Retained earnings	4,356,900
Treasury stock, common, 1,000 shares	18,000

The following transactions and events happened in 20X9, in chronological order:

a. A cash dividend of $38,000 was declared and paid.
b. 4,000 additional common shares were issued for land. The land was valued at $50,000, while recent transactions in common shares indicated a value of $75,000.
c. Treasury shares (common), 500 shares were bought at $12,500.
d. Preferred shares, 500 shares, were purchased and retired for $130 per share
e. Treasury shares, 600 shares were reissued at $15 per share
f. A common stock dividend of 10% was issued. Treasury shares were considered ineligible for the stock dividend, by order of the Board of Directors. The stock dividend resulted in a number of whole shares issued, but 350 shares had to be issued in the form of fractional share rights, still outstanding at year-end. The dividend was valued at $40 per share.
g. Net income for the year was $1,450,000.

Required:

1. From item (a), specify the amount of cash dividend to the preferred shareholders, and the dividend to the common shareholders.

2. Calculate the final balance in the equity accounts.

3. From item (b), justify the value used to record the common shares issued.

⭐⭐ **A13-19 Property Dividend Recorded—Common and Preferred Shares:** The records of Frost Corporation showed the following at the end of 20X4:

Investment in shares of Ace Corporation (500 shares at cost)	$ 10,000
Preferred shares, $1.20, cumulative, non-participating, no-par value (10,000 shares issued and outstanding)	$230,000
Common shares, no-par value (50,000 shares issued and outstanding)	240,000
Retained earnings	125,000

The preferred shares are in arrears for 20X3 and 20X4.

On 15 January 20X5, the Board of Directors approved the following resolution: "The 20X5 dividend, to shareholders of record on 1 February 20X5, shall be $1.20 per share on the preferred and $1 per share on the common; the dividends in arrears are to be paid on 1 March 20X5, by issuing a property dividend using the requisite amount of Ace Corporation shares. All current dividends for 20X5 are to be paid in cash on 1 March 20X5." The shares of Ace Corporation were selling at $60 per share on 15 January 20X5.

Required:

1. Compute the amount of the dividends to be paid to each class of shareholder, including the number of shares of Ace Corporation and the amount of cash required by the declaration. Assume that divisibility of the shares of Ace Corporation poses no problem and that the use of Ace Corporation shares is a property dividend, not a spinoff.

2. Give journal entries to record all aspects of the dividend declaration and its subsequent payment.

3. Explain how your solution would be different if the transaction were accounted for as a spinoff.

⭐⭐ **A13-20 Stock Dividend Recorded—Dates Cross Two Periods:** The records of Victoria Corporation showed the following balances on 1 November 20X5:

Share capital, no-par, 40,000 shares	$344,300
Retained earnings	592,100

On 5 November 20X5, the Board of Directors declared a stock dividend to the shareholders of record as of 20 December 20X5, of one additional share for each five shares already outstanding; issue date, 10 January 20X6. The appropriate market value of the shares was $12.50 per share. The annual accounting period ends 31 December. The stock dividend was recorded on the declaration date with a memo entry only.

Required:

1. Give entries in parallel columns for the stock dividend assuming:

   Case A Market value is capitalized.
   Case B $10 per share is capitalized.
   Case C Average paid in is capitalized.

2. Explain when each value is most likely to be used.

3. In respect to the stock dividend, what should be reported on the balance sheet at 31 December 20X5?

4. Explain how the financial statements as of 31 December 20X5 would be different if the stock dividend were recognized on the declaration date.

★★ **A13-21 Stock Dividend and Stock Split—Effects Compared:** Ellis Frank Corporation has the following shareholders' equity:

Common share capital, no-par, 130,000 shares outstanding	$ 310,000
Retained earnings	2,500,000
Total shareholders' equity	$2,810,000

The corporation decided to quadruple the number of common shares currently outstanding (to 520,000 shares) by taking one of the following alternative and independent actions:

a. Issue a 300% stock dividend (390,000 additional shares) and capitalize retained earnings on the basis of $4 per share.
b. Issue a 4-for-1 stock split.

Required:

1. Give the entry that should be made for each alternative action. If none is necessary, explain why. On the stock split, the old shares are called in, and the new shares are issued to replace them.
2. For each alternative, calculate the components of the shareholders' equity immediately after the change. For this requirement, complete the following schedule, which is designed to compare the effects of the alternative actions; explain and compare your results.

	Before Change	After Stock Dividend	After Stock Split
Shares outstanding			
Share capital	$	$	$
Retained earnings	$	$	$
Total shareholders' equity	$	$	$

★★ **A13-22 Stock Split—Adjustments:** NovaCor Limited had the following shareholders' equity on 31 December 20X8:

$2 Preferred shares (50,000 shares issued and outstanding)	$ 700,000
Common shares (160,000 shares issued and outstanding)	320,000
Retained earnings	1,345,000
Accumulated other comprehensive income	82,000
Total shareholders' equity	$2,447,000

The preferred shares are cumulative, non-participating, and convertible into three common shares. Net income for 20X8 had been $307,000. Basic earnings per share was calculated as $1.29:

Net income	$307,000
Preferred dividend entitlement (50,000 shares × $2)	100,000
Earnings available for common dividends	$207,000
Earnings per share ($207,000 ÷ 160,000 shares)	$ 1.29

During 20X8, the company paid the $2 per share preferred dividends and also paid $1.00 per share dividends to common shareholders. Dividends are reported in total and per share in the financial statements.

On 1 April 20X9, NovaCor executed a 4-for-1 split of its common shares. On 15 July 20X9, the company repurchased 22,000 common shares from one of the company's founders at $11.00 per share.

Required:

1. Prepare the journal entry to record the 20X9 share repurchase.
2. Post-split, how many common shares would the holder of 5,000 preferred shares receive on conversion?

3. When the company prepares its comparative financial statements for 20X9, what amount will be reported for 20X8 earnings per share? What amount would be reported for 20X8 cash dividends per common share?

4. Explain any other ways, in addition to the recalculation of earnings per share, that the 20X8 comparative amounts and disclosures would be changed, when presented in the 20X9 financial statements.

★★★ **A13-23 Stock Dividends and Splits; Fractional Share Rights:** UMG Corporation reported balances in shareholder's equity:

Common shares (unlimited shares authorized; 500,000 shares issued)	$14,000,000
Retained earnings	26,533,100

Each of the following cases is independent:

Case A The Board of Directors declared and distributed a 14% stock dividend, to be recorded at the market value of the common shares, $37 per share.

Case B The Board of Directors approved and distributed a 3-for-1 stock split.

Case C The Board of Directors declared and distributed a 6% stock dividend. The dividend resulted in the distribution of 28,000 whole shares and 12,000 fractional share rights allowing the acquisition of 2,000 whole shares. The dividend was valued at the average price paid for common shares to date. These fractional share rights were 75% exercised, but 25% were allowed to lapse.

Required:

1. For each case, prepare entries, or memo entries, to reflect the transactions.

2. For each case, calculate the closing balances in shareholders' equity accounts.

3. Comment on the differences and/or similarities between the results in requirement (2).

★★★ **A13-24 Stock Dividend with Fractional Share Rights—Entries and Reporting:** The accounts of Amick Corporation provide the following data at 31 December 20X1:

Share capital, no-par; authorized shares unlimited; issued and outstanding, 40,000 shares	$360,000
Retained earnings	300,000

- On 1 May 20X2, the Board of Directors of Amick Corporation declared a 50% stock dividend (i.e., for each two shares already outstanding, one additional share is to be issued) to be issued on 1 June 20X2. The stock dividend is to be recorded at distribution and capitalized at the average of contributed capital per share at 31 December 20X1.

- On 1 June 20X2, all of the required shares were issued for the stock dividend except for those represented by 1,300 fractional share rights (representing 650 full shares) issued.

- On 1 December 20X2, the company honoured 1,000 of the fractional share rights by issuing the requisite number of shares. The remaining fractional share rights were still outstanding at the end of 20X2.

Required:

1. Give the required entries by Amick Corporation at each of the following dates:
   a. 1 May 20X2 (memo entry)
   b. 1 June 20X2
   c. 1 December 20X2

2. Prepare the shareholders' equity section of the balance sheet at 31 December 20X2, assuming net income for 20X2 was $30,000.

3. Assume instead that the fractional share rights specified that (a) two such rights could be turned in for one share without cost or (b) each right could be turned in for $2.50 cash. On 1 June 20X2, 1,300 share rights were issued and recorded as in requirement (1). On 1 December 20X2, 900 rights were turned in for shares, 200 rights for cash, and the remainder (200 rights) lapsed. Give the entry to record the ultimate disposition of all the fractional share rights.

 A13-25 Equity; Retirement and Stock Dividend: Davison Enterprises reported the following description of shareholder's equity on 31 December 20X6:

Contributed Capital
    Preferred shares, $1, no-par, 100,000 shares authorized,
        cumulative, redeemable at company's option at $107
        plus dividends in arrears. Each preferred share is
        convertible into 10 common shares.

Issued and outstanding, 20,000 shares	$2,040,000
Common shares, no-par, 100,000 shares authorized and 80,000 issued and outstanding	640,000
Contributed capital on retirement of common shares	120,000
	2,800,000
Retained earnings	1,600,000
	$4,400,000

The following transactions took place in 20X7: There were no dividends in arrears.

20 Feb. Redeemed 1,000 preferred shares at the call price.
28 Feb. Declared $100,000 in dividends. Specify the distribution of the dividend between common and preferred shares.
31 Mar. Retired 8,000 common shares for $12 per share.
2 Apr.   Declared and distributed a 3% stock dividend on the common shares, valued at $11.50 per share. Fractional share rights were issued for 200 of the shares.
30 Apr. 40% of the fractional share rights were exercised, and the remainder lapsed.

Required:

1. Journalize the listed transactions.
2. Prepare the revised contributed capital section of the balance sheet, reflecting the entries in requirement (1). Net income was $820,000 for the year.

 A13-26 Comparative Retained Earnings—Appropriations and Reporting: The records of Hawken Supply Corporation provided the following annual data at 31 December 20X4 and 20X5 (assume all amounts are material):

	20X4	20X5
Current items (pre-tax)		
a. Sales revenue	$240,000	$260,000
b. Cost of goods sold	134,000	143,000
c. Expenses	71,000	77,000
d. Discontinued operation (before tax effect)	7,000	2,000
e. Cash dividend declared and paid	20,000	—
f. Stock dividend issued	—	30,000
g. Increase in restriction for bond sinking fund	10,000	10,000
h. Increase in bond sinking fund	12,000	15,000
i. Error correction; expense of prior year understated	6,000	—

Balances, 1 January

j. Restriction for bond sinking fund	70,000	?
k. Unappropriated retained earnings	160,000	?
l. Appropriation for plant expansion	65,000	?
m. Bond sinking fund	75,000	?
n. Bonds payable	100,000	?

Income taxes: Assume an average rate of 45% on all items.

Required:

1. Prepare a comparative single-step income statement for years 20X5 and 20X4. Include EPS disclosures on the assumption that there were 10,000 common shares outstanding.

2. Prepare a comparative statement of retained earnings for the years 20X5 and 20X4. Include note disclosure for the restrictions and appropriations.

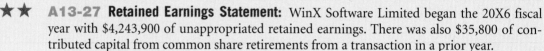

A13-27 Retained Earnings Statement: WinX Software Limited began the 20X6 fiscal year with $4,243,900 of unappropriated retained earnings. There was also $35,800 of contributed capital from common share retirements from a transaction in a prior year.

WinX has three share classes authorized and outstanding: Preferred A shares, Preferred B shares, and common shares. WinX has a 35% tax rate.

During the year, WinX distributed a 2-for-1 stock split. Common shares, with a total average issuance price of $346,700, were repurchased and retired for $519,000. Preferred B shares, with an average issuance price of $250,000, were retired for $247,500.

WinX reported $650,000 of pre-tax income before discontinued operations, but had a $911,000 pre-tax loss on discontinued operations.

The company paid $65,000 of dividends during the period. This represented the entire stated dividend on the remaining Preferred B shares (a total of $42,000 of dividends) and a partial payment of the Preferred A dividends. There are 110,000 Preferred A shares outstanding, with a $1 cumulative dividend. No common dividends were declared or paid.

WinX had a retroactive change in accounting policy in 20X6. The company changed from FIFO to average cost as a method of inventory valuation. This decreased opening inventory, and increased prior years' cost of goods sold, by $120,000, pre-tax.

Required:

Prepare the 20X6 retained earnings statement, in good form. Include disclosure notes. Comparative numbers need not be provided. (Hint: Some of the transactions and events listed above do not affect the retained earnings statement.)

A13-28 Retained Earnings Statement and Equity: Below are selected accounts from Unplugged TV Limited, at 31 December 20X9. The accounts have not been closed for the year but transactions have been correctly recorded.

Common shares	$1,635,200
Class A preferred shares	1,050,000
Cash dividends, common shares	240,000
Treasury stock, common	67,600
Accumulated other comprehensive income, unchanged in 20X9	54,600
Contributed capital on preferred share retirement	4,500
Retained earnings, 1 January 20X9	9,970,400
Stock dividend, common shares	469,800
Stock dividend distributable, common shares	120,800
20X9 net income before discontinued operations	765,900
Fractional common share rights outstanding	21,500

Excess on common share retirement (shares retired for $62,000 while average cost was $46,000)	16,000
Discontinued operations, gain, net of tax	8,400
Error correction, net of tax (increases prior earnings)	46,200
Cash dividends, preferred shares	88,500

Required:

1. Prepare the 20X9 retained earnings statement, in good form. Comparative figures need not be disclosed.
2. Prepare the shareholders' equity section of the balance sheet as of 31 December 20X9.

★ **A13-29 Other Comprehensive Income:** Praxior Corporation reports the following information at the end of 20X8 (in thousands):

Net income	$ 14,560
Unrealized losses on available-for-sale investments arising during 20X8	1,756
Gains realized during 20X8 on available-for-sale investments; amounts had previously been recorded as unrealized	235
Opening retained earnings	253,900
Opening accumulated other comprehensive income	95,000

Required:

1. Describe the nature of accumulated other comprehensive income, and the three common sources of other comprehensive income.
2. Draft two alternative presentation alternatives that may be used to show the changes in accumulated other comprehensive income in the 20X8 financial statements:
   a. Changes in OCI shown as an add-on to the income statement.
   b. Changes in the balance sheet OCI account shown as a separate statement.

★ **A13-30 Other Comprehensive Income:** The following information is from the annual report of Reliable Tires Limited (in thousands):

Statement of income and comprehensive income, net of income tax	**20X8**
Net income	$ 3,036
Other comprehensive income	
Change in unrealized gains and losses on available-for-sale securities	(89)
Change in unrealized foreign currency translation gains and losses	(144)
Change in gains and losses on derivatives designated as cash flow hedges	(57)
Total comprehensive income	$ 2,746
Other information:	
Retained earnings	
Balance at beginning of year	$10,473
Accumulated other comprehensive income	
Balance at the beginning of the year	$ 578
Net income	$ 3,036

Required:

1. Describe the nature of accumulated other comprehensive income, and the sources of accumulated other comprehensive income illustrated in the information above.

2. Calculate the closing balance in retained earnings and accumulated other comprehensive income, based on the information above.

3. Recast the information given above to illustrate a separate statement shown for the changes in the OCI account. Which presentation alternative has proven more popular in practice?

4. What additional information does the company have to disclose with respect to the balance in OCI at the end of the year?

★★   **A13-31 Shareholders' Equity:** Use appropriate data from the information given below to prepare the shareholders' equity section of the balance sheet for Croton Corporation at 31 December 20X5. Explain the meaning of each of the items disclosed in the company's shareholders' equity section.

Preferred shares, no-par value, $6, unlimited number authorized, cumulative and fully participating; 9,000 shares issued and outstanding	$105,000
Bonds payable, 7%	200,000
Stock subscriptions receivable, preferred shares	6,000
Common shares, no-par, unlimited number authorized; 5,000 shares issued and 4,900 outstanding	250,000
Discount on bonds payable	1,000
Retained earnings	290,000
Treasury shares, 100 common shares	5,600
Unrealized exchange gain on translation of foreign subsidiary's financial statements	70,500
Fractional common share rights	3,200
Contributed capital on common share retirement	1,900
Preferred shares subscribed, 100 shares	10,000

★★★ **A13-32 Entries and Shareholders' Equity:** On 1 January 20X5, Mersery Limited had the following shareholders' equity:

Series A preferred shares, no-par, $6, cumulative; 160,000 shares issued and outstanding	$16,400,000
Series B preferred shares, no-par, $2, cumulative, participating in dividends with common shares to an additional $1 after the common shares have received a $.50 matching dividend; 100,000 shares issued and outstanding	9,500,000
Common shares; 800,000 issued and outstanding	28,400,000
Contributed capital on retirement of Series B preferred shares	22,000
Retained earnings	11,600,000
	$65,922,000

Dividends are one year in arrears on the Series B preferred shares.
The following events and transactions took place during 20X5:

15 January	Issued 40,000 common shares for machinery with an appraised value of $1,650,000; the shares were estimated to be worth $40 per share.
30 January	25,000 Series A preferred shares were retired for $105 per share.
15 February	Dividends of $1,500,000 were declared and paid (indicate the amount of dividend for each share class).
31 March	15,000 Series B preferred shares were retired for $106 per share.
30 April	60,000 common shares were retired for $42 per share.

30 June	Dividends of $1,200,000 were declared and paid (indicate the amount of dividend for each share class).
14 November	A stock dividend of 10% was declared and issued on the common shares. The Board of Directors agreed that the dividend would be recorded at the market value of the common shares, $43.25. The dividend involved issuing fractional share rights that, if entirely exercised, would result in the issuance of 6,000 common shares.

Required:

1. Record all transactions in general journal form.
2. Prepare the shareholders' equity section of the balance sheet at 31 December 20X5. Assume income for the year was $2,475,000.

★★★ **A13-33 Shareholders' Equity:** Howard Corporation is a publicly owned company whose shares are traded on the TSE. At 31 December 20X4, Howard had unlimited shares of no-par value common shares authorized, of which 15,000,000 shares were issued. The shareholders' equity accounts at 31 December 20X4 had the following balances:

Common shares (15,000,000 shares)	$230,000,000
Retained earnings	50,000,000

During 20X5, Howard had the following transactions:

a. On 1 February, a distribution of 2,000,000 common shares was completed. The shares were sold for $18 per share.

b. On 15 February, Howard issued, at $110 per share, 100,000 of no-par value, $8, cumulative preferred shares.

c. On 1 March, Howard reacquired and retired 20,000 common shares for $14.50 per share.

d. On 15 March, Howard reacquired and retired 10,000 common shares for $20 per share.

e. On 31 March, Howard declared a semi-annual cash dividend on common shares of $0.10 per share, payable on 30 April 20X5, to shareholders of record on 10 April 20X5. (Record the dividend declaration and payment.) The preferred share dividend will be paid on schedule in October.

f. On 15 April, 18,000 common shares were acquired for $17.50 per share and held as treasury stock.

g. On 30 April, 12,500 of the treasury shares were resold for $19.25 per share.

h. On 31 May, when the market price of the common was $23 per share, Howard declared a 5% stock dividend distributable on 1 July 20X5, to common shareholders of record on 1 June 20X5. Treasury shares were not given the stock dividend. The stock dividend was recorded only on distribution. The dividend resulted in fractional share rights issued, that, when exercised, would result in the issuance of 2,300 common shares.

i. On 6 July, Howard issued 300,000 common shares. The selling price was $25 per share.

j. On 30 September, Howard declared a semi-annual cash dividend on common shares of $0.10 per share and the yearly dividend on preferred shares, both payable on 30 October 20X5, to shareholders of record on 10 October 20X5. (Record the dividend declaration and payment.)

k. On 31 December, holders of fractional rights exercised those rights, resulting in the issuance of 1,850 shares. The remaining rights expired.

l. Net income for 20X5 was $25 million.

Required:

Prepare journal entries to record the various transactions. Round per-share amounts to two decimal places.

★★ **A13-34 Transactions, Cash Flow Statement:** The following data is related to Truro Ltd.:

	20X9	20X8
Preferred shares, no-par	$ 1,000,000	$ 1,500,000
Common shares, no-par	31,395,000	26,000,000
Preferred shares subscribed	2,000,000	0
Common share fractional rights	0	287,000
Contributed capital on lapse of rights	57,400	0
Contributed capital on preferred share retirement	61,000	0
Retained earnings	10,625,000	7,940,000
Subscriptions receivable, preferred shares	(1,200,000)	0

During the year, the following transactions took place:

a. Preferred shares were retired.
b. Cash dividends were paid.
c. The common share fractional rights converted into common shares (80%) and the remainder (20%) lapsed.
d. Common shares plus $1 million cash were issued to acquire a patent that was valued at $4,000,000.
e. Contracts were signed to issue preferred shares with a total consideration of $2,000,000. The prospective shareholders paid $800,000 and will pay the balance within 12 months.
f. Net income was $3,400,000.
g. Additional common shares were issued for cash.
h. Retained earnings was reduced by $124,300 as the result of an error correction affecting prior periods.

Required:

1. Show the retained earnings T-account, beginning with the opening balance and going to the closing balance. Label all items that caused the change in the account.
2. Prepare the investing and financing sections of the CFS, in as much detail as possible with the information given.

★★ **A13-35 Cash Flow Statement:** The following data relates to Ottawa Limited:

31 December	20X5	20X4
Preferred shares, no-par	$ 520,000	$ 460,000
Common shares, no-par	8,438,350	6,840,000
Common share fractional rights	8,750	—
Contributed capital on preferred share retirement	29,000	22,000
Contributed capital on common share retirement	—	96,000
Retained earnings	3,867,000	3,911,500

TRANSACTIONS DURING THE YEAR:

1. Preferred shares were issued for $100,000 during the year. Share issue costs of $2,000 were charged directly to retained earnings. Other preferred shares were retired.
2. On 31 December 20X4, there were 570,000 common shares outstanding.
3. A total of 20,000 common shares were retired on 2 January 20X5 for $18 per share.
4. There was a 10% stock dividend on 1 April 20X5. This dividend was capitalized at $17.50, the market value of common shares. The stock dividend resulted in the issuance of fractional rights for 3,200 whole shares. Of these, 2,700 whole shares were subsequently issued and fractional rights for a remaining 500 shares are still outstanding at the end of the year.

5. Cash dividends were declared during the year.

6. Common shares were issued in June 20X5 for land. The transaction involved issuing 3,000 common shares for land valued at $52,000. The land value was used to record the transaction.

7. Common shares (46,000 shares) were issued for cash on 30 December 20X5.

8. Net income was $1,200,000 in 20X5.

Required:

Prepare the financing activities section of the CFS based on the above information.

CHAPTER 14

Complex Debt and Equity Instruments

INTRODUCTION

When accountants prepare financial statements, a major task is to classify and organize the accounts into categories. Unfortunately, some things are hard to classify. For example, RONA Inc. has $6 million in Class D *preferred share capital*, entitled to a 4% cumulative dividend. The company is required to buy back $1 million in shares, at book value, every year. These shares don't seem to be a permanent, residual equity interest: the company is required to repay the investment. RONA classifies these preferred shares as debt.

Financial instruments that have characteristics of *both* debt *and* equity are called *hybrid financial instruments*. In this chapter, classification and accounting for hybrid financial instruments will be examined. Criteria will be reviewed that help determine whether a security is debt or equity *in substance*.

Another topic in this chapter is accounting for options, whether they are granted as compensation to employees, provided to suppliers or customer to cement relationships, or provided to existing shareholders to preserve their interests. Sometimes these options are recorded, but often they are simply disclosed. The cost of employee stock options

can be considerable. RONA has options for over 3 million shares outstanding, mostly to employees, that allow the purchase of shares at an average price in the range of $8 per share. Since market value was over $20 per share, it's obvious that the option holders are receiving something of value. Representational faithfulness dictates that this value has to be reported in the financial statements. Other forms of long-term compensation are also reviewed, and patterns of accounting policy in this area are established.

This chapter also examines the use of derivative financial instruments to mitigate financial risk, specifically the use of hedges and swaps. The use of derivatives significantly alters the risk profile of a company, and their inclusion in the financial statements is not simple.

In the Appendix to this chapter, the various forms of *financial restructuring* are reviewed. When a company is in financial distress, debt may be settled for less than the amount owing, in cash or other assets, or lenders may accept share capital instead of their existing claims and become the residual risk takers.

THE DEBT-TO-EQUITY CONTINUUM

Throughout most of the 20th century, the distinction between debt financing and share-holders' equity was clear. Debt financing was an amount borrowed, at some specific interest rate, payable at a fixed time in the future or at the option of the lender. Shareholders' equity was any investment in shares, plus residual interests accruing through retained earnings or capital transactions. The legal form of debt and equity was unmistakable, and substance generally followed legal form.

Accountants traditionally relied on the legal nature of capital instruments for classification. If there was a stock certificate, the instrument was accounted for as equity; if there was a debt contract or agreement, the instrument was accounted for as a liability. This rule worked well as long as debt and equity conformed to expectations: that is,

- Debt carried a firm commitment to interest payments and repayment of capital at maturity, and
- Equity was a residual interest in net assets with rights only to dividends as declared and no guaranteed return of capital.

Unfortunately, there came to be too many forms of financing that didn't fit comfortably into these two simple categories. The financial markets support a continuum of investments, with features that range from pure debt to pure equity, with a lot of grey in the middle. Corporations (and the capital markets) have been very inventive in designing new investment vehicles that have characteristics of both debt and equity. These new types of securities are called **hybrid securities**.

For example, **income bonds** are bonds that pay interest, but *only when the corporation has earned a certain amount of income or operating cash flow* in the year. This isn't the guaranteed return on capital that is normally associated with debt. Then there are preferred **redeemable shares,** as reported by RONA. Since they have to be bought back for cash, they are really more like a liability.

Convertible debt, convertible at the investor's option, presents another accounting classi-fication dilemma. The issuing company allows the investor to convert the principal portion of the bond into a certain number of common shares on certain dates. The issuing company usually hopes that the bond will be converted prior to maturity, but can't force conversion. Investors will convert only if the shares are worth more money. Perhaps the company will avoid having to repay principal, if share prices increase, but maybe it will have to repay the debt, if share prices are soft. This is a contingency, and obviously hard to place into debt-or-equity slots.

The old method of classifying debt and equity on the balance sheet is not effective when the formerly clear boundary between debt and equity is bridged by hybrid securities.

Balance Sheet Classification

To deal with the reporting problems of hybrid securities, the accounting profession has developed a set of comprehensive standards for reporting hybrid securities and other com-plex financial instruments. This approach for financial instruments is new, and is a work in progress for the worldwide accounting profession, including Canada.

FINANCIAL INSTRUMENTS—GENERAL PRINCIPLES

General Measurement Rules

In Chapter 12, we discussed the general measurement rules that pertain to financial liabilities. The rules are:

Initial measurement	Fair value (likely present value)
Subsequent measurement:	Amortized cost using the effective interest method
Derecognition:	When extinguished: a. Discharged by paying the creditor, or b. Legally released from primary responsibility for the liability either by process of law or by the creditor

Classification Requirements for Hybrid Instruments

Financial instruments must be classified as liability or equity in accordance with the *substance* of the contractual arrangement. If the financial instrument is part debt and part equity, *the component parts are classified separately.* These requirements are an important application of the qualitative characteristic of substance over form: if it looks like a duck and it quacks like a duck, then it should be classified as a duck, even when it has a sign around its neck that says it's a moose! That is, balance sheet classification depends on the nature of the instrument as debt or equity and not on its name or label.

Furthermore, payments to investors for the use of capital should be presented in accordance with the nature of the financial instrument as a liability or as equity. Payments that are associated with financial liabilities should be presented on the income statement, and payments associated with equity instruments should be presented on the retained earnings statement. Gains and losses associated with debt retirement are reported on the income statement. Gains and losses associated with equity are capital transactions and are *not* reported on the income statement.

Tax Status Unaffected It is important to remember that the accounting classification will not change the tax classification of an investment vehicle, because the tax classification is established by Canada Revenue Agency rulings. Thus, interest payments on instruments that legally are debt but in substance are equity will be tax deductible as interest even if the interest is reported as a deduction from retained earnings in the balance sheet.[1]

Similarly, if an "equity" item is classified as debt in the financial statements, and "dividend" payments are reported on the income statement, the "dividends" will not be a tax-deductible expense. They will be treated as dividends for tax purposes; that is, they will not be taxed to a corporate recipient. However, their inclusion on the income statement will provide a source of permanent differences in the calculation of the provision for taxes. Accounting for permanent (and temporary) differences between accounting income and taxable income is discussed in Chapter 15.

Debt versus Equity Accounting Implications

Assume that a company raises $100,000 by issuing a financial instrument that will pay $6,000 per year to the investor. At the end of the fifth year, the company retires the financial

---

[1] An exception is that the interest paid on income bonds generally is not tax deductible. This is a specific provision of the *Income Tax Act*, and the tax treatment is not affected by the accounting treatment.

instrument in a transaction in the open market, buying it back at market value of $109,500. The financial statements are affected by whether the instrument is classified as debt or equity. The impact of each classification can be summarized as follows:

Event	Liability Classification	Equity Classification
Issuance	Increases long-term liabilities	Increases shareholders' equity
Annual $6,000 payment	Increases interest expense; decreases net income and decreases retained earnings	Reduces retained earnings as a dividend distribution; no impact on income statement
Annual $6,000 payment on CFS	In operations section	In financing section
Payment of $9,500 "premium" at retirement	Recorded as a loss on the income statement	Reduces shareholders' equity directly; no impact on income statement
$100,000 "repayment" of initial investment	Decreases liabilities	Decreases shareholders' equity

There are two major differences between these alternative classifications:

1. Reported income is changed by interest payments and gains and losses on retirement when the classification is a liability. In contrast, these items bypass the income statement if the classification is equity. For firms that jealously guard reported earnings, cash flow from operations, and related trends, this distinction is important.

2. The balance sheet classification (i.e., as debt or equity) of the item may be crucial to some corporations. The debt-to-equity ratio is often used in loan covenants to help control a major risk to lenders: the amount of debt that a company can issue. If debt-to-equity ratios are close to their contractually agreed maximums, then a new financial instrument issued and classified as equity is good news indeed; one classified as a liability is not. The classification rules attempt to ensure that classification follows substance, not form, to limit the potential for manipulation.

CLASSIFICATION RULES

To classify a financial instrument, it is essential to look at the payment arrangements. A basic characteristic of debt is that the creditors have a legal right to receive payments. In most ordinary debt arrangements, the debtor is obligated both to pay regular interest amounts and to repay the principal amount at a fixed and known time. Some debt has no fixed maturity, such as demand loans or lines of credit from a bank, but the lenders have the option of demanding their money back. The crucial aspect of debt is that *the creditors can demand payment.*

Equity investors, on the other hand, cannot demand payment; both the payment of dividends and the redemption or repayment of the amount invested is at the option of the company (or, more precisely, of the Board of Directors). If, at the end of the day, the investors get their money back, or can get their money back if they want to, then the financial instrument is substantively a liability.

Therefore, to determine whether a complex financial instrument is debt or equity in *substance,* we need to ask the following questions:

1. Is the periodic return on capital (i.e., cash interest or dividend payment) mandatory?

2. Is the debtor legally required to repay the principal in cash, either at a fixed, predetermined date (or dates), or at the option of the creditor?

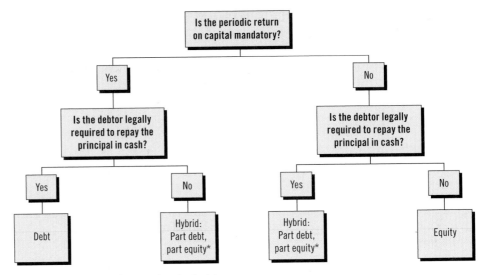

EXHIBIT 14-1

CLASSIFICATION OF FINANCIAL INSTRUMENTS

*Note: Hybrid securities may have one element valued at zero.

Classification depends on the answers to these two questions, as is illustrated in Exhibit 14-1:

- If the answer to *both* of these questions is "yes," then the financial arrangement is entirely a financial liability for accounting purposes and must be reported as such both on the balance sheet (for the present value of the future payments) and on the income statement (for the periodic interest payments).
- If the answer to both of these questions is "no," then the instrument is equity.
- If the answer is "yes" to one and "no" to the other, the capital raised by the financial instrument must be split between debt and equity. (The value assigned to either the debt or equity portion may be zero, however, if its expected present value is zero.)

The accountant must examine substance, not form. For example, a financial instrument may be described on paper as a debt obligation (form) but carry no legally enforceable claim for payment by the creditor (substance); in this case, the "debt" is really equity, with the following reporting implications:

1. The "interest" payments are reported as dividends on the retained earnings statement and on the cash flow statement.

2. The proceeds received by the debtor will be classified as share equity on the balance sheet.

SPECIFIC EXAMPLES OF FINANCIAL INSTRUMENTS CLASSIFICATION

Retractable Preferred Shares

Description Most preferred shares have a call provision, whereby the corporation can call in the shares and redeem them at a given price *if the company wishes*. The call price is specified in the corporate bylaw governing that class of share. Preferred share call provisions give management more flexibility in managing the corporation's capital structure than would be the case without a call provision. These shares are redeemable at the company's option and are equity.

Some preferred shares include the provision that the shares *must* be redeemed on or before a specified date (**term preferred shares**), or an option to redeem can be exercised *at*

term preferred shares

preferred shares that must be redeemed on or before a specified date *the option of the shareholder* (**retractable shares**). When redemption is required or is at the option of the holder, then the mandatory final cash payout effectively makes the preferred shares a liability. The key is that cash repayment must either be contractually required, or at the option of the *investor*.

Effect of Escalation Clause Sometimes, a preferred share issue may not have a direct or explicit requirement for the company to repay. Instead, the repayment obligation may be established indirectly through its terms and conditions. For example, suppose that a redeemable preferred share issue requires the company to triple the dividend rate after five years, or double the redemption price after five years. No prudent Board of Directors would leave the shares outstanding past year five at their significantly higher cost. The escalation clause clearly indicates that the shares will be redeemed before the escalation. These shares will be classified as debt.

Reporting Preferred shares are likely to be classified as debt if any one of the following conditions exists:

1. Redemption is contractually required; or

2. Redemption can be forced by the investor; or

3. Terms of the shares are such that redemption is essentially forced by the terms of the shares, even if the entity is financially sound.

Dividends Classic dividends are a legal liability only when declared, and the classification of preferred shares as a liability does not alter this. However, if dividends are cumulative *and must be paid in cash at redemption*, then dividends are accrued as time passes.

When preferred shares are classified as debt, *their dividends are reported on the income statement*, as a financing expense, not the retained earnings statement.

Required Redemption at a Premium If preferred shares *must be redeemed* at a value higher than book value, the redemption premium should be accrued over the life of the shares using the effective interest method. For instance, assume that redeemable preferred shares were issued at $100 but have to be bought back for $110 at the end of five years. Each year, the company must accrue a portion of the premium, and expense it as a cost of financing.

Reporting Example According to *Financial Reporting in Canada 2006*, a total of 22 companies out of the 200 surveyed disclosed preferred shares as debt. For example, Tembec Inc. shows $17 million of redeemable preferred shares, described as follows (emphasis added):

> Series 2 Class B shares redeemable at any time by the Company and, commencing on June 26, 2011, *at the option of the holder*, the redemption price being equal to the issue price plus declared and unpaid dividends. The Series 2 Class B shares are entitled to a preferential and non-cumulative dividend equal to the dividend yield percentage paid on the common shares.

The holder will be able to demand redemption of these shares. This is an important characteristic of debt. Therefore, Tembec does not include these shares in its shareholders' equity section. Instead, they are shown above shareholders' equity.

Tembec's financial statements and disclosure notes include no indication that any dividends were paid. The provisions of the preferred shares are that dividends will be "equal to the dividend yield percentage of the common shares." In other words, preferred dividends will not be paid unless common dividends are paid. None were. If preferred dividends had been paid, they should be shown as part of interest expense rather than in the statement of retained earnings. Six companies with preferred share liabilities in the *Financial Reporting in Canada 2006* survey reported dividends as "interest expense."

Differential Reporting Private companies sometimes issue preferred shares, redeemable at the shareholder's option in various circumstances, as part of tax-planning exercises. However, the intent is to retain the equity investment. If the company qualifies for differential reporting, the shares can be classified as equity.

Other Redeemable Shares

"Redeemable" does not automatically mean that shares are liabilities. Preferred shares that are redeemable *at the company's option* are not a liability. The company cannot be forced to pay cash, since redemption is voluntary. Redemptions that can be avoided do not create a liability. Also, preferred shares that are *convertible into common shares* are clearly equity.

Perpetual Debt

perpetual debt

a type of debt whose principal does not have to be repaid; yields an interest stream of income to investors

Description Perpetual debt is debt whose principal never has to be repaid, or is highly unlikely ever to be repaid. In general, perpetual debt provides the holder with a contractual right to receive interest, but the principal (1) never has to be repaid, (2) has to be repaid only in the indefinite future, or (3) has to be repaid only in very unlikely situations, such as upon liquidation of the company. For many years, Air Canada had outstanding perpetual debt (in foreign currencies, at very low interest rates) of about $1 billion. The company was obligated to pay this liability only upon the final dissolution and liquidation of the company but was allowed to pay it back at any interest repricing date. The company redeemed the debt without waiting for liquidation.

Reporting Although the principal amount of perpetual debt is an obligation on liquidation, like equity, its due date is in the infinite future. Therefore, the present value of this amount is zero. However, the interest payments represent obligations at fixed dates. The lender will be willing to pay for the interest stream, and it is the interest stream that generates loan proceeds. Therefore, accounting standards require that perpetual debt should be classified as a liability, valued at the present value of the stream of future interest payments.

For example, assume that a $1,000,000, 10% perpetual debt instrument is sold to yield 10%. The present value of the principal, which never has to be repaid, is zero. The present value of the interest, $100,000 a year in perpetuity, is $1,000,000 (that is, $100,000 ÷ 0.10). Thus, the bond sells for the value of the interest stream only. The interest stream is clearly a liability, because it must be paid. Therefore, the $1,000,000 is classified as a liability. The principal portion, with its equity overtones, has an assigned value of zero.

Private Companies and Shareholder Loans

An obvious form of debt that will not be repaid can be found in private corporations, particularly in small family corporations, where the controlling shareholder(s) often "lend" significant sums of money to the corporation. There is no intent to repay. These loans often are reported on the balance sheet as liabilities, because there is a legal debt contract. However, lenders typically consider shareholder loans as a part of equity capital because of the intent. This intent may be formalized in covenants or other contracts to protect lenders.

Convertible Debt

General Description One of the most common hybrid securities is convertible debt. Bonds often are issued by a corporation with the provision that they may be converted by the holder into shares (usually, common shares) at a specified price or ratio of exchange. For example, Axcan Pharma Inc. describes an issue of convertible debentures as follows in its annual financial statements (in thousands of U.S. dollars):

> Convertible subordinated notes, 4.25%, interest payable semi-annually starting October 15, 2003, convertible into 8,924,113 common shares, maturing April 15, 2008   <u>$125,000</u>
>
> The noteholders may convert their notes during any quarterly conversion period if the closing price per share ... exceeds 110% of the conversion price in effect on the thirtieth trading date ... The noteholders may also convert their notes upon the occurrence of specified corporate transactions or if the company has called the notes for redemption. ...

Companies often issue long-term debt that may be converted into common shares at the bond's maturity date, or during a period of time preceding the maturity date (e.g., for the last four years of the bonds' outstanding period). There are often various conversion windows that specify a particular ratio for conversion. For example, an investor might get 10 common shares for every $1,000 bond if it was converted within the first five years of a 15-year bond issue's life, 7.5 shares for conversion in the sixth through tenth year, but only five common shares during years 11 through 15.

The conversion ratio is expressed either in the number of shares per bond, or in a price per share. For example, a bond that is convertible into 20 common shares per $1,000 bond is the same as one that is convertible at a price of $50 ($1,000 ÷ $50).

Characteristics of Convertible Debt A key element of convertible bonds is that, in issuing the bonds, management fully expects (or hopes) that the conversion privilege will eventually be attractive to the investors: the investors will convert at or before the maturity date, and therefore the company will never have to repay the principal amount of the bonds.

Conversion of a bond becomes attractive when the market price of the share entitlement rises above the conversion price. For example, suppose that an investor has a $1,000 bond (purchased at par) that is convertible into 25 shares of common stock (i.e., the conversion price is $40). If the market price of the common shares is $46, the investor can make a profit of $6 per share (less transaction costs) by converting the bonds and then selling the shares on the open market:

Market value of shares obtained on conversion ($46 × 25)	$1,150
Less: cost of bond	<u>1,000</u>
Profit from conversion	<u>$ 150</u>

The market recognizes this reality, and therefore the market price of the bonds will increase to follow the conversion value of the shares. Therefore, once the market price of the shares rises above the conversion price, the bonds will sell at a price that is related to the value of the conversion privilege rather than at a price related to the merits of the debt instrument. In the eyes of the market, the bond ceases to trade as debt, and effectively is traded as equity.

forced conversion

whereby the issuer (the corporation) calls in a senior security for conversion to common shares when cash value is less than share value, ensuring shares will be issued

Forced Conversion A convertible debenture can often be called for redemption by the company prior to maturity; Axcan had this right in the example quoted earlier. The point of the redemption option is that management can **force conversion** before maturity if the market price is above the conversion price of the shares. By forcing early conversion, the company makes sure that the conversion takes place and cash repayment will not be necessary.

Nature of Convertible Debt As should be apparent from the foregoing discussion, a convertible bond with a fixed conversion price per share has elements of both debt and equity. Bonds with a conversion privilege will sell at a higher price (and lower interest yield) than bonds of equivalent terms and risk without a conversion privilege. This fact has become particularly obvious in recent years as innovative capital markets have divided convertible debentures into their two components (pure debt and share option) and traded them separately.

Convertible Debt with a Floating Conversion Price Per Share Convertible debt may be issued where the number of shares to be issued on conversion is not fixed by contract, but rather is based on the market value of the shares on the conversion date. If this is the case, the conversion option has no intrinsic value to the investor, because the investor has no upside benefit. For example, if a $1,000,000 bond were convertible into shares at the market value of shares on the conversion date and this value was $80, then 12,500 shares would be issued. If the market value were $82, then 12,195 shares would be issued. This type of bond has no equity component and is all debt.

The reason for this conclusion is that if the price is not fixed, the risk and reward of changing share prices stays with the company. The lender has no upside, nor downside risk. The liability will always trade in financial markets as a pure liability, with no option attached. Essentially, when the conversion option is at the company's choice and the price is based on the fair value of the day of conversion, the company could just as well issue new shares in the market and then use the proceeds to pay the principal. The dollar amount of the liability is not altered by this type of conversion option. The company must deliver shares that will satisfy the dollar amount of the liability.

CONCEPT REVIEW

1. What is a hybrid financial instrument?
2. What two questions must be answered to aid in classifying a financial instrument as debt or equity?
3. What is the distinguishing characteristic that causes retractable preferred shares to be reported as debt rather than as shareholders' equity?

CONVERTIBLE DEBT, CONVERSION AT THE INVESTOR'S OPTION

Convertible debt that is convertible at the option of the investor at a fixed conversion price is really two things:

1. A promise to pay interest and principal, and

2. An **option contract** that gives the investor the right to use that principal to buy a certain number of common shares.

The *substance* of the investment is reflected if these two elements are recognized separately in the financial statements. Thus, accounting standards require that at issuance, *if a liability includes an option on shares, the proceeds from issuance must be divided between the liability and the option, and the two recorded separately.*

Initial Recognition Assume that Tollen Corporation sells $100,000 of 8% convertible bonds for $106,000. The market interest rate on the day of issuance is 10%. Each $10,000 bond is convertible into 100 common shares on any interest date after the end of the second year from the date of issuance. Conversion is at the option of the investor. Also assume that it is appropriate to assign a value of $92,418 to the bond and $13,582 to the conversion privilege.

(Measurement of these amounts will be analyzed shortly.) A discount of $7,582 is recorded: the difference between the $92,418 net proceeds attributable to the bond and its $100,000 face value. The issuance will be recorded as follows:

Cash	106,000	
Discount on bonds payable*	7,582	
Bonds payable		100,000
Contributed capital: common share conversion rights		13,582
*$100,000 − $92,418		

The account, *common stock conversion rights*, is an equity account that will be reported as contributed capital on the balance sheet. In later years, the amount in that account will be transferred to share equity if and when the conversion rights are exercised, or transferred to other contributed capital if the conversion rights lapse.

Using this approach, the substance of the transaction is recognized. Both bonds *and* an option were issued, and both are now reflected in the financial statements. Accounting for the debt will reflect an effective interest rate that approaches the true interest rate on the debt. Finally, the proceeds received for the equity portion of the instrument are reflected in equity.

Conversion When convertible bonds are submitted for conversion, the first task is to update any accounts relating to bond premium or discount, accrued interest, and foreign exchange gains and losses on foreign currency–denominated debt. Following these routine adjustments, the balance of the liability account (and related unamortized premium or discount) that pertains to the converted bonds must be transferred to the share account. As well, the proportionate balance of the stock option account must also be transferred to the share account.

book value method

accounting for a transaction using book values as a reference point

Book Value Method The conversion can be recorded using the **book value method**. The book value of the debt is transferred to equity. For example, return to the Tollen bonds, illustrated earlier. Assume that all of the $100,000 Tollen bonds payable are converted to 1,000 common shares on an interest date. Assume that on this date, the stock price is $140 per share, and calculations show that $4,550 of discount remains unamortized after updating the discount account. The entry to record the conversion is:

Bonds payable	100,000	
Contributed capital: common share conversion rights	13,582	
Discount on bonds payable		4,550
Common shares		109,032

Market Value Method An alternative approach is the **market value method**. Under the market value method, the conversion is recorded *at the value of the shares that are issued on conversion.* This approach is supported by the various provincial and federal corporations' acts, which generally stipulate that shares should be recorded at their **cash equivalent value**, which is the amount that would be received if the company issued the shares for cash rather than through conversion. In our example, the shares are assumed to have a value of $140 each. The cash equivalent value of the 1,000 shares issued on conversion is $140,000, which will be recorded as follows:

Bonds payable	100,000	
Contributed capital: common share conversion rights	13,582	
Loss on conversion of bonds	30,968	
Discount on bonds payable		4,550
Common shares		140,000

An argument in favour of the market value method is that the transaction is not simply a trade—the exchange of debt for equity represents a change of risk for both the issuer and the holder, and therefore is a substantive exchange. Substantive exchanges (such as barter transactions) are normally accounted for at market values in order to reflect the economic consequences of the exchange.

However, if the market value method is used, a company will nearly always record a loss. The "loss" arises from the retirement of debt at an opportunity cost (the value of the shares issued) that is higher than the carrying value of the debt. The loss is charged to income through the income statement, thereby depressing earnings. Remember, if the shares are worth *less* than their redemption price, the investors will opt to get their money back. Thus, a gain on the transaction would be genuinely unusual.

The market value method is not often found in practice, no doubt because companies do not like charging income with a loss on a change in capital structure. Many accountants view the conversion as the culmination of a single transaction that started when the convertible bonds were issued. Therefore, the book value method is more appropriate, since it values shares at the actual resources received on the bond issue, adjusted for amortization to date of conversion.

Companies with earnings management agendas should be watched in this regard; there are no accounting pronouncements in this area and policy can be set internally.

Repayment If the market value of underlying shares is less than face value, investors will request repayment and the conversion rights will expire. If this happens at maturity, all discount or premium accounts will be zero. The entries for the Tollen bonds are:

Bonds payable	100,000	
Cash		100,000
Contributed capital: common share conversion rights	13,582	
Contributed capital: lapse of rights		13,582

Measurement Measurement of the debt versus equity components is a major issue because there are no separate objective prices provided by arm's-length market transactions. Standards suggest that either of two methods might be used:

1. The **incremental method** values the conversion option as the issuance price less the present value of a comparable *non-convertible* bond. This method was used in the Tollen Corporation example above. The present value of the cash flows of an 8%, five-year, $100,000 bond (assuming annual interest payments) is $92,418 at an effective interest rate of 10%. Subtracting $92,418 from the net proceeds of $106,000 leaves $13,582 attributable to the conversion option.

2. The **proportional method** requires calculation of both the present value of a comparable bond *and* a separate fair value for the option. Relative percentage values are used to divide the issuance proceeds between debt and equity. Options embedded in a convertible bond do not trade separately on the stock market, and determining fair value for the option is challenging. Fair value can be estimated using an option pricing model or by reference to the fair value of a similar option, if one exists. Option models are in common use by financial institutions; the Black-Scholes model is one of the most well known. Another example is the binomial option pricing model. Option pricing models price an option based on many factors, including the share price of the option contract, length of the option, current market value of the stock, volatility of stock price, expected dividends, and the risk-free interest rate. (See the disclosure of these factors in Exhibit 14-5 later in the chapter, in note 11.) Option pricing models are explained in many finance texts.[2]

---

[2] The Appendices to Sections 3861 and 3863 of the *CICA Handbook* (par. A9) illustrate application of a version of the Black-Scholes model.

Example Assume that Easy Company issues $1,000,000 of $1,000 bonds dated 1 January 20X2, due 31 December 20X4 (i.e., three years later), for $1,002,000. Interest at 6% is payable annually and each bond is convertible at any time up to maturity into 250 common shares (i.e., at a conversion price of $4). When the bonds are issued, the prevailing interest rate for similar debt without conversion options is 9%.

Using the *incremental* method, the amount of the proceeds that is attributable to the liability is measured as the present value of the cash flow, using the market rate of interest of 9%:

Face value [$1,000,000 × (P/F, 9%, 3)]	$772,180
Interest [($1,000,000 × 6%) × (P/A, 9%, 3)]	151,877
Total liability component	$924,057

The liability component is then subtracted from the total proceeds to find the value attributable to the conversion feature:

Proceeds of bond issue	$1,002,000
Liability component	924,057
Equity component	$ 77,943

The issuance of the convertible bonds will be recorded as follows:

Cash	1,002,000	
Discount on convertible bonds		
($1,000,000 − $924,057)	75,943	
Convertible bonds payable		1,000,000
Contributed capital: common share conversion rights		77,943

If the *proportional* method is used, then the bond is valued *and* an option pricing model is used to assign a value to the conversion feature. Assume in this case that the option pricing model produced a value of $84,655 for the conversion feature. Allocation of the $1,002,000 proceeds is as follows:

	Market Value	Proportion	Allocation
Liability component	$ 924,057	91.6%	$ 918,000
Stock option component	84,655	8.4	84,000
Total	$1,008,712	100.0%	$1,002,000

Using the allocation approach, the bond issuance would be recorded as follows:

Cash	1,002,000	
Discount on convertible bonds		
($1,000,000 − $918,000)	82,000	
Convertible bonds payable		1,000,000
Contributed capital: common share conversion rights		84,000

Valuation Concerns A contentious issue, though, is the reliability of the values used to price the two components. For a reference price to be established for a bond, one would have to establish the interest rate that the market would charge for a bond with similar terms and similar security, excluding the conversion feature. This may be straightforward, but perhaps not: perhaps credit would not be readily available on conventional terms, which is why convertible bonds were issued.

The value of the conversion option is also in dispute. Will an options pricing model, such as the Black-Scholes model, produce a "good" reference price for the conversion feature? Option pricing models were not developed to price such embedded, long-term options. Furthermore, the results cannot be verified on any kind of an after-the-fact basis, because the option is never separately traded.

Impact on Income An interesting aspect of the allocation of the proceeds is the impact on future income. Because some of the proceeds are allocated to equity, a discount is recorded. The size of the discount varies with the pricing and allocation methods used. The discount is amortized over the life of the bond, using the effective interest method, as illustrated in Chapter 12. This will decrease net income.

The amount allocated to the common share conversion rights stays in the contributed capital section of shareholders' equity permanently. The conversion rights account is *either folded into the common share account, if the option is exercised, or is part of other contributed capital, if the option is not exercised.*

Remember that the higher the value that is allocated to the option, the higher the discount. The higher the discount, the more interest expense is recognized, which will lower income. This effect may influence the allocation model adopted by management when the bond proceeds are initially recorded. For example, if there is a corporate bias to maximize net income, a model that minimizes the amount allocated to the common share conversion rights account will likely be chosen.

Reporting Example Refer to the excerpts from the Crew Gold Corporation financial statements in Exhibit 14-2. The balance sheet shows a convertible bond at $194,567, and an equity account of $15,676 related to the debt. The disclosure notes indicate that the bonds are convertible into common shares at the investor's option.

EXHIBIT 14-2

CREW GOLD CORPORATION

Selected Financial Statement Disclosures

Year ended June 30, 2006
(in thousands of U.S. dollars)

From the balance sheet:	2006	2005
Long-term debt		
Convertible bonds	$194,567	$3,113
Shareholders' equity		
Equity component of convertible debt	$ 15,676	$ 76

From Note 1, significant accounting policies

The convertible bonds issued during the years ending June 30, 2006 and 2004 have been segregated into their debt and equity components. The financial liability component, representing the value allocated to the liability at the time of inception, is recorded as a long-term liability. The remaining component, representing the value ascribed to the holders' option to convert the principal amount into common shares, is classified in shareholders' equity as "Equity component of convertible bonds".

EXHIBIT 14-2   *(cont'd)*

These components have been measured at their respective fair values on the date the bonds were issued. The finance costs associated with the issue of the convertible bonds are held as deferred financing costs and amortized over the period of the liabilities. Over the term of the debt obligation, the debt component is accreted on a straight line basis to the face value of the instrument by recording an additional accretion expense.

From Note 10, convertible bonds:

On December 15, 2005 the Company issued through a private placement directed towards institutional investors, Norwegian Kroner ("NOK") 1,320 million ($194.5 million) five-year senior convertible bonds. The bonds were issued in denominations of NOK500,000 and rank pari passu among themselves. After deducting financing costs of NOK53.3 million (US$7.8 million) net proceeds were NOK1,266.7 million (US$186.7 million).

These bonds bear a 6% coupon, payable annually in arrears. The principal portion of the bonds is convertible, at the option of the holder and subject to request for conversion pursuant to the conditions of the agreement, into common shares of the Company at a conversion price of NOK11.00 per share. The maximum number of shares that may be issued on conversion is 120 million. In the period from issue until June 30, 2006, 45,454 shares were issued following conversion of bonds. If the bonds are not converted, the principal portion is fully repayable in NOK on December 15, 2010.

Source: www.sedar.com, Crew Gold Corporation, Audited Annual Financial Statements, October 10, 2006.

Convertible Debt with a Floating Conversion Price per Share The previous example involved a bond with a fixed conversion price per share. If the conversion option was based on the market value of the common shares on the conversion date, then the option has no value to the investor. Such a convertible bond is classified entirely as debt.

CONCEPT REVIEW

1. Why might a convertible bond issued at a price above par end up with a discount recorded on the books?

2. Where is the account common share conversion option reported on the balance sheet? What happens to this account on bond conversion? Repayment?

3. When bonds convert to common shares, why are companies unlikely to use the market value method to report the conversion?

4. Describe the incremental method and the proportionate method used to allocate a portion of convertible bond proceeds to the conversion option.

CONVERTIBLE DEBT, CONVERSION AT THE ISSUER'S OPTION

The preceding discussion dealt exclusively with debt that is convertible at the investor's option. Corporations may also issue convertible debt that is convertible at the corporation's option.

Debt that is convertible at the issuer's option will either be:

1. Classified entirely as debt, or

2. Divided between debt (present value of interest payments) and equity (present value of principal).

Conversion Price Fixed or Floating   Standard setters have determined that when the number of shares (price per share) required to settle the obligation varies with changes in fair value, the principal is a *financial liability* of the entity. If the number of shares (the price per share) is fixed, then the principal is equity.

If the conversion price is fixed, the debenture holder is participating in the residual interest of the company. If the company does well and the fair value of a share is higher than the conversion price on the conversion date, the lenders benefit. The critical values were set on the loan date, not the conversion date, and risk passes to the lender. Therefore, the principal amount is not a financial liability. The principal must be classified as shareholder's equity. On the other hand, if the conversion floats, there is no transfer of risk and the amount is a liability.

Interest Obligation   If the company *must* pay interest in cash, the interest portion of the issue proceeds is a liability. If the company can issue shares at fair value in full payment of interest, the interest is also a liability and is recorded as such. However, if the bond agreement allows the company to issue shares at a *fixed price* in payment of interest, then this interest portion of the debt is equity. Risk falls on the debenture holder when the price per share is set, because the holder's ultimate benefit from interest payments will depend on the market value of the shares, and is not on a fixed monetary amount.

To summarize:

Bond Terms—Bond Convertible at Issuer's Option	Classification
Conversion price fixed, (bond indenture establishes the number of shares or the price per share)	Present value of principal is equity
Conversion price depends on market value of shares at the time of conversion	Present value of principal is debt
Interest that must be paid in cash	Present value of interest is debt
Interest that the company has the option of paying in a fixed number of shares, or by using a fixed price per share	Present value of interest is equity
Interest that the company has the option of paying in a variable number of shares, using current market prices to establish value	Present value of interest is debt

Annual Entries   Each period that the bond is outstanding, two adjustments have to be made:

1. Interest expense has to be recognized on the outstanding interest liability. The annual payment (which is labelled interest) reduces the interest liability. This results in an interest expense far lower than the interest actually paid.

2. A **capital charge** is recorded that will increase the shareholders' equity account to par over the life of the bond. The amount is determined using interest-based (present value)

calculations.[3] The capital charge reduces retained earnings, and thus decreases one equity account (retained earnings) and increases another (the equity account related to the bond). The capital charge does not change net income.

Note that *when the bond is initially issued at par*, the capital charge plus the interest expense will approximate the interest paid, and the total of the two represents the cost of capital for the financial instrument.

Example Suppose that Gagnon Ltd. issues a $100,000, 8%, four-year debenture at par, repayable at maturity at Gagnon's option in a fixed number of common shares (fixed conversion price). Interest is payable annually, in cash. The market interest rate is 8%. The present value of the debenture can be disaggregated as follows:

Principal [$100,000 × (P/F, 8%, 4)]	$ 73,503
Interest [$8,000 × (P/A, 8%, 4)]	26,497
Total	$100,000

Since the conversion price is fixed, the principal is equity. Since the interest must be paid in cash, it is a liability.

Accounting on Issuance When the bond is issued, the entry will be:

Cash	100,000	
Interest liability on debenture		26,497
Share equity—debenture		73,503

Annual Entries for Interest and Capital Charge As time passes, interest will be accounted for by the effective interest method, calculated only on the *outstanding balance of the interest liability*. The carrying amount of the interest liability will be increased by 8% each year, and the $8,000 annual payment of interest will reduce the liability. At the end of the first year, Gagnon will make the following entries to record the interest expense and the interest payment:

Interest expense ($26,497 × 8%)	2,120	
Interest liability on debenture		2,120
Interest liability on debenture	8,000	
Cash		8,000

The amortization of the interest liability over the four-year period is shown in the schedule in the top half of Exhibit 14-3.

Each year, the share equity portion of the debenture will also be increased by 8% of its opening balance in order to bring the balance in the equity account up to the maturity value

---

[3] The company may use a different accrual method, but must increase the equity account to par by the end of the bond's life.

> ### EXHIBIT 14-3
>
> ### CONVERTIBLE DEBT AT ISSUER'S OPTION, FIXED CONVERSION PRICE
> #### Amortization of Interest Liability
>
> | Year | Beginning Balance of Interest Liability | Interest Expense at 8% | Payment | Ending Balance of Interest Liability |
> |------|------|------|------|------|
> | 1 | $26,497 | $2,120 | $8,000 | $20,617 |
> | 2 | 20,617 | 1,649 | 8,000 | 14,266 |
> | 3 | 14,266 | 1,141 | 8,000 | 7,407 |
> | 4 | 7,407 | 593 | 8,000 | 0 |
>
> #### Equity Component
>
> | Year | Beginning Equity | Capital Charge @ 8% | Ending Equity |
> |------|------|------|------|
> | 1 | $73,503 | $5,880 | $ 79,383 |
> | 2 | 79,383 | 6,351 | 85,734 |
> | 3 | 85,734 | 6,859 | 92,593 |
> | 4 | 92,593 | 7,407 | 100,000 |

by the end of the bond term. The offset is a direct charge to retained earnings. For the first year, for example:

Retained earnings ($73,503 × 8%)	5,880	
Share equity—debenture		5,880

The increase in the equity account, to par value by the end of year 4, is shown in the schedule in the second half of Exhibit 14-2. (The capital charge would be shown net of tax on the retained earnings statement. In year 1, with a tax rate of 40%, the reduction to retained earnings is reported as $3,528 ($5,880 × (1 − .4).)

Because the bonds are issued at par, a useful check of accuracy is possible. The interest expense ($2,120) plus the charge to retained earnings ($5,880) will equal interest paid ($8,000). Each year, interest expense will decline and the charge to retained earnings will increase. That is,

Year	Interest Expense	Capital Charge	Total (Equivalent to Interest Paid If Bond Issued at Par)
1	$2,120	$5,880	$8,000
2	1,649	6,351	8,000
3	1,141	6,859	8,000
4	593	7,407	8,000

Accounting at Maturity If, at maturity, the company elects to redeem the bonds in cash, the entry will be a debit to share equity—debenture and a credit to cash. If, instead, the company chooses to satisfy its obligation by issuing common shares, the balance in the debenture equity account will be transferred to common share equity. Since the charge to retained earnings increases the share equity—debenture account annually, the amount transferred will be the initial valuation plus the cumulative annual charge. That is, one of the following entries is made:

Share equity—debenture	100,000	
Common shares		100,000

or,

Share equity—debenture	100,000	
Cash		100,000

Redemption for cash would be a rare event.

CONCEPT REVIEW

1. Under what circumstances is the principal portion of a convertible bond that is convertible at the issuer's option reported as shareholders' equity rather than as debt?

2. Under what circumstances is the interest portion of a convertible bond that is convertible at the issuer's option reported as shareholders' equity rather than as debt?

3. How is annual interest expense measured for a convertible bond, convertible at the issuer's option, where the present value of interest has been recorded as a liability and the present value of principal has been recorded as equity?

4. For a convertible bond, convertible at the issuer's option, where the present value of principal has been recorded as equity, what is the purpose of the capital charge?

STOCK OPTIONS

stock option

a derivative instrument allowing the holder to purchase a specified number of shares of a company at a specified price at or during a specific period

Stock options are financial instruments that give the holder the right to buy shares at a fixed price. If the exercise price of the option is above the value of the share, the option has no value. When options are first issued, they usually have an exercise price that is equal to or higher than the current market price of the shares. Only when the share price rises above the exercise price does the option itself have intrinsic value.

For example, suppose that Mercurial Limited issues stock options to its employees. Each option permits the employee to buy one Mercurial common share for $5 in two years' time. When the options are issued, the market price of Mercurial's shares is $4.

Options are said to be **in-the-money** when the common share price rises above the $5 exercise price; say, to $8. Options that are in-the-money on the exercise date will be exercised, as the investor will be able to buy an $8 share for $5. The market value of the rights during the waiting period, before the options are exercisable, reflects investors' collective expectations concerning the market value on the exercise date. If the market price of the common shares is less than $5 on the expiration date, the rights will expire unexercised.

derivative instruments

derivative instruments are designed to transfer risk by setting the conditions of an exchange of financial instruments at a particular time at fixed terms; derivative instruments derive their values from the underlying equity or debt instruments

Stock options are a form of **derivative instrument**. They are derivative because their value arises or is *derived* solely from the value of the primary equity shares that they can be used to buy. A bond that is convertible to common shares at a set price has an embedded stock option, and as illustrated in the last two sections, an embedded stock option gives rise to an equity component.

Stock Rights and Warrants

Corporations often issue **stock rights** that provide the holder with an option to acquire a specified number of shares in the corporation under prescribed conditions and within a stated future time period. Stock rights that are issued as an attachment to other securities (usually to bonds) are sometimes called **stock warrants**. A common distinction between stock rights and stock warrants is that stock rights often have a short life while warrants are valid for longer periods of time and often have no expiry date. The accounting issues are the same, however. Stock rights and warrants may be exercised to acquire additional shares from the corporation, sold at the market value of the rights (if transferable), or allowed to lapse on the expiration date (if any).

Recipient Accounting for Stock Rights

The issuance of stock rights raises accounting issues for both the recipient and the issuing corporation. For the recipient, stock rights received on existing shares held as an investment have no additional cost, so the current carrying value of the shares already owned is allocated between the original shares and the rights received, based on the current market values of each.

An investor may buy rights or warrants. They may be purchased on the open market, or they can be purchased as part of a **basket offering** of securities, such as a bond issued with detachable warrants. If an investor *buys* the rights, either directly or as part of a basket purchase, then they are recorded by the investor as an asset until the rights are exercised, at which time they are a component of the cost of the shares acquired. If the rights are allowed to expire, then any cost associated with them is expensed.

Issuer Accounting for Stock Rights

For the issuing company, there are two general accounting patterns for rights. One involves recognition, and the other involves memorandum entries regarding the rights.

Recognition   Assume that a corporation issues rights allowing the holder(s) to acquire common shares in four years' time at an acquisition price of $20 per share, which is the current market price of the common shares. The corporation issues 100,000 rights, and specifies that it takes five rights to acquire a share, so 20,000 shares could be issued if the rights are exercised. The corporation receives $18,000 for the rights.

The relevant dates are the (1) announcement date, (2) issuance date, or grant date, (3) exercise date, and (4) expiration date. Consider the following entries:

Announcement date:		
Memorandum: 100,000 stock rights approved, allowing purchase of 20,000 shares at $20 in four years' time.		
Issuance date; rights sold for a total of $18,000		
Cash, etc.	18,000	
Contributed capital: stock rights outstanding		18,000

At exercise, assuming that the current market price of the common shares was $28 and all rights were exercised:

Exercise date:		
Cash (20,000 shares × $20)	400,000	
Contributed capital: stock rights outstanding	18,000	
Common shares		418,000

Alternatively, assuming that the current market price of the common shares was $18 and all rights expired:

Expiry date:		
Contributed capital: stock rights outstanding	18,000	
Contributed capital, lapse of stock rights		18,000

Notice that the stock rights outstanding account ends up in one of two places: *either folded into the common share account, if the rights are exercised, or as part of other contributed capital, if the rights are not exercised.* Both of these accounts are equity accounts and both are elements of contributed capital. Notice also that the current fair value of the shares on the exercise date, $28, is not reflected in the entry that records exercise of the options. Financial statement users would often like to judge the terms of the rights offering, as approved by the Board of Directors. Details of all options are disclosed in the financial statements so anyone can make these calculations. But comparison of issuance price versus market value requires some digging!

Valuation Issues In the example above, the company has sold its rights to a second party, and the cash price has established fair value for the options. Options and rights, if issued for non-cash consideration, can be valued at the fair value of the consideration received or the fair value of the options issued, whichever is more reliably determined. This is known as the **fair value–based method**. The fair value of the consideration received might be the value of legal services received, or other time, effort, or property given to the corporation in exchange for options. This can often be very difficult to value. The fair value of the options issued can be estimated using option pricing models, but can be equally challenging to determine.

The options are worth *the risk-adjusted present value of the difference between the market value and the option price on the day the rights are exercised.* If an individual has the right to buy 10,000 shares for $10 in eight years' time, the "perfect" valuation would be to predict the market price—accurately—in eight years' time, and discount the gain to today's dollars at an appropriate interest rate. Assume that the market price were to be $42 in the future. The individual would have a gain of $320,000 (that is, 10,000 shares × ($42 − $10)). If the appropriate discount rate were 8%, the present value of this option would be $172,886 (that is, $320,000 × (P/F, 8%, 8) = $320,000 × .54027). Unfortunately, there is no crystal ball available to predict that future stock market price. Determining a risk-adjusted eight-year discount rate is another challenge.

The fair value of options can be established by use of an option pricing model, such as Black-Scholes model or the binomial pricing model. We've already mentioned some of the potential problems associated with using option pricing models for financial instrument valuation—these concerns are valid in this context as well. However, it is better to be imprecise than to give up.

Memorandum Entries What happens if the rights are issued for no consideration, or no measurable consideration, either to existing shareholders, lenders, employees, or whomever? How could you make the first entry if there were no proceeds on the sale of the rights? In the absence of any value for the options, the second alternative for accounting for rights is memorandum entries only.

At the date of announcement and the date of issuance, a memorandum entry is recorded. On the exercise date, the cash received for the shares is recorded, but the financial statements do not directly acknowledge that cash received is not current market value. For example, assume that rights were issued as described in the prior example, except that they were issued to existing shareholders and no price was charged. There would be memorandum entries on authorization and issuance, but no journal entry until exercise:

Exercise date:		
Cash (20,000 shares × $20)	400,000	
Common shares		400,000

If, instead, the rights were allowed to expire, a further memorandum entry would be recorded.

Do the rights have value? Sometimes their terms are highly speculative, and thus their value is small. In these circumstances, little is lost by the memorandum approach. In other situations, rights appear to be an important consideration to all parties, and use of the memorandum approach is troubling. Measurement is a substantive issue in this context.

Which situations follow which pattern? The situations can be summarized as shown in Exhibit 14-4. Further explanations follow, keyed to the numbers in the exhibit.

EXAMPLES OF STOCK OPTION REPORTING

Memorandum Entries

1—Issuance of Stock Rights to Existing Shareholders Rights may be issued in advance of a planned sale of common shares to give current shareholders the opportunity to maintain their relative voting position in the company (**pre-emptive rights**). Rights may also be issued on a financial reorganization. No consideration (or payment) is received by the company. This situation follows the memorandum alternative.

EXHIBIT 14-4

ACCOUNTING PATTERNS FOR STOCK OPTIONS

Ref #	MEMORANDUM	Ref #	RECOGNITION
1.	Issued to existing shareholders	3.	Issued as fractional shares on a stock dividend; dividend recorded at market or stated value
2.	Issued as a "poison pill"	5.	Issued on issuance of debt, whether detachable or not. Also includes convertible financial instruments; fair value method used
3.	Issued as fractional shares on a stock dividend; dividend recorded as a memo	6.	Issued as compensation to outside parties; fair value of rights or of services received
4.	Issued in a non-compensatory stock option plan for employees	7.	Issued in a compensatory stock option plan for employees: fair value method used

Note disclosure of the terms of option contracts accompanies both accounting treatments.

Note: These numbers are not sequential because they refer to the numbered explanations in the chapter material.

Example Assume that Sax Corporation has 30,000 common shares outstanding. On 1 January 20X2, the company decides to raise equity capital and increase its outstanding common shares 50% by issuing 15,000 additional shares. Existing shareholders are to be given the right to buy shares in proportion to their existing holdings. Assume that current shareholders are issued stock rights, one right for every share held. Two stock rights entitle the holder to purchase one common share at a price of $30 per share (the market price on 1 January 20X2). The rights are formally issued on 1 March 20X2, and expire on 1 September 20X2. On the issue date of the rights, the share price is $32 per share. The rights trade at an average price of $1.50 per right between the issue and expiration dates. On the expiration date of the rights, the share price is $34 per share.

Journal entries to reflect various transactions involving the stock rights are as follows:

1 January 20X2—announcement date: memorandum entry

1 March 20X2—issuance date: memorandum entry

1 July 20X2—1,000 stock rights are exercised by a shareholder

Cash (1,000 rights ÷ 2 = 500 shares) × $30	15,000	
Common shares, no-par (500 shares)		15,000

Subsequent exercises of stock rights would be recorded similarly, valued at the cash received for the shares. No recognition is given to the market value of shares on the exercise date. A memorandum entry would be required if shareholders allow rights to lapse.

2—Rights Issued as a "Poison Pill" Corporations trying to make themselves less attractive as a takeover target will sometimes issue rights that would make it far more expensive for an outsider to gain control. These rights are issued to existing shareholders for no consideration and are recorded by memorandum approach only.

Example Kinross Gold Corporation adopted a Rights Plan in 2006, described as follows:

Under the Plan, one right is issued for each common share of the Company. The rights will trade together with the common shares and will not be separable from the common shares or exercisable unless a take-over bid is made that does not comply with the Permitted Bid requirements. In such event, such rights will entitle shareholders, other than shareholders making the take-over bid, to purchase additional common shares of the Company at a substantial discount to the market price at the time.

In the event of a hostile takeover bid, the *current shareholders* not involved in the takeover bid would be allowed to buy shares at significantly reduced prices. This would greatly increase the shares outstanding and severely dilute the value of the shares held by the parties backing the takeover bid. They are not entitled to exercise rights, unless the bid is a "Permitted Bid." These poison pill rights are recorded only as a memo in the books. Disclosure is prominent, to scare off the wolves!

3—Stock Rights Issued with a Stock Dividend Rights issued as fractional shares may follow the recognition pattern, or the memorandum pattern, depending on how the underlying stock dividend is recorded. If the stock dividend is recorded at market value, or some other stated value, such as average capital paid in to date, then fractional share rights are recorded, as illustrated in Chapter 13. If the stock dividend is recorded in a memorandum entry only, the rights are also recorded by memorandum only. This practice was illustrated in Chapter 13; take a moment to look at the examples there.

4—Non-Compensatory Stock Options Issued to Employees Some public companies allow all employees to buy shares at a modest discount from market value, often equal to the typical broker's fee. The employee receives no special benefit from this arrangement. The plan is called a **non-compensatory stock purchase plan**. To qualify, standards require that the plan must be open to all employees, offer only a modest discount from market price, and not fix the exercise price for more than 31 days. Non-compensatory plans are accounted for using the memorandum approach. Shares issued are recorded at the cash price received, which would be very close to market value.

Recognition Required

5—Stock Rights Issued with Other Financial Instruments Corporations sometimes issue debt that is packaged together with detachable stock warrants. The intent of the warrants is to increase the attractiveness of the debt and to permit the investor to participate in the future growth of the corporation through share purchase. As well, it provides the corporation with a source of additional capital in the future, if the market value of the shares rises above the exercise price of the option.

Stock rights (or warrants) that are issued in conjunction with debt have two important characteristics that differentiate them from convertible debt:

1. The warrants usually are *detachable*, which means that they can be bought and sold separately from the debt to which they were originally attached, and

2. The warrants can be exercised without having to trade in or redeem the debt.

On issuance, a portion of the bond price is allocated to the warrants. The allocation is credited to a contributed capital (owners' equity) account, calculated based on the market values of the two securities on the date of issuance (the *proportional method*). If only the warrants have a readily determinable market value, the bonds are valued at the difference between the total bond price and the market value of the warrants (the *incremental method*).

Example Embassy Corporation issues $100,000 of 8%, 10-year, non-convertible bonds with detachable stock purchase warrants. Nuvolari Corporation purchases the entire issue. Each $1,000 bond carries 10 warrants. Each warrant entitles Nuvolari to purchase one common share for $15. The bond issue therefore includes 1,000 warrants (100 bonds × 10 warrants per bond). The bond issue sells for 105 exclusive of accrued interest. Shortly after issuance, the warrants trade for $4 each.

1. *Proportional method* (both securities have market values). Shortly after issuance, the bonds were quoted at 103 ex-warrants (that is, without warrants attached).

Market value of bonds ($100,000 × 1.03)	$103,000
Market value of warrants ($4 × 1,000)	4,000
Total market value of bonds and warrants	$107,000
Allocation of proceeds to bonds [$105,000 × ($103,000 ÷ $107,000)]	$101,075
Allocation of proceeds to warrants [$105,000 × ($4,000 ÷ $107,000)]	3,925
Total proceeds allocated	$105,000

Issuance entry

Cash	105,000	
Bonds payable		100,000
Contributed capital: detachable stock warrants		3,925
Premium on bonds payable		1,075*

*$101,075 − $100,000

2. *Incremental method* (only one security has a market value). Assume that no market value is determined for the bonds as separate securities. The warrants trade for $4 each.

Issuance entry		
Cash	105,000	
Bonds payable		100,000
Contributed capital: detachable stock warrants		4,000*
Premium on bonds payable		1,000**
*(1,000 warrants) × ($4)		
**Value allocated to bonds less the face value of the bonds: ($105,000 − $4,000) − $100,000		

Under the incremental method, the warrants are valued at market value. The remaining portion of the proceeds ($101,000) is allocated to the bonds. The amount of premium recorded equals the difference between the amount allocated to the bonds and face value. Subsequent to issuance, the stock warrant account is true to pattern: it is either folded into the common share account when shares are bought on exercise of the warrant, or it is closed out to another contributed capital account on expiry.

6—Compensation to Outside Parties A company sometimes wants to conserve cash during the early stages of its life and therefore issues shares or stock rights as payment for professional services. This situation follows the recognition alternative.

Example Assume that GT Ltd. issues 500 stock rights to Laura Brown as a director's fee. Two rights entitle Brown to purchase one common share for $30. The rights were issued on 1 March 20X2, expire on 31 December 20X2, and are exercised by Brown on 1 July 20X2 when the shares are trading for $36.50.

There are two alternatives for rights valuation:

1. The value of the rights could be assessed using an option pricing model.

2. The value of the rights could be assessed through the fair value of the services received.

In Brown's case, assume that the Black-Scholes model produced a value of $1,000. The fair value of services received might be the comparable director's fee that others received, if any. Assume that other directors were paid $800 cash.

Neither valuation method is ideal. The Black-Scholes model rests on certain assumptions, and the values produced cannot be readily verified for options that are not traded. The value of the services received—in this case, director's fees—might not exist, or be easily verifiable.

Let's assume that the director's fee is the most objective value for these options. The entries to record issuance and exercise are:

1 March 20X2—issuance date		
Administrative expense (director's fees)	800	
Stock rights outstanding		800
1 July 20X2—exercise date		
Cash (250 shares × $30)	7,500	
Stock rights outstanding	800	
Common shares, no-par (250 shares)		8,300

The market value of the shares on the date the common shares were issued, $36.50, is not recognized. If the options were to expire, the entry would be:

Stock rights outstanding	800	
Contributed capital: lapse of stock rights		800

7—Compensatory Stock Options Issued to Employees **Compensatory employee stock option plans** are those that are intended to compensate the employee for current performance or to provide an incentive for future performance. They are usually granted only to specific employees—senior management, perhaps—and can involve significant discounts from market price. Corporations must recognize these stock option plans by using the fair value–based method.

The fair value method uses an option pricing model (e.g., the Black-Scholes method or the binomial method) to measure the fair value of the option on the measurement date. The *measurement date* is the date on which the terms of the option, specifically, the option price, is determined. It is the date on which the compensation cost is determined.

ETHICAL ISSUES

For many years, companies followed the disclosure alternative for all employee stock options and aggressively resisted attempts by standard setters to force recognition. This resistance was based on the concern that the value of options could not be measured with certainty, but also caused by the fact that the additional compensation expense would be material and decrease profits. Standard setters were aided in their efforts to force recognition in the aftermath of accounting scandals such as Enron, WorldCom, and the like. Fairly or not, public opinion labelled corporate management as greedy and self-serving. Stock options were viewed as adding additional incentive for management to behave in inappropriate ways. Recognition of stock options was viewed as one way to reign in inappropriate behaviour. The representational faithfulness of financial statements has been enhanced as a result, although concerns about accurate measurement remain.

For example, suppose that an employee is granted options for 5,000 common shares at an option price of $20 per share. The options **vest** immediately, meaning that the employee can exercise the options whether employment continues or not. The options are exercisable immediately, which means that the shares can be purchased at any time. Using an option pricing model, the company determines that the fair value of the option is $48,000. The grant date is the measurement date because the options are vested, and the cost of the option is recorded as follows:

On the measurement date:		
Compensation expense	48,000	
Contributed capital: common share options		
outstanding		48,000

More often, the options do not vest immediately. Vesting might occur a few years after the options are granted. The reason for delayed vesting is to provide incentive for the employee to continue working for the company for a specified period of time.

When vesting occurs later, the *compensation expense is allocated over the vesting period.* For example, suppose that the 5,000 share options do not vest until four years after they have been granted. In that case, only one-quarter of the expense is recorded in each year:

On the measurement date, and then annually:		
Compensation expense ($48,000 ÷ 4)	12,000	
Contributed capital: common share options		
outstanding		12,000

After this entry is made four times, $48,000 of total compensation expense is recorded and there is a $48,000 balance in the contributed capital account. The $48,000 estimate remains constant over all four years. The fair value is not subsequently adjusted for changes in option pricing variables.

When the options are exercised, the contributed capital amount is moved into the common share account:

At exercise:		
Cash (5,000 shares × $20)	100,000	
Contributed capital: common share options outstanding	48,000	
Common shares		148,000

Not all options are exercised. Options may *lapse* because the options expire before the common share price rises above the option price. If the options lapse, the amount recorded as contributed capital remains, but its classification is changed to indicate that the options have expired:

If the options lapse:		
Contributed capital: common share options outstanding	48,000	
Contributed capital: share options expired		48,000

Forfeitures are treated differently. **Forfeiture** occurs when an employee fails to satisfy the conditions for exercising the options and the option expires. For example, an employee may leave the company prior to the vesting date. When forfeiture occurs, it means that the original amount of recognized compensation expense was overstated. The forfeiture is treated as a correction of an estimate—compensation expense is *credited* in the period in which the forfeiture occurs:

If the options are all forfeited:		
Contributed capital: common share options outstanding	48,000	
Compensation expense		48,000

An example of an option program disclosure is included in Exhibit 14-5, in note 11. We have illustrated only the simplest type of employee stock options. It is sufficient to have a general understanding of the accounting approach used for employee compensatory stock option plans. There are many more sophisticated types of options, and many more accounting complications. For example, vesting may not occur all at once (*cliff vesting*), as in the previous example, but may accrue gradually (*graded vesting*). In that case, the allocation method is more complex. As well, accounting standards require that, in some circumstances, probabilities of forfeiture be estimated in advance and subsequently adjusted as the estimates change.

CONCEPT REVIEW

1. Orville Corporation routinely gives stock options to its executives in lieu of higher salaries. What financial statement elements will change as a result of these options?

2. Explain how rights can be used as a poison pill, to lower the likelihood of a hostile takeover.

3. Pasty Limited issues common stock warrants as part of an issue of debentures (which are not convertible). The exercise price of the warrants is less than the market price of the common shares when the bonds are issued. Should any part of the proceeds of the bond issue be credited to shareholders' equity? Explain.

LONG-TERM COMPENSATION PLANS

Stock options are not always an appealing form of compensation. Employees may prefer to have cash, and may not want company shares. They may not be willing or able to manage the process of buying shares under an option plan and then selling shares to raise cash. When stock prices go down, instead of up, both employees and employers may be dissatisfied with the level of compensation that results. When stock prices shoot high, shareholders may be concerned with the excessive returns inadvertently granted to employees. For example, the CEO of Precision Drilling Trust cashed in options in 2005, and had personal income of $55 million. This is an extremely high level of compensation.

stock appreciation rights

a form of long-term compensation, often in lieu of stock options, where recipients are awarded a cash payment equal to the increase in common stock price over a particular period

Types of Long-term Compensation Plans As a result, many other forms of long-term compensation for employees have been created. Some of the more common alternatives are summarized in the chart, below. They include long-term bonuses, deferred compensation plans, and **stock appreciation rights** (SARs). Employee stock options, reviewed in the last section, have been included for completeness. Specific plans are described in the examples that follow. Keep in mind, though, that the major variables from an accounting perspective are:

1. Does the employee receive cash or shares?

2. Is the amount of the compensation established initially, or does it change annually, based on set criteria?

Compensation Scheme	Employee Receives	Description
Long-term bonus/ Deferred compensation plan—cash	Cash	Amount paid for achieving performance objectives; objectives may be for one year (amount known) or recalculated each year over a period of time (amount recalculated based on several variables); not paid immediately but rather after a period of years of employment
Long-term bonus/ Deferred compensation plan—shares	Shares	As above, only payment in shares
SARs—employee option	Cash or perhaps shares (at the employee's option)	Employee receives positive difference between set reference price of shares and later fair value of shares; share price is hoped to increase over a period of employment; value may be taken in cash or perhaps the employee may take value in shares instead if desired.
SARs—employer option	Cash or perhaps shares (at the company's option)	As above, only it is the company's choice as to whether cash or shares are distributed
Stock option	Shares	Employee has right to buy shares at a set price

Accounting Policy for Long-term Compensation Plans Accounting for the long-term compensation plan can follow several patterns:

1. The plan involves distribution of shares, and the value of the option is estimated *once*, when the options are granted; the value is accrued over the vesting period. If the plan vests immediately, the amount is recorded in full. The accrual increases an equity account, and results in an expense that decreases net income. This was illustrated for employee stock

options in the prior section. All long-term compensation plans that involve the payment of shares (that is, the employer cannot be forced to pay cash) use this pattern.

2. The plan involves a cash payment, and the value of the payment is known at the inception of the plan. This involves simple accrual, over the vesting period, of a cash bonus. The accrual increases a liability account, and results in an expense that decreases net income.

3. The plan involves a cash payment, but the likely amount to be paid must be subject to a new estimate each year. The annual accrual is a portion (straight-line accrual) of the estimated cost, with the cumulative amount adjusted to reflect any new estimate of the total paid.

With reference to the long-term compensation plans identified above, the following accounting policies are used:

Compensation Scheme	Amount	Financial Statement Elements	Accrual
Long-term bonus/Deferred compensation plan—cash	Cash to be paid estimated or set at inception New estimate of cost annually	Expense and Liability	Recorded over period to vesting (likely vests on payment date); if new estimate is different than old, cumulative balances are calculated and adjusted annually
Long-term bonus/Deferred compensation plan—shares	Option pricing model on date of grant	Expense and Equity	Recorded over period to vesting; no adjustment of initial estimate
SARs—employee option	Cash to be paid estimated at each year-end as (Fair value − Reference price) × number of shares Estimate adjusted annually	Expense and Liability	Recorded over period to vesting; since remeasured annually, cumulative balances are recalculated and adjusted annually
SARs—employer option	Option pricing model on date of grant	Expense and Equity	Recorded over period to vesting; no adjustment of initial estimate
Stock option	Option pricing model on date of grant	Expense and Equity	Recorded over period to vesting; no adjustment of initial estimate

Examples Long-term compensation contracts and their accounting are illustrated in the examples that follow.

Case 1 The employee is awarded a long-term bonus of $120,000 cash at the beginning of the 20X7 fiscal year, which will be paid at the end of 20X9 if the employee is still with the employer at that time. Since the employee would lose the bonus if he or she left the employer, it is not vested until payment. Accrual is over the period that must be worked prior to the payment:

Annual entry		
Compensation expense ($120,000 ÷ 3)	40,000	
Long-term bonus liability		40,000

If the employee leaves the employer prior to payment, the cumulative balances are reversed and a cost recovery (negative expense) is recorded on the income statement.

Case 2 The employee is awarded long-term compensation at the beginning of the 20X7 fiscal year, which will be paid at the end of 20X10 if the employee is still with the employer at that time. This bonus is for 150 units in a common pool, and the value of the pool is estimated annually based on a formula that includes return on investment, stock price, and sales growth. At the end of 20X7, each unit is estimated to be worth $650; at the end of 20X8, $800; at the end of 20X9, $350; and at the end of 20X10, $750. Cumulative balances are calculated afresh each year, and the annual entry reflects correction of estimates. Accrual is over the period that must be worked prior to the payment:

20X7 entry:		
Compensation expense (150 units × $650) ÷ 4	24,375	
Long-term compensation liability		24,375

In 20X8, to arrive at the measurement amount:

1. Calculate new value of the units (150 units × $800)	$120,000
2. Calculate the cumulative amount that should have been recorded to date ($120,000 × 2 years ÷ 4 years)	$ 60,000
3. Determine the balance now recorded (above)	24,375
4. Calculate adjustment required ($60,000 − $24,375)	$ 35,625

20X8 entry:		
Compensation expense	35,625	
Long-term compensation liability		35,625

In 20X9, the value of a unit declines and compensation expense is negative for the year. The value of the units is $52,500 (150 units × $350). The cumulative balance should be $39,375, or $52,500 × (3 years ÷ 4 years). The balance is now $60,000, so negative compensation expense (cost recovery) of $20,625 is recorded:

20X9 entry:		
Long-term compensation liability	20,625	
Compensation expense − cost recovery		20,625

In 20X10, the final accrual is made and the compensation is paid. The value of a unit is $750, or $112,500 in total for 150 units. All of this should be recorded and paid at this point (4 years ÷ 4 years). The entry:

20X10 entry:		
Compensation expense		
($112,500 − prior balance, $39,375)	73,125	
Long-term compensation liability	39,375	
Cash		112,500

Case 3 The employee is granted a deferred compensation award at the beginning of the 20X7 fiscal year, which will be turned over to the employee at the end of 20X8 if the employee is

still with the employer at that time. The award will be in the range of 8,000 to 10,000 common shares, with the number of shares dependent on the company's common share price at the end of 20X8. The benefit is valued at $62,000 using an option pricing model. This amount is accrued over 20X7 and 20X8, and the pattern is identical to that used for options.

Annual entry:		
Compensation expense ($62,000 ÷ 2)	31,000	
Contributed capital: common share options outstanding		31,000

At exercise:		
Contributed capital: common share options outstanding	62,000	
Common shares		62,000

Case 4 The employee is awarded 10,000 units of stock appreciation rights (SARs) at the beginning of 20X7. The employee will receive a payment at the end of the 20X9 year, if the employee is still with the employer at that time. The value of the SARs units will be equal to the fair value of the shares in 20X9, less some reference price, which is often the fair value of the shares when the SARs were granted. Thus, the employee receives a cash payment equal to the appreciation in stock price over the life of the SARs. Assume that the reference price is $10 per share. Stock price at the end of 20X7 is $18; at the end of 20X8, $13; and at the end of 20X9, $15. The terms of these SARs state that the employee may take cash or common shares, at the employee's option. When recording, *the company must assume that cash will be paid if it is the employee's option to receive cash.* The entries make an annual accrual with an adjustment for the cumulative balance:

20X7 entry:		
Compensation expense		
(10,000 units × ($18 − $10) × (1 year ÷ 3 years))	26,667	
Long-term compensation liability		26,667

20X8 entry:		
Long-term compensation liability		
(10,000 units × ($13 − $10) × (2 years ÷ 3 years))		
= $20,000 versus $26,667 recorded	6,667	
Compensation expense (cost recovery)		6,667

20X9 entry; employee takes cash:		
Compensation expense (10,000 units ×		
($15 − $10) × (3 years ÷ 3 years) = $50,000		
versus $20,000 recorded	30,000	
Long-term compensation liability	20,000	
Cash		50,000

If shares were issued, the credit would be made to common shares rather than cash.

Note that when the market value of the shares falls below the reference price, the balance in the contributed capital account is then zero, and compensation expense recorded to date is reversed. Cumulative compensation expense recorded cannot fall below zero.

Case 5 The employee is awarded 10,000 units of stock appreciation rights (SARs) at the beginning of 20X7. The terms are identical to those in case 4, except that in 20X9, it is the employer's choice as to whether cash or an equivalent value in common shares given to the employee at the end. Since the employer cannot be forced to pay cash, the compensation agreement is accounted for as a stock option, as illustrated in the prior section and case 3. An option pricing model would be used to value the SARs arrangement, and the cost would be recorded over three years.

Additional Complications Compensation plans are quite complex, and the accounting standards that govern their measurement, recognition, and disclosure are equally complex. There are rules that deal with estimating forfeitures and measurement if the value of the award changes after vesting, as well as rules that address indexed plans, combination plans, plan modifications, and so on. This section has looked at the overall patterns, rather than the detailed rules for the many possible situations.

CONCEPT REVIEW

1. What do employees receive under a SARs compensation plan?
2. When there is a long-term compensation plan, under what circumstances is a liability versus a contributed capital account recorded?
3. Why do some long-term compensation contracts require new measurement of cumulative amounts annually, and others do not?

DERIVATIVES

General Nature of Derivatives

Corporations issue certain types of securities that are neither debt nor equity in themselves, but that set terms and conditions for future exchange of financial instruments. There are many types of such derivative instruments in the market, which have value because of shifts in value of the underlying security. Stock options are one example. By themselves, stock rights represent neither an obligation of the corporation nor a share interest in the corporation; their value is derived from the value of the underlying security that can be acquired by exercising the option.

Standards define a derivative as a financial instrument or contract that has three characteristics:

1. The value of the derivative changes in response to the change in the underlying primary instrument;
2. It requires no initial net investment, or a very small investment; and
3. It is settled at a future date.

There are three essential types of derivatives:

1. Options;
2. Forward contracts; and
3. Futures contracts

Options An option is the right to buy or sell something in the future. A **call option** is the right to buy something at a given price in the future, and a **put option** is the right to sell something at a given price in the future. Options may be for commodities or financial instruments. For example, a company may issue a call option to buy 20,000 tonnes of coal at a given price at a given time. Alternatively, the company may purchase a put option to sell 1,000 shares of another company, now held as an investment, at a given price at a given time, if the company wishes.

In the language of options, one party to the contract is said to *write the option*, which means that the company has an obligation to perform if the other party makes a demand under the option contract. The other party to the option contract has the choice whether it acts or not, (it has the *option* to act or not) so no enforceable obligation is created for the second company. Of course, the terms of the option must be agreed to by both companies!

Forward Contracts A **forward contract** is an obligation to buy or sell something in the future. Both the price and the time period are specified, and there is no way to avoid the transaction. For example, if a company agrees to sell 12,000 shares (now held as an investment) at $60 per share in 60 days, with no ability to avoid the transaction, this is a forward contract. If the transaction would take place only if the company wanted, then it would be an option.

Futures Contracts A **futures contract** is also an obligation to buy or sell something in the future. Both the price and the time period are specified, and there is no way to avoid the transaction. Futures contracts differ from forward contracts, though, in that they are traded on stock markets, brokers exist that act as collection and delivery agents, and the company usually has to put some money upfront, collateral in the form of a **margin**. For example, if a company agrees to buy US$1,000 for Cdn$1,200 in 60 days, through a bank that requires an initial payment of $120, this would be a futures contract and $120 is the margin.

margin

in futures contracts, a portion of the transaction value placed upfront with the broker as collateral

Accounting Recognition

Accounting standards require that companies:

- Recognize derivatives on the balance sheet when the company becomes a party to the contract;
- Classify the derivative investment as a trading investment;
- After initial recognition, remeasure derivatives at their fair values; and
- Recognize gains and losses from the changed fair value, and gains and losses at settlement, in the period in which they arise, unless the derivative is a hedge.

Although a derivative should be recorded when it is acquired (i.e., the company becomes a party to the contract), it often has no cost and a zero fair value at that time. Therefore, the initial value assigned to a derivative is often zero. The intrinsic value (and the usefulness) of a derivative is derived from future changes in the value of the underlying primary instrument. The value of the derivative changes as those underlying values change. This change in fair value is recognized in income.

Example Assume that Bent Limited agrees to a futures contract to buy 4,000 shares of Resto Limited for $30 per share in 60 days. The broker requires a 10% payment, or $12,000, on margin. (This contract is not a hedge; accounting for hedges is explained below.) Bent records the payment for the contract:

Derivative investment—trading	12,000	
Cash		12,000

The shares of Resto are trading at $34 after 30 days, and the company has a gain because it can buy shares for $120,000 that are worth $136,000. The gain on the contract is recorded to reflect fair value and an additional $160 ($136,000 \times 10\% = \$1,360 - \$1,200 = \$1,600$) is required on margin.

Derivative investment—trading (($34 − $30) × 4,000)	16,000	
Gain on derivative instrument		16,000
Derivative investment—trading	1,600	
Cash		1,600

When the shares are purchased, they have a fair value of $31 per share, and are classified as available-for-sale investments. A loss of $3 ($34 − $31) per share is recorded, and then the contract is closed out.

Loss on derivative instrument	12,000	
Derivative investment—Trading		
(($31 − $34) × 4,000)		12,000
Available-for-sale investment—Resto Ltd. shares		
($31 × 4,000 shares)	124,000	
Cash [($30 × 4,000 shares) − $13,600]		106,400
Derivative investment—trading (balance)		17,600

Note the subsequent changes in the fair value of the available-for-sale shares will be classified in accumulated other comprehensive income until realized. The classification of derivatives as trading investments dictates that gains and losses are included in net income.

Hedges

If an investor speculates in derivatives, the risk is *high* because derivatives essentially bet on future price changes. However, the real point of derivatives is to reduce risk. Derivatives often are used as **hedges**—as a way to offset risk to which the company would otherwise be exposed. Hedged risks can include changes in exchange rates, interest rates, securities, and commodities (e.g., fuel, grain, nickel, gold). For an item to be a hedge, the company must first have risk in an area, and then put a hedge in place to counter the risk. That is, a loss on a primary instrument will offset a gain on a hedge instrument and vice versa. To match the related gains and losses, both must be recognized in income concurrently.

Example Suppose that Clix Incorporated sells goods to a U.S. customer. The selling price is stated in U.S. dollars. Assume that the amount of the sale is US$100,000, and that the U.S. dollar is worth Cdn$1.10 at the date of sale. Clix now has an account receivable (a primary financial asset) for US$100,000. On Clix's books, the receivable will be translated into Canadian dollars at the current exchange rate and reported at Cdn$110,000. Now, suppose that while Clix is waiting for the customer to pay, the exchange rate changes to US$1.00 = Cdn$1.02. The value of the receivable drops to Cdn$102,000; Clix has suffered a loss of $8,000 due to the exchange rate change.

Clix can protect itself by creating an offsetting financial liability for US$100,000. Any loss on the receivable will be exactly offset by a gain on the liability. It is possible that, in the normal course of business, the company will incur U.S. dollar–denominated liabilities, such as by buying from a U.S. supplier and having to pay in U.S. dollars. Even if the offset is not exact, the gains and losses will tend to cancel out.

More commonly, however, a company will go to its bank and arrange a *forward contract* to pay the bank US$100,000 on the due date of the receivable. That is, the company will receive US$100,000 from the customer, and will pay US$100,000 to the bank. The bank agrees to the value (the price the bank will pay) for the U.S. dollars *when the contract is signed* and accepts the risk that exchange rates will change.

A forward contract is a common type of hedge. The bank will charge a small fee for this service, but the fee is like an insurance policy—a small expense will eliminate the risk of a large loss. Although Clix would realize a gain if the value of the U.S. dollar went the other way, most companies prefer to avoid the risk of loss even though it means avoiding the possibility of gain. Hedging is widely practised in international business transactions.

Criteria for Hedge Accounting The substance of a hedge is that the company is protected from gains or losses on the risk being hedged. *Hedge accounting* is voluntary, and happens only after an element is designated as a hedge. Since there are so many ways to hedge, the designation of a hedge is largely left to management. A financial statement element such as a derivative is a hedge when a company has:

1. An established policy for risk management that involves hedging;

2. Identified the risk that is being hedged;

3. Designated the financial statement element as a hedge; *and*

4. Established reasonable assurance that the hedge will be effective.

All these criteria must be met for hedge accounting to be used.

Accounting Implications of Hedge Accounting Once this designation is made, accounting standards require that the gain or loss on a hedge be recorded in net income *at the same time* that the gain or loss on the item being hedged is recognized. This simultaneous recognition of gains and losses allows for offset, and therefore the substance of the hedge is reflected in the financial statements.

In the Clix example given above, Clix would recognize both a $8,000 loss on the primary financial statement element—the $110,000 receivable, now worth $102,000—*and* an $8,000 gain on the hedging instrument. The result is no change to bottom line net income.

Sometimes it will happen that the exchange exposure is hedged by an item that does not immediately generate exchange gains, and then the offset accounting treatment must be managed carefully. For example, assume that Clix had the US$100,000, and also had a purchase order outstanding to buy inventory in U.S. dollars. Clix designates the purchase order as a hedge of the receivable, since Clix plans to use the US$100,000 receivable to pay for the inventory, and the timing of collection and payment coincide.

If there is an $8,000 loss on the account receivable, there will be *no offsetting gain on the payable that will result from the purchase order because it isn't recorded until the inventory is delivered.* The hedge is still effective, but the accounting records don't reflect it. In this case, the $8,000 loss on the receivable is not recorded on the income statement. Instead, it is recorded as an element of accumulated other comprehensive income, on the balance sheet, until the transaction takes place.

Interest Rate Swaps

Another common hedge is an interest rate swap. Firms with a large volume of debt will attempt to create a balanced assortment of interest rates within their debt portfolio. That is, they will try to arrange an appropriate blend of fixed and floating interest arrangements. A **fixed interest rate** is one that will not change over its term. A **floating interest rate** is typically related to prime interest rates in Canada and the U.S. or to LIBOR (London Inter-Bank Offering Rate) internationally. As its name implies, a floating rate will change, or float, as basic market interest rates change.

It's important to have a balanced portfolio because interest rates are volatile. If they were stable, then borrowing costs could be predicted with confidence. If firms knew that interest rates would go down, then they would borrow with a floating rate and benefit when interest rates declined. If firms knew that interest rates would increase, then they would lock in as much borrowing as possible at current low rates. The difficulty is that interest rates are hard to predict so a blend is deemed prudent. An interest rate swap is a hedge of interest rate risk, one of the types of **cash flow hedge**.

cash flow hedge

a hedge of the exposure to variability in cash flows associated with interest payments and certain unrecognized commitments; results in changes in fair value of the hedge being recognized in other comprehensive income

Mechanics of an Interest Rate Swap The essence of an interest rate swap is that two companies agree to pay each other's interest cost. One company has floating rate debt outstanding but would prefer to have fixed rate debt, while a second company has fixed rate debt but would prefer floating rate debt. Normally, each company would have access to both fixed rate and floating rate loans in its home markets, but the cost may vary. Each chooses the most advantageous rate in its particular market. The advantage of interest rate swaps is not only that floating rate can be traded for fixed rate, and vice versa, but also that swaps give companies access to capital in other markets (generally, in foreign markets) that they could not access directly or easily.

Interest rate swaps are arranged through financial institutions, as futures contracts. The institutions do not actually make one-to-one pairings, although when the swaps were first invented, this was common. Instead, financial institutions form pools of fixed and floating rate capital that can be swapped. The other important function of the intermediaries is to guarantee the payments; the whole deck of cards collapses if one party is insolvent or misses a payment. For this reason, only firms with solid credit ratings can be parties to swap arrangements.

Assume, for example, that Firm A and Firm B both need $100 million in debt capital. Firm A has ready access to fixed rate debt at a relatively low interest rate but would prefer to have floating rate debt. Firm B, in a different capital market, has access to floating rate debt at very favourable terms, but would prefer a fixed interest rate. Each firm borrows at the most favourable terms in its local capital market and then agrees to swap payments. Firm A pays Firm B's floating rate interest, while Firm B pays Firm A's fixed rate interest.

Each firm expenses only the interest that it pays. Thus, the income statement reports the results of the interest rate swap: floating rate expense for Firm A, at whatever dollar amount is paid, and fixed rate for Firm B.

Accounting Implications of an Interest Rate Swap

The fair value of a swap contract will change when interest rates change and is calculated using present value–based valuation techniques. The financial instrument rules indicate that changes in fair values are included in income as they arise. However, changes in the fair value of the hedged loan are not reflected in the financial statement. No offset would occur. Therefore, special accounting rules are needed to ensure that net income is not changed by gains and losses on a hedged position. *The change in the fair value of the swap caused by interest rate changes is recorded in accumulated other comprehensive income and not on the income statement.* (Note that if changes in fair value are caused by changes in credit risk of the company, this is not a hedged risk and then net income may be affected)

Other Swaps

Other types of risk can also be swapped, most noticeably foreign exchange risk. If one company is due to receive U.S. dollars and another one due to pay U.S. dollars, they can, with the help of an intermediary, agree to exchange the foreign currency and eliminate the exchange risk. Again, the accounting treatment ensures that gains and losses generated by the *risk* are offset by the gains and losses of the *hedge*.

CONCEPT REVIEW

1. Explain the difference between a derivative financial instrument and a primary financial instrument.

2. What are the three classifications of derivative instruments?

3. How should a derivative financial liability be measured at the balance sheet date after the derivative is acquired?

4. When are gains and losses from derivative instruments recognized?

CASH FLOW STATEMENT

The cash flows relating to complex financial instruments must be reported in the cash flow statement (CFS) in a manner that is consistent with their substance. The net proceeds from the issuance of any financial instrument will be reported as a financing activity, with the nature of the instrument disclosed in the notes to the financial statements. If an instrument is a hybrid that consists of both equity and liability components, then the individual components should be reported together on the CFS. Since conversions do not involve cash flow, they are not reported on the CFS.

Cash flows for interest and dividends must be reported in a manner that is consistent with their substance. For example, all payments that are related to debt in *substance* should be included in cash flow from operations even if the *form* of the payments is that they are dividends.

As an example, consider the balance sheet accounts of YTR Limited:

	20X5	20X4
Term preferred shares	—	$ 3,000,000
Convertible bonds payable	$ 8,000,000	—
Discount on bonds payable	245,000	—
Common stock conversion rights	457,000	—
Stock rights outstanding	—	55,000
Common shares	13,800,000	13,645,000

Convertible bonds were issued in 20X5. Discount amortization in 20X5 was $15,000. The term preferred shares were redeemed during the year, at par. Stock rights were issued to a law firm for legal services performed in 20X4 and were exercised in 20X5. There were no other common share transactions.

As a result of these transactions, the CFS would report:

1. In financing, as a source of funds, proceeds on issuance of convertible bonds, $8,197,000. The bonds were originally allocated $7,740,000 of the original proceeds. (That is, $8,000,000 less $260,000; the original discount before this year's amortization.) In addition, proceeds of $457,000 were allocated to the equity account, $7,740,000 + $457,000 = $8,197,000.

2. In financing, as a use of funds, redemption of preferred shares, $3,000,000.

3. In financing, as a source of funds, sale of common shares, $100,000. The common shares account has actually increased by $155,000 (or, $13,800,000 − $13,645,000). However, this represents not only the cash received on the sale of shares, but also the rights account, $55,000, that was transferred to common shares. Only the cash portion is shown on the CFS.

4. In operations, add-back of the non-cash interest expense caused by discount amortization, $15,000.

The key to preparing a CFS is to reconstruct the changes to the various accounts, looking for cash flow. This cash flow is reportable. In operating activities, one must examine sources of revenue and expense that *do not reflect the underlying cash flow*. Discount and premium amortization, and gains and losses from retirements must be adjusted.

DISCLOSURE

The financial instruments described in this chapter are subject to common disclosure requirements. That is, information must be disclosed in the following general categories:

1. The accounting policy used for reporting each type of financial asset and financial liability.

2. The fair value for each class of financial asset or financial liability, presented in such a way that enables the user to compare the fair value with the reported carrying value. The methods used to measure fair values should be disclosed.

3. The nature and extent of risks arising from financial instruments, including, as appropriate, credit risk, liquidity risk, and market risk.

With respect to risk, note the following interpretations:

- Credit risk: the risk that one party will fail to discharge the obligation.
- Liquidity risk: the risk that a company will encounter difficulty in meeting obligations associated with financial liabilities.
- Market risk: the risk that cash flows attached to a financial instrument will fluctuate because of changes in market prices. This may be caused by fluctuations in currency prices, interest rates, or other factors.

Critical to these general categories is the requirement that financial instruments be completely described. This would include the principal amount, amounts issued or retired, options issued and retired, maturity date, share price, early settlement options, futures contracts, forward contracts, scheduled future cash commitments, stated interest rate, effective interest rate, repricing dates, collateral, currency, payment dates, interest rates, security, and conditions. Companies are also required to disclose their *policy for financial risk management*, including hedging policy.

To say that these disclosures are extensive is an understatement. The more complex the situation, the more extensive the disclosure. The emphasis is on terms and conditions, and also on the risk associated with recognized and unrecognized financial instruments.

Reporting Example Extracts from the financial statements of Russel Metals Inc. are shown in Exhibit 14-5. Notice that:

1. In the significant accounting policy note, the company reports that it uses hedge accounting for derivative instruments in accordance with its risk management policy, when the derivatives are designated as hedges and when they are effective as hedges. Gains and losses on hedged amounts are included in income in the same period as those related to the hedged items.

2. Note 12 on financial instruments indicates that the company uses foreign exchange forward contracts and currency swaps to manage risk. This note also reviews the identified risk categories, action taken to manage risk, and the fair value of financial instruments.

3. Note 11 contains information on the company stock option plan for directors and employees, and also a deferred share unit (DSU) plan. The DSU plan allows cash payments to directors for the market value of shares at the redemption date. A total of $1.6 million has been expensed for these plans in the current year. There is extensive disclosure of the options outstanding and the assumptions used in the option pricing model used for valuation.

EXHIBIT 14-5

RUSSEL METALS INC.

Selected Financial Statement Disclosures

Year ended December 31, 2006

From the summary of significant accounting policies:

m) *Derivative financial instruments*

The Company uses foreign exchange contracts to manage foreign exchange risk on certain committed cash outflows, primarily inventory purchases. When the derivative instruments have been designated and are highly effective at offsetting risks, hedge accounting is applied. Hedge accounting requires that gains and losses on the hedge instrument are recognized through income in the same period or manner as the item being hedged. Realized and unrealized foreign exchange gains and losses not designated as a hedge are included in income. Derivatives are not entered into for speculative purposes and the use of derivative contracts is governed by documented risk management policies.

EXHIBIT 14-5 *(cont'd)*

The Company formally documents all relationships between hedging instruments and hedged items, as well as its risk management objective and strategy for undertaking various hedge transactions. This process includes linking all derivatives to specific firm commitments or forecasted transactions. The Company assesses, both at the inception of the hedge and on an ongoing basis, whether the derivatives that are used in hedging transactions are highly effective in offsetting changes in the cash flows of hedged items.

From Note 11, Shareholders' equity:

d)   The Company has a shareholder-approved share option plan, the purpose of which is to provide the directors and employees of the Company and its subsidiaries with the opportunity to participate in the growth and development of the Company. The number of common shares that may be issued under the share option plan is 5% of the current issued and outstanding common shares. The options are exercisable on a cumulative basis to the extent of 20% per year of total options granted, except that under certain specified conditions the options become exercisable immediately. The consideration paid by employees for purchase of common shares is added to share capital.

The following is a continuity of options outstanding:

	Number of Options		Weighted Average Exercise Price	
	2006	**2005**	**2006**	**2005**
Balance, beginning of the year	1,869,466	1,793,816	$11.12	$ 6.52
Granted	865,000	856,000	25.88	15.85
Exercised	(710,833)	(768,350)	9.23	5.71
Expired and forfeited	(9,600)	(12,000)	19.20	6.75
Balance, end of the year	2,014,033	1,869,466	$18.09	$11.12
Exercisable	326,233	275,666	$20.29	$11.87

. . .

The Black-Scholes option-pricing model assumptions used to compute compensation expense under the fair value-based method are as follows:

	2006	**2005**	**2004**
Dividend yield	5%	5%	5%
Expected volatility	29%	25%	29%
Expected life	5 yrs	7 yrs	7 yrs
Risk free rate of return	5%	5%	5%
Weighted average fair value of options granted	$5.05	$2.93	$1.89

e)   The Company has established a Deferred Share Unit (DSU) plan for its directors. A DSU entitles the holder to receive, upon redemption, a cash payment equivalent to the market value of a common share at the redemption date. DSUs are credited to the director accounts on a quarterly basis and vest immediately. At December 31, 2006, there were 20,981 DSUs outstanding (2005: 18,024).

f)   Total compensation cost for stock-based compensation is as follows:

(millions)	**2006**	**2005**	**2004**
Stock options	$3.4	$1.5	$0.8
Deferred share units	0.2	0.3	0.1
	$3.6	$1.8	$0.9

continued on next page

EXHIBIT 14-5 *(cont'd)*

From Note 12, Financial instruments

12. Financial Instruments

a) *Fair value*

The fair value of long-term debt as at December 31, 2006 and 2005 is estimated based on the last quoted trade price, where it exists, or on the current rates available to the Company for similar debt of the same remaining maturities. The fair value of the Company's debt at December 31, 2006 was $194.5 million (2005: $197.9 million)....

As at December 31, 2006 and 2005, the estimated fair value of other financial assets, liabilities and off balance sheet instruments approximates their carrying values.

b) *Credit risk*

The Company, in the normal course of business, is exposed to credit risk relating to accounts receivable from its customers. This risk is mitigated by the fact that its customer base is geographically diverse and in different industries. The Company is also exposed to credit risk from the potential default by any of its counterparties on its foreign exchange forward contracts and the fixed-for-fixed cross currency swaps. The Company mitigates this risk by entering into forward contracts and swaps with members of the credit facility syndicate.

c) *Interest rate risk*

The Company is not exposed to significant interest rate risk. The Company's long-term debt is at fixed rates. The Company's bank debt, if any, that is used to finance working capital, which is short-term in nature, is at floating interest rates.

d) *Foreign exchange risk*

The Company uses foreign exchange contracts with maturities of less than a year to manage foreign exchange risk on certain future committed cash outflows. As at December 31, 2006, the Company had outstanding forward foreign exchange contracts in the amounts of US$16.5 million and € nil, maturing in the first half of 2007 (2005: US$58.7 million and € 2.9 million). The foreign exchange gain on U.S. denominated financial assets and liabilities included in 2006 operating earnings from continuing operations was $1.7 million (2005: $1.6 million; 2004: $2.3 million).

The Company has designated US$75 million of the Senior Notes as a hedge of its net investment in foreign subsidiaries.

Source: www.sedar.com, Russell Metals Inc., Audited Annual Financial Statements, February 19, 2007.

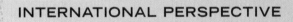

INTERNATIONAL PERSPECTIVE

The set of financial instruments standards, including the standards governing derivatives and hedges, come into play for publicly accountable companies during year-ends beginning in the 2007 fiscal year. Certain aspects of them, including classification of hybrid financial instruments and disclosure provisions, have been in effect for several years. However, the whole project is an integrated unit, covering investments, financing vehicles, and risk management tools. Implementation of this series of standards is expected to affect most reporting entities.

If companies are not publicly accountable, they do not have to apply the complete range of these standards at this time. The AcSB is in the process of determining an appropriate reporting strategy for these companies.

The financial instrument project has been a joint project of the Canadian Accounting Standards Board, the U.S. FASB, and the IASB. Because the standards were developed as a joint project, there are few substantive differences, in relative terms, between Canadian and international standards. However, differences do exist. For example, the international standards do not allow use of the proportionate method when determining the debt and equity portions of a convertible bond, convertible at the investor's option. IAS 32 also deals with the presentation of derivatives on a company's own equity accounts, a topic not dealt with in the Canadian standards. Other technical differences exist. There is ongoing work in the area of disclosures for financial instruments, and various other specific projects, which may decrease the differences between these standards.

The broad models for accounting for stock-based payments are similar between Canadian and international standards, but again there is a list of differences. These differences include guidelines in the international standards for dealing with plan modifications, but not in the Canadian standards, required recognition of stock plans with only minor price reductions offered to employees under international standards, different rules for measurement of cash-based settlement plans, and many more. The result is a daunting list in such a complex area.

RELEVANT STANDARDS

CICA Handbook:
- Section 3855, Financial Instruments—Recognition and Measurement
- Section 3861, Financial Instruments—Disclosure and Presentation
- Section 3862, Financial Instruments—Disclosures
- Section 3863, Financial Instruments—Presentation
- Section 3865, Hedges
- Section 3870, Stock-Based Compensation and Other Stock-Based Payments

IASB:
- *IAS* 32, Financial Instruments: Disclosure and Presentation
- *IAS* 39, Financial Instruments: Recognition and Measurement
- *IFRS* 2, Share-Based Payments

SUMMARY OF KEY POINTS

1. Financial instruments must be classified on the balance sheet in accordance with their substance, not necessarily their form. If there are two component parts to a financial instrument, the two components are separately recognized on issuance.

2. Annual payments associated with a financial instrument that is classified as debt are presented on the income statement; annual payments associated with a financial instrument classified as an equity instrument are presented on the retained earnings statement.

3. Classification of a financial instrument is driven by the contractual arrangements covering principal at maturity and contractual arrangements for annual payments, if any. If the company can be required to pay cash, then the component is a liability.

4. Preferred shares are likely to be classified as debt if the investor can force repayment (i.e., they are retractable) or if the shares have a due date (i.e., are term preferred shares) or if the shares have an unfavourable escalation clause that dictates repayment.

5. Bonds that are convertible into shares based on the current market value of shares on the conversion date have no equity component and are classified as debt. If the conversion rate is fixed, an equity component exists.

6. Bonds that are convertible into common shares at the *investor's* option embody two financial instruments: a liability and an option contract on common shares. The two

components are recognized separately on issuance, and classified accordingly. To measure the equity portion of a bond, either the incremental or the proportional method can be used. The incremental method is with reference to the bond price only while the proportional method uses both the bond price and a stock option model valuation.

7. Bonds that are convertible into a fixed number of common shares at the *company's* option will be classified as equity as to their principal and as a liability as to their annual cash interest component.

8. Bonds that are convertible into common shares at the *company's* option will be classified as a liability if the number of shares to be issued (price per share) is dependent on share price at the conversion date.

9. When a bond that is convertible at the company's option has an equity component, the equity component is increased to par value over the life of the bond through a capital charge, and interest expense is a constant percentage of the interest liability.

10. Stock options provide the holder with an option to acquire a specified number of common shares at a specific price, at a specific time.

11. Stock options may be recognized on issuance and recorded as an element of shareholders' equity. On issuance of the underlying shares, the options account is folded into the share account. If the options lapse, the option account becomes contributed capital.

12. In some circumstances, stock options may be accounted for through disclosure, by a memorandum entry approach.

13. Options are commonly recognized in the financial statements when options are granted as compensation to outside parties, as fractional rights in a stock dividend that is recognized itself, as warrants on the issuance of bonds, as part of a convertible bond, or when stock option plans involve compensation.

14. Options are commonly disclosed when granted to existing shareholders, issued in a stock dividend that is also given memorandum treatment, and for employee stock options that do not involve compensation expense.

15. Compensatory employee stock option plans are accounted for using the fair value–based method. The options must be valued using an option pricing model. Compensation is recognized over the vesting period.

16. Long-term compensation plans that require cash payments, or cash payments at the option of the employee, result in an expense and a liability, accrued over the vesting period.

17. If the amount of a long-term cash compensation award is unknown, a new estimate is made annually, and balances are corrected prospectively (that is, the new estimate is applied to the current and future periods.)

18. Long-term compensation plans that involve distribution of shares, or shares at the option of the company, result in an expense and an equity element, with the amount estimated at inception using an option pricing model. This value is accrued over the vesting period and not remeasured.

19. Derivatives are contracts that specify an exchange of financial instruments at a specified price. Derivatives include options, forward contracts, and futures contracts. They can be used to hedge various types of risk, including interest rate risk and exchange risk.

20. Derivative contracts are recorded at fair value. Gains and losses from changes in fair value are reported on the income statement.

21. If a financial instrument is designated as a hedge, then gains and losses on the hedge will be recognized in income at the same time as gains and losses on the risk being hedged, so they are offset on the income statement. Under certain conditions, gains and losses on hedges are recorded in accumulated other comprehensive income.

22. The cash flows relating to financial instruments should be reported on the CFS in a manner that is consistent with the substance of the payments, both for payments *on*

capital (i.e., interest and dividends) and repayments *of* capital (i.e., principal and share buybacks).

23. A company must disclose the accounting policy, fair value, and nature and extent of risks associated with financial instruments. Financial instruments must be fully described in the disclosure notes.

KEY TERMS

basket offering, 852
book value method, 843
call option, 864
capital charge, 848
cash equivalent value, 843
cash flow hedge, 867
compensatory employee stock option
    plans, 858
convertible debt, 835
derivative instruments, 852
fair value–based method, 853
fixed interest rate, 867
floating interest rate, 867
forced conversion, 841
forfeiture, 859
forward contract, 865
futures contract, 865
hedges, 866
hybrid securities, 835
in-the-money, 851

income bonds, 835
incremental method, 844
margin, 865
market value method, 843
non-compensatory stock purchase
    plan, 856
option contract, 842
perpetual debt, 840
pre-emptive rights, 854
proportional method, 844
put option, 864
redeemable shares, 835
retractable shares, 839
stock appreciation rights, 860
stock options, 851
stock rights, 852
stock warrants, 852
term preferred shares, 838
vest, 858

REVIEW PROBLEM

Each of the following cases is independent. Each illustrates a different aspect of hybrid securities. Assume in each case that the company is public.

A. Convertible Bonds

On 1 January 20X1, Amershi Limited issues $1,000,000 face amount of 8%, five-year, convertible debentures. Interest is payable semi-annually on 30 June and 31 December. The debentures are convertible at the investor's option at the rate of 20 common shares for each $1,000 bond. The market rate of interest for non-convertible bonds of similar risk and maturity is 6%. The net proceeds received by Amershi amounted to $1,250,000.

Required:

1. Record the issuance of the bonds on 1 January 20X1 using the incremental method to value the conversion option.
2. Prepare the journal entries for interest expense on 30 June 20X1 and 31 December 20X1. Assume that Amershi uses effective interest amortization for bond premium and discount.
3. Indicate how all amounts relating to the bonds will be shown on Amershi's financial statements for the year ending 31 December 20X1.
4. Assume that the holders of $300,000 face value bonds exercise their conversion privilege on 1 January 20X4, when the market value of the common shares is $65. Prepare the journal entry to record the conversion, using the book value method.

B. Subordinated Convertible Debentures

On 1 January 20X5, Bateau Incorporated issued $10,000,000 face amount of 8%, 10-year, subordinated convertible debentures at face value in a private placement. The debentures pay interest annually, in cash, on 31 December. At maturity, Bateau Incorporated has the option of issuing common shares to redeem the bonds instead of paying cash. The bonds are convertible into 50 common shares for each $1,000 of the bonds' face value.

Required:

1. Record the issuance of the bonds on 1 January 20X5.
2. Record the interest expense and payment on the first interest date of 31 December 20X5. Also record the related equity transfer.

REVIEW PROBLEM—SOLUTION

A. Convertible Bonds

1. The first step is to calculate the present value of the cash flows at the market rate of 6%, using semi-annual interest periods:

Principal [$1,000,000 × (P/A, 3%,10)]	$ 744,090
Interest [$40,000 × (P/F, 3%,10)]	341,208
	$1,085,298

Journal entry to record issuance, incremental method

Cash	1,250,000	
Bonds payable		1,000,000
Premium on bonds payable		85,298
Common share conversion rights		164,702

2. Entries for interest expense during 20X1:

30 June 20X1

Interest expense ($1,085,298 × 3%)	32,559	
Premium on bonds payable	7,441	
Cash		40,000

Liability balance: $1,085,298 − $7,441 = $1,077,857

31 December 20X1

Interest expense ($1,077,857 × 3%)	32,336	
Premium on bonds payable	7,664	
Cash		40,000

3. Bond-related items on 20X1 financial statements:

Income statement

Interest expense	$ 64,895

Balance sheet
  Long-term debt

Bonds payable	$1,000,000
Premium on bonds payable	70,193*
	$1,070,193

  Shareholders' equity

Common share conversion rights	$ 164,702

Cash flow statement
  Financing activities

Proceeds from issuance of convertible bonds	$1,250,000

*$85,298 − $7,441 − $7,664 = $70,193

4. Conversion of $300,000 face value bonds into 6,000 common shares on 1 January 20X4:

The present value of the retired bond on 1 January 20X4:

Principal [$300,000 × (P/A, 3%,4)]	$266,547	$744,090
Interest [$12,000 × (P/F, 3%,4)]	44,605	341,208
		$311,152

Bonds payable	300,000	
Premium on bonds payable	11,152	
Common share conversion rights ($164,702 × 3/10)	49,411	
Common shares		360,563

B. Subordinated Convertible Debentures

1. Interest:

These debentures pay interest annually, in cash; the present value of this cash flow is recorded by Bateau as a liability, using the market rate of interest:

$$\$800,000 \times (P/A, 8\%, 10) = \$5,368,064$$

Principal:

The company has the option of issuing a fixed number of shares instead of cash to redeem the bonds at maturity. The principal portion of the debt is credited to shareholders' equity:

Cash	10,000,000	
Interest liability on subordinated debentures		5,368,064
Share equity—subordinated debentures		4,631,936

2. *Entry to record interest expense on 31 December 20X5*

Interest expense ($5,368,064 × 8%)	429,445	
Interest liability on subordinated debentures		429,445

Entry to record interest payment on 31 December 20X5

Interest liability on subordinated debentures	800,000	
Cash ($10,000,000 × 8%)		800,000

Entry to transfer retained earnings to share equity—debentures

Retained earnings ($4,631,936 × 8%)	370,555	
Share equity—subordinated debentures		370,555

QUESTIONS

Q14-1   Historically, what factors have dictated classification of a financial instrument as debt or equity? How is the classification made when based on the financial instruments rules?

Q14-2   What is a financial instrument? Give three examples.

Q14-3   What is a hybrid financial instrument? Give an example.

Q14-4   Assume a company issues a financial instrument for $50,000 in 20X2 and retires it through an open market purchase for $56,000 in 20X5. In each of the intervening years, an annual payment of $2,500 was paid to the investor. How will the financial instrument affect income in each of the years if it is classified as debt? As equity?

Q14-5   Explain appropriate financial statement classification of retractable preferred shares.

Q14-6 Define convertible debt (convertible at the investor's option) and the accounting approach adopted for this financial instrument.

Q14-7 Explain how to account for convertible debt, convertible at the investor's option if the conversion option specifies that the shares to be issued depends on the fair value of shares at the conversion date.

Q14-8 Explain two different ways to value the conversion option associated with convertible debt at the investor's option.

Q14-9 What happens to the common share conversion rights account, created when convertible debt is issued, when the bond is actually converted? What if the bond is repaid in cash instead?

Q14-10 How is convertible debt classified if it is convertible at the issuer's option into a fixed number of shares? If it is convertible at the investor's option into a fixed number of shares?

Q14-11 Sometimes, a convertible bond convertible at the company's option is recorded entirely as debt, and sometimes it is recorded partially as debt and partially as equity. Under what circumstances is the latter treatment appropriate?

Q14-12 Is a bond convertible at the issuer's option into common shares ever recorded entirely as equity? Explain.

Q14-13 If a $400,000, 8% bond, convertible at the issuer's option, is issued at par and $76,400 of the issuance price is attributable to the interest obligation, how much interest expense will be recorded in the first year? How much "interest" is paid to the investor? What amount will be debited directly to retained earnings?

Q14-14 What is the distinction between stock rights and warrants?

Q14-15 If share rights are recognized on issuance, what happens to the share rights account if the share rights are exercised? Allowed to lapse? Compare this to the treatment of the common share conversion option account associated with convertible bonds.

Q14-16 Explain three occasions when share rights are not formally recognized in the financial statements, but are disclosed only. Why is disclosure appropriate some of the time?

Q14-17 When would a long-term compensation contract, payable after three years, result in an equity account being recognized in the first year? A liability?

Q14-18 Assume that a long-term cash bonus is agreed to with an employee group. It will vest over five years, and be paid at the end of the fifth year. The amount is estimated to be $400,000 at the end of year 1, $175,000 at the end of year 2, and $400,000 at the end of year 3. What is the compensation expense recognized in the third year?

Q14-19 Can compensation expense under a long-term performance reward program be negative? Explain.

Q14-20 Explain the terms of a SARs program for employees.

Q14-21 Define a derivative, and a hedge.

Q14-22 What is the difference between a futures contract and a forward contract?

Q14-23 When a company has a put option on shares of another company, and the price of the shares declines, will the company report a gain or a loss? Explain.

Q14-24 Assume that a Canadian company sells a product to a U.S. customer, and that the sale is denominated in U.S. dollars. What kind of a derivative instrument will eliminate the exchange risk? How will the transaction balance and the derivative instrument be reflected in the financial statements?

Q14-25 What is the purpose of a swap? If a company enters into a swap arrangement and the fair value of the swap changes, will net income change? Explain.

Q14-26 What areas of disclosure are required for financial instruments?

CASE 14-1

ON-THE-CREST LTD.

On-the-Crest Ltd. (OCL) is a company operating in the used-vehicle industry. OCL derives its revenue from selling, licensing, and servicing software products for car dealers, from the sale of products to car dealers, and the sale of used vehicles. Both through internal growth and acquisitions, OCL revenue has grown at the rate of 25% per year for each of the last five years. An initial public offering is planned in the next fiscal year.

Ida Wong, the audit partner, is seeking a summary memo from the senior in charge of the audit (see Exhibit 1). Ida has a meeting scheduled with Bill Valarian, CFO of OCL, tomorrow and needs to be aware of major reporting issues.

Required:

Review the notes and prepare a memo outlining accounting and reporting issues and alternatives. This memo will be the basis for the meeting with Bill Valarian.

EXHIBIT 1

ON-THE-CREST LTD.

Notes

From:	Audit Senior
To:	Ida Wong, Audit Partner
Re:	Potential accounting issues—On-the-Crest Ltd. (OCL)

The following issues have come to light during the audit and may impact on the financial statements of OCL:

Convertible Debt

At the beginning of the current year, OCL issued $7 million of 7.25% debt with interest payable semi-annually on 30 June and 31 December. Bond issue costs were $300,000, which are being amortized over 10 years. The maturity date is 10 years from issuance unless either of the following options is exercised:

a. On the date of the IPO, the lender can submit the bond for repayment, and OCL may choose to repay the liability in cash or in OCL shares. The number of OCL shares to be issued is based on the chosen IPO price.

b. After the debt has been outstanding for 36 months, there is a 2-week period during which the lender can submit the bond for repayment in cash.

The $7 million proceeds on issuance of debt were recorded in a long-term liability account.

> ## EXHIBIT 1 *(cont'd)*

Options Granted to a Supplier

OCL issued options to Software Supply Company (SSC) for 40,000 OCL shares. The options were issued in order to ensure that SSL made OCL a priority customer for the coming period, as SSL's services are critical for modifications to software that OCL provides to car dealers. The options are non-revocable and are exercisable six months after any IPO. If there is no IPO, the options are to be repurchased and retired at a price based on a set formula. The presence of these options has been disclosed in the financial statements.

Available-for-Sale Investment

To utilize idle cash, OCL made a $350,000 investment in the shares of Motors Company (MC), a public company also in the automotive industry. This acquisition took place in the prior fiscal year, and an unrealized loss of $100,000 was recognized at the end of last year because market value had declined to $250,000. Market price is unchanged at the end of the current fiscal year, and OCL is unwilling to sell the investment until market prices rebound. OCL is confident this will occur in the next two to five years.

Exchange Rate Hedge

OCL placed an order with a Japanese supplier during the year when the exchange rate was ¥1 = $0.0095. On the delivery date, the exchange rate was ¥1 = $0.0090. OCL paid for the merchandise 90 days later when the exchange rate was ¥1 = $0.0104. However, OCL had hedged the account payable at a rate of ¥1 = $0.0085 and paid $161,500 to the exchange broker for the required yen. The inventory was recorded at the cash cost of $161,500.

Convertible Preferred Shares

In the fourth quarter of the current fiscal year, OCL issued $1.7 million of convertible preferred shares in a private placement. Under the terms of the share agreement, the $1.7 million investment will automatically be converted into 600,000 common shares of OCL on the commencement of trading of OCL common shares on the TSE. There are no provisions for alternate arrangements if common shares are not traded on the TSE; the preferred shares would remain as preferred shares if OCL did not go public. The preferred shares have no preference rights to assets on the dissolution of the company, but have a stated cash dividend of $100,000 per year. The dividend is paid quarterly, and on conversion, OCL must pay the dividend up to date in cash including arrears, if any, whether declared or not. All the $1.7 million proceeds are recorded in the equity account, preferred shares. No dividend was due; none was declared or recorded in the current fiscal year.

Pricing Agreement

For the first time, OCL provided certain price and payment incentives to customers in order to spur demand. OCL extended payment terms from the current 30 days to 60 days, and specified that if pre-agreed list prices to *end consumers* are not realized, OCL would provide rebates. For example, assume OCL sold a product to a customer for $100 and expected it to be resold to the final customer for $165. If the final sale were to be priced at $155, OCL has agreed to accept $90 ($100 − ($165 − $155)). OCL has accrued an allowance for all amounts expected to be lost under the guarantee, based on market research.

CASE 14-2

SUNBEAM MINING CORPORATION

Sunbeam Mining Corp. (SMC) is a private corporation engaged in developing a gold mining site in northern Ontario. The CEO of SMC is Leslie Morantz, a well-known personality in speculative mining activities. Mr. Morantz is personally involved in SMC's financial strategy. Sixty percent of the voting common shares of SMC are owned by 287457 Ontario Limited, which is Mr. Morantz's personal holding company. The shares were issued to 287457 Ontario Ltd. in consideration for rights to the site; 287457 held the site mining option. The actual development of the mine site is the responsibility of SMC's president, Adam Evan, who is an experienced mining executive whom Mr. Morantz hired away from the Chilean operations of Noranda in 20X5.

SMC is known as a "junior mining company"; it has a single mine site and is still in the development stage. As is common with such companies, almost all costs incurred in the development process are capitalized; amortization of the capitalized costs will not begin until production actually gets underway. The site development is proceeding according to plan, but production is not expected to begin for at least 18 months.

Mr. Morantz plans to have SMC issue shares to the public in an initial public offering once the extent of the gold field has been determined and the economic feasibility of the site has been demonstrated, probably in early 20X8. Currently, however, all development costs are being financed through private sources. The primary sources of financing are as follows:

- The Ontario Teachers' Pension Fund (Teachers') (which devotes 5% of its investment portfolio to providing venture capital) purchased 20% of the SMC common shares for $5 million. In addition, Teachers' purchased 2,000 shares of convertible preferred shares for another $10 million. The preferred shares carry a variable dividend based on the prime interest rate plus 2%; the dividend is cumulative. The preferred shares are convertible into common at Teachers' option at any time prior to 1 July 20X12, after which SMC can call the preferred shares and issue common shares (on a one-to-one basis) in full payment.

- A loan from the Canadian Bank (CB) of 40,000 ounces of gold (i.e., 100 standard 400 ounce bars), advanced to SMC by the bank on 2 January 20X6. Gold is priced in U.S. dollars, and its price at the date of the loan was US$350 per ounce. Therefore, the dollar value of the gold loan was US$14 million at issuance. At SMC's request, the bank paid the principal in the equivalent amount of Canadian dollars, which was Cdn$16.8 million (at an exchange rate of US$1.00 = Cdn$1.20). The loan must be repaid in five annual instalments beginning on 31 December 20X9. Each instalment payment is 8,000 ounces of gold (i.e., 20 bars) plus accrued interest on that instalment, calculated at 6% per annum compounded from 2 January 20X6. If SMC wishes, the company may pay the instalments in the equivalent amount of cash (at the market price of gold at the date of repayment) rather than in gold.

    The bank requires regular, monthly cash flow statements prepared on a budget versus actual basis, with estimated costs to complete development. The bank holds a first and floating charge against the assets of SMC. The bank also prohibits dividend payments prior to maturity of the first instalment of the loan (that is, no dividends can be paid until 20X10).

- $5,000,000 in subordinated debentures were issued to 287457 Ontario Ltd. on 15 July 20X5. The debentures are subordinated to the bank loan. The debentures bear interest at 9% per annum. No principal or interest payments are due until the mine becomes productive, and then the debenture is repayable at 10% per year, plus accrued interest (beginning when commercial production commences), compounded on each $500,000 principal payment.

The 20% of the common shares that are not owned by Mr. Morantz and by Teachers' are owned by Mr. Evan; these were issued to him in 20X5 as an inducement for him to leave Noranda and join SMC.

Mr. Morantz has retained Emilia Chow to prepare SMC's financial statements for the year ending 31 December 20X6. He has instructed her to give him a report concerning her proposed financial statement presentation prior to her actual preparation of the statements. The report should succinctly outline her recommendations on presentation and disclosure of SMC's financing arrangements and other related matters.

At 31 December 20X6, the price of gold was US$360, and the value of the U.S. dollar was Cdn$1.15.

Required:

Assume that you are Ms. Chow. Prepare the report.

CASE 14-3

CREATIVE TRADERS LIMITED

Creative Traders Ltd. (CTL) is a Canadian publicly traded company that conducts business in several countries, using a variety of currencies. The notes to the financial statements pertaining to fair values of financial instruments for the past year, the year ended 31 December 20X1, are shown in Exhibit 1. CTL is quite thorough in explaining its exposure to risk of foreign currency fluctuations, interest rate changes, and changes in the fair value of financial instruments. Some of these risks are managed through derivatives.

Fair values have been included in the disclosure notes but not recorded, up to the current year. This coming year, derivatives will be recognized on the balance sheet at fair value. Changes in fair value are to be included in net income.

You are a professional accountant in the financial reporting group at CTL. A report for the audit committee has been requested, as a basis for discussion at an upcoming meeting. Specifically, you've been asked to quantify the impact of recording derivatives. You also must explain why recording is required, given that the contracts are executory in nature. Finally, your report should explain any concerns about accurately measuring fair value.

Required:

Prepare a report addressing the issues raised.

(Judy Cumby, adapted)

EXHIBIT 1

CREATIVE TRADERS LIMITED NOTES TO THE FINANCIAL STATEMENTS 31 DECEMBER 20X1

Note 8: Financial Instruments (all numbers are in millions)

Foreign Exchange Risk

The Company's global operations require active participation in foreign exchange markets. Currency exposures primarily relate to assets and liabilities denominated in foreign currencies, as well as economic exposure, which is derived from the risk that currency fluctuations could affect the dollar value of future cash flows

EXHIBIT 1   *(cont'd)*

related to operating activities. The company uses financial instruments, which are not reflected on the balance sheet, to regulate the cash flow variability of local currency costs or selling prices denominated in currencies other than the Canadian dollar.

The Company had forward contracts and options to buy, sell, or exchange foreign currencies with a Canadian dollar equivalent of $11,017 at 31 December 20X1 and $6,866 at 31 December 20X0. These contracts and options had various expiration dates, primarily in the first quarter of the next year. The net unrealized loss based on the foreign exchange rates at 31 December 20X1 was $(146). The net unrealized gain based on the foreign exchange rates at 31 December 20X0 was $45.

Interest Rate Risk

Interest rate risk reflects the sensitivity of the Company's financial condition to movements in interest rates. To manage the Company's exposure to interest rate risks, the Company has entered into various interest rate contracts. Neither the notional principal amounts nor the current replacement value on these financial instruments are carried on the consolidated balance sheet. The notional principal amounts on all types of interest derivative contracts at 31 December 20X1 totalled $1,052 with a weighted-average remaining life of 6.8 years. At 31 December 20X0, the notional principal amounts totalled $1,299 with a weighted-average remaining life of 6.3 years.

Fair Value of Financial Instruments

The fair value of the foreign currency and interest rate derivatives at December 31 were:

	Carrying Value	Gain	Loss	Fair Value
20X1				
Derivatives relating to:				
Foreign currency	NIL	$441	$(587)	$(146)
Interest rates	NIL	32	(7)	25
20X0				
Derivatives relating to:				
Foreign currency	NIL	$173	$(128)	$45
Interest rates	NIL	2	(20)	(18)

The following table presents the carrying amounts and estimated fair values of the Company's other financial instruments as at 31 December 20X1 and 20X0 for which the carrying amounts are different from their fair values:

December 31	Carrying Value 20X1	Fair Value 20X1	Carrying Value 20X0	Fair Value 20X0
Financial Liabilities				
Long-term debt (including current portion)	$3,476	$3,800	$3,476	$2,905
Other				
Convertible preferred securities; reported as debt	$327	$315	$327	$281

ASSIGNMENTS

 A14-1 Financial Instruments—Identification: Financial statement elements can be:

Assets (A)
Financial assets (FA)
Liabilities (L)
Financial liabilities (FL)
Equities (E)

Classify each of the following items from the point of view of the issuing company. An item can be more than one thing—for example, cash is an asset and a financial asset.

1. Contributed capital
2. Asset retirement obligation
3. Accounts payable to suppliers
4. Property, plant, and equipment
5. Bonds payable
6. Accumulated amortization, buildings
7. Common shares
8. Accounts receivable
9. Treasury stock
10. Bank loans payable
11. Inventory
12. Term preferred shares
13. Preferred shares convertible to common shares
14. Leasehold improvements
15. Warranty repair obligation
16. Exchange contract to buy foreign currency
17. Goodwill
18. Retained earnings
19. Loans receivable
20. Short-term investment in common shares of another company

★★ **A14-2 Impact of Debt versus Equity:** Laffoley Corporation needs to raise $7,000,000 in order to finance a planned capital expansion. It has investigated two alternatives:

1. Issue $7 million of preferred shares at par. The shares can be redeemed at the company's option at the end of 10 years for a price estimated to be in the region of $7,200,000. Annual (cumulative) dividends would amount to $420,000.

2. Issue bonds, which the company can buy back on the open market at the end of 10 years; analysts estimate that it would cost $7,200,000 to reacquire the $7,000,000 issue. Annual interest would amount to $600,000.

Required:

1. Assume Laffoley's tax rate is 30%. What is the *after-tax* annual cost of the two alternatives?

2. Provide journal entries to record issuance, annual dividends, or interest (for one year only) and retirement of both the shares and debt.

3. Assume that net income, before interest and tax, in Year 10 was $2,000,000. The tax rate was 30%. Calculate net income if equity were outstanding in Year 10, and retired at the end of the year. Calculate net income if debt were outstanding in Year 10 and retired at the end of the year.

★ **A14-3 Classification:** A description of several financial instruments follows:

 a. Series D shares, voting, annual $4 non-cumulative dividend, redeemable at the investor's option for $60 per share.

b. Subordinated notes payable, bearing an interest rate of 4%, interest reset every five years with reference to market rates; principal due to be repaid only on the dissolution of the company, if ever, although may be repaid at the company's option on interest repricing dates.

c. Series B preferred shares, annual $6 cumulative dividend, convertible into four common shares for every $100 preferred share at the investor's option, redeemable at $32 per share at the company's option in 20X10.

d. Subordinated 8% debentures payable, interest payable in cash semi-annually, due in the year 20X8. At maturity, the face value of the debentures may be converted, at the company's option, into common shares at a price of $12.50 per share.

e. Subordinated 8% debentures payable, interest payable semi-annually, due in the year 20X8. At maturity, the face value of the debentures may be converted, at the company's option, into common shares at the market price at that time. Interest may also be paid in shares using the market value of shares at the interest payment date.

Required:

Classify each financial instrument as debt, equity, or part debt and part equity. Explain your reasoning.

★★ **A14-4 Classification:** Description of several financial instruments follows:

Case 1 Series A first preferred shares, carrying a fixed cumulative dividend of $2.10 per share increasing by $4.20 in 20X8. The shares are redeemable at the company's option at a price of $45 per share until 31 December 20X7 and at a price of $75 thereafter.

Case 2 Convertible subordinated notes payable, entitled to annual interest at 3%. At maturity, the debentures may, at the company's option, be paid out in cash or converted into common shares at the set exchange price of $30 per share.

Case 3 Convertible subordinated debentures payable, entitled to annual interest at 4.5%. At maturity, the debentures may, at the company's option, be paid out in cash or converted into common shares using an exchange ratio governed by the market value of shares at the conversion date.

Case 4 Series F first preferred shares, carrying a fixed cumulative dividend of $3 per share per annum, redeemable at the company's option at $40 per share.

Case 5 Class C Series 1 shares, carrying a dividend entitlement equal to $4 per share or an amount equal to common share dividends, whichever is higher, redeemable at the investor's option at $110 per share. The company may, at its option, redeem the shares with class A common shares instead of cash, valued at their current market value.

Case 6 Convertible subordinated debentures payable, entitled to annual cash interest at 4.5%. At maturity, the debentures may, at the company's option, be paid out in cash or converted into common shares using an exchange price of $20 per share. Interest may also be paid in shares valued at $20 per share at the company's option.

Case 7 Series B first preferred shares, carrying a fixed cumulative dividend of $1.00 per share. The shares must be redeemed by the company at a price of $21 per share, plus dividends in arrears, if any, in 20X4.

Required:

Explain why each of the above items is a financial instrument. Classify each as a financial asset, financial liability, equity instrument, or part debt and part equity.

★★ **A14-5 Classification:** Elkridge Corporation issued the following financial instruments in 20X4:

1. *Convertible debentures* issued at 103. The debentures require interest to be paid semi-annually at a nominal rate of 7% per annum. The debentures are convertible by the holder at any time up to final maturity at a ratio of 10 common shares for each $1,000 principal amount.

2. *Convertible debentures* issued at par. The company is required to pay interest in cash quarterly at a nominal rate of 8% per annum. At maturity, Elkridge can repay the debentures in cash or issue common shares for the principal amount at $20 per share.

3. *Redeemable preferred shares* issued to Elkridge's founding family. The shares carry an obligation for the company to pay annual cash dividends at the rate of $12 per share. On or after 1 July 20X8, the preferred shareholders can require the company to repurchase the shares at the original issue price plus any accrued unpaid dividends.

Required:

Discuss the appropriate financial statement classification of each of these financial instruments.

★★ **A14-6 Convertible Debt:** Marjorie Manufacturing Limited issued a convertible bond on 2 July 20X5. The $5 million bond pays annual interest of 8%, each 30 June. Each $1,000 bond

is convertible into 50 shares of common stock, at the investor's option, on 1 July 20X10, up to 1 July 20X15, after which time each $1,000 bond may be converted into 45.6 shares until bond maturity on 30 June 20X20. Market analysts have indicated that, had the bond not been convertible, it would have sold for $4,240,000, reflecting a market interest rate of 10% annually. In fact, it was issued for $5,325,000.

Required:

1. Provide the journal entry to record the initial issuance of the bond. Justify the amount allocated to the conversion privilege.

2. Assume that market analysts have ascertained that a reasonable value for the conversion option would be $1,250,000. Repeat requirement (1) using the proportionate method.

3. Verify the $4,240,000 price of the bond, and explain the approach that would have been used to value the conversion option.

4. Calculate the interest expense that would be recorded in the first 12 months of the bond if the bond were recorded as in requirement (1).

5. Would more or less interest expense have been recorded if the conversion options were not recognized and the proceeds above par value ($325,000) assigned to a premium account? Explain, do not calculate.

★★ **A14-7 Convertible Debt:** Renouf Corporation issued convertible bonds in January 20X6. These bonds were convertible to common shares of Renouf at the holder's option at their

maturity date. The bonds had a par value of $4 million and were issued for $4,300,000. The bonds would have been issued for $3,900,000 had they not been convertible. The bonds were outstanding for 10 years, and, at their maturity date, one-half the bonds were converted to 20,000 shares of common stock, according to the conversion terms. The other half of the bonds were paid out in cash at par value.

Required:

1. Explain why convertible bonds are hybrid instruments.

2. Explain how the conversion option can be valued.

3. Provide the journal entry to record the financial instrument on issuance.

4. Provide the journal entry to record the disposition of the bond at maturity.

5. Why is it unexpected to have part of a bond issue convert and part be paid out in cash on the same date?

★★ **A14-8 Convertible Debt, Issuer's Option:** Miner Manufacturing Company issued a $450,000, 6%, five-year bond at par. The bond pays interest annually at year-end. At maturity, the bond can be repaid in cash or converted to 60,000 common shares at Miner's option. The market interest rate is 6%.

Required:

1. Calculate the portion of the bond relating to principal and interest.
2. Provide the entry made to record issuance of the bond.
3. Provide the entries to record interest expense and the annual payment each year for five years.
4. Provide the entries to record the charge to retained earnings each year for five years.
5. Provide the entry to record the maturity of the bond assuming that shares were issued.

 A14-9 Convertible Debt, Issuer's Option: Sui Ltd. issued a 10-year, $2,000,000 debenture with a nominal interest rate of 10%; cash interest is paid semi-annually. The market rate of interest for debt of similar size, risk, and term is 8%. The obligation can be satisfied by the issuer at maturity either by cash or by issuing common shares. The debenture was issued for $2,271,813. If shares are issued at maturity, the shares are valued at $40.

Required:

1. Classify this debenture as debt or equity. Explain your reasoning.
2. Provide the entry to record issuance of the debenture.
3. What amount(s) pertaining to this debenture will be shown on the balance sheet at the end of the second year (after adjustments)? Sui uses effective interest amortization.
4. Give the entry to record conversion to common shares at maturity. The average market value of common shares at this time was $62.
5. Suppose instead that the $2,000,000 debenture was convertible into common shares using a value of 105% of the average market value of common shares in the five trading days prior to conversion. Explain how that difference would affect your treatment of the debenture. Calculations are not necessary.

 A14-10 Convertible Debt, Issuer's Option: BT Corporation issued $5,000,000 of convertible bonds on 1 January with the following terms:

- Bonds mature in five years' time.
- Annual interest, 6%, is paid each 31 December.
- Bonds are convertible to 400,000 common shares at maturity, or can be repaid in cash, at BT's option.

Current market interest rates are 6%. The bond sells for par.

Required:

1. Calculate the present value of the bond at the market interest rate of 6%. Assign a value to the interest and the principal portions of the bond.
2. Provide the journal entry to record issuance of the bond.
3. Provide a schedule to show interest expense and amortization of the liability over the life of the bond.
4. How much is charged to retained earnings because of the principal portion of the bond in the first year? Calculate the charge for each year of the bond's life and the balance of the equity account at maturity.
5. Provide the journal entry that would be recorded at maturity if common shares were issued. Also provide the entry that would be made if cash were paid.

 A14-11 Convertible Bonds, Investor's Option: Montreal Limited was authorized to issue $10 million of 10-year, 7½% convertible bonds due 31 December 20X12. Bond interest is paid semi-annually, each 30 June and 31 December. Each $1,000 bond is convertible into

25 shares of Montreal's no-par common stock, at the investor's option, at any time beginning on 1 January 20X10. Other information is as follows:

- The bonds were sold in a public offering on 1 July 20X5, for $11,450,000. The market interest rate was 8% on the day of issue. On this date, there were 7.5 years until maturity.
- Any discount or premium is to be amortized using the effective interest method.
- On 1 January 20X9, the Board of Directors authorized a 3-for-2 stock dividend, recorded in memorandum form only. In accordance with the terms of the bond indenture, the conversion ratio for the bond was adjusted accordingly.
- On 1 January 20X10, $3,000,000 of the bonds converted to common shares.

Required:

1. Record the bond issuance on 1 July 20X5.
2. How many shares would each $1,000 bond receive after the stock split?
3. Record the bond conversion on 1 January 20X10. Indicate the number of shares issued.
4. Show the values on the balance sheet immediately after the conversion. Assume that the common share account had a balance of $35,000,000 prior to the conversion.

★★ **A14-12 Convertible Bond, Investor's Option:** Bixon Corp. Ltd. issued convertible bonds payable on 1 January 20X1, when the market interest rate was 10%. The bond indenture stated:

> $7,500,000 of 8% subordinated convertible debentures payable, interest payable semi-annually, convertible at the investor's option in 10 years' time into class A common shares of the company at the rate of 70 shares for each $1,000 bond issued.

The bonds were issued for net proceeds of $7,400,000.

Required:

1. At what price would the bonds be issued if they were not convertible?
2. How could the option be valued?
3. Provide the entry to record issuance of the bond on 1 January 20X1.
4. Provide the journal entry to record interest payment and interest expense on 30 June 20X1. Use the effective interest method to record discount amortization.
5. Provide the entry to record bond conversion to common shares at maturity, on 31 December 20X10.
6. Assume instead that the bond was repaid at maturity. Provide all entries to record the repayment/bond maturity.

★★★ **A14-13 Convertible Bonds—Classification:** You are the assistant to the vice-president of finance for a Canadian public company that manufactures and distributes food products.

The company issued convertible debentures in 20X6, at 101. These $15,000,000 convertible debentures are described as follows:

a. The adjustable rate convertible subordinated debentures, Series 1, due 1 April 20X18, bear interest at a rate that is the greater of 5%, or 1% plus the percentage that two times the common share dividend paid in the previous six months is of the conversion price.
b. The debentures are convertible at the holders' option into common shares of the company at a conversion price of $35 per common share, on or before the last business day prior to the maturity date of the debentures or the last business day prior to redemption.

Required:

1. How should the debenture be classified? Justify your conclusion.

2. Assume that the bond, if not convertible, would have sold for $13,200,000. Provide the initial entry to record the issuance.

3. Assume that option pricing models indicate that the option was worth $2,600,000. Repeat requirement (2) using the proportionate method.

4. Provide the appropriate entry at maturity assuming that (a) the bonds were all converted into common shares, and (b) the bonds were paid out in cash. Assume that the bond was initially recorded as in requirement (3).

★★ **A14-14 Convertible Bond—Alternatives:** APT Limited is considering raising needed capital in the money market, and has two bond options under consideration:

> **Bond #1** $20,000,000 6% 10-year bond, interest paid semi-annually. At maturity, the bond may be repaid in cash or converted to 110,000 APT common shares at APT's option.

> **Bond #2** $20,000,000 5¾% 10-year bond, interest paid semi-annually. At any time after the fifth year, the bond may be repaid in cash or converted to 110,000 APT common shares at the investor's option.

Bond #1 and Bond #2 are expected to sell at par. Bond #2 would sell for $19,628,000 without the conversion option, reflecting a market interest rate of 6%.

Required:

1. Provide a journal entry to record the issuance of each bond.

2. Calculate interest expense and/or the capital charge to equity for each bond for the first 12 months. Use effective interest amortization.

3. Provide the entry to record the conversion of bond #2 to common stock at the end of its eighth year.

★★★ **A14-15 Convertible Debt, Comprehensive Scenarios:** NewTech Ltd. has a 31 December fiscal year-end. The company issued convertible bonds on 1 July 20X4. The $5,000,000 bonds pay annual interest of 8% each 30 June and mature on 30 June 20X19. At the investor's option, each $1,000 bond is convertible into 50 shares of common stock on the bond's maturity date.

Bond market analysts indicated that if the bonds had not been convertible, they would likely have sold for $4,597,000. They were in fact issued for $5,350,000.

Required:

1. Provide the journal entry to record the initial issuance of the bond.

2. Provide the entry to record interest at 31 December 20X4, using the effective interest method. (Hint: you will need the IRR implicit in the bond price.)

3. Assume that, at the time of issuance, an option pricing model indicated that the conversion feature was likely worth $900,000. Using this and the $4,597,000 price for the bond, repeat requirement (1).

4. Assume that, instead of being convertible at the investor's option, the bond was convertible at the issuer's option at the current market price of the common shares on the maturity date. Explain what difference this would make to your response to requirements 1 and 2. No calculations are needed; explain only.

5. Assume that, instead of being convertible at the investor's option, the bond was convertible at the issuer's option at the set price of $50 per share. Explain what difference this would make to your response to requirements (1) and (2). No calculations are needed; explain only.

★★★ **A14-16 Convertible Debt, Three Cases:** The following cases are independent:

Case A

On 1 January 20X5, MediaCom Limited issued a financial instrument:

> Bonds payable, $6,000,000, 8%, due in 20 years' time. The bonds pay interest semi-annually each 30 June and 31 December. The bonds were issued at par. The bonds are convertible at the company's option into common shares at the rate of six shares for each $100 bond, but not until they have been outstanding eight years. The company may, at its discretion, repay the bond for cash in lieu of shares.

Required:

What would appear on the income statement and balance sheet with respect to the bonds for the year ended 31 December 20X5? Provide accounts and amounts. The company uses the effective interest method.

Case B

On the 31 October 20X4 balance sheet, ABC Company reported the following:

Debt		
Convertible bond payable, 10%,		
due 31 October 20X7	$4,000,000	
Less: discount	(371,468)	
		$3,628,532
Equity		
Contributed capital: common share		
conversion rights		$ 345,000

Interest is paid *annually* on 31 October and the bonds were originally valued to yield 14%.

Required:

Provide entries on 31 October 20X5 to record interest and show the conversion of the bonds to common shares on this date. Use the effective interest method to record discount amortization. The bond was converted into 500,000 common shares.

Case C

On 1 November 20X4, ABC Company issued a convertible bond with the following terms:

1. $6,500,000 par value, 7% interest paid semi-annually on 1 November and 1 May.
2. Convertible in 15 years time into 795,000 common shares at the investor's option.

The bond sold for $6,400,000 when the market interest rate was 8%.

Required:

Provide entries on issuance and on 31 December 20X4, ABC's year-end. The company uses effective interest method for bond discount.

★★★ **A14-17 Convertible Debt, Issuer versus Investor Option:** AMC Limited issued five-year, 8% bonds for their par value of $500,000 on 1 January 20X1. Interest is paid annually. The bonds were convertible to common shares at the rate of 50 common shares for every $1,000 bond.

Required:

1. Assume that the bonds were convertible at the investor's option and that the conversion option was valued at $37,908.
    a. Provide the journal entry on issuance.
    b. Calculate interest expense for each year of the bond's five-year life. Use an interest rate of 10% for this requirement.
    c. Provide the journal entry to record maturity of the bond assuming shareholders convert their bonds to common shares.

2. Assume that the bonds were convertible at the option of AMC Ltd.
    a. Calculate the portion of the original proceeds relating to principal and interest.
    b. Provide the journal entry on issuance.
    c. Calculate interest expense for each year of the bond's five-year life.
    d. Calculate the charge to retained earnings for each year of the bond's five-year life.
    e. Provide the journal entry to record maturity of the bond assuming shareholders convert their bonds to common shares.

 A14-18 Debt with Warrants Attached: Ferguson Memorials Limited issued a $1,000,000, 5% annual interest non-convertible bond with detachable stock purchase warrants. One warrant is attached to each $1,000 bond and allows the holder to buy two common shares for $28 each at any time over the next 10 years. The existing market price of Ferguson shares is $18. The bond issue sells for 104.

Required:

1. Assume that, shortly after the bond is issued, bonds alone are selling for 102. Record the issuance of the bond.

2. Repeat requirement (1) assuming that there is no market value for the bond but that warrants begin to trade for $32 each.

3. Repeat requirement (1) assuming that warrants are selling for $32 each and the bond alone is selling for 102.

4. What is the difference between a convertible bond and a bond with detachable warrants?

5. Assume that the warrants were recorded as in requirement (1). Further assume that 60% of the warrants are exercised and the remaining 40% are allowed to lapse. Provide journal entries to record the exercise and lapse.

 A14-19 Stock Rights—Identification: In each of the cases below, indicate whether the stock rights would be recognized or simply disclosed (memorandum entries).

1. Rights issued to a lawyer who provided services worth $10,000 on the incorporation of the company.

2. Warrants issued with bonds.

3. Rights issued for fractional shares on a stock dividend recorded at market value.

4. Rights embedded in convertible debt.

5. Rights issued to all employees of a company allowing them to buy limited numbers of shares at 98% of current fair market value.

6. Rights issued to existing shareholders as a poison pill, to discourage takeover bids for the company.

7. Rights issued to senior executives as part of a stock option plan: the exercise price is equal to the current market value on the date of grant.

8. Rights issued to existing shareholders to allow them to buy a *pro rata* number of shares in connection with a new issuance of common shares to the public.

A14-20 Rights—Recognition: Maritime Corp. is a junior mining company on the Toronto Stock Exchange. The common share price of Maritime fluctuates in value. Recent swings went from a high of $16 to a low of $0.30. Maritime issued stock rights on 1 September 20X5 to a consultant, in exchange for a project completed over the last year. The consultant estimated her time was worth $37,000, but the company estimated that it could have had the necessary work done for about $31,000 cash. The rights specified that 4,000 common shares could be bought for $0.20 per share at any time over the next 20 years. The market price of common shares was $1.50 on the day the rights were issued. At the same time options were issued to the consultant, identical rights were issued to the company president, under an employee stock option plan. The options were vested immediately. An option pricing model valued each set of stock options of $35,000.

Required:

1. Provide journal entries to record issuance of the two sets of rights. Justify values used.
2. Assume that, two years later, when the market price of the shares was $14, the consultant exercised her rights. Provide the appropriate entry.
3. Assume that, 10 years later, when the market price of the shares was $0.10, the president's rights expired. Provide the entry, if any.

 A14-21 Stock Options: HGTL Corporation has a stock option incentive plan for its top managers. It includes the following terms:

a. Each manager who qualifies receives the right to buy 5,000 HGTL common shares at an option price of $12 per share.
b. The option is non-transferable and expires five years from the issuance date.
c. The option cannot be exercised until three years from the issuance date.

Manager Houle was given such an option award on 1 January 20X5. He exercised his options on 1 January 20X8. An option pricing model indicated that the options were worth $36,000 on 1 January 20X5. The market value of common shares was $12 on 1 January 20X5.

Required:
Provide entries to record the option at the date of grant, the exercise date, and any other annual entries needed with relation to the grant.

 A14-22 Stock Options: Ming Limited has an executive stock option plan as follows: Each qualified manager will receive, on 1 January, an option for the computed number of common shares at a computed price. The number of option shares and the option price are determined by the Board of Directors, with advice from the compensation committee.

The options are non-transferable. They must be held for two years prior to exercise, and expire six years after the date of issuance. An individual must be an employee of the company on the exercise date in order to exercise the options.

On 1 January 20X3, manager Smoke was given options for 1,200 shares at $60. Option pricing models produced a value for the option of $30,000 on 1 January 20X3. The market value of common shares was $12 on 1 January 20X3. Ms Smoke exercised 1,000 of the options on 3 January 20X6. She did not exercise the remaining 200 options because she left the company late in 20X6.

Required:
Provide all entries relating to Ms Smoke's options.

 A14-23 Stock Options: Cambello Corporation is authorized to issue unlimited numbers of common shares, of which 75,000 have been issued at an average price of $75 per share. On 1 January 20X3, the company granted 2,000 stock options to each of its three senior executives. The stock options provide that each individual will be eligible to purchase, no earlier than 31 December 20X7, 2,000 common shares at a base option price of $140 per share. The options are non-transferable.

One individual who received the options exercised the options on 31 December 20X7, when the share price was $167. The second individual did not exercise her options. The share price fell to $105 in 20X8 and her options lapsed. The third individual left the company in early 20X6 and his options were forfeit.

Required:

Prepare the entries to record the granting of the options and the exercising, lapsing, and forfeit. Assume that all the options together were valued at $90,000 when issued.

★★ **A14-24 Stock Appreciation Rights:** TVest Co. issues 500,000 SARs to its eight-member top management group. These SARs allow the managers to receive either shares or cash, at their choice, after holding the SARs for five years. The value of the SARs is calculated as the difference between the $38 per share fair market value of 500,000 common shares on the date the SARs were issued, and the fair market value on the date of exercise.

Market values of common shares at the end of year 1, $42; year 2, $39; year 3, $40; year 4, $55; and year 5, $57.

Required:

1. Why are SARs issued instead of common stock options?
2. How much compensation expense would be recorded in each of years 1 to 5?
3. What would appear on the balance sheet at the end of each of years 1 to 4?
4. What entry would be made on the maturity of the SARs, assuming the managers elected to take cash?
5. What entry would be made on the maturity of the SARs, assuming the managers elected to take shares?
6. Describe how the accounting for this compensation scheme would be different if the company, rather than the managers, could decide whether to issue cash or shares for the compensation at maturity.

★ **A14-25 Long-Term Compensation:** Able Co. had compensation plans in effect for senior managers that included three long-term compensation elements. Balance sheet accounts at the end of 20X4:

Liability—Deferred performance units	$320,000
10,000 units outstanding to managers; units have been outstanding for two years and must be held for three more years until payment.	
Liability—SARs plan	$ 70,000
40,000 shares are under SARs agreement, where the reference share price is $45 and the current market value of shares is $52; the SARs have been outstanding for one year and must be held for a total of four years before exercise.	
Contributed capital—employee share options outstanding	$336,000
35,000 shares are under option at an exercise price of $42. The options were valued using a binomial valuation model and determined to be worth $560,000. The options have been outstanding for three years and must be held for a total of five years before they can be exercised.	

Required:

1. Describe the likely features of the three kinds of compensation plans Able appears to offer.

2. Assume no new compensation entitlements were offered in 20X5. The deferred performance units were valued at $86 per unit in 20X5, and the common share price was $60. Give the entries to record compensation expense related to the above plans.

★★ **A14-26 Long-Term Compensation:** Mercury Limited issued long-term compensation contracts as follows:

1. Mercury issued 40,000 SARs to its three top executives at the beginning of 20X3. These SARS allow the executives to receive either shares or cash, at their choice, after holding the SARs for three years. The value of the SARs is calculated as the difference between the market value of common shares on the date the SARs were issued, or $16, and the market value on the date of exercise. All executives exercised their SARs at the end of 20X5 and elected to receive cash.

2. Mercury issued 40,000 SARs to its three top executives at the beginning of 20X3. These SARS allow the executives to receive either shares or cash, at Mercury's choice, after holding the SARs for three years. The value of the SARs is calculated as the difference between the market value of common shares on the date the SARs were issued, or $16, and the market value on the date of exercise. The SARs were valued at $210,000 using an option pricing model. The value of the SARs was paid out in shares in 20X5.

3. Mercury issued long-term compensation units at the beginning of 20X3, to be paid out in cash after four years. The 25,000 units issued are valued annually based on balanced scorecard metrics. At the end of 20X3, each unit is estimated to be worth $8; and then $9 (20X4), $13 (20X5), and $16 (20X6).

4. Mercury issued long-term compensation units at the beginning of 20X3, to be paid out in shares after four years. The 20,000 units issued are valued annually based on balanced scorecard metrics. At the end of 20X3, each unit is estimated to be worth $8; and then $9 (20X4), $13 (20X5), and $16 (20X6). All units were paid out in shares. An option pricing model valued the compensation units at $260,000 in 20X3.

Market values of common shares at the end of 20X3, $19; 20X4, $24; and 20X5, $22.

Required:

1. Provide the journal entries for 20X3, 20X4, and 20X5.
2. What would appear on the balance sheet at the end of 20X4?

★★ **A14-27 Sale of Shares, Share Rights Issued, and Some Lapses—Entries:** Snowden Corporation has outstanding 100,000 common shares, no-par value. On 15 January 20X4, the company announced its decision to sell an additional 50,000 unissued common shares at $15 per share and to give the current shareholders first chance to buy shares proportionally equivalent to the number now held. To facilitate this plan, on 1 February 20X4, each shareholder was issued one right for each common share currently held. Two rights must be submitted to acquire one additional share for $15. Rights not exercised lapse on 30 June 20X4.

Required:

1. Give any entry or memorandum that should be made in the accounts of Snowden Corporation on each of the following dates:
   a. 1 February 20X4, issuance of all the rights. At this date, the shares of Snowden Corporation were quoted on the stock market at $15.50 per share.
   b. 27 June 20X4, exercise of 98% of the rights issued.
   c. 30 June 20X4, the remaining rights outstanding lapsed.
2. Repeat requirement (1) assuming that the rights were sold by the company for $62,000 to outside investors on 1 February 20X4.

★ ★ ★ **A14-28 Share Rights and Warrants:** On 31 December 20X2, the shareholders' equity section of Morristown Corporations' balance sheet was as follows:

Common shares, no-par, unlimited shares authorized, issued and outstanding, 4,543,400 shares	$16,876,400
Contributed capital: common share warrants outstanding, 12,300 warrants allowing purchase of three shares each at a price of $26 per share	110,000
Contributed capital: employee share options outstanding	161,000
Retained earnings	34,560,900
Total shareholders' equity	$51,708,300

There were 46,000 options outstanding to employees allowing purchase of one share each for $19; the options were exercisable at a variety of dates.

TRANSACTIONS DURING THE YEAR:

a. Options were issued to existing shareholders as a poison pill in the case of a hostile take-over. Options allowing purchase of two shares for each existing share held at a price of $1 each were issued, to be exercisable only under certain limited conditions.

b. Warrants outstanding at the beginning of the year were exercised in full. The market value of the shares was $40.

c. Employees exercised some outstanding $19 share options and 10,000 shares were issued. Remaining employee share options were not exercised in the current year. The market value of the shares was $40.

d. A 10% stock dividend was declared and issued, resulting in the issuance of 458,000 shares and 10,300 fractional share rights for a total of 1,030 shares issued. The dividend was valued at market value, $42 per share. Each fractional share right had a market value of $4.20.

e. Of the fractional share rights, 8,300 were exercised and 2,000 were allowed to lapse.

f. Options were issued for proceeds of $45,000, allowing purchase of 40,000 shares at a price of $35 per share.

g. One-quarter of the options issued in (f), above, was exercised. The market value of the shares was $48.

h. At the beginning of the year, options were granted to employees allowing purchase of 25,000 shares at $48, the current market value. The options are exercisable in six years. The fair value of the options was $72,000.

Required:

1. Provide journal entries for each of the transactions listed above.

2. Prepare the shareholders' equity section of the balance sheet, reflecting the transactions recorded in requirement (1).

3. What items would appear on the cash flow statement in the financing activities section as a result of the changes in the equity accounts documented in requirement (2)?

★ **A14-29 Derivatives:** Treetoo Limited wishes to buy 10,000 shares of YCo, a publicly traded company. Treetoo enters into a contract, through a broker, to buy the shares in 40 days at a price of $3 per share, the current fair value. The broker requires a 10% margin to be maintained at all times. After 10 days, at the fiscal year-end, the price of the YCo shares is $4 per share, and is $4.50 per share at the end of 40 days. At that time the shares are purchased and the contract is closed out.

Required:

1. Is this a forward contract or a futures contract? Explain.

2. What risk is the company hedging?

3. Prepare journal entries to record the inception of the contract, the change in its fair value at year-end and the additional margin payment, and its maturity.

⭐ **A14-30 Derivatives:** Starco Corp. wishes to purchase 5,000 shares of Gertrom Ltd., a publicly traded company. Starco contracts to buy the shares from a related party, Unit Ltd., for $62 per share in 90 days' time. The fair value was $62 per share on this day. One month later, at year-end, the fair value of the Gertrom shares is $54 per share, and it is $55 per share at the end of 90 days. At that time, the shares are bought and the contract is closed out.

Required:

1. Is this a forward contract or a futures contract? Explain.
2. What risk is the company hedging?
3. Prepare journal entries to record the inception of the contract, the change in its fair value at year-end, and its maturity.

⭐ **A14-31 Derivatives:** Notting Hill Limited issued a $10 million, 6% bond in 20X2 at par. The treasury group at Notting Hill would have preferred a blend of fixed and floating rate financing, but the floating rate financing offered was at rate of 7%, based on current market interest rates. Accordingly, the company locked in the 6% fixed rate bond financing. Notting Hill entered into an interest rate swap for half of the interest obligation, effectively turning $5 million of principal into floating rate financing.

Required:

1. Explain how a swap changes the fixed financing cost to a partially floating rate.
2. What risk is the company hedging?
3. Assume that the value of the swap increases after being held for one year. Why would this happen? What financial statement elements would be recorded?

⭐⭐⭐ **A14-32 Equity, Comprehensive:** Acer Corporation reported the following balances in shareholder's equity at 1 January 20X1:

Share equity—8% bonds ($10,000,000 par value). Bonds are convertible at maturity into common shares at the company's option.	$ 5,002,490
Convertible $8, no-par preferred shares, 60,000 shares outstanding; convertible into 8 common shares for every 3 preferred shares outstanding.	6,060,000
Class A no-par common shares, unlimited shares authorized, 915,000 issued and 899,000 outstanding	32,940,000
Common share warrants, allowing purchase of 90,000 shares at $32.50	660,000
Contributed capital: employee share options outstanding*	160,000
Contributed capital on preferred share retirement	55,000
Retained earnings	116,300,000
Less: Treasury shares, 16,000 common shares	(512,000)

*Forty thousand common stock options are outstanding to certain employees allowing purchase of one share for every two options held at a price of $27.50 per share. These options are vested and expire in 20X4.

The following events took place in 20X1:

a. Common shares were issued to employees under the terms of existing outstanding share options. 16,000 options were exercised when the share market value was $45.

b. Options were issued in exchange for a piece of land, appraised at $75,000. The options allow purchase of 100,000 shares at $15 each in five years' time. The market value of the shares was $46 on this date. The option was valued at $71,000 using the Black-Scholes option pricing model.

c. 40,000 common shares were acquired and retired at a price of $47 each.

d. 10,000 treasury shares were acquired at a price of $44 per share.

e. A cash dividend was declared and paid. The annual dividend for the preferred shares and $1 per share for the common shares were both declared and paid.

f. 24,000 preferred shares were converted to common shares.

g. The annual capital charge on the share equity 8% bonds was recorded.

h. Two-thirds of the common share warrants outstanding at the beginning of the year were exercised when the market value of the shares was $49.50; the remainder lapsed.

i. Options were granted to employees at the beginning of the year, allowing purchase of one share for every two options held at a price of $35. Fifty thousand options were issued. These options become vested at the beginning of 20X5. The fair value of the options was $720,000.

j. 10,000 preferred shares were retired for $107 each.

k. 20,000 treasury shares were sold for $32 each.

l. A 10% stock dividend was declared and issued. Treasury shares were not eligible for the stock dividend. The Board of Directors decided that the stock dividend should be valued at $30 per share. Most of the dividend was issued in whole shares; however, 41,000 fractional shares allowing acquisition of 4,100 whole shares were issued.

Required:

1. Provide journal entries (or memo entries) for the events listed.

2. Calculate the closing balance in each of the equity accounts at 31 December 20X1, reflecting the entries in requirement (1). Net income for the year was $6,200,000.

★★★ **A14-33 Cash Flow Statement—Individual Transactions:** The following cases are independent:

Case A

Information from the 31 December 20X5 balance sheet of Holdco Limited:

	20X5	20X4
Bonds payable	$5,000,000	$ —
Discount on bonds payable	234,000	—
Common stock conversion rights	695,000	—

Convertible bonds were issued during the year. Discount amortization was $14,000 in 20X5.

Case B

Information from the 31 December 20X5 balance sheet of Sellco Limited:

	20X5	20X4
Bonds payable	$ 5,000,000	$10,000,000
Discount on bonds payable	160,000	346,000
Common stock conversion rights	695,000	1,390,000
Common shares	$17,000,000	7,100,000

One-half of the bonds converted to common shares during the period. Other common shares were issued for cash. Discount amortization during the year was $26,000.

Case C

Information from the 31 December 20X5 balance sheet of Buyco Limited:

	20X5	**20X4**
Stock rights outstanding	$ 240,000	$ 295,000
Common shares	9,000,000	6,550,000

During the year, 10,000 stock rights originally valued at a price of $5.50 were exercised, and 10,000 common shares were issued for the exercise price of $14. One million stock rights, allowing existing shareholders to acquire common shares at one-tenth the then-current fair value in the event of hostile takeover, were also issued during the year. Other common shares were sold for cash.

Case D

Information from the 31 December 20X5 balance sheet of Bothco Limited:

	20X5	**20X4**
Bonds payable	$ —	$10,000,000
Discount on bonds payable	—	26,450
Common stock conversion rights	—	1,390,000
Contributed capital, lapse of conversion right	1,390,000	—

Bonds payable matured in the year, but were redeemed in cash at par, and not converted.

Required:

For each case, indicate appropriate disclosure on the cash flow statement. Be sure to state whether an item is classified in the operating, investing, or financing sections. Assume use of the indirect method of presentation for the operating section.

CHAPTER 15

Accounting for Corporate Income Tax

INTRODUCTION

Suncor Energy Inc. reported 2005 pre-tax earnings of $1,987 million. The company had to pay $39 million to the government in income taxes. Yet the income statement showed income tax expense of $742 million. On the right side of Suncor's balance sheet, the second largest single item (after retained earnings) was a *future income tax* liability of $3,545 million, amounting to 21% of total assets or 41% of net assets. How did Suncor avoid paying so much income tax in 2005 and instead report $3.5 billion in long-term tax liabilities?

Accounting for corporate income tax might seem rather straightforward. After all, the exact amount of income tax for each year is computed on the corporation's income tax return. Why is income tax expense usually different (and sometimes vastly different) from the actual taxes paid in a year?

The difference arises from an accounting practice known as *interperiod income tax allocation*. There are some revenues and expenses that are recognized in one year on the tax return but in other years for accounting purposes. Using tax allocation, the income tax expense recognized for any one year is based on the revenues and expenses recognized for accounting purposes in that same period, regardless of what amount is calculated on the tax return as that year's tax liability. As a result, a company's income tax *expense* usually differs from the amount of tax actually *payable* to the government. The difference between income tax expense and income tax payable results in an account known as *future income tax liability* (or *asset*).

There are two distinct but interacting aspects of interperiod income tax allocation. The first arises when the tax basis for assets and liabilities is different from the carrying value for accounting. That issue is the subject of this chapter.

The second aspect of interperiod income tax allocation relates to the recognition of future benefits of tax loss carryforwards. This aspect is explored in the following chapter.

One other aspect of accounting for income taxation is the *investment tax credit*, a special tax provision intended to encourage certain types of capital investment by businesses. This specialized topic is discussed in the Appendix to this chapter.

One important note about the chapter title: only corporations are subject to income tax because only corporations are recognized as legal entities. The profits of partnerships and proprietorships are taxed to the owners. Income tax expense does not appear on the financial statements of either partnerships or proprietorships.

INCOME TAX PROVISION VERSUS EXPENSE

provision for income tax

the expense (or recovery) of income tax charged to the income statement

It is common in practice for companies to label income tax expense in the income statement as the **provision for income tax.** This is a somewhat confusing label because we usually use "provision" to indicate an estimated liability, such as "Provision for Warranty Costs" in the liabilities section of a balance sheet.

Companies use the term "provision" for income tax expense because when a company has a loss for tax purposes, the income statement entry for income tax may be a credit rather than a debit. Rather than switch the income statement label from "expense" to "benefit," companies use the vague term "provision" to fit all circumstances. This practice might be viewed as sloppy terminology, but it is not apt to cause confusion to readers and it is easier to use.

In this book, in order to avoid confusion between the income statement item and the tax liability, we henceforth will typically use the title "income tax expense," even when the expense is a credit (i.e., a benefit).

INTERPERIOD TAX ALLOCATION—INTRODUCTION

Interperiod tax allocation deals with allocating tax expense to an appropriate year, irrespective of when it is actually paid. A company adopts those accounting policies that management perceives will best satisfy the objectives of financial statement users and preparers. One broad objective of accounting standards and accounting policies is to measure net income, which usually is the result of many accruals, interperiod allocations, and estimates. In contrast, the major objective of the *Income Tax Act* and Regulations is to generate revenue for the government.

Because it is easier and more objective to assess tax when cash is flowing, tax policy generally includes revenues and expenses in taxable income on the basis of cash flows rather than accounting allocations. Some important exceptions relate primarily to inventories, capital assets, and multiperiod earnings processes (e.g., revenue from long-term contracts), but cash flows are crucial. In addition, the *Income Tax Act* exempts certain types of income from taxation and prohibits the deduction of certain types of expenses.

Differences between Taxable and Accounting Income

Both accounting income and taxable income are the net result of matching revenues and expenses (and gains and losses) of a period. Most items of revenue and expense are recognized in the same period for both accounting and tax purposes. But there are some differences. These differences can be categorized as:

- Permanent differences;
- Temporary differences.

permanent differences

wherein an item enters into the reconciliation of taxable income but does not create future income tax; can be a revenue, gain, expense, or loss

Permanent Differences A **permanent difference**[1] arises when an income statement element—a revenue, gain, expense, or loss—enters the computation of either taxable income or pre-tax accounting income but never enters into the computation of the other. For example, dividend income received from another tax-paying Canadian corporation is included in accounting income but is not included in taxable income. Such dividends are tax-exempt revenue. They are a permanent difference because they are not subject to taxation.

Similarly, a company may sell land that it has held for a long time. Since land is a capital asset, the gain from selling the land is known as a *capital gain* for tax purposes. The full amount of the gain will be recognized on the company's income statement, but only 50% of

---

[1] The term "permanent differences" does not appear in accounting standards. Instead, standards refer to these types of tax-accounting difference as "other than temporary differences"— a negative definition because the definition explains what the difference is *not*. *Permanent differences* is the usual name that is used in accounting practice, for greater simplicity and clarity.

a capital gain is included in taxable income. Therefore, the 50% of a capital gain that is *not* taxed is a permanent difference.

Certain types of expense are not deductible for tax purposes. A common example is golf club dues paid by a corporation. The *Income Tax Act* specifically identifies golf club dues as non-deductible for tax purposes, but they are a legitimate expense if the corporation believes they should be part of, say, a sales or marketing effort. Therefore, the difference between pre-tax accounting income and taxable income that arises from golf club dues is a permanent difference.

There also may be deductions that are allowed in computing taxable income that have no equivalent for accounting income. In some years, for example, companies have been permitted to deduct tax depreciation, called capital cost allowance or CCA, based on an amount higher than the cost basis of the assets (e.g., the CCA rate could be based on 150% of the specified asset's cost). Since accounting depreciation expense can never exceed 100% of an asset's cost, the excess CCA was a permanent difference.

temporary differences

wherein an item of revenue, expense, gain, or loss arises in determining accounting income in one period and taxable income in another period; creates future income tax on the balance sheet; determined by comparing accounting balance sheet carrying values with tax values (a balance sheet approach)

Temporary Differences A **temporary difference** arises when the tax basis of an asset or liability differs from its accounting carrying value. Temporary differences can also be called **timing differences**; the distinction is whether the underlying tax treatment is described with reference to the resulting income statement (timing) effect, or balance sheet (temporary) effect. A temporary difference originates in the period in which it first enters the computation of either taxable income or accounting income, and reverses in the subsequent period when that item enters into the computation of the other measure. An item can either:

- be included in accounting income first, and then included in taxable income in a subsequent period, or
- enter into the calculation of taxable income first, and then be included in accounting income in a later period.

Origination and Reversal Revenue on a long-term contract may be recognized on a percentage-of-completion basis for accounting purposes. For income tax purposes, the recognition of revenue can be delayed until the contract is completed, provided that the contract lasts no more than two years. The revenue recognized in the first year will enter into the determination of net income, thereby giving rise to an originating temporary difference. In the following year, assuming that the contract has been completed, the revenue (and related expenses) will be included in taxable income; including the revenue in taxable income reverses the temporary difference:

- A temporary difference is said to *originate* when the difference between accounting recognition and tax treatment first arises, or when a recurring temporary difference *increases* the accumulated balance of temporary differences.
- A temporary difference is said to *reverse* when the accumulated temporary differences are *reduced* by the "catch-up" recognition for tax and accounting.

Other Examples Another example is deferred development costs. For income tax purposes, development costs can be deducted when incurred. For financial reporting, however, the deferred development costs may be recognized in determining net income only in later periods, as amortization. The temporary difference relating to development costs originates when the costs are deducted on the tax return and reverses over several future years as the deferred costs are amortized for accounting purposes.

Similarly, temporary differences arise from the difference between accounting amortization and CCA deducted for tax purposes. This is the most complex example, because the temporary difference arises from the fact that the historical cost of the capital assets is being allocated simultaneously for accounting and tax purposes, but in different patterns. Straight-line amortization is commonly used for reporting purposes by Canadian corporations, but CCA usually follows a declining-balance pattern of allocation. The temporary difference arises not from the fact that amortization expense is deducted for tax purposes but not for accounting, but rather from the fact that the amortization expense usually is less than CCA in the early years of an asset's life, giving rise to *originating* temporary differences. In later years, as CCA declines, the straight-line amortization becomes larger than CCA and the temporary difference *reverses*. The CCA/amortization temporary difference is the most common type of temporary difference.

Exhibit 15-1 lists some of the more common types of permanent differences and temporary differences.

EXHIBIT 15-1

EXAMPLES OF PERMANENT AND TEMPORARY DIFFERENCES

Permanent Differences

- Dividends received by Canadian corporations from other taxable Canadian corporations
- Equity in earnings of significantly influenced investees
- 50% of capital gains
- Golf club dues
- 50% of meals and entertainment expenses
- Interest and penalties on taxes
- Political contributions

Temporary Differences

- Amortization for accounting purposes; CCA for tax
- Amortization of capitalized development costs for accounting; immediate deduction for tax
- Amortization of capitalized interest for accounting; deducted when paid for tax
- Writedown of inventories or investments for accounting; loss recognized only when realized for tax
- Gains and losses on inventories valued at net realizable value for accounting; taxed when realized
- Instalment sales income recognized for accounting at time of sale; taxed when cash received
- Bad-debt expenses recognized in year of sale for accounting; tax deductible when uncollectible
- Percentage-of-completion accounting for contracts; completed contract reporting for tax (for contracts lasting no more than two years)
- Warranty costs accrued for accounting in period of sale; tax deductible when paid
- Bond discount or premium, amortized for accounting but taxable expense or revenue only when the principal is settled at maturity

---

CONCEPT REVIEW

1. Explain why accounting income is different from taxable income.

2. What is a permanent difference? Give an example.

3. A company deducts warranty expense in 20X0 on the income statement but pays warranty claims in 20X1. In what year does this temporary difference originate? In what year does it reverse?

CONCEPTUAL ISSUES IN INTERPERIOD TAX ALLOCATION

Interperiod income tax allocation has long been very contentious. Conceptually, there are three basic underlying issues:

1. The extent of allocation

2. The measurement method

3. Discounting

Before illustrating the mechanics of tax allocation, we will briefly address each of these three issues.

Extent of Allocation

Extent of allocation refers to the range of temporary differences to which interperiod tax allocation is applied. The three basic options are:

1. No allocation—the taxes payable method

2. Full allocation—the comprehensive tax allocation method

3. Partial tax allocation—the partial tax allocation method

taxes payable method

the method of accounting for income tax wherein income tax expense is recognized as the amount of income tax paid or payable for the current period; contrasted with tax allocation

Taxes Payable Method The **taxes payable method** recognizes the amount of taxes assessed in each year as the income tax expense for that year: income tax expense = current income tax. This is also known as the *flow-through method* because the actual taxes paid "flow through" to the income statement. Advocates of the taxes payable method argue that income tax is an aggregate measure, applied to the overall operations of the company as a whole, and that it is artificial to disaggregate the income tax amount as though each item of revenue and expense were taxed individually. As well, the taxes payable method corresponds with the actual cash outflow for income tax. If cash flow prediction is a primary objective of financial reporting, the taxes payable method may be superior to earnings measured by using full allocation.[2]

Viewed in the aggregate, temporary differences in a stable or growing company typically reverse and originate each year, with new originating temporary differences replacing those that are reversing. Taxes payable advocates argue that these aggregated temporary differences are "permanent" and will never result in a real cash flow. They also argue that the "future liability" that is created through tax allocation is not an obligation in the sense that the government does not view it as an amount currently owing.

comprehensive tax allocation

wherein all temporary differences are allocated between current and future periods regardless of likelihood or timing of reversal; temporary differences create future income tax on the balance sheet

Comprehensive Tax Allocation Those accountants who support **comprehensive tax allocation** are in the clear majority. They argue that a future cash flow impact arises from all temporary differences, no matter how far in the future that impact occurs. Tax "saved" this year via an early tax deduction will have to be "paid" in a future year when the expense is recognized for accounting but cannot be deducted for tax. Furthermore, they argue that it is a serious violation of the matching concept to recognize a revenue or expense in net income without simultaneously recognizing its inevitable future income tax effect. And while aggregate temporary differences may not decline, the individual temporary differences that make up the aggregate do in fact reverse, even if they are replaced by new temporary differences.

---

[2] On the other hand, one research study suggests that "deferred tax information leads to superior forecasts of future tax payments and that deferred tax data enhance prediction of future cash flows." Joseph K. Cheung, Gopal V. Krishnan, and Chung-ki Min, "Does Interperiod Income Tax Allocation Enhance Prediction of Cash Flows?", *Accounting Horizons* (December 1997), pp. 1–15.

Partial Tax Allocation Partial tax allocation takes the middle ground by arguing that some temporary differences merit allocation while others do not. While the recommended criteria may vary, the general idea is that material non-recurring temporary differences that are likely to reverse in the near future should be accorded tax allocation.

On the other hand, temporary differences that are recurring or that are uncertain of reversal should not be subject to allocation. Recurring temporary differences (such as NBV/UCC) create no "real" future cash flow impact because they net out—e.g., the CCA on newly purchased assets offsets declining CCA on old assets. Non-recurring temporary differences that may not reverse in the foreseeable future should not be subject to tax allocation because the cash flow timing and measurement are uncertain.

Canadian Reporting Requirements Canadian and international GAAP require comprehensive allocation for all public and publicly accountable corporations. Private corporations can elect to use differential reporting if all of their shareholders agree. The taxes payable method is used under differential reporting, as will be discussed near the end of this chapter.

Example The following example illustrates the two tax allocation bases—comprehensive tax allocation and the taxes payable method—that are now found in Canada.

A corporation has pre-tax income in each of three years of $1,000,000. Included in income in the first year is a gain of $600,000 that is not taxable until the third year. That is, there is a gain on the 20X1 income statement that will not be taxed until the money is collected in 20X3. This means that there is an account receivable of $600,000 on the accounting books. The tax basis of this account receivable is zero. Taxable income therefore will be $400,000 in 20X1, $1,000,000 in 20X2, and $1,600,000 in 20X3. Assuming an income tax rate of 40%, the taxes due for each period are $160,000 in 20X1, $400,000 in 20X2, and $640,000 in 20X3. This information is summarized as follows:

	20X1	20X2	20X3
Income before taxes (accounting basis)	$1,000,000	$1,000,000	$1,000,000
20X1 accounting gain that is taxable in 20X3	− 600,000		+ 600,000
Taxable income	$ 400,000	$1,000,000	$1,600,000
Tax rate	× 40%	× 40%	× 40%
Income tax assessed for the year	$ 160,000	$ 400,000	$ 640,000

If the taxes payable method is used, each year's full tax assessment *flows through* to net income:

	20X1	20X2	20X3
Net income before income tax	$1,000,000	$1,000,000	$1,000,000
Income tax expense	160,000	400,000	640,000
Net income	$ 840,000	$ 600,000	$ 360,000

In the view of most accountants, matching to the year of assessment distorts net income because the income tax relating to the $600,000 gain is reported in 20X3, while the gain itself is reported in 20X1. The corporation's apparent net income has declined significantly from 20X1 through 20X3, but the difference is due solely to the fact that the tax on part of 20X1's net income tax is included in income tax expense for 20X3.

When the comprehensive tax allocation method is used, the $240,000 income tax impact of the $600,000 gain is recognized in the same period (for accounting purposes) as the gain itself:

	20X1	20X2	20X3
Income before income tax	$1,000,000	$1,000,000	$1,000,000
Income tax expense:			
Current	160,000	400,000	640,000
Future	240,000	—	(240,000)
	400,000	400,000	400,000
Net income	$ 600,000	$ 600,000	$ 600,000

The entry to record the income tax expense in each year is:

20X1
Income tax expense (I/S)	400,000	
Income tax payable (B/S)		160,000
Future income tax liability (B/S)		240,000

20X2
Income tax expense (I/S)	400,000	
Income tax payable (B/S)		400,000

20X3
Income tax expense (I/S)	400,000	
Future income tax liability (B/S)	240,000	
Income tax payable (B/S)		640,000

The future income tax liability will be shown on the balance sheet at the end of 20X1 and 20X2, and then is *drawn down in* 20X3 when the temporary difference *reverses* and the tax actually becomes due. Notice the distinction in terminology:

- A temporary difference *reverses*, while
- The future income tax liability/asset that relates to the temporary differences is *drawn down.*

CONCEPT REVIEW

1. What is the flow-through method of accounting for income tax expense?
2. Why does comprehensive tax allocation result in better matching?
3. What kinds of temporary differences are usually omitted in partial tax allocation?

Measurement Method

When the effects of temporary differences are measured, should the tax rate be:

1. The rate in effect at the time that the temporary difference *first arises* (the deferral method), or

2. The rate that is *expected to be in effect* when the temporary difference reverses (the liability method)?

This is the *measurement method* issue.

Deferral Method   The **deferral method** records the future tax impact by using the corporation's effective average tax rate in the year that the temporary difference first arises, or *originates*. Advocates of the deferral method argue that interperiod income tax allocation is simply a method of moving expense from one period to another, and that the best measure of that expense is the effect that it had in the year that the temporary difference originated. The implication of the deferral method is that the balance sheet credit (or debit) for future income taxes is simply a deferred credit (or deferred debit), and should not be accorded the status of a liability (or asset). Future income tax credits and debits on the balance sheet are simply a necessary result of matching and improving income measurement. Conceptually, the focus is on the income statement.

**liability method/
accrual method**

for corporate income tax; records the future tax impact of temporary differences by using the tax rate that will be in effect in the year of reversal; the future tax impact is recorded on the balance sheet, and is updated as the tax rates change

Liability Method   In contrast, the **liability** (or **accrual**) **method** uses the tax rate that will be in effect in the year of *reversal*. Proponents of this view argue that ultimate realization of the amount of the temporary difference depends on the tax rates in effect when the temporary differences reverse, and thus the amounts to be realized bear no necessary relationship to the tax rates in effect when they originated. Conceptually, the emphasis is on measurement of the future cash flow impact, and the future amount to be paid is viewed as a liability. The focus, therefore, is on the balance sheet.

How can the tax rate in the year of reversal be projected? Prediction of future tax rates is a very tenuous proposition, and might also tempt a company's management to use a high or low prediction that has a desired impact of increasing or decreasing net income. Therefore, the practical solution is that only *enacted* rates of tax will be used. Note that if this year's tax rate is 40%, and the tax rate for next year has already been enacted and is, say, 42%, then 42% is used to measure the balance in future income tax.

Effect of Tax Rates   In a world of stable tax rates, there would be no difference between the two methods. But tax rates are not always stable. Tax rates in Canada are subject to annual adjustment by the governments (federal and provincial), including the use of surtaxes (that is, an extra tax calculated as a percentage of the basic income tax at the statutory rate).

What happens when tax rates change? Under the deferral method, no consequence for tax allocation arises from a change in tax rates. In contrast, the liability method requires that the liability be adjusted to reflect each year's *best estimate* of the future tax liability arising from temporary differences. Therefore, every time there is a change in the corporate tax rate, companies must increase or decrease the balance sheet amount for the future tax liability or asset. The offset to the adjustment is the income tax expense in the income statement.

Canadian Reporting Requirements   The CICA Handbook requires the use of the liability method.

Example   In the earlier example, the tax rate was assumed to be constant throughout the three years. The problem becomes more interesting, however, if tax rates change while a temporary difference exists. We will illustrate the impact of the liability and deferral methods using the same example but with a modification in the tax rates:

- Net income before income taxes is $1,000,000 in each of 20X1, 20X2, and 20X3.

- A gain of $600,000 is included in accounting income in 20X1 but is not subject to tax until 20X3.
- The income tax rate in 20X1 is 40%; during 20X2, the rate is reduced by act of Parliament to 30%, which remains in effect for both 20X2 and 20X3.

The calculation of income tax payable under this revised scenario is as follows:

	20X1	20X2	20X3
Income before taxes (accounting basis)	$1,000,000	$1,000,000	$1,000,000
20X1 accounting gain that is taxable in 20X3	− 600,000		+ 600,000
Taxable income	$ 400,000	$1,000,000	$1,600,000
Tax rate	× 40%	× 30%	× 30%
Income tax payable	$ 160,000	$ 300,000	$ 480,000

Entries for the two methods are shown parallel:

Liability Method			**Deferral Method**		
20X1					
Income tax expense	400,000		Income tax expense	400,000	
Income tax payable		160,000	Income tax payable		160,000
Future income tax liability		240,000	Deferred income tax		240,000

The entries are identical except for the name of the future tax account. It is called deferred income tax under the deferral method, and is classified on the balance sheet between long-term liabilities and shareholders' equity.

Liability Method			**Deferral Method**		
20X2					
Future income tax liability	60,000				
Income tax expense	240,000		Income tax expense	300,000	
Income tax payable		300,000	Income tax payable		300,000

Using the liability method, the future income tax account must be adjusted to reflect the tax rate change. The temporary difference of $600,000 now will result in taxation of only $180,000 (that is, the $600,000 temporary difference × 30%) instead of $240,000 ($600,000 × 40%). Therefore, we must reduce the balance of the future income tax liability by $60,000. The tax expense recorded is the *net amount* of the payable ($300,000) and the reduction in future income tax ($60,000). The tax expense of $240,000 is an effective tax rate of 24%, which is neither the old rate nor the new rate. It is a residual.

Under the deferral method, deferred income tax balances are not changed when the tax rate changes, and the payable is all that is recorded.

Liability Method			Deferral Method		
20X3					
Income tax expense	300,000		Income tax expense	240,000	
Future income tax liability	180,000		Deferred income tax	240,000	
Income tax payable		480,000	Income tax payable		480,000

In 20X3, the temporary difference is reversed because the gain enters taxable income. The future income tax or deferred income tax is reversed at its carrying value, $180,000 or $240,000, respectively. This time, the tax expense for the deferral method is the residual.

Note that the differences in the two methods relate to the adjustment needed (or not!) to future income tax when there has been a change in the tax rate.

Discounting

A final conceptual issue is whether future income tax balances should be discounted to present values. If the future tax consequence of a temporary difference is a liability, then the time value of money can be taken into account. If a corporation delays paying large amounts of income tax by taking advantage of completely legal provisions of the *Income Tax Act* (such as large CCA deductions), then the balance sheet credit represents, in effect, an interest-free loan from the government.[3]

In general, GAAP requires that future monetary assets and liabilities be shown at their discounted present value. Non-interest-bearing loans normally are discounted at an imputed rate of interest. Therefore, many accountants argue that future tax assets and liabilities also should be discounted in order to measure these monetary assets and liabilities in a manner that is consistent with the measurement of other monetary items.

Despite the strength of the theoretical arguments in favour of discounting, practical problems get in the way. There are difficulties in determining the interest rate to be used in discounting, and the timing of reversals is particularly problematic as they depend on accounting policy and management judgements.

Largely as the result of the many estimates that must be made in order to apply discounting, no country at present applies discounting to interperiod tax allocation.

CONCEPT REVIEW

1. What is the essential difference between the deferral method and the liability method of tax allocation?

2. A company records a future income tax liability in 20X1. In 20X2, the income tax rate changes. In 20X4, the future tax liability is drawn down and disappears. In what year is the impact of the rate change recognized, using the liability method?

3. What is the recommendation of the *CICA Handbook* with respect to discounting of future income tax amounts?

---

[3] Bear in mind, however, that the government does not view the amount as owing to it. The liability is an accounting construct, not a "real" liability; the government cannot demand payment in the event of the company's financial distress.

APPROACH TO INCOME TAX QUESTIONS

We will approach income tax questions in three steps:

Step 1—calculate taxable income and income tax payable.

Step 2—determine the change in future income tax.

Step 3—combine income tax payable with the change in future income tax to determine tax expense for the year.

After finishing these three steps, current year disclosure and account balances can be determined. Note that this approach is often called the balance sheet approach, as it is driven by balance sheet accounts—income tax payable and future income tax. This three-step approach provides a robust calculation methodology that also provides proof of balance sheet accounts. We'll look at a shortcut approach later in the chapter that can be used when tax rates have not changed.

Step 1—Calculate Taxable Income and Income Tax Payable

To calculate taxable income, adjust accounting income for temporary and permanent differences. Such differences are typically identified in the data, and have to be sorted into permanent and temporary differences, and those items that are added back versus subtracted. Start with accounting income, and identify the differences. If the item is:

- An expense now on the income statement, but is not tax deductible, it must be added back (e.g., amortization, fines).
- A revenue now on the income statement, but not taxable, it is subtracted (e.g., dividend revenue).
- An expense not on the income statement but allowable for tax purposes, it is subtracted (e.g., CCA).
- A revenue that is taxable but not on the income statement, it is added (e.g., collections of accounts receivable that are taxable this year but were income statement revenue in a prior year).

After calculating taxable income, multiply by the tax rate to obtain income tax payable.

Example The following facts pertain to accounting and taxable income for Mirage Limited in 20X1, Mirage's first year of operations:

- Net income before taxes is $825,000; there are no extraordinary items or discontinued operations.
- Net income includes dividends of $150,000 received from an investment in a taxable Canadian corporation that Mirage reports on the cost basis.
- In determining pre-tax accounting income, Mirage deducted the following expenses:
  - Golf club dues of $25,000
  - Accrued estimated warranty expense of $150,000
  - Depreciation of $200,000 (Mirage owns capital assets of $1,600,000, which are being depreciated straight-line over eight years).
- For tax purposes, Mirage deducts the following expenses:
  - Actual warranty costs incurred of $100,000
  - Capital cost allowance (CCA) of $300,000.
- The tax rate is 40%.

[handwritten annotation: not allowed to deduct]

The intercorporate dividend is a permanent difference, because it is not taxable income. The golf club dues are also a permanent difference because this expense is not deductible for tax purposes. There are two types of temporary differences in this example: warranty costs and CCA/depreciation.

When accounting income is adjusted for permanent differences, the result is *accounting income subject to tax*. In this example, the result is $700,000. Temporary differences are then included, to yield taxable income. Multiplying by the tax rate gives tax payable.

Pre-tax accounting income		$ 825,000
Permanent differences		
Intercorporate dividends		−150,000
Golf club dues		+ 25,000
Accounting income subject to tax		700,000
Temporary differences		
Warranty expenses accrued, not tax deductible	+150,000	
Warranty costs incurred, tax deductible	−100,000	+ 50,000
Depreciation, not tax deductible	+200,000	
Capital cost allowance (CCA), tax deductible	−300,000	−100,000
Taxable income		$ 650,000
Tax rate		× 40%
Income tax payable		$ 260,000

Exhibit 15-2 summarizes the calculation of taxable income for each of the three years of our example: 20X1, 20X2, and 20X3. Data is assumed for 20X2 and 20X3. Each column shows the adjustments for the two types of temporary differences: warranty costs and CCA/depreciation. Income tax payable is calculated from taxable income.

If the *taxes payable method* is used, analysis stops at this point. Tax expense is equal to tax payable, and no other financial statement elements are created.

Step 2—Determine the Change in Future Income Tax

To determine the change in future income tax, we will calculate the required balance in future income tax, for each source of temporary difference. We'll then compare this required

---

EXHIBIT 15-2

MIRAGE LIMITED CALCULATION OF TAXABLE INCOME

	20X1	20X2	20X3
Net income, before tax	$ 825,000	$ 900,000	$ 725,000
Permanent differences			
Intercorporate dividends	−150,000	−100,000	−125,000
Golf club dues	+ 25,000	0	0
Accounting income subject to tax	700,000	800,000	600,000
Timing differences			
Warranty expense	+150,000	+200,000	+160,000
Warranty claims paid	−100,000	−140,000	−230,000
Depreciation	+200,000	+200,000	+200,000
Capital cost allowance (CCA)	−300,000	−240,000	−180,000
Taxable income	$ 650,000	$ 820,000	$ 550,000
Enacted tax rate	40%	44%	45%
Income tax payable	$ 260,000	$ 360,800	$ 247,500

closing balance to the existing balance, and get the adjustment needed. To establish an appropriate format, we'll use a table for this calculation. The following example table has some data filled in for a capital asset example, which we'll explain as we proceed:

Column	[1] Tax Basis	[2] Accounting Basis	[3] Temporary Difference	[4] Future Tax Liability	[5] Opening Balance	[6] Adjustment
20X4 (30% tax rate)						
Capital asset	$172,000	$190,000	$(18,000)	$(5,400)	0	$(5,400)
20X5 (40% tax rate)						
Capital asset	$136,000	$160,000	(24,000)	(9,600)	$(5,400)	(4,200)

In this table, negative numbers and credits are entered in brackets, while unbracketed numbers are positive numbers or debits.

Future income taxes are caused when the carrying value (book value) of an asset or liability is different for tax versus accounting. This table records *tax carrying values* (column 1), *accounting carrying values* (column 2), takes the difference between them (column 3), multiplies this difference by the tax rate (column 4), compares that to the existing balance in the future income tax account (column 5), and calculates the difference as the needed adjustment (column 6).

Looking at the table, column by column:

Column 1—If there were a set of books kept for tax purposes, this would be the balance in the capital assets account. In this example, a capital asset was bought for $200,000 at the beginning of 20X4, and $28,000 of CCA was charged for tax purposes in 20X4. CCA, of course, is tax depreciation, so cost less accumulated CCA is $172,000. Looking vertically down this column, CCA was $36,000 in 20X5, bringing tax book value down to $136,000. These amounts are assets, so the numbers are not in brackets.

Column 2—This is the net book value of capital assets on the books of the company. This $200,000 asset had $10,000 of depreciation in 20X4 and $30,000 in 20X5. Net book value is therefore $190,000 in 20X4 and $160,000 in 20X5. Again, the amounts are assets, and are not in brackets.

Column 3—Column 3 is calculated by subtracting column 2 from column 1. Notice that the difference is negative, because column 2 is the larger number; the column 3 amount is in brackets because it is negative.

Column 4—Column 4 is calculated by multiplying column 3 by the enacted tax rate. This is 30% in 20X4 ($18,000 × 30%) and 40% in 20X5. This is in brackets; it keeps its character as a negative number, which means it will be a credit on the balance sheet. Column 4 is important—it's the *closing balance sheet position* of future income tax, and thus reflects the correct balances for financial position.

Column 5—Column 5 is the opening balance in the future income tax account. In 20X4, it is zero, assuming that this is the first year of the temporary difference. The opening balance sheet will provide this information if it is not the first year. (Or it might have to be calculated: opening tax basis less opening accounting basis multiplied by the opening tax rate.) In subsequent years, the opening balance is the closing balance of the prior year. That is, the $5,400 opening balance in 20X5 is the closing balance in 20X4. In our case, the 20X5 opening balance was a credit, and is thus in brackets.

Column 6—This is the adjustment column, and is the difference between the desired balance (4) and the current balance (5). It can be either a debit or a credit. In our case, we need the credit balance in the account to grow each time, so additional credits, in brackets, are needed. *These amounts are part of the journal entries prepared in step 3.*

Naturally, this analysis can be done without the table format. However, the information is logically organized in the table, and we will use this presentation in this text. Most of the table columns are mechanical, and no great computational challenge. The problematic columns are the first two—determining the tax basis and accounting basis of temporary differences.

Determining the Accounting Basis Think about these common temporary differences, and identify the balance sheet account that is related to the item:

Source of Temporary Difference	Related Balance Sheet Account
Depreciation and amortization	Net book value of capital assets, or other deferred charges
Inventory writedowns	Inventory
Revenue	Accounts receivable or deferred revenue
Warranty	Warranty liability
Bond discount and premium amortization	Net bond liability

At this stage in your accounting studies, there should be little problem in establishing the value of these types of accounts, based on information provided.

Determining the Tax Basis The tax basis is more complicated, and warrants some further analysis. We have already seen that for capital assets, the tax balance sheet would show cost less accumulated CCA charged. Cost less accumulated CCA is referred to as unclaimed capital cost, or UCC. As another example, assume that inventory is written down from cost of $400,000 to market value of $375,000 on the books. The accounting basis is $375,000, but the expense is not allowable for tax purposes and the inventory has a tax basis of $400,000 until sold.

With respect to assets:

- For monetary assets (i.e., receivables), the tax basis of a taxable asset is its accounting carrying value less any amount *that will enter taxation in future periods.*
- For non-monetary assets, the tax basis is the tax-deductible amount less all amounts *already deducted* in determining taxable income of the current and prior periods.

With respect to liabilities:

- For monetary liabilities, the tax basis is the accounting carrying value less any amount *that will be deductible for income tax in future periods.*
- For non-monetary liabilities (e.g., unearned revenue), the tax basis is its carrying amounts less any amount that *will not be taxable in future periods.*

An important aspect of these definitions of tax basis is that they all relate to future impacts on taxable income. That is, the tax bases are determined with respect to the past and future impact on taxable income.

Application The following examples apply these rules:

- Company A has an interest-bearing investment, on which the company accrues $15,000 of interest receivable at the end of the fiscal year. The interest is reported as revenue in A's income statement but will not be taxed until received in the next year. The tax basis of the interest receivable is *zero*: the carrying value of $15,000 less the amount that will be taxable in the future, which is the full $15,000.
- Company B has capital assets. The tax basis of this non-monetary asset is the tax-deductible amount, its full cost, less accumulated tax deductions to date, or accumulated CCA.
- Company C has a $45,000 warranty liability. The accounting liability is established because an expense is charged on the books, some of which is paid in the current

period, but $45,000 of which will be paid in the future. For tax purposes, warranty claims are deducted when paid—in the future. The tax basis is the accounting carrying value, $45,000, less amounts that will be deducted in the future, the whole $45,000. Therefore, the tax basis is *zero*.

- Company D has a $75,000 unearned revenue account. The cash was received, and is taxable, in this period. It will be recognized on the income statement later, when earned. The tax basis is *zero*: the accounting carrying value of $75,000 less the amount already included in taxable income; it will therefore not be taxable again in the future.

You must carefully reason your way through these definitions, then do a reality check: *for balance sheet items other than capital assets, the tax basis is often zero.* If there is a non-zero tax basis for an account related to a temporary difference, check your logic carefully! A non-zero result is plausible but relatively rare other than for capital assets and asset writedowns.

Permanent Differences   Permanent differences do not create future income tax. However, there may be balance sheet accounts that relate to permanent difference (e.g., prepaid golf club dues). If this is the case, the tax basis is equal to the accounting basis.

For example, suppose that a company has been fined $2,000 for a building code infraction. The fine is not yet paid and the company carries it as a current liability. Fines are not deductible for income tax purposes. Therefore, the tax basis of the fine is $2,000.

Clearly, the fine is a permanent difference and will have no tax impact. The fine has already been included in accounting income, since it has been accrued. For a monetary liability, the rule is that the tax basis is the accounting value ($2,000) less the amount that will be deductible for tax purposes (zero) so the tax basis is $2,000.

Since the tax basis is equal to the accounting basis for permanent differences, future income taxes are always zero for these items, and we simply exclude them from the table.

The equation becomes more complicated when an asset is partially tax deductible. For example, certain intangible assets such as purchased goodwill and purchased subscription lists are classified as eligible capital property for tax purposes, and 75% of the cost is subject to CCA at a declining-balance rate of 7%. The other 25% of the cost is not tax-deductible and therefore is a permanent difference. The tax basis is determined separately for the two components that make up the accounting carrying value. The cost of these assets must be broken down, with 75% included in calculations of future income tax, and 25% excluded.

Example   To illustrate the calculation of future income tax balances and adjustments, we will continue the Mirage Limited example.

At the end of 20X1, the tax bases and the accounting carrying values are as follows:

	Tax basis dr. (cr.)	Carrying value dr. (cr.)
Capital assets	$1,300,000	$1,400,000
Accrued warranty liability	0	(50,000)

The tax basis of the capital assets is the cost less accumulated CCA claimed: $1,600,000 − $300,000 = $1,300,000. Similarly, the carrying value of the capital assets is the cost less accumulated depreciation. Since 20X1 is the first year of operations and the year in which the assets were acquired, the carrying value is $1,600,000 − $200,000 = $1,400,000.

The carrying value of the warranty liability is the year-end balance in the accrual account: $150,000 − $100,000 = $50,000. The tax basis for a monetary liability is the accounting carrying value less the amounts that will be deducted for tax purposes in the future. Therefore, the tax basis of the warranty liability is $50,000 − $50,000 = $0.

These values are entered in the table in Exhibit 15-3, in columns 1 and 2. Columns 3 to 6 are completed by applying the 40% tax rate, entering the zero opening balances for this first year of operation, and then subtracting.

Return to Exhibit 15-2 and note the facts assumed for 20X2 and 20X3. In 20X2, Mirage Limited claims CCA of $240,000 and $140,000 in warranty costs on its tax return, while recognizing $200,000 in depreciation and $200,000 in accrued warranty expense on its income statement. Return to Exhibit 15-3 and note the tax and accounting bases. The carrying value of the capital assets declines to $1,200,000, while the tax basis declines by the amount of the 20X2 CCA, to $1,060,000. The difference is $140,000. At the 20X2 tax rate of 44%, the balance of the future tax liability relating to the CCA/depreciation temporary difference is $140,000 × 44% = $61,600 credit at 20X2 year-end. For the warranty liability, the temporary difference is $110,000 at the end of 20X2. That is, the opening warranty liability on the books was $50,000. This is increased by 20X2 expense of $200,000, and decreased by payments of $140,000. The accounting liability is $110,000 at the end of 20X3. The tax basis is still zero. At 44%, the balance in the future income tax asset is $48,400. Opening balances are carried down from the closing balances of 20X1, and the required adjustment is calculated.

The year 20X3 continues, with the data included in calculating taxable income from Exhibit 15-2. CCA was $180,000, reducing the tax basis to $880,000. Depreciation was $200,000, and the accounting basis is now $1,000,000. The warranty liability on the books began at $110,000. It was increased by warranty expense of $160,000, and reduced by claims paid of $230,000, to end the year at $40,000. The tax basis is zero, since claims will be deducted when paid. Arithmetically, the row is extended, noting the tax rate is now 45%.

It is important to notice at this point that the adjustment for each year is the result of two factors:

1. *The effect of the change in the tax rate on opening temporary differences.* In 20X2, for example, the tax rate increased by 4%, and the opening temporary differences were $100,000 for capital assets, so this change in the tax rate increases future income tax by $4,000.

2. *The effect of current-year temporary differences.* In 20X2, depreciation was $200,000, while CCA was $240,000. The impact of this is to reduce future income tax by $17,600 (($200,000 − $240,000) × 44%).

Thus, the $21,600 credit adjustment in the table is the result of both factors. You do not need to separately calculate them, but you can prove the adjustment if necessary.

EXHIBIT 15-3

MIRAGE LIMITED FUTURE INCOME TAX TABLE

	[1] Tax Basis dr. (cr.)	[2] Carrying Value dr. (cr.)	[3] = [1] − [2] Temporary Difference Deductible (Taxable)	[4] = [3] × t Future Tax Asset (Liability) at Yr.-end Rate	[5] = prev. [4] Less Beginning Balance dr. (cr.)	[6] = [4] − [5] Adjustment for Current Year dr. (cr.)
20X1—40%						
Capital assets	$1,300,000	$1,400,000	$(100,000)	$(40,000)	0	$(40,000)
Accrued warranty liability	0	(50,000)	50,000	20,000	0	20,000
20X2—44%						
Capital assets	1,060,000	1,200,000	(140,000)	(61,600)	$(40,000)	(21,600)
Accrued warranty liability	0	(110,000)	110,000	48,400	20,000	28,400
20X3—45%						
Capital assets	880,000	1,000,000	(120,000)	(54,000)	(61,600)	7,600
Accrued warranty liability	0	(40,000)	40,000	18,000	48,400	(30,400)

What Tax Rate? In the table, the tax rate that must be used is the enacted tax rate for the expected year of reversal. In our example, all rates were enacted in the year to which they pertain, as is normal practice. Thus, the 20X1 rate is used to measure future income tax at the end of 20X1, and so on. However, if the 20X2 rate were enacted in 20X1, then the 20X2 enacted rate would be used to measure future income tax at the end of 20X1.

After all, future income tax is a liability, and if the temporary differences will reverse and cause income tax when the rate is 44%, then this is the best measurement of the future cash outflow. Our prior comments on tax rates still stand—a future tax rate must be enacted to be used. This is to enhance reliability.

Also note that in 20X1, even if the 20X2 tax rates were enacted, only the 20X1 rates can be used to determine income tax payable in step 1. That's the whole meaning of the current-year tax rate—it dictates income tax payable!

Step 3—Combine Income Tax Payable with the Change in Future Income Tax to Determine Tax Expense for the Year

Our final step is to combine the calculation of tax payable with the change in the future income tax accounts to produce tax expense. This can be done in a schedule but is easily summarized in a journal entry, where there is:

1. A credit to tax payable, from step 1;

2. Debits and credits to future income tax accounts from step 2; and

3. A debit to tax expense, to balance.

Note that it is appropriate to maintain separate future income tax accounts for all temporary differences; financial statement presentation will differ for the accounts, as we will see. If there are four sources of temporary differences in your table in Step 2, you will have four line items for future income tax in your journal entry now.

Example Refer to the entries in Exhibit 15-4, based on the Mirage example. In each year, there is a credit to tax payable and debits and credits to the future tax accounts, and tax expense is debited to balance the entry.

EXHIBIT 15-4

MIRAGE LIMITED TAX JOURNAL ENTRIES

Income tax journal entry, 20X1

Income tax expense	280,000	
Future income tax asset—current	20,000	
Future income tax liability—long term		40,000
Income tax payable		260,000

Income tax journal entry, 20X2

Income tax expense	354,000	
Future income tax asset—current	28,400	
Future income tax liability—long term		21,600
Income tax payable		360,800

Income tax journal entry, 20X3

Income tax expense	270,300	
Future income tax liability—long term	7,600	
Future income tax asset—current		30,400
Income tax payable		247,500

BALANCE SHEET ELEMENTS

Future Income Tax Liabilities

Future income tax liabilities are created when tax paid is less than accounting accrual-based expense. This occurs when revenue is recognized on the books but is not taxable until a later period. An accounting asset, such as an account receivable, exists and its tax basis is zero. Future income tax liabilities are also created when tax expense deductions precede accounting expense deductions. For example, a declining-balance CCA results in higher expense in early years than straight-line accounting depreciation expense. As a result, UCC (unclaimed capital cost) is less than net book value. Future income tax liabilities result.

Future Income Tax Assets

Future income tax assets are created when tax is effectively prepaid. That is, tax on revenue is paid before the revenue is reflected on the books. For example, unearned revenue might appear on the accounting books, but deposits may be taxable when received. Tax is therefore paid before revenue is recognized for accounting purposes. A future tax asset is also created when expenses are on the accounting income statement before they are tax deductible, as for accrued warranty liabilities and the related expenses.

Rule of Thumb Future income tax often (not always) appears on the balance sheet on the opposite side from the balance sheet account to which it relates. For example, a future income tax asset is created by a warranty liability. Accounts receivable and inventory often result in future tax liabilities, and so on. Be careful, though—capital assets cause the future income tax credit that appears on many companies' balance sheets, but only if CCA and amortization follow certain "typical" patterns (that is, if cumulative CCA is more than cumulative amortization.) If amortization exceeds CCA to date, the result will be a future income tax asset.

Recognition Limits There are special concerns when future income tax is a debit balance. As you know, assets must represent future economic benefits, and those benefits must be probable. Future income tax assets are realized when future years come to pass, and temporary differences reverse in taxable income. If the company is in financial distress, these future years may not come to pass, and future income tax assets cannot be recognized. Such debits on the balance sheet are limited to the amount that is "more likely than not to be realized." This is a greater than 50% probability of use. We will explore this issue in more depth in the next chapter.

Classification

When future income tax assets or liabilities are reported on a balance sheet in which current and long-term assets and liabilities are segregated, they must be classified as either current or long term. The classification rules state that:

- Future income tax is a current element (current asset or current liability) if the related balance sheet account is a current asset or a current liability.
- Future income tax is a long-term element if the related balance sheet account is long term.

The classification of future income tax balances as current or long term *does not depend on the period of reversal.* A temporary difference relating to a long-term asset or liability might reverse in the next year, or not. The key to classification of future income tax balances is the classification of its related asset or liability.

Netting The future income taxes relating to all long-term assets and liabilities are lumped together and netted as a single amount for the same taxable company and the same taxing government. Similarly, current future income tax assets and liabilities should also be grouped together and shown net as a single amount. Long-term and current future income tax may not be netted.

Since consolidated financial statements include several taxable entities, it is quite possible to show a future tax *asset* and a future tax *liability*, in either current or non-current classifications (or both). For example, the company might have a net non-current future tax liability relating to the parent company, but a net non-current future tax asset relating to a subsidiary.

Income taxes currently receivable or payable should be shown separately and not combined (or netted) with future income tax balances on the face of the balance sheet.

Example Vancouver-based CHC Helicopters operates in 35 countries around the world. As a result of the far-flung tax jurisdictions in which the company operates, the company shows four different amounts for future income tax in its 2006 balance sheet (in thousands):

Future income tax assets (current)	$ 26,859
Future income tax assets (non-current)	39,848
Future income tax liabilities (current)	8,852
Future income tax liabilities (non-current)	180,001

CONCEPT REVIEW

1. What is the distinction between *current* future income tax balances and *long-term* future income tax balances?

2. A corporation has two types of temporary differences relating to non-current assets. One type of temporary difference gives rise to a future tax liability, while the other gives rise to a future tax asset. Under what circumstances would the asset and liability be shown separately on the balance sheet?

DISCLOSURE

General Recommendations

The general recommendations for disclosure of the components of the provision for income tax expense are as follows:

- The amount of income tax expense or benefit that is included in net income before discontinued operations and extraordinary items should be reported separately in the income statement; income tax expense should not be combined with other items of expense.

- The amount of income tax expense that is attributable to future income taxes should be disclosed, either on the face of the statements (i.e., in the income statement or cash flow statement) or in the notes.

- The amounts of income tax expense that relate to each of discontinued operations, extraordinary items, and capital transactions should be disclosed.

Example These disclosure standards, applied to the Mirage example, would result in the following disclosure on the income statement:

	20X1	20X2	20X3
Income before income tax	$825,000	$900,000	$725,000
Income tax expense			
Current	260,000	360,800	247,500
Future	20,000	(6,800)	22,800
	280,000	354,000	270,300
Net income	$545,000	$546,000	$454,700

This disclosure breaks income tax expense down into the portion that is paid during the year, and the portion that relates to future income tax. This breakdown could also be shown in the disclosure notes or the cash flow statement.

On the balance sheet, two future income tax amounts would be disclosed. Future income tax related to the warranty, a current liability, is shown as a current asset. The future income tax related to the non-current capital assets is disclosed as a long-term liability. The balances are from column 4 in the table, Exhibit 15-3:

	20X1	20X2	20X3
Current assets:			
Future income tax	$20,000	$48,400	$18,000
Long-term liabilities:			
Future income tax	$40,000	$61,600	$54,000

Sources of Temporary Differences Canadian public companies are also required to disclose the nature of temporary differences. Exhibit 15-5 presents the disclosure given by Canadian National Railway Company. CNR describes four types of temporary differences that resulted in income tax assets totalling $411 million at year-end 2005. A much larger temporary difference is the liability relating to "properties" (i.e., tangible capital assets). For balance sheet presentation, the long-term future tax asset is deducted from the two long-term future tax liabilities totalling $5,163 million, yielding a net liability of $4,752 million.

Notice that CNR used the older term *deferred income tax liability* rather than "future income tax," even though the company is using the liability approach.

Also notice that the one big amount relates to "properties and other." This is due to the CCA-depreciation difference, and is typical of companies that have a high level of tangible capital property, such as the Suncor example cited at the beginning of the chapter. In CNR's case, the accumulated future income tax due to the CCA-depreciation difference amounts

---

EXHIBIT 15-5

CANADIAN NATIONAL RAILWAY COMPANY
DISCLOSURE OF TEMPORARY DIFFERENCES

December 31 [in millions]	2005	2004
Deferred income tax assets		
Workforce reduction provisions	$ 51	$ 86
Personal injury claims and other reserves	234	197
Post-retirement benefits	117	115
Losses and tax credit carryforwards	9	278
	411	676
Deferred income tax liabilities		
Net prepaid benefit cost for pensions	168	121
Properties and other	4,995	4,914
	5,163	5,035
Total net deferred income tax liability	$4,752	$4,359

Source: www.sedar.com, Canadian National Railway Company, Audited Annual Financial Statements, February 6, 2006.

to 25% of the properties as reported on CNR's balance sheet. A little later in this chapter, we will discuss a possible interpretation of this amount.

Reconciliation of Effective Tax Rates The tax status of the corporation may not be obvious to the financial statement users. The reason is that the income tax expense (including both current and future taxes) reported by the company on its financial statements may appear to bear little resemblance to the expected level of taxes under the prevailing statutory tax rate.

For private companies, the difference between the actual tax expense and the statutory tax rate can readily be explained to the small number of stakeholders if they need to know. In a public company, however, there is no way for an individual investor or creditor to know what factors caused the variation in the tax rate.

Therefore, *public companies* are required provide a reconciliation between the statutory tax rate and the effective tax rate that the company is reporting. The reconciliation can be either in percentages or in dollar terms.

There are two general categories of causes for variations in the rate of tax:

1. Permanent differences, which cause items of income and/or expense to be reported in accounting income that are not included in taxable income, and

2. Differences in tax rates, due to
   a. Different tax rates in different tax jurisdictions;
   b. Special taxes levied (and tax reductions permitted) by the taxation authorities; or
   c. Changes in tax rates relating to temporary differences that will reverse in future periods.

Temporary differences themselves are *not* a cause of tax *rate* variations. Future income tax expense is included in the total reported income tax expense.

Exhibit 15-6 shows an example of the reconciliation for Power Corporation of Canada. This company provides its reconciliation in percentages. The 2005 reconciliation begins by showing that the statutory rate that Power normally would be expected to pay is 35.5%. However, the effective rate was reduced by the fact that net income included non-taxable investment income and earnings of affiliates—both are permanent differences. Some of Power's consolidated earnings were taxed in other jurisdictions, which reduced the effective tax rate by 3.5%. These permanent differences reduce Power's effective tax rate to 26.4%.

Accountant's versus Analyst's Concepts of Effective Tax Rate The accounting standard definition of effective tax rate (e.g., 26.4% in Power Corporation's disclosure) includes

---

EXHIBIT 15-6

POWER CORPORATION OF CANADA EFFECTIVE TAX RATE DISCLOSURE

The following table reconciles the statutory and effective tax rates:

	2005	2004
Combined basic federal and provincial tax rates	35.5%	35.6%
Non-taxable investment income	(4.2)	(5.0)
Earnings of affiliates	(0.8)	(1.3)
Lower effective tax rates on income not subject to tax in Canada	(3.5)	(3.0)
Miscellaneous, net of Large Corporation Tax	(0.6)	0.2
Effective income tax rate	26.4%	26.5%

Source: www.sedar.com, Power Corporation of Canada, Audited Annual Financial Statements, March 29, 2006.

future income tax. On the other hand, financial analysts usually view the effective tax rate as the amount of current taxes divided by pre-tax earnings, which is quite different from effective tax rate as defined by accounting standards.

CNR, for example, had 2005 earnings before income tax of $2,337 and income tax expense of $781. The $781 consisted of $234 in current tax and $547 in future tax. The statutory rate was 36.2%, while the "effective rate," using the accounting definition, was 33.4% after removing permanent differences but retaining the future income tax expense. Analysts, in contrast, would look at only the $234 in current tax expense, for an effective rate of 10%.

SHORTCUT APPROACH

In some cases, a shorter computational approach may be used to account for income tax. We recommend this approach only if the income tax rate has not changed from the prior year—this shortcut gets cumbersome with a change in tax rates. However, if the facts support the shortcut, it will save time.

The steps are as follows:

Step 1—Calculate taxable income and income tax payable.

Step 2—Determine the change in future income tax through a direct calculation.

Step 3—Combine income tax payable with the change in future income tax to determine tax expense for the year.

Only Step 2 has changed. The table need not be prepared; all that is needed is a direct calculation of the change in future income tax balances. Remember that the adjustment that flows from the table has two components—a change to opening future income tax balances because of the tax rate change, and the current year increase. If the tax rate has not changed, there is no adjustment of opening future income tax balances, and the current-year increase is all that is needed. The balance in future income tax can be tracked with a simple T-account.

In Step 2, to determine the change in future income tax for the year, the calculation is:

> Change in future income tax = the temporary difference during the year (accounting revenue or expense less the tax revenue or expense) × tax rate.

To illustrate the shortcut method, we will calculate the tax amounts for KelCo. Facts are as follows:

	20X2	20X3	20X4
Income before income tax	$242,000	$934,000	$1,361,000
Depreciation	230,000	230,000	230,000
CCA	287,000	197,000	312,000
Tax-free dividend revenue	—	75,000	—
Non-tax-deductible expenses	32,000	—	—
Tax rate	40%	40%	40%

The first step in the solution is to calculate taxable income and income tax payable for each year:

	20X2	20X3	20X4
Accounting income	$242,000	$934,000	$1,361,000
Permanent differences			
Dividend revenue	—	(75,000)	—
Non-deductible expenses	32,000	—	—
Temporary differences			
Depreciation	230,000	230,000	230,000
CCA	(287,000)	(197,000)	(312,000)
Taxable income	217,000	892,000	1,279,000
Tax rate	40%	40%	40%
Income tax payable	$ 86,800	$356,800	$ 511,600

The second step is to determine the change in future income tax each year. There is only one source of future income tax, the depreciation/CCA on capital assets. In 20X2, CCA is $57,000 ($287,000 − $230,000) larger than depreciation. This translates into a $22,800 ($57,000 × .4) increase (credit) in a future income tax liability. Since this is the first year, the balance in future income tax is also $22,800.

In 20X3, depreciation is larger than CCA by $33,000 ($230,000 − $197,000). This will reduce the credit balance in the liability by $13,200 ($33,000 × .4). The balance in future income tax liability is now $9,600 ($22,800 − $13,200). This $9,600 balance can be proven as the cumulative temporary differences multiplied by the tax rate. In this example, we have total depreciation over the two years of $460,000, versus $484,000 of CCA, for a $24,000 cumulative difference, multiplied by the tax rate of 40% to again give $9,600.

In 20X4, CCA is larger than depreciation, this time by $82,000 ($312,000 − $230,000). This will increase the future income tax liability by $32,800 ($82,000 × .4). The balance in future income tax liability is now $42,400 ($9,600 + $32,800) (also $796,000 of cumulative CCA versus $690,000 of cumulative depreciation = $106,000 × .40 = $42,400).

The last step is to prepare the tax entries, which determine the tax expense for the year:

20X2
Income tax expense	109,600	
Future income tax ($287,000 − $230,000) × .4		22,800
Income tax payable		86,800

20X3
Income tax expense	343,600	
Future income tax ($230,000 − $197,000) × .4	13,200	
Income tax payable		356,800

20X4
Income tax expense	544,400	
Future income tax ($312,000 − $230,000) × .4		32,800
Income tax payable		511,600

With this information, appropriate financial statement disclosure may be prepared.

Evaluation This method may seem far simpler, and indeed it is. Remember, though, that it is to be used only when the tax rate does not change—and, in the business world, changing tax rates are a fact of life. (The problem can be done with the shortcut method if the tax rate changes by also preparing a separate calculation of the effect of the tax rate change on opening future income tax. However, the possibility for error starts to become high, and the table approach is far more reliable.) The other significant advantage of the table approach is that the future income tax account is proven each year, with the difference between tax and accounting basis backing up the integrity of this account. It is important to have such proof for all financial statement elements.

DIFFERENTIAL REPORTING

Applicability As we explained in Chapter 1, a Canadian corporation that is not publicly accountable may elect to use differential reporting alternatives for certain reporting issues. Income tax accounting is one of those issues.

A corporation is not publicly accountable if none of its securities are traded in the public securities markets—that is, it is a private corporation. But certain types of enterprises are publicly accountable even if their securities are not publicly traded. These businesses include regulated enterprises (including rate-regulated businesses) and corporations owned by governments (i.e. crown corporations). Therefore, only non-regulated private non-government corporations can adopt differential reporting under the provisions of the *CICA Handbook*.

To apply differential reporting, all of the corporation's shareholders must agree unanimously, in writing. The consent requirement applies to the holders of non-voting shares as well as to voting shares.

Accounting Method Qualifying corporations may elect to use the taxes payable method of accounting for income taxes instead of comprehensive allocation.

Income tax paid is equal to income tax expense. There is no interperiod allocation of income taxes, and there are no future income tax amounts reported on the balance sheet.

Differential reporting for income taxes is an all-or-nothing affair. A company cannot decide to use future income tax accounting for some types of temporary differences while using the taxes payable basis for other types.

Disclosure In the accounting policies note, a company should disclose the fact that it is using the taxes payable method under the provisions of the differential reporting rules. The *CICA Handbook* also recommends disclosure of the company's significant tax policies, such as revenue recognition methods, applicable CCA rates, deductibility of pension costs, and deduction policy for costs that may be capitalized for accounting purposes.

In addition, the company should reconcile its income tax expense to the average statutory income tax rate. This disclosure is similar to that described above, with the important exception that the impact of temporary differences is not included in the reconciliation. The reconciliation would include items such as:

- Large corporations' tax;
- Non-deductible expenses;
- Non-taxable gains, including the non-taxable portion of capital gains; and
- The amount of deductible temporary differences for which a future tax asset has not been recorded.

CASH FLOW STATEMENT

The impact of income tax accounting on the cash flow statement is clear: all tax allocation amounts must be reversed out of transactions reported on the cash flow statement. The cash flow statement must include only the actual taxes paid.

When the indirect method of presentation is used for operating cash flow, future tax assets and liabilities that have been credited (or charged) to income must be subtracted from (or added back to) net income. That is, the change in future income tax is an add-back or deduction in operating activities. The change in income tax payable is another adjustment in operating activities. When the direct method of presentation is used, the cash used for (or provided by) income taxes must include only the taxes actually paid (or payable) to the government and tax refunds actually received (or receivable) from the government.

IS FUTURE INCOME TAX A LIABILITY?

Future (deferred) income tax accounting has been with us for about 60 years. Prior to 1987, it was called deferred income tax because the concept is based on income measurement concepts: matching tax expense with each period's net income. The tax expense relating to the current year's net income is recognized in the current year but deferred to future years. The concept was changed by the FASB in 1987 to embrace the new standard-setting emphasis on the balance sheet rather than the income statement.[4] The AcSB and the IASB adopted the revised U.S. approach in 1997.

It is possible to raise many questions about the validity of the future income tax concept. Future income tax is an allocation of an amount that arises largely from other allocations. It seems firmly grounded on the income statement concepts of revenue-expense recognition and matching, even though the FASB has strained mightily to justify income tax allocation under the asset-liability definitional approach. Even the name of basic concept, income tax *allocation*, is derived from an income statement approach rather than a balance sheet approach.

The most important question, however, is the validity of viewing future income tax credits as a true liability when they arise as the result of major recurring temporary differences. We observed earlier in this chapter that the major single cause of temporary differences is the difference between two other allocations: depreciation for accounting versus CCA for tax. In aggregate, these temporary differences will not reverse as long as the company continues to invest in replacing its physical assets.

One important aspect of the liability definition is that *a liability represents an existing obligation*. But to whom is this obligation owed? Defenders of tax allocation argue that future income tax is similar to a warranty liability—the obligation is real even though the specific parties to whom the liability will be fulfilled cannot be specifically identified. It is true that a warranty requires a cash outflow to as-yet-unknown parties. However, any income tax liability must be owed to specific known government jurisdictions. The other party is known precisely, but there is no current obligation for future taxes. The government does not consider the amount that we show as future income tax liabilities to be owing.

The reality of having to pay out cash in the future as recurring temporary differences (e.g., depreciation-CCA differences) are reversed depends on the joint occurrence of two conditions:

1. The asset basis of the temporary differences (i.e., the capital assets being depreciated) must shrink before there can be a net reversal, precipitating an actual cash outflow, and

2. The company must be earning taxable income while the net reversals are occurring.

While it is possible for these two conditions to co-exist, co-existence is unlikely. Asset bases contract when old assets are not being replaced, and that usually happens when the company is in decline. If a company is in decline it is unlikely to be generating taxable income.

---

[4] In the process of changing to a balance sheet approach, the FASB has made tax allocation much more difficult to understand and to apply in practice, with some ludicrous results such as inflating imputed goodwill in a business combination in order to offset a notional future income tax liability.

Accounting standards call for recognizing a contingent liability when a cash flow is *more likely than not* to be realized. It can be argued that, at best, future income tax liabilities relating to recurring temporary differences should be disclosed as a contingent liability because the conditions necessary to precipitate a cash flow are not likely to occur—the liability is neither likely to occur, nor is the amount of future cash flow measurable.

INTERNATIONAL PERSPECTIVE

Timing or Temporary Differences?

Worldwide, "timing differences" is the common name given to items that affect both accounting and tax, but in different periods. In 1987, the U.S. accounting standards dropped that term and introduced the term "temporary differences" when the FASB significantly revamped its income tax allocation standard. The U.S. was the only country to change terminology through 1997. However, in a 1996 exposure draft, the CICA's Accounting Standards Board proposed that the new terminology (and a new approach to income tax allocation) be used in Canada as well. In late 1997, the AcSB issued a new section of the *CICA Handbook*, Section 3465, that superseded the previous Section 3470. The new section changed Canadian practice from the use of the *timing differences* approach to the use of the *temporary differences* approach.

The name has been changed because the definition has also been changed. Tax allocation has been altered from an income statement viewpoint to a balance sheet viewpoint. Instead of allocating differences in the timing of recognition of revenues, expenses, gains, and losses, the AcSB requires that, for any corporation constrained by GAAP, any difference between the tax basis of an asset or liability and its balance sheet carrying value will be subject to tax allocation.

Extent of Allocation

In other countries, comprehensive allocation is almost universally used. An important exception is the United Kingdom, where partial allocation is required. Under the U.K. approach, future (or deferred) income tax is recognized only for timing differences that are likely to reverse within the foreseeable future, generally interpreted as within three years. Some timing differences—most notably, those relating to tangible capital assets—would not be recognized.

Partial allocation has been the accepted method in the United Kingdom for many years. However, a proposed change in the standard may move the United Kingdom closer to comprehensive allocation.

Impact of Allocation

Income tax allocation has a significant impact only in countries that permit accounting income to differ from taxable income. The U.S., Canada, and the United Kingdom are major countries that do not require accounting-tax conformity. Many other countries require corporations to report the same income for accounting purposes as they report for tax purposes.

However, the accounting-tax conformity rule applies only to taxable entities and only when home-country accounting standards are being applied. Consolidated financial statements do not represent any taxable entity. If consolidated statements are prepared using international standards, accounting-tax conformity may no longer exist and interperiod tax allocation may become significant in the consolidated statements even though future income taxes don't exist in the separate-entity financial statements.

Some countries do not permit different revenue and expense recognition practices for financial reporting and tax purposes, and in those countries (e.g., Italy, Sweden) interperiod tax allocation has no role.

Measurement Method

There is a large variation in practice among major industrialized countries. Some (e.g., the U.S., the United Kingdom, Australia) require the liability method, a few (such as France) require the deferral method, and others (e.g., Germany, Switzerland, the Netherlands) permit either method.[5]

RELEVANT STANDARDS

CICA Handbook:
- Section 3465, Income Taxes
- Section 3290, Contingencies

IASB:
- *IAS* 12, Income Taxes

SUMMARY OF KEY POINTS

1. The amount of taxable income often differs from the amount of pre-tax net income reported for accounting purposes.

2. The difference between taxable income and accounting income arises from two types of sources: *permanent* differences and *temporary* differences.

3. Permanent differences are items of revenue, expense, gains, or losses that are reported for accounting purposes but never enter into the computation of taxable income. Permanent differences also include those rare items that enter into taxable income but are never included in accounting income.

4. Temporary differences arise when the tax basis of an asset or liability is different from its carrying value (i.e., its accounting basis) in the financial statements.

5. The objective of *comprehensive interperiod income tax allocation* is to recognize the income tax effect of every item when that item is recognized in accounting net income. Alternatives to comprehensive allocation are the *taxes payable method (flow-through method),* and *partial tax allocation.*

6. When the item of revenue, expense, gain, or loss first enters the calculation of *either* taxable income or accounting income, it is an *originating* temporary difference.

7. A temporary difference *reverses* when it is recognized in the other measure of income. For example, if an item is recognized first for tax purposes and later for accounting purposes, the temporary difference originates when the item is included in the tax calculation and reverses when the item is recognized for accounting.

8. Under the liability method of tax allocation, the tax effect is recorded at the currently enacted rate that will apply in the period that the temporary difference is expected to reverse. The current rate is used if no future years' tax rates are enacted.

9. Under the liability method, the balance of future income tax assets and liabilities must be adjusted to reflect changes in the tax rate as they are enacted.

10. Future income taxes are not discounted.

11. Accounting for income tax involves calculating tax payable, calculating the change in the future income tax accounts, and then combining all elements to determine tax expense.

---

[5] This information is derived from the Reference Matrix that accompanies *TRANSACC: Transnational Accounting,* 2nd edition, edited by Anne d'Arcy and Dieter Ordelheide (London: MacMillan Press, 2001).

12. Future income tax is calculated as the difference between the tax basis and the accounting carrying value of related balance sheet accounts, multiplied by the enacted tax rate.

13. Future income tax assets and liabilities are classified as *current* assets/liabilities if the temporary differences relate to current assets or liabilities. Future income tax balances that relate to long-term assets and liabilities are reported as long-term assets and liabilities.

14. Within each classification of current and non-current, future income tax balances relating to different items are netted and reported as a single amount. Current and non-current future tax liability balances may not be netted against each other.

15. Companies that qualify for differential reporting may use the taxes payable method for income tax. No future income tax is recorded, and tax expense equals tax paid.

16. *Public companies* must explain in a note the difference between the effective tax rate reported in the financial statements and the statutory rate. In this context, the effective tax rate is the income tax expense (including future taxes) divided by the pre-tax net income. Public companies must also disclose sources of temporary differences.

17. The cash flow statement will include only the amounts of taxes actually paid or received for the year. All allocations, whether for temporary differences or for tax-loss carryforwards, must be reversed out.

KEY TERMS

accrual method, 906
comprehensive tax allocation, 903
deferral method, 906
interperiod tax allocation, 900
liability method/accrual method, 906
partial tax allocation, 904

permanent difference, 900
provision for income tax, 900
taxes payable method, 903
temporary difference, 901
timing differences, 901

REVIEW PROBLEM

The following information pertains to Suda Corporation at the beginning of 20X1:

	Tax basis	Accounting basis
Equipment	$400,000 UCC	$500,000
Deferred development costs	0	$200,000

At the beginning of 20X1, Suda had a balance in its future income tax liability account of $105,000, pertaining to both the amounts above. That is, there is $35,000 related to equipment and $70,000 to the deferred development costs. The enacted income tax rate (combined federal and provincial) at the end of 20X1 was 35%.

The following information pertains to the next three years:

	20X2	20X3	20X4
Net income (including amortization)	$200,000	$160,000	$100,000
New equipment acquired	—	100,000	—
Amortization expense on equipment	65,000	70,000	75,000
CCA claimed	80,000	74,000	69,000
Amortization of development costs	40,000	50,000	45,000
Development costs incurred (deductible for tax purposes)	50,000	30,000	70,000
Income tax rate (enacted in each year)	35%	38%	38%

Required:
For each of 20X2, 20X3, and 20X4, calculate:

1. The income tax expense that would appear on Suda's income statement.

2. The balance of the future income tax liability or asset account(s) that would appear on Suda's balance sheet.

REVIEW PROBLEM—SOLUTION

Calculation of taxable income and tax payable

	20X2	20X3	20X4
Net income	$200,000	$160,000	$100,000
Plus amortization on equipment	65,000	70,000	75,000
Less CCA	(80,000)	(74,000)	(69,000)
Plus amortization of development costs	40,000	50,000	45,000
Less development costs incurred	(50,000)	(30,000)	(70,000)
Taxable income	$175,000	$176,000	$ 81,000
Tax rate	35%	38%	38%
Tax payable	$ 61,250	$ 66,880	$ 30,780

Calculation of tax basis and carrying value

	Equipment		Development costs	
	Tax basis	Carrying value	Tax basis	Carrying value
20X1 ending balances	$400,000	$500,000	0	$200,000
Additions	—	—		+ 50,000
CCA & Amortizations	(80,000)	(65,000)		(40,000)
20X2 ending balances	320,000	435,000	0	210,000
Additions	+100,000	+100,000		+ 30,000
Amortizations	(74,000)	(70,000)		(50,000)
20X3 ending balances	346,000	465,000	0	190,000
Additions				+ 70,000
Amortizations	(69,000)	(75,000)		(45,000)
20X4 ending balances	$277,000	$390,000	0	$215,000

Calculation of changes in future income tax liability

	Year-end tax basis dr. (cr.)	Carrying value dr. (cr.)	Temporary difference deductible (taxable)	Future tax asset (liability) at yr.-end rate	Less beginning balance dr. (cr.)	Adjustment for current year dr. (cr.)
20X2—35%						
Equipment	320,000	435,000	(115,000)	(40,250)	(35,000)	(5,250)
Development costs	0	210,000	(210,000)	(73,500)	(70,000)	(3,500)
				(113,750)		
20X3—38%						
Equipment	346,000	465,000	(119,000)	(45,220)	(40,250)	(4,970)
Development costs	0	190,000	(190,000)	(72,200)	(73,500)	1,300
				(117,420)		
20X4—38%						
Equipment	277,000	390,000	(113,000)	(42,940)	(45,220)	2,280
Development costs	0	215,000	(215,000)	(81,700)	(72,200)	(9,500)
				(124,640)		

Tax entries

20X2

Tax expense	70,000	
Tax payable		61,250
Future income tax—equipment		5,250
Future income tax—development costs		3,500

20X3

Tax expense	70,550	
Future income tax—development costs	1,300	
Future income tax—equipment		4,970
Tax payable		66,880

20X4

Tax expense	38,000	
Future income tax—equipment	2,280	
Future income tax—development costs		9,500
Tax payable		30,780

1. Income tax expense

	20X2	**20X3**	**20X4**
Current	$61,250	$66,880	$30,780
Future	8,750	3,670	7,220
Income tax expense	$70,000	$70,550	$38,000

2. Future income tax liability balance
   Per table, column [4] above. Each year's balance will be reported as a single long-term credit amount, as follows:

20X2	$113,750
20X3	$117,420
20X4	$124,640

APPENDIX

THE INVESTMENT TAX CREDIT

General Nature

The *Income Tax Act* provides for *investment tax credits* for (1) specified types of expenditures for capital investment and (2) qualifying research and experimental development expenditures. The expenditures that qualify for the investment tax credit are matters of government policy and change from time to time. By giving a tax credit, the government can influence companies to increase investments in certain types of facilities and in selected geographic areas by effectively reducing their cost. The expenditures that qualify vary on three dimensions:

1. Type of expenditure

2. Type of corporation

3. Geographic region

A tax credit is a direct, dollar-for-dollar offset against income taxes that otherwise are payable. The advantage of a tax *credit* (instead of a tax *deduction* for the expenditures) is that the amount of the tax credit is not affected by the tax rate being paid by the corporation. For example, if a $100,000 expenditure qualifies for a 7% tax credit, the tax reduction will be $7,000 regardless of whether the corporation is paying taxes at 25%, 38%, 45%, or any other rate.[6]

To realize the benefit of a tax credit, it usually is necessary for the qualifying corporation to have taxable income and to generate income tax payable. If there is not sufficient tax payable in the year of the qualifying expenditures, the tax credit can be carried back three years and forward 20 years. Certain types of corporations may be eligible to receive the credit in cash, even if there is not enough tax due within the current and carryback periods to completely utilize the tax credit.

Accounting Treatment

In theory, there are two possible approaches to accounting for the investment tax credit (ITC):

1. The *flow-through approach*, whereby the ITC for which the corporation qualifies is reported as a direct reduction in the income tax expense for the year; or

2. The *cost-reduction approach*, in which the ITC is deducted from the expenditures that give rise to the ITC; the benefit of the ITC is thereby allocated to the years in which the expenditures are recognized as expenses.

Perhaps not surprisingly, the *CICA Handbook* recommends the cost reduction approach, although the U.S. rules allow either approach and the topic has seen its share of controversy over the years.

Expenditures Reported as Current Expenses

The government often grants ITC for research and development expenditures. Some of those expenditures will not qualify for the defer-and-amortize approach for development costs and will be charged to expense in the period in which they are incurred.

Investment tax credits that relate to expenditures that are reported as expenses in the income statement are permitted to flow through to the income statement.

The ITC on current expenses may be recognized in either of two ways:

1. As a reduction in income tax expense; or

2. As a reduction of (or offset against) the expense that gave rise to the ITC.

---

[6] Depending on the type of capital expenditure and the location of the enterprise, the investment tax credit may range from 7% to 35%.

The second method may seem more consistent with the cost-reduction approach, but it is contrary to the general principle that revenues and expenses should not be shown net of taxes. In practice, the first approach (of deducting the ITC from income tax expense) is more common. Since the ITC will reduce the effective tax rate being paid by the corporation, a public corporation will treat the ITC as a tax rate reduction and will include it in its tax rate reconciliation.

Expenditures Capitalized or Deferred

If the ITC qualifying expenditures are for a capital asset or are for development costs that can be deferred and amortized, then the ITC itself is deferred and amortized on the same basis as the asset. This can be accomplished either by reducing the capitalized cost of the asset or by separately deferring and amortizing the ITC:

EXHIBIT 15-A1

RECORDING THE INVESTMENT TAX CREDIT

Illustrative Data

1   *May 20X5*
Purchased eligible transportation equipment (30% CCA rate) costing $100,000, to be amortized straight-line over 10 years, no residual value, with a half-year's amortization in the year of acquisition for both accounting and tax purposes.

31   *December 20X5*
Pre-tax income (after amortization on new equipment), $150,000. Investment tax credit ($100,000 × 7%; not included in previous amounts), $7,000. The tax rate is 40%.

Entries for 20X5

a. *1 May—purchase qualified equipment*

Equipment	100,000	
Cash		100,000

b. *31 December—record ITC*

Income tax payable	7,000	
Deferred investment tax credit		7,000

c. *31 December—record amortization expense*

Amortization expense ($100,000 × 1/10 × 1/2)	5,000	
Accumulated amortization		5,000

d. *31 December—record amortization of investment tax credit for 20X5*

Deferred investment tax credit ($7,000 × 1/10 × 1/2)	350	
Amortization expense		350

e. *31 December—record income tax on 20X5 earnings**

Income tax expense ($150,000 × 40%)	60,000	
Future income liability		
($13,950 × $4,650) × 40%		3,720
Income tax payable		56,280

*See Exhibit 15-A2 for the calculations of these amounts.

Investment tax credits related to the acquisition of assets would be either:

1. Deducted from the related assets with any amortization calculated on the net amount; or

2. Deferred and amortized to income on the same basis as the related assets.

For the second approach, the *CICA Handbook* makes no recommendation concerning the classification of the deferred ITC on the balance sheet. One option is to include it as a non-current deferred credit. There is no requirement for separate disclosure. Another option would be to deduct the deferred ITC from the balance of the asset. This second approach seems more consistent with the cost-reduction theory than the first, but either may be used in practice.

EXHIBIT 15-A2

REPORTING THE INVESTMENT TAX CREDIT

Calculation of income tax expense

Tax and accounting cost of asset	
Capital cost of equipment	$100,000
Less: investment tax credit of 7%	7,000
Net capital cost	$ 93,000
Accounting income	$150,000
Amortization	
[($100,000 ÷ 10 × 1/2 year) − ($7,000 × 1/10 × 1/2)]	+ 4,650
CCA ($93,000 × 30% × 1/2 year*)	− 13,950
Taxable income	$140,700
Tax rate	× 40%
Current tax due before ITC	$ 56,280
Less investment tax credit ($100,000 × 7%)	7,000
Income tax payable	$ 49,280
Current income tax	$ 56,280
Future income tax liability [($13,950 − $4,650) × 40%]	3,720
Income tax expense	$ 60,000

*Assuming that only a half-year's deduction for CCA is claimable in the first year, as is usual.

Income Statement reporting, year ended 31 December 20X5

Amortization expense ($5,000 − $350 amortization of ITC)		$ 4,650
Pre-tax income		$150,000
Income tax expense—current (from above)	$ 56,280	
—future (from above)	3,720	60,000
Net income		$ 90,000

Balance Sheet reporting, 31 December 20X5

Equipment (at cost)		$100,000
Accumulated amortization	$ 5,000	
Deferred investment tax credit ($7,000 − $350)	6,650*	11,650
Reported carrying value		$ 88,350
Income tax payable (from above)		$ 49,280
Future income tax liability (from above)		$ 3,720

*Or may be classified as a deferred credit.

For income tax purposes, the ITC is deducted from the tax basis of the asset.[7] The effect is as follows:

- For expenditures that are deferred and capitalized for accounting purposes but are deducted immediately for tax purposes (e.g., development costs), a temporary difference is created because the cost (net of ITC) is being deducted immediately but is charged to income via amortization over several years; and
- For capital assets, the tax basis and the accounting basis start out the same (i.e., both reduced by the amount of the ITC benefit), but temporary differences arise from any differences between CCA and amortization.

Exhibits 15-A1 and 15-A2 demonstrate the relevant accounting procedures. Exhibit 15-A1 contains the basic data and illustrates the journal entries used to record the qualifying expenditure and the ITC. Exhibit 15-A2 shows the impacts on the financial statements. The exhibits assume that the deferred ITC is deducted from the asset on the balance sheet.

RELEVANT STANDARDS

CICA Handbook:
- Section 3805, Investment Tax Credits

SUMMARY OF KEY POINTS

1. The investment tax credit (ITC) is a direct reduction of income taxes that is granted to enterprises that invest in certain types of assets or in research and development costs.

2. There are two possible approaches to accounting for ITCs: (1) the flow-through approach and (2) the cost reduction approach.

3. The *CICA Handbook* recommends using the cost reduction approach, wherein the ITC is deducted (either directly or indirectly) from the asset or expense that gave rise to the ITC.

4. ITCs on expenditures that are reported as current expenses are usually deducted from income tax expense rather than from the functional expense itself.

5. When qualifying expenditures are made to acquire an asset (including deferred development costs), the ITC can either be (1) deducted from the asset's carrying value, with depreciation based on the net amount or (2) deferred separately and amortized on the same basis as the asset itself.

QUESTIONS

Q15-1   How can differences between accounting and taxable income be classified? Define each classification.

Q15-2   XTE Corporation (a) uses straight-line amortization for its financial accounting and accelerated amortization on its income tax return and (b) holds a $50,000

---

[7] Actually, it's a bit more complicated, because the accounting deduction is made in the year of purchase while the deduction from the tax base occurs only in the year(s) in which the ITC is *realized*, which is always at least one year later than the expenditure. We will ignore this additional temporary difference in this discussion.

equity investment in another Canadian company. XTE receives dividends annually. What kind of tax difference is caused by each of these items? Explain.

Q15-3   Temporary differences are said to "originate" and "reverse." What do these terms mean?

Q15-4   Give three examples of a permanent difference, and three examples of a temporary difference.

Q15-5   Explain the alternative options for the extent of allocation possible in dealing with interperiod tax allocation. Which alternative is Canadian practice?

Q15-6   Sometimes the taxes payable method is called the flow-through method. Why might this name seem appropriate? What are the advantages of this method? When is this method generally accepted in Canada?

Q15-7   Why is the balance in a future income tax liability account not discounted?

Q15-8   Thertot Limited reported $100,000 of income in 20X4, $300,000 of income in 20X5, and $500,000 of income in 20X6. Included in 20X4 income is an expense, $50,000, that cannot be deducted for tax purposes until 20X6. Assume a 40% tax rate. How much income tax is payable in each year? How much income tax expense will be reported? Why are the total three-year payable and total three-year expense equal?

Q15-9   ATW Corporation has completed an analysis of its accounting income, taxable income, and the temporary differences. Taxable income is $100,000, and there are two temporary differences, which result in (a) a future income tax asset of $15,000 and (b) a future income tax liability of $20,000. The income tax rate for the current period and all future periods is 32%. There were no future income tax assets or future income tax liabilities as of the beginning of the current year. Give the entry to record income tax.

Q15-10   A company has $100,000 in originating temporary differences in 20X6, its first year of operation. The temporary differences give rise to a future income tax liability. The tax rate is 35% in 20X6. In 20X7, there were no new temporary differences, but the tax rate increases to 46%. If the liability method is used, at what amount will future income taxes be shown on the 20X7 balance sheet?

Q15-11   A company reports a $1,000,000 revenue (on account; a long-term account receivable was recognized) in accounting income in year 1. It is taxable income when collected in year 4. What is the accounting carrying value of the receivable at the end of year 1? The tax basis? Assuming that the tax rate is 40% in years 1 and 2, and 35% in years 3 and 4, what will be the balance in the future income tax account at the end of each year?

Q15-12   A company bought $500,000 of capital assets at the beginning of year 1. Year 1 amortization was $100,000 and CCA was $50,000. What is the tax basis of the assets at the end of year 1? The accounting carrying value? If the tax rate is 20%, what is the balance in the future income tax account at the end of year 1?

Q15-13   When do balance sheet items have a different accounting carrying value and tax basis?

Q15-14   Do permanent differences cause the accounting carrying value and tax basis of the related balance sheet item to differ? Explain.

Q15-15   On the balance sheet, are future income taxes debits or credits? Explain. Is a debit to a future income tax account always a decrease, and a credit always an increase? Explain.

Q15-16   Assume that a company reports a future income tax liability of $500,000. The enacted tax rate goes down. How will the balance sheet account change if the liability method is used?

Q15-17   How are future income taxes classified on the balance sheet as current or non-current items? Can different future income tax amounts be netted?

Q15-18 What kinds of differences cause a company to report taxes at a rate different than the statutory rate?

Q15-19 What is an investment tax credit?

Q15-20 Explain two different approaches to account for an investment tax credit for a capital asset. Which method is current Canadian practice?

Q15-21 How might an ITC received because of qualifying expenditures for capital assets be reported on the balance sheet?

CASE 15-1

SUNCOR ENERGY INC.

Cyril Bouchard is a senior account manager for a large Canadian bank. The bank is considering the possibility of syndicating a large debenture issue for Suncor Energy Inc. Suncor is heavily involved in the oil sands development in northern Alberta. Cyril has been given the task of analyzing Suncor's financial performance. When the bank's account managers or analysts are reviewing any customer's financial statements, the bank's policy is to remove the effects of income tax allocation in order to enhance the usefulness of the statements for such analytical procedures as evaluating earnings and measuring debt:equity ratios.

Cyril has assigned you, David Kim (a management trainee), the task of evaluating Suncor's financial statements both with and without the effect of FIT. Cyril also would like your comments on the likelihood of Suncor's accumulated FIT being reversed in the foreseeable future.

Condensed versions of Suncor's income statement, balance sheet, and cash flow statement are presented in Exhibits 1 to 3. Exhibit 4 shows an excerpt from Note 9, Income Taxes.

Required:
Prepare a memo from David Kim to Cyril Bouchard.

EXHIBIT 1

SUNCOR ENERGY LTD.
Statement of Earnings (condensed)

(in millions of dollars)

	31 December 2006	31 December 2005
Revenues	15,829	11,129
Expenses		
Purchases of crude oil and products	4,723	4,184
Operating, selling and general	2,998	2,417
Depreciation, depletion, and amortization	695	568
Other expenses	3,607	2,108
	12,023	9,277
Earnings before income taxes	3,806	1,852
Provision for income taxes		
Current	20	39
Future	815	655
	835	694
Net earnings	2,971	1,158

EXHIBIT 2

SUNCOR ENERGY LTD.
Balance Sheet
(in millions of dollars)

	31 December 2006	31 December 2005
Assets		
Current assets		
Cash and cash equivalents	521	165
Accounts receivable	1,050	1,139
Inventories	589	523
Income taxes receivable	33	6
Future income taxes	109	83
Total current assets	2,302	1,916
Property, plant and equipment, net	16,189	12,966
Deferred charges and other	290	267
Total assets	18,781	15,149
Liabilities and Shareholders' Equity		
Current liabilities		
Short-term debt	7	49
Accounts payable and accrued liabilities	2,111	1,830
Taxes other than income taxes	40	56
Total current liabilities	2,158	1,935
Long-term debt	2,385	3,007
Accrued liabilities and other	1,214	1,005
Future income taxes	4,072	3,206
	9,829	9,153
Shareholders' equity		
Share capital	794	732
Contributed surplus	100	50
Cumulative foreign currency translation	(71)	(81)
Retained earnings	8,129	5,295
Total shareholders' equity	8,952	5,996
Total liabilities and shareholders' equity	18,781	15,149

EXHIBIT 3

SUNCOR ENERGY LTD.
Statement of Cash Flows (condensed)
(in millions of dollars)

	31 December 2006	31 December 2005
Cash flow from operating activities	4,564	2,348
Cash used in investing activities	(3,489)	(3,113)
Cash flow provided by financing activities	(719)	844
Increase in cash and cash equivalents	356	79
Effect of foreign exchange on cash and cash equivalents	—	(2)
Cash and cash equivalents at beginning of year	165	88
Cash and cash equivalents at end of year	521	165

EXHIBIT 4

SUNCOR ENERGY LTD.
Future Income Taxes

(in millions of dollars)

	31 December 2006	31 December 2005
Future income tax assets:		
Employee future benefits	12	7
Asset retirement obligations	32	19
Inventories	59	67
Other	6	(10)
	109	83
Future income tax liabilities:		
Excess of book values of assets over tax values	4,413	3,490
Deferred maintenance shutdown costs	43	51
Employee future benefits	(88)	(87)
Asset retirement obligations	(203)	(162)
Other	(93)	(86)
	4,072	3,206

Source: www.sedar.com, Suncor Energy Inc., Audited Financial Statements, March 8, 2007.

CASE 15-2

DEEP HARBOUR LIMITED

Deep Harbour Limited (DHL) is a private company owned by Daniel Lalande. Lalande started the company in 20X1, and DHL has reported reasonably consistent growth in profits from fiscal 20X1 to 20X7. The company is in the plastic moulding business, making everything from toys to dashboards.

The year ended 30 November 20X8 has been challenging for DHL. The company invested $8.2 million in new injection moulding machinery in February 20X8. This meant a two-week scheduled production shutdown to allow for installation and training. The two weeks stretched to five weeks when last-minute replacement parts were delayed at the U.S. border. The machinery was fully operational in late March 20X8; however, additional costs were incurred.

DHL has used the taxes payable method to account for corporate income taxes, but now has to adopt comprehensive tax allocation. The Chartered Bank of Canada (CBC) provided a $7 million 10-year term loan for the new equipment, but insisted that certain covenants be met with financial results measured using specific required policies. DHL has no differences from required accounting policies except for the tax accounting policy.

DHL must meet the following two balance sheet ratios under the terms of debt covenants:

1. The current ratio must exceed 1-to-1.
2. The total debt-to-equity ratio must be less than 4-to-1 (all non-equity credit accounts included in the numerator).

If covenants are breached, the loan may be called for repayment with 30 business days' notice. In practical terms, it is likely that a breach would result in higher financing costs, now prime plus 1/2%.

DHL has asked you, a public accountant, to review the financial statements and adjust the balance sheet for the effects of the new income tax policy. DHL is aware that this policy will be applied retrospectively, and thus will affect comparative retained earnings statements.

For now, though, DHL would like the balance sheet implications quantified. Management understands that any change to future income tax changes the retained earnings balance.

The draft balance sheet is shown in Exhibit 1, calculation of taxable income is in Exhibit 2, and other information is in Exhibit 3.

DHL has also asked you to evaluate (and make changes for) any other accounting policies that might concern you. DHL has no wish to fall afoul of CBC's judgements in any credit review process.

Required:

Prepare a report that responds to the concerns raised.

EXHIBIT 1

DHL BALANCE SHEET AS OF 30 NOVEMBER 20X8

(in thousands)

Assets	
Current	
Accounts receivable	$ 2,690
Inventory, at lower of cost or market	513
Prepaid expenses	219
Investment tax credit receivable	1,200
	4,622
Capital assets, net of depreciation	12,850
	$17,472
Current Liabilities	
Bank operating line of credit	$ 295
Accounts payable and accrued liabilities	3,071
Deferred investment tax credit, net of amortization	
(written off straight line over 4 years)	900
	4,266
Long-term debt	7,500
Shareholders' equity	5,706
	$17,472

EXHIBIT 2

DHL TAXABLE INCOME YEAR ENDED 30 NOVEMBER 20X8

(in thousands)

Accounting income	$2,252
Depreciation (including $3.5 on capitalized interest)	1,306
Capital Cost Allowance[1]	(404)
Inventory writedown to LCM[2]	40
Interest capitalized	(35)
Non-deductible entertainment and marketing expenses	84
Amortization of deferred investment tax credit	(300)
Taxable income	2,943
Income tax payable (@ 42%)	1,236
Less: Investment tax credit	1,200
Net tax payable	$ 36

[1] UCC at the end of 20X8, correctly calculated, was $9,100. This includes the new machinery net of the investment tax credit.

[2] Tax deductible when inventory is sold.

EXHIBIT 3

DHL OTHER INFORMATION

1. DHL has paid $120,000 of tax instalments in 20X8, recorded as prepaid expenses on the 30 November 20X8 balance sheet.
2. No tax expense or liability has been recorded for 20X8 as yet. Accounting income was closed to retained earnings on a pre-tax basis to prepare the balance sheet in Exhibit 1.
3. DHL offers a six-month warranty on certain products. In past years warranty expense had been expensed when claims were paid, since the warranty was new and not easily estimable. However, DHL has now had three years' experience with the warranty program and can safely estimate that the warranty liability at the end of 20X8 is in the $60,000 to $80,000 range.
4. DHL capitalized $35,000 of interest on the bank loan for the period that the new equipment was being installed. Capitalized interest is deductible for tax purposes when paid.
5. A full year's amortization was charged on all assets, including the new machinery. This machinery is being amortized straight-line over its expected life of 10 years. A full year's depreciation is charged in the first year.

CASE 15-3

CANADIAN PRODUCTS LIMITED

Canadian Products Limited (CPL) is a large public Canadian company. Recently the president issued a public letter to standard setters and to the Ontario Securities Commission (OSC) complaining about Canadian tax standards:

> We at CPL are very concerned that our current operating performance and debt-to-equity position are grossly misstated due to the Canadian standards for accounting for income tax. These standards do not reflect the economic reality of our tax position.

> Our future income tax balances arise because we are allowed to amortize our capital assets far more rapidly for tax purposes than they actually wear out. Thus, deductible expenses for tax purposes exceed our book expenses. Last year, our tax expense exceeded taxes payable by $17.2 million. When combined with prior amounts, we have a cumulative difference of $190.6 million, and this difference is expected to continue to increase.

> We estimate that this year's $17.2 million would not possibly be required to be repaid for at least 12 years—and perhaps never if we continue to expand. I understand that if we followed U.K. rules, using partial allocation, we wouldn't have to expense this amount at all this year. The U.K. approach seems far more realistic.

> We are also disturbed that discounting is not allowed for future tax amounts. If we had any other non-interest-bearing, long-term liability on our books, discounting would be considered appropriate. This inconsistency in the way supposedly analogous liabilities are treated highlights the fact that the future income tax liability is, in fact, different.

> We urge standard setters and market regulators to take a second look at the standards governing accounting for corporate income taxes.

Required:
Evaluate this statement, looking at both sides of each issue raised.

(CGA-Canada, adapted)

ASSIGNMENTS

★ **A15-1 Terminology Overview:** Listed below are some terms frequently used in relation to income tax accounting. Brief definitions are also listed. Match the definitions with the terms.

TERM
1. Future income tax liability
2. Taxes payable method
3. Interperiod income tax allocation
4. Liability method
5. Permanent difference
6. Taxable income
7. Income tax expense
8. Temporary difference
9. Partial allocation
10. Intraperiod income tax allocation

BRIEF DEFINITIONS
A. Income tax payable plus net future tax amounts attributable to this year.
B. The approach in which tax expense is equal to income taxes assessed by the taxation authorities.
C. Approach used to measure the effect of temporary differences; current tax rates are used for originating differences and existing balances are updated when tax rates change.
D. Amount of tax related to current and past accounting income that is not due this year.
E. Sources of future income tax, focusing on balance sheet differences between the tax and accounting values.
F. An allocation of the income tax provision across two or more accounting periods.
G. An amount used to compute income tax payable.
H. An allocation of the income tax provision among the major components in the financial statements.
I. A difference between taxable income and accounting income that never will reverse.
J. An approach in which only some differences between tax and accounting bases are recognized.

★ **A15-2 Explanation of Tax Alternatives:** Briefly respond to each of the following:

1. The taxes payable method is often supported by those who want financial statements to portray cash flow. Why?
2. Supporters of the taxes payable method suggest that future income taxes are meaningless. Why do they feel this is true?
3. Partial tax allocation involves recognizing some temporary differences as deferred or future income taxes but not recognizing others. What kinds of temporary differences are likely to cause recognition of future income tax?
4. What are the major problems when attempting to discount future income tax?

★ **A15-3 Income Tax allocation—Two-Year Period:** Star Corporation provided the following data related to accounting and taxable income:

	20X4	20X5
Pre-tax accounting income (financial statements)	$200,000	$220,000
Taxable income (tax return)	120,000	300,000
Income tax rate	30%	30%

There are no existing temporary differences other than those reflected in this data. There are no permanent differences.

Required:

1. How much tax expense would be reported in each year if the taxes payable method was used? What is potentially misleading with this presentation of tax expense?

2. How much tax expense and future income tax would be reported using comprehensive tax allocation and the liability method? Why is the two-year total tax expense the same in requirements (1) and (2)?

★ **A15-4 Income Tax Allocation—Three-Year Period; Rate Change:** Bhutani Inc. had pre-tax net income of $100,000 in each of 20X1, 20X2, and 20X3. The 20X1 income included $40,000 that was not taxable until 20X3. Bhutani's income tax rate was 35%.

Required:

1. How much tax expense would be reported in each year if the taxes payable method is used?

2. How much tax expense and future income tax would be reported in each year using comprehensive tax allocation?

3. Assume that the government changed the income tax rate to 30%, effective for 20X2 and following years. What income tax expense and future income tax would be reported in each of the three years, using comprehensive income tax allocation?

★★ **A15-5 Income Tax Allocation—Two-Year Period:** Lonesome Limited reported the following information (in thousands) for 20X6 and 20X7:

	20X6	20X7
Income from continuing operations, before unusual item, discontinued operation, and income tax	$30,000	$25,000
Unusual item—gain on sale of capital assets (before income tax)	8,000	
Gain from discontinued operations, before income tax		10,000

Lonesome's income tax rate is 30%. The 20X6 unusual gain is not taxable until 20X7. The 20X7 gain on discontinued operation is fully taxable in 20X7.

Required:

1. Prepare a partial income statement in good form for 20X6 and 20X7, starting with "Income from continuing operations, before unusual item, discontinued operation, and income tax," using two different methods:
   a. Taxes payable method
   b. Comprehensive tax allocation

2. Explain the circumstances under which Lonesome Limited could use the taxes payable method and still be within Canadian GAAP.

★ **A15-6 Temporary Differences:** Listed below are six independent sources of future income tax. For each item, indicate whether the future income tax account on the balance sheet would be a debit or a credit.

Item	Debit or Credit
a. Accelerated amortization (CCA) for income tax and straight-line amortization for accounting	_____
b. Estimated warranty costs: cash basis for income tax and accrual basis for accounting	_____
c. Sales revenue when payment is deferred: cash basis for tax purposes but recognize on delivery for accounting	_____
d. Construction contracts: completed-contract for income tax and percentage-of-completion for accounting	_____
e. Unrealized loss: loss recognized only on later disposal of the asset for income tax but market value (LCM) recognized for accounting	_____
f. Rent revenue collected in advance: cash basis for income tax, accrual basis for accounting	_____

★★ **A15-7 Income Tax Allocation, Alternatives:** The financial statements of Dakar Corporation for a four-year period reflected the following pre-tax amounts:

Solution

	20X4	20X5	20X6	20X7
Income Statement (summarized)				
Revenues	$110,000	$124,000	$144,000	$164,000
Expenses other than depreciation	(80,000)	(92,000)	(95,000)	(128,000)
Depreciation expense (straight-line)	(10,000)	(10,000)	(10,000)	(10,000)
Pre-tax accounting income	$ 20,000	$ 22,000	$ 39,000	$ 26,000
Balance Sheet (partial)				
Machine (four-year life, no residual value), at cost	$ 40,000	$ 40,000	$ 40,000	$ 40,000
Less: Accumulated Depreciation	(10,000)	(20,000)	(30,000)	(40,000)
	$ 30,000	$ 20,000	$ 10,000	$ 0

Dakar has a tax rate of 40% each year and claimed CCA for income tax purposes as follows: 20X4, $16,000; 20X5, $12,000; 20X6, $8,000; and 20X7, $4,000. There were no future income tax balances at 1 January 20X4.

Required:

1. For each year, calculate net income using the taxes payable method.
2. For each year, calculate the future income tax balance on the balance sheet at the end of the year using the liability method of tax allocation. Also calculate net income using the liability method of tax allocation.
3. Explain why the tax allocation method is usually viewed as preferable to the taxes payable method.

★ **A15-8 Temporary Difference:** Cheney World Enterprises Inc. undertook a major modification of its assembly process in 20X4. Restructuring costs incurred during 20X4 totalled $24 million. These costs will legitimately be deducted in computing Cheney's taxable income for 20X4. For accounting purposes, however, the costs will be amortized on a straight-line basis over the next three years, 20X5 through 20X7. Cheney's income tax rate is 35%.

Required:

1. Determine both the tax basis and the accounting basis for these costs at 31 December 20X4.

2. Compute the amount of the temporary difference as of the end of 20X5.

3. What will be the balance of future income tax asset or liability relating to these costs that will be shown on the balance sheet at each year end, 20X4 through 20X7? How much of the future income tax will be shown as a current item?

★ **A15-9 CCA-Depreciation Differences:** Olivetti Corporation acquired new equipment for $400,000 in 20X4. For accounting purposes, the equipment will be amortized over four years, straight-line, with a full-year's depreciation in the first year. For income tax purposes, Olivetti can take CCA over three years: $200,000 in 20X4, $125,000 in 20X5, and $75,000 in 20X6. Olivetti's income tax rate is 30%.

Required:
For each 31 December, 20X4 through 20X7, determine:

1. The tax basis for the equipment.
2. The accounting basis for the equipment.
3. The amount of the temporary difference relating to the equipment.
4. The amount future income tax expense.
5. The balance of future income tax asset or liability that would be shown on the balance sheet.

★★ **A15-10 Cumulative CCA-Depreciation Differences:** Agnew Corporation started operations in 20X1. The company acquired equipment in the first year for a price of $90,000. The equipment will be amortized for accounting purposes over three years on a straight-line basis (with a full year's depreciation in the year of acquisition). For determining income tax payable, the company can deduct one-half of the purchase cost as CCA in the first year, one-third in the second year, and one-sixth in the third year.

The company's 20X1 startup was successful, and in 20X2 the company bought identical equipment for $96,000. In 20X3, a third set of equipment was acquired for $99,000. The pattern of depreciation and CCA is proportionately the same for each acquisition. Agnew's tax rate is 30%.

The company's management plans to continue the same level of investment for the foreseeable future, as long as the company remains profitable.

Required:

1. Determine the temporary difference relating to the tax versus accounting bases of the equipment (that is, CCA versus accounting amortization) for each of 20X1 through 20X3. What is the accumulated balance of the temporary difference at the end of each year?

2. What is the balance of the *future income tax* account at the end of each year?

3. What will happen to the accumulated temporary differences and future income tax if Agnew continues to maintain its current level of investment in equipment, replacing each asset as it comes to the end of its useful life?

4. What conditions will be necessary to cause the timing difference balance to decline in future years?

5. Under what conditions will reversal of the accumulated timing differences cause a cash outflow?

★★ **A15-11 Cumulative Temporary Differences:** At the end of 20X3, Tustian Limited's balance sheet showed equipment at total cost of $4,000,000. The equipment was being amortized at 10% per year, straight-line, and was 40% depreciated at the end of 20X3. The income tax files showed unclaimed capital cost (UCC) for the equipment of $1,100,000. Tustian's balance sheet also showed an asset of $800,000 for unamortized development costs. The development costs had been incurred in previous years and had been deducted for income tax purposes in those prior years.

In 20X4, Tustian acquired an additional $600,000 in equipment while scrapping equipment that originally cost $400,000. The CCA rate for Tustian's equipment is 20%. Total CCA claimed for 20X4 was $280,000. Tustian amortized $100,000 of the development costs.

Tustian pays income tax at a rate of 40%.

Required:

1. Determine the cumulative temporary differences relating to equipment and development costs at the end of each of 20X3 and 20X4.

2. What is the balance of the *future income tax* account at the end of each year?

3. What are the accounting basis and the tax basis of the equipment and of the development cost at the end of each of 20X3 and 20X4?

4. If Tustian maintains its capital asset base by reinvestment and renewal in future years, when will the future income tax balance begin to decline? Explain.

★ **A15-12 Tax Calculations:** The records of Tina Corporation, at the end of 20X4, provided the following data related to income taxes:

a. Expense in 20X4, $80,000, properly recorded for accounting purposes but not tax deductible at any time.

b. Investment income in 20X4, $350,000, properly recorded for accounting purposes but not taxable at any time.

c. Estimated expense, $130,000; accrued for accounting purposes at the end of 20X4; to be reported for income tax purposes when paid at the end of 20X5.

d. Gain on disposal of land, $480,000; recorded for accounting purposes at the end of 20X4; to be reported as a capital gain for income tax purposes at the end of 20X6.

Accounting income (from the financial statements) for 20X4, $800,000; the income tax rate is 35%. There were no future tax amounts as of the beginning of 20X4.

Required:

1. Are the individual differences listed above permanent differences or temporary differences? Explain why.

2. Prepare the journal entry to record income tax at the end of 20X4.

3. Show the amounts that will be reported on (a) the balance sheet and (b) the income statement for 20X4.

★ **A15-13 Tax Calculations:** Beetle Corporation reported accounting income before taxes as follows: 20X4, $75,000; 20X5, $88,000. Taxable income for each year would have been the same as pre-tax accounting income except for the tax effects, arising for the first time in 20X4, of $1,800 in rent revenue, representing $300 per month rent revenue collected in advance on 1 October 20X4, for the six months ending 31 March 20X5. Rent revenue is taxable in the year collected. The tax rate for 20X4 and 20X5 is 30%, and the year-end for both accounting and tax purposes is 31 December. The rent revenue collected in advance is the only difference, and it is not repeated in October 20X5.

Required:

1. Is this a temporary difference? Why or why not?
2. What is the accounting carrying value for the unearned rent at the end of 20X4? The tax basis? Explain.
3. Calculate taxable income, and income tax payable, and prepare journal entries for each year-end.
4. Prepare a partial income statement for each year, starting with pre-tax accounting income.
5. What amount of future income tax would be reported on the 20X4 and 20X5 balance sheets?

★ **A15-14 Tax Calculations:** The pre-tax income statements for VCR Corporation for two years (summarized) were as follows:

	20X5	20X6
Revenues	$740,000	$800,000
Expenses	640,000	685,000
Pre-tax income	$100,000	$115,000

For tax purposes, the following income tax differences existed:

a. Revenues on the 20X6 income statement include $45,000 rent, which is taxable in 20X5 but was unearned at the end of 20X5 for accounting purposes.
b. Expenses on the 20X6 income statement include membership fees of $40,000, which are not deductible for income tax purposes.
c. Expenses on the 20X5 income statement include $32,000 of estimated warranty costs, which are not deductible for income tax purposes until 20X6.

Required:

1. What was the accounting carrying value and tax basis for unearned revenue and the warranty liability at the end of 20X5 and 20X6?
2. Compute (a) income tax payable, (b) future income tax table and (c) income tax expense for each period. Assume an average tax rate of 30%.
3. Give the entry to record income taxes for each period.
4. Complete income statements to include income taxes as allocated.
5. What amount of future income tax will be reported on the balance sheet at each year-end?

★ **A15-15 Tax Calculations:** Yuan Incorporated recorded instalment sales revenue of $80,000 in 20X1 and $100,000 in 20X2. The revenue is not taxable until collected. Of the year 20X1 revenue, $60,000 was collected in 20X2 and the remaining $20,000 collected in 20X3. Of the year 20X2 revenue, $68,000 was collected in 20X3 and the rest in 20X4. Yuan's accounting earnings before income tax for the three years was as follows:

20X1	$200,000
20X2	300,000
20X3	240,000

On 1 January 20X1, the enacted rate for all years was 40%. During 20X3, the rate was revised to 36%.

CGA-Canada, adapted.

Required:

Prepare the necessary journal entries to record income tax for the years 20X1, 20X2, and 20X3.

(CGA-Canada, adapted)

★ **A15-16 Tax Calculations:** STC started operations on 1 January 20X5. Information on the first two years of operations is as follows:

	20X5	20X6
Accounting income before income tax	$45,000	$60,000
Amortization expense on tangible capital assets	20,000	20,000
Capital cost allowance	12,000	24,000
Equity in earnings of subsidiaries (not taxable)	15,000	20,000
Income tax rate	34%	34%

The company accurately estimated the actual 20X6 data in 20X5. The 20X7 and later income tax rate of 40% was enacted in 20X5 to take effect in 20X7. That is, STC knew that $4,000 of the 20X5 temporary difference would reverse in 20X6, and the remainder in 20X7 or better.

Required:

Prepare all income tax journal entries for 20X5 and 20X6.

(CGA-Canada)

★ **A15-17 Future Income Tax, Change in Tax Rates:** DCM Metals Limited has a 31 December year-end. The tax rate is 30% in 20X4, 35% in 20X5, and 42% in 20X6. The company reports income as follows:

20X4	$550,000
20X5	123,000
20X6	310,000

Taxable income and accounting income are identical except for a $300,000 revenue reported for accounting purposes in 20X4, and reported one-half in 20X5 and one-half in 20X6 for tax purposes. The revenue is related to a long-term account receivable, taxable only when collected.

Required:

Compute tax expense and future income tax on the balance sheet for 20X4, 20X5, and 20X6.

★★ **A15-18 Future Income Tax, Change in Tax Rates:** Stacy Corporation would have had identical income before tax on both its income tax returns and income statements for the years 20X4 through 20X7, except for a capital asset that cost $120,000. The operational asset has a four-year estimated life and no residual value. The asset was depreciated for income tax purposes using the following amounts: 20X4, $48,000; 20X5, $36,000; 20X6, $24,000; and 20X7, $12,000. However, for accounting purposes, the straight-line method was used (that is, $30,000 per year). The accounting and tax periods both end on 31 December. Income amounts before depreciation expense and income tax for each of the four years were as follows:

	20X4	20X5	20X6	20X7
Accounting income before tax and depreciation	$60,000	$80,000	$70,000	$70,000
Tax rate	30%	30%	40%	40%

Required:

1. Explain why this is a temporary difference.
2. Calculate the accounting carrying value and tax basis of the asset at the end of each year.
3. Reconcile pre-tax accounting and taxable income, calculate income tax payable and tax expense, compute the balance in the future income tax account, and prepare journal entries for each year-end.

⭐⭐ **A15-19 Future Income Tax, Change in Tax Rates:** The Bevis Company has a future income tax liability in the amount of $80,000 at 31 December 20X4, relating to a $200,000 receivable. This sale was recorded for accounting purposes in 20X4 but is not taxable until the cash is collected. In 20X5, $100,000 is collected. Warranty expense in 20X5 included in the determination of pre-tax accounting income is $75,000, with the entire amount expected to be spent and deductible for tax purposes in 20X6. Pre-tax accounting income is $650,000 in 20X5. The tax rate is 30% in 20X5.

Required:

1. What is the accounting carrying value, the tax basis of the account receivable, and the warranty liability, at the end of 20X4 and 20X5? What was the enacted tax rate at 31 December 20X4?
2. Calculate taxable income and income tax payable, compute the balance in the future income tax accounts, and prepare journal entries for year-end 20X5.
3. Calculate the future income tax that would be reported on the balance sheet at the end of 20X5.

⭐⭐ **A15-20 Tax Calculations; Change in Tax Rates:** On 1 January 20X3, Highmark Corporation reported the following amounts on the balance sheet:

Current: Future income tax (debit)	$ 16,000
Long-term: Future income tax (credit)	$120,000

On this date, the net book value of capital assets was $1,750,000 and undepreciated capital cost was $1,450,000. There was a warranty liability of $40,000. Taxable income of $500,000 (in total) in 20X1 and 20X2 had resulted in the payment of $195,000 of income tax.

In 20X3, accounting income was $170,000. This included non-tax-deductible expenses of $42,000, dividend revenue of $12,000, depreciation of $75,000, and a warranty expense of $39,000. Warranty claims paid were $51,000 and CCA was $99,000.

Required:

Provide the journal entry to record tax expense in 20X3. The enacted tax rate was 41% in 20X3.

⭐⭐ **A15-21 Tax Calculations—Tax Rate Change:** The income statements for Lemond Corporation for two years (summarized) were as follows:

	20X4	20X5
Revenues	$200,000	$180,000
Expenses	181,000	152,000
Pre-tax accounting income	$ 19,000	$ 28,000
Taxable income (per tax return)	$ 47,000	$ 28,000

The income tax rate is 40% in 20X4 and 35% in 20X5. The 20X5 tax rate was enacted in 20X5. For tax purposes, the following differences existed:

a. Expenses (given above) on the 20X4 and 20X5 income statements include golf club dues of $10,000 annually, which are not deductible for income tax purposes.

b. Revenues (given above) on the 20X5 income statement include $10,000 rent revenue, which was taxable in 20X4 but was unearned for accounting purposes until 20X5.

c. Expenses (given above) on the 20X4 income statement include $8,000 of estimated warranty costs, which are not deductible for income tax purposes until paid in 20X6.

Required:

1. Explain whether each difference is a permanent or temporary difference.
2. Calculate income tax payable for each year.
3. Calculate income tax expense for each of 20X4 and 20X5. Also calculate the balance in the future income tax account at the end of 20X4 and 20X5.

★★

A15-22 Tax Calculations—Tax Rate Change: The records of Morgan Corporation provided the following data at the end of years 1 through 4 relating to income tax allocation:

	Year 1	Year 2	Year 3	Year 4
Pre-tax accounting income	$58,000	$70,000	$80,000	$88,000
Taxable income (tax return)	28,000	80,000	90,000	98,000
Tax rate	30%	35%	40%	40%

The above amounts include only one temporary difference; no other changes occurred. At the end of year 1, the company prepaid an expense of $30,000, which was then amortized for accounting purposes over the next three years (straight-line). The full amount was included as a deduction in year 1 for income tax purposes. Each year's tax rate was enacted in each specific year—that is, the year 2 tax rate was enacted in year 2, etc.

Required:

1. Calculate income tax payable for each year.
2. Calculate income tax expense.
3. Comment on the effect that use of the liability method has on income tax expense when the income tax rate changes.

★★ **A15-23 Tax Rate Change, Two-Stage:** At the end of 20X4, Varna Ltd. had accumulated temporary differences of $500,000 arising from CCA/amortization on tangible capital assets. The balance of the future income tax liability account was $200,000. Over the next three years, Varna experienced the following:

	20X5	20X6	20X7
Accounting income, before income taxes	$200,000	$220,000	$250,000
Expenses not deductible for computing income tax	8,000	10,000	6,000
Temporary differences*	44,000	50,000	52,000

*excess of tax-deductible expenses over expenses recognized in accounting income

The tax rate was 40% for taxation years 20X4 and 20X5, 34% for 20X6, and 30% for 20X7.

Required:

1. Calculate income tax expense for each year, 20X5, 20X6, and 20X7. Assume that the rates for 20X6 and 20X7 were enacted year by year. Distinguish between current income tax expense and future income tax expense. State any additional assumptions that you make.

2. Assume instead that the rates for 20X6 and 20X7 were enacted in 20X5. How, if at all, would this affect income tax expense in each of the three years?

A15-24 Tax Calculations: Reno Limited, in the first year of its operations, reported the following information regarding its operations:

a. Income before tax for the year was $1,300,000 and the tax rate was 35%.
b. Depreciation was $140,000 and CCA was $67,000. Net book value at year-end was $820,000, while UCC was $893,000.
c. The warranty program generated an estimated cost (expense) on the income statement of $357,000 but the cash paid out was $264,000. The $93,000 liability resulting from this was shown as a current liability. On the income tax return, the cash paid is the amount deductible.
d. Entertainment expenses of $42,000 were included in the income statement but were not allowed to be deducted for tax purposes.

In the second year of its operations, Reno Limited reported the following information:

a. Income before income tax for the year was $1,550,000 and the tax rate was 37%.
b. Depreciation was $140,000 and the CCA was $370,000. Net book value at year-end was $680,000, while UCC was $523,000.
c. The estimated costs of the warranty program were $387,000 and the cash paid out was $342,000. The liability had a balance of $138,000.

Required:
Prepare the journal entry to record income tax expense in the first and second year of operations. The second-year tax rate was not enacted until the second year.

(CGA-Canada, adapted)

 A15-25 Tax Calculations: Renon Corporation uses the liability method of tax allocation At 1 January 20X6 Renon Corporation had the following balances, events, and transactions:

a. Income before income tax and before item (c) (below) was $1,440,000.
b. In 20X6, depreciation was $170,000 and CCA was $35,000. At the beginning of the year, the net book value of capital assets was $2,695,000, while the UCC was $1,205,000. This was the only temporary difference prior to 20X6.
c. There was an extraordinary item (a loss of $638,000), resulting from a fire at the processing plant. Only $425,000 of the loss was tax deductible; the remainder was a permanent difference between accounting and taxable income.
d. The company received dividends of $65,000 from another Canadian company. These were included in income but were not taxable.
e. The company had $140,000 in advertising expenses, which were included in income but were not deductible for tax purposes.

The tax rate for the year was 45%; in all previous years the tax rate was 35%. The 45% rate was enacted in 20X6.

Required:

1. Prepare the required income tax entry for 20X6.
2. Prepare the bottom section of the income statement, beginning with income before income tax and extraordinary item.
3. If the company were to use *partial* tax allocation, instead of *comprehensive* tax allocation, describe how the income tax expense would likely change and why.

★★ **A15-26 Tax Calculations, Rate Change:** In its first year of operations, Sobhy Corporation reported the following information:

a. Income before income taxes was $1,000,000.
b. The company acquired capital assets costing $900,000; depreciation was $150,000 and CCA was $90,000.
c. The company recorded an expense of $200,000 for the one-year warranty on the company's products; cash disbursements amounted to $80,000.
d. The income tax rate was 35%.

In the second year, Sobhy reported the following:

a. Legislation was enacted that changed the tax rate to 40%.
b. Income before income tax was $1,200,000.
c. Depreciation was $150,000; CCA was $162,000.
d. The estimated warranty costs were $250,000 while the cash expenditure was $220,000.
e. Entertainment expenses of $40,000 included on the income statement were not deductible for tax purposes.

Required:
Prepare the journal entries to record income tax expense for the first and second years of operation.

★★ **A15-27 Tax Calculations, Rate Change:** Golf Incorporated, which began operations in 20X3, uses the same policies for financial accounting and tax purposes with the exception of warranty costs and franchise fee revenue. Information about the $60,000 of warranty expenses and $90,000 franchise revenue accrued for book purposes is provided below:

	20X3	20X4	20X5
Warranty cost for book purposes	$60,000	—	—
Warranty cost for tax purposes (claims paid)	15,000	$20,000	$25,000
Franchise fee revenue, book, on account	90,000	—	—
Franchise fee revenue, tax, cash received	9,000	51,000	30,000
Effective tax rate	38%	40%	45%
Income before tax	$75,000	$90,000	$80,000

Required:
Prepare journal entries to record taxes for 20X3 to 20X5. The company uses the liability method. Separate future income tax accounts are used for each source of temporary differences. The tax rate for a given year is not enacted until that specific year.

(CGA-Canada, adapted)

★★ **A15-28 Tax Calculations:** A. Grossery Limited is a wholesale grocery distributor formed in 20X4, with warehouses in several locations in southern Ontario. The company uses the liability method of tax allocation. In fiscal 20X4, the company had net operating income before tax of $30,000 and an extraordinary gain of $100,000 (before tax). The following items were included in the determination of net income:

a. Depreciation on buildings and equipment owned of $50,000. The assets' original cost was $650,000.
b. Pension expense of $44,747. Pension amounts paid were $48,395. There is a deferred pension asset on the balance sheet of $3,648 as a result.
c. Amortization of capitalized leased assets and interest expense on the lease liability totalled $14,300; the assets' lease payments in 20X4 amounted to $21,000.

In calculating the amount of income tax owed to the government in 20X4, the following factors must be taken into account:

a. CCA amounts to $80,000 for 20X4.

b. Pension costs are tax deductible at the time of *funding*.

c. The capitalized leases are taxed as operating leases. That is, cash lease costs are tax deductible and depreciation, interest, etc., recognized for accounting purposes are not tax deductible. Over time, cash payments will equal the total of these expenses, but the timing of expense recognition is different. The net accounting carrying value for lease-related amounts at the end of 20X4 was a net debit of $6,700. The tax basis was zero.

d. The extraordinary gain will be taxable in 20X7, when proceeds are collected.

e. The tax rate is 40%.

f. Golf club dues of $20,000 are included in the net operating income of $30,000.

g. Tax instalment payments during the year amounted to 75% of the payable amount.

Required:

Prepare the final sections of the income statement for 20X4, starting with income from operations before tax. Clearly support your calculations of income tax and other amounts. Also show what would appear on the balance sheet and cash flow statement in relation to tax for 20X4. Use the direct method in the operating activities section.

 A15-29 Classifying Balance Sheet Future Income Tax: The following information pertains to deForest Limited for the year ending 31 December 20X2:

a. The carrying value of deForest's inventory was $260,000 at the end of 20X2; the tax basis was $300,000.

b. deForest records a liability for the amount of vacation time that employees have earned but have not yet taken. Salaries paid to vacationing employees are deductible for tax purposes only when paid. The liability balance on the books at the end of 20X2 was $100,000.

c. The company is amortizing the discount on bonds issued three years previously. The principal amount of the bonds is due in 20X5. The amortization is not deductible for tax purposes, but the excess of face value over issue price will be deductible when the bonds are repaid in 20X5. The original amount of the discount was $20,000. Of that amount, $12,000 remains unamortized at the end of 20X2.

d. Total accumulated depreciation for accounting purposes is $200,000; and accumulated CCA for income tax purposes is $450,000. The related tangible capital asset has a five-year useful life and an original cost of $600,000.

e. The enacted income tax rate is 30%.

Required:

1. Calculate the future income tax amounts relating to each of these four items.

2. How would these amounts be reported on the company's 31 December 20X2 balance sheet?

3. Would your response to requirement (2) change if you knew that some of the depreciation/CCA difference would reverse next year? Explain.

 A15-30 Tax Expense; Comprehensive: At the end of 20X8, Sharon Corporation reported the following items in the financial statements:

Future income tax—current (liability)	171,000
Future income tax—long term (liability)	456,000

In 20X8, the company reported $214,500 of taxable income. It also reported a $450,000 long-term receivable, taxable when collected. The first future income tax account relates to this receivable. Capital assets, with a net book value of $3,700,000, had a lower UCC and thus caused the second future income tax account above.

In 20X9, Sharon reported accounting income of $900,000. Collections on the long-term receivable amounted to $300,000. There were non-deductible entertainment expenses of $24,000. Depreciation was $240,000 and CCA was $300,000. The tax rate was 39%.

Required:

1. Prepare a journal entry to record tax expense in 20X9. Tax rates were enacted in the year to which they pertain.

2. What would appear on the balance sheet at the end of 20X9 with respect to income tax? Give accounts and amounts.

★★ **A15-31 Tax Expense; Comprehensive:** Liquid Limited reported income before income tax of $175,900 in 20X9. The tax rate for 20X9 was 38% and was enacted during the year. The enacted tax rate at the end of the previous year was 35%.

At the end of 20X8, the balance sheet of Liquid included the net book value of depreciable capital assets of $795,000, long-term accounts receivable of $120,000, and a warranty liability of $49,000. Long-term receivables represent taxable income when collected.

In 20X9, dividends (tax free) received from taxable Canadian corporations were $16,000. Non-deductible entertainment expenses were $30,000. UCC was $480,000 at the beginning of the year. In 20X9, CCA was $50,000, and depreciation expense was $63,000.

During 20X9, long-term receivables of $42,000 were collected. There were no new long-term receivables. The warranty expense of $71,400 was equal to the warranty claims paid.

Required:

1. Calculate income tax expense for 20X9.

2. List the balance sheet accounts and their classification in the balance sheet as of the end of 20X9.

★★★ **A15-32 Income Tax Expense and Future Income Tax; Comprehensive:** Darragh Limited reported the following in 20X2:

- Income before tax and extraordinary items of $500,000.
- Extraordinary loss of $50,000. (This amount is 20% tax deductible in the current year. The remainder is a permanent difference.)
- Tax-free dividend income of $45,000.
- Depreciation of $125,000. Net book value was $5,200,000 at the beginning of the year, and $5,075,000 at the end of the year.
- CCA was $166,000 in 20X2.
- Collection of long-term receivables, $250,000. These amounts are taxable as received, but were included in accounting income when initially set up in 20X1.
- There were $100,000 of new long-term accounts receivable at the end of the year. The revenue related to these amounts is included in accounting income in 20X2.
- Warranty expense of $56,000 was equal to claims paid. However, there was an opening warranty liability of $32,000. This is a 12-month warranty.
- The 20X2 tax rate is 40%.

At the end of 20X1, the following things were reported:

- Future income tax, a credit of $92,500, related to the $250,000 long-term accounts receivable.
- Future income tax, a credit of $555,000, related to capital assets (Hint: Consider this amount when determining opening UCC).
- Future income tax, related to the warranty.

Required:

1. Prepare the bottom section of the income statement, beginning with income before income tax and extraordinary items.

2. Show the balance sheet items as they would be presented on the balance sheet, in good form.

★ ★ ★ **A15-33 Tax Calculations, Comprehensive:** Crandall Corporation was formed in 20X1. Relevant information pertaining to 20X1, 20X2, and 20X3 is as follows:

	20X1	20X2	20X3
Income before income tax	$100,000	$100,000	$100,000
Accounting income includes the following:			
Depreciation (assets have a cost of $120,000)	10,000	10,000	12,000
Pension expense*	5,000	7,000	10,000
Warranty expense	3,000	3,000	3,000
Dividend income	2,000	2,000	3,000
Taxable income includes the following:			
Capital cost allowance	25,000	15,000	7,000
Pension funding (amount paid)	7,000	8,000	9,000
Warranty costs paid	1,000	4,000	3,000
Tax rate—enacted in each year	40%	44%	48%

*Pension amounts are tax deductible when paid, not when expensed. Over the long term, payments will equal total expense. The tax basis for the pension will always be zero. For accounting purposes, there will be a balance sheet asset account asset called "deferred pension cost" for the difference between the amount paid and the expense, since the amount paid is higher.

Required:
Prepare the journal entry to record income tax expense for each year.

★ ★ ★ **A15-34 Tax Calculations, Comprehensive:** At the beginning of 20X1, Farcus Corporation had the following future tax accounts:

Future tax asset—current $19,600

Warranty expense to date has been $126,000; claims paid have been $70,000. There is a $56,000 warranty liability included in short-term liabilities on the balance sheet.

Future tax liability—long term $497,000

The net book value of capital assets was $2,276,000 at the beginning of 20X1; UCC was $856,000. Over time, CCA has been $1,420,000 higher than depreciation.

INFORMATION RELATING TO 20X1 AND 20X2:

	20X1	20X2
Net income before extraordinary item	$625,000	$916,000
Extraordinary gain (Note 1)	—	14,000
Items included in net income		
Golf dues	8,000	9,000
Tax penalties, not tax deductible	3,000	1,000
Depreciation	287,000	309,000
Warranty expense	22,000	41,000
Percentage-of-completion income (reported for the first time in 20X1) (Note 2)	17,000	10,000
Other information		
CCA	395,000	116,000
Warranty claims paid	16,000	50,000
Completed-contract income (used for tax purposes)	0	27,000
Tax rate—enacted in each year	40%	42%

Notes

(1) $4,000 is the tax-free portion of the gain. The remainder is fully taxable.

(2) The construction-in-progress inventory is classified as a current asset.

Required:

1. Indicate the amount and classification of all items that would appear on the balance sheet in relation to income tax at the end of 20X1 and 20X2. Assume no tax is paid until the subsequent year.

2. Draft the bottom section of the income statement for 20X2, beginning with "Income before extraordinary item." Show all required disclosures. Include comparative data for 20X1.

★★ **A15-35 Investment Tax Credit (Appendix):** Pegasus Printing began operations in 20X4, and has bought equipment for use in its printing operations in each of the last three years. This equipment qualifies for an investment tax credit of 14%. Information relating to the three years is shown below:

	20X4	20X5	20X6
Income before income tax	$165,000	$456,000	$468,000
Income tax rate	25%	25%	25%
Equipment eligible for ITC	$ 40,000	$689,000	$450,000
Estimated life of equipment	10 years	13 years	12 years

a. Income before tax includes non-deductible advertising expenditures of $20,000 each year.

b. Equipment is depreciated straight-line over its useful life for accounting purposes, assuming zero salvage value. A full year of depreciation is charged in the year of acquisition. CCA claims in 20X4 were $12,000; 20X5, $135,000; and 20X6, $216,000.

Required:

1. Calculate the depreciation expense in each of the three years, net of the investment tax credit amortization.

2. Calculate taxes payable in each of the three years. Note that depreciation added back is net depreciation, as calculated in requirement (1).

3. Calculate tax expense for each year, using Canadian standards (cost reduction) to account for the investment tax credit.

4. Calculate tax expense, using the flow-through approach for all tax amounts.

5. Why is the cost reduction approach preferable?

6. Show how capital assets, and the deferred investment tax credit, would be presented on the balance sheet at the end of 20X4.

CHAPTER 16

Accounting for Tax Losses

INTRODUCTION

In its 2006 annual report, Quebec-based ADF Group[1] reported accumulated tax loss carryforwards totalling approximately $150 million. These carryforwards can be used to reduce income taxes in future years. The company reported that the value of these carryforward benefits was $44 million. ADF's total assets were $53 million. Should ADF recognize the value of these tax benefits as an asset, thereby increasing its asset base by over 80%?

When a corporation's taxable "income" is actually a loss, the corporation can use that loss to reduce past and future income taxes. A loss will normally have tax benefits, but the benefits may not be *realized* in the period of the loss. Should future benefits be *recognized* in the year of the loss in order to achieve matching, or should their recognition be delayed in the interests of conservatism?

This chapter begins with an explanation of the income tax benefits that arise from a loss. Then we will discuss the issue of when and how to recognize those benefits.

---

[1] ADF Group Inc. designs, engineers, and fabricates complex steel structures.

TAX BENEFITS OF A LOSS

Accounting income is converted to taxable income by making appropriate adjustments for all temporary and permanent differences. This is true whether the accounting records report a net income or a net loss. Accounting income may become a taxable loss, and an accounting loss may become taxable income or a taxable loss, depending on the nature of the permanent and temporary differences. When a corporation prepares its tax return and finds it has a taxable loss, the corporation is entitled to offset the loss against past and future taxable income as follows:

- The loss can be *carried back* for three years for a refund of tax previously paid.
- Any remaining loss can be *carried forward* for 20 years to reduce taxes that would otherwise be payable.

If the sum of the previous three years' plus the next 20 years' taxable income turns out to be less than the loss, any remaining potential benefit is lost.

It is simple to account for the tax benefits of the loss *carrybacks*; the taxes recovered are recognized on the income statement as a tax recovery in the loss year, and the refund receivable is shown on the balance sheet as a current asset. Recognition occurs in the period of the loss because there is no uncertainty about whether or not the company will actually receive the benefit. Accounting for loss carrybacks will be demonstrated in the next section.

However, if the carrybacks do not fully utilize the loss, a recognition problem arises. Income taxes can be reduced in *future* periods as a result of the tax loss carryforward. Should the benefit of reduced future taxes be recognized in the period of the loss, or only in the period in which the benefits are realized? Since the future benefits arise from the current year's loss, the matching principle suggests that the benefits should be matched to the loss that created the benefits, and should be recognized in the loss year. The general principle, therefore, is that the tax benefits of tax losses should be recognized in the period of the loss, *to the extent possible.*

The actual amount of the benefit can be *measured* with reasonable assurance. For example, if a company has a tax loss of $1 million and the tax rate is 35%, the potential benefit of the tax loss is a reduction of past and future income taxes of $1 million $\times$ 35%, or $350,000. There will be some variation due to changes in tax rates from year to year, but the major part of the benefit is readily estimable.

What is not certain is whether the benefits of any carryforwards will actually be *realized.* In order to realize the benefit, the company must have enough taxable income during the carryforward period to use up the loss carryforward. Basically, the carryforward benefit is a contingent gain—a benefit will be realized only *if* something happens in the future. The conservatism principle suggests that contingent gains should not be recognized prior to their realization. However, the CICA, FASB, and IASB all have chosen to favour matching over conservatism. Current accounting standards require recognition of the contingent gain whenever management decides that it is *probable* (i.e., greater than 50% probability) that the future benefits will be realized.

Tax Loss versus Tax Benefits

To avoid confusion, it is necessary to keep track separately of the amount of the tax *loss* and the amount of the tax *benefit.* The **tax loss** is the final number of taxable loss on the tax return. The **tax benefit** is the total present and future benefit that the company will be able to realize from the tax loss through a reduction of income taxes paid to governments. Basically, the tax benefit is equal to the tax loss multiplied by the tax rate. Put another way, *the tax loss is the gross amount and the tax benefit is the tax savings.* Since tax rates can change, keeping track of the gross amount is essential for calculating the tax savings.

TAX LOSS CARRYBACKS

A tax **loss carryback** entitles the corporation to recover income tax actually paid in the previous three years. For example, assume that Fabian Corporation was established in 20X1.

For the first four years, the company was moderately successful, but in the fifth year it suffered a tax loss of $500,000. Fabian's taxable income for the first five years was as follows:

Year	Taxable Income	Tax Rate	Income Tax Paid
20X1	$100,000	40%	$ 40,000
20X2	240,000	40	96,000
20X3	160,000	35	56,000
20X4	300,000	37	111,000
20X5	(500,000)	38	—

The loss will be carried back to the preceding three years to recover tax previously paid. Normally, the loss is carried back to the earliest (oldest) year first, and then applied to succeeding years until the loss is used up. The year 20X1 is outside the three-year carryback period, and therefore the loss can be carried back only as far as 20X2. The tax recovery will be as follows:

Year	Carryback	Tax Rate	Tax Recovery
20X2	$240,000	40%	$ 96,000
20X3	160,000	35	56,000
20X4	100,000	37	37,000
Totals	$500,000		$189,000

In this example, the carryback completely utilizes the 20X5 tax loss of $500,000. Note that the tax is recovered at the rate at which it was originally paid. The tax rate in the year of the loss (i.e., 38% for 20X5) is irrelevant for determining the amount of tax recoverable via the carryback. Fabian will record the benefit of that carryback as follows:

Income tax receivable (B/S)	189,000	
Income tax expense (recovery) (I/S)		189,000

The *credit* to income tax expense reflects the fact that it is a recovery of taxes paid in earlier years. A company will usually label this amount as "provision for income tax" or "income tax recovery" in its income statement. If any part of the tax loss is attributable to discontinued operations or extraordinary items, the recovery must be allocated to the relevant components of income, as was described in Chapter 3 for *intraperiod* allocation.

In 20X3, the tax rate was 35%; in 20X4 it had increased to 37%. The company would maximize its recovery by applying more of the carryback to 20X4 instead of 20X3; there is no requirement in the *Income Tax Act* to apply the carryback sequentially. If the company follows a recovery maximization strategy, the carryback would be applied as follows:

Year	Carryback	Tax Rate	Tax Recovery
20X2	$240,000	40%	$ 96,000
20X4	260,000	37	96,200
Totals	$500,000		$192,200

Maximizing the carryback tax recovery is a viable strategy, but it is a bit of a gamble because if the company has a loss in 20X7, the 20X4 carryback potential will have already been used up and the 20X3 tax is then out of reach because it is no longer within the allowable carryback period of three years. Therefore, companies usually apply the carryback sequentially even if there may be an advantage to applying the carryback non-sequentially, to the years that had the highest tax rate.

TEMPORARY AND PERMANENT DIFFERENCES IN A LOSS YEAR

Step 1: Calculate Taxable Income

The first step in doing a tax question is always to calculate taxable income. This involves adjusting accounting income for permanent and temporary differences. Temporary differences continue to originate and/or reverse, regardless of whether the company is experiencing profits or losses. Permanent differences are likewise the same, whether accounting and/or taxable income are positive or negative. Indeed, it is quite possible for temporary differences and permanent differences to convert a pre-tax accounting profit to a tax loss. For example, assume the following facts for Michelle Limited for the fiscal year ending 31 December 20X8:

- Net income before taxes of $90,000, after deducting amortization expense of $150,000.
- CCA totalling $280,000 deducted on the tax return.
- Net book value of capital assets of $1,700,000 and undepreciated capital cost (UCC) of $1,200,000 on 1 January 20X8, a temporary difference of $500,000 that is reflected in an accumulated future income tax liability balance of $200,000 at 1 January 20X8.
- Non-deductible golf club dues of $10,000.
- Taxable income in the three-year carryback period of $360,000.
- Tax rate of 40% in the current and previous years.

Michelle Limited's taxable income for 20X8 will be computed as follows:

Accounting income	$ 90,000
Permanent difference:	
Golf club dues	+ 10,000
Temporary difference:	
Amortization	+150,000
CCA	−280,000
Taxable income (loss)	$ (30,000)

Step 2: Determine Future Income Tax

The next step is to determine the change to future income tax caused by current-year temporary differences and/or any change in the tax rate. This is normally done with a table, but since the tax rate did not change this year, the shortcut approach can be used.

The difference between CCA and amortization yields a temporary difference of $130,000 (i.e., $150,000 − $280,000). This temporary difference increases the future income tax liability by $52,000 (i.e., $130,000 × 40%).

The $30,000 tax loss creates a potential tax benefit of $12,000 (at 40%).

Step 3: Journal Entries

The third step is to prepare the journal entries. These entries reflect temporary differences, income tax payable, if any, and the disposition of the tax loss.

The $52,000 of future income tax arising from temporary differences is recorded as follows:

Income tax expense (I/S)	52,000	
Future income tax liability—capital assets (B/S)		52,000

The $30,000 tax loss is carried back, which results in a tax recovery (@ 40%) of $12,000:

Income tax receivable—carryback benefit (B/S)	12,000	
Income tax expense (I/S)		12,000

If these two entries are combined, the summary entry to record the provision for income tax will be:

Income tax expense	40,000	
Income tax receivable—carryback benefit	12,000	
Future income tax liability—capital assets (B/S)		52,000

The bottom of the income statement will show:

Income before income tax		$90,000
Income tax expense (Note 1)		40,000
Net income		$50,000
Note 1:		
Future income tax	$52,000	
Recovery of amounts paid in prior years	(12,000)	
Income tax expense	$40,000	

Adjusting Temporary Differences

In the Michelle Limited example above, the temporary difference created a tax loss of $30,000. Since the company had available taxable income in the carryback period against which the loss can be offset, good tax strategy calls for taking the maximum allowable CCA in 20X8 in order to obtain a refund of taxes previously paid.

Suppose instead that the company did not have taxable income in the preceding three years. A tax loss in 20X8 would not permit the company to realize any tax benefit in 20X8 because there would be no possibility of receiving a tax refund. In a sense, the tax loss would go to waste unless the company generates profits in the carryforward period, never a sure thing.

Instead of having a tax loss, the company can simply reduce the amount of CCA that it deducts on its tax return for 20X8 by $30,000, from $280,000 to $250,000. CCA is an *optional* deduction; in any year, a company can deduct anywhere from zero to the maximum percentage allowed by tax regulations. A company will have a higher amount of undepreciated capital cost (and CCA) in *future years* if it claims less CCA in the *current year*. Companies make these decisions based on advice from their tax-planning advisors.

1. How many years can a tax loss be carried back? How many years into the future can it be carried forward?

2. What is the difference between the tax loss in a particular year and the tax benefit of the loss?

3. Why do companies usually apply a loss carryback sequentially (i.e., to the earliest year first), even if the tax refund might be slightly larger if they applied it to the carryback year that had the highest tax rate?

TAX LOSS CARRYFORWARDS

In the Fabian Corporation example earlier in the chapter, the tax benefit of the $500,000 tax loss in 20X5 was fully realized through the carryback. But suppose instead that the loss in 20X5 was $1,000,000. Then the carryback could utilize only $700,000 of the loss:

Year	Carryback	Tax Rate	Tax Recovery
20X2	$240,000	40%	$ 96,000
20X3	160,000	35	56,000
20X4	300,000	37	111,000
Totals	**$700,000**		**$263,000**

The tax benefit ($263,000) relating to $700,000 of the $1 million tax loss is realized through the carryback; the tax benefit is both *recognized* and *realized* in 20X5. After the carryback, there is a carryforward of $300,000 remaining. The tax benefit of the **loss carryforward** cannot be realized until future years, when the carryforward is applied against otherwise taxable income.

loss carryforward

to carry a tax loss forward to apply against taxable income of up to 20 subsequent years after a year in which a taxable loss is incurred; will avoid tax otherwise payable

The accounting question is whether the future tax benefit of the carryforward can be *recognized* in 20X5, the period of the loss. Companies often want to recognize the benefits of a loss carryforward because that recognition decreases the apparent accounting loss. The income tax recovery is a credit entry in the income statement, reducing the amount of the reported loss. Recognition will also either (1) reduce the future tax liability or (2) create an asset on the balance sheet if there is no future tax liability to offset it against.

The Basic Principle—"More Likely Than Not"

The criterion for recognizing the future benefits is simply a matter of probability. If it is probable that the carryforward will be realized, then the benefit is recognized. On the other hand, if realization is unlikely, then the potential benefit should not be recognized. The threshold under Canadian and U.S. standards is whether it is *more likely than not* that the benefit will be realized. Conceptually, it is simple: a 51% probability of realization requires recognition; 49% probability means no recognition. In practice, estimation is more difficult.

In deciding whether the probability is greater than 50%, management may consider possible tax-planning strategies, including such actions as:

- Reducing or eliminating CCA in the year of the loss and future years;
- Amending prior years' tax returns to reduce or eliminate CCA; or
- Recognizing taxable revenues in the carryforward period that might ordinarily be recognized in later periods.

Whether or not the over-50% criterion has been met is obviously a matter of judgement. In theory, there should be objective evidence as to the likelihood of realization.

Evidence of Likelihood

The AcSB has provided some guidelines to help managers (and auditors) decide whether the criterion of "more likely than not" has been met. Favourable evidence to support recognition includes the following:

- A strong earnings history, interrupted only by an unusual event that caused the loss;
- Enough accumulated temporary differences to absorb the unrealized loss as the temporary differences reverse; or
- Existing contracts or back orders that will generate more than enough taxable income to absorb the loss.

On the other hand, the criterion of "more likely than not" will *not* be met if:

- The company has a history of tax losses expiring without being used.
- A change in the company's economic prospects indicates that losses may continue for the next few years.
- There are pending circumstances that, if not resolved in the company's favour, will impair the company's ability to operate profitably (e.g., significant patent infringement lawsuits or potential major environmental impacts caused by the company's operations).

Canadian standards suggest that "objective evidence" should be found to verify management's judgement. However, it is not clear just what constitutes verifiable evidence of something that will happen in the future.

Reducing CCA

Two tax-planning strategies by which a company can increase the likelihood of realizing the benefits of a carryforward are (1) reducing or eliminating capital cost allowance deductions in the current and future years and (2) amending prior years' tax returns to reduce or eliminate CCA.

Earlier in this chapter, we pointed out that a company can reduce its tax loss by reducing or eliminating CCA in a loss year. The lower the loss, the more likely that its tax benefits can be realized. The key to this strategy is that CCA not claimed is not lost. CCA is an *optional deduction* for tax purposes. It is limited to a maximum, but there is no minimum. If a company chooses not to claim CCA in a year, the undepreciated capital cost (UCC) remains unchanged—except for additions to and retirements from the class—and CCA on the undiminished balance remains available as a deduction in future years.

One way of increasing the likelihood that a company will fully utilize a carryforward is to eliminate CCA in the carryforward years. In some industries, CCA is very large, both in absolute amount and in relation to net income. Not claiming CCA has the effect of increasing taxable income, against which the carryforward can be used. After the carryforward benefits have all been realized, the company can resume deducting full CCA to reduce its future net income.

A further strategy is to *amend prior years' returns* to reduce or eliminate CCA. The relevant time frame is the three previous years, those to which carrybacks apply. If CCA is reduced in those years, taxable income increases. If taxable income increases, more of the carryback can be used. Indeed, it may be possible to reduce prior years' CCA enough to completely use up the tax loss as a carryback. The CCA that is removed from prior-year tax returns is restored to the balance of UCC and available for deduction in future years.

The *Income Tax Act* imposes various restrictions on the amendment of prior years' returns, and these need not concern us here. But "playing around" with CCA is a fully legitimate way of either reducing a tax loss or using it up in prior and subsequent years.

Reassessment in Years Subsequent to the Loss Year

Once the future tax benefit of a tax loss carryforward has been recognized as an asset, the asset is subject to review at each balance sheet date. If the probability of realization drops to 50% or less, the future income tax asset should be reduced. There is nothing unusual about this requirement; assets are generally subject to review and to writedown if their value has been impaired. If an asset is unlikely to recover its carrying value, either through use or through sale, it should be written down.

The potential benefit of a tax loss carryforward may be recognized not only in the year of the loss, but also in years subsequent to the loss year. Management may decide that the 50% probability threshold is not attained in the year of the loss and therefore will not recognize the tax loss carryforward benefits. In any subsequent year (that is, prior to actually realizing the benefits), management may decide that the probability of realization has increased to over 50%. When the probability is judged to become greater than 50%, the future benefit of a prior year's tax loss carryforward should be recognized in that year. Previous years are not restated.

Examples of Recognition Scenarios

We can illustrate the various basic recognition points by means of a simple illustration. Suppose that Parravano Limited has been in business for five years, and incurs a loss of $500,000 in 20X5. The company has no temporary or permanent differences, and therefore the pre-tax accounting loss is the same as the loss for income tax purposes. The history of the company's earnings since the company began operations is as follows:

Year	Taxable Income (Loss)	Taxes Paid (Recovered)
20X1	$100,000	$40,000
20X2	(60,000)	(24,000)
20X3	140,000	56,000
20X4	30,000	12,000

The tax rate has been constant at 40% from 20X1 through 20X5.

In 20X5, Parravano incurs a loss of $500,000. A further loss of $100,000 occurs in 20X6.

In 20X5, Parravano can carry back $170,000 of the loss to recover taxes paid in 20X3 and 20X4, a total of $68,000. A carryforward of $330,000 remains, the potential tax benefit of which is $132,000 ($330,000 × 40%). Recognition of the future benefits of the carryforward depends on management's conclusions regarding the likelihood of realizing the benefits. The following scenarios illustrate recognition of the benefits of tax loss carryforwards under various possible assumptions concerning the likelihood of realization. The entries under each scenario are summarized in the "Direct Recognition" columns of Exhibit 16-1.

Scenario 1: Assuming future realization is judged to be probable in each year of the losses. If the probability of realizing the future tax benefit of the carryforward is judged to be more than 50%, the potential $132,000 benefit of the $330,000 20X5 carryforward is recognized in the year of the loss. The entry to record taxes for 20X5 will be as follows, assuming a 40% tax rate:

Entry in loss year 20X5
Income tax receivable—carryback benefit (B/S)   68,000
Future income tax asset—carryforward benefit (B/S)[1]   132,000
     Income tax expense (recovery) (I/S)   200,000

[1] $330,000 × 40% = $132,000

The total income tax expense (recovery) account on the 20X5 income statement (i.e., $68,000 + $132,000 = $200,000) is equal to 40% of the tax loss for 20X5 ($500,000 × 40%). The full potential tax benefit of the loss has been *recognized*, although only $68,000 will be *realized* in the current year.

In 20X6, the $40,000 potential tax benefit of the $100,000 loss will also be recognized, if management believes that the loss carryforwards from both years are likely to be realized within the carryforward period:

Entry in loss year 20X6		
Future income tax asset—carryforward benefit (B/S)[1]	40,000	
Income tax expense (recovery) (I/S)		40,000
[1] $330,000 × 40% = $132,000		

Scenario 2: Assuming future realization is judged to be improbable in 20X5, but becomes probable in 20X6. Now, suppose instead that, due to Parravano's erratic earnings history, realization of the benefit of the carryforward is judged to be unlikely. The entry to record the tax benefit in 20X5 would then be limited to the amount of tax recovered through the carryback:

Entry in loss year 20X5		
Income tax receivable—carryback benefit (B/S)	68,000	
Income tax expense (recovery) (I/S)		68,000

In the following year, 20X6, Parravano Limited has a loss for both accounting and tax purposes of $100,000. Since there is no available taxable income in the carryback period, the $100,000 tax loss will be carried forward. The company now has two carryforwards that have been neither realized nor recognized:

- $330,000 from 20X5, expiring in 20X25, and
- $100,000 from 20X6, expiring in 20X26.

The total carryforward is $430,000.

However, suppose that Parravano obtained a large contract late in 20X6. The 20X6 operating results do not yet reflect the profit that will be generated by the contract, but the contract is expected to boost earnings considerably in 20X7 and the next several years. Therefore, management decides when preparing the 20X6 financial statements that it is more likely than not that the full benefit of tax loss carryforwards from both 20X5 and 20X6 will be realized within the carryforward period.

Assuming a continuing tax rate of 40%, the future tax benefit of the total $430,000 carryforward is $172,000. Since, in management's judgement, the criterion of "more likely than not" has now been satisfied, the future benefit is recorded as an asset:

Recognition in 20X6 of future benefits		
Future income tax asset—carryforward benefit (B/S)[1]	172,000	
Income tax expense (recovery) (I/S)		172,000
[1] $430,000 × 40% = $172,000		

When the future benefit of $172,000 is recognized in the income statement, the 20X6 pre-tax loss of $100,000 will be converted into a net *income* of $72,000 simply as the result of recognizing the still-unrealized tax loss carryforward benefit:

Net income (loss) before income tax	$(100,000)
Provision for income taxes (recovery)	(172,000)
Net income (loss)	$ 72,000

Scenario 3: Partial recognition. In Scenario 2, we assumed that Parravano recognized all of the accumulated tax benefits in 20X6. It is possible, however, that management may decide only part of the benefit is more likely than not to be realized. Suppose, for example, that Parravano management decided in 20X6 that the benefits from only $200,000 of the accumulated tax loss carryforwards had a probability of greater than 50% of being realized. At a tax rate of 40%, the entry to record the recognition in 20X6 will be:

Recognition in 20X6 of future benefits		
Future income tax asset—carryforward benefit (B/S)[1]	80,000	
Income tax expense (recovery) (I/S)		80,000
[1] $200,000 × 40% = $80,000		

The benefits from the remaining $230,000 tax loss carryforward can be recognized in a later period (within the carryforward period), if the probability of realization becomes greater than 50%.

Scenario 4: Reduction of previously recognized benefit. Like any other asset, the future income tax asset that arises from recognizing the future benefit of a tax loss carryforward must continue to have probable future benefit. If an asset no longer is likely to be recoverable or realizable, it must be written down to its probable future benefit. If the probable future benefit is zero, the asset must be completely written off. If the probable future benefit is greater than zero but less than the originally recorded amount, the balance should be reduced accordingly.

For example, return to the Scenario 1 entry for 20X5, when Parravano recorded a $132,000 future income tax asset because of a loss carryforward in 20X5:

Income tax receivable—carryback benefit (B/S)	68,000	
Future income tax asset—carryforward benefit (B/S)	132,000	
Income tax expense (recovery) (I/S)		200,000

But suppose that in 20X6, Parravano experiences an additional loss of $100,000. The total tax loss carryforward is now $430,000: $330,000 from 20X5 plus $100,000 from 20X6. When preparing the 20X6 financial statements, Parravano's management decides that the future benefit of only $200,000 of the tax loss carryforward is more likely than not to be realized in the carryforward period. The future income tax asset of $132,000 must be reduced to the lower amount of probable recovery: $200,000 × 40% = $80,000. The entry to reduce the balance of the future income tax asset is $52,000, the amount necessary to reduce the balance from $132,000 to $80,000:

Income tax expense (I/S)	52,000	
Future income tax asset—carryforward benefit (B/S)		52,000

There is nothing final about the estimate of future recovery. The probability of realizing the benefit is evaluated at each balance sheet date until the carryforward expires. In future years within the carryforward period, Parravano may decide that the probability of realization of the full carryforward benefit has become more likely than not. If that happens, then the future income tax asset can be increased to reflect the higher probable amount.

Impact of Recognition Assumption on Net Income

The only difference between these four scenarios is the estimated probability of realizing the loss carryforward benefits. The earnings impacts of these different scenarios are summarized in Exhibit 16-2. Depending on management's realization estimates, the after-tax net loss in 20X5 varies from $(300,000) to $(432,000). In 20X6, the bottom line varies from a loss of $(152,000) to a net income of $72,000. Indeed, the potential net loss in 20X6 could be as high as $(192,000) if all of the previously recognized carryforward benefits were deemed improbable of realization.

EXHIBIT 16-1

COMPARISON OF METHODS FOR RECORDING TAX LOSS CARRYFORWARD BENEFITS

Scenario	Year	Direct Recognition			Using Valuation Account		
1a. C/B + full recognition of 20X5 C/F benefit	**20X5**	IT rec.—C/B FIT asset—C/F IT exp. (recovery)	68,000 132,000	 200,000	IT rec.—C/B FIT asset—C/F IT exp. (recovery)	68,000 132,000	 200,000
1b. Full recognition of 20X6 C/F benefit	**20X6**	FIT asset—C/F IT exp. (recovery)	40,000	 40,000	FIT asset—C/F IT exp. (recovery)	40,000	 40,000
2a. C/B, but no recognition of C/F benefit	**20X5**	IT rec.—C/B IT exp. (recovery)	68,000	 68,000	IT rec.—C/B FIT asset—C/F IT exp. (recovery) IT exp. (recovery) Val. allow.—FIT asset	68,000 132,000 132,000	 200,000 132,000
2b. Recognize full 20X5 + 20X6 C/F benefit	**20X6**	FIT asset—C/F IT exp. (recovery)	172,000	 172,000	FIT asset—C/F IT exp. (recovery) Val. allow.—FIT asset IT exp. (recovery)	40,000 132,000	 40,000 132,000
3a. C/B but no recognition of C/F benefit	**20X5**	IT rec.—C/B IT exp. (recovery)	68,000	 68,000	IT rec.—C/B FIT asset—C/F IT exp. (recovery) IT exp. (recovery) Val. allow.—FIT asset	68,000 132,000 132,000	 200,000 132,000
3b. Partial recognition of C/F benefit	**20X6**	FIT asset—C/F IT exp. (recovery)	80,000	 80,000	FIT asset—C/F IT exp. (recovery) IT exp. (recovery) Val. allow.—FIT asset	40,000 52,000	 40,000 52,000
4a. Same as scenario 1, above—full recognition	**20X5**	IT rec.—C/B FIT asset—C/F IT exp. (recovery)	68,000 132,000	 200,000	IT rec.—C/B FIT asset—C/F IT exp. (recovery)	68,000 132,000	 200,000
4b. Only $200,000 of total C/F benefit is now deemed probable	**20X6**	IT expense FIT asset—C/F	52,000	 52,000	FIT asset—C/F IT exp. (recovery) IT expense Val. allow.—FIT asset	40,000 92,000	 40,000 92,000

EXHIBIT 16-2

COMPARISON OF NET INCOME UNDER
DIFFERENT RECOGNITION SCENARIOS

Scenario		20X5	20X6
1	Income (loss) before income taxes	$(500,000)	$(100,000)
	Income tax expense (recovery)	(200,000)	(40,000)
	Net income (loss)	$(300,000)	$ (60,000)
2	Income (loss) before income taxes	$(500,000)	$(100,000)
	Income tax expense (recovery)	(68,000)	(172,000)
	Net income (loss)	$(432,000)	$ 72,000
3	Income (loss) before income taxes	$(500,000)	$(100,000)
	Income tax expense (recovery)	(68,000)	(80,000)
	Net income (loss)	$(432,000)	$ (20,000)
4	Income (loss) before income taxes	$(500,000)	$(100,000)
	Income tax expense (recovery)	(200,000)	52,000
	Net income (loss)	$(300,000)	$(152,000)

These scenarios demonstrate two points: (1) the importance of management's estimates of the probability of recognition, and (2) the potential range of earnings management that is possible under the "more likely than not" rule for recognition. Financial statement readers should be wary of income tax "recoveries" that are recognized but not realized. These recoveries may well be reversed in future years, with resulting impacts on reported net earnings.

USING A VALUATION ALLOWANCE

valuation allowance

in accounting for assets of uncertain realization, the asset is recorded in its entirety, and then reduced to the value that is "more likely than not" to be realized by means of a valuation allowance, which is a contra account to the asset

In the example above, we increased or decreased the balance of the future income tax asset directly. An alternative approach is to record the full amount of the potential future benefit and then use a **valuation allowance** to adjust for the probability of realization. The entries, using a valuation allowance, are summarized in the final columns of Exhibit 16-1.

As an analogy, think of accounts receivable. The full amount of accounts receivable is always recorded in the accounts, and then an allowance for doubtful accounts is used to reduce the balance to its estimated realizable value. The same principle can be applied to future tax benefits of tax loss carryforwards. Return to the Parravano example. In every scenario, the full amount of the future tax benefit is recorded in 20X5, the loss year:

Future income tax asset—carryforward benefit[1]	132,000	
Income tax expense (recovery)		132,000

[1] $330,000 × 40%

A valuation account is then considered, depending on the amount of recovery that is *probable*.

Scenario 1: Full recovery is probable. No valuation allowance is needed in this situation because management estimates that the company probably can realize the full benefit of the tax loss carryforward.

Scenario 2: Recovery is improbable at first, becoming probable in a later year. The full amount of the future benefit is recorded, as shown in the entry above. However, in 20X5, management believes that the probability of recovery is less than 50%. None of the future benefit should appear on the 20X5 balance sheet. An allowance for the full amount is required:

Income tax expense (recovery)	132,000	
Valuation allowance—FIT asset		132,000

When the company prepares a balance sheet for 20X5, the valuation allowance will completely offset the FIT asset and none of the asset will appear on the balance sheet.

In 20X6, none of the 20X5 loss carryforward is used, and the company has an additional loss carryforward of $100,000. The full future benefit of the 20X6 loss is recorded (at 40%):

Future income tax asset—carryforward benefit	40,000	
Income tax expense (recovery)		40,000

The future income tax asset and its related valuation account now appear as follows:

Future income tax benefit relating to 20X5	$132,000
Future income tax benefit relating to 20X6	40,000
Total potential future benefits	172,000
Less: valuation allowance	(132,000)
Balance prior to year-end 20X6 adjustment	$ 40,000

At the end of 20X6, management decides that full realization of the benefits now is more probable than not. Therefore, the valuation allowance is reduced to zero in order to permit the full future value of the asset (i.e., $172,000) to appear on the 20X6 balance sheet:

Valuation allowance—FIT asset	132,000	
Income tax expense (recovery)		132,000

Scenario 3: Partial recognition. Return to the 20X5 year, where a future tax asset of $132,000 has been recognized because of the $330,000 tax loss. In 20X6 management decides that only $200,000 of the carryforward is likely to be utilized within the carryforward period. A valuation allowance is needed to reduce the balance sheet amount from the full benefit of $132,000 to the probable recovery of $80,000, an adjustment of $52,000:

Income tax expense	52,000	
Valuation allowance—FIT asset		52,000

Only the net amount of $80,000 will be reported on the 20X6 balance sheet:

Future income tax asset—carryforward benefit	$132,000
Valuation allowance—FIT asset	(52,000)
Balance reported on 31 December 20X6 balance sheet	$80,000

Scenario 4: Reduction of previously recognized benefit. In this scenario, the benefit is fully recognized (at $132,000) in the year of the loss, 20X5. No valuation allowance is created because management feels that realization of the benefits is likely.

In 20X6, the company has another loss of $100,000. The potential future benefit of this loss is recognized:

Future income tax asset—carryforward benefit	40,000	
Income tax expense (recovery)		40,000

The gross accumulated tax loss carryforward is now $430,000 (that is, $330,000 + $100,000) and the total recorded future income tax asset is $172,000 (i.e., $132,000 + $40,000).

At this point, management decides that the company probably will realize the benefits of only $200,000 of the total carryforward. The benefit is $200,000 × 40% = $80,000. Therefore, the valuation allowance is credited for $92,000 to bring the reported FIT asset balance down from $172,000 to the estimated probable realizable value of $80,000:

Income tax expense	92,000	
Valuation allowance—FIT asset		92,000

Write-Off of Expired Carryforward Benefits When a company reaches the end of the carryforward period for any tax loss, any remaining FIT asset balance must be written off. When an allowance account is used, the expired portion of both the FIT asset and the valuation account must be written off.

For example, suppose that Parravano has not been able to utilize any of the tax loss carryforwards from 20X5 and 20X6. Assume that in recognition of this fact, the company had already credited the valuation account for the full amount of the benefits relating to those two years, $172,000. The carryforward period for the 20X5 loss ends 20 years later, in 20X25. At the end of 20X25, the 20X5 potential benefit of $132,000 must be eliminated:

Valuation allowance—FIT asset	132,000	
Future income tax asset—carryforward benefit		132,000

Both accounts will still contain the $40,000 balance relating to 20X6, but that amount will have to be eliminated in the following year (20X26) when the carryforward period for the 20X6 loss expires.

Use of the Valuation Allowance Method The valuation allowance method may seem more cumbersome than simply recognizing or not recognizing the future income tax asset represented by a tax loss carryforward. However, many companies prefer the valuation allowance method because it keeps track of the full tax loss carryforward benefits. They are comfortable with the valuation allowance method because it is consistent with the approach used for other financial statement elements such as accounts receivable and inventory LCM valuations.

According to *Financial Reporting in Canada 2006*, 120 of the 200 surveyed companies disclosed unrecognized tax loss carryforward benefits in 2004. Of the 120, 81 used a valuation allowance. This indicates the popularity of the method. Of course, one reason for its popularity is that U.S. standards *require* use of the valuation allowance method. Therefore, any Canadian companies that report into the U.S. necessarily will use a valuation allowance.

The high incidence of unrecognized tax loss carryforwards also gives an indication of how prevalent loss carryforwards are in Canadian businesses!

WHICH TAX RATE?

Which tax rate should be used to record the amount of a future tax asset or liability? Canadian, U.S., and international standards all require that future tax assets and liabilities should be recognized at the rate(s) that are expected to be in effect when the temporary differences reverse or the tax loss carryforward benefits are realized. In most instances, that will be the rate that is enacted at the balance sheet date. However, if Parliament has approved a rate change that will take effect in one or more future years, the future benefits of tax loss carryforwards should be measured at the substantially enacted rates for those future years in which the benefits are expected to be realized. Given the difficult of estimating exactly which year the benefits will be realized, companies may need to make adjustments to the recorded FIT asset for the carryforwards.

Tax Rate Changes

Once a future income tax asset has been recorded for a tax loss carryforward, the balance of that account must be maintained at the tax rate that is expected to be in effect when the carryforward is utilized. As noted above, the usual presumption is that the substantially **enacted tax rate** will be used.

In Scenario 1, above, Parravano recorded the full amount of the tax benefit from its $330,000 accumulated tax loss carryforwards in 19X5. Parravano will have a future income tax asset of $132,000 on its balance sheet, recorded at a 40% tax rate.

Suppose that the tax rate goes down to 38% before Parravano actually uses any of the carryforward. The asset will have to be revalued to $330,000 × 38%, or $125,400. This change will be included as part of the annual re-evaluation of the FIT asset or liability. If the carryforward benefit is the only component of Parravano's FIT asset, the writedown would be recorded as follows:

Income tax expense ($132,000 − 125,400) (I/S)	6,600	
Future income tax asset—carryforward benefit (B/S)		6,600

If, instead, the tax rate goes up, the increase in the asset account will be *credited* to income tax expense.

CONCEPT REVIEW

1. What is the basic criterion for recognizing the benefit of a tax loss carryforward prior to its realization?

2. What tax rate should be used to recognize the future benefits of a tax loss carryforward?

3. Is it possible to recognize the future benefits of tax loss carryforwards in years subsequent to the loss year? If so, explain the necessary circumstances. If not, explain why not.

4. Once the future benefit of a tax loss carryforward has been recognized, does the asset always remain on the balance sheet until the benefit has been realized?

BASIC ILLUSTRATION

To illustrate the recognition of tax loss carryforward benefits over a series of years, we will start with a fairly simple example that has no other types of temporary differences. To keep things moderately interesting, however, we will include tax rate changes.

Assume the following information for Dutoit Limited:

	20X1	20X2	20X3	20X4
Net income before tax	$100,000	$(300,000)	$150,000	$250,000
Taxable income*	100,000	(300,000)	150,000	250,000
Tax rate	45%	40%	42%	43%

*Prior to including any tax loss carrybacks or carryforwards.

The first year of operations for Dutoit was 20X1. Assume that the tax rate for each year is determined during that year. For example, we do not know in 20X2 that the tax rate for 20X3 will be 42%. Dutoit does not use a valuation allowance.

Assuming Realization Is Not Likely

We will first assume that at no point does management believe that there is greater than a 50% probability that the company will be able to realize the benefits of any unused tax loss carryforward. This is a pessimistic assumption, of course, but in an uncertain environment, management may really not know if the company will have a profitable year until it is well underway.

20X1   The income tax is simply the taxable income times the tax rate:

Income tax expense ($100,000 × 45%)	45,000	
Income tax payable		45,000

20X2 $100,000 of the loss can be carried back to 20X1, to recover the prior year's taxes paid:

Income tax receivable—carryback benefit	45,000	
Income tax expense (recovery)		45,000

There is an unrecognized tax loss carryforward of $200,000.

20X3   Taxable income prior to deducting the tax loss carryforward is $150,000. The tax loss carryforward of $200,000 more than offsets the otherwise-taxable income for 20X3. No taxes will be due, and no income tax expense will be recorded or reported. There is a tax loss of $50,000 still unused.

For the sake of clarity, two entries can be made in a year where a loss carryforward is used. The first entry records income tax as though there were no loss carryforward:

Income tax expense ($150,000 × 42%)	63,000	
Income tax payable		63,000

Of course, the income tax payable does not have to be paid, so the second entry eliminates it, recording the use of the loss carryforward:

Income tax payable	63,000	
Income tax expense (recovery)		63,000

The company should show the offsetting effects of the two opposite income tax expenses on 20X3 earnings. The disclosure could be either on the face of the income statement or in the notes. If income statement presentation is used:

Net income		$150,000
Income tax expense (recovery):		
Income tax on current year's earnings	$63,000	
Tax reduction from tax loss carryforward	(63,000)	—
Net income		$150,000

20X4 There is $250,000 of taxable income, on which $250,000 × 43%, or $107,500, of tax would be paid. The remaining $50,000 carryforward is used, reducing the taxes otherwise due by $50,000 × 43%, or $21,500. The net amount owing is $86,000:

Income tax expense	107,500	
Income tax payable		107,500
Income tax payable	21,500	
Income tax expense (recovery)		21,500

The breakdown of income tax expense may be included in the notes or in the income statement. The income statement will show:

Income before income tax		$250,000
Income tax expense (recovery)		
Tax on current earnings	$107,500	
Recovered through loss carryforward	(21,500)	86,000
Net income		$164,000

Notice that in each year, the carryforward is applied against taxable income in that year at the current rate. *The tax rate in the year of the loss is irrelevant.*

Assuming Realization Becomes Likely

Now, let's re-examine the situation assuming instead that, in 20X3, Dutoit's management judges that it will be more likely than not that the benefits of the remaining carryforward will be realized.

The entries in 20X1 and 20X2 will not change. In 20X3, however, $150,000 of the carryforward is used to reduce 20X3 taxable income to zero. The remaining $50,000 carryforward is also recognized. The benefit of the full $200,000 carryforward is *recognized*, even though the benefit of only $150,000 is *realized* in that year by applying it against the taxable income in that year. The entries for 20X3 now are:

Income tax expense	63,000	
Income tax payable (unchanged)		63,000
Future income tax asset—carryforward benefit	21,000	
Income tax payable	63,000	
Income tax expense (recovery)		84,000

The full benefit of the $200,000 carryforward has been *recognized* in 20X3. Income tax expense is a net credit on the income statement of $21,000, the unrealized portion of the carryforward.

Income before income tax		$150,000
Income tax expense (recovery):		
Income tax on current earnings	$ 63,000	
Recovery from tax loss carryforward	(84,000)	(21,000)
Net income		$171,000

The income statement may simply reflect the $21,000 recovery, but such minimal disclosure is not helpful when trying to interpret the financial statements!

In 20X4, the remaining $50,000 of tax loss carryforward is used, but it has already been *recognized*. The result, therefore, is that the balance of the future income tax (FIT) asset goes from $21,000 at the beginning of 20X4 to zero at the end of the year. The entries are:

Income tax expense	107,500	
Income tax payable ($250,000 × 43%)		107,500
Income tax payable ($50,000 × 43%)	21,500	
Future income tax asset—carryforward benefit		21,000
Income tax expense (recovery)		500

In the entry above, the credit to the FIT asset is the amount recorded. The change in the tax rate has made the loss carryforward worth an extra $500 ($50,000 × 1% = $500) which is credited to income tax expense.

EXTENDED ILLUSTRATION

In this illustration of accounting for the tax benefits of tax losses, we will assume that (1) the company has one type of temporary difference relating to capital assets, (2) a loss arises in the second year, and (3) the income tax rate changes in the third and fourth years. The facts for Birchall Incorporated are as follows:

- In 20X1, Birchall begins operations and acquires equipment costing $1 million.
- The equipment is being amortized straight line at 10% (i.e., at $100,000 per year), and the company's policy is to expense a full year's amortization in the year of acquisition.
- Birchall claims CCA of $350,000 in 20X1, $200,000 in 20X2, $150,000 in 20X3, and $100,000 in 20X4.
- The tax rate is 40% in 20X1 and 20X2. During 20X3, Parliament increases the tax rate to 42%, applicable to 20X3 and following years, and, in 20X4, the rate is changed to 43%.
- Birchall's earnings before income tax for 20X1 through 20X4 are as follows:

20X1	$ 300,000
20X2	$(600,000) (loss)
20X3	$ 200,000
20X4	$ 600,000

The first step is to calculate taxable income, shown in Exhibit 16-3. In 20X1, taxable income is $50,000. At 40%, the current tax payable is $20,000.

EXHIBIT 16-3

EXTENDED ILLUSTRATION—CALCULATION OF TAXABLE INCOME, INCOME TAX PAYABLE, AND FUTURE INCOME TAX TABLE

	20X1	20X2	20X3	20X4
Tax Rate (t)	40%	40%	42%	43%
Accounting income (loss) subject to tax	$300,000	$(600,000)	$200,000	$600,000
Temporary difference:				
+ Amortization	100,000	100,000	100,000	100,000
− CCA	(350,000)	(200,000)	(150,000)	(100,000)
Taxable income (loss) for current year	$ 50,000	$(700,000)	$150,000	$600,000
Income tax payable (before loss carryforward use)	$ 20,000		$ 63,000	$258,000

Future Income Tax Table

	[1] Year-End Tax Basis dr. (cr.)	[2] Year-End Carrying Value dr. (cr.)	[3] = [1] − [2] Temporary Difference Deductible (taxable)	[4] = [3] × t Future Tax Asset (Liability) at Yr.-End rate	[5] = prev. [4] Less Beginning Balance dr. (cr.)	[6] = [4] − [5] Adjustment for Current Year dr. (cr.)
20X1 [t = 40%]: Capital assets	$650,000	$900,000	(250,000)	$(100,000)	0	$(100,000)
20X2 [t = 40%]: Capital assets	450,000	800,000	(350,000)	(140,000)	$(100,000)	(40,000)
20X3 [t = 42%]: Capital assets	300,000	700,000	(400,000)	(168,000)	(140,000)	(28,000)
20X4 [t = 43%]: Capital assets	200,000	600,000	(400,000)	(172,000)	(168,000)	(4,000)

Next, the change in future income tax is calculated. This is done in table format, also in Exhibit 16-3. The initial cost of the capital assets (i.e., equipment) was $1,000,000. In 20X1, Birchall deducts CCA of $350,000 on its tax return and amortization of $100,000 on its income statement. As a result, the *tax basis* of the capital assets at the end of 20X1 is $650,000 (i.e., $1,000,000 − $350,000) while the accounting carrying value is $900,000; a temporary difference of $250,000 exists. At the 40% enacted tax rate, the future income tax (FIT) liability for the capital assets is $100,000. Combining these two elements gives Birchall's 20X1 income tax expense of $120,000:

Income tax expense	120,000	
Income tax payable		20,000
Future income tax liability—capital assets		100,000

In 20X2, Birchall has a loss. The accounting loss (pre-tax) is $600,000, but the loss for tax purposes is $700,000 after adding back amortization and deducting CCA (Exhibit

16-1). Of the tax loss, $50,000 can be carried back to 20X1 to claim a refund of the $20,000 paid in that year. The remaining $650,000 of the tax loss will be carried forward.

The tax basis of the capital assets declines to $450,000 (after the 20X2 CCA of $200,000), while the carrying value declines to $800,000 (after deducting another $100,000 of amortization) at the end of 20X2. The temporary difference relating to the capital assets therefore is $350,000, resulting in a FIT liability of $140,000 at the end of 20X2. The year-end FIT liability is an increase of $40,000 over the previous year. These components can be summarized as follows:

- Tax loss is $700,000, of which $50,000 is carried back and $650,000 is carried forward.
- FIT liability relating to capital assets increases by $40,000.
- Birchall has a receivable for tax recovery (carryback) of $20,000.

From this point on, we must make assumptions about the probability of realizing the benefits of the $650,000 carryforward.

Situation 1: Assuming Probability of Realization is ≤ 50%
20X2

If realization is *not* likely, the components already identified above are recorded as follows for 20X2:

Income tax expense	20,000	
Income tax receivable—carryback benefit	20,000	
Future income tax liability—capital assets		40,000

Exhibit 16-4 shows the journal entries to record income tax expense.

EXHIBIT 16-4

EXTENDED ILLUSTRATION—SITUATION 1 CARRYFORWARD
REALIZATION PROBABILITY ≤ 50%
INCOME TAX JOURNAL ENTRIES

Income tax journal entry, 20X1

Income tax expense	120,000	
Future income tax liability—capital assets		100,000
Income tax payable		20,000

Income tax journal entry, 20X2

Income tax expense	20,000	
Income tax receivable—carryback benefit	20,000	
Future income tax liability—capital assets		40,000

Income tax journal entries, 20X3

Income tax expense	91,000	
Future income tax liability—capital assets		28,000
Income tax payable ($150,000 × .42)		63,000
Income tax payable	63,000	
Income tax expense—carryforward benefit		63,000

Income tax journal entries, 20X4

Income tax expense	262,000	
Future income tax liability—capital assets		4,000
Income tax payable ($600,000 × .43)		258,000
Income tax payable	215,000	
Income tax expense—carryforward benefit		215,000

20X3

In 20X3, taxable income is $150,000, as is shown in the third numeric column of Exhibit 16-3. This permits Birchall to use some of the tax loss carryforward to offset the otherwise taxable income. The entries to record income tax expense can be condensed into a single entry, but it may be more helpful to present them as two separate entries so we can see what is going on:

1. The income tax expense for 20X3 earnings would be, without the carryforward, the tax payable on taxable income of $150,000 plus the change in the FIT liability. The tax basis of the capital assets is $300,000, and the carrying value is $700,000, which yields a temporary difference of $400,000. The tax rate is changed to 42% in 20X3, which means that the ending balance of the FIT liability should be $168,000 (that is, $400,000 × 42%). The entry to record the income tax expense without the carryforward is:

Income Income tax expense	91,000	
Future income tax liability—capital assets		
($168,000 − $140,000)		28,000
Income tax payable ($150,000 × 42%)		63,000

2. Applying $150,000 of the carryforward against the taxable income eliminates the amount of tax payable and reduces income tax expense:

Income tax payable ($150,000 × 42%)	63,000	
Income tax expense—carryforward benefit		63,000

The result for 20X3 is that net income tax expense of only $28,000 is recognized. At the end of 20X3, there is an unused gross tax loss carryforward of $500,000:

20X2 tax loss	$ 700,000
Carryback to 20X1	− 50,000
Carryforward used in 20X3	−150,000
Remaining carryforward at end of 20X3	$ 500,000

20X4

For 20X4, taxable income is $600,000. In this year, CCA is equal to amortization, and therefore there is no change in the amount of temporary difference relating to the capital assets. However, there is a change in the tax rate, from 42% to 43%, and there is a change in the FIT liability. The FIT liability is $400,000 × 43% = $172,000, an increase of $4,000 over the 20X3 year-end FIT liability. The $500,000 loss carryforward is used to reduce income tax payable. The entries to record income tax expense are:

Income tax expense	262,000	
Income tax payable ($600,000 × 43%)		258,000
Future income tax liability—capital assets		4,000
Income tax payable	215,000	
Income tax expense—carryforward benefit		215,000

As the result of these three entries, the net income tax expense reported on the income statement is $47,000 ($262,000 − $215,000). The series of entries for this scenario is summarized in Exhibit 16-4.

Situation 2: Assuming Probability of Realization is >50%

20X1

No change from the prior example. See Exhibit 16-5 for a summary of the entries for this situation.

EXHIBIT 16-5

EXTENDED ILLUSTRATION—SITUATION 2 CARRYFORWARD REALIZATION PROBABILITY 50%

Future income tax table:

	Year-End Tax Basis dr. (cr.)	Year-End Carrying Value dr. (cr.)	Temporary Difference Deductible (Taxable)	Future Tax Asset (Liability) at Yr.-End Rate	Less Beginning Balance dr. (cr.)	Adjustment for Current Year dr. (cr.)
20X1 *[t = 40%]:*						
Capital assets	$650,000	$900,000	(250,000)	$(100,000)	0	$(100,000)
20X2 *[t = 40%]:*						
Capital assets	450,000	800,000	(350,000)	(140,000)	$(100,000)	(40,000)
Carryforward benefit	n/a	n/a	650,000	260,000	0	260,000
				120,000		
20X3 *[t = 42%]:*						
Capital assets	300,000	700,000	(400,000)	(168,000)	(140,000)	(28,000)
Carryforward benefit	n/a	n/a	500,000	210,000	260,000	(50,000)
				42,000		
20X4 *[t = 43%]:*						
Capital assets	200,000	600,000	(400,000)	(172,000)	(168,000)	(4,000)
Carryforward benefit	n/a	n/a	0	0	210,000	(210,000)
				(172,000)		

Income tax entries:

20X1

Income tax expense	120,000	
Future income tax liability—capital assets		100,000
Income tax payable		20,000

20X2

Future income tax asset—carryforward benefit	260,000	
Income tax receivable—carryback benefit	20,000	
Future income tax liability—capital assets		40,000
Income tax expense (recovery)		240,000

20X3

Income tax expense	91,000	
Future income tax liability—capital assets		28,000
Income tax payable		63,000
Income tax payable ($150,000 × 42%)	63,000	
Future income tax asset—carryforward benefit		50,000
Income tax expense (recovery) ($650,000 × (42% − 40%))		13,000

20X4

Income tax expense	262,000	
Future income tax liability—capital assets		4,000
Income tax payable ($600,000 × 43%)		258,000
Income tax payable ($500,000 × 43%)	215,000	
Future tax asset—carryforward benefit		210,000
Tax expense (recovery) ($500,000 × (43% − 42%))		5,000

20X2

If realization is more likely than not, then a tax asset will be recognized for the carryforward. In 20X2, the future benefit of the carryforward of $650,000 is recognized at the then-enacted rate of 40%. The income tax entry is:

Future income tax asset—carryforward benefit		
($650,000 × 40%)	260,000	
Income tax receivable—carryback benefit	20,000	
Future income tax liability—capital assets		40,000
Income tax expense (recovery)		240,000

This entry reflects that three things are going on:

1. Recognition of carryback benefits of $20,000;

2. Change in the temporary difference for equipment of $40,000 (credit); and

3. Recognition of the future benefits of the carryforward of $260,000.

The loss carryforward can be included in the future income tax table, as shown in Exhibit 16-5. Refer to 20X2. The loss carryforward is included as a positive number in column 3; the first two columns are left blank. Each year the *remaining* gross tax loss carryforward is entered in column 3 and the rest of the table is completed as usual. Capital asset data is included in Exhibit 16-5 for the sake of completeness. Note that column 4 shows the balance sheet position at year-end. The balance sheet at the end of 20X2 will show a single amount, a non-current future income tax *asset* of $120,000:

FIT asset—carryforward benefit	$260,000
FIT liability—capital assets	(140,000)
FIT asset (non-current, net)	$120,000

20X3

In 20X3, there is initial taxable income of $150,000, after adjusting accounting income for the additional $50,000 temporary difference relating to capital assets but before applying the tax loss carryforward. There is a net change in the FIT—capital assets of $28,000 (see Exhibit 16-5). Applying $150,000 of the tax loss carryforward against the $150,000 taxable income reduces the tax loss carryforward to $500,000 (column 3) and the recorded amount to $210,000 (column 4). This is an adjustment of $50,000 (column 6). Again, we will record the results as two separate entries—the first as though there were no loss carryforward, and the second recording loss usage.

20X3		
Income tax expense	91,000	
Future income tax liability—capital assets		28,000
Income tax payable		63,000
Income tax payable ($150,000 × 42%)	63,000	
Future income tax asset—carryforward benefit		50,000
Income tax expense (recovery) ($650,000 ×		
(42% − 40%))		13,000

The second entry reflects the impact of the change in tax rates on the opening loss carryforward. Use of $150,000 of the loss carryforward clearly eliminates $63,000 of tax payable. This is the debit. The table tells us to credit the loss carryforward FIT asset by $50,000, to arrive at the correct closing balance. To make the journal entry balance, a further $13,000 credit to tax expense is needed. This amount can be proven as the change in the tax rate (2%, or 42% − 40%) multiplied by the *opening* tax loss of $650,000. In other words, the tax loss carryforward is more valuable because the tax rate increased, and tax expense is credited to reflect this.

20X4

In 20X4, there is taxable income of $600,000, tax payable (before any loss carryforward is used) of $258,000, and an increase in the FIT—capital assets account of $4,000, as is shown in Exhibit 16-5. The entire remaining tax loss carryforward of $500,000 is used. Therefore, the entries to record income tax expense for 20X4 are:

Income tax expense	262,000	
Future income tax liability—capital assets		4,000
Income tax payable ($600,000 × 43%)		258,000
Income tax payable ($500,000 × 43%)	215,000	
Future tax asset—carryforward benefit		210,000
Tax expense (recovery) ($500,000 × (43% − 42%))		5,000

The FIT table shows no remaining loss carryforward at the end of 20X4, and this account must be reduced by $210,000 to zero. Again, the increase in tax rate has caused an adjustment to tax expense because of the higher value of the opening tax less carryforward. This is the $5,000 remaining credit.

On the balance sheet at the end of 20X4, only the FIT—capital assets remains, at a credit balance of $172,000: $400,000 accumulated temporary differences at a tax rate of 43%.

Comparison of Results The earnings impact of the above scenarios is summarized in the partial income statements shown in Exhibit 16-6. When the probability of realization is less than or equal to 50%, matching is not achieved. The income tax expense in each year has no relationship to the pre-tax earnings, except in the first year.

When the probability of realization is greater than 50%, however, the full benefits of the tax loss are recognized in the year of the loss, thereby matching the benefits in the year that the loss arose. Of course, it may seem a little odd to be talking about the "benefits" of a loss. A loss itself is not beneficial, but at least it can have some favourable consequences if the company is able to utilize the tax loss carryforward.

EXHIBIT 16-6

COMPARISON OF RESULTS
IMPROBABLE VERSUS PROBABLE REALIZATION OF TAX
LOSS CARRYFORWARD BENEFITS

Probability ≤ 50% (Exhibit 16-4):	20X1	20X2	20X3	20X4
Earnings (loss) before income tax	$300,000	$(600,000)	$200,000	$600,000
Income tax expense (recovery)	120,000	20,000	91,000	47,000
Net income (loss)	$180,000	$(580,000)	$109,000	$553,000
Probability > 50% (Exhibit 16-5):				
Earnings before income tax	$300,000	$(600,000)	$200,000	$600,000
Income tax expense (recovery)	120,000	(240,000)	78,000	257,000
Net income (loss)	$180,000	$(360,000)	$122,000	$343,000

Reporting Objectives

We have already pointed out that the matching doctrine is well served if the benefit of a loss carryforward is reported in the loss year. For example, assume that a company had an accounting and taxable loss of $100,000 in 20X2, and then accounting and taxable income of $100,000 in 20X3. The tax rate is 40%. It seems appropriate reporting to show both years net of $40,000 tax, and report an after-tax net loss of $60,000 in 20X2 and an after-tax net income of $60,000 in 20X3. It is understood that the $40,000 benefit of the loss carryforward can be recorded in 20X2 before it is realized in 20X3 as long as realization is probable.

However, what if realization is not probable? In this case, the 20X2 net loss would be reported as $100,000, and the benefit of the loss carryforward would be recorded in 20X3. This would result in net tax expense of zero in 20X3, and reported net income would be $100,000. While the $100,000 loss is greater in 20X2 than the after-tax $60,000 alternative, the $100,000 20X3 reported results are greater, as well. Management may prefer the "bounce" and be prepared to take a "big bath" in 20X2.

The swing caused by recognition may be even more pronounced. For example, assume that the $100,000 loss in 20X2 is followed by two years of breakeven results. If the probability of loss carryforward use shifts to "probable" in one of these years, $40,000 of net income will be reported, reflecting recognition of the loss carryforward future income tax asset. In this case, a positive trend in earnings can be manufactured by reassessment of probability. Alternatively, two or three years of loss carryforward may be recognized in one particular year, increasing results materially.

The reporting decision is based on the probability of realization. Probability is assessed by management, with the decision reviewed by external auditors. Accounting standards provide some guidance for evaluating probability, but auditors must proceed with great caution, given the magnitude of tax expense.

DISCLOSURE

Income tax expense relating to continuing operations should be shown on the face of the income statement. The amount of income tax expense may include benefits from either carrybacks or carryforwards, but there is not a requirement that those benefits be disclosed on the face of the income statement. Information on tax losses is confined to the disclosure notes, and consists only of the following:

- The current and future tax benefit from tax loss carrybacks and carryforwards, segregated between (1) continuing operations and (2) discontinued operations and extraordinary items.
- The amount and expiry date of *unused* tax losses. There is no disclosure of how much of the unused (i.e., *unrealized*) tax loss carryforwards for each year have already been *recognized* in net income.

Public companies must disclose the nature of items that create future income tax. Therefore, recognized tax losses must be specifically identified. Public companies also must reconcile their effective tax rate with the statutory rate. Companies usually also disclose the amounts of tax loss carrybacks and carryforwards that were used during the year.

The problem with most disclosures is that it is very difficult, and often impossible, for a reader to figure out whether an income tax recovery has been *realized* or merely *recognized*. Recourse to the notes, to the effective tax rate disclosure, and to the cash flow statement may provide clues, but often the information relating to income tax assets and liabilities is so summarized that it is impossible to figure out the details.

Disclosure Example

Nortel Networks Corporation had a net loss of over $2.6 billion for 2005 and net income of $0.03 in 2006. Nortel's 2006 balance sheet showed net deferred tax assets of over $4.0 billion—more than 20% of total assets!

Exhibit 16-7 shows parts of Nortel's income tax disclosure. Nortel reports potential tax benefits of loss carryforwards of $4,609 million. This is largely offset by a valuation allowance of $4,431 million (some of which applies to the investment tax credits). The company reports unused operating tax loss carryforwards of over $8.5 billion, as well as $5.0 billion in capital loss carryforwards. Note that about 30% of the operating loss carryforwards never expire. This is because other countries, including the U.S., have more liberal policies for loss carryforwards. Nortel is a transnational corporation with most of its business in tax jurisdictions outside Canada.

Notice, by the way, that Nortel uses the older terminology of *deferred* income taxes rather than *future* income taxes. This is acceptable terminology, although it is used by only about 6% of the companies surveyed by *Financial Reporting in Canada 2006*. "Deferred" is the more common terminology worldwide, however.

EXHIBIT 16-7

TAX LOSS CARRYFORWARD DISCLOSURE EXAMPLE
NORTEL NETWORKS CORPORATION

(in millions of U.S. dollars)

8. INCOME TAXES (excerpts)

The following table shows the significant components included in deferred income taxes as of December 31:

	2006	2005
Assets:		
Tax benefit of loss carryforwards	$4,609	$4,486
Investment tax credits, net of deferred tax liability	1,358	1,174
Provisions and reserves	750	786
Post-retirement benefits other than pensions	288	306
Plant and equipment	216	96
Pension plan liabilities	622	610
Deferred compensation	153	256
Shareholder lawsuit settlement	746	—
	8,745	7,714
Valuation allowance	(4,431)	(3,429)
	4,314	4,285
Liabilities:		
Provisions and reserves	104	108
Plant and equipment	35	34
Unrealized foreign exchange and other	133	206
	272	348
Net deferred income tax assets	$4,042	$3,937

As of December 31, 2006, Nortel had the following net operating carryforwards (in millions), which are scheduled to expire in the following years:

	Net operating losses	Capital losses
2006–2008	$ 65	$ 8
2009–2011	2,133	—
2012–2018	640	7
2019–2025	3,154	—
Indefinitely	2,547	4,970
	$8,539	$4,985

Differential Reporting

Companies that have elected to use differential reporting will report on a taxes payable basis in a loss year as well as in profitable years. Differential reporting for income tax is an accounting policy choice, and thus cannot be changed opportunistically year by year, even though a company might like to report a future tax benefit to reduce an after-tax loss.

When differential reporting is used, only the amount of taxes actually recovered through carrybacks in the loss year will be reported as income tax recovery. When carryforwards are used to reduce taxes in following years, the reduced amount of tax actually paid is reported as income tax expense.

Disclosure requirements remain in effect, however. The company must disclose the amount and expiry date of unused tax losses carried forward.

EVALUATION OF FUTURE BENEFIT ACCOUNTING

The Canadian standard for accounting for the future benefit of a loss carryforward is consistent with U.S. and international practice. It is interesting to note, however, that the current U.S. position is the result of intense lobbying by the U.S. business community. When the U.S. first moved to the temporary differences approach, all future tax assets were prohibited, including those that arose from temporary differences as well as those that might arise from tax loss carryforwards. But the outcry was so intense that the FASB backed down and, in a sense, went to the opposite extreme by permitting *all* future tax assets to be recognized, as long as the probability of realization was *judged by management* to be greater than 50%. Both positions were rationalized within the FASB's conceptual framework, which suggests that the framework is rather flexible.

The supporters of early recognition believe that, conceptually, future tax benefits should be matched to the loss that gave rise to those benefits. They argue that if benefits are recognized only when realized, net income in those future periods will be distorted.

However, many observers are troubled by the recognition of tax loss carryforward benefits well in advance of their realization. The principal concern is that future tax assets do not satisfy the basic definition of an asset. There has been no transaction that establishes the corporation's right to receive the future benefit; realization of the benefits is contingent on generating sufficient taxable income in the future. And, clearly, the government does not recognize any claim owing to the company.

The recognition of unrealized tax assets for tax loss carryforwards has the effect of reducing the apparent accounting loss. The effect of an operating loss is softened by this practice and gives financial statement users the perception that the loss isn't as bad as it really is, since the benefit of a carryforward has not been realized and there is no certainty that the benefit ever will be realized.

> ### ETHICAL ISSUES
>
> Management must estimate the probability of realizing future tax benefits. There is a lot of management discretion involved. Although auditors challenge management's probability estimates, accounting standards give few effective levers to the auditor. If the likelihood of realization is marginal, management may prefer to delay recognition to one or more periods following the loss. This will enhance net income in those future periods.
>
> As well, when the primary source of the loss is discontinued operations or extraordinary items, the ability to delay recognition of the benefit to a later period offers an opportunity to management to increase net income before discontinued operations and extraordinary items because intraperiod allocation applies only in the year of the loss.
>
> The recognition of future tax benefits from loss carryforwards, plus the ability to remeasure those benefits within the carryforward period, is an ethical morass.

INTERNATIONAL PERSPECTIVE

The U.S. FASB initiated the asset-liability approach to accounting for income taxes, and also originated the rather liberal treatment of loss carryforwards. The IASB and the Canadian AcSB followed the FASB lead after about a 10-year delay. However, few other countries have adopted the FASB/IASB/CICA approach. Most countries permit the recognition of loss carryforwards only upon realization.

Of course, the primary purpose of international standards is to harmonize financial reporting across financial markets, so that all companies can report in financial markets other than that of their home country. Thus, it would appear that all international reporting would have to use the methods described in this chapter in order to conform to international standards. While that may be true on the surface, the fact is that companies can be more conservative in their appraisal of realization probabilities, depending on the prevailing ethos in their home country. In a country that has very conservative accounting practices, almost all companies will view the probability of future recognition as being less than likely. Thus, the future benefit of the carryforwards will not be recognized, even though they might have been recognized in similar circumstances if the reporting company is based in the U.S. or in Canada. The influence of the home country accounting environment cannot be overlooked.

As well, international standards do not contain the phrase "more likely than not." The international standard (IAS 12) has more conservative wording, that the benefits of tax loss carryforwards should recognized only "to the extent that it is probable" that future profits will be sufficient.

IAS 12 does not define "probable," but it is interesting that when the IASB revised its standard on discontinued operations, it explicitly rejected the FASB approach of "more likely than not" in that context. Instead, the international standard requires "high probability." By extrapolation, it seems probable that when the IASB and FASB work together to revise income tax accounting over the next few years, a company's ability to recognize the future benefits of tax loss carryforwards may become more restricted.

RELEVANT STANDARDS

CICA Handbook:
 • Section 3465, Income Taxes
IASB:
 • *IAS* 12, Income Taxes

SUMMARY OF KEY POINTS

1. In Canada, tax losses may be carried back and offset against taxable income in the three previous years. The company is entitled to recover tax paid in those years. The tax recovery is based on the tax actually paid and not on the tax rate in the year of the loss.

2. If the three-year carryback does not completely use up the tax loss, a company is permitted to carry the remaining loss forward and apply it against taxable income over the next 20 years.

3. The future benefits of tax loss carryforwards should be recognized in the year of the loss if there is a greater than 50% probability that the benefits will be realized.

4. The likelihood of realizing the tax benefits of a loss carryforward can be increased by reducing the corporation's claim for CCA on its tax return in the carryback and carryforward years.

5. Future benefits of unrecognized tax loss carryforwards may be recognized in years following the loss if the probability of realization shifts to be greater than 50%.

6. Management reporting objectives may bias the probability assessment to allow loss carryforward recognition in particular years to emphasize an earnings recovery or other favourable trends.

KEY TERMS

enacted tax rate, 968
loss carryback, 955
loss carryforward, 959

tax benefit, 955
tax loss, 955
valuation allowance, 965

REVIEW PROBLEM

Dezso Development Limited is a Canadian-controlled company. The company has a 31 December fiscal year-end. Data concerning the earnings of the company for 20X6 and 20X7 are as follows:

	20X6	20X7
Income (loss) before income taxes	$(90,000)	$30,000
Amounts included in income		
Investment income	$ 1,000	$ 2,000
Depreciation expense—capital assets	30,000	30,000
Amortization expense—development costs	20,000	22,000
Amounts deducted for income tax		
Capital cost allowance	nil	35,000
Development expenditures	25,000	15,000
Income tax rate	38%	37%

Other information:

• Taxable income and the income tax rates for 20X2 through 20X5 are as follows:

Year	Taxable income (loss)	Tax rate
20X2	$ 7,000	40%
20X3	13,000	40
20X4	9,000	40
20X5	(12,000)	41

• At 31 December 20X5, capital assets had net book value of $570,000, and undepreciated capital cost of $310,000.
• At 31 December 20X5, the balance sheet showed an unamortized balance of development costs of $200,000 under "Other Assets."
• The investment income consists of dividends from taxable Canadian corporations.

Required:

1. For each of 20X6 and 20X7, prepare the journal entry or entries to record income tax expense. Assume that management judges that it is more likely than not that the full benefit of any tax loss carryforward will be realized within the carryforward.

2. Show how the future income tax amounts would appear on the 20X6 year-end balance sheet.

3. Suppose that early in 20X8, management decided that the company was more likely than not to use only $10,000 of the remaining gross tax loss carryforward.

a. Show the entry that would be made to reduce the carryforward benefit. *Use a valuation account.*

b. What impact would this entry have on the 20X8 financial statements for Dezso Development Limited?

REVIEW PROBLEM—SOLUTION

1. (a) 20X6 Tax Expense

The taxable income or loss can be calculated as follows:

	20X6	20X7
Accounting income (loss) before tax	$(90,000)	$30,000
Permanent difference: investment income	(1,000)	(2,000)
Accounting income (loss) subject to tax	(91,000)	28,000
Depreciation	30,000	30,000
CCA	nil	(35,000)
Amortization of development costs	20,000	22,000
Development cost expenditures	(25,000)	(15,000)
Taxable income (loss)	$(66,000)	$30,000

The 20X5 tax loss will have been carried back to 20X2 ($7,000) and 20X3 ($5,000). After the 20X5 tax loss has been carried back, there remains $17,000 taxable income in the carry-forward period for the 20X6 loss:

Year	Taxable Income	Used in 20X5	Available in 20X6	Tax Receivable @ 40%
20X2	$ 7,000	$ 7,000)	—	—
20X3	13,000	(5,000)	$ 8,000	$3,200
20X4	9,000	—	9,000	3,600
20X5	(12,000)	12,000	—	—
			$17,000	$6,800

The gross carryforward that remains after the carryback is $66,000 − $17,000 = $49,000. Assuming that realization of these benefits is more likely than not and that the enacted tax rate remains at 38% when the 20X6 statements are being prepared, the carryforward benefit is $49,000 × 38% = $18,620:

The adjustments for the temporary differences for both years are summarized in the table below.

	Year-End Tax Basis dr. (cr.)	Year-End Carrying Value dr. (cr.)	Temporary Difference Deductible (Taxable)	Future Tax Asset (Liability) at Yr.-End Rate	Less Beginning Balance dr. (cr.)	Adjustment for Current Year dr. (cr.)
20X6 [t = 38%]:						
Capital assets	310,000	540,000	(230,000)	$(87,400)	$(106,600)[(1)]	$19,200
Development costs	0	205,000[(3)]	(205,000)	(77,900)	(82,000)[(2)]	4,100
Carryforward benefit	n/a	n/a	49,000	18,620	0	18,620

[(1)] ($570,000 − $310,000) × .41
[(2)] ($200,000) × .41
[(3)] $200,000 + $25,000 − $20,000

	Year-End Tax Basis dr. (cr.)	Year-End Carrying Value dr. (cr.)	Temporary Difference Deductible (Taxable)	Future Tax Asset (Liability) at Yr.-End Rate	Less Beginning Balance dr. (cr.)	Adjustment for Current Year dr. (cr.)
20X7 [t = 37%]:						
Capital assets	275,000	510,000	(235,000)	$(86,950)	$(87,400)	450
Development costs	0	198,000	(198,000)	(73,260)	(77,900)	4,640
Carryforward benefit	n/a	n/a	19,000	7,030	18,620	(11,590)

Putting all of these elements together gives us the following 20X6 summary of income tax expense:

Income tax receivable—carryback benefit	6,800	
Future income tax asset—carryforward benefit	18,620	
Future income tax liability—capital assets	19,200	
Future income tax liability—deferred development costs	4,100	
Income tax expense (recovery)		48,720

(b) 20X7 Tax Expense

The taxable income for 20X7 is $30,000, as calculated previously. No tax is due for 20X7 because there is an available tax loss carryforward of $49,000. After applying $30,000 of the carryforward against 20X7 taxable income, a carryforward of $19,000 remains. At the newly enacted tax rate of 37%, the FIT asset related to the carryforward is $7,030. In recording the income tax expense for 20X7, the balance of the FIT-carryforward account must be reduced from its beginning balance of $18,620 (debit) to an ending balance of $7,030 (debit), a credit adjustment of $11,590.

The adjustments for all types of temporary differences are summarized in the preceding table. The entry to record income tax expense, exclusive of the loss carryforward, is:

Income tax expense	6,010	
Future income tax liability—capital assets	450	
Future income tax liability—deferred development costs	4,640	
Income tax payable ($30,000 × .37)		11,100

The entry to record loss carryforward use:

Income tax expense[1]	490	
Income tax payable ($30,000 ×.37)	11,100	
Future income tax asset—carryforward benefit (per table)		11,590

[1] This is the reduction in value of the opening tax loss because of a 1% decline in the tax rate; ($49,000 × 1%)

2. 20X6 Balance Sheet Presentation

All three of the 20X6 temporary differences are non-current. Therefore, they will be combined into a single net amount when the balance sheet is prepared. The net amount is:

FIT asset—carryforward benefit	$ 18,620 dr.
FIT liability—capital assets	(87,400) cr.
FIT liability—deferred development costs	(77,900) cr.
FIT liability, non-current	$(146,680) cr.

3. (a) Adjustment to FIT-carryforward benefit

The remaining carryforward at the beginning of 20X8 is $19,000, as determined in the answer to part 1(b), above. At the enacted rate of 37%, the remaining carryforward benefit is $7,030 (that is, $19,000 × 37%). A valuation account must be created to reduce the *reported* balance of the benefit to $3,700 (i.e., $10,000 × 37%), an adjustment of $3,330:

Income tax expense ($7,030 − $3,700)	3,330	
Valuation allowance—FIT asset		3,330

Note that the amount of the gross *recorded* benefit (before the valuation allowance) will remain at $7,030.

(b) Financial Statement Impact

There will be two effects:

• Income tax expense will be increased by $3,330.

- The future income tax asset relating to the tax loss carryforward benefit will be reduced to $3,700 on the balance sheet.

Future income tax asset—carryforward benefit	$7,030
Less valuation allowance	3,330
Net asset	$3,700

QUESTIONS

Q16-1   What is the benefit that arises as a result of a tax loss?

Q16-2   Over what period can a tax loss be used as an offset against taxable income?

Q16-3   Why do companies usually use tax losses as carrybacks before using them as carryforwards?

Q16-4   When do *recognition* and *realization* coincide for tax losses?

Q16-5   Why is it desirable to recognize the benefit of a tax loss carryforward in the period of the accounting loss? Under what circumstances would such a benefit be *realized*?

Q16-6   What criteria must be met to *recognize* the benefit of a tax loss carryforward in the period of the accounting loss?

Q16-7   ABC Company has a taxable loss of $100,000. The tax rate is 40%. What is the benefit of the tax loss?

Q16-8   A company reports an accounting loss of $75,000. Depreciation for the year was $216,000, and CCA was $321,000. The company wishes to maximize its tax loss. How much is the tax loss?

Q16-9   Refer again to the data in Question 16-8. Assume instead that the company wishes to minimize its taxable loss/maximize taxable income. How much is the taxable income (loss)? Explain.

Q16-10   Explain why a company might choose not to claim CCA when it reports (a) accounting income and (b) an accounting loss.

Q16-11   Define the term "more likely than not."

Q16-12   What strategies can be used to increase the likelihood that a tax loss carryforward will be used?

Q16-13   Provide three examples of favourable evidence in assessing the likelihood that a tax loss carryforward will be used in the carryforward period.

Q16-14   A company has a tax loss of $497,000 in 20X4, when the tax rate was 40%. The tax loss is expected to be used in 20X6. At present, there is an enacted tax rate of 42% for 20X5. The government intends to increase the tax rate to 45% in 20X6, but no legislation concerning tax rates has yet been drafted. At what amount should the tax loss carryforward be recorded, if it meets the appropriate criteria to be recorded?

Q16-15   A company recorded the benefit of a tax loss carryforward in the year of the loss. Two years later, the balance of probability shifts, and it appears that the loss will likely not be used in the carryforward period. What accounting entry is required if a direct adjustment is made (i.e., not to a valuation account)?

Q16-16   A company did not recognize the benefit of a tax loss carryforward in the year of the loss. Two years later, the balance of probability shifts, and it appears that the loss will likely be used in the carryforward period. What accounting entries are required in each year if a valuation account is used?

Q16-17 How will income change if a tax loss carryforward, previously recognized, is now considered to be unlikely?

Q16-18 A company has recorded a $40,000 benefit in relation to a $100,000 tax loss carryforward. The tax rate changes to 35%. What entry is appropriate?

Q16-19 Give three objections to the practice of recording a tax loss carryforward prior to realization.

Q16-20 What disclosure is required in relation to tax loss carryforwards?

CASE 16-1

SIGMA AUTO PARTS LTD.

Sigma Auto Parts Ltd. is an Ontario-based manufacturer of automobile parts. The Canadian operations supply automotive components and parts to three U.S. and two Japanese auto manufacturers. Approximately 30% of Sigma's worldwide sales is generated by its Canadian operations.

The company has large operating subsidiaries in the U.S., Mexico, Germany, and the Czech Republic. Sigma has recently established an operating subsidiary in the People's Republic of China to supply both international and domestic manufacturers in that country.

Sigma is a Canadian private company. However, the German subsidiary does have an outstanding public issue of non-voting common shares that are traded on the Frankfurt exchange. Generally, financing is obtained through a combination of retained earnings, debt, and private equity placements in each subsidiary's home country, with the exception of China (as explained below). The company reports in Canadian GAAP, using U.S. dollars as the reporting currency.

Angelo Zhang has recently been promoted to the position of chief accountant at the Sigma head office in Windsor, Ontario. The newly appointed chief financial officer, Jean Adams, has asked Mr. Zhang to review several reporting issues and advise her on appropriate treatments. The specific issues are as follows:

1. Earlier in the year, a Canadian supplier claimed the right to terminate its obligations to supply Sigma with certain stainless steel products at the prices stated in two standing supply contracts with Sigma. The supplier has continued to supply the products, but invoiced Sigma at market prices rather than at the contracted prices. Sigma has continued to pay the supplier, but only at the contract prices. The accumulated differential between the invoiced market prices and the contract prices has been accumulating for several months and now amounts to about $30 million. Sigma and the supplier have agreed to submit their disagreement to binding arbitration. The arbitration hearing is expected to be held late in the following fiscal year.

2. Sigma is building new manufacturing facilities in the Czech Republic to replace some older facilities that have become obsolete. The new facilities should be ready within two years, whereupon operations will be transferred to the new facilities and the old site will be abandoned. Recent legislation in the Czech Republic makes Sigma responsible for demolition and site restoration costs in the event that the old facilities cannot be sold to a buyer that is willing to bear the costs of demolition or rebuilding. The currently estimated costs are $25 million for demolition and $10 million for site restoration (at the current exchange rate).

3. The U.S. operations have experienced profitability problems over the past several years. The decline of some of the U.S. auto manufacturers has taken its toll on the auto parts industry. The auto companies have been forcing suppliers' prices down, a situation that has led to the bankruptcy of one major U.S.–based auto parts manufacturer. For a while, Sigma U.S. was just about breaking even on an accounting basis, but was in an operating loss position for tax purposes. However, for each of the most recent two years, Sigma's U.S. subsidiary has reported a significant loss for both accounting and tax pur-

poses. In view of the basic strength of Sigma's cutting-edge operations and the strength of its worldwide operations, Jean Adams's predecessor felt confident in fully recognizing the income tax benefits that will be derived from any tax loss carryforwards. Now, however, the situation is not so clear-cut. It may be quite a while before the industry settles and Sigma is able to return the U.S. operations to profitability.

4. Generally speaking, the subsidiaries in each country are financed locally rather than through significant direct investment from Canada. An exception is the new subsidiary in China; substantial direct foreign investment was necessary in order to quickly establish the company and also to obtain certain government approvals and tax benefits. Total direct investment in China currently is $103 million and is likely to increase over the next couple of years. The Chinese new yuan is tied to a basket of foreign currencies, of which the U.S. dollar represents the largest proportion. Due to the weakening of the U.S. dollar, the yuan has been gradually increasing in value.

5. During the current year, Sigma's German division issued €150 million of 7% unsecured subordinated debentures on a private placement basis. The debentures mature in five years and are not redeemable prior to maturity. Upon maturity, Sigma has the option of issuing non-voting common shares, the number of shares dependent on their market value at the time.

Required:

Assume that you are Angelo Zhang. Prepare the report to Ms Adams.

CASE 16-2

ELLIS INGRAM CORPORATION

Ellis Ingram Corporation (EIC) is a manufacturer of household appliances. The company is privately held with a broad shareholder group. The company has sizable loans outstanding, and audited financial statements are required to assess compliance with loan covenants, related to the current ratio and return on assets. Differential reporting may not be used under the terms of the loan agreements. A material component of management compensation is bonus payments, a fixed portion of net income.

After several years of positive earnings, EIC is reporting sizable losses in 20X5. These losses relate to a strike that shut down EIC's major manufacturing facility. While the operation was shut down, many customers found other suppliers. EIC is slowly regaining market share. Market projections are cautious for 20X6, as consumer demand is expected to be soft, and EIC's customer base is still impaired. No bonuses will be paid in 20X5. Lenders have agreed to a one-year exclusion on debt covenants related to return on assets for 20X5, but 20X6 profits will be carefully watched.

EIC has provided the following information with respect to operating results:

	(in thousands)	
	20X5	**20X4**
Accounting income (loss) before income tax	$(31,420)	$6,145
Income tax instalments paid during the year	nil	2,030
Income tax payable at year-end	?	177
Future income tax, a long-term liability, with respect to capital assets with a net book value of $6,950 at the end of 20X4 and $6,200 at the end of 20X5 (no additions in 20X5)	?	917
Impairment of goodwill, recorded on the income statement but not tax-deductible	8,410	nil
Other non-deductible expenses	540	357
Effective tax rate	41.6%	44.3%

EIC reported total taxable income of $2,680 in 20X3 and 20X2 combined, on which income tax of $1,187 was paid. No CCA will be claimed in 20X5.

A major issue for management and the Board of Directors of EIC is the probability assessment of loss carryforward use at the end of 20X5. In order to facilitate discussion, you, a public accountant, have been asked to prepare financial statement results for both alternatives—likely and not likely—and comment on the implications of the choice for 20X6. Your analysis must include all tax amounts and necessary calculations. You have also been asked to analyze the status of the gross profit on the late-20X5 sale of merchandise to Luciano Limited. If adjustment is needed, you are to revise the reported financial results (see Exhibit 1).

Required:

Prepare the requested analysis.

EXHIBIT 1

Data on Sale to Luciano Limited

EIC entered into two related transactions with Luciano Limited, a long-time supplier, at the instigation of Luciano, in December 20X5. EIC sold $2,050,000 of product to Luciano. Credit terms were 20 days, and Luciano paid on time, in late December. The cost of these goods was $1,685,000. EIC also purchased goods with a retail price of $2,100,000 from Luciano. Luciano likely booked a profit of 35% on the goods. EIC has paid for the merchandise, which is still in inventory. The goods are expected to be sold in February 20X6. EIC has recently been alerted that Luciano is under scrutiny by the SEC for transactions of this nature. (Luciano is the Canadian subsidiary of a U.S. public company)

The accounting policy for this sale has yet to be determined, but will be discussed at the next Board of Directors meeting. The profit will be taxable in 20X5 regardless of when it is recognized for accounting purposes.

From a recent article in the financial press:

> Recent SEC scrutiny has focused on barter and "round trip" transactions. In barter transactions, two companies swap products, with each company recognizing revenue on the transaction, at the fair value of the goods exchanged. GAAP states that revenue must be deferred on these transactions if the transaction does not represent the end of the earnings process. Another similar type of transaction is called "round tripping." One company sells a product to another company, for cash, which then turns around and sells equivalent product back to the company at a similar cash price. Both companies recognize revenue. The SEC is of the opinion that gross profit on these round-trip transactions must be deferred until the product is eventually sold to outside, final customers.

CASE 16-3

GAMMA SHOE COMPANY LIMITED

The Gamma Shoe Company Limited is experiencing financial difficulties. Earnings have been declining sharply for the past several years, and the company has barely maintained positive earnings for the past three. In the current year, the company is expected to report a substantial loss for the first time in almost 30 years. A tax loss will also be reported.

Gamma is a large, multinational corporation with manufacturing plants in 19 countries and retail operations in 47 countries. It is the largest shoe company in the world, generating billions of dollars in sales. The company is wholly owned by the Gamma family, and, in the past, the company has refused to publicly reveal any aspects of its finances.

The business was started in Hungary by Ray Gamma, who was a master shoemaker. He established his own facility for quality mass-produced shoes, which he sold through retail stores around the country. In 1940, Ray and his family escaped from the war zone and fled to Canada with only some personal possessions. In Canada, he established a new shoe company to supply shoes and boots to the military, and his expertise at shoe manufacturing led his company to become a prime government contractor and to expand rapidly.

After the end of the war, Ray converted his productive capacity to domestic shoes and boots, but encountered difficulty in getting access to established shoe stores due to restrictive trade practices by his competitors. Therefore, he established his own chain of shoe stores to sell only Gamma shoes. Over the next 15–20 years, the business expanded literally around the world, with particular prominence in Europe and the Americas.

Last year, Ray Gamma relinquished the position of CEO and retained only the position of chairman of the Board of Directors. Ray's son, Able, was named the new CEO. Able was distressed by the downward slide that the company had taken in recent years, and set about re-organizing its operations. Indeed, the huge loss that is expected for 20X8 relates largely to losses from discontinued operations, as well as to the costs of some other re-organization initiatives that the Board has approved at Able's urging.

The company did succeed in issuing $100 million of 25-year bonds as a private placement early in 20X8 at a net price of 103. Part of the understanding with the bondholders was that the company would seek additional equity capital as soon as possible. The bond indenture contains very strict limits on the issuance of further debt and on the payment of cash dividends.

One source of equity capital would be to issue non-voting shares to the public, but the Board of Directors would prefer private placements of equity shares if at all possible. Able and Ray have been negotiating with a U.S. pension fund manager about issuing a class of special shares. The pension fund would be able to demand redemption of the shares if the company did not achieve targeted profitability, solvency, and liquidity ratios within five years.

As part of the reorganization, the Gamma Board has approved Able's suggestion that the company divest itself of its U.S. tanning operations.* Able is actively seeking a buyer, but as yet has been unsuccessful due to the relatively high cost of making leather in the U.S., compared to Argentina or Mexico. The amount to be realized is unknown, but will probably be less than net book value. Able is also thinking of selling off all of the company's other U.S. operations in order to reduce the company's vulnerable assets under the U.S.'s *Helms-Burton* law; Gamma uses the shell of a confiscated U.S. manufacturing plant in Cuba. No decision has been made on any additional sell-off of U.S. assets, however.

Ray is demanding that the Hungarian government return a factory in Hungary that was confiscated during the war. The government is willing to sell the factory to Gamma, but Ray insists that it be given back. Its equipment is very old and outmoded.

The company's international credit arrangements are managed globally by Megabank Canada, which leads a consortium of international banks that deal collaboratively with Gamma. The retail operations in each country are financed locally through operating lines of credit (in local currency), while Megabank provides the financing directly to Gamma for most of its physical facilities in the various countries. Generally speaking, Gamma's retail stores are rented, while Gamma's manufacturing facilities are owned.

Able has engaged Maria Pan as a consultant to assist the company in its reorganization. Able wants Maria to report on not only the operational aspects of the company's reorganization, but also the accounting implications of the company's position and actions.

Required:

Assume that you are Maria Pan. Respond to Able Gamma's request regarding accounting implications.

---

*Tanning is the process of turning animal hides into leather. It is a very smelly process.

ASSIGNMENTS

 A16-1 Income Tax Explanation: Cheshire Corporation reported the following items with respect to income tax in the 20X4 financial statements:

Future income tax, current asset	$ 3,700
Future income tax, non-current liability	129,600

The 20X4 income statement shows the following income tax expense:

Income tax expense:	
Current	$37,500
Future (all non-current)	19,500
Impact of loss carryforward	(41,300)
	$14,500

The disclosure notes indicate that there is an unrecognized loss carryforward in the amount of $357,500. No tax loss carryforwards have been recorded as assets. The tax rate is 40%.

Required:

1. Explain the components of the 20X4 income tax expense. Why is there income tax expense if there is a loss carryforward?

2. Give an example of a balance sheet account that could have caused a current asset FIT account, and a non-current liability FIT account.

3. Why would the loss carryforward not have been recognized in its entirety in 20X4? What would change (amounts and accounts) if it could be recognized?

4. What would the opening balance in the two future income tax accounts have been?

5. How much tax is currently payable? How much tax would have been payable if there had been no loss carryforward?

 A16-2 Loss Carryback/Carryforward: The income statements of Bromley Corporation for the first four years of operations reflected the following pre-tax amounts:

	20X4	20X5	20X6	20X7
Revenue	$250,000	$310,000	$360,000	$500,000
Expenses	240,000	390,000	320,000	400,000
Pre-tax income (loss)	$ 10,000	$ (80,000)	$ 40,000	$100,000

There are no temporary differences other than those created by income tax losses. Assume an income tax rate of 34% for all four years.

Required:

1. Give entries to record income tax expense for each year, assuming that Bromley management believes in 20X5 that there is a 40% probability of realizing the benefits of the carryforward prior to their expiry. Show computations.

2. Repeat requirement (1) for 20X5 through 20X7, assuming that management believes in 20X5 that Bromley is almost certain to realize the benefits of the carryforward (and doesn't change their minds). Show computations.

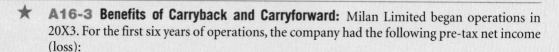 **A16-3 Benefits of Carryback and Carryforward:** Milan Limited began operations in 20X3. For the first six years of operations, the company had the following pre-tax net income (loss):

Year	Taxable income	Tax rate
20X3	$ (30,000)	44%
20X4	180,000	45%
20X5	220,000	43%
20X6	(650,000)	40%
20X7	70,000	36%
20X8	150,000	38%

There have been no permanent or temporary differences between pre-tax accounting income and taxable income.

In 20X6, management was less than 50% certain that any tax carryforward would be realized. Management decided in 20X7 that full realization of carryforward benefits was more likely than not, and did not change that opinion in 20X8.

Required:

For each year, determine:

1. Income tax currently payable (receivable)

2. Income tax expense (recovery)

3. Net income (loss)

★ **A16-4 Carrybacks and Carryforwards in Successive Years:** Yang Enterprises Limited was founded at the beginning of 20X0. For the first 10 years, the company had the following record of taxable income and loss (before considering any tax loss carryforwards or carrybacks):

Year	Taxable Income (Loss)
20X0	$ 30,000
20X1	45,000
20X2	25,000
20X3	(70,000)
20X4	15,000
20X5	(115,000)
20X6	(40,000)
20X7	30,000
20X8	60,000
20X9	180,000

The company had no permanent or temporary differences in any of the 10 years. The income tax rate was 40% from 20X0 through 20X5. In 20X6, the government enacted new legislation that called for reducing the rate to 37% for 20X6 and to 34% for 20X7 and beyond. In each year, management believed that the company was more likely than not to realize the benefit of any tax loss carryforwards.

Required:

Calculate income tax expense for each year, 20X0 through 20X9.

★ **A16-5 Loss Carryback; Entries and Reporting:** Tyson Corporation reported pre-tax income from operations in 20X4 of $80,000 (the first year of operations). In 20X5, the corporation experienced a $40,000 pre-tax loss from operations. Future operations are highly uncertain. Assume an income tax rate of 45%. Tyson has no temporary or permanent differences.

Required:

1. Assess Tyson's income tax situation for 20X4 and 20X5. How should Tyson elect to handle the loss in 20X5?

2. Based on your assessments in requirement (1), give the 20X4 and 20X5 income tax entries.

3. Show how all tax-related items would be reported on the 20X4 and 20X5 income statement and balance sheet.

★ **A16-6 Loss Carryforward, Valuation Allowance:** The pre-tax earnings of Cranston Limited for the first three years were as follows:

	20X3	20X4	20X5
Revenues	$ 550,000	$600,000	$650,000
Expenses	665,000	575,000	615,000
Earnings (loss) before income taxes	$(115,000)	$ 25,000	$ 35,000

The company had no permanent or temporary differences in any of the three years. The income tax rate was constant at 30%.

In 20X3 and 20X4, the prospect for future earnings was highly uncertain. In 20X5, Cranston management decided that the future outlook for the company was quite good, and that significant earnings would be generated in the near future.

Required:

1. Restate the above income statements to reflect income tax effects for each year.

2. Show any amounts relating to income taxes that would be reported on Cranston's balance sheet in each of the three years.

3. Prepare journal entries to record income taxes in each year. The company's accountant has recommended using the valuation allowance approach to recording tax loss carryforward benefits.

★★ **A16-7 Loss Carryforward, Valuation Allowance, rate change:** Immen Corporation had the following taxable and pre-tax accounting income:

	20X1	20X2	20X3	20X4
Earnings (loss) before taxes	$(200,000)	$(30,000)	$20,000	$130,000
Tax rate	40%	40%	36%	36%

Assume that 20X1 is the first year of operations for the company. Tax rates are enacted in the year in which they become effective.

In 20X2, the company won some major contracts that management believed would bring the company into profitability. Therefore, management decided at the end of 20X2 that it was more likely than not that 60% of the unused tax loss carryforward would be used within the carryforward period. In 20X4, management further decided it was more likely than not that the full 100% of the unused carryforward would be realized.

Required:

1. Prepare the journal entries to record the provision for income tax for each year. Do not use a valuation allowance.

2. Prepare the journal entries to record the provision for income tax for each year. Use a valuation account.

3. Present the lower part of the income statement, showing pre-tax earnings, income tax provision, and net earnings after tax.

4. Calculate the effective tax rate for each year.

★★ **A16-8 Recognition of Loss Carryforward:** Chinmoy Corporation experienced an accounting and tax loss in 20X5. The benefit of the tax loss was realized in part by carryback. The remainder was left as a tax loss carryforward but was not recognized as management felt that there was considerable doubt as to its eventual recognition. The gross tax loss carryforward amounted to $274,500. In 20X6, a further accounting and tax loss was recognized. This time, the tax loss was $86,000, and the benefit of the tax loss carryforwards was still not recorded. In 20X7, the company recorded accounting income. The taxable income prior to using the loss carryforward was $55,000. There were no permanent or temporary differences. The tax rate was 34% in 20X7. The enacted tax rate for 20X8 was 36%, enacted in 20X8.

Required:

1. Record 20X7 tax entries assuming that the likelihood of using the remaining tax loss carryforwards is still considered to be less than 50%.

2. Assume that in 20X8 accounting and taxable income was $450,000. Record income taxes.

3. Record 20X7 tax entries assuming that the probability of using the remaining tax loss carryforwards is considered to be greater than 50% for the first time.

4. Again assume that accounting and taxable income in 20X8 was $450,000, but that the entries from requirement (3) were made. Record 20X8 income tax.

★ **A16-9 Calculate a Loss Carryback and Its Benefit, Temporary Differences:** Tyler Toys Limited uses the liability method of tax allocation. Tyler reported the following:

	20X3	20X4	20X5	20X6
Accounting income before tax	$10,000	$15,000	$(40,000)	$10,000
Depreciation expense (original cost of asset, $75,000)	6,000	6,000	6,000	6,000
Golf club dues	3,000	4,000	3,000	4,000
CCA (maximum available claim)	3,000	6,000	12,000	10,000
Tax rate—enacted in each year	20%	20%	30%	35%

Required:

1. Calculate taxable income each year, and the tax payable. Tyler claims the maximum CCA each year.

2. How much of the loss could Tyler use as a tax loss carryback? How much tax refund will it receive? How much is the tax loss carryforward? How much is the tax benefit?

★ **A16-10 Recording Temporary Differences, Loss, Rate Change:** Refer again to the data in A16-9.

Required:

Provide the journal entry to record the benefit of the tax loss in 20X5 assuming that the tax loss is first used as a tax loss carryback and the remainder is available as a tax loss carryforward. Be sure to adjust the long-term future income tax account for the temporary difference between depreciation and CCA, and also the change in tax rates. What condition has to be met to record the loss in 20X5?

★★ **A16-11 Loss Carryforward, Temporary Difference:** Bean Corporation began operations in 20X3. In its first year, the company had a net operating loss before tax for accounting purposes of $60,000. Depreciation was $84,000, and CCA was $96,000. The company claimed CCA in 20X3. In 20X4, Bean had taxable income before the use of the tax loss carryforward of $240,000. This was after adding back $84,000 of depreciation and deducting $120,000 of CCA. The income tax rate is 40% in both years. Capital assets had an original cost of $990,000 in 20X3.

Required:

1. Prepare a journal entry or entries to record income tax in 20X3 and 20X4 assuming that the likelihood of using the tax loss carryforward is assessed as probable in 20X3. Also prepare the lower section of the income statement for 20X3 and 20X4.

2. Repeat requirement (1) assuming that the likelihood of using the tax loss carryforward is assessed as improbable.

3. Which assessment—probable or improbable—seems more logical in 20X3? Discuss.

★★ **A16-12 Loss Carrybacks and Carryforwards, Rate Change:** Wilderness Tours Limited has experienced the following accounting and taxable income:

	Accounting Income	Taxable Income*	Tax Rate
20X4	($66,000)	($42,000)	30%
20X5	40,000	30,000	34
20X6	70,000	62,000	32
20X7	30,000	(68,000)	25

Before applying any available tax loss carryforwards

The differences between accounting and taxable income are caused by permanent differences between accounting and tax expenses. All tax rates are enacted in the year to which they relate. Wilderness Tours does not use a valuation account.

Required:

1. Record income tax for 20X4 through 20X7 assuming that the future use of tax loss carryforwards is considered to be unlikely.

2. Repeat requirement (1) assuming that the use of tax loss carryforwards is considered to be more likely than not in the loss year.

★ **A16-13 Future Tax Asset Revaluation; Rate Change:** MacLeod Lumber Limited reports the following asset on the balance sheet at 31 December 20X5:

Future tax asset, loss carryforward $306,000

This asset reflects the benefit of a tax loss carryforward recorded in 20X4. It was not used in 20X5. The enacted tax rate was 34%. In 20X6, the enacted tax rate changes to 36%.

Required:

1. Record 20X6 tax entries if MacLeod reported accounting and taxable income of $60,000 in 20X6. The use of the tax loss carryforward is still considered to be probable.

2. Record 20X6 tax entries if MacLeod reported accounting and tax losses of $300,000 in 20X6. The use of the tax loss carryforward is still considered to be probable.

★★ **A16-14 Future Tax Assets and Loss Carryforwards; CCA:** Ling Enterprises was formed in 20X4, and recorded an accounting loss of $45,000 in its first year of operations. Included in the accounting loss was dividend revenue of $20,000 and depreciation expense of $50,000. The CCA claim was calculated as $40,000. The tax rate was 40%. Capital assets had an original cost of $210,000 in 20X4.

Required:

1. Can Ling record the benefit of the tax loss in 20X4? Why or why not?

2. Provide the tax entry in 20X4 assuming that the benefit of the tax loss carryforward cannot be recorded and CCA is claimed.

3. Should Ling claim the CCA in 20X4? Explain the circumstances under which it would be wise to claim CCA.

4. Repeat requirement (2) assuming that the benefit of the tax loss carryforward can be recorded and CCA is claimed.

5. Assume that in 20X5 Ling reported $163,000 of accounting income before tax. The tax rate was 40%. This included dividend revenue of $20,000 and depreciation of $50,000. CCA was $70,000 and was claimed. Record taxes in 20X5 assuming that:
   a. 20X4 taxes were recorded as in requirement (2).
   b. 20X4 taxes were recorded as in requirement (4).

★★ **A16-15 Loss Carryback/Carryforward; Temporary Difference:** Creek Limited shows the following on its 31 December 20X4 balance sheet:

Future income tax liability, long term	$870,000

All this income tax liability relates to the difference between the NBV and UCC of capital assets. At 31 December 20X4, NBV is $9,630,000 and UCC is $7,455,000.

In 20X2, 20X3, and 20X4, the company has reported a total taxable income of $324,750 and paid taxes of $81,450.

In 20X5, Creek reported an accounting loss before tax of $480,000. Depreciation of $67,500 is included in this calculation. No CCA will be claimed in 20X5. The enacted tax rate was 40% in 20X5.

Required:

1. Calculate the tax loss in 20X5.

2. How much of the tax loss can be used as a loss carryback? What will be the benefit of this loss carryback?

3. How much of the loss is available as a tax loss carryforward? What is the benefit of this tax loss carryforward?

4. Under what circumstances can the benefit of the tax loss carryforward be recorded as an asset?

5. Record income tax for 20X5 assuming that the tax loss carryforward can be recorded.

6. Record income tax for 20X5 assuming that the tax loss carryforward cannot be recorded.

7. Assume that accounting and taxable income was $150,000 in 20X6, and the enacted tax rate was still 40%. Prepare the journal entry to record income tax in 20X6 assuming that the tax loss carryforward (a) was recorded in 20X5 as in requirement (5), and (b) was not recorded in 20X5 as in requirement (6).

★ **A16-16 Loss Carryback/Carryforward, Valuation Allowance:** Ultima Corporation had the following pre-tax earnings:

Year	Pre-Tax Income (Loss)
20X1	$ 50,000
20X2	75,000
20X3	30,000
20X4	(395,000)

The tax rate was 30% in all years. The company has no permanent or temporary differences. Management predicts that only $100,000 of the carryforward will be utilized within the carryforward period.

In 20X5, Ultima has pre-tax earnings of $60,000. The tax rate for 20X5 is 30%. In 20X5, Parliament increases the rate for 20X6 and following years to 34%. In view of the profit in 20X5, management decides that Ultima is likely to realize the full benefits of the tax loss carryforward.

Required:

1. Assume that Ultima *does not* use a valuation account for its future income tax assets. Prepare the journal entry to record income tax expense for each of 20X4 and 20X5.

2. Assume that Ultima *does* use a valuation account. What balances relating to future income tax will appear on Ultima's books at the end of 20X4 and 20X5?

★★ **A16-17 Loss Carryback/Carryforward:** Munificence Limited had the following pre-tax income and losses:

Year	Pre-Tax Income (Loss)	Tax Rate
20X2	$ 180,000	34%
20X3	220,000	34
20X4	340,000	34
20X5	170,000	32
20X6	(1,340,000)	30
20X7	150,000	30
20X8	380,000	27

The tax rates are those effective for the year indicated. The rates were enacted the year prior to the year in which they became effective. Taxable income (loss) equalled accounting income (loss) in each year. Munificence does not use a valuation allowance.

Required:

1. Prepare the entry to record income tax expense for 20X6. At the end of 20X6, management estimates that there is greater than a 50% probability of realizing the benefits of only $200,000 of the loss carryforward.

2. Prepare the income tax expense entries for 20X7 and 20X8. In 20X7, management decides that the probability of realizing the benefits of the remaining loss carryforward is greater than 50%.

★ **A16-18 Loss Carryback/Carryforward, Valuation Allowance:** The following information pertains to Sandstrom Corporation:

- From 20X1 through 20X3, Sandstrom had pre-tax earnings totalling $150,000.
- In 20X4, Sandstrom had a pre-tax loss of $550,000.
- The company has no permanent or temporary differences.
- The income tax rate was 40% from 20X1 through 20X4.
- In 20X4, a rate of 38% was enacted for 20X5 and a rate of 36% was enacted for 20X6 and following years.
- In 20X4, management predicted that the benefits of only $200,000 of the tax loss carryforward were probable of realization in the carryforward period. Management also estimated that pre-tax earnings for 20X5 would be no more than $60,000.
- Actual pre-tax earnings in 20X5 were $80,000. Management estimated that only $120,000 of the tax loss carryforward was probable of realization.
- Pre-tax 20X6 earnings were $100,000. Management decided that it was highly probable that the full benefit of the remaining tax loss carryforward would be realized.

Required:

Sandstrom uses a valuation account for its future income tax assets. What are the balances in FIT-related accounts for each of 20X4, 20X5, and 20X6?

★ **A16-19 Loss Carryback/Carryforward; Entries:** Decker Limited began operations in 20X5 and reported the following information for the years 20X5 to 20X9:

	20X5	20X6	20X7	20X8	20X9
Pre-tax income	$10,000	$12,000	$15,000	$(106,000)	$13,000
Depreciation	10,000	10,000	10,000	10,000	10,000
Capital cost allowance	10,000	18,000	14,000	0	0

The income tax rate is 40% in all years. Assume that Decker's only depreciable assets were purchased in 20X5 and cost $200,000.

Required:

1. Prepare the journal entries for income taxes for 20X8 and 20X9. In 20X8, Decker's opinion was that realization of the loss carryforwards was more likely than not.

2. What is the balance of future income tax at the end of 20X9? Show calculations.

 A16-20 Loss Carryback/Carryforward; Rate Change: In the years 20X2 through 20X4, Dashmill reported a total of $259,000 of taxable income. The enacted tax rate during those years was 32%. At the end of 20X4, Dashmill reported a future income tax liability related to capital assets. The net book value of these assets was $650,000, while the UCC was $438,000 at the end of 20X4.

During 20X5, Dashmill Corporation recorded an accounting loss of $436,000, after depreciation expense of $42,000. No CCA was claimed in 20X5. In 20X5, the enacted rate changed to 35% for both 20X5 and 20X6.

In 20X6, Dashmill reported income before tax of $350,000. Depreciation of $43,000 was equal to the CCA claim.

Required:

1. Determine after-tax net income for 20X5 and 20X6 assuming that the benefit of the tax loss carryforward can be recognized in 20X5.

2. Repeat requirement (1) assuming that the benefit of the tax loss carryforward cannot be recognized in 20X5.

  A16-21 Loss Carryforward, Temporary Differences; Rate Change, Entries: The Village Company manufactures and sells television sets. The company recorded warranty expense of 2% of sales for accounting purposes. The following information is taken from the company's books:

(in thousands)	20X5	20X6	20X7	20X8	20X9
Sales	$3,000	$6,000	$8,000	$10,000	$15,000
Actual warranty claims paid	60	80	200	90	75
Accounting income (loss) before taxes	nil	(980)	nil	2,000	4,000
Depreciation	600	600	600	600	600
Capital cost allowance	600	nil	500	450	400
Dividend revenue	nil	20	20	nil	nil

Net book value of depreciable assets at 31 December 20X5: $7,600,000. Undepreciated capital cost at 31 December 20X5: $5,600,000. There is a future liability of $800,000 with respect to this temporary difference. There is no taxable income remaining to absorb loss carrybacks prior to 20X5.

The tax rate is 40% in 20X5 through 20X7 and increases to 45% for 20X8 and 20X9. Tax rates are enacted in the year to which they pertain. There are no other sources of temporary differences.

Required:

Give journal entries to record income taxes for 20X6 to 20X9 inclusive. Realization of the loss carryforward is considered to be more likely than not in 20X6.

 A16-22 Loss Carryback/Carryforward; Temporary Differences; Rate Change: You have been asked to account for income taxes for Melissa Corporation.

At 31 December 20X4 the net book value of capital assets was $560,000 and the undepreciated capital cost was $345,000. In addition, there was a $400,000 accounts receivable on the company's balance sheet. This receivable had been set up in 20X4 upon the recognition of revenue. The revenue will not be taxable until the receivable is collected. Melissa has always been a profitable company and has had accounting and taxable income in each of the last three years. Taxable income totalled $74,000 over the last three years. The tax rate has been stable at 42%.

In 20X5, Melissa recorded its first-ever accounting loss, reporting a loss of $486,000. This included revenue on the collection of a life insurance policy on the company president, who died in a mountain climbing accident in the year. The $200,000 revenue is not taxable now or in any future period. Depreciation expense was $40,000. No CCA was claimed. No portion of the 20X4 account receivable was collected. The tax rate, enacted in 20X5, was 40%. Melissa management felt that the company was assured of realizing the tax loss carryforward in future years.

In 20X6, Melissa returned to financial health and reported accounting income of $266,000. Non-deductible advertising expenses were $23,000. Depreciation was $56,000, and CCA was $70,000. Of the receivable recorded in 20X4, $125,000 was collected. The tax rate, enacted in 20X6, was 46%.

Required:

Calculate tax expense for 20X5 and 20X6. Your answer must include a calculation of income tax payable, the table that explains the adjustment needed to determine future income tax for the year, and journal entries to record income tax expense.

 A16-23 Loss Carryback/Carryforward; Temporary Differences; Rate Change: On 1 January 20X6, Primary Incorporated commenced business operations.

At 31 December 20X8, you are involved in preparing the financial statements. The following information is available to you:

	20X6	20X7	20X8
Income (loss) before tax	$407,400	($639,000)	$1,000,000
Tax rate (enacted in each year)	35%	38%	41%
Depreciation expense			
(asset cost was $970,000)	65,000	65,000	65,000
Capital cost allowance	350,000	0	287,000
Dividends received (non-taxable)	10,000	75,000	10,000
Non-deductible expenses	19,000	20,000	20,000

Required:

1. Prepare journal entries to record tax for 20X6, 20X7, and 20X8. Your entries should be in good form, and all calculations should be shown. Assume that the loss carryforward in 20X7 is considered likely of recognition.

2. How would your answer differ if the taxes payable method were used? Describe, do not calculate.

 A16-24 Loss Carryback/Carryforward; Temporary Differences; Rate Change: On 1 January 20X1, Wassabe Incorporated commenced business operations. The following information is available to you:

	20X1	20X2	20X3	20X4
Income (loss) before tax	$110,000	($604,000)	$ 65,000	$100,000
Tax rate (enacted in each year)	34%	32%	30%	28%
Depreciation (historical cost of assets, $4,100,000)	216,000	200,000	190,000	190,000
Capital cost allowance	250,000	0	100,000	190,000
Rental revenue recognized*	65,000	—	—	—

*Rental revenue is recognized as earned for accounting purposes, in 20X1. It is recognized as collected for tax purposes in 20X3.

Required:

Prepare journal entries to record tax for 20X1, 20X2, 20X3, and 20X4. Your entries should be in good form, and all calculations should be shown. Assume that the tax loss carryforward in 20X2 is considered unlikely of recognition but that in 20X3 the balance of probability shifts and, in 20X3, the loss is considered likely to be used.

A16-25 Loss Carryback/Carryforward, Rate Change; Comprehensive: Dexter Limited began operations in 20X5 and reported the following information for the years 20X5 to 20X9:

	20X5	20X6	20X7	20X8	20X9
Pre-tax income	$ 8,000	$15,000	$ 9,000	$(95,000)	$ 6,000
Depreciation	10,000	10,000	10,000	10,000	10,000
CCA	10,000	18,000	14,000	0	0
Net book value	90,000	80,000	70,000	60,000	50,000
UCC	90,000	72,000	58,000	58,000	58,000

Required:

1. Prepare journal entries to record income taxes in each year, 20X5 through 20X9. Assume that realization of the tax loss carryforward benefits is more likely than not and the tax rate is 40% in all years.

2. Repeat requirement (1) assuming that the tax rate is now 40% in 20X5 and 20X6, 43% in 20X7, 45% in 20X8, and 47% in 20X9. Tax rates are enacted in the year to which they pertain.

3. Return to the facts of requirement (1) (the tax rate is 40%). Repeat your journal entries for 20X8 and 20X9 assuming that use of the tax loss carryforward is deemed to be unlikely in 20X8, but likely in 20X9.

★★ **A16-26 Loss Carryback/Carryforward, Temporary and Permanent Differences, Use in Subsequent Year:** Dynamic Limited reported the following 20X5 income statement:

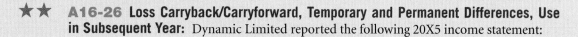

DYNAMIC LIMITED

Income Statement

For the year ended 31 December 20X5

Revenue	$2,715,000
Cost of goods sold	1,396,000
Depreciation	160,000
General and administrative expenses	75,000
Other	60,000
	1,691,000
Income before tax	$1,024,000

OTHER INFORMATION:

a. There is an $80,000 accrued rent receivable on the balance sheet. This amount was included in rental income (revenue) this year, but will not be taxed until next year. This is the first time such an accrual has been made.

b. The CCA claim for 20X5 is $301,000. At the beginning of 20X5, UCC was $2,165,000 while net book value was $2,916,000. The balance in the related future income tax liability was $300,400 (cr.)

c. Revenue includes dividends received of $40,000, which are not taxable at any time.

d. Other expenses include non-deductible entertainment expenses of $60,000.

e. The balance sheet shows an asset account called "future income tax asset $30,000," which is the benefit of a $75,000 loss carryforward, recorded in 20X3.

Required:

Prepare the journal entry or entries to record tax in 20X5. Show all calculations. The tax rate is 40%.

(CGA-Canada, adapted)

 A16-27 Loss Carryback/Carryforward, Comprehensive, Rate Change: Chingolo Corporation was incorporated in 20X5. Details of the company's results are presented below:

	20X5	20X6	20X7
Income (loss) before tax	$ 30,000	($100,000)	$ 50,000
Depreciation expense	40,000	40,000	40,000
Capital cost allowance claimed	50,000	0	50,000
Dividend income	5,000	5,000	5,000
Tax rate	37%	37%	37%
Net book value, end of year	360,000	320,000	280,000
UCC, end of year	350,000	350,000	300,000

Required:

1. Prepare journal entries for tax for 20X5, 20X6, and 20X7. Assume that realization of the benefit of the loss carryforward is more likely than not in 20X6. The company does not use a valuation allowance.

2. Repeat requirement (1), assuming that the tax rate is 37% in 20X5, but is changed to 39% in 20X6 and to 43% in 20X7. All tax rates are enacted in the year in which they are effective.

3. Revert to the facts of requirement (1) (i.e., 37% tax rate in each year). Assume that the use of the unused tax loss carryforward is considered unlikely in 20X6, and is still unlikely in 20X7, other than the loss carryforward actually utilized in 20X7. Provide journal entries for 20X5, 20X6, and 20X7.

 A16-28 Loss Carryback/Carryforward, Comprehensive, Valuation Allowance: Refer to the data and the requirements of A16-27.

Required:

Repeat requirement (3) for A16-27 assuming that the company uses a valuation account for its future income tax assets.

 A16-29 Tax Losses: Subsequent Recognition and Revaluation; Valuation Allowance: Partinni Limited reports the following items on the balance sheet at 31 December 20X4:

Future income tax, loss carryforward	$784,000 dr.
Future income tax, capital assets	340,000 cr.
Net future tax asset, long term	$444,000 dr.

The loss carryforward had been recorded in 20X4. The enacted tax rate was 35% at the end of 20X4, and the net book value of capital assets was $2,650,000, while the UCC was $1,587,500.

In 20X5, Partinni reported accounting income of $27,000. Depreciation, the only temporary difference, was $80,000, while CCA of $90,000 was claimed. In 20X5, the enacted tax rate changed to 30%. Probability assessment regarding the loss carryforward did not change.

In 20X6, the enacted tax rate changed to 32%. Partinni reported accounting income of $17,000. Depreciation of $20,000 was expensed, and no CCA was claimed. Because of continued low profitability, the company reluctantly decided in 20X6 that the probability of using the remaining tax loss carryforward in the carryforward period now had to be considered low.

Required:

1. Record income tax entries for 20X5 and 20X6. Assume that a valuation account is not used.

2. Repeat the entries for 20X6 assuming that a valuation account is used.

★★ **A16-30 Tax Losses; Intraperiod Allocation, Income Statement:** At the beginning of 20X4, Caprioli Tracking Corporation (CTC) had a future income tax liability (long term) on its balance sheet of $60,000. The future income tax balance reflects the tax impact of gross accumulated temporary differences of $95,000 relating to CCA/Depreciation and $55,000 relating to pension costs. The tax expense has been higher (that is, CCA and pension funding have been higher) than the accounting expense (that is, depreciation and pension expense). Over the past three years, taxes have been due and paid as follows:

Year	Taxable Income	Taxes Due
20X1	$60,000	$22,000
20X2	20,000	7,600
20X3	40,000	16,000
		$45,600

In 20X4, CTC suffered the first loss in its history due to a general economic turndown. The accounting loss amounted to $200,000 before taxes, including an extraordinary loss (fully tax deductible) of $80,000 before taxes. In computing accounting income, CTC deducted depreciation of $10,000 per year. On its 20X4 tax return, CTC elected to take no CCA, and therefore the 20X4 loss for tax purposes was as follows:

Accounting income (loss)	$(200,000)
Depreciation	10,000
Pension expense (not deductible)	30,000
Pension funding (deductible)	(60,000)
Taxable income (loss)	$(220,000)

The income tax rate, which had gradually increased over several years to 40% in 20X3, remained at 40% for 20X4 taxable income. In 20X4, Parliament enacted legislation to reduce the income tax rate to 36% for 20X5 and following years.

In management's judgement, it is more likely than not that any tax loss carryforward will be fully utilized in the carryforward period.

Required:

Prepare the lower part of the CTC income statement for 20X4, starting with "earnings before income tax and extraordinary item."

A16-31 Explain Impact of Temporary Differences, Tax Losses: You are the new accountant for Cooker Chemicals Limited (CCL). You have been asked to explain the impact of income tax on the financial statements for the year ended 31 December 20X5. You discover the following:

- CCL's product development expenses of $1 million have been deferred, to be amortized over the anticipated product life of four years starting two years from now.
- CCL had depreciation expense of $365,000 in 20X5 but claimed no CCA. In the past, CCA charges have been significantly higher than depreciation, resulting in a $547,800 future income tax liability on the balance sheet.
- In 20X5, CCL had a loss for tax purposes of $2 million. The company's tax rate is 40%, constant since incorporation 10 years ago.
- In the past several years, accounting and taxable income have been steady but unimpressive in the range of $150,000 to $250,000. CCL is aware that management has to make significant strategic changes to combat disastrous operating results this year. In particular, CCL is faced with the need to upgrade capital assets to remain competitive. However, raising money for this venture will be very difficult.

Required:
Explain the income tax impacts of the above and describe how results would be reported on the company's financial statements.

(ICAO, adapted)

 A16-32 Tax Losses, Temporary Differences: The 20X6 records of Laredo Incorporated show the following reconciliation of accounting and taxable income:

Net income per the financial statements	$124,000
Plus (minus)	
Dividend revenue	(2,900)
CCA in excess of depreciation	(42,300)
Warranty payments in excess of expense	(500)
Non-tax-deductible expenses	2,900
Taxable income	$ 81,200

In 20X5, Laredo Inc. had reported an operating loss, the tax benefit of which was fully recognized in 20X5 through loss carryback and recognition of a future tax asset.
Selected balance sheet accounts at the end of 20X5

Future income taxes (current asset; regarding warranty amounts)	$ 320
Income tax receivable (current asset)	16,400
Future income tax (long-term asset; loss carryforward)	20,000
Future income tax (long-term liability)	48,000
Warranty liability	1,000
Net book value of capital assets, after depreciation of $41,000	618,000

UCC at the end of 20X5 was $468,000. Depreciation expense in 20X6 was $41,000. The enacted tax rate in 20X5 was 32%. The enacted tax rate in 20X6 was 38%.

Required:
Present the lower portion of the 20X6 income statement. Also include the tax entries for 20X6.

(ASCA, adapted)

 A16-33 Tax Losses, Temporary Differences: Boom Corporation was incorporated in 20X4. Its records show the following:

	20X4	20X5	20X6
Pre-tax income (loss)	—	$(1,700,000)	$ 900,000
Non-deductible expenses	—	40,000	50,000
Amortization of capital assets	$ 25,000	150,000	250,000
Capital cost allowance	25,000	—	500,000
Net book value of depreciable fixed assets*	225,000	3,070,000	2,870,000
Undepreciated capital cost (UCC)*	225,000	3,220,000	2,770,000
Tax-free revenue	4,000	10,000	12,000
Enacted income tax rate (at year-end)	38%	40%	45%

*As calculated at the end of the year, after appropriate recognition of acquisitions and the yearly charge for depreciation or CCA.

Required:

1. Present the lower portion of the 20X4 through 20X6 income statements. Assume that the likelihood of tax loss carryforward realization is considered to be more probable than not in all years.

2. Repeat requirement (1) assuming that the likelihood of tax loss carryforward realization is considered to be indeterminable in all years.

(ASCA, adapted)

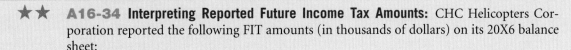 **A16-34 Interpreting Reported Future Income Tax Amounts:** CHC Helicopters Corporation reported the following FIT amounts (in thousands of dollars) on its 20X6 balance sheet:

	Dr./(Cr.)
FIT assets, current	$ 26,859
FIT assets, non-current	39,848
FIT liabilities, current	(8,852)
FIT liabilities, non-current	(180,001)
	$(122,146)

The income statement showed income tax expense of $10,940. The cash flow statement showed an add-back in operating activities of $4,550. In the disclosure note for income taxes, the company reported an FIT asset for "losses carried forward" of $41,463 as one of the components of the overall future income tax amounts. The note also reported tax loss carryforwards (in millions) as follows:

Non-capital losses relating to Canadian operations	$117.0
Non-capital losses relating to Dutch operations	28.7
Non-capital losses relating to other foreign operations	10.2
	$152.9

The company stated that it had "provided a valuation allowance in respect of $21.4 million of the non-capital losses."

The note also disclosed that during the year, "legislation was substantively enacted in the Netherlands to reduce the corporate income tax rate from 34.5% to 30.0%."

Required:

1. Explain why CHC shows four different balance sheet amounts for FIT instead of just one net liability of $122,146.

2. How much of the non-capital (that is, operating) tax loss carryforward has been *recognized*?

3. What is the apparent average tax rate that CHC used to calculate the tax benefits of the tax loss carryforwards?

4. Suppose that the amount of Dutch loss carryforwards did not change during 20X6. What was the balance of Dutch income tax assets (before deducting the valuation allowance) at both the beginning and the end of the year?

 A16-35 Integrative Problem, Chapters 12–16: FTC Corporation showed the following items on its 31 December 20X6 balance sheet:

Bonds payable, 9.25%, due 31 December 20X16	2,000,000
Discount on bonds payable	81,967
Future income tax—long-term liability	116,000
$8 cumulative preferred shares, callable at $105, authorized 200,000 shares, issued and outstanding, 144,000 shares	14,940,000
Common shares, authorized unlimited shares, issued and outstanding, 733,000 shares	12,210,000
Retained earnings	14,639,500

During 20X7, the company reported the following transactions:

1. On 15 January, 3,000 common shares were purchased as treasury shares for $19.25 per share.

2. On 28 February, dividends were declared and paid sufficient to allow a $1.50 per share dividend on the common shares. No dividend had been declared or paid during 20X4, 20X5, or 20X6. Dividends on different share classes should be debited to separate dividend accounts, which will be closed to retained earnings at year-end.

3. On 21 March, 24,000 preferred shares were retired at the redemption price. On the same date, all the common treasury shares were resold for $22 per share.

4. On 31 July, 2,000 common shares were repurchased and retired. The company paid $16.25 for the shares.

5. The bonds payable had been issued on 1 January 20X4 to yield 10%. Interest was due annually on 31 December. On 1 August 20X7, 40% of the bond issue was retired for 102 plus accrued interest to the date of sale. Bond discount amortization was recorded to the date of redemption for the redeemed bonds using straight-line amortization. (Note: First, determine original proceeds on issuance and total annual discount amortization. Round all calculations to the nearest dollar.)

6. Bond interest was paid, and bond discount amortization recorded, on 31 December, for the remaining bonds.

Required:

1. Journalize the transactions listed above.

2. To raise capital for a needed expansion, FTC is investigating the possibility of issuing a convertible bond. The $5,000,000 bond, with a 20-year term, would have an interest rate of 6% paid annually at year-end. The market interest rate is 10%. The bond would be issued at par. The bond would be convertible at maturity to common shares at the investor's option.

   Provide the journal entry that would be made to record the bond issuance. Explain how interest expense would subsequently be calculated.

3. FTC uses the liability method of tax allocation to record corporate income taxes. Future income tax of $116,000 consisted of two elements, recorded at the enacted tax rate of 32%:

Net book value ($6,790,000) versus undepreciated capital cost ($5,227,500)	500,000 cr.
Tax loss carryforward ($1,200,000 gross)	384,000 dr.
Net future income tax, non-current	116,000 cr.

In 20X7, income before tax but after all transactions recorded in requirement (1) was $431,000. Depreciation was $203,000, while CCA was $412,000. Advertising expense, not deductible for income tax purposes, was $25,000. The enacted tax rate for 20X7 changed to 34% in 20X7. At the same time, the enacted tax rate for 20X8 changed to 33%.

Record entries for income tax for 20X7. (Note: Disregard the effect of bond discount amortization and the gain or loss on bond retirement for these calculations although both are temporary differences.)

4. Repeat requirement (3) assuming that the loss carryforward was unrecorded at the end of 20X6, and the likelihood of its further realization was still considered to be low at the end of 20X7.

CHAPTER 17

Accounting for Leases

INTRODUCTION

Le Château Inc., Canadian clothing manufacturer and retailer, reports liabilities of about $4.3 million for capital lease obligations on its 2007 balance sheet. This amount is equal to about 30% of the company's total long-term debt. How does this amount arise, and how does it affect the company's annual financial reporting?

Most people are familiar with the general concept of a lease, whether it is through leasing an apartment, a car, or an office. Basically, a lease is an arrangement whereby the person or company that owns an asset agrees to let another person or company use the asset for a period of time at a stated (or determinable) amount of rent. The owner is called the *lessor*, while the renter is the *lessee*.

Accounting for a lease may not appear at first to be a big problem. After all, the lessee is paying rent to the lessor, so on the surface it would appear that the lessee simply recognizes rent expense on the income statement, while the lessor reports rent revenue. However, things are not always what they seem.

In accounting, a basic principle is that we should attempt to report transactions in accordance with their economic substance rather than their legal form. Often, the economic substance of a lease is that the lessor is really giving use of the asset over most of the asset's useful life in return for a full repayment of the cost of the asset, plus interest. When that happens, the lessor is really acting as a financial intermediary that is financing the asset for the lessee. The principle of reporting *substance over form* therefore leads us to account for the asset as though it were a purchase financed fully by debt. Therein lies the complication.

The purpose of this chapter is to explain the circumstances under which a lease is treated as a form of financing instead of a simple rental agreement, and how a financing lease should be reported. In this chapter, we look at the general substance of leases, and we examine accounting by the lessee in detail. Accounting by the lessor is discussed in the Appendix to this chapter.

DEFINITION OF A LEASE

A lease is a contract that gives the rights to use a tangible asset in return for the payment of rent. In the commonly used sense of the term, a lease is a fee-for-usage contract between an owner of property and a renter. The asset's owner is the lessor, and the renter is the lessee. The lease specifies the terms under which the lessee has the right to use the owner's property and the compensation to be paid to the lessor in exchange.

Leased assets can include both real property and personal property. *Real property* means real estate: land and buildings. *Personal property* includes much more than the property that belongs to a person; it is any property that is not real property, and includes both tangible assets (such as machinery, equipment, or transportation vehicles) and certain intangibles (such as patents).

WHY LEASE? THE LEASING CONTINUUM

Short-Term Leases

Suppose you want to rent a car. If you rent a car for one hour, you will pay a very high rate. If you rent for one day, you will pay a high rate, but the rate will be considerably less than the hourly rate times 24. If you rent for a month, the rate per day will be much lower than the rate to rent for one day. And if you rent for three years, a very low rental rate per day can be obtained. As the rental term lengthens, the daily rent goes down because more and more of the risk of ownership is transferred to the lessee. At some point in this sliding scale of automobile rental payments, the lessee essentially agrees to pay for the car via the rent payments.

Why do companies lease assets instead of buying them? A short-term lease is used to obtain temporary use of an asset without having to buy it. This is appropriate when there is no long-term need for an asset, or when the lessee's business is volatile and there is not a constant need for a certain type of asset. A short-term lease that gives the lessee temporary use of an asset is called, in accounting, an **operating lease**.

Because an operating lease provides only a relatively short-term return to the lessor, the lessor bears the risk of ownership. If the lessee returns the asset after only a short rental period and the lessor cannot find another lessee, then the lessor will incur the costs not only of maintaining the asset but also of watching it sink slowly into obsolescence. Consequently, the longer the lease term, the lower the daily rental cost.

Long-Term Leases

At the other end of the leasing continuum, long-term leases give the lessee substantially all of the benefits of ownership. The lessee also has to bear most of the risks of ownership. For example, the lessee is committed to the lease contract even if the asset becomes obsolete.

When a lease transfers substantially all of the benefits and risks of ownership to the lessee, the lessee might as well have purchased the asset outright. Indeed, purchasing the asset would give more flexibility—there are no restrictions on what the owner does with an asset.

In accounting terms, a lease that transfers substantially all of the benefits and risks of ownership to the lessee is called a **capital lease**. A little later in this chapter, we will explain the criteria for deciding whether a lease is a capital lease. First, however, we will look at operating lease accounting.

OPERATING LEASES

An operating lease is one that gives the lessee the right to use the asset for only a relatively short period of its useful life, such as renting a car or truck for a day, a month, or a year. Accounting for operating leases is not complicated. The lessee makes periodic lease payments that are accounted for as normal expense items by the lessee. Meanwhile, the lessor credits the payments to an income account such as leasing revenue (or *other income* if leasing is not one of the company's mainstream business activities). If a lessee rents space for $1,000 a month, the lessee's entry would be as follows:

Rent expense	1,000	
Cash		1,000

It is important to remember that the length of "term" is a relative phrase when it comes to asset leasing; a 10-year lease is short term when it applies to leasing a building that may last for 60 years.

Uneven Payments

The only catch with operating leases is that sometimes the lease payments are not even. When rental space is very scarce, for example, the lessee may have to make an initial lump-sum payment to the landlord in order to obtain space.[1] If there is an unusually large payment at the beginning (or inception) of the lease, the special payment is amortized over the period of time that the lessee is required to make lease payments. This period of time is called the **initial lease term**. The lease may be renewable, but since there is no obligation on the part of the lessee to renew the lease, the amortization must end with the initial term.

An alternative arrangement that also occurs, particularly for real estate rentals, is that the lessor will "forgive" lease payments (or operating cost payments) for a limited period of time at the beginning of the lease. For example, in a market that has excess supply, a lessor may attract a lessee by agreeing that lease payments will not begin until six months after the lease starts. These forgiven payments also are amortized over the initial term of the lease by charging the contractual monthly lease payments to income and then amortizing the forgiven amounts over the full initial lease term.

For example, assume that Woody's Limited leases space in an office building for five years for an annual rental of $100,000. Because the office rental market is "soft," the lessor agrees that Woody's need not begin paying rent until the second year; the first year's rent is forgiven. The substance of this deal is that Woody's agrees to pay a total of $400,000 for five years; this averages out to an effective rental rate of $80,000 per year. For the first year, there is no cash flow for rent, but Woody will record an expense of $80,000, which is offset by a deferred credit:

Rent expense	80,000	
Deferred rent liability		80,000

For each of the next four years, the $80,000 will be amortized to rent expense, thereby reducing rent expense from the cash outflow of $100,000 to the average annual expense of $80,000. The entries on Woody's books will be:

Rent expense	80,000	
Deferred rent liability	20,000	
Cash		100,000

The deferred rent will be reported as a current liability on the balance sheet, usually combined with other deferred credits and accrued liabilities.

---

[1] Such payments sometimes are known as *key money* and may be prohibited in some jurisdictions, particularly in those with rent controls on residential properties.

A fundamental question is: *when is a lease an operating lease?* Current accounting standards answer this question only indirectly: a lease is an operating lease when it is not a capital lease! Therefore, in order to understand the rather fuzzy distinction between an operating lease and a capital lease, we must examine the criteria for defining capital leases.

GUIDELINES FOR DEFINING CAPITAL LEASES

The more challenging type of lease (for accountants) is one in which the lessor agrees to purchase an asset (of any type) and to lease it immediately to the lessee for substantially the full economic life and value of the asset. When that happens, the lessor is not interested in enjoying the benefits of ownership, even though the lessor will have legal title. Instead, the objective of such a transaction is to provide financing to the lessee to permit the lessee to acquire the asset without actually buying it.

This type of lease is called a "capital lease" in accounting. A capital lease is reported in accordance with its substance as a financing instrument rather than as a simple rental. Most of the rest of this chapter will deal with accounting for capital leases.

Financial Reporting

The financial reporting of capital leases is very different from that for operating leases. There can be a significant impact on the financial statements if a lease is reported as a capital lease. Accounting standard setters have developed criteria to help financial statement preparers (and auditors) decide whether a lease qualifies as a capital lease for financial reporting. In Canada, these criteria are only guidelines; the basic criterion is judgemental: *do the terms of the lease transfer substantially all of the benefits and risks of ownership from the lessor to the lessee?*

Conditions of Leasing Canadian and international standards state that, normally, a lease should be assumed to transfer substantially all of the benefits and risks of ownership to the lessee when at least one of the following conditions is present at the inception of the lease:[2]

- There is reasonable assurance that the lessee will obtain ownership of the leased property at the end of the lease term. This would occur (1) if the lease provides for automatic transfer of title to the lessee at the end of the lease, or (2) if the lessee is entitled to exercise a *bargain purchase option.*
- The lessee will receive substantially all of the economic benefits expected to be derived through use of the leased property. Since assets are most productive in the earlier years of their lives, this condition is presumed to be satisfied if the lease term is at least 75% of the asset's economic life.
- The lessor will be assured of recovering the investment in the leased property, plus a return on the investment, over the lease term. This condition is presumed to be satisfied if the present value of the *minimum net lease payments* is equal to at least 90% of the fair value of the asset at the inception of the lease.

Definitions Some definitions are needed in order to apply these criteria:

- A **bargain purchase option** exists when there is a stated or determinable price given in the lease that is sufficiently lower than the expected fair value of the leased asset at the option's exercise date to make it likely that the lessee will exercise the option. Even if the lessee does not really want the asset after the end of the lease term, it would be advantageous to exercise the option and then resell the asset at its higher fair value.
- The **lease term** includes:
  - All terms prior to the exercise date of a bargain purchase option;
  - All bargain renewal terms; and
  - All renewal terms at the *lessor's* option.

---

[2] The U.S. FASB has the same criteria, but they are *rules;* if any *one* of the criteria is satisfied, then the lease *must* be reported as a capital lease; if none is satisfied, then the lease *must* be reported as an operating lease.

- **Bargain renewal terms** are periods for which the *lessee* has the option of extending the lease at lease payments that are substantially less than would normally be expected for an asset of that age and type.
- A **guaranteed residual value** is an amount that the lessee agrees to assure the lessor can get for the asset by selling it to a third party at the end of the lease term. In essence, it may also represent an option for the lessee to buy the asset but without obligating the lessee to exercise the option. If the lessee chooses not to buy the asset from the lessor, the lessor can sell it for whatever the market will bear, but any deficiency in the sales proceeds must be provided by the lessee.
- **Minimum net lease payments** means all payments over the *lease term*, as described above (that is, including bargain renewal terms), *net* of any operating or executory costs that are implicitly included in the lease payment, *plus* any guaranteed residual value. A bargain purchase price also is included.

It is important to deduct operating costs from the lease payments to find the net lease payments. For example, if the lessor pays insurance on the asset, the lessor includes an estimate of the cost of insurance premiums when setting the lease payments. The insurance is not a cost of *acquiring* the asset; however, it is a cost of *using* the asset. Therefore, any operating costs that are implicitly included in the lease payments must be estimated and subtracted in order to find the present value of the payments that represent, in substance, the cost of acquiring the asset.

Minimum net lease payments also do not include any amounts for **contingent lease payments**, which are additional payments that are based on subsequent events, such as rent calculated on a percentage of a lessee's gross sales revenue.

- The lessee's **incremental borrowing rate (IBR)** is the interest rate that the lessee would have to pay if it obtained financing through the bank (or other credit sources) to buy the asset, and is determinable with reasonable assurance.[3]
- The **implicit lease interest rate** is the interest rate that discounts the minimum net lease payments to equal the fair value of the leased property at the beginning of the lease. It is the internal rate of return (IRR) for the lease, which is known to people in finance as the *lessee's implicit rate*.
- The interest rate used for discounting net lease payments is the lower of (1) the *lessor's* interest rate implicit in the lease, if known by the lessee, and (2) the *lessee's* IBR. In most cases, the lessor's rate is not known or is an after-tax rate that is not appropriate for the lessee's accounting.

Economic versus Useful Life   The *economic* life of an asset is the maximum number of years that it can be economically productive. The *useful* life to a particular company may be shorter. For example, desktop computers may be useful for six years, but a company may choose to keep its desktop computers no more than four years in order to stay up to date. The economic life is six years, while the useful life is four years. Useful life can never be longer than economic life.

Fair Value Ceiling   In no case should the asset be recorded at higher than its fair value. Consider a simple example. Suppose that a lessee agrees to pay the lessor $100,000 at the end of each year for four years. The fair value of the asset being leased is $300,000, and the asset has a four-year useful life. The lessee's IBR is 10%. The lessor's implicit interest rate is 9%. If the lessee's IBR of 10% is used for discounting the lease payments, the present value of the lease payments will be $316,987:

$$PV = \$100,000 \times (P/A, 10\%, 4) = \$316,987$$

---

[3] In finance literature, the incremental borrowing rate is sometimes called the *borrowing opportunity rate,* or *BOR.*

Using the lessor's implicit rate of 9%, the PV will be $323,972. If the lessee uses either its IBR or the lessor's implicit rate, the book value of the asset will be higher than the fair value of the asset. In such a case, the lessee would use a rate that discounts the lease payments to the $300,000 fair value of the asset. The equation is:

$$\$300,000 = \$100,000 \times (P/A, \, i, \, 4)$$

and must be solved for the value of i. The interest rate that solves this equation is 12.6%.[4]

Example of a Capital Lease

In order to illustrate these various definitions, consider the following example. Assume that Rosie Incorporated enters into a lease for equipment. The terms of the lease and the characteristics of the equipment are as follows:

- The current purchase price of the equipment is $700,000. The expected economic life of the equipment is 20 years.
- The initial lease term is eight years; Rosie cannot cancel the lease during this period.
- Lease payments during the initial lease term are $100,000 per year. These payments include property taxes and insurance costs that are estimated to be $5,000 per year.
- At the end of the initial lease term, Rosie can elect to renew the lease for two successive four-year terms at an annual rental of $40,000 per year, including estimated property taxes and insurance of $4,000 per year.
- Eight-year-old equipment of this type has a fair value of approximately $350,000, and can be leased for about $54,000 per year, net.
- If Rosie does not exercise the renewal options, the asset reverts to the lessor and will be physically removed from Rosie's premises. Following the second renewal term (that is, after 16 years), the asset will automatically revert to the lessor, although the lessor may elect not to physically remove the asset.
- All lease payments are due at the *beginning* of each lease year.
- If Rosie went to the company's friendly local bank manager, the company would be able to borrow the money to buy the equipment at an interest rate of 10%.
- Rosie does not know the lessor's interest rate implicit in the lease.

In this example, there is no purchase option and therefore there is no *bargain purchase option*. It is normal for there to be no bargain purchase option.

Minimum Lease Payments   The *minimum net lease payments* for the *initial lease term* of eight years are $95,000 per year: $100,000 minus the estimated $5,000 for operating or executory costs. Similarly, the minimum net lease payments for the renewal terms are $36,000: $40,000 minus $4,000 estimated operating costs.

Bargain Renewal Option   The existence of a bargain renewal option is determined in either of two ways. The first is by comparing the renewal lease payments to the fair value of a used asset of that age. If we discount the $36,000 annual net lease payments for the eight years of the two renewal periods, we get a present value at the beginning of the ninth year of $211,263. The example states that equipment of that type and age normally has a fair value of $350,000. The present value of the renewal is only 60% of the fair value, and therefore the renewal periods can be considered to be bargain renewal terms.

---

[4] The implicit rate can quickly be calculated with a financial calculator or with an Excel spreadsheet. An explanation for using Excel for present value and implicit interest calculations can be found on this book's Online Learning Centre.

The second approach is to compare the renewal payments in the lease with the normal net lease payments charged for that type of equipment. The normal net lease payments of $54,000 are 50% higher than Rosie's renewal of $36,000, which again supports the conclusion that the renewals are bargain renewal terms.

Lease Term Since the renewal terms are bargain renewal terms, the *lease term* is the initial lease term of eight years plus the two 4-year renewal terms, or 16 years.

Residual Value The example makes no explicit provision for a residual value, either guaranteed or unguaranteed. However, after 16 years, the lessor may elect to leave the equipment for Rosie to dispose of. Since 16 years is 80% of the asset's estimated economic life, it is likely to have little value to the lessor. Therefore, the lessor may well decide not to bother with the expense of removing it and may simply let Rosie keep it. It is important to note that this is an option of the lessor; if it were the lessee's option, then the lease would effectively have a purchase option of $0.

If Rosie believes that the equipment will be essentially useless after 16 years, then there may be a cost to physically remove the asset. This cost, if estimable, would be included as an additional cost of the lease; in effect, it would be a negative residual value.

Discount Rate The *incremental borrowing rate* is stated in the example to be 10%.

Comparison to Guidelines The terms of the lease can be compared to the three guidelines for determining whether substantially all of the risks and rewards of ownership have been transferred to the lessee:

1. There is no bargain purchase option and no automatic reversion of the asset to the lessee at the end of the lease.

2. The lease term, including bargain renewal terms, is 16 years. This lease term constitutes 80% of the asset's estimated 20-year economic life. Therefore, it appears that Rosie will have the use of the asset over 75% of its economic life.

3. The discounted present value of the minimum net lease payments over the 16-year lease term at Rosie's IBR of 10% is $656,056:

> PV = $95,000 (P/A due, 10%, 8) + $36,000 (P/A due, 10%, 8) (P/F, 10%, 8)
> PV = $557,500 + $98,556
> PV = $656,056

The discounted present value of the minimum net lease payments is equal to 94% of the fair value of the equipment of $700,000. Therefore, the 90% guideline is met. Notice that if the bargain renewal periods had not been included, the present value of the net lease payments for only the *initial* lease term would amount to about 80% of the asset's fair value. Therefore, it is important to determine whether or not the renewal terms are bargain renewals.

Applying the guidelines, it appears that the lease satisfies not just one, but two of the guidelines. Therefore, this lease would be reported as a *capital lease*.

INFORMAL CRITERIA FOR CAPITAL LEASES

While standard setters have provided criteria for lease classification that are based on the nature of the lease contract itself, professional judgement still is required. The basic issue is whether, *in substance*, the risks and benefits have been transferred from the lessor to the lessee.

One criterion that is not explicitly cited by the standard setters but that is very useful in practice is to look at the *nature of the lessor*. The nature of the lessor may be key in determining whether the lease is capital or operating.

For example, if the lessor is the leasing subsidiary of a bank, it should be clear that the lease is not an operating lease. Financial institutions have financial assets, not operating assets (except for their own tangible operating assets, of course) on their balance sheets. A bank's leasing division will not assume the risks of owning an asset, even though it has title to many thousands of them through lease contracts. One can be assured that, from the point of view of the bank, the lease is a capital lease no matter how ingenious the drafting may have been to try to avoid the accounting capital lease criteria.

In order to fully realize the tax advantages that often are the driving force behind capital leases, a lessor must qualify as a lessor under the income tax regulations. That means that a lessor must derive at least 90% of its revenues from lease transactions. Any company that meets this criterion is a financial intermediary. Any lease that such a financial institution enters into can be assumed to be a capital lease, even if none of the three capital lease criteria are met.

CONCEPT REVIEW

1. What is the basic criterion that determines whether a lease is a capital lease?

2. When are operating lease rental payments allocated (as expense) to periods other than those in which the payments are made?

3. List the three guidelines that help financial statement preparers decide whether a lease is a capital lease.

4. Define the following terms:
   • bargain renewal options
   • incremental borrowing rate
   • lease term

5. How can the nature of the lessor influence the lessee's accounting for a lease?

LONG-TERM LEASES: PROS AND CONS

Some people argue that long-term leasing has several advantages over buying an asset. However, the perceived advantages to the lessee also have offsetting disadvantages. For each purported advantage we will look at the apparent benefits first (PRO), and then at the related disadvantages (CON).

Off–Balance Sheet Financing

Pro: If a company enters a long-term lease and that lease does not qualify as a capital lease for accounting purposes, the company effectively has obtained financing for an asset without having to show the asset (and any related liability) on its balance sheet. For example, airlines often use leasing in this manner by entering into operating leases that last for several years but don't last long enough for the lease to qualify as a capital lease. Lessees may view off–balance sheet financing as an advantage because they effectively incur debt that doesn't appear on the balance sheet.

Con: The shorter the lease, the greater the cost to the lessee. In shorter leases, more of the risk remains with the lessor. The lessor does not accept this risk out of generosity. The cost is passed back to the lessee in the form of higher annual lease payments and/or heavy cancellation penalties if the lessee does not renew. Therefore, a lessee may obtain "off–balance sheet" financing but at a real economic cost in higher expenses and operating cash flow expenditures.

100% Financing

Pro: A financial institution will not lend the full amount of the purchase price to a buyer. Normally, financing can be obtained for no more than 75% or 80% of the cost of the asset. In contrast, a lease can effectively provide full financing, since there is no substantial down payment to be made at the inception of the lease.

Con: This advantage exists only for assets that are readily transferable if the lessee defaults (e.g., automobiles, airplanes), and only to lessees that have high credit ratings. For other assets and less creditworthy lessees, the lessor covers the risk by forward-weighting the lease payments, meaning that most of the cash flow for lease payments is in the early years of the lease. Also, since lease payments are payable at the beginning of each period, the first payment is, in effect, a down payment.

Protection against Obsolescence

Pro: The shorter the lease term, the easier it is for the lessee to stay up to date with the latest technology. If a new product or process becomes available, the lessee can refuse to renew the existing lease and move to the newer product instead. An alternative is for the lessor to provide upgrade privileges in the lease. For example, an existing leased photocopier may be replaced by a newer model, or a leased automobile may be "rolled over" to a new model every second or third year. Such lease arrangements do help the lessee guard against obsolescence.

Con: Flexibility comes at a price. The risk of obsolescence falls on the lessor, and the lessor will compensate for the added risk by charging higher lease payments. Lessor-provided upgrades can help provide flexibility, but they do lock the lessee into the lessor's product. As well, automatic upgrades are expensive. Many companies find it much less costly to skip a product generation unless it is crucial to be on the cutting edge of technology.

Protection from Interest Rate Changes

Pro: Lease payments are always determined on the basis of fixed interest rates, even when the lease contains contingent payments based on other variables (e.g., gross revenues from use of the asset). Therefore, a long-term or capital lease can protect the lessee from interest rate fluctuations.

Con: If the lessee's business fluctuates in response to economic conditions, it may be better to use variable-rate loans from financial institutions to finance the assets. When the economy is down, interest rates are down, thereby not locking the company into a high implicit interest rate.

Transfer of Income Tax Benefits

The transfer of income tax benefits from the lessee to the lessor is perhaps the driving force behind the bulk of direct financing leases. The legal owner of an asset can deduct CCA on the tax return. But the owner may not be able to use the CCA deduction, or the full benefit of that deduction. Some examples of such a situation are:

- The owner is a non-profit organization, such as a school, hospital, or charity.
- The owner is a for-profit business, but either is losing money or is not earning enough to use the full amount of the available CCA.
- The owner is profitable, but pays taxes at a lower rate than potential lessors.

The last item is particularly important in the Canadian context, because manufacturers pay lower effective tax rates than do financial institutions.

If any of these conditions exist, then the CCA is more valuable to a lessor than to the potential user of the asset. Lessors calculate their return on investment on an after-tax basis, and most of the benefit of a reduction in the lessor's taxes will be passed on to the lessee in the form of lower lease payments. Therefore, the asset can often be leased for a cash flow present value that is less than the amount the lessee would pay to buy the asset.

CONCEPT REVIEW

1. What is meant by off–balance sheet financing?
2. Who holds title to (i.e., legally owns) a leased asset?
3. How can a lease be used to transfer CCA tax benefits from the lessee to the lessor?

ACCOUNTING FOR CAPITAL LEASES

If a long-term lease qualifies as a capital lease for accounting purposes, the general approach is to record the asset on the books of the lessee as though it had been purchased and financed by instalment debt. An outline of the accounting is as follows:

- The present value of the lease payments is determined by using:
  - The lower of the lessee's IBR or the lessor's implicit rate, if known, and
  - *Net* lease payments for the initial term, plus net lease payments for any bargain renewal terms, plus any renewal terms at the *lessor's* option, plus any *guaranteed* residual value or any bargain purchase price.
- The present value is recorded as the cost of the asset and is classified as a tangible capital asset. *The recorded cost cannot be higher than the asset's fair value.*
- The offsetting credit is to a *lease liability* account.
- Interest is accrued for each period, charged to interest expense and credited to the lease liability account (or to accrued interest payable).
- Lease payments are debited to the lease liability account.
- The asset is amortized by following the company's normal amortization policy for that type of capital asset. However, the amortization period cannot exceed the lease term unless the lease contains a bargain purchase option or automatic transfer of title at the end of the lease. Otherwise, the asset will be amortized over the lease term (including bargain renewal terms).

The leased asset is accounted for as though it was owned, and the payments are treated as payments on an instalment loan. Once the present value is recorded as an asset and a liability, *there is no connection between the asset and the liability in the subsequent accounting.*

CAPITAL LEASE ILLUSTRATION—BASIC EXAMPLE

To begin our illustration of accounting for capital leases for the lessee, we will use this example:

Lessee Limited wishes to acquire equipment that has an expected economic life of five years and a fair value of $55,000. Instead of buying the asset outright, the company enters into a lease with a bank's leasing subsidiary. The terms of the lease are as follows:

- The initial lease term is three years.
- The lease begins on 2 January 20X2.
- Payments over the initial lease term are $22,000 per year, payable at the end of each lease year (that is, on 31 December 20X2, 20X3, and 20X4).
- Lease payments include insurance costs that are estimated to be $2,000 per year for the three years of the initial lease term.

- At the end of the initial lease term, the lease is renewable for another two years *at Lessee Limited's option* for $6,000 per year, including insurance. The cost of insurance in year 4 and thereafter is estimated to be $1,000 per year. The normal rental cost of three-year-old equipment of this type is almost $10,000 per year.
- There is no *guaranteed* residual value, and the asset reverts to the lessor at the end of the lease.
- If Lessee Limited had purchased the asset, the company would have drawn on its bank line of credit, which bears interest at 12% per annum.

In this example, the important elements for analysis are as follows:

- The *lease term* is five years: the initial lease term of three years plus the bargain renewal term of two years.
- The *minimum net lease payments* are $20,000 for each of the first three years and $5,000 per year for the fourth and fifth years (that is, the estimated insurance cost must be subtracted or netted out to determine the net lease payments).
- Lessee Limited's *incremental borrowing rate* is 12% per annum.

Under the accounting guidelines, this lease is a capital lease for the following reasons:

- The lease term is five years, which exceeds 75% of the equipment's estimated five-year economic life.
- The present value of the minimum net lease payments at the lessee's IBR is $54,051, which exceeds 90% of the $55,000 fair value of the equipment:

PV = $20,000 (P/A, 12%, 3) + $5,000 (P/A, 12%, 2) (P/F, 12%, 3)

PV = $48,037 + $6,014

PV = $54,051

To clinch matters, the lessor is a financial intermediary whose business is the financing of assets through leases.

Accounting for the Lease

Before attempting the accounting by Lessee Limited, an amortization table should be constructed, similar to those illustrated in Chapter 12. An amortization table for this example is shown in Exhibit 17-1. The end-of-year cash flows are placed in the fourth column, and the present value (@12%) is placed at the beginning of the second column ("outstanding balance"). The principal amount outstanding during the year 20X2 is the full present value of $54,051. In general journal form, the lease will be recorded on the books on 2 January 20X2 as follows:

Asset under capital lease	54,051	
Lease liability		54,051

Interest Interest is calculated on that amount at the same rate used to discount the payments, 12%. The first year's interest is $6,486, which means that of the first $20,000 lease payment, $6,486 is charged to interest expense and the remainder of $13,514 reduces the outstanding principal balance. The entry to record the accrued interest is:

Interest expense	6,486	
Lease liability		6,486

EXHIBIT 17-1

LEASE AMORTIZATION SCHEDULE—END-OF-YEAR PAYMENTS
(ANNUITY IN ARREARS)

Year	Outstanding Balance	Interest @ 12%	End-of-Period Cash Flow	Incr/(Decr) in Balance	Ending Balance
20X2	$54,051	$ 6,486	$20,000	$(13,514)	$40,537
20X3	40,537	4,865	20,000	(15,135)	25,402
20X4	25,402	3,048	20,000	(16,952)	8,450
20X5	8,450	1,014	5,000	(3,986)	4,464
20X6	4,464	536	5,000	(4,464)	(0)
Totals		$15,949	$70,000	$(54,051)	

When the cash payment is made, the entry is:

Insurance expense	2,000	
Lease liability	20,000	
Cash		22,000

Since the cash payment includes an implicit amount for insurance, the estimated insurance amount must be debited separately to an expense account. Note that the debit is for the originally *estimated* amount and not for the actual amount, even if the lessee subsequently learns that the lessor actually paid a different amount for insurance. The reason is that the estimate was used to determine the net lease payments, which then were discounted to find the present value. The only way that the liability accounting will work out is to stick to the predetermined *net lease* payments, even though the actual cost to the lessor may be different.

In this illustration, the interest is credited directly to the lease liability account. Alternatively, the accrued interest could have been credited to *accrued interest payable*, in which case the credit for the cash payment would have to be broken down between interest and principal. In practice, it is simpler just to credit accrued interest directly to the lease liability account; then the cash payments can be credited to the lease liability without having to figure out how much of the payment gets credited to which account.

Amortization The two entries illustrated above for the 31 December 20X2 year-end are those for the liability. In addition, there must be an entry to amortize the asset. The asset will be amortized over the lease term in accordance with whatever method is used for that type of asset under Lessee Limited's accounting policies. Amortization is based on the recorded discounted present value of the asset, minus any guaranteed residual value.

The amortization period is the minimum lease term as defined above (that is, including bargain renewal terms), and not just the initial lease term. If we assume that Lessee Limited's accounting policy for this type of asset is to amortize it on the straight-line basis with a full year's amortization taken in the first year, then the amortization of the leased equipment on 31 December 20X2 will be $10,810 (i.e., $54,051 ÷ 5). The entry will be:

Amortization expense	10,810	
Accumulated amortization		10,810

Exhibit 17-2 shows the remaining entries to record both the liability and the asset amortization over the entire five-year lease term. It is important to note that the amortization of

EXHIBIT 17-2

LESSEE'S ENTRIES TO RECORD CAPITAL LEASE—BASIC EXAMPLE

	Dr.	Cr.	Lease Liability Balance—Cr.
2 January 20X2			
Asset under capital lease	54,051		
Lease liability		54,051	54,051
31 December 20X2			
Interest expense	6,486		
Lease liability		6,486	60,537
Insurance expense	2,000		
Lease liability	20,000		40,537
Cash		22,000	
Amortization expense	10,810		
Accumulated amortization		10,810	
31 December 20X3			
Interest expense	4,865		
Lease liability		4,865	45,402
Insurance expense	2,000		
Lease liability	20,000		25,402
Cash		22,000	
Amortization expense	10,810		
Accumulated amortization		10,810	
31 December 20X4			
Interest expense	3,048		
Lease liability		3,048	28,450
Insurance expense	2,000		
Lease liability	20,000		8,450
Cash		22,000	
Amortization expense	10,810		
Accumulated amortization		10,810	
31 December 20X5			
Interest expense	1,014		
Lease liability		1,014	9,464
Insurance expense	1,000		
Lease liability	5,000		4,464
Cash		6,000	
Amortization expense	10,810		
Accumulated amortization		10,810	
31 December 20X6			
Interest expense	536		
Lease liability		536	5,000
Insurance expense	1,000		
Lease liability	5,000		0
Cash		6,000	
Amortization expense	10,811		
Accumulated amortization		10,811	
2 January 20X7			
Accumulated amortization	54,051		
Asset under capital lease		54,051	
(to record the return of the asset to the lessor)			

the asset has no connection with the accounting for the outstanding liability; there is no correspondence between the asset amortization and the debt amortization.

Exhibit 17-2 includes a column that shows the accumulated balance of the total lease liability account, assuming that the accrued interest is added to the lease liability (instead of being recorded in a separate "accrued interest" account). The year-end interest accruals increase the balance, while the lease payments reduce the balance. The final lease payment, on 31 December 20X6, reduces the balance to zero.

Financial Statement Impacts

Balance Sheet At the end of 20X2, the outstanding balance in the lease liability account is $40,537, as shown on the amortization schedule in Exhibit 17-1. This liability must be classified as a current liability to the extent that it will be reduced within the next fiscal year.

Of the $40,537 balance, the amount that will be paid within the next year is the amount *of that balance* that will be paid with the next lease payment (i.e., on 31 December 20X3). Exhibit 17-1 shows that the next payment will reduce the outstanding liability by $15,135, to a balance of $25,402. Therefore, the liability balance will be classified on the balance sheet as follows:

Current liability	$15,135
Long-term liability	25,402
Total	$40,537

It may be tempting to classify $20,000 as the current portion because that is the amount of cash that will be paid within the next fiscal year. However, the total payment includes a substantial component of interest expense that pertains to the year 20X3 and that therefore has not yet been accrued. The current liability, therefore, is not how much cash will be paid in the next year, but rather *how much of the year-end liability balance* will be paid in the next year.

On the asset side, the leased equipment will be shown either separately or as a part of the general equipment account. Similarly, the accumulated amortization will be shown either separately or combined with the accumulated amortization of similar assets. As usual, of course, the equipment can be shown net of accumulated amortization on the face of the balance sheet with the gross amount and accumulated amortization shown in a note to the financial statements.

Income Statement The income statement will include amortization expense ($10,810), interest expense ($6,486), and insurance expense ($2,000). Each of these expenses can be combined with similar costs; the expenses relating to leased assets need not be reported separately. The interest expense for the lease will, however, be included with other long-term interest, which is reported separately from interest on short-term obligations.

Cash Flow Statement On the cash flow statement, the amortization expense ($10,810) will be added back as an adjustment to net income for determining the cash flow from operations (if the indirect approach to operating cash flow is used). As well, the principal component of the lease payment ($20,000 − $6,486 interest = $13,514 principal) is shown in the financing activities section as an outflow.

Notes to Financial Statements The notes should disclose the commitment for future capital lease payments, both in total and individually for each of the next five years. The payments due under all of the reporting enterprise's capital leases can be added together and reported in the aggregate, of course.

Future Income Taxes

Leases normally are taxed in accordance with their legal form. The tax deduction is the amount of lease payments made during the tax year. The fact that a lease may be accounted for as a capital lease is of no interest to Canada Revenue Agency.

Therefore, a lease that is reported by the lessee as a capital lease will be taxed as an operating lease. This difference in treatment will give rise to a *temporary difference*. Accounting for future income taxes and temporary differences is explained in Chapter 15.

CONCEPT REVIEW

1. Why must operating and executory costs be subtracted from capital lease payments before the lease payments are capitalized?
2. What impact does lease capitalization have on a company's total assets and on its debt-to-equity ratio?
3. Over what period should the lessee amortize a leased asset?

CAPITAL LEASE ILLUSTRATION—EXTENDED EXAMPLE

The basic example that is illustrated above has two important assumptions built into it— (1) the lease payments are at the end of each year and (2) the lease year coincides with the company's fiscal year. We will now present a similar example, but with these two simplifying assumptions removed.

Assume that Lessee Limited needs to acquire equipment that has a fair value purchase price of $55,000. The company elects to acquire this equipment through a lease from its bank's leasing subsidiary. The terms of the lease are as follows:

- The initial lease term is three years.
- The lease begins on 1 April 20X2.
- Payments over the initial lease term are $20,500 per year, payable at the *beginning* of each lease year (that is, starting on 1 April 20X2).
- Lease payments include insurance costs that are estimated to be $2,000 per year for the three years of the initial lease term.
- At the end of the initial lease term, the lease is renewable for another two years *at Lessee Limited's option* for $4,200 per year, including insurance. The cost of insurance in year 4 and thereafter is estimated to be $1,000 per year. The normal rental cost of three-year-old equipment of this type is almost $10,000 per year.
- The asset reverts to the lessor at the end of the lease; there is no *guaranteed* residual value.
- If Lessee Limited had purchased the asset, the company would have drawn on its bank line of credit, which bears interest at 12% per annum.
- Lessee Limited's fiscal year ends on 31 December.

In this extended example, the important elements for analysis are as follows:

- The *lease term* is still five years: the initial lease term of three years plus the bargain renewal term of two years.
- The *minimum net lease payments* are now $18,500 for each of the first three years and $3,200 per year for the fourth and fifth years (as in the earlier example, the estimated insurance cost must be subtracted or "netted out" to determine the net lease payments).
- Lessee Limited's *incremental borrowing rate* is 12% per annum.

The present value of the minimum net lease payments, at 12%, is $54,077:

> PV = $18,500 (P/AD, 12%, 3) + $3,200 (P/AD, 12%, 2) (P/F, 12%, 3)
> PV = $49,766 + $4,311
> PV = $54,077

The annual lease payments are less than in the earlier example, but the present value is almost the same because the payments now are at the *beginning* of each lease year instead of at the end.

Accounting for the Lease

On 1 April 20X2, Lessee Limited will record its acquisition of the asset and the related obligation as follows:

Asset under capital lease	54,077	
Lease liability		54,077

Simultaneously, a cheque for $20,500 will be issued to the lessor:

Insurance expense	2,000	
Lease liability	18,500	
Cash		20,500

Since the first payment is made at the inception of the lease, the principal balance outstanding during the first lease year is only $35,577 (i.e., $54,077 − $18,500). The interest expense over the life of the lease clearly will be less than in the earlier example because the outstanding balance is always less.

The amortization schedule for the lease liability is shown in Exhibit 17-3. In order to show the initial amount of the obligation (and the historical cost of the asset), the first line of the amortization schedule shows the establishment of the liability on 1 April 20X2 and the immediate cash outflow for the first net lease payment, all of which reduces the principal amount outstanding.

EXHIBIT 17-3

LEASE AMORTIZATION SCHEDULE—BEGINNING OF LEASE YEAR PAYMENTS (ANNUITY DUE)

Lease Year Ending 31 March*	Outstanding Balance	Interest @ 12%	1 April Payment	Incr/(Decr) in Balance	Ending Balance
20X2*	**$54,077**		**$18,500**	**$(18,500)**	**$35,577**
20X3	35,577	$4,269	18,500	(14,231)	21,346
20X4	21,346	2,562	18,500	(15,938)	5,408
20X5	5,408	649	3,200	(2,551)	2,857
20X6	2,857	343	3,200	(2,857)	(0)
Totals		$7,823	$61,900	$(54,077)	

*Lease inception—no accrual period for interest

At the end of Lessee Limited's fiscal year, the accounts must be adjusted to record accrued interest, as well as to record asset amortization and (if material) to allocate the insurance expense. The adjusting entries on 31 December 20X2 will appear as follows, *assuming* that the company follows a policy of allocating amortization on a monthly basis:

Interest expense	3,202	
Lease liability		3,202
($35,577 × 12% × 9/12 year = $3,202)		
Amortization expense	8,112	
Accumulated amortization		8,112
($54,077 ÷ 5 years × 9/12 year = $8,112)		
Prepaid expenses	500	
Insurance expense		500
($2,000 × 3/12 year)		

Adding accrued interest of $3,202 to the lease liability will bring the total liability at 31 December 20X2 to $38,779. The portion that will be paid during the next fiscal year will be classified as a current liability. The current portion consists of two components:

Principal reduction portion of the payment to be made on 1 April 20X3	$14,231
Plus accrued interest to the balance sheet date, 31 December 20X2	3,202
Current portion of 31 December 20X2 lease liability	$17,433

The principal reduction can be obtained directly from the amortization schedule (Exhibit 17-3), while the accrued interest is the amount recorded above. The interest portion can also be obtained from the amortization schedule as 9/12 of the 20X3 lease year interest of $4,269. It is worth reiterating that the current portion is *not* the cash flow in the next year (i.e., the $18,500 net lease payment). The current portion of the fiscal year-end liability balance is the accrued interest to date plus the principal reduction during the next year.

On 1 April 20X3, the second payment will pay the accrued interest as of 20X2 year-end, plus the additional accrued interest for the first three months of 20X3, and the remainder will reduce the principal balance. The accrued interest for the first three months is based on the present value of the remaining lease payments after the last payment was made, or $35,577 @ 12% × 3/12 = $1,067 (or $4,269 interest for 20X3 from Exhibit 17-3 × 3/12). The entry will appear as follows:

Interest expense	1,067	
Lease liability		1,067

Then, the payment can be recorded:

Insurance expense	2,000	
Lease liability	18,500	
Cash		20,500

The interest expense for the first three months is *not* based on the liability balance at year-end, which already includes nine months of accrued interest. In the amortization table, we have assumed that the interest compounds only annually, when the payments are made. This assumption is normal. If payments are made monthly, the amortization schedule is calculated with implicit monthly compounding, using the nominal annual IBR divided by 12 as the monthly interest rate. In making the journal entries to accrue interest and record the payments, therefore, it is essential to use the same compounding periods as in the amortization schedule. It is not a matter of materiality; it simply is a matter of balancing out at the end.

The implicit lease interest is calculated on the basis of the lease year (from 1 April through 31 March), which is then allocated as interest expense to the fiscal year:

- The $4,269 interest that is shown in the amortization schedule (Exhibit 17-3) for the lease year ending 31 March 20X3 is allocated 9/12 (i.e., $3,202) to fiscal year 20X2 and 3/12 ($1,067) to fiscal year 20X3.
- Next lease year's interest of $2,562, is allocated 9/12 (or $1,921) to fiscal 20X3, which brings the interest expense for the fiscal year ended 31 December 20X3 to $2,988 ($1,067 + $1,921).

The allocation of lease-year interest to fiscal years is illustrated in Exhibit 17.4.

EXHIBIT 17-4

ALLOCATION OF INTEREST EXPENSE TO FISCAL YEARS

Lease Payment	Implicit Interest*			Allocation for Accounting Fiscal Year	
				Interest Expense	Year-End
1 April 20X2	0	=	0		
				= 3,202	31 Dec. 20X2
			3,202		
1 April 20X3	4,269	=	1,067		
				= 2,988	31 Dec. 20X3
			1,921		
1 April 20X4	2,562	=	641		
				= 1,128	31 Dec. 20X4
			487		
1 April 20X5	649	=	162		
				= 419	31 Dec. 20X5
			257		
1 April 20X6	343	=	86		
				= 86	31 Dec. 20X6
Total interest	7,823		7,823	7,823	

*From Exhibit 17-3

Insurance expense is allocated to the fiscal years in a manner similar to interest expense. Any operating costs that are included in the gross lease payment would be allocated, if they are material.

The full set of journal entries to record the leased asset and the lease liability over the entire five-year lease term is shown in Exhibit 17-5. To the right of the journal entries is a running tabulation of the balance in the lease liability account, assuming that the accrued interest is recorded directly in the lease liability account. Interest accruals increase the balance (at the 12% p.a. interest rate times the balance following the preceding lease payment), while each payment decreases the balance. The liability balance at the end of each fiscal year is the *total* liability; on the balance sheet, the total will be divided into current and long-term portions, as described above.

EXHIBIT 17-5

LESSEE'S ENTRIES TO RECORD CAPITAL LEASE—EXTENDED EXAMPLE

	Dr.	Cr.	Lease Liability Balance—Cr.
2 April 20X2			
Asset under capital lease	54,077		
Lease liability		54,077	54,077
Insurance expense	2,000		
Lease liability	18,500		35,577
Cash		20,500	
31 December 20X2			
Interest expense	3,202		
Lease liability		3,202	38,779
($35,577 × 12% × 9/12)			
Amortization expense	8,112		
Accumulated amortization		8,112	
(for 9/12 year)			
Prepaid expenses	500		
Insurance expense		500	
1 April 20X3			
Interest expense	1,067		
Lease liability		1,067	39,846
Insurance expense	2,000		
Lease liability	18,500		21,346
Cash		20,500	
31 December 20X3			
Interest expense	1,921		
Lease liability		1,921	23,267
($21,346 @ 12% × 9/12)			
Amortization expense	10,815		
Accumulated amortization		10,815	
(for a full year)			
1 April 20X4			
Interest expense	641		
Lease liability		641	23,908
($21,346 @ 12% × 3/12)			
Insurance expense	2,000		
Lease liability	18,500		5,408
Cash		20,500	

EXHIBIT 17-5 *(cont'd)*

LESSEE'S ENTRIES TO RECORD CAPITAL LEASE—EXTENDED EXAMPLE

	Dr.	Cr.	Lease Liability Balance—Cr.
31 December 20X4			
Interest expense	487		
Lease liability		487	5,895
($5,408 @ 12% × 9/12)			
Amortization expense	10,815		
Accumulated amortization		10,815	
1 April 20X5			
Interest expense	162		
Lease liability		162	
($5,408 @ 12% × 3/12)			6,057
Insurance expense	1,000		
Lease liability	3,200		2,857
Cash		4,200	
31 December 20X5			
Interest expense	257		
Lease liability		257	3,114
($2,857 @ 12% × 9/12)			
Amortization expense	10,815		
Accumulated amortization		10,815	
Prepaid expenses	250		
Insurance expense	250		
Prepaid expenses		500	
(to adjust the prepaid insurance from a balance of $500 to a balance of $250 to reflect the lower cost in the fourth lease year)			
1 April 20X6			
Interest expense	86		
Lease liability		86	3,200
($2,857 @ 12% × 3/12)			
Insurance expense	1,000		
Lease liability	3,200		0
Cash		4,200	
31 December 20X6			
Amortization expense	10,815		
Accumulated amortization		10,815	
1 April 20X7			
Amortization expense	2,705		
Accumulated amortization		2,705	
(amortization for the final three months)			
Insurance expense	250		
Prepaid expenses		250	
Accumulated amortization	54,077		
Asset under capital lease		54,077	
(return and write-off of asset)			

1. How should the current portion of the lease liability be determined?

2. When lease payment dates do not coincide with the company's reporting periods, how is interest expense calculated?

NON-CAPITAL LEASES: OPERATING LEASES REVISITED

At the beginning of this chapter, we stated that operating leases are relatively short-term leases that provide the lessee with temporary use of an asset. By assuming only temporary use of the asset, the lessee avoids many of the risks of ownership, including obsolescence. This relief from risk comes only at a price, however. Lessors will pass the cost of their ownership risk on to the lessee through a higher rental cost. In general, the shorter the lease for a particular asset, the higher the cost per period will be.

In accounting, operating leases are not defined directly and substantively, but rather are defined indirectly: *a lease is accounted for as an operating lease if it is not judged to be a capital lease.*

Operating lease treatment therefore is the "default" treatment for leases that fail to meet the basic criterion of conveying substantially all of the risks and benefits of ownership to the lessee, or for which there is no objectively determinable basis for arriving at a present value for the lease.

The problem with this approach is that it leads to an all-or-nothing approach to capitalization: if one of the guidelines is satisfied, the whole lease is capitalized, but if none of the guidelines is satisfied, then none of the lease is capitalized. This has led to a number of capitalization-avoidance techniques and to the development of a whole industry dedicated to devising ways of leasing assets to companies while avoiding the capitalization criteria. Three common methods of avoiding capitalization are:

1. Base a large part of the lease payment on contingent rent.

2. Insert a third party between the lessee and the lessor.

3. Shorten the lease term, but impose a substantial penalty for non-renewal.

Contingent Rent Contingent rent is rent that depends on specified future events. Leases for retail space offer a common example of contingent rent—in addition to a basic rent, the lessee (i.e., the retailer) often agrees to pay a percentage of the store's gross sales to the lessor. The capitalization criteria apply to minimum net lease payments. When there are contingent rental payments, their probable future value is ignored when the lease is being evaluated as a possible capital lease. Therefore, the larger the amount of rental that can be made dependent on future events, the lower the minimum net lease payments will be.

Inserting a Third Party This can occur in a number of ways. The most common is for the lessee to form a separate company, the purpose of which is to lease assets to the operating company. The separate company enters into the formal lease agreement with the lessor, obligating itself to pay for the full cost of the asset over the lease term, and then enters into a year-by-year lease with the operating lessee.

This approach will not work under GAAP if the intermediate company is a subsidiary of the operating company because the operating company will be required to consolidate the leasing subsidiary (if the operating company does not qualify for differential reporting). Instead, the intermediate company will be a company that has the same owners as the operating company. Companies under common ownership are not combined in Canadian reporting (or in other countries), and therefore the operating company need not report the asset or the obligation on its balance sheet even though the lessor may clearly have entered into a capital lease.

Shortening the Lease Term The third approach is probably the most common. Corporations may lease major and crucial operating assets under lease agreements that provide for a year-by-year renewal (at the lessee's option) or for lease terms that are considerably shorter than the economic life of the asset. Operating leases can be the result of a well-thought-out strategic positioning, but quite often they are deliberate attempts to obtain assets through off–balance sheet financing.

For example, airlines commonly lease a significant part of their fleets through leases that run five to seven years. Since an airplane, properly maintained, can last for a very long time, there is no way that a seven-year lease will qualify as a capital lease. But without the aircraft, the airline cannot operate, and so at least a core of aircraft must be leased continuously. But by leasing everything in sight, the airline (or other such company) can avoid showing the lease obligations on the balance sheet. This practice is usually known as "cleaning up the balance sheet."

Financial statement users need to be wary of such off–balance sheet financing arrangements. A company that owns its essential assets, or leases them through capital leases, will show higher total assets (and thus a lower return on assets) and a higher debt-to-equity ratio than will a company that uses operating leases. But the user must not be misled into concluding that the company that owns its assets is the weaker performer. In fact, the company that owns its assets may be in a substantively stronger financial position. Short-term leases come at a higher price, so a "clean" balance sheet may hide a weak operating performance.

There is widespread international dissatisfaction about perceived shortcomings in the reporting of operating leases among users and professional accountants alike. To consider alternatives and new approaches to lease accounting, the IASB and FASB have jointly established a new international working group to review lease accounting. We will discuss this initiative at the end of the chapter, in the International Perspective section.

SALE AND LEASEBACK

It is not unusual for a company to sell an asset and simultaneously lease it back. This type of transaction is, appropriately, called a sale and leaseback. Sale and leasebacks are most common for buildings. The asset is converted from an owned asset to a leased asset.

A sale and leaseback gives an immediate cash inflow to the seller. The cash can be used to retire debt (particularly any outstanding debt on the asset, such as a mortgage or a collateral loan) used for operating purposes, or any other purpose that management wishes (e.g., paying a dividend).

The seller must evaluate the lease and identify it as either a capital lease or an operating lease. The criteria for this judgement are exactly as described in earlier sections of this chapter.

The sale portion of the deal is initially recorded just like any other sale, with a gain or loss recorded for the difference between the net proceeds from the sale and the asset's net book value. The gain or loss will not ordinarily be recognized in income in the year of the sale, however. If the lease is a capital lease, any gain or loss is deferred and amortized on the same basis as the amortization of the leased asset. The objective of this treatment is to prevent income manipulation. A company cannot enter into a sale and leaseback arrangement in order to recognize a gain in the period of the sale.

If the lease is an operating lease, the gain or loss also should be deferred and amortized in proportion to rental payments over the lease term. But since an operating lease term is likely to be rather short, the gain or loss will flow into income more quickly than if the lease is deemed to be a capital lease.

There is one exception to the defer-and-amortize rule. When the fair value of the property is less than its carrying value at the time of the transaction, the loss should be recognized immediately.

An interesting aspect of sale and leaseback is that it can result in the enhancement of reporting income over a period of years. This opportunity arises when a company enters into a sale and leaseback arrangement for a building that it owns but only partially occupies. Suppose, for example, that a company occupies only 10% of a building. If the company sells the building at a profit and then leases back just the portion that it occupies, the full gain can be deferred and amortized. The amortized gain may more than offset the lease payments, thereby enhancing reported net income over the lease period.

Example of Sale and Leaseback

Assume that Vendeur Limited owns a building in central Montreal. Vendeur enters into an agreement with Bailleur Incorporation, whereby Vendeur sells the building to Bailleur and simultaneously leases it back. The details are as follows:

- The historical cost of the building is $10,000,000; it is 60% depreciated on Vendeur's books.
- Bailleur agrees to pay Vendeur $8,500,000 for the building.
- Bailleur agrees to lease the building to Vendeur for 20 years. The annual lease payment is $850,000, payable at the *end* of each lease year.
- There is no guaranteed residual value.
- Vendeur will pay all of the building's operating and maintenance costs, including property taxes and insurance.
- The effective date of the agreement is 1 January 20X1.
- Vendeur's incremental borrowing rate is 9%.
- Bailleur's interest rate implicit in the lease is computed after tax, and is not disclosed to Vendeur.

The building has a net book value, after accumulated depreciation, of $4,000,000. Since the selling price is $8,500,000, Vendeur realizes a gain of $4,500,000 on the transaction. However, this gain is not recognized in income but instead is deferred. The journal entry to record this sale on 1 January 20X1 is:

Cash	8,500,000	
Accumulated depreciation, building	6,000,000	
Building		10,000,000
Deferred gain on sale and leaseback of building		4,500,000

The gain on the sale will be amortized over the 20-year lease term, *regardless of whether the lease qualifies as a capital lease or as an operating lease.* It is necessary, however, to determine whether the lease is a capital lease for financial reporting purposes. Applying the three tests:

1. Is it likely that the lessee will obtain ownership of the leased property at the end of the lease? *No.*

2. Will the lessee receive substantially all of the economic benefits of the building? *Uncertain. The building was 60% depreciated at the time of the sale, indicating that it is not a new building. The 20-year lease term could be 75% of the remaining economic life of the building.*

3. Is the lessor assured of recovering the investment in the leased property, plus a return on the investment, over the lease term? *Probably, because the present value of the lease payments is $7,759,264 at 9%, which is at least 90% of the sales price of the building.*

Since at least one of the criteria for evaluating the lease as a capital lease is satisfied, the leaseback should be recorded as a capital lease. Using Vendeur's IBR of 9% yields a present value of the 20-year stream of end-of-year payments equal to $7,759,264. The lease is recorded as follows:

Building under capital lease	7,759,264	
Lease liability		7,759,264

At the end of 20X1, Vendeur will:

- Record the interest expense (at 9%).
- Pay the $850,000 annual lease payment to Bailleur.
- Amortize the asset.
- Amortize the deferred gain.

The interest expense and the lease payment will be recorded as follows:

Interest expense	698,334	
Lease liability		698,334
Lease liability	850,000	
Cash		850,000

Assume that Vendeur uses declining-balance amortization for its buildings, at a rate that is double the straight-line rate. Since the lease term is 20 years, the straight-line rate would be 5%. Therefore, the declining-balance rate is 10% per annum. The entry to record amortization of the leased building will be as follows:

Amortization expense, leased building	775,926	
Accumulated amortization, leased building		775,926

Finally, the deferred gain on the sale must be amortized. The gain should be amortized in proportion to the amortization of the leased asset, and not in proportion to the lease payments. Since the asset amortization is at 10% declining balance, the gain must similarly be amortized:

Deferred gain on sale and leaseback of building	450,000	
Amortization expense, leased building		450,000

The amortization of the gain is *credited* to the amortization expense charged for the asset. The reason is that the sale and leaseback transaction had the effect of taking a building with a $4,000,000 book value and rerecording it on Vendeur's books at $7,759,264, close to its fair value. By offsetting the gain against the asset amortization, the amortization expense is reduced to $325,926, which is closer to the amount the building depreciation would have been if it had not been sold.

If the stream of lease payments had been discounted at a lower rate (7.75%, to be exact), the capitalized value of the asset would have been $8,500,000, the same as its selling price. Ten percent amortization applied to $8,500,000 yields $850,000, which when reduced by the $450,000 amortization of the gain results in net amortization of $400,000, exactly the amount that would have been recognized had the building not been sold.

CONCEPT REVIEW

1. What is contingent rent?

2. Why may a company attempt to structure a lease in order to avoid having it classified as a capital lease for financial reporting purposes?

3. If a company sells an asset at a gain and then leases the asset back, how should the gain be recognized for financial reporting purposes?

CASH FLOW STATEMENT

Lease capitalization has an interesting impact on the cash flow statement. If a lease is reported as an operating lease, the lease payments are deducted as an expense in determining net income. Since the expense does represent a cash flow, the impact of the lease payments stays in the cash flow from operations.

If a lease is capitalized, on the other hand, the effects on the cash flow statement are quite different:

- Although the initial lease agreement is viewed, in substance, as a purchase, the transaction does not show up on the cash flow statement as an investing activity because it is a non-cash transaction—a lease obligation is exchanged for a leased asset.
- As the asset is amortized, the amortization expense is included in net income. On the cash flow statement, however, amortization is added back to net income to determine cash flow from operations.
- The portion of each year's payments that represents interest expense must be segregated on the cash flow statement, as part of interest expense relating to long-term obligations.
- The principal repayment portion of the lease payments is shown as a financing activity (that is, as a reduction of a liability).

The overall effect of lease capitalization is to remove the lease payments from operating cash flow and reclassify them as financing activities. Over the life of the lease, the full amount of the net present value of the net lease payments is lifted out of operations (by adding back the amortization) and instead is classified as a reduction of debt.

DISCLOSURE OF LEASES

Operating Leases

In the notes to the financial statements, lessees should disclose the company's obligation for operating lease payments for each of the next five years and for the five-year period in total. Operating leases that are on a year-by-year basis, with no obligation beyond the forthcoming year, are usually not included in the disclosure because there is no obligation beyond the current year. In *Financial Reporting in Canada 2006*, the authors reported that 168 of their 200 surveyed companies disclosed the existence of operating leases. Of the 168, all but three reported the operating lease obligations for each of the next five years. One hundred and twenty-two also reported the aggregate payments for the following five years.

Capital Leases

A company's rights to leased assets are different from its rights to owned assets. A company can sell, modify, or otherwise dispose of owned assets without restriction. Owned assets can also be used as collateral for a loan. Leased assets, on the other hand, belong to the lessor. The lessee does not have the same rights of ownership, even though the lessee bears substantially all of the risks and benefits of ownership.

In order to make it clear that some assets shown on the balance sheet have been obtained through capital leases, both the leased assets and the related lease obligations should be reported separately, either on the face of the balance sheet or in a note.

Of course, the current portion of the lease liability should be shown separately, as has been described earlier in this chapter.

Accounting standards also recommend other disclosures:

- The minimum lease payments for the next five years, both by year and in the aggregate
- The details of capital lease obligations, including interest rates and expiry dates
- Any significant restrictions imposed on the lessee by the lease agreement
- The amount of amortization of leased assets
- The interest expense relating to lease obligations

Companies may combine the amortization of leased assets with amortization of other tangible capital assets, and the interest expense can be combined with interest paid on other long-term obligations. Therefore, separate disclosure is not really required.

Disclosure Examples

Disclosure practice is spotty, at best. The authors of *Financial Reporting in Canada 2006* found that 70 companies (out of a sample of 200) disclosed the existence of capital leases. Most of the companies (90%) did disclose the amount of capital lease liabilities, but only 61% disclosed the amount of assets under capital lease and accumulated amortization. Only 63% disclosed the payments year by year.

An example of a capital lease disclosure note is shown in Exhibit 17-6. Le Château Inc. shows the lease payments for the next three years, which is as far as the leases extend, totalling $4,642. The amount that constitutes interest is deducted, leaving a residual of $4,339. This amount is the present value of the remaining lease payments, and is divided between the current portion and the long-term portion on Le Château's balance sheet. The current portion is then subtracted to yield the amount of $2,288 that is the long-term liability. Both the current and long-term amounts are shown on the face of the company's balance sheet.

EXHIBIT 17-6

LE CHÂTEAU INC. CAPITAL LEASE DISCLOSURE

7. CAPITAL LEASE OBLIGATIONS

The future minimum lease payments required under the capital lease agreements are as follows:

	$ (thousands)
2008	2,234
2009	1,376
2010	1,032
Total minimum lease payments	4,642
Amount representing interest at rates varying between 5.6% and 6.4%	303
	4,339
Less: current portion (shown as current liability on the balance sheet)	2,051
Long term	2,288

The fair value of fixed rate capital leases is based on estimated future cash flows discounted using the current market rate for debt of the same remaining maturities. The fair value of these capital leases approximates the carrying value.

Source: www.sedar.com, Le Château Inc., Audited Annual Financial Statements, April 28, 2006.

ETHICAL ISSUES

Leasing offers multiple opportunities for managers to commit actions that are explicitly intended to mislead financial statement users. The most obvious and widespread is the simple expedient of leasing long-term assets through relatively short-term leases. Accounting standards were not intended to make lease reporting an *option*. The intent was to *require* companies to report leases according to their substance.

In practice, though, managers often do choose the reporting method for long-term leased assets. By careful structuring of lease provisions, management (with the encouragement of the leasing industry) can obtain long-term use of assets while still reporting the leases as operating leases.

For managers who are trying to meet short-term profit goals, this practice has two primary advantages. When leases are classified as operating leases:

- Both the leased assets and the related liabilities are kept off the balance sheet.
- The lease-related expenses flowing onto the income statement will be lower in the early years of the lease contracts.

This is a practice known as "window dressing"—making the financial position of the company look better than it really is. Since the intent is to mislead financial statement readers, it clearly is an unethical practice.

Leasing also provides an opportunity for unethical behaviour through the use of related parties. Leasing through a related third party, such as through a company controlled by an officer or shareholder of the lessee, provides an opportunity for the third party to skim off profits through inflated lease payments.

Finally, sale-and-leaseback arrangements provide an opportunity to manipulate earnings. This can be done by (1) either selling an entire asset and then leasing only part of it back, or (2) leasing it via a series of operating leases that permit the selling company to recognize gains from the transaction in the current year.

INTERNATIONAL PERSPECTIVE

Capitalization of long-term leases has become a widely accepted practice worldwide. Similar to the Canadian standard, the international standard says that leases that transfer substantially all of the risks and benefits of ownership to the lessee should be capitalized. The international criteria are substantially the same as those in the Canadian standard. However, the international criteria are stated rather more broadly and include some additional criteria that were explicitly excluded in the Canadian standard. The most significant additional guideline recommends capital lease treatment if the leased assets are so specialized that only the lessee can use them without major modifications. In contrast, the Canadian standard rejects that criterion on the basis that the concept of "specialized" is too imprecise to be applied reliably.

International standards do not use the term "capital lease." Instead, the IASB calls them "finance leases," which makes sense because the leases provide financing for acquisition of the asset. Also, it fits with the original finance industry terminology of "financial leases." The term "capital lease" was invented by the U.S. FASB.

Looking Ahead

Leasing is a huge industry. The volume of world leasing finance was estimated at US$582 billion for 2005.[5] The IASB observes:

> The boards have been told that investors and other users of financial statements routinely make adjustments to the financial statements for analytical purposes using incomplete footnote disclosures, raising question about the usefulness of the current lease accounting model.[6]

---

[5] *IASB Insight*, March 2007, page 10.

[6] Ibid.

As a result, the IASB and FASB are reconsidering all aspects of lease accounting and have undertaken a joint examination of lease accounting. The two boards established the International Working Group on Lease Accounting at the end of 2006.

The working group began work in early 2007. The group consists of 18 members from 10 countries. Most members are from either the leasing industry (e.g., Singapore Aircraft Leasing; GE Energy Financial Services) or major lessees (e.g., Canadian Pacific Railway; Wal-Mart Stores Inc.; Qantas Airways). The working group is providing suggestions and feedback to the IASB and FASB staffs.

The IASB plans to publish a discussion paper in 2008. In due course, we can expect an extensive overhaul of lease accounting standards.

RELEVANT STANDARDS

CICA Handbook:
- Section 3065, Leases

IASB:
- *IAS* 17, Leases

SUMMARY OF KEY POINTS

1. A lease is an agreement that conveys from a lessor to a lessee the right to use real property, plant, or equipment for a contracted price per period.

2. The shorter the term of the lease, the higher the cost per period. As the lease term lengthens, the cost per period goes down because more of the risk of ownership (e.g., obsolescence) is borne by the lessee.

3. A lease that transfers substantially all of the risks and benefits of ownership to the lessee is called a capital lease. There are three guidelines used to determine whether a lease is a capital lease: (1) does the lessee enjoy the use of the asset over most of its economic life (usually, at least 75%); (2) is the lessee essentially buying the asset through lease payments that amount to at least 90% of the cost of the asset; or (3) does the lease contain a bargain purchase option (or other transfer of title to the lessee)?

4. Capital leases are recorded by the lessee as though the asset had been purchased; the net lease payments over the lease term are discounted, usually at the lessee's incremental borrowing rate, and the present value is recorded as both an asset and a liability. Once recorded, the asset and the liability are accounted for independently.

5. The asset is amortized in accordance with the lessee's policy for assets of that type, except that the amortization period is limited to the minimum lease term (including bargain renewal terms) unless there is a bargain purchase option or other transfer of title to the lessee.

6. The liability is accounted for as an instalment loan with blended payments. Interest expense is calculated at the same rate as was used for discounting the payments, and the excess of payments over interest expense reduces the outstanding liability balance.

7. The current portion of the lease liability consists of (1) accrued interest to the balance sheet date plus (2) the amount of principal that will be paid over the next year.

8. Capital leases are usually *taxed* as operating leases. As a result, temporary differences usually result in future income tax liabilities.

9. Leases that are not capital leases are recorded as *operating leases*, wherein the lease payments ordinarily are recognized as an expense for the period.

10. One of the principal motivations for leasing is income taxation: if the lessor can receive greater benefits from the CCA tax shield than can the lessee, then the savings to the lessor are returned to the lessee through lower lease payments, thereby reducing the cost of the asset.

11. A sale and leaseback arrangement is an agreement in which the owner of an asset sells it to a lessor and simultaneously leases it back. The subsequent lease is accounted for as either capital or operating, as for other leases; any gain or loss on the sale is deferred and amortized over the lease term, except for a loss that reflects a decline in the fair value of the asset, in which case the loss is recognized immediately.

12. The amount of capital lease obligations and assets held under capital leases should be separately disclosed. Companies should also disclose their commitments under operating leases and under capital leases for each of the next five years, and in aggregate.

13. There is growing dissatisfaction about the all-or-nothing aspect of lease capitalization. International accounting standards, including those of Canada, may be altered in the future to require capitalization of all leases of greater than one-year duration.

KEY TERMS

bargain purchase option, 1009
bargain renewal terms, 1010
capital lease, 1007
contingent lease payments, 1010
contingent rent, 1026
direct-financing lease, 1038
guaranteed residual value, 1010

implicit lease interest rate, 1010
incremental borrowing rate (IBR), 1010
initial lease term, 1008
lease term, 1009
minimum net lease payments, 1010
operating lease, 1007
sales-type lease, 1038

REVIEW PROBLEM

Orion leased a computer to the Lenox Silver Company on 1 April 20X5. The terms of the lease are as follows:

• Lease term (fixed and non-cancellable)	three years
• Estimated economic life of the computer	five years
• Fair market value at lease inception	$5,000
• Bargain purchase offer	none
• Transfer of title	none
• Guaranteed residual value by lessee, 1 April 20X8	$2,000
• Lessee's normal depreciation method*	straight line
• Lessee's incremental borrowing rate	11%
• Executory costs included in lease payments	none
• Initial direct costs	none
• Annual lease payment, beginning of each lease year	$1,620
• Lessor's implicit interest rate	unknown to lessee
• Lessee's fiscal year-end	31 December

*Lenox Silver Company charges a half-year depreciation in the year of acquisition and a half-year in the year of disposition, regardless of the actual dates of acquisition and disposal.

Required:

1. Classify the lease from the perspective of the lessee.
2. Provide entries for the lease from 1 April 20X5 through 31 December 20X6.

3. Show how the leased asset and the lease obligation will be shown on the lessee's balance sheet at 31 December 20X6.

4. Suppose that at the end of the lease, the lessor tells the lessee to dispose of the asset, and to keep any proceeds in excess of the guaranteed residual value. Provide entries for the lessee on 1 April 20X8, assuming that the lessee sells the asset for $2,100 and remits the required $2,000 payment to the lessor.

REVIEW PROBLEM—SOLUTION

1. Discounting the minimum lease payments, which include the guaranteed residual value of $2,000, yields:

P = $1,620 (P/A due, 11%, 3) + $2,000(P/F, 11%, 3)
= $4,394 + $1,462 = $5,856

Using the guidelines provided by the *CICA Handbook*, the lease qualifies as a capital lease because the present value of the minimum lease payments, $5,856, exceeds 90% of the fair value of the leased property. The lease does not contain a transfer of title, and the lease term is only 60% of the estimated useful life of the asset; these are the other two guidelines provided by the *CICA Handbook*. Only one criterion needs to be met. Clearly, since the present value of the lease payments exceeds the asset's fair value, the lessee is agreeing to pay the entire cost of the asset; the lease is a capital lease.

2. The asset and the offsetting liability must be capitalized. The capitalized value of the leased asset cannot be greater than the asset's fair value, and therefore the fair value of $5,000 must be used instead of the present value of $5,856. Note that the lessor's implicit interest rate cannot be used because it is not known. But even if it were known (or assumed) and was lower than the lessee's IBR, it still could not be used because using a lower rate would increase the present value even further beyond the fair value. The entries at the inception of the lease will be:

1 April 20X5—inception of the lease

Asset under capital lease	5,000	
Lease liability		5,000

1 April 20X5—first payment

Lease liability	1,620	
Cash		1,620

Since the lessee's IBR yields a present value that is higher than the fair value of the asset, it cannot be used for further accounting for the lease. Instead, the implicit rate *to the lessee* must be calculated by solving the following equation for *i*, the implicit interest rate:

P = $1,620 (P/A due, *i*%, 3) + $2,000 (P/F, *i*%, 3)

By using a computer spreadsheet, a financial calculator, or trial and error, the implicit rate of 24.55% can be found. This rate must then be used to accrue the interest and to record the components of the annual lease payments. The amortization table for the lease obligation is as follows:

Year	Beginning Balance	Interest Expense @ 24.55%	Cash Payment	Reduction of Principal	Ending Balance
20X5	$5,000	0	$1,620	$1,620	$3,380
20X6	3,380	$830	1,620	790	2,590
20X7	2,590	636	1,620	984	1,606
20X8	1,606	394	2,000	1,606	0

The entries to record the amortization, interest accrual, and payments through 31 December 20X6 are shown below.

31 December 20X5—adjusting entries

Amortization expense	500	
Accumulated amortization		500
[($5,000 − $2000) ÷ 3 × 1/2 = $500]		
Interest expense	622	
Lease liability		622
[($5,000 − $1,620) × 24.55% = $830 × 9/12 = $622]		

1 April 20X6—interest accrual

Interest expense	208	
Lease liability		208
[($5,000 − $1,620) × 24.55% = $830 × 3/12 = $208]		

1 April 20X6—second payment

Lease liability	1,620	
Cash		1,620

31 December 20X6—adjusting entries

Amortization expense	1,000	
Accumulated amortization		1,000
[($5,000 − $2000) ÷ 3]		
Interest expense	477	
Lease liability		477
[$636 (from amortization table) × 9/12]		

3. The lessee's balance sheet at 31 December 20X6 will include the following amounts:

Capital assets

Asset under capital lease	$5,000
Less accumulated amortization	(1,500)
	$3,500

Current liabilities

Current portion of capital lease liability	$1,461
[$477 accrued interest at 31 December 20X6, plus	
$984 principal portion of the next payment	
(from amortization table)]	

Long-term liabilities

Obligation under capital lease (from amortization table)	$1,606

4. 1 April 20X8—sale of asset

Cash (received from sale)	2,100	
Lease liability	2,000	
Accumulated amortization	3,000	
Asset under capital lease		5,000
Cash (paid to lessor)		2,000
Gain on disposal of leased asset		100

This entry assumes that adjustments have already been made to (1) accrue the last of the interest and (2) record amortization for 20X8.

APPENDIX

ACCOUNTING FOR LEASES BY LESSORS

Introduction

The main body of this chapter has dealt extensively with accounting by lessees. Lessor accounting really is just the reverse of lessee accounting. The concepts are not significantly different, except that the lessor has a lease *receivable* where the lessee has a lease *liability*. This appendix takes a brief look at lessor accounting.

Lessors: A Specialized Industry

Any company can be a lessee. In theory, any company could also be a lessor. In practice, however, lessors constitute a highly concentrated specialized industry. In accounting text-books, we don't examine specialized industries. Banks, insurance companies, mutual funds, regulated public utilities, real estate development companies, and private investment companies are all examples of specialized industries. Lessors fit into that same category.

Not just any company can be an effective lessor. The specialized nature of leasing is the result of the *Income Tax Act*. Only companies that derive at least 90% of their revenue from leasing are permitted to deduct CCA in excess of rental revenue—a crucial aspect of success-ful lessor activity. Lessors are financial intermediaries. Often, they are subsidiaries of broader financial institutions, such as chartered banks or asset-based lending institutions. *There are no publicly listed lessors in Canada.*

Classification as a Capital Lease

For a lease to be reported as a capital lease by the lessor, the same general definition applies as for lessees. A capital lease is one that transfers substantially all the asset's benefits and risks from the lessor to the lessee.

The guidelines for deciding whether a lease is a capital lease are the same for the lessor as for the lessee, as we discussed in the main body of this chapter. However, there are two addi-tional guidelines for lessors:

1. There is no significantly higher credit risk associated with the lease than there is with similar receivables; *and*

2. The lessor can reasonably estimate the amounts of any unreimbursable costs that will be paid by the lessor (and which therefore are implicitly included in the lessee's lease payments).

In considering whether the general guidelines for capital leases are satisfied, the defini-tions are essentially the same as for lessees:

- *Minimum lease term* includes bargain renewal terms, terms prior to the exercisability of a bargain purchase option, and renewal terms at the *lessor's* option.
- *Minimum net lease payments* include lease payments during bargain renewal terms, any bargain purchase option price, and any *guaranteed* residual value including any residual value that is guaranteed by a third party.

The interest rate used for discounting the net lease payments by the lessor is the *rate implicit in the lease*. The implicit rate is the rate that discounts the cash flow stream to a net present value that is equal to the cash value of the asset.

For example, assume a lessor enters into a lease contract and buys an asset for $1 million, which then is immediately transferred to the lessee for 24 months, with *monthly* payments of $50,000 at the end of each month. Assuming that there is no residual value at the end of the 24 months, the interest rate implicit in the lease is the rate that will discount the stream of 24 monthly $50,000 payments to equal the $1 million purchase price:

$$\$1,000,000 = \$50,000 \ (P/A, \ i, \ 24)$$
$$i = 1.5131\% \ per \ month$$

The monthly implicit interest rate will then be used by the lessor in accounting for the lease.

In practice, lessors normally use an *after-tax* implicit rate. Therefore, from a practical standpoint, the lessor's implicit interest rate in the lease is usually not known to the lessee. Even if the lessor's implicit rate is known, it still wouldn't be relevant for the lessee because it is an after-tax rate and the lessee must account for the lease on a pre-tax basis.

After-tax accounting is rather complex and will not be discussed further. In order to clarify the *principles* underlying lease accounting by the lessor, the following examples will use the *pre-tax* implicit interest rate.

Direct-Financing Lease and Sales-Type Lease Once a lease is classified as a capital lease to the lessor, a secondary classification must be made. A lessor's capital lease may be either a **direct-financing lease** or a **sales-type lease**.

In a direct-financing lease, the lessor is acting purely as a financial intermediary. The profit of a financial intermediary is derived solely from the interest implicit in the lease payments.

In contrast, a sales-type lease is used by a manufacturer or a dealer as a means of selling a product. There are two profit components in a sales-type lease: (1) the profit (or loss) on the sale and (2) interest revenue from the lease.

Each of these types of capital leases is discussed and illustrated in the following sections. We will demonstrate two methods of recording:

1. The *net method* of recording the lease, which is similar to the basis used for accounting by lessees.

2. The *gross method* of recording, a different basis of bookkeeping that is usually used by lessors because it has a level of detail that improves control.

First, however, we will take a brief look at lessor accounting for operating leases.

Operating Leases

If a lease does not qualify as a capital lease, then it must be reported as an operating lease. The characteristics of accounting for an operating lease are as follows:

- The assets that are available for leasing are shown (at cost) on the lessor's balance sheet.
- The assets are amortized in accordance with whatever policy management chooses for each type of asset.
- Lease revenue is recognized as the lease payments become due (or are accrued, if the payment dates do not coincide with the reporting periods).
- Lump-sum payments (e.g., payments by the lessee at the inception of the lease) are amortized over the initial lease term.
- Initial direct costs (that is, the direct costs of negotiating and setting up the lease) are deferred and amortized over the initial lease term proportionate to the lease revenue.

Essentially, lease revenue is recognized on a straight-line basis, matched with amortization expense on the asset and amortization of any initial lease costs. The cost (and accumulated amortization) of assets held for leasing should be disclosed, as should the amount of rental revenue included on the income statement.

Accounting for operating leases by the lessor is not complicated. The greater challenge comes with capital leases.

DIRECT-FINANCING LEASES—NET METHOD

Example

To illustrate the net method accounting for a direct-financing lease, assume that in December 20X1 Capital Leasing Corporation (CLC) signs an agreement with Lessee Limited for the lease of a piece of equipment. The lease contains the following provisions:

- The initial lease term is three years.
- The lease begins on 2 January 20X2.
- Payments over the initial lease term are $20,000 per year, payable at the *end* of each lease year (i.e., the first payment will be on 31 December 20X2).
- At the end of the initial lease term, the lease is renewable for another two years at Lessee's option for $5,000 per year. The normal rental cost of three-year-old equipment of this type is $10,000 per year.
- There is no *guaranteed* residual value, although CLC estimates the *unguaranteed* residual value at $3,000 after five years.

Note that this is the same as the *basic example* we used earlier for lessee accounting, except that we netted out the insurance expense for simplicity.

CLC will pay $55,000 cash for the equipment. The equipment will be delivered by the third-party vendor directly to Lessee on 2 January 20X2.

The implicit interest rate in the lease is the amount that will discount the five end-of-year lease payments and the estimated residual value to a present value of $55,000:

$$\$55,000 = \$20,000 \, (P/A, i, 3) + \$5,000 \, (P/A, i, 2) \, (P/F, i, 3) + \$3,000 \, (P/F, i, 5)$$

The implicit rate is 12.67% per annum.[7]

After we find the implicit interest rate, we can see whether the lessor is recovering at least 90% of the fair value of the asset:

$$P = \$20,000 \, (P/A, 12.67\%, 3) + \$5,000 \, (P/A, 12.67\%, 2) \, (P/F, 12.67\%, 3)$$
$$P = \$53,348$$

The present value of the minimum lease payments is 97% of the $55,000 fair value of the equipment. This clearly is a capital lease.

Notice that the unguaranteed residual value is the only difference between (1) the 90% test and (2) the formula for finding the implicit interest rate. A lease will fail the 90% test only when the unguaranteed residual value is very large.

As well, this lease is a capital lease because the lease (including the bargain renewal term) is for substantially all of the asset's economic life. This is indicated by the low estimated residual value at the end of five years. Assuming normal credit risk, CLC does not bear any significant risk of ownership. Even if Lessee Limited elects not to renew at the end of the initial three-year lease term, CLC has little risk because it will end up holding an asset with a value that is substantially greater than CLC's unrecovered cost, as we will see shortly.

---

[7] The implicit interest rate was determined by entering the cash flows in an Excel worksheet and letting the computer find the implicit rate. This approach is highly recommended and is explained on this book's Online Learning Centre.

> ### EXHIBIT 17-A1
>
> ## LESSOR'S AMORTIZATION SCHEDULE—END-OF-YEAR PAYMENTS (ANNUITY IN ARREARS)
>
> | Year | Beginning Balance | Interest @ 12.67% | 31 December Cash Flow | Incr/(Decr) in Balance | Ending Balance |
> |------|------|------|------|------|------|
> | 20X2 | $55,000 | $ 6,967 | $20,000 | $(13,033) | $41,967 |
> | 20X3 | 41,967 | 5,316 | 20,000 | (14,684) | 27,284 |
> | 20X4 | 27,284 | 3,456 | 20,000 | (16,544) | 10,740 |
> | 20X5 | 10,740 | 1,361 | 5,000 | (3,639) | 7,101 |
> | 20X6 | 7,101 | 899 | 8,000* | (7,101) | 0 |
> | Totals | | $18,000 | $73,000 | $(55,000) | |
>
> *The 20X6 cash flow consists of the $5,000 net lease payment plus $3,000 estimated residual value (unguaranteed).

The one difference in accounting between lessees and lessors is the subtle distinction relating to residual value. For *lessees*, only a residual value that is guaranteed by the lessee is included in the cash flow stream for accounting purposes. *Lessors*, however, would include the estimated residual value of the asset regardless of whether it is guaranteed or unguaranteed.[8]

Given the implicit rate of interest and the periodic cash flows, an amortization schedule for CLC can be constructed as illustrated in Exhibit 17-A1. The first line on the amortization schedule is the cash outflow (on 2 January 20X2) for the asset, a negative cash flow of $55,000. The figures for cash flow in the remaining lines are the lease payments as outlined above. The 20X6 cash flow is a combination of the $5,000 lease payment and the $3,000 estimated *unguaranteed* residual value.

At the inception of the lease, CLC will make the following entry:

2 January 20X2		
Lease receivable	55,000	
Cash		55,000

In return for spending $55,000 on the asset (which never crosses CLC's premises or books), CLC has acquired the right to receive a series of payments, the present value of which is $55,000. *Legally*, CLC holds title to the equipment, and CLC will be able to take CCA on the equipment for income tax purposes. In substance, however, the only asset that CLC will report on its balance sheet is the financial asset, *lease receivable*.

At the end of the next fiscal period, CLC will accrue interest revenue on the receivable, using the implicit rate of 12.67%. Assuming that the next fiscal year ends on 31 December 20X2, a full year's interest will be accrued:

31 December 20X2		
Lease receivable	6,967	
Interest revenue		6,967

---

[8] For the 90% test, though, only a *guaranteed* residual value is included.

The receipt of the lease payment on 31 December 20X2 will be recorded as a reduction of the lease receivable:

31 December 20X2		
Cash	20,000	
Lease receivable		20,000

The balance in the lease receivable account following the first payment will be $41,967 (that is, $55,000 plus $6,967 interest minus $20,000 payment). This amount corresponds with the ending balance for 20X2 that is shown in the last column of Exhibit 17-A1.

This method of accounting corresponds with that normally used by lessees. At all times, the balance in the lease receivable account is the present value of the remaining lease payments, plus accrued interest to date.

CURRENT VERSUS LONG-TERM BALANCES

Earlier in this chapter, the separation of the lessee's lease liability into current and long-term portions was illustrated. *If* the lessor uses a current/long-term classification, the same principle will apply: the current portion is the amount by which the principal will be reduced during the next fiscal year, plus any interest accrued *to date.*

However, a lessor may not use a balance sheet format that classifies items as current or long term. Companies that engage in direct-financing leases are financial institutions (e.g., bank subsidiaries, finance companies, or specialized leasing companies), and financial institutions do not classify their assets and liabilities on the basis of current versus non-current. Therefore, the classification of the current portion of the receivable balance is generally not an issue for lessors.

Example—Gross Method

Now, we will use the gross method to record the same example that we just used for the net method. The amortization table is the same as that shown in Exhibit 17-A1.

Over the life of the lease, CLC will receive a total cash inflow of $73,000; $65,000 from lease payments plus the $8,000 estimated residual value. The present value of the future cash flow is $55,000. The $18,000 difference between the gross cash flows and the discounted present value is the interest income (or *finance revenue*) that will be reported by CLC. This is no different than using the net method, as shown in the interest column of Exhibit 17-A1. However, the initial entry, using the gross method, is as follows:

2 January 20X2		
Lease payments receivable	73,000	
Cash		55,000
Unearned finance revenue		18,000

On the balance sheet, the $18,000 unearned finance revenue will be deducted from the gross lease payments. Only the net present value of $55,000 will be reported as an asset.

At the end of 20X2, interest will be accrued at the 12.67% implicit rate. Earned finance revenue for 20X2 is $55,000 × 12.67% = $6,967 (rounded). Instead of adding the accrued interest to the lease receivable, it is *deducted* from the unearned finance revenue:

31 December 20X2		
Unearned finance revenue	6,967	
Finance revenue		6,967

The effect of this entry is to reduce the offset account by $6,967. The balance of unearned finance revenue drops from $18,000 to $11,033. As a result, the net lease receivable shown on the 31 December 20X2 balance sheet will increase from $55,000 to $61,967.

On 2 January 20X3, the first lease payment will be made. The full amount of the lease payment will be credited to the lease receivable:

2 January 20X3		
Cash	20,000	
Lease payments receivable		20,000

After the payment is received and recorded, the net balance of the lease receivable is $41,967:

Lease payments receivable, 31 December 20X2	$73,000
Payment received, 2 January 20X3	20,000
Remaining lease payments receivable	53,000
Unearned finance revenue ($18,000 − $6,967)	11,033
Net lease receivable	$41,967

This is exactly the same amount as shown in Exhibit 17-A1 at the end of the first row, following the first payment. Thus, there is no difference in reporting between the net and gross bases.

Exhibit 17-A2 summarizes the entries that CLC will make over the term of the lease. The net lease receivable following each lease payment is exactly the same as shown in Exhibit 17-A1. There is absolutely no difference in financial reporting between the net and gross bases.

This example assumes that CLC actually realized the expected $3,000 residual value at the end of the lease. In reality, it is highly unlikely that the lessor would realize exactly the estimated amount of an unguaranteed residual value.

Any excess or deficiency in the realized residual value at the disposal date will be recognized immediately in net income. If a decline in the residual value was estimated prior to the disposal date, then any anticipated loss would be recognized by a reduction in the lease present value and the unrealized finance revenue. Anticipated gains are not recognized until realized upon disposal.

CONCEPT REVIEW

1. What two additional guidelines exist for a lessor to account for a lease as a capital lease that do not exist for a lessee?

2. What interest rate does the lessor use for accounting for a capital lease?

3. When does the lessor include the residual value in the cash flow stream for accounting purposes?

Why Use the Gross Method?

Since the gross and net methods yield the same results, and since the net method is simpler and corresponds to the method used by lessees, one might wonder why the gross method is used at all.

EXHIBIT 17-A2

LESSOR RECORDING OF CAPITAL LEASE—GROSS METHOD

	Dr.	Cr.	Net* Lease Receivable Balance—Dr.
2 January 20X2			
Lease payments receivable	73,000		
Cash		55,000	
Unearned finance revenue		18,000	$55,000
31 December 20X2			
Unearned finance revenue	6,967		
Finance revenue		6,967	$61,967
2 January 20X3			
Cash	20,000		
Lease payments receivable		20,000	$41,967
31 December 20X3			
Unearned finance revenue	5,316		
Finance revenue		5,316	$47,284
2 January 20X4			
Cash	20,000		
Lease payments receivable		20,000	$27,284
31 December 20X4			
Unearned finance revenue	3,456		
Finance revenue		3,456	$30,740
2 January 20X5			
Cash	20,000		
Lease payments receivable		20,000	$10,740
31 December 20X5			
Unearned finance revenue	1,361		
Finance revenue		1,361	$12,101
2 January 20X6			
Cash	5,000		
Lease payments receivable		5,000	$ 7,101
31 December 20X6			
Unearned finance revenue	899		
Finance revenue		899	$ 8,000
2 January 20X7			
Cash	8,000		
Lease payments receivable		8,000	nil
(to record the final lease payment of $5,000 plus the residual value of $3,000)			

*Net lease receivable is the debit balance of lease payments receivable minus the balance of unearned finance revenue.

Like almost all of the accounts shown on any company's balance sheet, the leases receivable account is a *control account*. The leases receivable is much like accounts receivable.

The balance sheet amount is a total; underlying that total is a large number of individual leases. For good internal control, an important characteristic of a control account is that it can easily be reconciled to the underlying subsidiary records. For leases receivable, that means that the receivables for the individual leases can be added up to verify the balance in the control account.

The gross method makes that reconciliation easier. Since the amounts in the lease payments receivable account are gross amounts, the balance can be verified by adding the remaining gross payments shown on all of the individual leases. Under the net method, by contrast, it is necessary to compute the present value of each lease at a particular point of time in order to perform the reconciliation. The gross method has the advantage of separating the control account function (via the lease payments receivable) from the revenue recognition function (via the unearned finance revenue).

Lessees are likely to have only a few leases, and the leases are incidental to their principal operations. Therefore, maintaining balances by the net method is no great problem for most lessees. Every lease that is reported as a capital lease will have its own amortization table, and summing the present values is fairly straightforward. Lessors, on the other hand, are specialized corporations whose main business is leasing. They will have thousands, perhaps tens of thousands, of individual leases. Some of the leases may be in arrears, and the present values may not correspond with their planned amortization schedules. Reconciliation on the net method would be a major headache. Therefore, the gross method is used.

Disclosure for Lessors

Lessors should disclose the following:

- The lessor's net investment (i.e., the lease payments receivable, less unearned finance revenue)
- The amount of finance income
- The lease revenue recognition policy

It may be also be desirable to disclose the following information:

- The aggregate future minimum lease payments receivable (that is, the gross amount)
- The amount of unearned finance income
- Any contingent rentals that have been taken into income
- The estimated amount of unguaranteed residual values
- Any executory costs included in minimum lease payments

CONCEPT REVIEW

1. Why do lessors usually use the gross method rather than the net method of accounting for capital leases?

2. Where does the *unearned finance revenue* account appear on the balance sheet?

SALES-TYPE LEASES

Basic Nature

A sales-type lease is a capital lease that, from the lessor's point of view, represents the sale of an item of inventory. Lessors in sales-type leases are manufacturers or dealers—they are not financial institutions and are not acting as financial intermediaries.

For the *lessee's* financial reporting, it doesn't matter whether the lessor is the producer of the product or is simply a financial intermediary. For the *lessor's* financial reporting, however, the distinction matters because a sales-type lease is viewed as two distinct (but related) transactions:

1. The sale of the product, with recognition of a profit or loss on the sale; and

2. The financing of the sale through a capital lease, with finance income recognized over the lease term.

There is absolutely nothing new in recording or reporting a sales-type lease, once the transaction has been recognized as being two separate but related transactions. The sale is recorded at the fair value of the asset being sold, with the asset received in return being the present value of the lease payments. The lease is then accounted for as a direct financing lease.

Example—Sales-Type Lease

Assume that on 31 December 20X1, Binary Corporation, a computer manufacturer, leases a large computer to a local university for five years at $200,000 per year, payable at the beginning of each lease year. The normal cash sales price of the computer is $820,000. The computer cost Binary Corporation (BC) $500,000 to build. The lease states that the computer will revert to BC at the end of the lease term, but a *side letter* from BC to the university states BC's intention not to actually reclaim the computer at the end of the lease.

The implicit interest rate that discounts the lease payments to the $820,000 fair value of the computer is 11.04%. Unless the cost of financing is well in excess of this rate, the lease can be assumed to be a capital lease. Because the lessor is the manufacturer of the product, and because the computer is carried on BC's books at a value that is less than fair value, the lease clearly is a sales-type lease.

The sale component of the transaction will be recorded as follows (using the gross method):

31 December 20X1		
Lease payments receivable	1,000,000	
Unearned finance revenue		180,000
Sales revenue		820,000
Cost of goods sold	500,000	
Computer inventory		500,000

The first payment (at the inception of the lease) will be recorded as:

31 December 20X1		
Cash	200,000	
Lease payments receivable		200,000

The income statement for 20X1 will include a gross profit of $320,000 relating to the lease transaction, which is the profit on the sale. The balance sheet on 31 December 20X1 will show a net lease receivable of $620,000: the gross lease payments of $1 million, minus the unearned finance revenue of $180,000, minus the first payment of $200,000.

In 20X2 and following years, the lease will be accounted for exactly as illustrated above for direct financing leases. Finance revenue (or interest income) will be accrued each reporting period at the rate of 11.04% on the net balance of the receivable and charged against the unearned finance revenue, while payments will be credited directly to the lease payments receivable account. The balance sheet will include the *net* balance of the receivable.

Estimating the Selling Price

In the example above, the implicit interest rate was obtained by finding the rate that discounted the lease payments to the cash selling price of $820,000. But, in practice, the fair value or "cash price" may not be so obvious. The problem arises because many products that are sold via sales-type leases are subject to discounts or special "deals" wherein the actual price is less than the stated list price. In theory, the lease payments should be discounted to equal the actual price rather than the list price. In practice, this is harder to do because the actual price is often hidden in the transaction.

Sometimes, the "true" selling price can be approximated by looking at the appropriateness of the implicit interest rate. For example, a common tactic in long-term automobile leasing is to advertise a very low rate of interest (e.g., 0.9%), a rate that clearly is below the market rate of interest. A super-low rate really represents a decrease in the price of the car. A potential lessee can see what price he or she is getting by discounting the lease payments at whatever rate the bank would be willing to finance the car (i.e., at the borrower's incremental borrowing rate).

Accounting standards offer no real assistance. The standards state that the sales revenue is the present value of the minimum lease payments computed at the interest rate implicit in the lease. This yields an equation that contains two unknowns—present value *and* implicit interest rate. In order to determine the implicit interest rate, the sales price must be known. In order to determine the sales price as a discounted present value, the interest rate must be known. One cannot compute a present value from an implicit interest rate.

The actual determination of the revenue split (and profit split) between the sale and the lease components of the transaction is a matter of considerable judgement. The split will affect (1) gross profit on the sale in the current period and (2) interest revenue in future periods. Management is likely to define the sales price in a way that best suits its reporting needs. If the statements are audited, the auditor must test the reasonableness of management's sales price definition.

Incidence of Sales-Type Leases

The incidence of sales-type leases in Canada is actually rather rare. There are a lot of manufacturers and/or dealers that do appear to sell their products through sales-type leases. Common examples are computers and automobiles. But a lessor will not be able to claim the full amount of CCA on leased assets if the CCA exceeds the lease payments received, *unless* the lessor qualifies as a lessor under the income tax regulations. To qualify, a lessor must obtain at least 90% of its revenue from leasing.

In order for the lessor to receive full tax advantage from the lease, companies that use leasing as a sales technique will either (1) form a separate corporation to carry out the leasing activity or (2) arrange for a third-party lender to provide the lease arrangements.

If a leasing corporation is formed, it may not be a "real" company in the sense that it is autonomous and has separate management; the lessor company may be no more than a filing cabinet full of lease agreements. If you lease a car, for example, you most likely will find that your monthly payments do not go to the dealer or to the manufacturer; they go to a finance company such as "Nissan Canada Finance Inc." The finance company then qualifies as a lessor for tax purposes. In substance, the auto dealer sells the car to the finance company, and the finance company then enters into a lease with the customer. From the viewpoint of the finance subsidiary, it is entering into a *direct-financing lease.*

Another option is for the manufacturer to go to an independent finance company and negotiate all of the leases through that company. The lessor and the manufacturer will establish an arm's-length sales price between them, and therefore the sales price of the product will be clear. The lease accounting is then all on the books of the lessor rather than the manufacturer. The lessor will account for the lease as a direct-financing lease.

In summary, sales-type leases entered into by a manufacturer or dealer are not common in Canada because the *Income Tax Act* effectively discourages the practice by granting favoured tax status only to qualified leasing companies.

CONCEPT REVIEW

1. What is the basic difference between a sales-type lease and a capital lease?

2. In a sales-type lease, why is it often difficult to determine objectively the sales price of the item being "sold"?

3. How common are sales-type leases in Canada?

INTERNATIONAL PERSPECTIVE

International standards for lessors are very similar to those described above. However, the standard does not use the terms "direct financing" and "sales-type." Instead, all leases are referred to as *finance* leases.

When a manufacturer or dealer enters into lease arrangements as a method of selling the product, the lessor should recognize "selling profit" in accordance with the usual practice for ordinary sales. If the fair value of the asset is not reliably determinable, then the present value of the future lease payments should be discounted at the market rate of interest. This seems to be a rather more reasonable approach than the impossible implicit rate approach required by Canadian standards.

SUMMARY OF KEY POINTS

1. A lessor treats a lease as a capital lease if, in addition to transferring substantially all of the risks and rewards of ownership to the lessee, two other criteria are both met: (1) the credit risk is normal and (2) all executory and operating costs included in the lease payments can be reasonably estimated.

2. The lessors' guidelines for determining when substantially all of the risks and benefits of ownership have been transferred are the same as for lessees.

3. Lessors must classify a capital lease as either a direct-financing lease or a sales-type lease. A direct financing lease arises when a lessor acts purely as a financial intermediary. A sales-type lease arises when a manufacturer or dealer uses leasing as a means of selling a product.

4. The lessor in a direct-financing lease recognizes revenue as finance revenue or interest revenue on a compound interest basis over the minimum lease term.

5. A sales-type lease has two profit components: (1) the profit or loss from the sale and (2) interest revenue from the lease financing.

6. The minimum lease term includes bargain renewal terms and all terms prior to exercisability of a bargain purchase option. The minimum net lease payments include all payments during the lease term (as defined above), less initial direct costs, executory costs, and operating costs, plus the guaranteed residual value, if any.

7. The interest rate used in lessor accounting for a capital lease is the rate implicit in the lease. The net method and the gross method give the same results in the financial statements. Lessors normally use the gross method of recording capital leases to facilitate control.

REVIEW PROBLEM

Orion leased a computer to the Lenox Silver Company on 1 January 20X5. The terms of the lease and other related information are as follows:

• Lease term (fixed and non-cancellable)	three years
• Estimated economic life of the equipment	four years
• Fair market value of the computer at lease inception	$5,000
• Lessor's cost of asset	$5,000
• Bargain purchase price	none
• Transfer of title	none
• Guaranteed residual value by lessee (excess to lessee) 1 January 20X8	$2,000
• Lessee's incremental borrowing rate	11%
• Collectibility of rental payments	assured
• Annual rental (1st payment 1 January 20X5)	$1,620

Required:

1. Provide entries for the lessor from 1 January 20X5 through 1 January 20X6, using the gross method of recording.

2. Provide the lessor's journal entry at the termination of the lease on 1 January 20X8, assuming that the asset is sold by the lessee on that date for $2,600.

REVIEW PROBLEM—SOLUTION

The lease is a capital lease because the lease term (three years) is 75% of the economic life of the asset. The lease is a direct-financing lease because the lessor's carrying value of the leased asset is equal to its fair value.

The lessor must account for the lease by using the interest rate implicit in the lease. The interest rate that discounts the lease cash flows to $5,000 is 24.55% (before tax) (solved by spreadsheet).

1. Lease entries, gross method

1 January 20X5—inception of lease

Lease receivable [($1,620 × 3) + $2,000]	6,860	
Unearned finance revenue		1,860
Cash, Inventory, etc.		5,000

1 January 20X5—first payment

Cash	1,620	
Lease receivable		1,620

31 December 20X5—interest accrual

Unearned interest revenue*	830	
Interest revenue		830

        *[($6,860 − $1,620) − $1,860] × 24.55% = $3,380 × 24.55% = $830

1 January 20X6—second payment

Cash	1,620	
Lease receivable		1,620

2. Termination of Lease

1 January 20X8—receipt of guaranteed residual value from lessee

Cash	2,000	
Lease receivable		2,000

The fact that the lessee was able to sell the asset for $2,600 is irrelevant for the lessor. The lessee gets to keep the extra $600.

QUESTIONS

Q17-1 At the beginning of the fiscal year, a tenant signs a three-year lease to rent office space at the rate of $1,000 per month. The first six months are free. How much rent expense should be recognized in the first year of the lease?

Q17-2 Under what circumstances is a lease normally considered a capital lease? What role does judgement play?

Q17-3 Give three reasons that a company might enter into a long-term lease instead of buying an asset outright.

Q17-4 A car dealer advertises a new car lease with the following terms:

- $3,500 cash paid by the customer at the beginning of the lease;
- Monthly payments of $229 for 48 months; and
- The customer is required to pay $2,650 at the end of the lease, and then owns the vehicle.

What is the substance of the lease contract?

Q17-5 Under what circumstances would a deferred rent liability appear on the balance sheet of a company that is a lessee in an operating lease?

Q17-6 Define the following terms, as used in lease accounting standards:

- bargain purchase option (BPO)
- lease term
- minimum net lease payments
- contingent lease payments
- bargain renewal term
- guaranteed residual value
- incremental borrowing rate
- interest rate implicit in the lease

Q17-7 Assume that a lessee signs a lease for a three-year term for $1,000 per year that has a renewal option at the lessee's option for a further three years for $1,000 per year. How long is the lease term, as defined by lease accounting standards?

Q17-8 How would your answer to Question 17-7 change if the renewal was at the lessor's option? If rental during the second term was $100 per year instead of $1,000?

Q17-9 A lessee signs a lease for a two-year term that requires a yearly payment of $14,000, which includes $2,500 for insurance and maintenance cost. At the end of the two-year term, there is a $1,000 BPO. How much are the minimum net lease payments?

Q17-10 Assume an asset has a fair market value of $48,500 and is leased for $10,000 per year for six years. Payments are made at the end of each lease term. Insurance costs included in this amount are $1,000, and there is a $6,000 guaranteed residual. What is the interest rate implicit in the lease for the lessee? Why is this not also the interest rate implicit in the lease for the lessor?

Q17-11 Assume a non-profit organization wished to acquire a particular asset. Why might it be cheaper to lease rather than buy the asset?

Q17-12 Assume a lease involves payments of $20,000 per year, net of insurance costs, and is properly capitalized on the lessee's books at a 10% interest rate for $135,180. How much interest would be recognized in the first year of the lease if the payments were made at the beginning of the period? The second year?

Q17-13 A lessee enters into a five-year capital lease with a five-year bargain renewal option, and then the asset is returned to the lessor. How long would the amortization period be for the asset? Assume that such an asset is expected to have a 12-year useful life.

Q17-14 How is the current portion of the lease liability determined if the lease payments are due and payable at the end of the fiscal year? How would your answer change if the payments were due at the beginning of the period?

Q17-15 What is a sale and leaseback? How are such transactions accounted for?

Q17-16 What is the general definition of a capital lease from the perspective of a lessor? What guidelines exist to classify a lease for the lessor?

Q17-17 What interest rate does the lessor use for discounting calculations associated with a lease?

Q17-18 From a lessor's view, a capital lease may be one of two types. Identify the types and distinguish between them.

Q17-19 Describe the nature of a sales-type lease. What kinds of entities offer such leases?

Q17-20 In a sales-type lease, how does separation of the sale component from the lease component affect revenue recognition in the current and future years?

CASE 17-1

SANDSUPPORT CORPORATION

Sandsupport Corporation (SC) is a privately owned company based in Alberta. The company provides support services for the oil and gas industry, especially for new exploration not only in Canada, but also in other countries such as Venezuela and Mexico.

Due to the ever-increasing worldwide demand for energy and the resultant increase in exploration activity, SC is planning a major expansion of its operational capacity. As part of this expansion, the company needs to acquire a significant amount of new equipment. In the past, the company has obtained external financing only through debt, mainly via private placements of secured first-mortgage debentures with pension funds and other institutional investors.

Additional financing will be needed to acquire the new equipment. However, management is hesitant about obtaining more straight debt financing due to restrictive covenants (e.g., on debt to equity ratio) that are in place for some of SC's existing debt. Therefore, management is considering three alternatives.

Leasing is the first possibility that management is considering. SC leases quite a lot of equipment to its clients on short-term leases for specific projects, and it seemed logical to look into leasing as way for SC to acquire the equipment. Management has been in contact with GWC Finance Corporation about negotiating a lease. Under the potential lease arrangements, GWC would purchase the equipment from its German manufacturer; the manufacturer would deliver the machinery directly to SC. SC would agree to a lease contract that would enable GWC to classify the lease as a capital lease, in accordance with its status as a tax-qualifying lessor. Since the equipment is quite specialized, the lease payments would be "front-loaded," with most of the total lease payments payable in the first five years. GWC has suggested that SC may be able to enter into an agreement with one of SC's major clients (e.g., Suncor or PetroCanada) for the client to guarantee a substantial residual value—enough to reduce the minimum lease payments to less than 90% of the equipment's fair value. SC would unofficially compensate the client through reduced fees for SC's services.

The second possibility would also involve leasing, but the lease would not be an obligation of SC. Instead, two SC shareholders would form a separate corporation and that corporation would enter into the lease with GWC. The new corporation would then lease the equipment to GWC with an initial lease term of five years. After the first five years, the lease would continue on a year-to-year basis automatically until the GWC lease expired. At that point, GWC would transfer title to the new corporation, which in turn would sell the equipment to SC for nominal consideration.

The third option involves the issuance of convertible preferred shares to the Alberta Teachers' Pension Plan. The proceeds of the share issue would be used to buy the equipment. SC has never previously used outside equity financing, but preferred shares seems to be a logical answer to the financing problem faced by SC. SC would be obligated to pay dividends annually at 8% of the paid-in value of the shares. Anytime after five years, ATPP could convert to common shares (for whatever number of common shares will amount to a current market value equal to the preferred shares' original paid-in value). As well, SC would be able to call the shares for redemption at any time after five years.

Management is very experienced at being a lessor, but not at all experienced at being a lessee. Therefore, the CFO has come to you for advice on the best route to take for the new financing. In particular, the CFO is concerned about the financial statement impact of these three alternatives.

Required:

Analyze the consequences of each of the above alternatives in a memo to your superior. Explain which one you would recommend for SC.

CASE 17-2

WHEELS ON WHEELS

Ontario provincial courts have ruled that municipalities must provide public transit for people with physical disabilities. Like many other Ontario municipalities, the town of Scofield has decided not to modify its existing buses to accommodate wheelchairs, but instead will establish a separate publicly supported service. Rather than operate the service as a public enterprise, the town council decided that this transit service should be "privatized" (that is, operated by a private business on behalf of the town).

Accordingly, the Scofield town council put out a call for proposals from private enterprises to provide the service. The winner of the contract was Peerless Transit Incorporated. Peerless is a private Ontario corporation owned by the Bishnoi family. The corporation engages in charter bus services in many localities in Ontario, including the provision of school bus services in some areas. Peerless had been operating a charter bus service in the Scofield area for about six years, and had demonstrated an ability to provide quality service at reasonable prices. Peerless had been sufficiently successful that two other charter bus operators decided to cease operations in the last couple of years. Peerless's gross revenues for the previous year were approximately $7 million.

The initial contract between Peerless and Scofield is for five years. The town will subsidize Peerless's service for people with physical disabilities. The subsidy will be based on the annual audited operating results. The amount of the subsidy will be the cost of operations, net of operating revenues, plus a profit margin calculated annually as 8% of the average of that year's beginning and ending net assets (i.e., total assets less liabilities) relating to the service. Peerless is to form a separate subsidiary to operate the new service ("Wheels on Wheels"), so that the net assets of the new services are not intermingled with those of Peerless's other operations.

Wheels on Wheels (WOW) will be able to charge fees for its services, but all fees must be approved by the Scofield town council. Fees for regular transportation must be similar to those charged by the town in its regular bus service, but charter operations using the alternate fleet (e.g., taking people with physical disabilities on a picnic) can charge market rate. Indeed, one of the criteria that the town will use in evaluating future contract renewals will be WOW's success in finding alternative revenue sources instead of relying too heavily on the town's subsidy.

To assist with start-up costs, the town will grant a substantial advance to WOW at the beginning of the contract. The advance will be offset against future subsidies.

WOW plans to acquire a small fleet of specially designed vehicles, each of which will accommodate eight wheelchairs. Vehicles of this type are already in widespread use in other towns and cities across the continent. The expected useful life of the vehicles is 18 years. WOW has several choices about how to acquire the vehicles. The first alternative is for the company to buy the vehicles directly from their Ontario manufacturer and pay for them by taking out a secured loan from the bank. A second alternative is for WOW to buy the vehicles directly, but to finance them by having Peerless (i.e., the parent company) take out a loan using its other buses as security, and then use the proceeds of the loan as a capital infusion into WOW. As a third alternative, the company could lease the vehicles for five years, with a renewal option should the town offer to renew the contract. Peerless has been in touch with an interested leasing company located in Buffalo, New York; the leasing company would benefit from the high tax depreciation deductions in the lease's early years and would pass this benefit back to Peerless through lease payments (in U.S. dollars) calculated on an after-tax basis. The fourth alternative would be to lease the vehicles on a year-by-year basis from the manufacturer; since the vehicles are in widespread use, the manufacturer is confident that the vehicles can be sold or rented elsewhere should Wheels on Wheels cease operations.

Peerless has identified a building in town to use as a storage and dispatch depot for the vehicles. The building can be purchased (with funds borrowed from the Peerless parent company) or can be leased for five years with a renewal option.

The president of Peerless, Aparna Bishnoi, is seeking advice on the best options to follow in setting up Wheels on Wheels. She is interested in both the cash flow and the accounting consequences of her alternatives.

Required:

Assume that you have been hired by Peerless Transit as an advisor. Write a report to Ms Bishnoi.

CASE 17-3

BLISS AIR LINE LIMITED

Start-Up

Michael Bliss is the President, CEO, and controlling shareholder of Bliss Air Line Limited (BALL). He started the company four years ago to provide low-cost charter service to holiday destinations. Although the airline is low cost, it is not no-frills; the airline's motto is "Travel with Bliss and have a ball!"

To obtain initial working capital, Michael sold a long-distance trucking company that he owned, and he invested the proceeds in BALL. The new company acquired four old Boeing 737-100 aircraft that had been decommissioned by other airlines and were parked in the Arizona desert. The purchase price was $10 million each. Approximately $1 million per plane was needed to get the planes ready for recertification and to equip the interior to Michael's satisfaction. The money for acquisition and refurbishment was provided by a collateral loan from GE Capital.

The airline was successful from the beginning, and in the second year the company bought three slightly newer airplanes, Boeing 737-300s, for $25 million each. These newer planes had not been decommissioned, and therefore they were able to enter service quickly to provide much-needed capacity in BALL's second summer season.

In the third year, BALL was again short of capacity and had to rent two more 737s from a major competitor that was no longer using them. The cost is $115,000 per month to rent.

It became apparent to Michael that the company would need much more capacity. As well, the rapidly rising cost of fuel, terminal charges, and overhead all pointed to a need to reduce operating cost per seat mile. The old 737-100s were much less efficient than the latest models. As well, new anti-pollution standards were being phased in, which would require the 737-100s to be either retired or re-equipped with new engines in three years.

Capital Structure

Due to the need for new capital for expanded operations, Michael decided to make BALL a public company. The capital structure was altered to provide for four classes of shares.

1. An unlimited number of voting common shares;
2. An unlimited number of restricted common shares;
3. 70,000 non-voting retractable preferred shares; and
4. An unlimited number of non-voting, cumulative, non-participating preferred shares.

The voting common shares have 100 votes each. The restricted common shares have one vote each.

After approval by the securities commissions, the company issued the following:

- 150,000 voting common shares to Michael Bliss in exchange for his existing BALL shares;
- 17,000,000 restricted common shares issued at $20 per share in an initial public offering; and
- 11,000 retractable preferred shares to GE Capital to replace the $44,000,000 collateral loan (i.e., for the first group of aircraft).

The restricted voting shares were listed on the Toronto Stock Exchange.

The retractable preferred shares carry an annual cumulative preference dividend of $220 per share. The shares are not callable for the first four years. After that, BALL can call any or all the shares for redemption at $4,100 per share. At any time, if BALL misses a dividend, GE Capital will have the right to demand redemption at $4,500 per share plus accrued dividends.

New Equipment

To provide additional capacity, the Board of Directors considered several possibilities. One was to buy new 737-700s outright. The planes cost $47 million each, and would be financed by secured long-term floating rate debt, privately negotiated with major U.S. and international lenders. Preliminary indications were that BALL could obtain the necessary financing at a current rate of 6.5%. Industry practice was to amortize that type of aircraft over 20 years, assuming a 10% residual value. Of course, the planes physically would last much longer if properly maintained, but obsolescence takes its toll.

A second alternative was to lease the new aircraft. A major leasing company indicated willingness to give BALL 14-year leases at $360,000 per month per plane. Of course, BALL could combine the two alternatives—buy some planes and lease others.

The new aircraft would be used not only for fleet expansion, but also to replace the old 737-100s, which soon would have to be retired. But to obtain more cash for operations (and new asset acquisition), the Board also was considering what to do with the three newer 737-300s. These planes had been purchased with instalment debt financing, and the Board thought it would be beneficial to "cash in" the ownership equity by entering into a sale-and-leaseback arrangement. Although the planes were becoming obsolete for top-tier airlines, they still were in demand by smaller airlines and by those in developing countries.

Professional evaluations indicated that BALL could sell the planes for a profit of about $2 million each, and then lease them back for four years at $125,000 per month.

Recommendations Needed

The end of the first fiscal year of public ownership is rapidly approaching. Before making any decisions about leasing and/or buying new planes, and about sale-and-leaseback of the 737-300s, Michael and the Board need a professional opinion on the financial statement implications. The CFO, Michelle Bliss, has retained you, FCGA, for advice on these issues. The Board also wants advice on any other financial statement issues that you see.

Required:

Write the report.

CASE 17-4

NATURAL BREWS INCORPORATED

Natural Brews Incorporated (NBI) is a Toronto microbrewery that began production in 1986. Amin Amershi is president and CEO of the company and owns 60% of the shares; the other 40% are owned by the brewmaster, Chor Lam. The shareholders' agreement between Amin and Chor gives the two partners equal voting power.

The shareholders' agreement also specifies that the net income of the company (before deducting salaries for either shareholder) shall be divided proportionately between the two shareholders. The shareholders can withdraw their respective share of earnings in the form of either salary or dividends or any combination thereof (whichever is better from a personal income tax standpoint), or they can leave any amount of earnings in the company. Earnings left in the company are added to each shareholder's investment for purposes of determining the proportionate share of next year's earnings.

The shareholders' agreement between Amin and Chor does not require audited financial statements. However, the agreement does specify that in measuring the earnings of NBI, the shareholders agree to abide by the recommendations of NBI's accounting advisor.

NBI has been very successful and profitable. The beer has sold well in major bars, clubs, and restaurants. In order to stress the quality image of the beer, promotional efforts have been directed entirely at "upscale" drinking establishments and their customers, with special emphasis on high-volume establishments. The success of NBI's products in licensed premises has led to a strong demand at the retail level as well.

Since both owners have been leaving substantial earnings in the company in recent years, NBI has virtually no debt and has accumulated earnings that were invested largely in temporary investments. In the current year, NBI liquidated most of the temporary investments and made some long-term investments. The first such investment was acquisition of a 35% interest in a major downtown club, Club Colby, which is also one of the largest single outlets for NBI products. The other 65% of Club Colby is owned by a three-person partnership that manages the club, as well as several other enterprises.

In an attempt to get some synergy with its investment in Club Colby, NBI also leased the premises of a defunct restaurant next to the club and agreed to pay $10,000 per month for the next two years for the premises. NBI entered into an agreement with Rolando Eric, an experienced restaurant manager, whereby Rolando will invest his own capital in the restaurant and manage it on behalf of NBI. Rolando and NBI will share equally in the profits. The restaurant holds a liquor licence and will, of course, feature NBI products on tap. The restaurant and Club Colby will engage in joint promotion and marketing.

In order to keep up with anticipated demand for its products, NBI purchased the entire net assets (i.e., assets and liabilities) of another, smaller microbrewery in Mississauga, Ontario, Foaming Fantasies Limited (FFL), as a going concern. FFL's assets consist of land, one building, brewing equipment, and accounts receivable; FFL liabilities are accounts payable, a mortgage on the building, and a bank operating loan. The net asset value of FFL on FFL's books at the date of sale was $150,000 (net of liabilities of $750,000); NBI paid the previous owner of FFL $250,000 cash. Amin and Chor plan to continue brewing FFL's largest selling brand but will discontinue its smaller brands. The capacity thus released will be used to produce one of NBI's brands.

NBI is also planning to acquire additional new capacity. NBI just paid $30,000 for a non-refundable option to purchase land adjacent to NBI's current facilities for $150,000; the option expires in 90 days but is transferable. One alternative that NBI is considering is to purchase the land, build an extension to the present building, and purchase all the necessary equipment. The estimated cost for the building and equipment is $400,000 and $200,000 respectively. NBI's bank has indicated a willingness to extend a 20-year mortgage for 75% of the cost of the land and building and to extend a five-year term loan for 80% of the cost of the equipment. The mortgage would bear interest at 10% for the first five years; the interest rate on the term loan would start at 8% but would be adjusted monthly to the prime rate plus .75%.

Alternatively, NBI can accept an arrangement with McKellar Development Corporation whereby McKellar would assume and exercise the option on the land, construct the new building, fully equip it, and then lease the completed facility to NBI. The lease payments would be $84,000 per year, in advance, for each of the first 10 years. NBI would be responsible for all property taxes, maintenance costs, and insurance. After the initial 10-year term, the lease payments would be renegotiated for another 10-year term, but the payments would not be less than $84,000. For income tax purposes, NBI would deduct the lease payments as an operating expense.

Required:

Assume the role of accounting advisor. Prepare a report to the shareholders in which you recommend specific accounting policies for NBI's recent activities as outlined above. Amin and Chor would also like your recommendation on whether NBI should buy and build the additional production capacity or enter into the lease arrangement with McKellar. Assume a tax rate of 40%, and a 6% cost of capital.

CASE 17-5

WRIGHT AIRCRAFT COMPANY LTD.

Wright Aircraft Company (WAC) manufactures small single- and dual-engine aircraft primarily for sale to individuals, flying clubs, and corporations. WAC is one of the pioneers in the industry and has developed a reputation as a leader in both small aircraft engineering and marketing innovations.

During the last few years, WAC has profitably leased an increasing number of its aircraft to flying clubs. The leasing activity currently represents a significant portion of WAC's annual volume. Details of the leasing arrangements with flying clubs are as follows:

1. The flying club signs a long-term agreement with WAC for the aircraft. The lease has a non-cancellable term of six to 10 years, depending on the type of aircraft being leased. Lease payments are normally made monthly. Properly maintained, an aircraft will last for 20 years or more. The lease requires the flying club to maintain the aircraft at its own expense.

2. The club is required to deposit with WAC an amount equal to 10% of the total lease payments for the term of the lease. The deposit is not refundable, but it is used in lieu of lease payments during the final 10% of the lease term.

3. A bank lends WAC an amount equal to the remaining 90% of the total gross lease payments, discounted at 12% per annum. The discounted amount is paid immediately to

WAC. As the lease payments are received from the flying club, WAC acts solely as an intermediary; WAC sends the lease payments directly to the bank as received.

4. The bank requires WAC to insure the leased aircraft for an amount at least equal to the outstanding balance of the loan.
5. The flying club signs WAC's bank loan agreement as a surety, thereby obligating itself directly to the bank if the club defaults on the lease payments. The agreement enables the bank to repossess the aircraft in case the flying club defaults on its lease payments.
6. At the end of the lease term, when all lease payments have been made and the bank loan has been fully repaid, the flying club may renew the lease indefinitely for $1,000 per year.

Required:

a. Assume that Wright Aircraft Company is a public company. Explain how WAC should account for the leases. Include in your discussion all factors presented in the case that have a bearing on your recommendations.
b. Assume that WAC is a private corporation that is wholly owned by members of the Wright family. The company is controlled and actively managed by the Wright brothers, sons of the founder, but other members of the family also own shares and rely on dividend income.

ASSIGNMENTS

★ **A17-1 Capital Lease Fundamentals:** Niko Limited signed a lease for a five-year term that requires yearly, beginning-of-year payments of $104,000, including $9,600 of annual maintenance and property taxes. Niko guarantees a residual value of $26,500 at the end of the lease term, although both parties expect the asset to be sold as used equipment for approximately $35,000 at that time.

Required:

1. How much are Niko's minimum lease payments, as defined for lease accounting purposes?
2. If Niko's IBR is 10%, what amount will Niko record as an asset?
3. How much will Niko record as an asset if the residual value is *unguaranteed*?
4. Suppose that the fair value of the leased asset is $375,000 at the inception of the lease. How would this fact affect the amount recorded for the leased asset?

★★ **A17-2 Terminology, Classification, Entries:** Burrill Limited has an 8% incremental borrowing rate at the local bank. On 1 January 20X1, Burrill signed the following lease agreement for a piece of equipment. The equipment has a fair value of $133,000 and a 12-year economic life. Other information is as follows:

- The non-cancellable lease is for eight years.
- The lease payment is $24,000 annually, payable at the beginning of each lease year.
- Lease payments include $4,000 of maintenance expense annually.
- At the end of the lease term, the leased asset reverts back to the lessor.

Other information:

- Burrill has a fiscal year that ends on 31 December.
- Burrill uses straight-line depreciation for similar capital assets.

Required:

1. For this lease, what is the:

   - lease term?
   - guaranteed residual value?
   - unguaranteed residual value?
   - bargain purchase option?
   - minimum net lease payment?
   - incremental borrowing rate?

   If these amounts do not exist in the above lease, enter "none" as your response. State any assumptions.

2. Is this lease an operating lease or a capital lease for the lessee? Explain your reasoning.
3. Prepare the journal entries for the first year of the lease on Burrill's books.
4. How would your answer change if the lease contained a clause that said that the lease could be cancelled at any time by either party? Explain.

★★ **A17-3 Terminology, Classification, Entries:** Canadian Leasing Company leased a piece of machinery to Ornamental Concrete Limited, with the following terms:

- The lease is for five years; Ornamental cannot cancel the lease during this period.
- The lease payment is $79,600. Included in this is $7,900 in estimated insurance costs.
- At the end of the five-year initial lease term, Ornamental can elect to renew the lease for one additional five-year term at a price of $29,500, including $2,500 of estimated insurance costs. Market rentals are approximately twice as expensive.
- At the end of the first or second lease term, the leased asset reverts back to the lessor.
- Lease payments are due at the beginning of each lease year.

Other information:

- Ornamental could borrow money to buy this asset at an interest rate of 10%.
- The equipment has a fair market value of $390,000 at the beginning of the lease term, and a useful life of approximately 12 years.
- The lease term corresponds to the fiscal year.
- Ornamental uses straight-line depreciation for all capital assets.

Required:

1. For this lease, what is the:

   - lease term?
   - guaranteed residual value?
   - unguaranteed residual value?
   - bargain purchase option?
   - bargain renewal terms?
   - minimum net lease payment?
   - incremental borrowing rate?'

   If these amounts do not exist in the above lease, enter "none" as your response. State any assumptions.

2. Is this lease an operating lease or a capital lease for the lessee? Why?
3. Prepare journal entries for the first year of the lease on Ornamental's books.

★   **A17-4 Operating Lease, Inducements:** The Association of Western Agricultural Producers leases space in an office complex and has recently signed a new, three-year lease, at the rate of $2,500 per month. However, the lessor offered four months "free" rent at the beginning of the lease as an inducement for the Association to sign the lease agreement.

The lease agreement was signed on 1 October 20X1, and the Association has a 31 December fiscal year-end. Rent is due on the first day of each month.

Required:

1. Prepare journal entries for the first six months of the lease, assuming adjustments are made monthly.
2. What amounts would be shown on the income statement and balance sheet for this lease as of 31 December 20X2?

★★   **A17-5 Terminology:** Lu Enterprises Limited is expanding and needs more manufacturing equipment. The company has been offered lease contracts for three different assets:

Lease 1   The machinery has a fair value of $116,000, and an expected life of 10 years. The lease has a five-year term, renewable for a further two years at the option of the lessee. Annual rental for the first term is $28,600, for the second, $11,500. Payments are made each 31 December. The first term rental includes $2,600 for maintenance and insurance, the second, $1,500. Lease payments are close to market lease rates for both the first and second terms. At the end of the second term, Lu can buy the asset for $1.

Lease 2   The machinery has a fair value of $550,000 and an expected life of six years. The lease has a five-year term. Annual rental is paid at the beginning of the lease year, in the amount of $104,300. Insurance and operating costs, approximately $16,500, are paid directly by Lu Enterprises in addition to the lease payments. At the end of the lease term, the machinery will revert to the lessor, which will sell it for an expected $75,000. If the lessor does not realize $75,000 in the sale, then Lu has agreed to make up the difference.

Lease 3   The machinery has a fair value of $55,000 and an expected useful life of five years. The lease has a one-year term, renewable at the option of the lessee, and an annual rental of $10,600, payable at the beginning of the lease term. If the lease is renewed, the annual rental does not change. If the lease is not renewed, the leased asset reverts back to the lessor. Annual payments include $1,400 of maintenance and insurance costs. If the machine is used for more than 3,000 hours per year, a payment of $7.40 per hour for each extra hour must also be made.

Lu has an incremental borrowing rate of 10%. Lu has been told that the interest rate implicit in Lease 1 is 8%, but Lu does not know the interest rates implicit in Leases 2 and 3.

Required:

1. For each lease, identify:

	#1	#2	#3
a. Lease term	___	___	___
b. Bargain purchase option	___	___	___
c. Unguaranteed residual	___	___	___
d. Guaranteed residual	___	___	___
e. Bargain renewal terms	___	___	___
f. Minimum net lease payments	___	___	___
g. Contingent lease payments	___	___	___
h. Interest rate to be used to discount the minimum net lease payments	___	___	___

If a term is not applicable for a particular lease, enter "N/A."

If a term is present, but its amount is not known, enter "?"

2. Classify each lease, and provide reasons for your response.

3. Provide the entry made at the beginning of each lease.

★★★ **A17-6 Residual Values and BPOs:** Return to the facts of A17-5.

Required:

1. Prepare amortization tables showing how the lease liability reduces over the lease term for leases 1 and 2.

2. Assume that leases 1 and 2 were entered into on 1 January 20X2. Lu has a 31 December fiscal year-end. Prepare journal entries for each lease for 20X2. Remember to deduct residual value when calculating amortization for Lease 2.

3. Prepare the entry to record exercise of the bargain purchase option for Lease 1. Prepare the entry to record the end of Lease 2, assuming that the asset is sold by the lessor for $60,000 and that Lu must make up the $15,000 shortfall. Record interest to the date of the transaction first. Note that in the transaction, the asset and the leased liability are removed from Lu's books.

★★ **A17-7 Lease Motives:** Consider each of the following lease arrangements:

1. Abbaz Corporation signs a two-year lease for office space in a large, downtown office complex. Abbaz plans to have a permanent presence in the downtown area but has moved office premises several times in the past 10 years, motivated by factors such as convenience, quality of building, and price.

2. The Vital Organ Donation Society, a non-profit organization, must acquire a vehicle. It has the authority to borrow money for this purpose but is also considering a five-year lease arrangement, with a subsequent renewal option at a very favourable price, which appears to be much cheaper than the borrowing option.

3. Cahil Limited plans to acquire manufacturing equipment that it could buy outright. Since the company has no spare cash, all the money would have to be borrowed. However, existing loans required the company to maintain a debt-to-equity ratio of no more than 2 to 1, and the company's balance sheet reflects a ratio very close to this limit now. Cahil is considering a three-year lease with a low annual charge but material per-year contingent usage charges.

4. Bagg Limited has just completed the construction of a new warehouse facility. It is considering two financing options: a 25-year commercial mortgage or a 25-year lease. Under the mortgage agreement, interest rates would be fixed for five-year periods but would be renegotiated when each five-year period expired. Under the lease agreement, title would pass to Bagg Corporation at the end of the lease. The lease payments would be renegotiated every 10 years.

5. Dimmins College is considering an arrangement whereby it will sell all its rare book collection to a leasing company, and immediately lease back the collection on a 20-year lease, with fixed payments for each of the 20 years. At the end of the lease period, the collection will again belong to the College.

6. Elias Limited is attempting to acquire a $400,000 piece of manufacturing equipment for its plant operation, which it believes will significantly reduce its operating costs over the next four years. The equipment would likely be obsolete at that time. The company's friendly banker has offered a four-year loan, for up to $360,000, at prime interest rates. A friendly leasing company has offered a four-year lease covering all the equipment cost. The lease requires equal payments each year; payments are at the end of each year.

Required:

In each example, explain the company's motive for entering into the lease arrangement.

★★ **A17-8 Capital Lease:** Roscoe Corporation leased computer equipment from Central Leasing Corporation on 1 January 20X1. The equipment had an expected life of five years and a fair market value of $32,500. The lease had the following terms:

a. Lease payments are $7,600 per year, paid each 31 December.
b. Insurance and maintenance costs included in the lease payments amount to $200 annually.
c. At the end of the lease term, the computer equipment reverts to Central Leasing Company, which will leave it with Roscoe.
d. The lease term is five years.'

Roscoe has an incremental borrowing rate of 7% and has not been told of the interest rate implicit in the lease. Roscoe uses straight-line depreciation and has a 31 December fiscal year-end.

Required:

1. Is this a capital lease or an operating lease for Roscoe? Explain.
2. Prepare an amortization schedule showing how the lease liability reduces over time.
3. Prepare journal entries for the first two years of the lease.
4. How much interest expense would be recognized in the 20X1 and 20X2 fiscal years if the lease had been dated 1 July 20X1?
5. If the fair market value of the equipment was $25,405, how much interest expense would be recognized in 20X1?

★★ **A17-9 Capital Lease; Quarterly Payments; Current/Non-Current Classification:** Packard Limited is planning on leasing 150 desktop computers from Hewlett Corporation. The list price for the computers is $2,000 each, or $300,000 in total. The lease will be for three years, starting on 1 October 20X4. The lease payments are $26,000 at the beginning of each quarter. Packard's incremental borrowing rate is 8% per annum. Packard's fiscal year ends on 31 December. The computers have an expected useful life of four years but will almost certainly have no market value at the end of the lease. Although it is not specified in the lease agreement, Packard's customary practice with such leases is to simply convey title to the computers at the end of the lease term, at a nominal payment by the lessee.

Required:

1. Prepare the journal entries to record the lease and lease payments for Packard's fiscal year ending 31 December 20X4.
2. What amounts relating to the lease liability will appear on Packard's 31 December 20X4 balance sheet?

★★ **A17-10 Capital Lease; Financial Statement Reporting:** Harbinger has entered into an agreement to lease specialized equipment from Doom Inc. for 10 years. Doom is a U.S.–based company that specializes in asset-based financing, including both loans and leases. The equipment would cost $1.4 million and last at least 12 years, if Harbinger were to buy it. The lease calls for Harbinger to make annual beginning-of-year lease payments of $180,000. Harbinger's incremental borrowing rate is 8%. At the end of the lease, Harbinger has the option of buying the equipment for $25,000. The lease term begins on 1 September 20X5. Harbinger will depreciate the equipment at a declining-balance rate of 20%. The company uses the half-year convention, taking half a year's depreciation in the year of acquisition and the year of disposal.

Required:

1. What amounts will appear on Harbinger's balance sheet, income statement, and cash flow statement for the year ending 31 December 20X5? Assume that Harbinger uses the indirect approach to present cash flow from operating activities.

2. Suppose that the lease payments were $200,000 instead of $180,000. What value would be assigned to the leased asset on Harbinger's balance sheet at the inception of the lease? Explain.

 A17-11 Capital Lease: Risley Limited leased a cement truck from Dominion Leasing Limited on 1 January 20X2. The cement truck had an expected life of 17 years and a fair market value of $219,000. The lease had the following terms:

a. Lease payments are $40,000 per year, paid each 1 January, for five years. These lease payments include $8,000 of expected insurance and maintenance costs.
b. At the end of five years, the lease is renewable at Risley's option for $20,000 per year, including $5,000 of expected insurance and maintenance costs, for a further eight years.
c. The asset reverts back to the lessor at the end of any lease term.

Risley knows that the annual rental for a cement truck is in the range of $38,000 annually. Risley has an incremental borrowing rate of 8% and has not been told the interest rate implicit in the lease. Risley uses straight-line depreciation and has a 31 December year-end.

Required:

1. Is this a capital lease or an operating lease for Risley? Explain.
2. Prepare an amortization schedule showing how the lease liability reduces over time.
3. Prepare journal entries for the first two years of the lease.

 A17-12 Calculations, Income Statement, Guaranteed Residual Value: On 2 January 20X2, Argos Corporation enters into a three-year agreement to lease materials-handling equipment from X-Sess Corporation. The fair value of the equipment is $140,000, and its expected useful life is four years. During the lease negotiations, Argos agreed to guarantee a residual value of $20,000 in exchange for a reduction in the quarterly lease payments. X-Sess's pre-tax implicit interest rate is 12%. Argos's incremental borrowing rate is 13%. The first quarterly lease payment was due at the inception of the lease.

Required:

1. What will be the amount of the annual lease payment?
2. Prepare an amortization table for the lease obligation.
3. What amounts relating to the lease will appear on Argos's income statement and balance sheet for the year ended 31 December 20X2?

 A17-13 Capital Lease: On 31 December 20X1, Lessee Limited entered into a lease agreement by which Lessee leased a jutling machine for six years. Annual lease payments are $20,000, payable at the beginning of each lease year (31 December). At the end of the lease, possession of the machine will revert to the lessor. However, jutling machines are expected to last for only six years, at the end of which time they typically disintegrate into dust.

At the time of the lease agreement, jutling machines could be purchased for approximately $90,000 cash. Equivalent financing for the machine could have been obtained from Lessee's bank at 14%.

Lessee's fiscal year coincides with the calendar year. Lessee uses straight-line depreciation for its jutling machines.

Required:

1. Prepare an amortization table for the lease, assuming that the lease will be capitalized by Lessee.
2. In general journal form, prepare all journal entries relating to the lease and the leased asset for 20X1, 20X2, and 20X3. Ignore income tax effects.
3. Repeat requirement (2) assuming that the fair market value of the equipment was $77,273 at the inception of the lease.

4. Return to the original facts of the situation. How would the amounts relating to the leased asset and lease liability be shown on Lessee's balance sheet at 31 December 20X4?

 A17-14 Capital versus Operating Lease, Judgement: Luong Enterprises Limited (LEL) leases a calvanizing machine from CIBC Leasing Corporation (a wholly owned subsidiary of CIBC), effective 1 February 20X1. The five-year lease calls for an initial payment of $20,000, followed by 19 equal quarterly payments of $6,000, payable at the end of each quarter of the lease term except the last. CIBC leasing will repossess the asset at the end of the lease term and sell it through a broker, which guaranteed CIBC a base price. The broker is not related to Luong.

At the time the lease agreement is signed, new calvanizing machines are selling in the $120,000–$125,000 range. Five-year-old machines generally can be purchased in the used-machine market for about 20% of the cost of a new machine.

Had LEL chosen to buy the machine rather than lease it, CIBC would have lent LEL 80% of the purchase price as a five-year loan with blended monthly payments at an interest rate of 12% per annum (3% per quarter).

LEL ordinarily depreciates its calvanizing machines at a rate of 20%, declining balance, and records a half-year depreciation in the year of acquisition. LEL's fiscal year ends on 31 December.

Required:

1. Is the lease a capital lease or an operating lease to Luong Enterprises? Explain the reasons for your answer.
2. Compute the amounts relating to the lease (and leased asset) that will appear in LEL's balance sheet on 31 December, 20X4 assuming that the lease is reported as:
   a. an operating lease
   b. a capital lease

 A17-15 Capital Lease; Quarterly Payments; Fair Value Limitation: Christal Corporation leased computer equipment from HP Leasing Limited for three years at $30,000 per quarter. The lease begins on 1 May 20X5. Payments are due at the end of each lease quarter (that is, the first payment will be due on 31 July 20X5). The fair value of the equipment is $300,000. Christal Corporation's fiscal year-end is 31 December, and its incremental borrowing rate is 8% per annum. The equipment will be amortized at a declining-balance rate of 30%. The first year's amortization of the leased asset will be proportional.

Required:

1. In general journal form, prepare the appropriate entries at the inception of the lease.
2. Using a financial calculator or a computer spreadsheet, calculate the interest rate implicit in the lease for the *lessee*.
3. What will be the lease liability balance (including accrued interest, if any) on 31 December 20X5?

 A17-16 Implicit Interest Rate; Amortization—Income Tax Effects: On 2 January 20X2, Weymouth Limited entered into a five-year capital lease for manufacturing equipment. Details of the lease are as follows:

- The leased asset is capitalized at $995,400.
- Amortization is straight line over the life of the lease with a full-year amortization in 20X2.
- Lease payments, made each 1 January, are $249,213, and include $10,500 of maintenance costs.

Required:

1. What interest rate did the lessee use to capitalize the lease?
2. Prepare a lease amortization schedule showing interest expense and the reduction of the liability over the lease term.
3. What is the total expense relating to the lease that will appear on Weymouth's income statement for each year?

★★★

A17-17 Capital Lease, Reporting: Videos to Go signed a lease for a vehicle that had an expected economic life of eight years and a fair value of $18,000. The lessor is the leasing subsidiary of a national car manufacturer. The terms of the lease are as follows:

- The lease term begins on 1 January 20X2, and runs for five years.
- The lease requires payments of $5,800 each 1 January, including $1,700 for maintenance and insurance costs.
- At the end of the lease term, the lease is renewable for three one-year periods, for $2,600 per year, including $2,100 for maintenance and insurance. The normal rental costs for a similar used vehicle would be approximately double this amount.
- At the end of any lease term, if Videos to Go does not renew the contract, the vehicle reverts back to the lessor. The lessor may choose to leave the vehicle with Videos to Go if its value is low.

Videos to Go does not know the interest rate implicit in the lease from the lessor's perspective but has an incremental borrowing rate of 12%. Videos to Go has a 31 December year-end and uses straight-line amortization for all assets.

Required:

1. Explain why this is a capital lease for the lessee.
2. Prepare a lease amortization schedule showing how the lease liability changes over the lease term.
3. Prepare journal entries for 20X2 and 20X3.
4. Show how the lease would be reflected on the balance sheet, income statement, and CFS for 20X2 and 20X3. Segregate debt between its short-term and long-term components. Use the indirect method for operating activities in the cash flow statement.
5. How much interest expense would be reported on the income statement in each year from 20X2 to 20X10 if Videos to Go had a 31 May fiscal year-end?

★★★

A17-18 Capital Lease, Calculate Rate: Toronto Grinding Corporation (TGC) wishes to acquire a new grinding machine. The machine is available for $20,000 cash. The firm does not have sufficient cash to purchase the asset but must find financing for it. The Royal Toronto Bank of Commerce has indicated a willingness to lend TGC up to $17,000 at 10% interest. However, the firm has decided instead to lease the machine through Montrealease.

The terms of the lease are that TGC will pay Montrealease $2,861 at the beginning of each year of the 10-year lease. TGC is to pay all costs of operating the machine, including maintenance, taxes, and insurance. At the end of the 10-year lease term, Montrealease will take possession of the machine unless TGC exercises its option to renew the lease for five more years at a cost of $610 per year paid at the beginning of each year.

Grinding machines of this type are normally expected to last about 15 years. TGC uses straight-line depreciation in its accounts and uses the half-year convention maximum CCA (currently 20%) for tax purposes. The lease term begins on 2 January 20X1. TGC's fiscal year ends on 31 December.

Required:

1. Prepare entries in general journal form to record all of the transactions and adjustments relating to the lease for TGC for 20X1 and 20X2.

2. Illustrate how lease-related accounts would appear on the TGC balance sheet on 31 December 20X2.

 A17-19 Lease Accounting, Amortization Schedule, Part Year, CFS: Access 3000 Limited has decided to lease computer equipment with a fair market value of $380,000. The lease is with the Imperial Leasing Company, the leasing subsidiary of a major Canadian bank. The terms of the lease are as follows:

- The initial lease term is four years, and it is effective 1 January 20X1.
- There is a renewal term at the lessor's option for a further two years.
- Payments are $84,000 annually, made at the beginning of each lease year. Each payment includes an estimated $4,000 for insurance.
- Payments during the renewal term are $28,000, including $1,000 for insurance. Payments are made at the beginning of the lease year.
- The computer equipment reverts to the lessor at the end of each lease term, but residual value at the end of the sixth year is likely negligible.
- If Access 3000 had not leased the equipment, it would have borrowed money to finance a purchase acquisition at an interest rate of 8%.

Required:

1. Is the lease a capital lease or an operating lease for Access 3000? Why?
2. Prepare a lease amortization schedule, showing interest expense and reduction of the liability over the lease term.
3. Prepare entries for Access 3000 for 20X1, assuming Access 3000 has a 31 December year-end. Use straight-line amortization.
4. Prepare entries for Access 3000 for the calendar year 20X1, assuming Access 3000 has a 31 March year-end.
5. If the fiscal year ended on 31 December, what would appear in relation to the lease on the cash flow statement for the year ended 31 December 20X1?

  A17-20 Capital Lease, Guaranteed Residual: Lessee Limited agreed to a non-cancellable lease for which the following information is available:

a. The asset is new at the inception of the lease term and is worth $32,000.
b. Lease term is four years, starting 1 January 20X1.
c. Estimated useful life of the leased asset is six years.
d. The residual value of the leased asset will be $6,000 at the end of the lease term. The residual value is guaranteed by Lessee Limited.
e. The declining-balance depreciation method is used for the leased asset, at a rate of 30% per year.
f. Lessee's incremental borrowing rate is 10%.
g. Four annual lease payments will be made each 1 January during the lease term, and the first payment, due at inception of the lease term, is $8,626, including $1,100 of maintenance costs.
h. Lessee has a 31 December fiscal year-end.

Required:

1. Is this an operating lease or a capital lease? Explain.
2. Prepare a table showing how the lease liability reduces over the lease term. Record the entries for 20X1.
3. Prepare the financial statement presentation of all lease-related accounts as they would appear in the financial statements of the lessee at 31 December 20X1. Include note disclosure. Ignore income taxes.

★★ **A17-21 Sale and Leaseback:** Central Purchasing Limited owns the building it uses; it had an original cost of $825,000 and a net book value of $450,000 as of 1 January 20X2. On this date, the building was sold to the Royal Leasing Company for $500,000 and simultaneously leased back to Central Purchasing Limited.

The lease has a guaranteed, 12-year term and required payments on 31 December of each year. The payments are $76,500, and the lease allows the property to revert to the lessee at the end of the lease. Central Purchasing could have mortgaged this property under similar terms at an interest rate of 9%. The Royal Leasing Company will pay property taxes estimated to be $6,200 per year. These costs are included in the lease payment. Central will pay maintenance and operating costs. The building is being amortized straight line, with an estimated remaining life of 15-years.

Required:

1. Prepare entries to record the sale and leaseback of the building.
2. Prepare year-end adjusting entries for 20X2.
3. Show how all amounts related to the sale and leaseback will be presented on the balance sheet, income statement, and cash flow statement in 20X2.

★★ **A17-22 Sale and Leaseback:** Sportco Limited is suffering temporary cash flow difficulties due to poor economic conditions. To raise sufficient capital to allow operations to continue until economic conditions improve, Sportco entered into an agreement with a major lease corporation, Leaseco Limited. On 1 January 20X2, Sportco sold its largest manufacturing property to Leaseco at its fair market value, $1,750,000. The property had a net book value of $250,000 at the time of the sale.

Sportco, in turn, leased back the property from Leaseco for 15 years. The annual rent was $175,000, due each year starting on 1 January 20X2. Sportco can repurchase the property from Leaseco at the end of the lease term. The repurchase price (stated in the lease contract) is $2,500,000, based on projected fair values for the property. The land value is estimated to be 40% of the total fair market value of the property, while the building represents the other 60%. Sportco amortizes its buildings at a declining-balance rate of 10%.

Sportco's incremental borrowing rate is 7%. Its financial statements are prepared in accordance with generally accepted accounting standards.

Required:

How should Sportco account for this transaction in its financial statements for the year ending 31 December 20X2? Be specific, and explain the approach that you have chosen. Ignore any income tax issues and disclosure issues.

(CICA)

★★★ **A17-23 Sale and Leaseback:** On 31 March 20X2, Supergrocery Inc. sold its major distribution facility, with a 30-year remaining life, to National Leasing Company for $9,000,000 cash. The facility had an original cost of $10,400,000 and accumulated depreciation of $3,600,000 on the date of sale.

Also on 31 March 20X2, Supergrocery signed a 20-year lease agreement with National Leasing Company, leasing the property back. At the end of the 20-year lease term, legal title to the facility will be transferred to Supergrocery. Annual payments, beginning on 31 March 20X2, are $875,000. Maintenance and repair costs are the responsibility of Supergrocery. Supergrocery has an incremental interest rate of 9%. The company uses straight-line depreciation and has a 31 December year-end. Supergrocery records a part-year's depreciation, based on the date of acquisition, whenever it buys capital assets.

Required:

1. Give the 20X2 entries that Supergrocery Incorporated would make to record the sale and the lease.

2. Give the entries Supergrocery would make in 20X3 and 20X4 in relation to this transaction.

3. Show how the balance sheet and income statement would reflect the transactions at the end of 20X2, 20X3, and 20X4. Do not segregate balance sheet items between short-term and long-term items.

A17-24 Capital versus Operating Lease: Bellanger Corporation has signed two leases in the past year. One lease is for computer equipment, the other for a vehicle.

The computer equipment has a fair market value of $27,400. Lease payments are made each 2 January, the date the lease was signed. The lease is a two-year arrangement, requiring payments of $11,500 per year on each 2 January, and can be renewed at the lessor's option for subsequent one-year terms up to three times, at a cost of $2,250 per year. At the end of any lease term, the equipment reverts back to the lessor. Annual maintenance and insurance costs are paid by the lessor, and amount to $500 per year for the first two years, and $250 per year thereafter. These costs are included in the lease payments.

Bellanger estimates that the equipment has a useful life of seven years, but acknowledges that since technology changes so quickly, the equipment would be out of date after seven years. On the other hand, management does not foresee the need to continually upgrade to state-of-the-art technology.

The vehicle lease is for a company car that has a list price of $22,700 but could be bought for a cash payment of $21,000. The annual lease payment, due at the end of each lease year, is $3,000. The lease required a one-time upfront payment of $4,000, due and paid on 1 January, the day the lease was signed. The lease is a four-year lease. If more than 25,000 kilometres are put on the car in any one-year period, a payment of $0.27 per extra kilometre must be paid in addition to the annual rental. All maintenance costs are covered by warranty.

At the end of the four-year lease agreement, Bellanger may, at its option, sign a further two-year lease agreement for the car at an annual rate of $2,400 per year, again payable at the end of the lease term. This is about the going rate for used-car leases. The annual rental includes $300 for maintenance costs.

If Bellanger does not renew the lease, or at the end of the second lease term, the vehicle reverts to the lessor, who will either sell the vehicle or re-lease it. The vehicle has an estimated 10-year useful life.

Bellanger uses 30% declining-balance depreciation for computer technology, and straight-line depreciation for vehicles. Bellanger has an 8% incremental borrowing rate.

Required:

1. Classify each lease as a capital or operating lease. Justify your response.

2. Show how each lease would be reflected in the financial statements—income statement, balance sheet, and cash flow statement—at the end of the first year. Assume that 32,000 kilometres were put on the car in this year and the additional contingent rental was paid by the end of the year.

A17-25 Operating and Capital Leases: Filmon Furnishings Limited is a small furniture company in Sudbury. The accountant is getting ready for the audit of the fiscal year ended 31 December 20X2 and must make appropriate adjustments to the Rental Expense account:

	Rental Expense
2 January 20X2	5,000
November 20X2	2,000
December 20X2	2,000
	$9,000

The payment on 2 January 20X2 related to a rental contract signed for a delivery van. The contract requires annual payments of $5,000 per year, each 2 January for four years. These payments include $600 for maintenance, but Filmon is responsible for insurance payments of $1,400 per year. At the end of the four-year rental contract, Filmon may choose to sign a second rental contract for $2,000 per year for two years, including $900 of maintenance. The normal rental cost of four-year-old vehicles is almost double this amount, excluding maintenance. At the end of the rental contract, the van must be returned to the renter. Its value would be very minimal at the end of the second rental contract, as the van would be almost worn out.

The payments in November and December 20X2 are monthly rental payments on the large, warehouse-style sales facility that represents Filmon's primary location. The warehouse itself is owned by a related company, Filmon Properties Limited, which the major shareholder of Filmon Furnishings Limited controls. The rental agreement, signed in January 20X2, requires three monthly payments of $2,000 in 20X2, payments of $3,500 per month in 20X3, and payments of $5,000 in 20X4, the final year of the rental agreement. The agreement states that no rent need be paid for the first nine months of 20X2. One payment is still owing, but not yet accrued, on 31 December 20X2.

Filmon has existing term loans with the Bank of Ontario at an interest rate of 8%.

Required:

1. Provide adjusting journal entries to correct the Rental Expense account and properly reflect the substance of the rental contracts on the books. Justify your decisions, where appropriate. Filmon amortizes all assets using the straight-line method.

2. Show how the rental contracts would be reflected on the income statement, balance sheet, and cash flow statement at 31 December 20X2. Be sure to segregate debt between long-term and short-term portions.

★★★ **A17-26 Cash Flow Statement Review:** Laker had the following information available at the end of 20X5:

Comparative balance sheets, as of 31 December

	20X5	20X4
Cash	$ 3,000	$ 800
Accounts receivable	3,500	2,590
Short-term investments*	4,000	6,000
Inventory	8,400	7,000
Prepaid rent	600	2,400
Prepaid insurance	420	180
Office supplies	200	150
Net lease receivable	25,000	35,000
Land and building	70,000	70,000
Accumulated amortization	(21,000)	(17,500)
Equipment	105,000	80,000
Accumulated amortization	(26,000)	(22,400)
Patent	9,000	10,000
Total assets	$182,120	$174,220
Accounts payable	$ 5,400	$ 6,400
Taxes payable	1,000	800
Wages payable	1,000	600
Short-term notes payable	2,000	2,000
Long-term notes payable	12,000	14,000
Bonds payable	80,000	80,000
Premium on bonds payable	4,060	5,170
Common shares	52,000	47,500
Retained earnings	24,660	17,750
Total liabilities and equity	$182,120	$174,220

*Not cash equivalents

Income statement information for year ended 31 December 20X5

	20X5	20X4
Sales revenue		$231,850
Cost of goods sold		149,583
Gross margin		82,267
Selling expenses	$15,840	
Administrative expenses	31,340	
Amortization expense	8,100	55,280
Income from operations		26,987
Gain on sale of short-term investments	800	
Lease finance revenue	5,080	
Interest expense	(13,350)	7,470
Income before taxes		19,517
Income tax expense		7,807
Net income		$ 11,710
Dividends paid		4,800
Increase in retained earnings		$ 6,910

Required:

Prepare a cash flow statement, using the indirect method to disclose operating activities.

 A17-27 Cash Flow Statement Review: Each of the following items must be considered in preparing a cash flow statement for Phillie Fashions for the year ended 31 December 20X6:

1. Capital assets that had a cost of $10,000 6½ years before and were being amortized straight-line on a 10-year basis, with no estimated scrap value, were sold for $3,125.

2. Phillie Company leased an asset to a customer, as a way of selling it, on 31 December 20X6. Phillie recognized a net receivable of $23,456, after the first payment of $8,700. The $8,700 payment was collected on 31 December. The gross profit on the sale was $5,670. There was unearned finance revenue of $6,200 over the lease term, which lasts four years.

3. During the year, goodwill of $5,000 was completely written off to expense.

4. During the year, 250 shares of common stock were issued for $32 per share.

5. Capital asset amortization amounted to $1,000, and patent amortization to $200.

6. Bonds payable with a par value of $12,000, on which there was an unamortized bond premium of $360, were redeemed at 103.

7. Phillie Company, as lessee, reported a net lease liability of $14,678 at the end of 20X6. In 20X5, the liability had been $15,766. The current portion of the liability was $2,410 each year.

Required:

For each item, state what would be included in the cash flow statement, whether it is an inflow or outflow, and the amount(s). Assume that correct entries were made for all transactions as they took place and that the indirect method is to be used to disclose cash flow from operations. In your response, use a three-column format as follows:

Operating/Investing/Financing	Inflow/Outflow	Amount

★★ **A17-28 Classification (Appendix):** Details of two leases follow:

Lease 1 is between the Canadian Leasing Company, as lessor, and the Office Supply Company, as lessee. Year-end payments are $34,000 each year for three years, and the Canadian Leasing Company will pay approximately $1,500 per year on insurance and maintenance contracts. At the end of the three-year lease contract, the leased asset will revert to the Canadian Leasing Company, which will sell it to a used-equipment dealer for approximately $35,000. The equipment had a list price of $95,000 at the beginning of the lease but could have been bought outright for $89,000. Office Supply Company has been in business for six years and has an acceptable credit rating.

Lease 2 is between the Ardmore Furniture Company, as lessor, and the Centurion Sales Company, as lessee. The lease is for office furniture with a list price of $80,000. Centurion is required to make 1 January payments of $7,500 each year for 15 years. These payments include $250 for insurance. At the end of the 15 years, the office equipment, which Ardmore manufactured at a cost of $52,000, will be relatively worthless. Centurion Sales is a new organization, with a poor credit rating and is unable to obtain a bank loan to buy the equipment outright.

Required:

Classify each of the above leases from the perspective of the lessor and describe the appropriate accounting treatment. State any necessary assumptions.

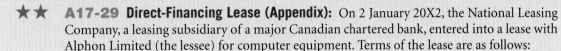 **A17-29 Direct-Financing Lease (Appendix):** On 2 January 20X2, the National Leasing Company, a leasing subsidiary of a major Canadian chartered bank, entered into a lease with Alphon Limited (the lessee) for computer equipment. Terms of the lease are as follows:

- The initial lease term is two years, with payments due each 31 December, at the end of each lease year.
- Payments are $16,000 per year, including $2,000 for maintenance costs.
- The lease is renewable for a further three years at the option of National Leasing Company, for $9,000 per year.
- At the end of the second lease term, the computer equipment will likely have a $1,000 value. National Leasing Company will resell the equipment at this time.
- National Leasing Company bought the equipment from Command Computers for $46,550 in order to lease it to Alphon.

Assume that the maintenance cost is paid by National Leasing Company to a third party every 31 December. Assume also that the National Leasing Company has a 31 December year-end.

Required:

1. What interest rate is implicit in the lease?
2. Prepare an amortization schedule that shows how the net lease receivable is reduced over the life of the lease.
3. Prepare journal entries to record the lease for 20X2 and 20X3 using the net method.
4. Prepare journal entries to record the lease for 20X2 and 20X3 using the gross method.

A17-30 Direct-Financing Lease (Appendix): On 31 December 20X1, Lessor Limited leased a jutling machine to a client for six years at $40,900 per year. Lease payments are to be made at the beginning of each lease year. Lessor purchased the machine for $200,000. Lessor negotiated the lease so as to receive a return of 9% on the investment. Lessor anticipates no significant salvage value or removal costs at the end of the lease term.

Required:

1. Prepare an amortization schedule for the lease receivable, assuming that the lease is a capital lease.
2. Prepare journal entries to record the lease transactions for 20X1 through 20X2, assuming that the lease receivable is recorded by Lessor on the net method.
3. Repeat requirement (2) but assuming instead that the lease receivable is recorded on the gross method.
4. How would the amounts relating to the lease be shown on Lessor's balance sheet at 31 December 20X3? Assume that the lessor has an unclassified balance sheet.

★★★

A17-31 Direct Financing Lease—Lessee and Lessor (Appendix): On 2 January 20X4, Yvan Limited entered into a five-year lease for office equipment from Jeffery Leasing Incorporation. The lease calls for annual lease payments of $100,000, payable at the beginning of each lease year. Yvan's incremental borrowing rate is 6%. The lessor's implicit rate in the lease is also 6%. The fair value of the equipment is $450,000. Yvan Limited amortizes office equipment on a straight-line basis.

Required:

1. Prepare the lease liability amortization schedule for Yvan Limited.
2. What amounts will appear on Yvan Limited's balance sheet, income statement, and cash flow statement as of 31 December 20X4?
3. Prepare the journal entries relating to the leased asset and the lease liability for 20X5 for Yvan Limited. Use the net method of recording the liability.
4. Prepare the journal entries relating to the lease for Jeffrey Leasing Incorporated for 20X5. Use the gross method of recording the leased asset.

★★ **A17-32 Direct Financing Lease—Lessee and Lessor (Appendix):** Sondheim Limited entered into a direct financing lease with New Age Leasing Corporation. The lease is for new specialized factory equipment that has a fair value of $3,200,000. The expected useful life of the equipment is 15 years, although its physical life is far greater. The initial lease term begins on 1 April 20X2 and runs for 10 years. Annual lease payments are $400,000, payable at the beginning of each lease year. After the initial lease term, Sondheim has the option of renewing the lease on a year-by-year basis for as long as Sondheim wishes. Since the equipment will be obsolete by that time, the renewal is set at $10,000 per year, which is expected to be a fair rental value for equipment of that age. Other information is as follows:

- Sondheim's incremental borrowing rate is 6%.
- The implicit pre-tax interest rate in the lease is 7%, but this rate is not known to Sondheim.
- Sondheim will amortize the equipment on a straight-line basis, charging half-year amortization in the first year.

Required:

1. Prepare the journal entries relating to the lease liability and the leased equipment for Sondheim for 20X2 including all appropriate adjusting entries. Use the net method of recording.
2. What amounts will appear on Sondheim's balance sheet and cash flow statement at 31 December 20X2? Assume that Sondheim uses the indirect approach to determining cash flow from operating activities.
3. Prepare the journal entries relating to the lease for New Age for 20X2. Use the gross method of recording. What is the net amount of lease receivable that will appear on New Age's balance sheet on 31 December 20X2?

★★ **A17-33 Sales-Type Lease (Appendix):** Jordin Company is an equipment dealer that sometimes uses leasing as a means to sell its products. On 1 January 20X1, Jordin leased equipment to Easten Corporation. The lease term was four years with annual lease payments of $5,769 to be paid on each 31 December. The equipment has an estimated zero residual value at the end of the lease term. The equipment was carried in Jordin's accounts at a cost of $20,000. Jordin expects to collect all rentals from Easten, and there were no material cost uncertainties at the inception of the lease. The implicit interest rate in the lease was 11%.

Required:

1. Why is this a sales-type lease for Jordin?
2. How much is the gross profit or loss recognized by Jordin? The finance revenue recognized over the life of the lease?

3. Assume that the implicit interest rate is 4% (not 11%). How much is the gross profit or loss recognized by Jordin? The finance revenue recognized over the life of the lease?

4. Give the entries made by Jordan Company (based on the 11% rate) at the inception of the lease. Use the gross method.

★★ **A17-34 Direct-Financing Lease; Lessor, Lessee (Appendix):** Parravano Incorporated has leased a serging machine from Xerox Leasing Corporation for annual beginning-of-year payments of $15,000 for 10 years. The lease term begins on 1 January 20X2. Parravano's fiscal year ends on 31 December. Parravano's incremental borrowing rate is 10% per annum. The fair value of a new serging machine is $102,000, including PST, GST, and delivery. The lease will be reported by both the lessee and the lessor as a direct-financing capital lease. Parravano depreciates its serging machines on the straight-line basis, using the half-year convention.

Required:

1. Show all amounts relating to the lease and the leased asset that will appear on the balance sheet and income statement of Parravano for the year ending 31 December 20X5.

2. Show all amounts relating to the lease that will appear on the balance sheet and income statement of Xerox Leasing Corporation at 31 December 20X5. The lessor uses the gross method of recording leases. The interest rate implicit in the lease is 10%.

★★★ **A17-35 Classification, Lessor and Lessee Financial Statements (Appendix):** Lessor and lessee agreed to a non-cancellable lease for which the following information is available:

a. Lessor's cost of the asset leased is $40,308. The asset is new at the inception of the lease term.
b. Lease term is three years, starting 2 January 20X3.
c. Estimated useful life of the leased asset is six years.
d. On 2 January 20X3, the lessor estimated that the residual value of the leased asset would be $6,000 on the renewal option date (see (h) below) and zero at the end of its useful life. The residual value is not guaranteed.
e. The straight-line depreciation method is used for the leased asset.
f. Lessee's incremental borrowing rate is 7.5%. Lessee has an excellent credit rating.
g. Lessor's interest rate implicit in the lease is 8%. Lessee does not know this rate.
h. Renewal option, exercisable on 2 January 20X6, is for three years with an annual payment of $1,200 each 1 January. No insurance costs are included, as these will be the lessee's responsibility in the renewal period. This is a bargain renewal option.
i. Title to the leased asset is retained by the lessor.
j. Lessor has no unreimbursable cost uncertainties.
k. Annual lease payments will be made each 2 January during the lease term, which is three years. Payments will include $1,100 of estimated insurance costs for the first three years.
l. The lessor paid $2,200 in initial direct costs.

Required:

1. Calculate the annual payment that would be required for the first three years of the lease term.
2. Is this an operating lease or a capital lease to the lessee? Explain. Compute the lessee's capitalizable cost of the leased asset.
3. What type of lease is this to the lessor? Explain.
4. Prepare an amortization schedule showing how the lessor's net lease receivable would reduce over the life of the lease.
5. Show all lease-related accounts as they would appear in the balance sheet and income statement of the lessee and the lessor at 31 December 20X3, for the year then ended. The lessor's balance sheet is unclassified.

CHAPTER 18

Pensions and Other Post-Retirement Benefits

INTRODUCTION

Many companies promise to provide their employees certain benefits after they retire. The most common form of *post-retirement benefit* is a pension. However, a company may also provide other post-retirement benefits such as life insurance or extended health care. These benefits are provided as compensation for employees' *pre-retirement* services. Post-retirement benefits are a form of deferred compensation. Therefore, the cost of post-retirement benefits should be recognized in the periods during which the employee is working. This is one of the most problematic measurements in accounting.

The challenges arise from the fact that the pension benefits will actually be paid far in the future; it is difficult to measure the *present cost* of those *future benefits*. Some of the projections that have to be made are retention rates, mortality rates, retirement trends, future interest rates, and rates of return on fund assets. Accounting for post-retirement benefits is an exercise in estimation and judgement.

To make matters more complicated, there are several different methods of measuring and allocating pension cost, known as *actuarial cost methods*. Every actuarial method allocates the future estimated cost of post-retirement benefits to the years

of an employee's service. However, each actuarial method provides a different funding pattern. (For those readers who want a better understanding of actuarial methodology, a unit in the Online Learning Centre illustrates the three basic actuarial methods.)

Pension plans are big business. For example, ACE Aviation Holdings, the parent company to Air Canada, reports total assets on the balance sheet of $13.4 billion at the end of 2006, and shareholders' equity of $1.6 billion. The disclosure notes to the financial statements show that the pension plan, whose assets and liabilities are not recorded by ACE, has assets of $11.8 billion and obligations of $13.2 billion, making it pretty much just as large as the employer operation. The pension plan is underfunded by $1.4 billion, only slightly less than the recorded equity of the employer company.

This chapter focuses primarily on accounting for pensions, but includes an example of other post-retirement benefits. The general structure of pension calculations and assumptions are analyzed, various components of pension expense are explored, and a spreadsheet is introduced that helps to organize pension data. The extensive disclosure requirements for post-retirement benefits are reviewed.

TYPES OF PENSION PLANS

There are two general types of pension plans:

1. Defined contribution plans, and

2. Defined benefit plans.

A **defined contribution plan** is one in which the employer (and often the employee) make agreed-upon (or *defined*) cash contributions to the plan each period, which are invested by a trustee on behalf of the employee. For example, a plan might provide that the employer will contribute 6% of the employee's salary to the pension plan each year. The pension that the employee eventually receives as a result of those contributions is a function of the trustee's investment success; the pension annuity is determined by the amount of accumulated contributions plus earnings on those contributions at the time that the employee retires.

A **defined benefit plan** is one in which the eventual *benefits* to the employee are stated in the pension plan. The benefits are normally calculated on the basis of the employee's salary at or near retirement and the length of her or his employment with the company. It is the employer's responsibility to pay for this pension. For example, a company may provide that an employee will receive an annual pension that is equal to 2% of the employee's final year's salary for each year of service. If the employee is earning $100,000 in the year before retirement and has worked for the company for 35 years, the annual pension will be:

Annual pension annuity = $100,000 × 2% × 35 years = $70,000

The essential difference between the two types of plans can be summarized as follows:

Type of Plan	Contributions	Benefits
Defined contribution	Fixed	Variable
Defined benefit	Variable	Fixed

Since defined benefit plans entitle the employee to a specified (or *defined*) pension, the challenge for the employer is to make payments into the plan that will eventually provide enough money to pay the pension. If the plan trustee is not very successful in investing the money, then the company will have to provide more money to make up any deficiency. On the other hand, investment returns that are larger than expected will reduce the employer's necessary contributions to the plan.

The task of figuring out how much the employer should contribute to a defined benefit plan is the task of the **actuary**. An *actuary* is a person who calculates statistical risks, life expectancy, payout probabilities, etc. Actuaries are typically employed by insurance agencies and other financial institutions. Actuarial science is a well-established and well-recognized profession, with a rigorous multi-stage qualification process.

PENSION VARIABLES

Contributory versus Non-Contributory

A **contributory pension plan** is one in which the *employee* makes contributions to the plan, in addition to those made by the employer. Defined contribution plans often are contributory. This works to the employees' advantage, since any amounts paid into a defined contribution plan will increase the eventual pension. The other alternative is that the pension plan is **non-contributory**; the cost of the pension is borne entirely by the employer, and the employee pays nothing.

Vesting

Pension plan benefits are said to be **vested** when the employee has the right to receive her or his pension entitlement even if she or he leaves the employer before retirement age. The pension is not actually paid until retirement, of course, but the funds in the pension plan are "earmarked" for that individual or rolled into the individual's RRSP. Many provinces require that benefits be vested under two separate circumstances:

1. Any contributions to a pension plan made by an *employee* are automatically vested.

2. The *employer's* contributions become vested when the employee has worked for the same employer for 10 years *and* has reached age 45. This is known as the 10+45 rule. An important effect of this rule is that it prevents an employer from getting rid of a long-term employee just prior to retirement in order to save on pension payouts.

Some provinces require much faster vesting of employer's contributions (e.g., after only two years in Ontario). Of course, employers may voluntarily commit themselves to faster vesting than provincial legislation requires.

Trusteed

Most pension plans are **trusteed**, which means that there is an independent **trustee** who receives the pension contributions from the employer (and, if appropriate, from the employee), invests the contributions in accordance with provincial regulations and agreed-upon guidelines, and pays out benefits to the pensioner. Trustees of pension funds are often financial institutions such as trust companies and banks; a pension trustee is not an individual person. Most plans are trusteed:

- A plan must be trusteed in order for the employer to be able to deduct pension plan contributions from taxable income.
- Trusteeship is required for a plan to be registered.
- From an accounting perspective, if a pension plan is not trusteed and instead is administered by the company, the company must report both the pension plan assets and the accrued pension liability on its balance sheet because the assets are under the control of the company. When a plan is administered by a trustee, however, the plan assets are beyond control of the company's managers; neither the plan assets nor the pension liability are reported on the employer's balance sheet.

Trusteeship does not absolve the employer of responsibility to ensure that a defined benefit pension plan is solvent and is able to pay out the benefits when they come due.

Registered

Pension plans normally are **registered** with the pension commissioner in the province of jurisdiction. The commissioner's office is responsible for seeing that the pension plan abides by pension legislation, including requirements for funding, reporting, trusteeship, actuarial valuation, and control over surpluses.

An important benefit of registration is that it also enables the company to deduct from taxable income amounts contributed to the plan. If the plan is not registered, the employer cannot deduct the pension contributions; tax deductions will come only when the pension is actually paid to the employee or when a pension annuity is purchased on behalf of the employee at the retirement date. Since pension contributions are material, this would delay the tax deduction for the company and would be highly undesirable!

1. Give two examples of post-retirement benefits other than pensions.

2. Explain the difference between a defined contribution pension plan and a defined benefit pension plan.

3. Why is trusteeship critical when accounting for pensions?

4. What is the risk to an employee if pension rights are not vested?

5. Who makes contributions to the pension plan if it is non-contributory?

DEFINED CONTRIBUTION PLANS

Defined contribution plans have been increasing in popularity with employers because they have lower financial risk. Defined contribution pension plans are relatively easy to deal with for accounting purposes. Because the amount of the contribution is known, there is little uncertainty about either the cash flow or the accounting measurement. The one uncertainty that does arise is that if the plan is not fully vested from the start of an individual's employment with the company, it will be necessary to estimate the probable portion of individuals who will stay with the company long enough for the pension to become vested.

Current Service Cost is Pension Expense

Aside from the one wrinkle of vesting, the contribution (i.e., the employer's annual cash outflow) is readily determinable from the terms of the pension plan. The accounting expense flows from the contribution; *the amount of the contribution is treated as an expense on the income statement.* The employer's required contribution for services rendered during the period is known as the *current service cost* for the period.

Ordinarily, the employer pays the full amount of the current service cost into the pension plan in the current year. However, sometimes payments are made after the fiscal year-end. If some of the funding for the current year's services is to be paid into the plan in future years, the current service cost is the amount of the current payments plus the present value of future payments. The difference between the present value of the year's contribution and the amount actually paid is recognized as a liability. The discount rate is based on market interest rates for high-quality debt instruments of similar amount and timing. Payments to be made within the next year are not discounted.

Example Suppose that Enterprise Fourchu Limité (EFL) pays $60,000 into the pension plan at the end of 20X1 for 20X1 services rendered. This is the simplest case, and the entry is straightforward:

Pension expense	60,000	
Cash		60,000

Be careful to expense only amounts relating to the *current* year's service; there may well be an agreement covering 20X2, but it would not be recorded as a liability in 20X1.

Now, assume that EFL has agreed to pay $60,000 at the end of 20X1 and *also* agrees to make another payment of $40,000 *relating to employees' 20X1 services* at the end of 20X4. Assuming an interest rate of 6%, the present value of the future payment is $40,000 \times (P/F, 6\%, 3) = \$33,585$. The entry to record 20X1 pension expense will be:

Pension expense	93,585	
Cash		60,000
Accrued pension liability		33,585

Other Elements of Expense for a Defined Contribution Plan

There may be three other elements of expense for a defined contribution pension plan, although *these elements are rare.* These elements are past service cost, interest expense, and plan earnings.

Past Service Cost When a pension plan is first established (or *initiated*), an employer may agree to make contributions in the future that relate to employees' past services. For example, when EFL first established the pension plan, the company might have agreed to contribute $5,000 into the pension plan for each year of an employee's prior employment. These costs are called *past service costs.* Past service costs are allocated in a rational and systematic manner over the period that the company expects to benefit. The most commonly used amortization period is the length of time that, on average, the employees are expected to continue working for the company. This period is called the *average remaining service period* (ARSP).

Interest Expense When an entity has obligations that must be made in future periods as a result of employee services rendered during the current period or past periods, the entity must recognize interest on those accrued contributions. This is part of pension expense, not a separate interest expense. Interest is calculated by using the same rate that was used in discounting the obligation in the first place. Note the $33,585 pension liability recognized by EFL, above. In 20X2 EFL will record interest of $33,585 \times 6\% = \$2,015$ as a part of pension expense.

Plan Earnings A defined contribution plan's assets, and the earnings on those assets, are normally entirely committed to paying pension benefits to employees, and thus no special accounting for the investment revenue is required, or allowed. In special circumstances, though, there may be *an unassigned surplus* of assets in the plan. This might happen if past service costs were being funded over a period of years, and contributions were higher than needed. That is, *in rare circumstances* there would be assets in a contributory pension plan that would really accrue to the company, not the employees. If this were to happen, then investment earnings *on the unassigned assets* (not total assets) would be calculated, and reduce pension expense.

DEFINED BENEFIT PLANS—STRUCTURE

A defined benefit pension plan consists of the pension fund assets, placed with a trustee, and the post-retirement obligation to employees. This asset and liability do not constitute an accounting entity, so there are no accounting statements for the pension fund itself. Instead, accountants grapple with how and when to report the asset and liability, and the changes in the asset and liability, in the financial statements of the sponsoring employer. While these issues are explored in depth as this chapter progresses, it helps at this point to have a clear view of the two "sides" to the pension fund itself.

Pension Plan Assets The assets of a pension fund increase when the employer or the employee makes contributions to the trustee, and when the assets generate return. The assets can decline if the plan generates a negative return, and assets also decline when benefits are paid to pensioners.

Pension Plan Obligation The obligation of a pension plan to its members is measured as the *expected present value* of payments to be made to members when they retire. It increases each year that the employee works, and earns more pension, and also increases annually for an interest component. It can increase or decrease when experience to date is different than the original estimate, and also increase or decrease when future estimates about mortality, future salary levels, and so on change. It will decrease when benefits are paid to retirees.

DEFINED BENEFIT PLANS—ACTUARIAL METHODS

Probability Factors

In a defined benefit plan, the future benefit is known, but the annual contributions that are necessary to provide that defined future benefit must be estimated. Such estimates are made using complex mathematical models called **actuarial cost methods,** which link the terms of the pension plan to annual contributions. In these actuarial cost methods, many factors must be taken into account in order to estimate the current cost of the distant benefit. A few of the more important ones are as follows:

- *Investment earnings.* The higher the earnings on the plan assets, the less that will have to be contributed to the plan. Because of the long time period involved, even a small change in the assumed interest rate can have a significant impact on the current contributions and accounting expense.

- *Future salary increases.* Since pension benefits are often tied to the employee's future earnings, it is necessary to estimate (or *project*) the future salary increases. Salary increases are always dependent, at least in part, on inflation rates. Therefore, it also is necessary to estimate future inflation rates.

- *Employee turnover.* Vesting does not usually occur immediately in defined benefit plans. Therefore, it is necessary to estimate what proportion of employees will stay long enough for vesting to occur.

- *Mortality rates.* Mortality may be connected with vesting; if an employee dies before vesting occurs, then there may be no liability. However, a pension plan may specify **death benefits** or **survivor benefits** that give lump-sum or continuing benefits to a surviving spouse, partner, and/or child. The mortality rate and the extent of any trailing entitlements must be estimated.

- *Life expectancy after retirement.* The longer a retired employee lives after retirement, the more must be paid out in pension. Some pension plans pass this risk on to insurance companies by purchasing a life annuity on behalf of the employee at retirement; then if the employee lives longer than expected, it is the insurance company's problem. In other cases, the pension fund retains the risk and it must be estimated by the actuary.

It is the job of the actuary to make all of the estimates necessary for the measurement of pension funding and pension cost. However, an accountant should be particularly concerned about the first two factors in the list above: (1) the return on plan assets and (2) the projected rate of salary increases, because these components have a significant impact on the accounting measurements.

Actuaries often are required to be quite conservative, and may estimate the return on plan assets on the low side and the projected rate of salary increases on the high side. The company need not use the same estimates for accounting purposes that are used by its actuaries for funding purposes.

death benefits

a component of pension plan contracts that allows for special lump-sum or continuing benefits to be paid to a beneficiary upon the death of a pension plan member

---

ETHICAL ISSUES

The estimates used by management for accounting must be *best estimates* and must be internally consistent. For example, since the return on plan assets, inflation rates, and salary increases are related over the long run, it would make little sense to use a high estimated return on plan assets (which would include a high inflation allowance) while also assuming a very low rate of increase in salaries (which would imply a low future inflation rate). There is always room for bias in estimates, and there may be a corporate motive to minimize or maximize pension amounts. This objective can sometimes be met through manipulation of estimates, and care must be taken when looking at the quality of best estimates.

Funding versus Accounting

In approaching the issue of pension accounting for defined benefit plans, it is extremely important to keep the accounting measurements separate from plan funding. **Funding** is the manner in which the actuary, on behalf of the employer, sets the necessary contributions to the plan. The accounting measurements determine pension expense, and do not have to be equal to funding. Similar factors and the same family of actuarial methods may be used for both—or not. Understanding pension accounting requires understanding pension funding, because they do interact.

Funding Approaches There are several actuarial cost methods that actuaries can use to calculate the cash contributions that a company must make. It is important to emphasize that no one method is "better" than another; all methods provide full funding of benefits.

However, there is a significant difference between various actuarial cost methods in the *pattern* of payments made to the trustee over an employee's working life. If one particular actuarial cost method requires higher cash contributions in the early years of an employee's tenure with the company, it could be viewed as more fiscally conservative. Other actuarial cost methods require the bulk of the funding later in the employee's working life. All methods are acceptable for funding under pension legislation, and all are used in practice.

The three basic actuarial cost methods that can be used for funding can be described briefly as follows:

1. The **accumulated benefit method** calculates the contributions that an employer must make in order to fund the pension to which the employee currently is entitled, based on the *actual* years of service to date and on the *current* salary.

2. The **projected benefit method** calculates the required funding based on the *actual* years of service to date but on a *projected* estimate of the employee's salary at the retirement date.

3. The **level contribution method** projects both the *final salary* and the *total* years of service, and then allocates the cost evenly over the years of service.

Clearly, the level contribution method involves more projections, and the accumulated benefit method involves fewer projections.

Basis for Pension Entitlements In a defined benefit pension plan, the annual pension paid may be based on a percentage of final year's salary. Pension plans that give pensions that are based on the final year's salary are called **final pay pension plans**. Different formulas to determine the pension are possible. For example, the pension could be calculated on the basis of:

flat benefit pension plan

a pension plan in which the employee is entitled to benefits based on years of service (rather than salary levels)

- **Flat benefit** per year of service, with no entitlement related to salary;
- Career average pay—that is, an average of the employee's earnings over the entire time spent with the employer;
- The best year's earnings (which permits employees to phase out toward the end of their careers); or
- An average of the last five (or three, or whatever) years' earnings.

BASIC EXAMPLE

To illustrate the three actuarial cost methods, consider a basic illustration of a defined benefit pension. Assume that an employee named Chris begins working for Celebrities Limited at age 30. Assume the following:

- Chris's starting salary is $25,000 per year.
- The normal retirement age at Celebrities is 65.
- The pension plan provides that an employee will receive an annual pension of 2% of the final year's salary for each year of service.
- The pension is fully vested from the date of employment.

Some additional estimates are needed, which are provided by the actuary:

- The estimated life expectancy after retirement is 14 years.
- The expected return on the investment in pension plan assets will be 6%.
- Chris's salary will increase by a compound average annual rate of 3%.
- Chris will work for Celebrities for 35 years, until normal retirement age.

Comparison of Methods

The calculation details for each of the three methods are explained in a unit on the Online Learning Centre. Exhibit 18-1 summarizes the funding required under each of the actuarial cost methods at selected ages.

EXHIBIT 18-1

COMPARISON OF FUNDING REQUIREMENTS FOR CURRENT SERVICE USING DIFFERENT ACTUARIAL COST METHODS

| Chris's Age | Allocated Funding under Each Method | | |
	Accumulated Benefit	Projected Benefit	Level Contribution
30	$ 679	$ 1,856	$4,227
35	1,207	2,484	4,227
40	2,111	3,324	4,227
45	3,645	4,448	4,227
50	6,228	5,953	4,227
55	10,551	7,966	4,227
60	17,748	10,660	4,227
64	26,786	13,458	4,227

The allocation patterns are very different, and yet each method results in full funding over the years of service. The accumulated benefit method and the projected benefit method both start with low payments and end with high payments. This pattern is most extreme with the accumulated benefit method. The level contribution method, as the name states, requires the same funding each year.

Bear in mind that the calculation is for just one employee, which is unrealistic. A company's overall pension funding requirement is calculated for the employee group as a whole. Employees just entering the workforce may have low pension amounts attributable to their service, which will offset the apparently dramatic increase in amounts for older employees. For an employee group as a whole, the relative difference in pension amounts between methods will level out if the employee group is stable and has an even age composition. However, the age and length-of-employment composition of employee groups are often unstable; there are usually more employees at the lower-experience levels of employment than at the senior levels. In practice, the differences between methods do not even out.

Remember, a company may use *any* actuarial cost method to determine funding.

Sensitivity to Assumptions

The calculations are extremely sensitive to basic assumptions within methods. If the assumed rate of salary increase is changed from 3% to 4%, for example, all of the costs in the table above would increase by almost 40%.

The interest rate sensitivity is also great. If the assumed interest rate were increased from 6% to 8% in the preceding example, the required contributions at age 35 would change as shown below for the three methods:

Interest Rate Assumed	@ 6%	@ 8%
Accumulated benefit method	$1,207	$ 635
Projected benefit method	2,484	1,305
Level contribution method	4,227	2,470

This highlights the need to use appropriate assumptions. As previously stated, the accounting standard requires use of "best estimate" assumptions that are internally consistent.

Accounting Actuarial Cost Method

current service cost

the actuarial present value of the pension entitlement earned by an employee group in a given year; part of pension expense

Accounting standards require the use of the *projected benefits method* to calculate the annual **current service cost**. Current service cost is a major component of each year's pension expense. Companies are all required to use the same actuarial cost method to ensure that a common measurement tool is used, and thus comparability is preserved. Generally, this method is felt to best measure the cost of entitlements earned during the period, and standard setters have been consistent in their preference for this method.

Note that if the pension plan is a flat benefit plan, where the eventual pension earned is based on years of service (e.g., $500 per year for every year worked, irrespective of final pay), then *either* the projected benefits method *or* the accumulated benefit method can be used to measure pension expense. This may sound like a big concession, but both of these actuarial cost methods result in the same annual funding requirement for a flat benefit plan, so the choice of method is not an issue.

Differences between Funding and Accounting Amounts

Life is easy (relatively speaking) when the current service cost for accounting is the same as the current service contribution for funding. When that happens, the debit to pension expense directly offsets the expenditure of cash for funding. For example, assume that Celebrities uses the same method (projected benefits method) and the same assumptions (best estimates) in its calculations for both accounting and funding. Refer to Exhibit 18-1. At the end of Chris's year 40, the entry to record the current service pension expense and the current service funding would appear as follows:

Pension expense	3,324	
Cash		3,324

Now suppose instead that Celebrities uses the accumulated benefit method for funding. The entry will no longer balance, because the amount recorded as expense ($3,324) is greater than the amount paid into the pension fund in that year ($2,111, from Exhibit 18-1). In order to balance the entry, the difference between these two amounts has to be credited to a credit account, often called an accrued benefit liability:

Pension expense	3,324	
Cash		2,111
Accrued benefit liability		1,213

If the accrued pension account has a debit balance, it is called an **accrued benefit asset**.

Interpreting the Liability

If the accumulated amount is a credit (that is, the cost is being charged to expense faster than contributions are being made to the plan), it is tempting to say that the company "owes" the pension plan and the pension plan is underfunded. However, an accrued liability *caused by a different actuarial cost method used for funding and accounting* should *not* be interpreted in this way. The funding is *appropriate for the actuarial method being used.*

CONCEPT REVIEW

1. Name three actuarial cost methods and specify what projections, if any, are involved for each one.

2. Which actuarial method is required for accounting measurements for a defined benefit plan?

3. What is the significance of an accrued benefit liability on the balance sheet?

DEFINED BENEFIT PENSION EXPENSE— LIST OF COMPONENTS

Pension expense for a defined benefit pension plan is the sum of *10* components. That is, in order to calculate pension expense, it is necessary to gather these components together and add them up. For convenience, we will group these into continuing components and special components.

The following five components are continuing because they either will always exist or are likely to exist as part of pension expense. These five components are the main focus of the following sections.

Continuing components:

1. Current service cost;

2. *Plus:* Interest on the accumulated accrued benefit obligation;

3. *Minus:* Expected earnings on plan assets;

4. *Plus:* Amortization of past service cost from plan initiation or amendment; and

5. *Plus* or *minus:* Amortization of excess actuarial loss (or gain).

Five special components arise only under certain circumstances. We will briefly explain each of these components later in the chapter.

Special components:

1. Amortization of the transitional obligation (or asset);

2. Any changes to the valuation allowance for pension plan assets;

3. Gain or loss on plan settlement or curtailment;

4. Any expense recognized for termination benefits; and

5. Any amount recognized as a result of a temporary deviation from the plan.

CONTINUING COMPONENTS

Current Service Cost

The first and most significant element of pension cost is the *current service cost.* The annual measurement of pension earned for work done during the year is the current service cost.

Accounting standards require that current service cost normally be measured using the projected benefits method. The actuary determines this figure and provides it in an actuarial report.

Interest on Accrued Benefit Obligation

The **accrued benefit obligation** is the present value of the post-retirement benefits that the employees have earned to date. Interest is calculated as the *opening accrued benefit obligation multiplied by the interest rate*. Alternatively, interest may be calculated by the actuary and provided in an actuarial report. Interest is included in pension expense.

Interest Rate The rate used for accruing interest on the obligation must be consistent with the rate used to discount the benefits to obtain the obligation in the first place. Accounting standards require that the rate used to discount the obligation should be based on market interest rates for high-quality debt at the balance sheet date. Terms should match. For example, if the pensions will, on average, be paid out in 20 years' time, then a 20-year interest rate should be used.

Expected Earnings on Plan Assets

Expected earnings on plan assets *reduces* the amount of pension expense. Just as pension expense is increased for interest on the obligation, it is decreased by earnings on fund assets. The higher the earnings, the lower the overall pension expense to the company.

The expected earnings are based on the *expected long-term rate of return on plan assets, multiplied by the opening balance of pension fund assets*. The rate of return may be equal to the rate used by the actuary for funding calculations, but if the actuary's rate is conservative (i.e., low), then a more realistic rate should be used by the company to calculate expected earnings for accounting purposes.

The value of the plan assets that is used in this calculation may be either (1) the *fair value* of the plan assets or (2) a *market-related value*. A market-related value is one that is based on fair values but that is not actually the current fair value. An example is a five-year moving average of share equity prices, which is commonly used by insurance companies.

Offsetting Effects Interest cost and expected earnings will tend to offset each other in the calculation of pension expense. However, the offset will be complete only *if*:

- The discount and earnings rates are identical;
- The same actuarial method is used for both accounting and funding;
- Assumptions underlying accounting measures are the same as those underlying the funding measures; and
- Pension amounts have been fully funded.

Very few companies will satisfy all four conditions, and therefore a complete offset of accrued interest and expected earnings is likely to be rare.

Actual versus Expected Return Being an estimate, the expected return on plan assets is likely to be incorrect, both over the long run and year by year. Some companies prefer to use *actual* earnings in pension expense, rather than the *expected* earnings, since the real earnings are known and reflect "economic reality." Some companies do use actual earnings on plan assets instead of expected earnings. However, actual earnings are volatile, and pensions are long-term arrangements, so use of expected return is felt to be preferable.

past service cost

the actuarial present value of pension benefits given in a newly introduced (or amended) pension plan for work already rendered by current employees

Past Service Cost from Plan Initiation

When a pension plan is first started, employees may be given pension entitlements for their employment prior to the initiation of the plan. In other words, the pension plan starts out with a substantial accrued benefit obligation from past service rendered by current employees. This beginning obligation is known as the **past service cost (PSC)**.

Recognition or Not? Past service cost is usually described as an incentive for existing workers in current and future periods. Therefore, restating past years is not appropriate, and the PSC is amortized over current and future periods of service. The status of the PSC on the balance sheet is more problematic. Liabilities are probable future sacrifices of economic resources based on past transactions. If the past service of employees is viewed as the past transaction, and employers have the obligation to meet the funding requirements of the pension plan for past service, which they do, then it seems that PSC is indeed a liability. The difficulty is what to debit. Is there an asset? A large current expense? Neither alternative seems to sit well. A further alternative is to debit accumulated other comprehensive income (OCI).

The accounting treatment followed in Canada is:

- The PSC liability is not recognized in the balance sheet;
- The PSC liability is amortized to expense over current and future periods; and
- The PSC liability is disclosed, along with the pension fund assets, in the disclosure notes.

Other alternatives are possible using international standards, and recognition of the net status of the plan is required in the U.S. We will return to this discussion as part of the larger issue of recognition of the overall financial position of the fund.

Amortization Period Past service cost is included in pension cost, amortized on a straight-line basis over an appropriate time period. The amortization period is the **expected period to full eligibility (EPFE)** of the employee group. The EPFE is the length of time that, on average, the current employee group must work to be entitled to full pension. EPFE may be compared to the **average remaining service period (ARSP)** of the employee group. The average remaining service period is the length of time that, on average, the current employee group is expected to stay on the job before retirement. For example, say that an employee is entitled to 2% of her final pay for each year worked, to a maximum of 60% of final pay. This takes 30 years. The employee is hired at age 25, and will likely work until she is 65. Her ARSP is her 40-year working life, but her EPFE is 30 years, because she has maxed out her pension entitlements at that point.

The EPFE of a group is a function of employee turnover, mortality rates, retirement age, average employee age, and employment expansion (or contraction) by the employer, among other things. EPFE (and ARSP) are stable if the workforce is stable. However, when employees retire, new employees of various ages are hired to replace them. *Therefore, the amortization period does not necessarily decline year by year.* EPFE and ARSP are re-evaluated periodically, and may increase, decrease, or remain the same, depending on the changing composition of the workforce. Notice that:

- If full eligibility occurs only at retirement, and pension benefits are earned right up to the last year, then EPFE is equal to ARSP. This is quite common.
- Full eligibility may be achieved when the employee has reached a certain age. For example, a pension plan may stipulate that an employee's pension benefits will be calculated on years of service and salary only up to age 65. At that point, if the employee keeps working, no additional pension benefits will accrue even if the employee does not retire. The period to full eligibility will then be the average age of the employee group at plan inception subtracted from the age at which full benefits are established.

Funding As always, it is important to distinguish between *accounting* for past service costs and *funding* of past service costs. For *funding* purposes, pension legislation often gives an employer a specific period, often up to 15 years, to fund any pension liability. Of course, the past service cost obligation will continue to grow because it will accrue interest, and therefore the company will have to make sufficiently large cash contributions to fund the past service cost plus interest.

The *funding* period is *not* the appropriate period of amortization for past service costs. EPFE is the choice for amortization.

Past Service Cost from Plan Amendment

From time to time, a company will amend its pension plan, usually to increase benefits as the result of labour agreements. When an existing plan is amended to increase benefits based on years of service to date, an additional unfunded obligation is established that relates to prior service. The liability that arises from a *plan amendment* is another source of past service cost (PSC).

Legislation usually requires that a company fund a deficiency that arises from plan amendments over a shorter period than that required for plan initiation. Often, any increase in the accrued pension obligation that arises from a plan amendment must be fully funded within five years (as contrasted with 15 years for plan initiation). Once again, though, the funding period is not relevant to the amortization period.

For accounting purposes, a company has two options:

1. Amortize PSC from amendments on the same basis as PSC from initiation—the expected period to full eligibility; or

2. Amortize PSC from amendments over the period to the next expected plan amendment.

The second option recognizes that plan amendments occur more or less regularly in many companies. When amendments occur with some regularity, it makes sense to amortize the additional pension plan obligation that arises from a plan amendment over a shorter period than that used for amortization of past service cost, which arises only once in the life of a pension plan.

Actuarial Gains and Losses

Previous sections of this chapter stressed that assumptions and estimates have a major impact on the measurement of pension expense. An interesting aspect of accounting estimates is that estimates are always wrong, and therefore adjustments must be made to correct for estimation errors.[1] There are two sources of estimation error that require adjustment, and give rise to **actuarial gains and losses**:

1. Recent experience gives rise to gains and losses that arise because actual figures are different from the assumptions made; these are known as **experience gains and losses**.

2. There are reasons to alter the assumptions about the future that underlie calculation of the accrued pension obligation; adjustments made for this reason are due to **changes in assumptions**.

Experience Gains and Losses Experience gains and losses reflect the extent to which measurements made in previous years have turned out to be incorrect due to errors in estimates or assumptions. The most obvious example is the return on plan assets; calculations may have assumed a 6% average return, but the actual return this year might have been 13%— or 1%. This difference results in an experience gain or loss. Other factors that may turn out to have been different than expected include employee turnover, retirement rates, employee earnings growth, etc.

Experience gains and losses relate to the *past*. They are the result of actual experience being different from the expectations upon which the actuarial cost was calculated in previous years, and they can relate to either the actuarial obligation or the plan assets, or both.

Changes in Assumptions In contrast, adjustments that arise from changes in assumptions are *forward looking*; they reflect changes in the accrued pension obligation that arise from

---

[1] This is not intended to suggest that accountants should not use estimates. Estimates are used because it is better to make an approximation than to ignore the economic realities completely. However, there are always estimation errors.

altering one or more of the assumptions about the future. Changes could be made to the expected return on plan assets (and thus the discount rate), the growth rate in projected earnings, employee turnover, early retirements, and so forth.

The pension benefit obligation will increase or decrease as a result of the required periodic actuarial revaluation. Pension legislation usually requires an employer to have an **actuarial revaluation** at least once every three years. The actuary looks at the actual performance factors since the preceding revaluation and at factors affecting future outlook, and restates the accrued pension obligation accordingly. If the pension obligation increases as the result of a revaluation, a loss occurs; if the pension obligation decreases, a gain occurs.

For *funding* purposes, deficiencies in plan assets that arise either from experience factors or from changes in assumptions have to be funded within a relatively short period of time, usually no more than five years. Surpluses that arise as the result of an actuarial revaluation (such as an unexpectedly high return on plan assets) cannot normally be withdrawn from the pension plan, but they may entitle the employer to take a **pension holiday** by temporarily reducing or eliminating payments for the current service funding requirements.

Amortization: The Corridor Method
Gains and losses that arise either from experience or from changes in assumptions are collectively known as actuarial gains and losses. Gains and losses may offset each other over time, as successive revaluations adjust both the pension funding and pension accounting to more closely correspond with economic facts and changed expectations. Some level of error is expected, given that the estimates are so sensitive to estimated variables. Actuarial gains and losses are included in pension expense in some fashion, usually using an amortization rule.

The amortization rule is popularly known as the **10% corridor method** for amortization. This calculation *is based on balances as of the beginning of each year.* This calculation allows that:

- *No amortization is needed* if the cumulative actuarial gains and losses are less than the 10% corridor.
- If the cumulative amount is outside the corridor, *only the excess is amortized.*
- The 10% corridor is defined as 10% of the *greater* of:
    1. The accrued benefit obligation at the beginning of the year; or
    2. The value of the plan assets at the beginning of the year.
- If amortization is required under this test, the recommended amortization period is the ARSP. (Note that the amortization period is ARSP, not EPFE.)

Example Assume that Maitland Packaging Limited has a pension plan that has been in effect for some time and is subject to an actuarial revaluation every two years. ARSP is 10 years. Other data relating to the plan at the beginning of 20X3 are as follows:

	Total	10%
Accrued pension obligation, beginning of 20X3	$100,000	$10,000
Value of plan assets, beginning of 20X3	120,000	12,000
Unamortized actuarial loss, beginning of 20X3		11,000

Since the unamortized actuarial loss is less than 10% of the *greater* of the pension obligation or pension plan assets, no amortization is required for 20X3.

Now, assume that an actuarial revaluation occurs at the end of 20X3. The result of the revaluation is that the pension plan has an additional actuarial loss of $7,000. The relevant information for the beginning of 20X4 is:

	Total	10%
Accrued pension obligation, beginning of 20X4	$110,000	$11,000
Value of plan assets, beginning of 20X4	130,000	13,000
Unamortized actuarial loss, beginning of 20X4 ($11,000 + $7,000)		18,000

The unamortized actuarial loss now exceeds the higher of the two 10% amounts, and therefore the *excess* must be amortized. For 20X4, amortization of $500 will be added to pension expense:

($18,000 − $13,000) ÷ 10 years ARSP = $500

The *unamortized* amount at the beginning of 20X5 is $17,500. This calculation does not imply an annual amortization of $500. Instead, amortization is *recalculated each year*. The amount of the excess will change every year (1) the amounts of the obligation and assets change and (2) any excess is amortized. For example, assume the following data for Maitland for 20X5:

	Total	10%
Accrued pension obligation, beginning 20X5	$125,000	$12,500
Value of plan assets, beginning of 20X5	150,000	15,000
Unamortized actuarial loss, beginning of 20X5 ($18,000 − $500)		17,500

Amortization for 20X5 will be $250 (assuming that ARSP continues to be 10 years):

($17,500 − $15,000) ÷ 10 years = $250

The unamortized loss at the beginning of 20X6 is $17,250. If either the pension obligation or the value of the plan assets increases to at least $172,500 by the beginning of 20X6, then no amortization will be required because the unamortized amount will not be in excess of the 10% corridor.

Other Alternatives *Amortization of the excess amount over the ARSP (as described above) is the minimum amortization;* a company may amortize a larger portion of its actuarial gains and losses if it wishes. In fact, a company can elect to write off the entire amount of actuarial gains and losses immediately.

If a company chooses to amortize a larger amount of its actuarial gains and losses, the same method should be used consistently. If any year's amortization under an alternative approach would be less than the minimum amount as defined above, then the minimum amount should be used instead. Furthermore, if a company elects to use a policy of immediate write-offs, the policy must be applied consistently to both gains and losses. This removes the temptation to recognize all gains immediately, but defer and amortize losses to the extent possible.

Summary of Amortization Periods

Amortization periods for the components of pension expense can be summarized as follows; continuing components have been described and the special component follows later in the chapter:

Pension Expense Continuing Components	Amortization Period
Past service cost from plan initiation	Expected period to full eligibility (EPFE)
Past service cost from plan amendment	Expected period to full eligibility (EPFE), or period to next expected amendment
Actuarial gains and losses	Minimum is excess over 10% corridor calculated annually; amortized over average remaining service period (ARSP), or Company may choose to recognize more than the minimum.
Special Components	
Transitional obligation or asset	Average remaining service period (ARSP)

CONCEPT REVIEW

1. List the five components that are typically part of pension expense.

2. What are the two situations that give rise to past service cost?

3. Over what period(s) could the additional accrued pension obligation arising from a plan amendment be amortized?

4. When must actuarial gains and losses be amortized?

5. What optional periods may be used for the amortization of actuarial gains and losses?

PENSION EXPENSE EXAMPLE

Refer to Exhibit 18-2 for data for Gertron Corporation. To calculate pension expense, it is necessary to gather together the five components discussed:

1. Current service cost, measured using the projected service method (given)	$ 556,700
2. Interest on accrued benefit obligation ($13,675,000 × 6%)	820,500
3. Expected return on plan assets ($8,010,000 × 5%)	(400,500)
4. Past service cost ($4,050,000 ÷ 10)	405,000
5. Actuarial gains and losses ($2,260,000 − (10% of $13,675,000)) = $892,500; $892,500/12	74,375
	$1,456,075

EXHIBIT 18-2

PENSION EXAMPLE DATA

Gertron Corporation has a defined benefit pension plan. The following data applies to the plan:

Current service cost for 20X5, measured using the projected service method	$ 556,700
Benefit payments to retired employees	134,800
Funding contributions made to the pension trustee in 20X5	1,030,000
Actual return on plan assets in 20X5	157,900

Expected return on plan assets, 5%
Interest rate related to long-term liabilities, 6%
Employee expected period to full eligibility, 10 years
Employee average remaining service life, 12 years

Balances, end of 20X4:

Accrued pension benefit obligation, end of 20X4	$13,675,000
Pension plan assets, market value, end of 20X4	8,010,000
Unrecognized past service cost	4,050,000
Unrecognized actuarial losses	2,260,000
Balance sheet accrued pension asset	645,000

Gertron uses the 10% corridor method for amortization of unrecognized actuarial gains and losses.

Highlights of the calculations:

- Interest and expected return are calculated on the opening balances. These figures may be provided by the actuary but often have to be calculated based on the information given.
- Amortization of the accumulated actuarial losses is subject to the 10% corridor. This is 10% of the accrued pension obligation (10% of $13,675,000), because the obligation is larger than pension assets. Note also that this calculation is done with *opening* balances, and *only* the portion of the unrecognized loss that is over the corridor is amortized.
- The amortization period is EPFE for past service and ARSP for actuarial gains and losses.
- Benefits paid to pensioners are not a component of pension expense because these amounts are accrued over the pensioner's working life; payment is not the event that triggers an expense.

If the funding amount is $1,030,000, the company would make an entry as follows:

Pension expense	1,456,075	
Cash		1,030,000
Accrued benefit asset		426,075

The ending balance of the accrued benefit asset, which appears on the balance sheet, is therefore $218,925 (the $645,000 opening balance, less $426,075).

Reconciliation It is possible to derive the closing balances in the major pension fund elements, and use these numbers to prove the $218,925 balance sheet account.

Accrued benefit obligation		
Opening balance		$13,675,000
Increase due to current service cost		556,700
Increase due to interest accrued		820,500
Decrease due to pension benefits paid to pensioners		(134,800)
Closing balance		$14,917,400
Pension fund assets		
Opening balance		$ 8,010,000
Increase due to actual investment income earned		157,900
Decrease due to pension benefits paid to pensioners		(134,800)
Increase due to contributions during the year		1,030,000
Closing balance		$ 9,063,100
Unamortized past service cost		
Opening balance		$ 4,050,000
Decrease due to current year amortization		(405,000)
Closing balance		$ 3,645,000
Unrecognized actuarial losses		
Opening balance		$ 2,260,000
Loss due to earnings results in the current year		
Expected earnings	$400,500	
Actual earnings	(157,900)	242,600
Decrease due to amortization		(74,375)
Closing balance		$ 2,428,225

Now, the net of these four accounts will be equal to the company's reported accrued benefit asset on the balance sheet:

Accrued benefit obligation:	$14,917,400 credit
Pension fund assets	$ 9,063,100 debit
Unamortized past service cost	3,645,000 debit
Unrecognized actuarial losses	2,428,225 debit
Accrued benefit asset	$218,925 debit

Notice that this balance sheet account is the net funded status of the plan ($14,917,400 less assets of $9,063,100; and underfunded by $5,854,300) *less the unrecognized past service cost and actuarial losses.* Since the latter two elements total over $6 million, the pension is reflected as an *asset* on the balance sheet.

SPREADSHEET ILLUSTRATION

One of the practical problems in pension accounting is simply keeping track of all of the different amounts that are involved, and a spreadsheet helps.

First Year   To begin the illustration, we will assume that the company, St. Mark Spas Limited (SMS) establishes a pension plan at the end of year 20X0, effective 1 January 20X1. The employees will receive pension entitlements for past years' service. The plan will be accounted for by the projected benefit method, using "best estimate" assumptions. Additional information is obtained from the pension plan trustee and from the actuary.

- The assumed earnings on plan assets and the interest rate for the pension obligation is 8%.
- At 31 December 20X0, the present value of the pension obligation for past service is $100,000 (at the 8% rate).
- The company will use the straight-line method for amortization.
- Both the ARSP and the EPFE are 10 years.
- Current service cost for the year 20X1 is $30,000, at 8%, using the projected benefit method.
- To adequately *fund* the current service cost and part of the past service cost, the company is required to make a cash contribution of $65,000 to the plan at the end of 20X1.
- Since there are no fund assets or actuarial gains or losses at the beginning of the year, expected return on fund assets is zero and there is no amortization of unrecognized actuarial amounts.

Pension expense for 20X1 is the sum of:

Current service cost (given)	$30,000
PSC amortization (straight-line over 10 years) ($100,000 ÷ 10)	10,000
Interest on the beginning-of-year accrued obligation ($100,000 × 8%)	8,000
Pension expense, 20X1	$48,000

Since $65,000 was paid, there will be a $17,000 ($65,000 − $48,000) accrued pension asset in the long-term assets section of the balance sheet.

Spreadsheet   Exhibit 18-3 shows one possible format for a pension plan worksheet. Refer to this exhibit as the explanation proceeds, below. The columnar arrangement is as follows:

- The first two numerical columns keep track of the amount of the pension obligation (credit) and the pension assets (debit).
- The next two columns keep track of the unamortized pension costs. In this example, there is a separate column for past service costs and actuarial gains, because they have a different amortization scheme. An additional column can be added for past service costs arising from plan amendments, if any.
- The next is a column for summarizing pension expense. The entries in this column will come from several of the preceding columns.
- Finally, there is a column for the balance sheet account of accrued benefit asset or liability. Pension expense will be a *credit* to this account, and pension funding will be a *debit*.

As an opening 20X1 position, the $100,000 pension obligation (credit, in brackets) and unrecognized past service cost (debit) are entered. They offset, and there is no opening balance sheet account on the company's books. That is, *the first four columns cross-add to equal the sixth column.*

First Year   Current service cost of $30,000 increases the liability (first column) and pension expense (fifth column), as does the $8,000 interest on the opening liability. PSC amortization of $10,000 decreases the unrecognized PSC (fourth column), and increases pension expense. The $65,000 funding contribution increases fund assets (second column) and the balance sheet account; pension expense, once complete, is transferred to the balance sheet account. The columns are then added. Note that the first four columns again add to equal the final column. This is the reconciliation of the balance sheet account, and proves that the spreadsheet is complete.

EXHIBIT 18-3

PENSION PLAN SPREADSHEET

	Memorandum Accounts				Statement Accounts	
	Values		**Unrecognized Pension Costs**			
	Accrued Pension Obligation dr./(cr.)	**Value of Plan Assets dr./(cr.)**	**Unamortized Actuarial Loss (Gain)**	**Past Service Cost**	**Pension Expense**	**Accrued Benefit Asset (Liability)**
20X1						
Beginning balances	$(100,000)			$100,000		
Current service cost	(30,000)				$30,000 dr.*	
Interest on obligation	(8,000)				8,000 dr.	
PSC amortization				(10,000)	10,000 dr.	
					48,000 dr.	$(48,000) cr.
Funding contribution		$ 65,000				65,000 dr.
Ending balance	**$(138,000)**	**$ 65,000**	**—**	**$ 90,000**		**$ 17,000 dr.**
20X2						
Current service cost	(35,000)				35,000 dr.	
Interest on obligation	(11,040)				11,040 dr.	
Actual return on assets		7,200	$ (7,200)			
Expected return on assets			5,200		(5,200) cr.	
PSC amortization				(10,000)	10,000 dr.	
					$50,840 dr.	(50,840) cr.
Funding contribution		68,000				68,000 dr.
Ending balance	**$(184,040)**	**$140,200**	**$ (2,000)**	**$ 80,000**		**$ 34,160 dr.**
20X3						
Current service cost	(32,000)				32,000 dr.	
Interest on obligation	(14,723)				14,723 dr.	
Actual return on assets		14,000	(14,000)			
Expected return on assets			11,216		(11,216) cr.	
Actuarial revaluation	22,000		(22,000)			
PSC amortization				(10,000)	10,000 dr.	
					$45,507 dr.	(45,507) cr.
Funding contribution		37,000				37,000 dr.
Ending balance	**$(208,763)**	**$191,200**	**$(26,784)**	**$ 70,000**		**$ 25,653 dr.**
20X4						
Current service cost	(43,000)				43,000 dr.	
Interest on obligation	(16,701)				16,701 dr.	
Actual return on assets		10,000	(10,000)			
Expected return on assets			15,296		(15,296) cr.	
Benefit payments	18,000	(18,000)				
PSC amortization				(10,000)	10,000 dr.	
Excess actuarial gain amortization			591		(591) cr.*	
					$53,814 dr.	(53,814) cr.
Funding contribution		68,000				68,000 dr.
Ending balance	**$(250,464)**	**$251,200**	**$(20,897)**	**$ 60,000**		**$ 39,839 dr.**

*[$26,784 − (208,763 × 10%)] ÷ 10 years = $591 amortization of excess.

Second Year For 20X2, there will be another calculation of current service cost. There now will be some earnings on the plan assets. SMS will receive a report from the pension plan trustee shortly after the end of the year that explains the investment activity and investment results. Assume the following:

- Current service cost is $35,000.
- The *actual* return on the plan assets was $7,200 (a return of approximately 11% on the $65,000 in the plan at the *beginning* of 20X2).
- SMS contributes $68,000 cash to the plan at the end of 20X2, in accordance with the actuary's calculations for funding.
- The value of the plan assets at the end of 20X2 is $140,200.

The *expected* return on the plan assets for 20X2 was 8% of the beginning-of-year plan assets of $65,000, or $5,200. The actual return was $7,200. The extra return of $2,000 above the expected return is an *experience gain*, which is one type of actuarial gain.

Actuarial gains/losses are not included directly in the calculation of pension expense. Instead, they are tracked in a separate schedule off the financial statements, and the accumulated actuarial gain/loss is subject to the 10% corridor test. At the *beginning* of 20X2, there was no actuarial gain or loss, and therefore the corridor test is not necessary for 20X2.

The calculation of 20X2 pension expense is as follows:

Current service cost	$35,000
Past service cost amortization	10,000
Interest on accrued obligation, beginning of year ($138,000 × 8%)	11,040
Expected earnings on plan assets ($65,000 × 8%)	(5,200)
	$50,840

The entries for the expense and funding payment are as follows:

Pension expense	50,840	
Accrued benefit asset/liability		50,840
Accrued benefit asset/liability	68,000	
Cash		68,000

Refer again to the spreadsheet in Exhibit 18-3. Find the following items:

- Current service cost of $35,000 increases the pension obligation and pension expense.
- Interest on the pension obligation of $11,040 also increases the pension obligation and pension expense.
- The actual return in plan assets of $7,200 increases fund assets *but is then entered as a credit in the unamortized gains and losses column*, column 3. Actual return is NOT part of pension expense.
- Expected return of $5,200 is also entered in column 3, as a debit, and is recorded as a reduction to pension expense. In column 3, this leaves the difference between actual and expected return. This is an experience gain (credit) of $2,000.
- As in 20X1, past service cost is amortized by $10,000, increasing pension expense and reducing the unamortized amount.
- Funding contributions of $68,000 increase fund assets and are entered as a debit in the final column.

- To complete the spreadsheet, pension expense is totalled and entered as a credit in the final column. The columns are totalled and cross-added. Again, the total of the first four columns equals the final column, the balance sheet pension account.

Third Year Assume the following additional facts for 20X3:

- Current service cost for accounting is $32,000, as calculated by the actuary.
- Actual return on the plan assets is $14,000.
- The first biennial actuarial revaluation occurs. Due to changes in assumptions, the accrued pension obligation is decreased by $22,000.
- SMS contributes $37,000 cash to the plan at the end of 20X3.

At the beginning of 20X3, there was an unamortized actuarial gain (i.e., an experience gain) of $2,000. A corridor test must be applied to this amount to see whether any amortization is needed in 20X3. Amortization is not necessary if the unamortized actuarial gain is less than 10% of the *higher* of the beginning-of-year accrued obligation and the beginning-of-year pension plan assets:

	Total	10%
Accrued pension obligation	$184,040	$18,404
Value of pension plan assets	140,200	14,020

The unamortized actuarial gain of $2,000 is well below the 10% limit of $18,404, and therefore no amortization is necessary. Bear in mind, however, that the company can choose to amortize this gain if it wishes to do so. Alternatively, the company may recognize the full amount of each year's gain (or loss) in the current year. Amortization using the corridor method is the *minimum* amortization required.

The calculation of pension expense is as follows:

Current service cost	$32,000
Past service cost amortization	10,000
Interest on accrued obligation, beginning of year ($184,040 × 8%)	14,723
Expected earnings on plan assets ($140,200 × 8%)	(11,216)
	$45,507

The entries for these amounts are as follows:

Pension expense	45,507	
Accrued benefit asset/liability		45,507
Accrued benefit asset/liability	37,000	
Cash		37,000

Spreadsheet Refer to Exhibit 18-3. The following items are entered on the spreadsheet:

- The current service cost of $32,000 and the interest on the accrued obligation of $14,723 are added to the obligation and to pension expense.

- *Actual* earnings on the plan assets of $14,000 are entered in column 2 (as an increase in the value of the plan assets) and in column 3 (unamortized actuarial gain).
- The *expected* earnings on plan assets of $11,216 partially offsets the actual actuarial gain in column 3, leaving only the difference between the expected and the actual in the unamortized column. Expected earnings are also entered in column 5, pension expense.
- The $22,000 gain from the actuarial revaluation *reduces* the pension obligation, and it also is entered in column 3 as a credit (gain) in the unamortized actuarial gain.
- The past service cost amortization of $10,000 reduces the unamortized amount and is a component of pension expense.
- The total pension expense is credited to the accrued benefit asset/liability, in the last column.
- The funding contribution is added to the pension plan assets and is debited to the accrued benefit asset/liability.

In 20X3, the expense is higher than the funding, and therefore the debit balance of the accrued benefit asset/liability is reduced by $8,507, to a debit balance of $25,653 ($34,160 − $8,507).

Fourth Year   During the fourth year, the SMS pension plan pays benefits to retired employees. Assume the following facts for 20X4:

- Current service cost is $43,000.
- Actual return on plan assets is $10,000.
- SMS contributes $68,000 to the plan.
- Benefits of $18,000 are paid to retirees by the trustee.
- Both ARSP and EPFE are still 10 years.

The first four lines of the 20X4 section at the bottom of Exhibit 18-3 are essentially the same as has been described above for 20X3—current service cost, interest, actual return on assets, and expected return on assets.

The fifth line introduces something new to our example—the payment of benefits. Benefits are paid by the trustee out of the plan assets, and therefore they represent a decrease in the value of the plan assets. As well, part of the pension obligation to these employees has been fulfilled, and the benefit payments reduce the accrued obligation as well. Benefit payments have no impact on pension *expense.*

The next line shows the amortization of past service cost; there is no change in this item from previous years.

At the beginning of 20X4, there is an accumulated actuarial gain of $26,784. This amount comprises experience gains arising from strong earnings on the plan assets, plus the $22,000 actuarial revaluation in 20X3. The corridor test must be applied to see whether we should amortize any of this gain.

The higher of the obligation and the assets *at the beginning of the year* is the $208,763 accrued obligation. Ten percent of that amount is $20,876. The accumulated actuarial gain is greater than that amount, and therefore amortization of the excess is necessary in 20X4. The amortization is $591:

[$26,784 − ($208,763 × 10%)] ÷ 10 years ARSP = $591

This amortization reduces the unamortized amount and is *credited* to pension expense (it is a gain) in Exhibit 18-3 in the seventh line for 20X4.

Summary of Spreadsheet Adjustments

Refer to the following table for a summary of spreadsheet items caused by continuing elements of pension expense.

Column	Normal Balance	Increase	Decrease	Either Increase or Decrease
Accrued pension obligation	Credit	• Current service cost • Interest on opening obligation	• Benefit payments to retirees	• Actuarial revaluation (credit this column if liability increases and debit this column if liability decreases)
Pension plan assets	Debit	• Annual funding contribution • Actual earnings	• Benefit payments to retirees	
Unamortized actuarial gains or losses	Debit if loss Credit if gain		• Amortization of opening balance, if any	• New actuarial revaluations (debit this column if liability increases and credit this column if liability decreases.) • Difference between actual fund earnings (credit this column) and expected earnings (debit this column)
Unamortized PSC	Debit	• Past service cost from plan initiation or amendment	• Amortization of opening balance	
Pension expense	Debit	• Current service cost • Interest on opening obligation • Amortization of PSC	• Expected earnings on plan assets	• Amortization of experience gains (decrease expense) or losses (increase expense)
Accrued benefit asset/liability	Debit if an asset and credit if a liability			• Credit for the expense amount • Debit for the funding amount

SPECIAL COMPONENTS OF PENSION EXPENSE

Transitional Amortization

When new pension standards came into effect in 2000, companies had to make certain adjustments to comply with these standards, plus companies were required to properly account for post-retirement benefits other than pensions. The net numerical sum of these changes was known as the *transitional asset* or *transitional obligation*, depending on whether the net change was an unamortized debit or credit balance. The transitional asset or obligation could be accounted for in either of two ways, **retrospectively** or **prospectively.**

If the transitional balance was accounted for retrospectively, the asset or liability was set up on the balance sheet, and the other side of the entry went to retained earnings. Prior years' financial statements could be retrospectively restated, tracing the effect of the altered post-retirement costs, or not restated at all; the company was given the choice. Alternatively, the transitional balance could have been accounted for prospectively, and left unrecognized until it was amortized into pension expense. This treated the transition amount like PSC, or unamortized actuarial gains or losses. If a transition amount was unrecognized, the balance was/is amortized over the ARSP. This is known as **transitional amortization.**

Valuation Allowance for Pension Plan Assets

We observed earlier in this chapter that a company may fund its pension plan faster than it accrues the liability. This can happen either because (1) the plan is funded by the level contribution method, while accounting is by the projected benefit method, or (2) the assumptions used by the actuary for funding are more conservative than the "best estimate" assumptions used for accounting.

When cash paid out for funding exceeds the accounting accrual for the obligation, an asset (i.e., accrued benefit liability) will accumulate and will be shown on the balance sheet. The amounts accumulated can be quite significant. For example, BCE Inc. reported a balance sheet pension asset of $1,110 million for 2006, up from $984 million in 2005.

Every asset on the balance sheet must be subject to occasional validity checks to ensure that the asset isn't overvalued and that the enterprise will obtain value from that asset in the future, either through sale or use. The same is true for pension assets shown on the balance sheet. Therefore, standards require that an enterprise limit the asset to the amount that can be realized in the future. That is, if there is doubt that the asset can be used by the company, it must be written down through a valuation allowance. Note that:

- Any required valuation allowance is charged against pension expense for the period.
- The valuation test is performed each year, and the allowance is increased or decreased as necessary.
- All increases and decreases to the valuation allowance flow through pension expense.

Gains and Losses on Plan Settlements and Curtailments

On occasion, an employer may end a pension plan. When a plan is ended, it is a **pension plan settlement**; the obligation to the pensionable group is settled by transferring assets to a trustee, and any deficiencies in funding are remedied.

More often, there is a partial settlement of a plan due to closing down a division or otherwise significantly restructuring or downsizing operations. If a plan continues but has significantly fewer persons in the eligible employee group, there has been a **pension plan curtailment**.

When a company goes out of business, a division is shut, or large numbers of employees are laid off, there is likely to be a substantial gain that arises from the fact that the pensions are closed out at the entitlement earned by the employee to date rather than at the entitlement projected in the actuarial estimates. That is, the accounting numbers are based on the projected benefits method but the legal obligation on settlement is based on the benefits accumulated to date (i.e., by the accumulated benefit method). On the other hand, the severance agreement may include special pension benefits that will increase the company's obligation and thereby result in a loss. It depends on the circumstances of the shutdown.

Gains and losses that arise from settlements or curtailments are not subject to amortization. Settlements relate to employees who are no longer with the company, and therefore the ARSP related to these employees is zero. Such gains and losses are recognized immediately.

> **pension plan curtailment**
>
> where a pension plan is partially settled due to a significant restructuring or downsizing of operations; the plan continues but has significantly fewer persons in the eligible employee group; usually involves recognizing an expense or gain as part of pension expense

Classification Classification of the gain or loss on settlement or curtailment will depend on circumstances. The gain or loss would be included in pension expense if a plan settlement arises in the continuing segments of the business. Usually, though, plan settlements (and curtailments) arise when a company restructures or discontinues some aspect(s) of its operations. When this happens, the costs associated with this business reorganization are presented separately, as *discontinued operations* on the income statement. Separate disclosure also is usually given to the costs of *restructuring*, typically as an unusual item. Therefore, pension plan gains and losses arising from discontinued operations or from major restructuring will be included with that item, wherever it is classified.

Termination Benefits

An employer sometimes offers special incentives to induce employees to retire, or to take early retirement. Enhanced retirement offers are called **termination benefits**. Since the special termination benefits are in addition to the benefits normally offered to employees, the cost of providing the special benefits has not been included in the actuarial calculations for the employee group, either for funding or for accounting purposes. Therefore, special termination benefits require recognition of extra costs.

The costs of special termination benefits are accrued in the financial statements as an expense and a liability, once employees have accepted the offer and the cost can be reasonably estimated. Since the employees are leaving the company, amortization of the cost over future periods is not appropriate. Of course, if the termination is involuntary, acceptance by the employee is not a condition and the accrual is made as soon as the decision is made and the cost can be reasonably estimated.

Special termination benefits may be offered as a part of a restructuring plan. Restructuring costs, including any termination benefits, are usually recognized separately as an unusual item in the company's income statement. Special termination benefits that are part of restructuring will be included with the restructuring cost on the income statement, rather than with the normal pension expense.

Temporary Deviations from the Plan

Temporary deviations from a plan arise primarily with respect to benefits other than pension plans. Sometimes a company has a cost-sharing arrangement for a post-retirement benefit such as extended health care. The company may bear most of the cost, but the retiree may contribute to the cost (partially as a way of discouraging excessive use of the resource). The cost of the benefit may be based on the cost of providing the benefit. If benefit costs are surprisingly large in a particular year, the company may decide to bear the unexpected costs instead of retrospectively charging the retirees. *The cost of temporary deviations from the plan should be charged to income immediately.*

CONCEPT REVIEW

1. Sometimes losses or gains from plan settlements, plan curtailments, and termination benefits are not included as part of pension expense on the income statement but are reported elsewhere on the statement. When (and where) would such losses or gains be reported separately from pension expense?

2. Under what circumstances will a company use a valuation allowance with respect to the balance sheet account for a pension plan asset (i.e., accrued benefit asset)?

3. When are temporary deviations from a plan recognized?

RECORDING THE NET PENSION PLAN STATUS

This chapter has shown that the net pension asset or liability on the balance sheet consists of the following elements:

	Pensions benefit obligation (credit)
−	Pension fund assets (debit),
+/−	Unrecognized amounts, such as PSC (debit) (or credit, if actuarial gains)
	Accrued benefit asset/liability (debit or credit)

Companies with underfunded plans and large unrecognized costs might actually show *pensions assets* on the balance sheet. The following might be typical early in the life of a pension plan, or after plan amendment:

Pension benefit obligation	$(675,000)
Pension fund assets	100,000
Unrecognized PSC	600,000
Accrued benefit asset	$ 25,000

That is, there are significant obligations, minimal assets, and major unamortized past service costs. The result is a pension asset, which seems counterintuitive: the pension fund is underfunded, but the balance sheet shows a pension fund asset?

Now, it may well be that the underfunded position of the plan is no cause for concern among pensioners. If the underfunded position is caused by past service from plan initiation or amendment, there is likely a 5, 10, or 15-year plan to address the underfunded position.

Nonetheless, there is an obligation of the company that will use future resources. It is not recorded on the balance sheet. There are those that feel strongly that the net underfunded position of the plan, which is $575,000 ($675,000 pension benefit obligation, less the fund assets of $100,000) should be recorded on the face of the balance sheet as a liability, with the offsetting debit in accumulated other comprehensive income.[2] Canadian standards require only that the $575,000 net status of the plan be disclosed, not recorded. Some of the arguments in favour of recording the net pension amount are:

1. The net position of the plan appears to meet the definition of a liability, since it is based on a past transaction (work done by employees to date), and it represents a probable sacrifice of future benefits (since the company as a going concern, it is obliged to meet pension obligations.)

2. Pension amounts are subject to certain estimates, but these estimates can be made in reliable enough form that recognition is appropriate.

3. Some research indicates that analysts and other users react differently to the underfunded status of the plan if it were recorded in the balance sheet, versus if it were simply disclosed in the notes. If this is true, then disclosure is not a good substitute for recognition.[3]

The amounts involved are material. For example, a report prepared by UBS Securities Canada Inc, indicates that pension fund deficits in the S&P/TSX 60 amounted to $20.5 billion at the end of 2005, up from $15 billion in 2004. The autoparts, forestry and manufacturing sectors, which are labour intensive, were particularly sensitive.[4]

Accounting standards in the U.S. now require recognition of the net status of the plan. A form of recognition is one of two alternatives currently available under international standards, with further reforms on the horizon. Canadian companies may have to accustom themselves to this approach.

PAYMENT OF BENEFITS

In all of the preceding discussion, there has been little mention of actual pension benefits paid to retired ex-employees. The reason is that the benefits payments are the responsibility of the pension plan (under control of the trustee), rather than of the employer. The employer must make up any deficiency in the pension plan due to higher average payouts than originally estimated, through the periodic actuarial revaluations (i.e., experience gains and losses), but these are the result of probabilistic outcomes rather than of specific payments to specific retirees.

The spreadsheet illustration in Exhibit 18-3 includes benefit payments in the fourth year of the pension plan. The payment of benefits reduces both the plan assets and the accrued obligation, but it does not affect pension expense.

OTHER POST-RETIREMENT BENEFITS

Post-retirement benefits may involve a lot more than pensions. Employers may include supplementary health care, prescription drug plans, dental benefits and various insurance plans for retirees. Because of universal health care in Canada, the cost of these benefits is less than in the United States. However, the cost of **other post-retirement benefits** (OPRBs) can still be substantial.

other post-retirement benefits

benefits (in addition to pensions) earned by employees during their working lives but paid during the post-retirement period; examples include supplementary health care, prescription drug plans, dental benefits, and various insurance plans

---

[2] Another alternative is that the entire pension obligation should be recorded as a liability, and pension fund assets reported as a separate long-term asset. This is an issue of reporting entity and will not be pursued in this discussion.

[3] Refer to the discussion in Picconi, Marc, "The Perils of Pensions: Does Pension Accounting Lead Investors and Analysts Astray?" *The Accounting Review*, 81, No. 4 (July 2006), pages 925–955.

[4] See Robinson, Allan, "U.S. accounting changes may affect Canadian firms," *The Globe and Mail*, September 29, 2006.

There are some practical differences between pensions and other post-retirement benefits, summarized as follows:

	Pensions	**Other Post-Retirement Benefits**
Use	Regular monthly payments with predictable or estimable increases until entitlements cease	Sporadic use from employee to employee and unpredictable cost increases
Beneficiary	Retired employee with usually some survivor rights	Retired employee and family members, as specified in the plan
Funding	Likely to be fully or mostly funded during the working life of the employee	Likely to be totally unfunded because contributions to unregistered plans are not tax deductible for the employer
Revaluations	Periodic as required by legislation	Likely more frequent to reflect changed cost estimates

The differences in usage of the plans, in particular, make cost estimation even more uncertain than the already-uncertain pension estimates. Nonetheless, the relevance of the information dictates that reliability be sacrificed, with appropriate disclosure of variables used.

For many years, the cost of OPRBs was accounted for on a *pay-as-you-go* basis. That is, when the benefits were actually paid out, or the health care premiums paid for employees after retirement, the amount would be expensed at that time. This method was obviously flawed, as the cost of the benefit was earned by the employee during employment, and the company had an obligation prior to the retirement period. Therefore, accounting standards now require that OPRBs be accounted for in a similar manner as pensions. That is, the annual expense is:

1. Current service cost;

2. *Plus* interest on the accrued obligation;

3. *Minus* expected earnings on segregated fund assets, if any;

4. *Plus* amortization of past service costs;

5. *Plus* or minus amortization of excess actuarial gains or losses.

Other special components may arise from time to time, and are accounted for as a pension plan. Since the rules came into effect in 2001, many companies selected prospective treatment, which resulted in a large transitional balance, amortized over the ARSP.

Example Review the spreadsheet in Exhibit 18-4, which reflects the following data for 20X8:

Opening OPRB liability	$175,000	Interest rate for assets	4%
Opening plan assets	10,000	Contribution paid to other post-retirement health care fund	$22,000
Opening unamortized transition amount	$150,000	Past service	None
Opening unamortized actuarial loss; corridor method is used	$18,700	Benefits paid by other post-retirement health care fund to retirees during the period	$24,000
Current service cost	$34,000	ARSP	None
Interest rate for obligation	6%		12 years
		Actual return on plan assets	$250

EXHIBIT 18-4

OPRB SPREADSHEET

20X8	Memorandum Accounts				Statement Accounts	
			Unrecognized			
	OPRB Obligation	Plan Assets	Actuarial G/L	Transition Amount	OPRB Expense	Accrued Asset(Liab)
Opening	$(175,000)	$10,000	$18,700	$150,000		$ 3,700*
Current service cost	(34,000)				$34,000	
Interest expense (6%)	(10,500)				10,500	
Expected earnings (4%)			400		(400)	
Actual return		250	(250)			
Amortization of transition amount (12 years)				(12,500)	12,500	
Amortization of actuarial gain outside corridor ($18,700 − $17,500)/12			(100)		100	
Contribution		22,000			—	22,000
Benefits paid	24,000	(24,000)			$56,700	(56,700)
Totals	$(195,500)	$ 8,250	$18,750	$137,500		$(31,000)

*Sum of first four columns

This spreadsheet follows the familiar pattern. Current service cost of $34,000 increases the obligation and the expense, as does the $10,500 interest calculated on the opening obligation balance. Expected earnings of $400 reduce the expense, and actual earnings increase the fund balance, while the difference between the actual ($250) and expected ($400) earnings is part of the unrecognized amount. The transition amount is amortized over the 12-year ARSP, reducing the unrecognized transition amount and increasing expense. The excess unamortized actuarial amount, based on the corridor method and opening balances, is amortized to the expense. Finally, cash paid to the fund increases the asset balance and affects the balance sheet account, and benefits paid reduce assets and the obligation.

CASH FLOW STATEMENT

In this chapter we have repeatedly pointed out that the cash flows relating to pensions are almost certainly different from the accounting expense. On the cash flow statement, the difference between pension expense and pension cash flow is an adjustment for "non-cash items." Cash paid to the pension fund during the year is required disclosure in the pension note.

DISCLOSURE RECOMMENDATIONS

The disclosure recommendations for post-retirement benefits are unusually extensive. The financial statements themselves include only two amounts relating to pensions and other post-retirement benefits:

1. On the income statement, the amount of expense relating to providing post-retirement benefits; and

2. On the balance sheet, the net *accrued benefit asset or liability* that reflects the difference between the accumulated accounting expense and the accumulated funding after unrecognized amounts are netted out.

These amounts provide little direct information about the nature of post-retirement benefits and the manner in which they are being recognized. Therefore, disclosure is the only viable way to assist users.

Basic Disclosures

Companies must disclose a complete description of their employee benefit plans. Disclosure also includes (1) important accounting policies and (2) measurements being used for pension accounting. The policy disclosures belong in the accounting policy note or description, along with other policy choices that the company has made. Several relevant policy disclosures are suggested, including:

- The amortization basis for past service costs;
- The method chosen for recognizing actuarial gains and losses (i.e., immediate recognition, amortization of full amounts, or the corridor method) and the period for amortization, if amortization is being used; and
- The valuation method for plan assets (i.e., market value or market-related value).

Measurement disclosures are extensive. A description of these required measurements spans seven pages in the accounting standard and will not be repeated here. Suffice it to say that all calculations and assumptions must be disclosed. *Some* major items:

1. Amount of the accrued benefit asset or accrued pension liability that has been included in the balance sheet, along with its balance sheet classification;

2. A reconciliation of pension amounts to the balance sheet account (that is, the first four spreadsheet columns, to equal the balance sheet account);

3. Amount of expense recognized for the period, and the components of the expense;

4. Actuarial present value of accrued pension benefits at the end of the period, and the changes in this amount during the year;

5. Fair value of the pension plan assets, measured at market value or a market-related value; also actual return for the year;

6. The resulting plan surplus or deficit (that is, item 4 less item 5);

7. Amount of funding contributions made by the company during the period;

8. Amount of contributions by employees, if any;

9. Amount of benefits paid;

measurement date

in pension accounting, the date on which the actuary determines the amount of the accrued benefit obligations and other key pension amounts

10. Important measurement information—the **measurement date**, date of the last valuation, discount rate, expected long-term rate on plan assets, the projected rate of compensation increase, and the assumed health care cost trend rate; and

11. For public companies only, the effect of a 1% change in health care cost trends.

This is a rather daunting list of disclosures, one that is unparalleled in any other standard. One might wonder just how a financial statement reader can use all this information. However, the recommended disclosures are an attempt to harmonize the disclosures with those required in other jurisdictions.

Disclosure Example

Rogers Communications provides an example of post-retirement benefit disclosure. Rogers's accounting policy note states:

Pension benefits:

The Company accrues its pension plan obligations as employees render the services necessary to earn the pension. The Company uses the current settlement discount rate to measure the accrued pension benefit obligation and uses the corridor method to amortize actuarial gains or losses (such as changes in actuarial assumptions and experience gains or losses) over the average remaining service life of the employees. Under the corridor method, amortization is recorded only if the accumulated net actuarial gains or losses exceed 10% of the greater of accrued pension benefit obligation and the value of the plan assets at the beginning of the year.

The Company uses the following methods and assumptions for pension accounting:

(i) The cost of pensions is actuarially determined using the projected benefit method prorated on service and management's best estimate of expected plan investment performance, salary escalation, compensation levels at the time of retirement and retirement ages of employees. Changes in these assumptions would impact future pension expense.

(ii) For the purpose of calculating the expected return on plan assets, those assets are valued at fair value.

(iii) Past service costs from plan amendments are amortized on a straight-line basis over the average remaining service period of employees.

Exhibit 18-5 shows the company's note relating to post-retirement benefits. Read it carefully. Note in particular:

- The plan is underfunded by $67 million at the end of 2006 but shows a $34 million pension *asset* on the balance sheet. This is because of unrecognized PSC and material actuarial losses.
- Pension expense includes $12 million amortization of actuarial gains.
- Information regarding the increase in the accrued benefit obligation and plan assets is provided.
- Key assumptions are provided, such as interest and asset return rates, and also wage increase assumptions.

EXHIBIT 18-5

ROGERS COMMUNICATIONS—PENSION DISCLOSURES

The Company maintains both contributory and non-contributory defined benefit pension plans that cover most of its employees. The plans provide pensions based on years of service, years of contributions and earnings. The Company does not provide any non-pension post-retirement benefits.

Actuarial estimates are based on projections of employees' compensation levels at the time of retirement. Maximum retirement benefits are primarily based upon career average earnings, subject to certain adjustments. The most recent actuarial valuations were completed as at January 1, 2004 for certain of the plans and January 1, 2006 for one of the plans. The next actuarial valuation for funding purposes must be of a date no later than January 1, 2007 for all of the plans.

continued on next page

EXHIBIT 18-5 *(cont'd)*

The estimated present value of accrued plan benefits and the estimated market value of the net assets available to provide for these benefits measured at September 30 for the year ended December 31 are as follows:

	2006	**2005**
Plan assets, at fair value	$545	$484
Accrued benefit obligations	612	575
Deficiency of plan assets over accrued benefit obligations	(67)	(91)
Employer contributions after measurement date	4	6
Unrecognized transitional asset	(28)	(38)
Unamortized past service cost	3	4
Unamortized net actuarial loss	122	151
Deferred pension asset	$ 34	$ 32

Accrued benefit obligations are outlined below measured at September 30 for the year ended December 31:

	2006	**2005**
Accrued benefit obligations, beginning of year	$575	$453
Service cost	24	15
Interest cost	32	30
Benefits paid	(22)	(19)
Contributions by employees	15	14
Actuarial loss (gain)	(12)	82
Accrued benefit obligations, end of year	$612	$575

Net plan expense is outlined below:

	2006	**2005**
Plan cost:		
Service cost	$ 24	$ 15
Interest cost	32	30
Actual return on plan assets	(40)	(67)
Actuarial loss (gain) on benefit obligation	(12)	82
Costs	4	60
Differences between costs arising during the year and costs recognized during the year in respect of:		
Return on plan assets	7	37
Actuarial loss (gain)	22	(74)
Plan amendments/prior service cost	1	1
Transitional asset	(10)	(10)
Net pension expense	$ 24	$ 14

The Company also provides supplemental unfunded pension benefits to certain executives. The accrued benefit obligation relating to these supplemental plans amounted to approximately $19 million at December 31, 2006 (2005 — $18 million) and related expense for 2006 was $4 million (2005 — $3 million).

(a) Actuarial assumptions:

	2006	**2005**
Weighted average discount rate for accrued benefit obligations	5.25%	5.25%
Weighted average discount rate for pension expense	5.25%	6.25%
Weighted average rate of compensation increase for pension expense and accrued benefit obligation	3.50%	4.00%
Weighted average expected long-term rate of return on plan assets	6.75%	7.25%

continued on next page

EXHIBIT 18-5 *(cont'd)*

Expected return on assets represents management's best estimate of the long-term rate of return on plan assets applied to the fair value of the plan assets. The Company establishes its estimate of the expected rate of return on plan assets based on the fund's target asset allocation and estimated rate of return for each asset class. Estimated rates of return are based on expected returns from fixed income securities which take into account bond yields. An equity risk premium is then applied to estimate equity returns. Differences between expected and actual return are included in actuarial gains and losses.

The estimated average remaining service periods for the plans range from 9 to 13 years. The Company did not have any curtailment gains or losses in 2006 or 2005.

. . .

Actual contributions to the plans are as follows:

	Employer	Employee	Total
2006	$28	$15	$43
2005	21	14	35

Expected contributions by the Company in 2007 are estimated to be $25 million.

Employee contributions for 2007 are assumed to be at levels similar to 2006 on the assumption staffing levels in the Company will remain the same on a year-over-year basis.

Expected cash flows:

Expected benefit payments for funded and unfunded plans for fiscal year ending:

2007	$ 26
2008	25
2009	26
2010	26
2011	26
	129
Next five years	133
	$262

Blue Jays and Fido each have defined contribution plans with total pension expense of $2 million in 2006 (2005 — $5 million).

Source: www.sedar.com, Rogers Communications Inc., Audited Annual Financial Statements, March 30, 2007.

CONCEPT REVIEW

1. What are the arguments in favour of recording the net status of a pension plan, without netting unrecognized amounts?

2. Name the five continuing components of the expense for a post-retirement benefit such as extended medical care.

3. What is the likely intent of requiring extensive disclosures for pension assumptions?

INTERNATIONAL PERSPECTIVE

There is surely no more complicated area in financial accounting than pensions, so it probably won't come as any surprise that there are technical and philosophical differences between the current Canadian standard, the U.S. standard, and the IASB counterpart. There are many broad similarities, but there are specific differences that may significantly affect given companies in given circumstances. Then, there is the whole issue of recording the net status of the plan.

IAS Overview

IAS 19 deals with a broader scope of employee benefits than the Canadian standard on post-retirement benefits; *IAS* 19 covers short-term benefits, profit sharing, and bonuses. However, treatment of these items in Canadian practice is consistent with the *IAS* standard. Canadian standards also require substantially more disclosure for all types of pension plans, especially in the areas of the effect of assumptions and cash flow for pension amounts.

IAS 19 does not state how past service in a defined *contribution* plan would be accounted for, so the Canadian rules are more comprehensive in this area. The standards follow generally similar patterns for defined *benefit* pension plans, requiring accrual of current service cost over the working life of the employee, using the projected benefit method. Past service costs are amortized, and the components of pension expense are broadly similar.

However, *IAS* 19 requires that past service cost be amortized over the period to vesting, not the EPFE, as required in Canada. Under *IAS* 19, the 10% corridor method *may be* used to determine appropriate amortization of accumulated beginning-of-the-year net actuarial gains or losses. However, companies may also record actuarial amounts as a lump sum in other comprehensive income and *never* amortize them to net income. This latter alternative is not part of Canadian practice.

Another difference relates to the measurement conventions used for pension fund assets and rates of return used on fund assets. The international approach bases asset values on market values and returns on expected market returns, with no provision to use market-related values or expected long-term rates of return. There are many other differences related to plan curtailment and settlement, multi-employer plans, measurement dates and the like.

Recording the Net Plan Status

As the chapter explained, current standards require that companies record, as a balance sheet element, plan obligations net of plan assets and also *net of unrecorded amounts*. U.S. requirements are that companies must record plan obligations net of fund assets. *Unrecorded amounts will no longer be netted out.* The U.S. standard involves recording the "other side" of the entry as accumulated other comprehensive income (OCI) in shareholders' equity (likely a debit, to offset a credit to a net pension liability). These unrecognized amounts would then be amortized (or **recycled**, in the standard's terminology) to net income over time. The U.S. is also looking at a long-run project to reconsider many aspects of pension accounting.

recycling

amortizing (or recognizing) amounts recorded in other comprehensive income into net income

Under current IASB standards, companies may follow *the current Canadian approach*, or they may follow *something like the U.S. approach*. One important difference with the latter, though, is that actuarial gains and losses recorded in OCI *would not* be recycled but would remain as a permanent element in accumulated OCI.

The IASB is also looking at short-run and longer-term pension accounting projects. One current project deals with the issue of recording the net status of the pension plan as a balance sheet element. It seems likely that the IASB will strengthen its position in this area, but alternatives may still be allowed, and it is not likely that the IASB standard will be identical to the U.S. position.

RELEVANT STANDARDS

CICA Handbook:
- Section 3461, Employee Future Benefits

IASB:
- *IAS* 19, Employee Benefits

SUMMARY OF KEY POINTS

1. In a defined contribution pension plan, the amounts to be paid into the pension plan fund are determined, and the eventual pension is a function of the amounts paid in and the earnings accumulated in the pension fund.

2. In a defined benefit pension plan, the retirement benefits are defined as a function of either years of service or employee earnings, or both, and the employer is responsible for paying enough into the fund that, combined with investment earnings, there will be enough to pay the pension to which the employee is entitled.

3. Pension plans are contributory when the employee pays into the plan.

4. An employee does not have ownership of pension assets until rights have vested. *Employee* contributions are always vested. In most provinces, vesting of *employer* contributions is legally required when an employee has reached the age of 45 and has worked for the company for 10 years, although many provinces have much shorter legal vesting requirements.

5. Pension plans normally are trusteed, wherein the employer pays required amounts into the pension plan and the trustee administers the plan, invests the contributions, and pays out the benefits.

6. Pension plans are usually registered with the pension commissioner in the province of jurisdiction. Employers can deduct their contributions to a pension plan from taxable income when a formal plan is both registered and trusteed.

7. There are several different ways in which an employer's annual contribution to a defined benefit pension plan can be calculated; these are known as actuarial cost methods for funding the pension plan. These methods are different with respect to the variables that are projected, and the funding patterns.

8. For a defined contribution plan, the annual expense is equal to the contribution made to the plan for current service. If past service is recognized, which is rare, then amortization of PSC and interest will also be included.

9. For a defined benefit pension plan, pension expense for a year is a combination of (1) current service cost, (2) plus interest on the accrued obligation, (3) minus the expected earnings on the plan assets, (4) plus amortization of past service costs, (5) plus or minus amortization of excess actuarial gains or losses. Other special components of pension expense may arise from time to time, such as amortization of transitional assets or liabilities.

10. For defined benefit pension plans, the projected benefit actuarial cost method must be used for recording current service cost. GAAP does not restrict the actuarial cost method that is permissible for funding.

11. Current service cost is an estimate of the cost of providing the pension entitlement that the employee earned in the current year of employment.

12. Past service cost is an estimate of the present value of retrospective pension entitlements relating to previous years' service when a new pension plan is instituted or

when an existing plan is amended. Past service costs are deferred and amortized over the expected period to full eligibility, which is often the estimated average remaining service life of the employee group. Service cost granted on improvement to an existing plan may alternatively be amortized over the period to the next expected amendment.

13. Pension expense is increased by interest on the opening balance of the pension benefit obligation, and reduced by expected earnings on opening plan assets.

14. Actuarial gains and losses arise either because actual experience is different from expectations or because assumptions about the future are changed, or both.

15. Actuarial gains and losses *must* be amortized only if the accumulated amount exceeds 10% of the higher of the accrued pension obligation or the value of the plan assets at the beginning of the year. Only the excess over the 10% corridor needs to be amortized, although a company may elect to amortize a larger amount. The amortization period is the average remaining service period (ARSP) of the employee group.

16. A company may choose to amortize actuarial amounts on a different basis than the corridor method, as long as the amortization is at least equal to the "corridor amortization." A company may also elect to recognize actuarial gains and losses in income in the period in which they arise.

17. Benefits paid to retirees reduce the value of the plan assets and reduce the accrued pension obligation. Benefits paid do not enter directly into the calculation of pension expense.

18. Because of the long time span involved in pension estimates, the current service and past service costs are very sensitive to the underlying assumptions used, including the interest rate assumption.

19. Different assumptions can be used for accounting and for funding, even if the same actuarial method is used for both. Best estimates must be used for accounting purposes.

20. The difference between accounting expense and funding cost are accumulated in a balance sheet account called an accrued benefit asset/liability. This account is equal to the *accumulated benefit obligation, netted with fund assets and all unrecognized amounts.*

21. A spreadsheet is a useful way to organize data needed for pension plan accounting. The spreadsheet tracks the pension benefit obligation, pension plan assets, unrecognized amounts, pension expense, and the balance sheet pension account.

22. Special components of pension expense include amortization of a transitional amount over the ARSP, any change in a valuation allowance needed to avoid overvaluation of the net pension asset, gains and losses on plan settlement or curtailment (unless part of a discontinued operation or unusual item), and adjustment for temporary deviations from a plan.

23. Some believe that the pension plan obligation, net of plan assets (but not net of unrecorded amounts) should be recorded as a balance sheet element based on the definition of a liability, the ability to measure the amounts reliably, and the improved usefulness of the financial statement for users.

24. Other post-retirement benefits include supplementary medical and dental plans for retirees. These benefits are accounted for in a similar fashion as pensions, with the cost accrued over the working life of the employee.

25. Companies must disclose the value of plan assets at market or market-related values. The accrued benefit obligation must also be disclosed along with a reconciliation of these two amounts, and unrecognized PSC and actuarial gains and losses, to the balance sheet accrued pension account.

26. Companies must provide extensive pensions disclosures with respect to accounting policies and measurement of estimates.

KEY TERMS

REVIEW PROBLEM

The following data relate to a defined benefit pension plan:

Accrued pension obligation, 1 January 20X6	$25,000
Long-term interest rate on debt	10%
Unrecognized past service cost from amendment dated 31 December 20X5 (not amortized in 20X5)	$10,000
Unrecognized transitional liability, original initial value: $7,000 at the transition date of 1 January 20X0; unrecognized amount at 1 January 20X6	4,000
Unrecognized actuarial gain, 1 January 20X6	4,700
Actual return on plan assets for 20X6	2,000
Fair value of plan assets, 1 January 20X6	16,000
Long-run expected rate of return on plan assets	10%
Average remaining service life of the employee group (also expected period to full eligibility)	14 years
Estimated interval between plan amendments	5 years
Funding payment at year-end 20X6	$ 4,000
Benefits paid to retirees in 20X6	5,000
Current service cost for 20X6	9,000

The company prefers to amortize the past service cost from plan amendments over a shorter time span.

Required:

1. Compute pension expense for 20X6.

2. Compute the accrued pension obligation at 1 January 20X7.

3. Compute the fair value of plan assets at 1 January 20X7.

4. Compute the unrecognized actuarial gain at 1 January 20X7. Also compute the amortization of the unrecognized actuarial gain for 20X7.

REVIEW PROBLEM—SOLUTION

1. Pension expense, 20X6

Current service cost (given)		$ 9,000
Interest ($25,000 × 10%)		2,500
Expected return on plan assets ($16,000 × 10%)		(1,600)
Amortizations:		
Past service cost: $10,000 ÷ 5 years	$2,000	
Transition liability: $7,000 ÷ 14 years	500	
Excess actuarial gain:		
[$4,700 − ($25,000 × 10%)] = $2,200 ÷ 14 =	(157)	2,343
		$12,243

2. Accrued pension obligation, 1 January 20X7

Obligation, 1 January 20X6	$25,000
Service cost, 20X6	9,000
Interest	2,500
Benefits paid	(5,000)
	$31,500

3. Fair value of plan assets, 1 January 20X7

Value at 1 January 20X6	$16,000
Actual earnings on plan assets	2,000
Funding contributions	4,000
Benefits paid	(5,000)
	$17,000

4. Unrecognized actuarial gain at 1 January 20X7

Unrecognized gain, 1 January 20X6	$ 4,700
Extra earnings on plan assets, 20X6:	
$2,000 actual − $1,600 estimated	400
Amortization, 20X6	(157)
	$ 4,943

Amortization, 20X7
Excess over corridor:

Higher of accrued obligation or plan assets,	
1 January 20X7 = $31,500	
10% × $31,500 = $3,150 corridor limit	
Amortization: ($4,943 − $3,150) = $1,793 ÷ 14 =	$ 128

Note: ARSP is assumed to continue to be 14 years. If the employee group is stable, with new employees entering the workforce to replace retiring employees, ARSP will be stable. ARSP will decline only if retiring workers are not being replaced by younger employees.

Pension Plan Spreadsheet (optional)

20X6	Pension Obligation	Plan Assets	Actuarial G/L	PSC and Transition Amount	Pension Expense	Accrued Asset (Liab)
		Memorandum Accounts			**Statement Accounts**	
			Unrecognized			
Opening	$(25,000)	$16,000	$(4,700) (gain)	$10,000 4,000 $14,000		$ 300*
Current service cost	(9,000)				$ 9,000	
Interest (10%)	(2,500)				2,500	
Actual return		2,000	(2,000)			
Expected return (10%)			1,600		(1,600)	
Amortization of PSC				(2,000)	2,000	
Amortization of transition amount				(500)	500	
Amortization of actuarial gain outside corridor			157		(157)	
Benefits paid	5,000	(5,000)			$12,243	(12,243)
Funding		4,000				4,000
Totals	$(31,500)	$17,000	$(4,943)	8,000 3,500 $11,500		$(7,943)

*Sum of first four columns

QUESTIONS

Q18-1 Distinguish between a defined contribution pension plan and a defined benefit pension plan. Why are defined contribution plans attractive to employers?

Q18-2 Distinguish between a contributory pension plan and a non-contributory pension plan.

Q18-3 Why is it logical that contributions made by an employee to a pension plan vest immediately, while an employer's contributions vest only after a certain period of time?

Q18-4 What is the advantage to a company to having a trusteed pension plan? What responsibilities does the trustee usually assume?

Q18-5 What is the incentive to the company for registering a pension plan?

Q18-6 Explain the impact each of the following variables would have on the current cost of a defined benefit pension plan:
a. an increased rate of return on investments held by the pension plan
b. lower than expected employee mortality rates
c. higher than expected employee turnover
d. a rollback of wages by 3%

Q18-7 Explain why pension accounting must be based on assumptions and estimates.

Q18-8 Explain three funding approaches that an employer can use for pension plans.

Q18-9 Assume that a pension plan must accumulate $700,000 by an employee's retirement age in order to fund a pension. Three different funding models have been used to project funding requirements for the first year. The estimates are $2,600, $6,300, and $1,100. Identify three different funding methods and the funding level most likely associated with each.

Q18-10 In each of the following circumstances, identify the funding method that an employer would likely find most appealing:
a. Conserve current cash balances.
b. Have equal cash requirements each year.
c. Use a funding pattern that could also be used to measure the pension expense.

Q18-11 Assume that a company used one actuarial cost method for accounting, and another for funding. An accrued benefit asset results. Which amount was higher, the accounting measure or the funding measure? What if an accrued benefit liability had been produced?

Q18-12 List and define the five continuing components of net pension expense.

Q18-13 List and define the five special components related to pension amounts.

Q18-14 How is interest on the accrued pension obligation measured?

Q18-15 What is a past service cost? How is it accounted for as part of pension expense?

Q18-16 Define the EPFE and explain when and why it is used as an amortization period.

Q18-17 Define the ARSP and explain when and why it is used as an amortization period.

Q18-18 How are earnings on fund assets, a component of pension expense, measured?

Q18-19 What is the difference between an experience gain or loss and a gain or loss caused by a change in assumptions? How are the two accounted for in the calculation of net pension expense? What alternatives exist?

Q18-20 A company follows the practice of amortizing actuarial gains and losses to pension expense when the amount is outside the 10% corridor. At the beginning of 20X4, the balance of unamortized actuarial gains was $27,000. If the opening values of pension assets and obligations were both $230,000 and the ARSP was 10 years, how much amortization would be expensed in 20X4?

Q18-21 When is a valuation allowance with respect to a pension fund asset required?

Q18-22 When are gains and losses related to pension plan settlements and curtailments recognized?

Q18-23 When are the costs of enhanced pension entitlements associated with termination packages included in income?

Q18-24 If a pension has a benefit obligation of $400,000, pension fund assets of $250,000, and unrecognized losses of $175,000, what will be the resulting balance sheet pension account?

Q18-25 There are suggestions for an altered definition of the compositions of the pension fund balance sheet account. Use the data in Q18-24 to illustrate the effect of the altered definition. That is, what would be the balance sheet pension account under the altered definition?

Q18-26 What justification is there for recording the net position of the pension plan, rather than the net position of the plan less unrecognized amounts?

Q18-27 Why are post-retirement benefits other than pensions less likely to be fully funded? What difference will this make in financial statement treatment?

Q18-28 What note disclosure is required for pensions?

Q18-29 How are plan assets valued for the purposes of disclosure?

CASE 18-1

BALANCE SHEET RECOGNITION ISSUES

For organizations with defined benefit pension plans, the actuary's estimate of the organization's obligation for pension benefits must be disclosed. The market value of pension plan assets available to satisfy that obligation is also disclosed in the notes to financial statements. Within accounting circles, there has been considerable debate as to whether it would be more appropriate to recognize the net status (pension assets less pension liabilities) of the plan as an asset or obligation on the face of the balance sheet instead of relying on disclosure. Consider, for example, the following conversation, between the chief financial officer (CFO) of a large corporation and a financial analyst (FA) from a brokerage firm:

FA: "I'm sick and tired of having to adjust liabilities on the balance sheet for footnote liabilities, such as the pension obligation! The obligation is that of the organization, not the pension fund, and it belongs, net of related plan assets, on the organization's balance sheet."

CFO: "I was under the impression that it was the extent of disclosure, not the form, that mattered to you analysts."

FA: "That's not the point. A balance sheet must be complete to be useful. It seems to me that the pension obligation meets any reasonable definition of a liability, and it belongs on the balance sheet along with other liabilities. Besides, some users might be misled because they expect the balance sheet to contain all liabilities."

CFO: "I have some concerns about putting the pension obligation on the balance sheet. For one thing, the pension fund is a separate legal entity. Take my organization for example. We have agreed with our union to work toward a goal of having the plan, which is currently underfunded, fully funded by 20X20. Our only obligation is to make contributions to the pension fund as suggested by the actuary in order to achieve our funding objective.

"Also, the benefit obligation is based on the *projected salaries* of our employees. If we used *current salaries*, with an actuarial method such as the accumulated benefit method, our pension obligation would reflect our current obligations and be much lower. This is what we'd have to pay if we terminated the plan at any point, and it makes more sense as a balance sheet position.

"I further have concerns that the obligation is too soft a number to warrant balance sheet recognition along with other liabilities. For example, consider our plan formula, which provides for an annual post-retirement pension benefit of 2% of the employee's career average earnings for each year of service, to be paid each year beyond retirement until death. All payments are fully indexed to cost-of-living increases after retirement. There are many uncertainties related to measurement.

"And one more thing. How is our auditor supposed to be able to express an opinion as to whether the obligation on the balance sheet is fairly presented? That means a lot of hours spent with the actuary, hours that our organization will have to pay for! Things are much simpler for the auditor when the obligation appears in a disclosure note only."

FA: "The need to make estimates about the future is not unique to pensions. I wonder whether the claim about uncertainties related to measurement is just an excuse you executives use to conceal your real concerns."

CFO: "Well, to be honest, our organization does have concerns about the economic consequences resulting from putting the net pension on the balance sheet. Our stock price could be adversely affected, not to mention our credit rating, borrowing capacity, and management compensation contracts."

FA: "It seems that the controversy regarding pension accounting continues!"

Required:

Discuss the issues raised.   (CICA, adapted)

CASE 18-2

CANDIDA LIMITED

Candida Limited is a Canadian public company in the business of exploration, production, and marketing of natural gas. It also has power generation operations. Earnings in 20X5 were $2.4 billion, and total assets were $24.1 billion.

You have recently begun work in the finance and accounting department. Your immediate task is to analyze and report on the pension information (see Exhibit 1) included in the last annual report. Your supervisor provided this information with a request:

> We have to prepare for an upcoming meeting of the audit committee. We have several new members of the committee, and the chairperson has suggested that we provide a brief report on Candida's pension issues to get everyone up to speed. It's been several years since we've discussed this issue in depth; this is the opportunity.
>
> Your report should include an explanation of defined benefit versus contribution plans (we have both but are curtailing the former), and the financial statement elements that relate to each plan. It will be necessary to explain the nature of the accrued pension benefit obligation for the defined benefit plans, and the pension plan asset balances, and relate these amounts to the $45 million pension asset we disclose on the balance sheet.
>
> We're particularly concerned about our potential pension position for 20X6, the coming year. We'll see an increase in compensation cost of about 5%, which will accordingly increase pension cost. On top of the large investment losses we experienced last year, this may mean serious increases in pension amounts. Your report should review the accounting treatment of the loss but also project our 20X6 pension expense. Finally, since our pension expense is likely going to be problematic next year, you should identify some key assumptions that Candida can consider to help reduce pension expense.

Required:
Prepare the report.

EXHIBIT 1

CANDIDA LIMITED SELECTED PENSION INFORMATION (IN MILLIONS)

Income Statement	20X5	20X4	20X3
Total expense for defined contribution plans	$12	$9	$ 6
Total expense for defined benefit plans	$12	$6	$10
Balance Sheet			
Accrued pension asset	$45	$7	$16

Disclosure Notes

For Defined Benefit Plans	20X5
Accrued benefit obligation	$228
Fair value of plan assets	113
Unamortized net experience loss	147
Unamortized past service cost	13

Current service cost was $7 in 20X5, and $3 in 20X4.
The company contributed $50 to all pension plans in total over 20X5.

Included in the above accrued benefit obligation of $228 is $14 of unfunded benefit obligation related to the Company's other post-retirement benefits.

Assumptions are as follows:	20X5	20X4
Discount rate	6.0%	6.5%
Rate of compensation increase	4.75%	3.0%
Expected rate of return on plan assets	6.2%	6.6%
Average remaining service life (and EPFE)	12 years	
Health care costs trend rate for next year	10%	

ASSIGNMENTS

★ **A18-1 Understanding Pension Terminology:** Match the brief definitions with the terms.

Terms:

1. Past service cost
2. Current service cost
3. Corridor method
4. Pension plan assets
5. Gains and losses on plan settlements
6. Expected period to full eligibility of pension rights
7. Pension benefit obligation
8. Actual return on plan assets
9. Accrued benefit asset/liability
10. Other post-retirement benefits
11. Interest rate on comparable debt instruments
12. Expected return on plan assets
13. Interest on accrued pension obligation

Brief Definitions:

A. Entitlements other than pensions applicable to retirees.
B. Cost of future pension benefits earned during the current accounting period.
C. The interest rate used to adjust for the time value of money in pension obligation calculations.
D. Balance sheet account caused by the difference between accounting expense and actual funding.
E. Evaluation of minimum need to amortize unrecognized actuarial gains and losses. Amortization is based on excess over 10% of opening pension assets or liability.
F. Resources set aside to provide future pension benefits to retirees.
G. Beginning value of pension plan assets multiplied by the expected rate of return on plan assets.
H. Length of time that the employee must work until full pension rights are earned; used for PSC amortization.
I. Actuarial determination of the value of retrospective pension benefits.
J. Pension obligation at the beginning of the current accounting period multiplied by an interest rate relating to long-term financing.
K. Not normally used to calculate pension expense; difference between this and expected creates an actuarial gain or loss.
L. Often part of discontinued operations, caused by eliminating or curtailing a pension plan.
M. Future pension benefits, evaluated using present value and actuarial expectations, including mortality, turnover, and the effects of current and future compensation levels.

★ **A18-2 Pension Accounting Terminology:** Define the following terms with respect to pension plans:

1. Defined contribution
2. Defined benefit
3. Contributory
4. Trusteed
5. Registered
6. Vested benefits
7. Actuarial cost method
8. Actuarial revaluation
9. Experience loss
10. Changes in assumptions
11. Projected benefits method
12. Level contribution method
13. Accumulated benefit method

★ **A18-3 Amortization Periods** Leung Industries Limited (LIL) has a defined benefit pension plan covering all employees. The pension obligation was $4,360,000 at the beginning of the current year, which is $260,000 higher than fund assets. Plan revaluation is done every three years, and plan improvements have been made approximately every six years.

Required:

1. LIL reports unamortized past service cost of $657,000, an unamortized transition balance of $35,700, past service cost from plan amendment of $344,000, and unamortized actuarial losses of $124,000 at the beginning of the current year. Explain how each of these amounts arose.
2. LIL has EPFE of 16 years, and ARSP of 19 years. Explain the meaning of each of these terms.
3. LIL uses the corridor method of amortizing actuarial gains and losses, and chooses policies that minimize amortization amounts on other amortizable amounts. Calculate the appropriate amortization of all balances to include in pension expense in the current year.

★ **A18-4 Defined Contribution Plan:** TGY Limited has a defined contribution plan for its 160 employees. The plan is trusteed, and each year the company makes an annual contribution, matching employee contributions to the plan to a certain maximum. The funds are invested for the employees by the pension fund trustee using pre-determined parameters.

The pension plan was established to target roughly 60% of final pay to employees as a pension, with survivor benefits or a minimum 10-year payout. Calculations were done based on mortality assumptions, and an expected 5% fund earnings rate. Based on these assumptions, TGY paid $234,000 to the fund in 20X7. At the end of 20X7, plan assets total $2,890,000.

Required:

1. What are the employees of TGY entitled to as a result of this pension? How is this different than a defined benefit plan?
2. What amount of pension expense would TGY report in 20X7?
3. If fund earnings were to be 8% in 20X8, instead of the 5% predicted, who would benefit? Explain.

★ **A18-5 Defined Contribution Plan:** Jianing Joyrides Limited (JJL) operates amusement parks in several locations. The company has a defined contribution plan for its senior employees. Five percent of each employee's monthly salary is deducted from his or her pay and is contributed to the pension plan. JJL pays an additional 5% of the employee's salary into the plan.

In August 20X2, a terrorist attack on another company's amusement park caused a precipitous drop in JJL's business for the remainder of the year. The duration of the dramatic downturn in business was unpredictable.

The drop in business caused a severe cash shortage. In order to help the company weather this crisis, the employees agreed that JJL could defer its share of the August–December pension plan contributions. Employee contributions were made on schedule. The company agreed to make three equal blended payments at the end of each of the next three years (that is, 20X3, 20X4, and 20X5), including interest at 6% from 31 December 20X2. The current interest rate on high-quality debt instruments of similar amount and timing is 4%. During the August–December period, salaries for the participating employees totalled $2 million. JJL's fiscal year ends on 31 December.

Required:

1. Calculate the amount of the delayed payments.

2. Prepare the journal entry to record pension expense for the last five months of 20X2.

3. Assume that salaries in 20X3 total $5 million. Calculate JJL's 20X3 pension expense.

★ **A18-6 Defined Contribution Plan:** Chen Ltd. established a defined contribution plan at the beginning of 20X9. The company will contribute 3% of each employee's salary annually, at the end of each year. Total salaries in 20X9 were $5.2 million.

When the plan was initiated, Chen promised to pay into the plan an amount of past service, calculated to be approximately $3.7 million at the beginning of 20X9. The funding was agreed to be $235,000 per year over 25 years. The expected period to full eligibility is 28 years and the average remaining service period (ARSP) of the employee group is 30 years. Chen uses a discount rate of 4% for its past service obligations.

Required:

Determine the amount of pension expense for 20X9. Note that past service cost is accounted for the same for both defined benefit and defined contribution plans.

★ **A18-7 Prepaid Pension Cost:** Morocco Corporation initiated a defined benefit pension plan on 1 January 20X5. The plan does not provide any retrospective benefits for existing employees. The pension funding payment is made to the trustee on 31 December of each year. The following information is available for 20X5 and 20X6:

	20X5	20X6
Current service cost	$150,000	$165,000
Funding payment	170,000	185,000
Interest on accrued pension benefit	10,000	15,000
Expected return on plan assets	10,000	18,000

Required:

1. Prepare the journal entry to record pension expense for 20X6.

2. What amount appears on the 31 December 20X6 balance sheet related to the pension?

(AICPA, adapted)

★ **A18-8 Accrued Pension Obligation and Pension Fund Assets:** Belfiori Limited reports the following data for 20X8:

Plan assets (at fair value)	
Balance, 1 January	$342,800
Balance, 31 December	344,100
Accrued pension obligation	
Balance, 1 January	$599,690
Balance, 31 December	704,200

The company has a contributory, defined benefit pension plan covering all employees over the age of 30.

Required:

1. How much did the pension plan assets change during the year? Give three items that would cause plan assets to change.

2. How much did the accrued pension obligation increase during the year? Give five items that would cause this amount to change.

3. Compute the amount of the underfunded (overfunded) net position of the pension plan for accounting purposes at the beginning and the end of the year. Explain what these amounts mean.

★★ **A18-9 Pension Expense:** HTR Resources Ltd. has a non-contributory defined benefit pension plan for its employees. At the beginning of 20X8, there is unrecognized past service cost of $3,300, unrecognized actuarial losses of $5,460, and an unrecognized transition cost of $1,080 (all amounts in thousands). The data for 20X8 is as follows:

Plan assets at fair market value, 1 January	$32,520
Actual return	2,760
Contributions made by employer	9,600
Pension benefits paid	(5,100)
Plan assets at fair market value, 31 December	$39,780
Projected benefit obligation, 1 January	$52,560
Current service cost	7,140
Interest cost	4,200
Past service cost arising during the year	390
Loss from actuarial changes, 31 December	180
Pension benefits paid	(5,100)
Projected benefit obligation, 31 December	$59,370

HTR uses expected return on plan assets in computing pension expense and amortizes gains or losses based on opening balances using the corridor method. ARSP is equal to EPFE and is 12 years. The expected rate of return on fund assets is 7%.

Required:

1. Compute the accrued/prepaid pension cost on the balance sheet at 1 January 20X8.

2. Prepare the 20X8 journal entry to record pension expense.

3. Compute the accrued/prepaid pension cost on the balance sheet at 31 December 20X8.
(CGA-Canada, adapted)

★★ **A18-10 Pension Expense:** Flex Fibres Ltd. has a non-contributory defined benefit pension plan for its employees. The data for 20X8 (in thousands) is as follows:

Unrecognized actuarial losses, 1 January	$ 2,700
Unrecognized past service cost, 1 January	1,500
Unrecognized transition cost, 1 January	600
Actual return	1,260
Contributions made by employer	3,150
Pension benefits paid	2,250
Plan assets at fair market value, 1 January	14,100
Projected benefit obligation, 1 January	22,800
Current service cost	3,000

Other information:
EPFE , 1 January   10 years

ARSP, 1 January	8 years
Estimated interest rate on long-term debt	5%
Expected return on plan assets	7%

Flex uses expected return on plan assets in computing pension expense. Opening balances of unrecognized amounts are amortized during the year over maximum periods.

Required:

1. Compute the pension expense for 20X8.

2. Compute the projected benefit obligation at 31 December 20X8.

(CGA-Canada, adapted)

★★ **A18-11 Pension Expense:** The following data relate to a defined benefit pension plan:

Accrued benefit obligation, 1 January 20X4	$187,500
Unrecognized actuarial gain, 1 January 20X4	35,250
Fair value of plan assets, 1 January 20X4	120,000
Unrecognized past service cost from 31 December 20X3 plan amendment	75,000
Actual return on plan assets for 20X4	15,000
Current service cost for 20X4	67,500
Contributions made by employer relating to 20X4	30,000
Pension benefits paid in 20X4	37,500
Expected return on plan assets	6%
Discount rate used for accrued benefit obligation	7%
EPFE and ARSP, 1 January 20X4	14 years
Normal interval between plan amendments	3 years

Required:

1. Compute the accrued benefit asset (or liability) on the balance sheet at 1 January 20X4.

2. Compute the pension expense for 20X4. The company uses the shortest period to amortize past service cost from amendments and the corridor method for unrecognized actuarial gains.

(CGA-Canada, adapted)

★ **A18-12 Pension Expense:** The 20X5 records of Jax Company provided the following data related to its non-contributory, defined benefit pension plan (in $ thousands):

a. Accrued pension obligation (report of actuary)

Balance, 1 January 20X5	$23,000
Current service cost	1,200
Interest cost	1,840
Pension benefits paid, 20X5	(400)
Balance, 31 December 20X5	$25,640

b. Plan assets at fair value (report of trustee)

Balance, 1 January 20X5	$ 2,408
Actual return on plan assets	190
Contributions, 20X5	3,214
Pension benefits paid, 20X5	(400)
Balance, 31 December 20X5	$ 5,412

Expected long-term rate of return on plan assets, 7%.

c. 1 January 20X5, balance of unamortized past service cost from plan amendment, $20,000. Amortization period remaining, 12 years.

d. There are no unamortized experience gains or losses at 1 January 20X5.

Required:

1. Compute 20X5 pension expense.
2. Give the 20X5 entry(ies) for Jax Company to record pension expense and funding.
3. What term could be used to amortize past service cost from plan amendment?
4. Prepare the required note disclosure of the amounts of pension fund assets and obligations. This schedule should include unrecognized amounts and sum to the balance sheet liability. Is the pension fund overfunded or underfunded from an accounting perspective?

★ **A18-13 Corridor Rule:** Dauphinee Corporation has a defined benefit pension plan. At the end of 20X5, the following information was included in the disclosure notes:

(in thousands)	
Accrued benefit obligation	$(6,490)
Plan assets	3,980
Unamortized actuarial loss	840
Unamortized past service cost	1,160
Accrued benefit liability	$ (510)

The average remaining service period was 18 years. The expected period to full eligibility was 16 years.

Required:
Using the corridor rule, determine the actuarial loss that must be included in 20X6 pension expense.

★ **A18-14 Corridor Rule:** Lowen Limited has a defined benefit pension plan. Data with respect to the plan, which was initiated in 20X0 (in thousands) is as follows:

	20X0	20X1	20X2	20X3	20X4
Plan assets (31 December)	$ 845	$1,210	$1,890	$2,005	$2,475
Accrued pension obligation (31 December)	1,050	1,450	1,620	2,345	2,810
New actuarial (gains)/losses arising during year	100	200	(175)	(316)	(60)
ARSP (years)	18	20	19	21	20

Required:

1. Using the 10% corridor rule, determine the actuarial gain or loss to be included in pension expense in each year from 20X0 to 20X4. Round any amortization to the nearest thousand.
2. Prepare a schedule of unamortized actuarial gains and losses carryforward, assuming use of the corridor rule, for each year from 20X0 to 20X4.

★ **A18-15 Corridor Rule:** Fenerty Fabrics has a defined benefit pension plan that arose in 20X3. The following information relates to the plan:

(in $ thousands)	20X3	20X4	20X5	20X6	20X7
Plan assets (31 December)	$500	$260	$320	$350	$200
Pension obligation (31 December)	450	410	360	330	356
New actuarial (gains)/losses arising in year	(46)	16	(45)	21	(4)
ARSP (years)	15	9	11	12	10

Required:

1. What alternatives does Fenerty have to account for its actuarial gains and losses? Explain.

2. For each year what amount would be included in pension expense if actuarial gains and losses were recognized in the year that they arose?

3. Calculate the amount of actuarial gain and loss that should be included in pension expense each year, assuming that the company follows the practice of amortizing actuarial gains and losses to pension expense when the amount is outside the 10% corridor. Note that the amortization is based on opening cumulative balances. Round to the nearest $100.

4. Prepare a schedule of unamortized actuarial gains and losses for carryforward, assuming that the company follows the accounting policy in requirement (3).

 A18-16 Pension Expense: The following data relate to a defined benefit pension plan:

Accumulated pension obligation, 1 January 20X5	$60,000
Initial total past service cost awarded 1 January 20X3 (relates to an employee group with an expected period to full eligibility of 10 years)	20,000
Reduction in pension liability from curtailing pension plan in 20X5, measured at 31 December 20X5	18,000
Discount rate	8%
Unrecognized experience gains and losses, net gain, 1 January 20X5	10,000
Current service cost, 20X5	14,000
Contributions, 20X5	16,000
Expected return, 20X5 (opening assets, $50,000)	4,000
Actual return, 20X5	6,000
EPFE and ARSP, 20X5	15 years

Required:

1. Provide the entry to record pension expense for 20X5. The company follows the practice of amortizing actuarial gains and losses to pension expense when the 1 January amount is outside the 10% corridor. The curtailment involves benefits to employees' irregular operations.

2. Repeat requirement (1) assuming that the company includes all actuarial gains and losses in pension expense in the year that they arise. For this part, the unrecognized experience gains and losses at 1 January 20X5 are zero.

★ **A18-17 Pension Expense:** Allspice Corporation has a non-contributory, defined benefit pension plan. The accounting period ends 31 December 20X9. Pension plan data to be used for accounting purposes in 20X9 are as follows (in $ thousands):

a. Pension plan assets

Balance, 1 January, at market value	$460,000
Actual return; gain (expected return, 6%)	6,000
Contribution to the pension fund by Allspice	51,800
Benefits paid to retirees	(3,400)
Balance, 31 December	$514,400

b. Projected benefit obligation

Balance, 1 January	$680,000
Current service cost	46,800
Interest cost	35,700
Loss due to change in actuarial assumptions, as of 31 December, 20X9	8,000
Pension benefits paid	(3,400)
Balance, 31 December	$767,100

Average remaining service period, eleven years.
Expected period to full eligibility, eight years

c. Company records
    1 January 20X9 unamortized amounts:
    Unamortized past service cost $56,000
    Unamortized actuarial gain/loss $45,400 (gain)

Required:

1. Calculate pension expense for 20X9. The company follows the practice of amortizing actuarial gains and losses to pension expense when the 1 January amount is outside the 10% corridor.

2. Calculate the amortization of relevant amounts for 20X9, and the unamortized amounts for carryforward.

3. Give the 31 December 20X9 entries to record pension expense and funding for Allspice.

 A18-18 Pension Spreadsheet: Tretmire Timber Corp. has a defined benefit pension plan. The following data pertain to the plan for the year 20X8:

Pension plan assets, 1 January	460,700
Projected benefit obligation, 1 January	582,400
Unrecognized past service cost, 1 January	91,600
Unrecognized actuarial losses, 1 January	75,700
Current service cost	80,500
Benefit payments to retired employees	72,000
Contributions to the pension fund	148,000
Actual return on plan assets	41,400

Other information:

Expected return on plan assets	6%
Interest rate on long-term debt	7%
EPFE and ARSP	13 years

Required:

Prepare the pension spreadsheet for 20X8. Round calculations to the nearest hundred.

(CGA-Canada, adapted)

 A18-19 Pension Spreadsheet: Okamura Construction Corp. has a defined benefit pension plan. Information concerning the 20X7 and 20X8 fiscal years are presented below:

From the plan actuary:

- Current service cost in 20X7 is $430,000 and in 20X8 is $488,000.
- Pension obligation is $4,975,000 at the beginning of 20X7.
- Unamortized past service cost at the beginning of 20X7 was $680,000.
- ARSP is 24 years and EPFE is 21 years at the beginning of 20X7; this is changed to 23 and 20 years, respectively, at the beginning of 20X8.
- Unrecognized actuarial loss at the beginning of 20X7 was $487,000.
- Benefits paid to retirees, $235,000 in 20X7 and $295,000 in 20X8.
- Actuarial revaluation at the end of 20X7 showed a $406,000 increase in the obligation. Revaluations take place every four years.

From the plan trustee:

- Plan assets at market value at the beginning of 20X7 were $3,705,000.
- 20X7 contributions were $510,000 and in 20X8, $525,000.
- Actual earnings were $276,000 in 20X7 and $80,000 in 20X8.

Other information:

- Interest rate on long-term debt, stable in 20X7 and 20X8, 6%.

- Expected rate of return on asset, stable at 4% in 20X7 and 20X8.
- The company uses the corridor method for actuarial losses, and amortizes excess amounts over the maximum period.

Required:

Prepare a spreadsheet for 20X7 and 20X8 that determines pension expense, and also the closing balance sheet position with respect to pensions. Round amounts to the nearest $100.

★★ **A18-20 Pension Expense; Spreadsheet:** Fox Company has a non-contributory, defined benefit pension plan adopted on 1 January 20X5. On 31 December 20X5, the following information is available:

For accounting purposes

- Interest rate used for discounting and asset return, 5%.
- Past service cost, granted as of 1 January, $200,000. This is also the accrued pension obligation on 1 January.
- EPFE is 14 years.
- Current service cost for 20X5, appropriately measured for accounting purposes, $67,000.

For funding purposes

- Funding was $99,500 for all pension amounts. The payment was made on 31 December.
- Actual earnings on fund assets, zero.

Required:

1. Compute pension expense for 20X5, and indicate what will appear on the balance sheet as of 31 December 20X5. The company follows the practice of amortizing actuarial gains and losses to pension expense when the 1 January amount is outside the 10% corridor.
2. Prepare a pension spreadsheet that summarizes relevant pension data.

★★ **A18-21 Pension Expense; Spreadsheet—Continuation:** Refer to the data and your solution to A18-20. Certain balances are needed to carry forward to this assignment. The interest rate remains at 5%. The following data pertains to 20X6:

- Current service cost for accounting was $96,000. Interest on the pension obligation was $13,850.
- Total funding of the pension plan was $118,000, on 31 December 20X6.
- Actual return on fund assets was $8,900.
- An actuarial revaluation was done to reflect new information about expected turnover rates in the employee population. This resulted in a $35,000 increase in the accumulated pension obligation, as of 31 December 20X6.
- A plan amendment resulted in a past service cost of $40,000 being granted as of 1 January 20X6 (31 December 20X5). The company prefers to amortize this amount in the shortest possible period of time and will begin amortization in 20X6.

Required:

1. Compute pension expense for 20X6 and indicate what will appear on the balance sheet as of 31 December 20X6. Assume that there will be five years until the next plan amendment. The EPFE was 13 years. The company follows the practice of amortizing actuarial gains and losses to pension expense when the 1 January amount is outside the 10% corridor.
2. Prepare a pension spreadsheet that summarizes relevant pension data.

★★

e**X**cel

A18-22 Pension Expense; Spreadsheet: Brian Limited sponsors a defined benefit pension plan for its employees. The following data relate to the operation of the plan for the years 20X3 and 20X4:

	20X3	20X4
Pension benefit obligation, 1 January	$638,100	?
Plan assets (fair value), 1 January	402,300	?
Accrued benefit asset/liability (credit), 1 January	74,000	?
Unamortized actuarial losses, 1 January	3,400	?
Unamortized past service cost, 1 January	158,400	?
Current service cost	39,000	$48,000
Expected rate of return	8%	8%
Actual return on plan assets	36,000	66,000
Amortization of past service cost	16,800	17,200
Annual funding contributions, at year-end	72,000	81,000
Benefits paid to retirees	31,500	154,000
Increase in pension benefit obligation due to changes in actuarial assumptions as of 31 December each year	85,590	43,620
Interest on pension benefit obligation	53,600	71,200
EPFE & ARSP	20 years	17 years

Required:

1. Do the corridor test to establish required amortization of actuarial gains and losses in 20X3 and 20X4, as needed. The company follows the practice of amortizing actuarial gains and losses to pension expense when the 1 January amount is outside the 10% corridor.

2. Prepare a spreadsheet that summarizes relevant pension data for 20X3 and 20X4. As part of the spreadsheet, calculate pension expense and the related balance sheet accrued benefit asset/liability for 20X3 and 20X4.

★★ **A18-23 Other Post-Retirement Benefits:** Hruska Corp. provides post-retirement benefits to its retirees for dental and supplementary health care. The following information relates to these benefits:

Benefit obligation, 1 January 20X6	$56,000
Current service cost for 20X6	16,000
Unrecognized transition cost, 1 January 20X6	35,000
Unamortized actuarial loss, 1 January 20X6	7,200
Fund assets, 1 January 20X6	7,000
Contributions to the benefit fund for 20X6	9,000
Benefit payments to retired employees for 20X6	12,000
Expected return on plan assets	6%
Actual return on fund assets	350
Discount rate for obligation	7%
ARSP, 1 January 20X6	20 years
Period between actuarial revaluations	2 years

Required:

1. Calculate the balance sheet position as of 1 January 20X6.

2. Compute the benefit obligation for post-retirement benefits at 31 December 20X6, and plan assets at 31 December 20X6.

3. Compute the appropriate expense for post-retirement benefits other than pensions for the year ended 31 December, 20X6. Hruska uses the corridor method with excess amounts amortized over the maximum period.

4. Prepare a reconciliation of the balance sheet position at 31 December 20X6.

Note: The solution to this question is based on a spreadsheet.

★★ **A18-24 Other Post-Retirement Benefits; Spreadsheet:** Lin Developments Ltd. provides post-retirement benefits to its retirees for supplementary health care, including prescription medication. Lin adopted the accounting standard in this area on a prospective basis, which meant that there was a transition amount of $245,000, to be amortized over 25 years. At the beginning of the current year, there is still $176,400 unamortized. Also unamortized is an actuarial and experience loss of $78,500, related primarily to unexpected cost increases in prescription medication.

Lin does not fund these health care benefits to any great extent. As a result, there is only $21,500 in the fund account at the beginning of the year, while the estimated obligation for supplementary health care benefits is $566,300. Actual earnings of the fund this year were $600. Contributions of $46,400 were made to the fund and benefits paid out were $43,900. In the current year, actuarial estimates indicate that current service cost is $67,800.

Required:

Prepare a spreadsheet for the current year that determines the expense for post-retirement benefits, and also the closing balance sheet position with respect to the benefits. Note that the long-term interest rate is 5%, assets earn 2% on average, and Lin uses the corridor method with amortization spread over the same period as was used for the transition account.

★ **A18-25 Pension Expense, Cash Flow:** Dixon Ltd. has a non-contributory, defined benefit pension plan. The interest rate on comparable long-term debt was 5%. Expected return on fund assets is 6%. The company wishes to use any shorter amortization period where possible. However, the company follows the practice of amortizing actuarial gains and losses to pension expense when the 1 January amount is outside the 10% corridor. Plan amendments are expected every five years. EPFE and ARSP are both 10 years. On 31 December 20X8 (end of the accounting period and measurement date), the following information was available:

1. Asset report of the trustee

Asset balance, 1 January 20X8	$ 840,000
Return on plan assets, actual	42,000
Cash received from employer	560,000
Pension benefits paid to retirees	nil
Balance, 31 December 20X8, at market	$1,442,000

2. Pension benefit obligation (actuary's report)

Balance, 31 December 20X7	$ 720,000
Past service cost (due to plan amendment on 1 January 20X8)	80,000
Balance, 1 January 20X8	800,000
Current service cost	520,000
Interest cost	40,000
Pension benefits paid	nil
Balance, 31 December 20X8	$1,360,000

Required:

1. Compute pension expense and unamortized amounts carried forward. The unamortized actuarial losses to 1 January amounted to $77,600. The $80,000 of PSC created on 1 January 20X8 is to be amortized beginning in 20X8.

2. The company uses the direct method to disclose operations on the cash flow statement. What amount will be shown as an outflow with respect to pensions?

A18-26 Pension Information, Interpretation: The following information relates to the pension plan of Daniels Corporation, which has a contributory defined benefit pension plan:

Financial Accounting Information, 20X5		Pension Fund Status 31 December 20X5	
Income Statement			
Pension expense:		Pension benefit obligation	$(1,820)
Current service cost	$200	Plan assets at fair value	1,017
Interest cost	120	Funded status	$ (803)
Return on plan assets	(176)		
Net amortization	163		
	$307		
Balance Sheet			
Accrued pension asset	$373		
Items not yet recognized in earnings			
Unamortized past service cost	$950		
Unamortized net loss	$226		

The information was prepared for the 20X5 annual financial statements and is accurate; the pension plan terms granted PSC entitlements in 20X2 when the plan was amended. The president of Daniels Corporation has asked for clarification of the following:

a. What likely caused the unrecognized net loss ($226) and why is it not recognized immediately?
b. What is the nature of the net amortization in the calculation of pension expense and why does it increase pension expense?
c. If the plan is underfunded by $803, why does the company show an accrued pension asset of $373 on the balance sheet, i.e., what does this $373 represent?
d. Which of the above measurements are dependent on estimates? Explain.
e. In general, how long is the amortization period for past service cost from plan amendment?

Required:
Respond to the requests of the company president.

 A18-27 Pension Expense, Explanation, Calculation: Neotech Industries (NI) was created in 20X0. The company is in the optical equipment industry. Its made-to-order scientific and medical equipment requires large investments in research and development. To fund these needs, Neotech made a public stock offering, completed in 20X4. Although the offering was reasonably successful, NI's ambitious management is convinced that the company must report a good profit this year (20X5) to maintain the current market price of its stock. NI's president recently stressed this point when he told his controller, "We need to report at least $1.1 million in pre-tax profit or our stock price will plummet!" NI's pre-tax profit was $1.1 million, before adjustments. However, appropriate pension accounting has yet to be resolved.

As of the beginning of fiscal year 20X5, NI instituted an employee pension plan with defined benefits. The plan is operated by a trustee. At the inception of the plan, the unfunded past service cost was $3,000,000. NI agreed to fund this amount through equal payments over 20 years, and made the first payment on 1 January 20X5. A 7% interest rate is appropriate and the funding is calculated as an annuity due. The payments were blended payments, including both principal and interest. For 20X5, current service cost was $650,000, funded at year-end. The expected period to full eligibility of employees covered by the plan is 24 years. No payments were made to pensioners during the year. NI has expensed all payments made to the trustee.

The president has also asked what estimates could be revised to minimize pension expense.

Required:

Respond to the issues raised and make appropriate recommendations. Your answer should include a recalculation of pre-tax income.

 A18-28 Pension Expense: In late 20X1, Joseph Abattoirs Limited established a defined benefit pension plan for its employees. At the inception of the plan, the actuary determined the present value of the pension obligation relating to employees' past services to be $1 million, as of the end of 20X1.

In each year following inception of the plan, the actuary measured the accrued pension obligation arising from employees' services in that year. These current service costs amounted to $80,000 in 20X1, $82,000 in 20X2, and $85,000 in 20X3. The costs were determined by using an actuarial cost method based on employees' projected earnings, prorated on services.

All actuarial obligations and funding payments were determined by assuming an interest rate of 6%, which is the maximum rate permitted by the provincial legislation. This rate is also management's best estimate of the long-term rate of return on plan assets. In accordance with provincial legislation, the past service cost was to be funded over 15 years, the maximum period allowed. Payments were to be made at the end of each year, beginning in 20X1. Current service costs were to be fully funded at the end of each year. The company would use any actuarial surpluses that arose to reduce the current year's payment, whereas any actuarial deficiencies would be funded over not more than five years.

In 20X4 the actuary conducted the mandatory triennial revaluation. The revaluation revealed that the plan assets at the end of 20X3 totalled $611,471. At this point, the average remaining service period of employees covered by the plan was 21 years. In conjunction with the actuary, management decided not to make any changes in assumptions, however, including the assumption that the long-term rate of return would be 6%. The actuary also determined that the current service cost for 20X4 was $87,500. There was an experience gain of $21,870 on the pension plan obligation, arising in 20X4. The actual plan earnings for 20X4 were $55,055.

The expected period to full pension eligibility is 20 years and has been stable at 20 years for the past four years.

Required:

Determine the amount of pension expense that should appear on the income statement of the company for 20X4. The company follows the policy of including all actuarial gains and losses in income in the year in which they arise.

(CICA, adapted)

 A18-29 Pension Expense: Computer Imaging Ltd. (CIL) established a formal pension plan 10 years ago to provide retirement benefits for all employees. The plan is non-contributory and is funded through a trustee, which invests all funds and pays all benefits as they become due. Vesting occurs when the employee reaches age 45 and has been employed by CIL 10 years.

At the inception of the plan, past service cost (PSC) amounted to $300,000. For accounting purposes, PSC is being amortized over 15 years (the EPFE of the employee group at the inception of the plan) on a straight-line basis. The past service cost is being funded over 10 years by level annual end-of-year payments calculated at 5%, which is a reasonable approximation of long-term borrowing rates (see actuarial report for the funding amount, following). Each year, the company also funds an amount equal to current service cost less actuarial gains or plus actuarial losses. The assumed average annual return on plan assets is projected at 6%.

At the beginning of 20X8, the accumulated actuarial obligation was $1,296,330. Opening unrecognized actuarial gains were $154,250. In 20X8, the average remaining service period of the whole employee group was estimated to be 20 years. Expected period to full eligibility was shorter than this, at 18 years.

The independent actuary's biennial revaluation report follows.

Computer Imaging Limited
Non-Contributory Defined Benefit Pension Plan
Actuarial Report, 31 December 20X8

Current Service Cost

Computed by the projected benefits method		$ 85,375

Actuarial revaluation

Experience gains for		
Mortality	$ 7,875	
Employee turnover	12,625	
Reduction in pension obligation due to layoffs	20,000	
Decrease in accumulated pension obligation due to increase in discount rate	29,500	
Net actuarial gains		$ 70,000

20X8 funding

Current service cost	$85,375	
Past service cost	38,853	
Less revaluation gains of 20X8	(70,000)	
Total cash contribution to plan		$ 54,228

Pension plan asset portfolio

Market value, 31 December 20X7	$1,375,790
Portfolio performance, 20X8	
Interest, dividends and capital gains	151,685
Market value, 31 December 20X8	$1,527,475
Investment performance for 20X8	11.025%

Required:

Calculate pension expense for 20X8, and the year-end balance of the accrued pension obligation. Also provide a calculation of the unrecognized actuarial gains and losses at the end of 20X8. The company follows the practice of amortizing actuarial gains and losses to pension expense when the 1 January amount is outside the 10% corridor.

 A18-30 Pension Expense; Spreadsheet: Markon Consultants Limited began a pension fund in the year 20X3, effective 1 January 20X4. Terms of the pension plan follow:

- The expected earnings rate on plan assets is 6%.

- Employees will receive partial credit for past service. The past service obligation, valued using the projected benefit actuarial cost method and a discount rate of 6%, is $216,000 as of 1 January 20X4.

- Past service cost will be funded over 15 years. The initial payment, on 1 January 20X4, is $20,000. After that, another $20,000 will be added to the 31 December current service funding amount, including the 31 December 20X4 payment. The amount of past service funding will be reviewed every five years to ensure its adequacy.

- The EPFE of the employee group earning past service is 20 years.

- Current service cost will be fully funded each 31 December, plus or minus any actuarial or experience gains related to the pension liability. Experience gains and losses related to the difference between actual and expected earnings on fund assets will not affect plan funding in the short run, as they are expected to offset over time.

Data for 20X4 and 20X5

	20X4	20X5
Current service cost	$51,000	$57,000
Funding amount, 1 January 20X4	20,000	—
Funding amount, 31 December	??	??
Actual return on fund assets	1,000	6,800
Increase in actuarial liability at year-end due to change in assumptions	—	16,000
EPFE and ARSP for all employees	26 years	25 years

Required:

1. Prepare a spreadsheet containing all relevant pension information. The company follows the practice of amortizing actuarial gains and losses to pension expense when the amount at the beginning of the year is outside the 10% corridor.

2. Prepare journal entries to record pension expense and funding for 20X4 and 20X5.

★★★ **A18-31 Pension Expense; Spreadsheet—Continuation:** Refer to the data, and your

solution, for A18-30 above. Certain balances carry forward. Further data for Markon Consultants related to 20X6 and 20X7 is as follows:

	20X6	20X7
Current service cost	$65,000	$72,000
Actual return on fund assets	12,610	11,440
Increase (decrease) in actuarial liability at year-end due to change in assumption	(5,000)	—
Pension benefits paid, at end of the year	12,000	23,000
EPFE for all employees	24 years	27 years

Required:

1. Prepare a spreadsheet containing all relevant pension information. The company follows the practice of amortizing actuarial gains and losses to pension expense when the amount at the beginning of the year is outside the 10% corridor.

2. Prepare journal entries to record pension expense and funding for 20X6 and 20X7.

★★ **A18-32 Pension Spreadsheet:** The following partial spreadsheet has been prepared:

	Memorandum Accounts				Statement Accounts	
			Unrecognized			
20X2	Pension Obligation	Plan Assets	Actuarial G/L	PSC	Pension Expense	Accrued Asset (Liab)
Opening	(25,590,000)	16,760,000	5,678,000	$675,000		(2,477,000)
Current service	(610,000)					
Change in assumptions as of December 31	540,000					
Actual earnings		867,000				
Closing balances						

Additional information:

1. EPFE and ARSP are 16 years for the general employee group and seven years for the group eligible for past service.

2. The appropriate interest rate is 6.5% for both the obligation and the plan assets.

3. The company uses the maximum amortization period for all amortizable amounts.

4. The company makes a contribution to the pension fund each December 31. This funding is equal to current service cost, plus $100,000 for past service cost, plus any actuarial loss (less any actuarial gain) related to the actuarial liability that has arisen during the period.

Required:
Complete the spreadsheet. Label any items added.

★★   **A18-33 Pension Spreadsheet:** The following partial spreadsheet has been prepared:

eXcel

20X3	Memorandum Accounts				Statement Accounts	
			Unrecognized			
	Pension Obligation	Plan Assets	Actuarial G/L	PSC	Pension Expense	Accrued Asset (Liab)
Opening balance	(476,100)	272,300	3,400 dr	158,400		??
Current service	(78,000)					
Interest						
Actual return		36,000				
Change in assumptions	(79,800)					
Funding		95,000				
Benefits paid	31,500					
Closing balances						
20X4						
Current service	(48,000)					
Interest						
Actual return		66,000				
Change in assumptions	(56,200)					
Funding		81,000				
Benefits paid	194,000					
Closing balances						

Required:
Complete the spreadsheet. Label any items added. The interest rate for all amounts is 6% and amortization period for all amounts, 15 years.

★★   **A18-34 Pension Spreadsheet:** The following partial spreadsheet has been prepared:

20X2	Memorandum Accounts				Statement Accounts	
			Unrecognized			
	Pension Obligation	Plan Assets	Actuarial G/L	PSC	Pension Expense	Accrued Asset (Liab)
Opening	(7,800,000)	4,210,000	988,500 dr	??		(538,500)
Current service	(510,000)					
Change in assumptions— actuarial revaluation	(45,000)					
Actual return		160,000				
PSC granted during year	(1,420,000)					
Closing balances						

Additional information:
• The interest rate is 5% for assets and 4% for the obligation.

- EPFE is 20 years at the beginning of 20X2, ARSP is 15 years, and there are five years between plan amendments. The new PSC granted during the year will not be amortized until 20X3.
- The company chooses amortization policies that are as long as possible in all circumstances.
- The company funds current service cost each December 31, plus $400,000 related to past service, plus any actuarial losses or minus any actuarial gains related to the pension liability that arose during the year.

Required:
Complete the spreadsheet. Label any items added.

★★★ **A18-35 Pension Expense, Multi-Year; Spreadsheet:** Drebus Entertainments Limited instituted a defined benefit pension plan in the year 20X2, effective 1 January 20X2. Terms of the pension plan follow:

- Current service cost will be fully funded each 31 December, plus or minus any actuarial or experience gains related to the pension obligation. Experience gains and losses related to the difference between actual and expected earnings on fund assets will not affect plan funding in the short run, as they are expected to offset over time.
- Employees will be granted past service. The past service obligation, valued using the projected benefit actuarial cost method, is $3,750,000 as of 1 January 20X2.
- Past service cost will be funded through payments of $480,000 made each 31 December beginning on 31 December 20X2.
- The EPFE of the employee group earning past service is 16 years.
- The assumed earnings rate on plan assets is 7%. This is also the long-term borrowing rate.

Data for the first three years of the plan are:

	20X2	20X3	20X4
Current service cost	$915,000	$975,000	$1,074,000
Actual return on fund assets	—	68,250	280,800
Increase (decrease) in actuarial liability at year-end due to change in assumptions	—	(67,500)	—
Benefits paid to employees, at end of year	—	15,000	52,500
ARSP (and EPFE) for all employees	10 years	14 years	17 years

Required:
1. Prepare a spreadsheet containing all relevant pension information. The company follows the practice of amortizing actuarial gains and losses to pension expense when the amount at the beginning of the year is outside the 10% corridor.
2. Prepare journal entries to record pension expense and funding for all years.

★★★ **A18-36 Comprehensive; Chapters 12, 13, 14, 17, 18:** Oilfield Multiservices Ltd (OML) offers oilfield operation services to the oil and gas industry in Alberta and Texas. OML owns no natural resource properties itself, but assists in exploration activities through cementing and stimulation services. The company has prepared draft financial statements (Exhibit 1). However, some transactions during the year have not been properly reflected in the financial statements (Exhibit 2). Additional information on financial statement elements are provided in Exhibit 3. OML is required, as part of its bond agreement, to maintain a minimum level of retained earnings of $30 million, and a maximum debt-to-equity ratio of 1.5. In the debt-to-equity ratio, the numerator is "total liabilities." Since a number of the transactions that have not been processed affect debt and/or equity, the CFO is concerned that these key financial targets continue to be met.

Required:

1. Provide journal entries to account for the information provided in Exhibits 2 and 3. None of the adjustments mentioned alter income tax expense, income tax payable, or future income tax. Round all adjustments to the nearest thousand. All amounts are given in thousands, except share volumes and per share amounts.

2. Prepare a revised balance sheet, income statement, and retained earnings statement.

3. Evaluate the key financial targets and suggest action for the coming year if there are concerns.

EXHIBIT 1

OILFIELD MULTISERVICES LTD.—DRAFT FINANCIAL STATEMENTS FOR THE YEAR ENDED 31 DECEMBER 20X7 (IN THOUSANDS)

BALANCE SHEET

Assets

Cash		$ 14,960
Accounts receivable		30,497
Inventory		1,958
Prepaid expenses and deposits		930
Current assets		48,345
Capital assets, net		78,441
Intangible assets		890
Suspense		8,338
Total assets		**$136,014**

Liabilities

Accounts payable and accrued liabilities		$ 19,511
Income tax payable		1,600
Current bank loan		12,100
Current liabilities		33,211
Lease liability		3,985
Long-term debt	30,000	
Premium	1,210	31,210
Future income tax		6,900
Accrued pension obligation		620
Total liabilities		75,926

Shareholders' equity

Preferred shares		5,100
Common shares		11,050
Contributed capital on common stock retirement		788
Stock options outstanding		450
Retained earnings		42,700
Total shareholders' equity		60,088
Total liabilities & shareholders' equity		**$136,014**

INCOME STATEMENT; YEAR ENDED 31 DECEMBER 2007

Sales	$146,560
Expenses	
Operating	103,490
Selling, general & administration	8,385
Interest	2,355
Amortization	8,420
	122,650
Income before tax	23,910
Income tax	5,950
Net income	**$ 17,960**

RETAINED EARNINGS STATEMENT; YEAR ENDED 31 DECEMBER 2007

Retained earnings, beginning of year	$27,965
Common share retirement	0
Dividends:	
Preferred dividends	0
Common share dividends	(3,225)
Stock dividends	0
Net income (loss) for year	17,960
Retained earnings, end of year	$42,700

EXHIBIT 2

OILFIELD MULTISERVICES LTD.—OUTSTANDING TRANSACTIONS

Note: Amounts are in thousands, except share volumes and per share amounts

1. Preferred dividends were declared but not paid. They have not yet been recorded. They should be included in "Accounts payable and accrued liabilities."

2. On 1 October 20X7, 865,000 common shares were re-acquired from a shareholder and retired. The $6,240 payment was debited to the "suspense" account, which now appears as an asset on the balance sheet.

3. No premium amortization on the bond has been recorded for 20X7.

4. No adjustment has been made for compensation expense inherent in stock option plans.

5. The $2,098 payment made to the pension trustee, was debited to the "suspense" account. No pension expense has been recorded in the 20X7 financial statements. The pension plan covers operating employees (85%) and administrative staff (15%).

6. A stock dividend of 10% was declared and distributed on 31 December on common shares. The Board of Directors agreed that this was to be capitalized at a value of $8 per share. The stock dividend has not yet been recorded.

7. The lease liability must be adjusted for interest and the current portion, which will be classified as part of the current liability "Current bank loan."

EXHIBIT 3

OILFIELD MULTISERVICES LTD.—ADDITIONAL INFORMATION

Note: Amounts are in thousands, except share volumes and per share amounts

1. Lease obligation

The lease obligation is the remaining portion of a 20-year capital lease with annual payments each 1 January of $612. The 1 January 20X7 payment was properly recorded. The interest rate used for lease capitalization was 7%. No interest has been recorded in 20X7, nor has the current portion of the lease liability been recorded.

2. Share information

Preferred shares—$6 cumulative no-par preferred shares outstanding, 51,000 shares outstanding during the entire year in 20X7.

Common shares—No-par common shares outstanding at the beginning of 20X7, 6,210,000 shares. During the year, 865,000 shares were retired on 1 October and a 10% stock dividend was declared and distributed on 31 December.

3. Bonds payable

- Long-term debt consists of
- Bonds payable, 6 1/4%, due 30 June 20X21 $30,000

Oilfield used straight-line amortization for the bond premium. The premium account has had a balance of $1,210 as of 1 January 20X7.

4. Outstanding stock options

Stock options have been outstanding during 20X7 for 265,000 shares. These options are held by senior administrative employees. They may be exercised for the first time on 1 January 20X9, and are being amortized over four years. The options were originally valued at $900 using the binomial option pricing model.

5. Pension information

According to a recent actuarial evaluation, the defined benefit pension plan had $8,475 in assets and $9,716 of accrued benefit obligation at the beginning of 20X7. The actual return on assets was $680, while $495 was expected. Current service cost in 20X7 was $1,700 using the projected benefits actuarial cost method. A long-term interest rate of 6% was considered appropriate to measure interest cost. The company uses the corridor method to evaluate the need to amortize actuarial gains and losses, and no amortization was needed in 20X7. Benefits paid to pensioners were $500. The unamortized balance of past service cost from plan adoption and amendment was $600 at the beginning of 20X7. The amortization period relating to this amount was 10 years at the beginning of 20X7.

(CGA-Canada, adapted)

CHAPTER 19

Earnings per Share

INTRODUCTION

References to earnings data expressed as earnings per share (EPS) are common in the financial press. For instance, in recent reports, BCE announced higher third-quarter profits at $0.84 per share, up from $0.44 in the prior comparative period; reports trumpeted quadrupled fourth-quarter EPS of $0.35 at Tim Hortons Inc, and CGI announced reported earnings of $0.18 per share, before $0.13 per share of restructuring costs. Earnings per share is clearly used to communicate information in financial markets.

Earnings per share is calculated in order to indicate each shareholder's proportionate share in the company's earnings. An absolute increase in net income is not, in itself, an adequate indicator because net income may go up as a result of increased investment. For example, a company may issue more shares for cash. The increased investment would be expected to generate additional earnings for the company. For an individual shareholder, the real question is whether net income increased *enough* to compensate for the increased number of shares outstanding. If the proportionate increase in net income was less than the proportionate increase in outstanding shares, then earnings attributable to each share will decline.

In this chapter, we demonstrate how to calculate basic EPS, which is defined as net income, less the claims of senior shares, divided by the weighted-average number of common shares outstanding. The chapter also addresses the intricacies of diluted EPS, a "what-if" statistic presented to give investors information about the potential decline in EPS if outstanding options and convertible securities were to result in the issuance of common shares. Finally, the uses and limitations of earnings per share data are explored.

REQUIREMENT TO REPORT EPS

Only public corporations are required to report EPS data, since EPS is used as an important communication and evaluation tool in public markets. EPS is far less relevant for most private companies. Nevertheless, it may be quite useful for private corporations that have a larger shareholder group, such as co-operatives and employee-owned companies, to present EPS as a routine part of their financial reporting. If EPS is calculated, a corporation must follow the rules established in the accounting standards.

EPS FIGURES

Companies must report two EPS numbers and disclose them on the income statement. Each is based on different measures of earnings and outstanding shares. The first EPS statistic is **basic earnings per share**, calculated on (1) earnings before discontinued operations and extraordinary items, and then (2) net income. The EPS effect of discontinued operations and/or extraordinary items is shown separately, although it can be shown in the disclosure notes.

basic earnings per share

earnings per share calculated as net income available to common shareholders (earnings less preferred share claims and other prior claims) divided by the weighted-average common shares outstanding

Basic EPS is useful for comparing a company's current performance with its past record. However, many companies have significant amounts of convertible securities and/or stock options outstanding, which raise the possibility of substantial change in the corporation's capital structure. Therefore, in order to provide a basis for useful forward predictions, diluted EPS must also be disclosed. **Diluted earnings per share** shows the maximum dilution to EPS that could occur if all potentially available dilutive common shares were issued—that is, if all dilutive stock options were exercised, and all dilutive convertible debt and convertible preferred shares were converted to common shares.

Diluted EPS must be calculated both on (1) earnings before discontinued operations and extraordinary items, and then (2) net income. The diluted EPS effect of discontinued operations and/or extraordinary items must be disclosed as well, although it can be shown in the disclosure notes.

BASIC EARNINGS PER SHARE

The basic earnings per share calculation for the year (or for an interim period, such as a quarter) is as follows:

$$\frac{\text{Net income available to common shareholders}}{\text{Weighted-average number of common shares outstanding}}$$

The following sections explain more fully both the numerator and denominator of the basic EPS calculation.

Net Income Available to Common Shareholders

The numerator, *net income available to common shareholders*, is the net income of the company, less claims to income that take precedence over the common share claim. The most usual prior claim to net income is the dividend entitlement of senior shares. In the context of EPS calculations, **senior shares** refer to those shares that have dividend claims with higher priority than common shares. Most preferred shares meet this criterion. The restricted dividend rights of senior shares are deducted from net income as follows:

- For *cumulative* senior shares, the annual dividend is subtracted from net income regardless of whether it has been declared for the year; any future dividend distributions to common shareholders can be made only after senior shares' dividends in arrears have been paid.

- For *non-cumulative* senior shares, only those dividends actually declared during the period are subtracted in determining the EPS numerator.

What happens if cumulative preferred share dividends go in arrears, and, say, three years' dividends are paid in year 3 to clear up the arrears and bring the shares up to date? In years 1 and 2, when no dividends were paid, the annual dividend entitlement would have been deducted from earnings in order to calculate basic EPS. In the third year, three years' dividends are paid, but *only the current year dividend is deducted* when calculating basic EPS. It would be double counting (or double deducting!) to take year 1 and year 2 dividends off *again*. So, for cumulative shares, the maximum deduction is one year's dividend. If shares are non-cumulative, a deduction is made for any and all dividends declared in the period. This represents their maximum claim to earnings.

If there are "senior" shares that participate in dividends with common, then they are not considered to be senior shares for the purpose of EPS calculation, regardless of whether they are called "preferred shares" or "senior shares" in the corporate charter. See the section on multiple classes of shares, following.

Other Adjustments While dividends on preferred shares are the most frequent adjustment to the earnings line in basic EPS, there is a possibility that more adjustments are needed.

- If preferred shares are retired during the period, a "loss" will be recorded directly in shareholders' equity, if the price paid is higher than the average issuance price to date. This was described in Chapter 13. This loss is not included in net income, but is included (subtracted) in the numerator of basic EPS.
- If there is a *capital charge* on a convertible bond that is recorded as a direct deduction from retained earnings, this amount is also subtracted in the numerator of basic EPS.

Remember, though, that some preferred shares are classified as debt on the balance sheet because they have the characteristics of debt—usually, these shares have fixed repayment terms. Dividends on these preferred shares must be deducted on the income statement, not the retained earnings statement. As a result, the number presented as net income may be after the preferred dividends. Be sure to understand the starting point; preferred dividends are deducted only once!

The important question is always *what are the earnings available to common share holders?* Increases or decreases to all equity accounts should be carefully reviewed before EPS is calculated.

Weighted Average Number of Shares

The denominator of the EPS calculation reflects the number of shares, on average, that were outstanding during the year. The denominator will include all classes of shares that have residual claim (last call) on dividends, regardless of the name given to them in the corporate charter or in the accounting records. The denominator is weighted by the proportion of the year that shares are outstanding. The result is **weighted average common shares outstanding (WACS)**.

To calculate the weighted average of outstanding shares, shares are weighted by the length of time they are outstanding during the period. If a corporation issues additional shares during the year, additional capital invested in the business should increase net income. Similarly, if the number of shares outstanding during the year is reduced through a share buy-back program, withdrawal of capital from the business can be expected to reduce net income. The intent of the EPS calculation is to reflect the relative effect on income after including the change in shares outstanding.

Example Assume that a company has 9,000,000 shares outstanding at the beginning of the year and issues an additional 3,000,000 shares on 1 September. There will have been 9,000,000 shares outstanding for the first eight months of the year, followed by 12,000,000 for the last four months. The weighted-average number of shares outstanding is 10,000,000. This can be calculated using a number of approaches. For example,

---

Method 1

9,000,000 shares outstanding for eight months: 9,000,000 × 8/12   =   6,000,000

12,000,000 shares outstanding for four months: 12,000,000 × 4/12 =   4,000,000

WACS   = 10,000,000

Method 2	Number of Shares	×	Months Outstanding	=	Weighted No. of Shares
	9,000,000		8		72,000,000
	12,000,000		4		48,000,000
	Total				120,000,000

WACS = 120,000,000 ÷ 12 months = 10,000,000

Method 3

9,000,000 shares outstanding for the full year: 9,000,000 × 12/12   =   9,000,000

3,000,000 shares outstanding for four months: 3,000,000 × 4/12   =   1,000,000

WACS   = 10,000,000

Each of these methods generates the same, correct answer and all are acceptable approaches. Illustrations will use the first method.

This calculation is done by full month (8/12, 4/12), although the most precise weighted average is based on days. Weighting by month provides a reasonable approximation, but calculations may have to be done more precisely if the approximation is not adequate in the circumstances. For instance, if outstanding shares fluctuated heavily during a month, daily averaging would be far more accurate.

Stock Splits and Stock Dividends

stock dividend

a dividend payable by issue of shares of the company's own common stock

If shares are issued as a **stock dividend** or a stock split, *they are not weight-averaged*. Instead, the stock dividend or stock split is treated as though it had been in effect for the whole period. It is also *adjusted through all prior years* disclosed as comparative data. That is, dividend shares and split shares are treated as though they have always been outstanding.

Remember, when a share dividend, split, or **reverse split** occurs, common share equity is not changed, nor is the composition of the broader capital structure affected (i.e., no change to long-term debt or other elements). There is no substantive change to the corporation's net asset structure. Splits and dividends do not bring new capital into the corporation and therefore cannot be expected to generate additional earnings. Earnings are simply split up into different-sized pieces.

reverse split

decrease in the number of shares outstanding with no change in the recorded capital accounts of the company; may be used to increase the market and book value per share of company shares

In order to assure comparability of EPS, *all* reported prior years' EPS numbers are restated to reflect splits and dividends. In the case of a two-for-one split, all prior EPS figures will be divided by two because one share outstanding in previous years is equivalent to two shares outstanding after the split. The denominator of the fraction doubles, so the product is halved.

Example The following example illustrates the calculation of WACS when there is a stock split or stock dividend.

- A corporation has 5,000 shares outstanding on 1 January, the beginning of the fiscal year.
- On 31 March, the conversion privilege on convertible bonds is exercised by the bondholders, resulting in an additional 2,400 shares being issued.
- On 1 September, the shares are split two-for-one.
- On 1 October, an additional 3,000 shares are issued for cash.

In this example, each share outstanding prior to 1 September is equivalent to two shares outstanding after that date. The denominator of the EPS calculation must be adjusted to reflect the shares outstanding at the end of the year, after the stock split. The discontinuity that occurs as the result of the stock split must be adjusted by multiplying the pre-September outstanding shares by the split factor (in this example, $\times$ 2) as follows:

WACS calculation:		
1 January–31 March (pre-split)	5,000 $\times$ **2** $\times$ 3/12	2,500
1 April–31 August (pre-split)	7,400 $\times$ **2** $\times$ 5/12	6,167
1 September–30 September	14,800 $\times$ 1/12	1,233
1 October–31 December	17,800 $\times$ 3/12	4,450
WACS		14,350

The 5,000 shares outstanding for the first three months are equivalent to 10,000 (5,000 $\times$ 2) shares after the split. Similarly, the 7,400 shares are multiplied by two to arrive at 14,800 post-split shares. Shares from the date of the split are *not* multiplied by two, because they are stated in post-split shares.

Post Year-End Split or Dividend If there is a stock dividend or stock split *after the end of the year* (in the next fiscal period), it is factored into the weighted-average calculation of the *current year*. This applies to stock dividends and splits that take place before the audit report is signed. Assume a company's fiscal year ends on 31 December 20X5. Thirty thousand common shares have been outstanding for the entire period. On 15 January 20X6, before the audit is complete, there is a reverse stock split, 1 for 3. The 30,000 shares become 10,000 shares. This 10,000 figure will be used for EPS calculations even though the split happened after the end of the year. After all, by the time the financial statements are released, the shareholders will be holding their new, smaller shares, and all data should be applicable to this new capital arrangement

Other Effects of a Split or Dividend A split or dividend will change the terms of all outstanding share commitment contracts. That is, *when there is a stock split or stock dividend, the number of shares into which each senior security is convertible is adjusted accordingly*. For example, if a $1,000 bond was convertible into four shares of common stock prior to a two-for-one split (i.e., a conversion price of $250), then it will automatically be convertible into eight shares (a conversion price of $125) after the split. There is *always* an anti-dilution provision to protect the holders of convertible securities and options. Option contracts will also be changed, increasing the number of shares offered and decreasing the option price.

Example: Basic EPS

Exhibit 19-1 shows the computation of basic EPS in a situation involving a simple capital structure that has non-convertible preferred shares. It is based on the following facts:

1. Capital structure:	
Common shares, no-par, outstanding on 1 January	90,000 shares
Common shares, sold and issued 1 May	6,000 shares
Preferred shares, no-par, $1.20 (cumulative, nonconvertible) outstanding on 1 January	5,000 shares
2. Earnings data for the year ending 31 December:	
Net income before discontinued operations	$147,000
Discontinued operations, net of tax	30,000
Net income	$177,000

> ## EXHIBIT 19-1
>
> ## BASIC EPS CALCULATION
>
> | | Earnings Available to Common Shares | Weighted-Average Number of Shares | Earnings per Share |
> |---|---|---|---|
> | **Earnings:** | | | |
> | Net income before discontinued operations | $147,000 | | |
> | Less preferred dividend entitlement: 5,000 shares × $1.20 | (6,000) | | |
> | Earnings available to common, before discontinued operations | 141,000 | | |
> | Discontinued operations | 30,000 | | |
> | Earnings available to common, after discontinued operations | $171,000* | | |
> | **Shares outstanding:** | | | |
> | 90,000 × 4/12 | | 30,000 | |
> | 96,000 × 8/12 | | 64,000 | |
> | Weighted average | | 94,000 | |
> | **EPS:** | | | |
> | Income before discontinued operations | $141,000 | 94,000 | $1.50 |
> | Discontinued operations | 30,000 | 94,000 | 0.32 |
> | Net income | $171,000* | 94,000 | $1.82 |
>
> *Or, $177,000 − $6,000

Exhibit 19-1 presents the computation of the weighted-average number of common shares outstanding during the year. The numerator is adjusted for preferred dividends. Remember that net income is *before* these dividends, and an adjustment is needed.

The two EPS figures of $1.50 and $1.82 must be reported on the face of the income statement. The $0.32 EPS figure for the discontinued operations may be reported either on the income statement or in the disclosure notes. Presentation on the income statement would look like this:

Earnings per share:	
Income before discontinued operations	$1.50
Discontinued operations	0.32
Net income	$1.82

Multiple Classes of Common Shares

As we saw in Chapter 13, Canadian corporations may have multiple classes of common, or residual, shares outstanding. These share classes *participate* in dividends. A primary reason for having two or more classes of common shares is to vary the voting rights between the different classes, normally in order to prevent the controlling shareholders from losing control to hostile investors.

The fact of multiple classes does not, in itself, mean that there is a difference in dividend privileges. *As long as the several classes share dividends equally, share for share, then they are all lumped together in the denominator of the EPS calculation.*

Unequal Dividend Entitlements If the sharing of dividends is *unequal*, more than one EPS statistic will be calculated. For example, assume that a corporation has two classes of common voting shares, Class A and Class B. Class A shares receive three times the dividend declared on Class B shares. If there were 20,000 Class A shares and 80,000 Class B shares outstanding throughout the year, then 140,000 shares ((20,000 Class A shares × 3) plus 80,000 Class B shares) would be used for WACS. If the result was $1 per share, basic EPS would be reported as $1 per share for Class B and $3 for Class A.

Complex/Unequal Dividend Entitlements Dividend arrangements often provide a base dividend, followed by participation in any remaining dividends declared. For example, assume now that both Class A and Class B common shares are entitled to receive a $1 per share dividend. After this amount, Class A shares are entitled to receive $2 per share in dividends for every $1 per share paid to Class B. Net income was $220,000. There were 20,000 Class A shares and 80,000 Class B shares outstanding throughout the year.

To keep it simple, also assume that there are no preferred shares, no shares issued or retired during the year, and no discontinued operations or extraordinary items included in net income.

To calculate basic EPS when the two share classes participate differently in dividend declarations, net income is assigned to the classes according to the base dividend, then *all* of the remaining net income is allocated according to the sharing arrangement. This allocation is based on a ratio, which is a combination of the number of shares outstanding in each class and their relative dividend entitlement. The result is two earnings pools, which are then divided by the number of shares for each respective pool. Finally, EPS for each pool is the additive sum of the base dividend and the entitlement to undistributed earnings. The calculations:

Step 1—Calculate earnings minus the base dividend

Net income is $220,000, and the base dividend is $100,000
    ($1 × (20,000 Class A shares plus 80,000 Class B shares))
Unallocated income is $120,000

Step 2—Allocate undistributed earnings to the share classes

Class A receives $120,000 × 40/120* = $40,000
Class B receives $120,000 × 80/120* = $80,000
A shares, in equivalent Class B shares = 40,000 (20,000 × 2)**
There are 80,000 Class B shares outstanding = 80,000
Fractions: A: 40 ÷ (40 + 80); B: 80 ÷ (40 + 80)

**There are 20,000 Class A shares outstanding, entitled to two times the Class B dividend.

Step 3—Determine per share amounts (from Step 2)

Class A: $40,000 ÷ 20,000 shares = $2
Class B: $80,000 ÷ 80,000 shares = $1

Step 4—Add base dividend to the Step 3 amounts

Class A: $1 + $2 = $3
Class B: $1 + $1 = $2

Basic EPS for each class reflects both the base dividend plus the dividend that would be received if *all income* were declared as dividends. The denominator would be a weighted average for each class if shares outstanding had changed during the period.

Declared or Not? This example assumes that the base dividend was declared. If the dividend is not declared, but is *cumulative*, then nothing changes. However, if the base dividend is *not cumulative*, then it is lost if it is not declared, and excess dividends over the base in future years would follow the (step 2) residual allocation. Therefore, if the base is not cumulative and is not declared, step 1 would not be required in the EPS calculation. In the vast majority of cases, the base dividend is cumulative, so all steps are needed.

CONCEPT REVIEW

1. What type of corporation is required to disclose earnings per share amounts?

2. What is the formula for basic earnings per share?

3. How does earnings available to common shares differ from net income?

4. Asquith Corporation has 2,000 common shares outstanding on 1 January 20X0, issues another 400 shares on 1 July 20X0, and declares a two-for-one stock split on 31 December 20X0. What is the weighted-average number of shares outstanding for the year? What is the impact of the stock split on prior years' EPS amounts?

5. List the steps in calculating basic EPS when there are multiple common share classes.

DILUTED EARNINGS PER SHARE

Earnings dilution occurs when additional shares are issued without a sufficient proportionate increase in the level of earnings. Diluted EPS is meant to reflect any potential for earnings dilution because of existing share contracts. It is based on the *hypothetical situation* of complete conversion of dilutive debt and equity instruments and options exercise. Diluted EPS is hypothetical in that it reflects the results of share transactions that have not really taken place but could take place in the future. It's often called a "what if" number—that is, what happens *if* all contingent claims to common shares were exercised?

Elements to Include To be specific, diluted EPS reflects the hypothetical earnings dilution that occurs if:

- Dilutive convertible senior securities outstanding at the end of the fiscal year are converted to common shares, *and*
- All dilutive options to purchase shares that are outstanding at the end of the fiscal year are exercised, *and*
- The (dilutive) convertible senior securities that actually converted during the year did so at the beginning of the fiscal year, *and*
- Shares issued because of (dilutive) share option contracts during the year were issued at the beginning of the year.

Convertible senior securities include debt and preferred shares, senior to common shares in their entitlement to interest or dividends. If these are convertible to common shares at some point in the future, or have been converted to common shares during the period, they will enter into the calculation of diluted EPS.

A **stock option** gives the holder the right to acquire a share at a stated price. Options sometimes are issued as a part of a package offering of securities (i.e., as a sweetener to attract buyers to a bond issue) and also are widely used as a form of executive compensation. There are various types of options, including stock rights, warrants, and employee stock options. In this chapter, the word "options" will be used to encompass all alternatives. If options were exercised and/or outstanding, they will be considered when calculating diluted EPS.

Dilutive Versus Anti-Dilutive Diluted EPS is meant to be a worst-case scenario. **Dilutive** elements are those that, when included in EPS calculations, cause a decrease in earnings per share. **Anti-dilutive** elements are those that cause EPS to increase. If conversion of senior securities or exercise of options would result in an *increase* in earnings per share, they are anti-dilutive, and are *excluded* from the calculation of diluted EPS. It is assumed that the investors holding anti-dilutive elements would not convert to common shares in these circumstances.

Diluted EPS Calculation

To calculate diluted EPS, adjustments are made to basic EPS for dilutive options and convertible securities.

Adjustment for Dilutive Options Options are dilutive when they are in the money. Options are said to be **in-the-money** *if the exercise price is lower than the market value of common shares.* For example, if an option contract specifies a share price of $34.50, and the share price is $50, then the options are in the money. If the share price is $20, the options are not in the money. *Options are dilutive when they are in-the-money.*

Treasury Stock Method Option adjustments are based on the **treasury stock method**—proceeds are assumed to be used to reacquire and retire common shares at the average market price during the period. Assume that 1,000 options are outstanding with an exercise price of $10. The average price of common shares during the year was $40, so these options are in the money. If the options were exercised, another 1,000 shares would be outstanding for the period, and the company would receive $10,000 ($10 × 1,000). In diluted EPS calculations, it is assumed that this $10,000 is used to repurchase and retire other common shares, also at the beginning of the year. Ten thousand dollars would buy 250 shares ($10,000 ÷ $40). The *denominator* of diluted EPS would be increased by 1,000 shares issued and decreased by 250 shares retired. Options are dilutive when the number of shares issued is greater than the shares retired; this occurs only when options are in-the-money.

Alternative Approach This is not the only way to handle options in EPS calculations. For instance, up to the end of 2000, Canadian standards required the assumption that option proceeds were invested. The *numerator* of the EPS fraction was increased by imputed after-tax earnings. The denominator was increased by shares issued.

Adjustment for Dilutive Senior Securities Bond and preferred share adjustments are based on the **if-converted method**—that is, the numerator and denominator are adjusted to reflect what would have been *if the securities were converted at the beginning of the period (or the date of issue, if later).* The numerator of the EPS fraction is adjusted for dividends or after-tax interest that would be saved if the bonds or preferred shares were converted. In other words, how would the numerator be different if the convertible bonds didn't exist? Interest expense would be eliminated. What if the preferred shares didn't exist? There would be no dividends. The effect to the denominator is straightforward in both cases. More shares would be outstanding!

Technicalities to note:

1. If there are a variety of conversion terms, perhaps depending on when the conversion were to take place, the most dilutive alternative must be used.

2. If the securities were issued during the year, the assumed conversion goes back only to the date of issue, not the beginning of the year.

3. If the conversion option lapsed during the year, or if the security was redeemed or settled during the year, the conversion is still included (if dilutive) for the period of time it was outstanding.

---

dilutive

in the calculation of diluted EPS, a security or option that would have the effect of decreasing EPS if converted or exercised; such instruments are included in the diluted calculation

---

if-converted method

in the context of diluted EPS calculations, the assumption that convertible securities actually converted at the beginning of the period, with the accompanying changes to net income or preferred dividends and number of shares outstanding

Calculation Rules To summarize the potential adjustments:

	Change to Numerator	Change to Denominator
Options—treasury stock method	None	1. Increase by shares issued 2. Decrease by shares retired (Proceeds ÷ market value)
Convertible bonds—if-converted method	Increase by after-tax interest avoided	Increase by shares issued
Convertible preferred shares—if-converted method	Increase by dividend claim avoided*	Increase by shares issued

*If there were any other items recorded in the financial statements, such as gains or losses on preferred share retirement, these items would have been adjusted when calculating the basic EPS numerator and also included in the numerator adjustment here.

Individual Effect Notice that convertible bonds and convertible preferred shares involve a change to the numerator *and* a change to the denominator. The **individual effect** of each convertible item is represented by this ratio. For instance, if there was $10,000 of after-tax interest on a bond that was convertible into 40,000 common shares, the individual effect would be $0.25 ($10,000 ÷ 40,000).

individual effect

in diluted EPS calculation, for each potentially dilutive element separately, the change to earnings entitlement divided by additional shares that would have to be issued; used to establish dilution or anti-dilution and sequence for convertible senior securities

Steps in Calculating Diluted EPS

The steps in calculating diluted EPS are listed in Exhibit 19-2. A flow chart of the process is shown in Exhibit 19-3. We'll explain these steps in the example that follows; refer to the list as the example progresses.

Diluted EPS Calculation: Example

Assume that a corporation has the following capital structure for all of 20X1:

- Convertible debentures: $1,000,000 maturity value, issued at 110; $100,000 of proceeds were attributable to the conversion option (and classified as shareholders' equity); 12% interest per annum, paid quarterly; convertible into 10 common shares for each $1,000 of bond maturity value at the option of the investor.
- Convertible preferred shares: 1,000 shares issued and outstanding; $150 annual per share dividend, cumulative; callable at $1,200 per share; convertible into common shares on a 5:1 basis until 20X5; convertible on a 10:1 basis thereafter.
- Common shares: 20,000 shares issued and outstanding all year.

Net income for 20X1 is $600,000. There are no discontinued operations or extraordinary items. The corporation's income tax rate is 40%. There are executive stock options outstanding all year, allowing purchase of 4,000 common shares at an option price of $50. The average market value of common shares during the period was $125. Interest expense for the year for the convertible bond was $120,000 ($1,000,000 × 12%).

Basic EPS for 20X1 is calculated at the top of Exhibit 19-4. Preferred dividends are deducted from net income to find the earnings available to common shares, and this amount is divided by 20,000 common shares outstanding.

EXHIBIT 19-2

STEPS IN CALCULATING DILUTED EPS

To Calculate Diluted EPS:

1. **Begin with the basic EPS numbers**, based on earnings before discontinued operations and extraordinary items. If there were no discontinued operations or extraordinary items, begin with the only basic EPS number available, basic EPS based on net income.

2. If any options were **exercised** during the period, **determine if the options exercised were in the money**, and thus dilutive. **Adjust the denominator** as though these shares were issued at the beginning of the period, using the **treasury stock method**.

3. **Identify options outstanding during the year**, the option price, and the average share price for the period. Determine if the options are in the money, and thus dilutive. **Adjust the denominator** as though these shares were issued at the beginning of the period, using the **treasury stock method**. If quarterly information is given, perform the calculations quarterly. Calculate a subtotal at this point.

4. **Identify any convertible senior debt or shares that actually converted** during the period. **Calculate the individual effect** of the converted securities, using the **if-converted method**. This adjustment moves the conversion back to the beginning of the year. The individual effect of potentially dilutive elements is the calculation of the change to the numerator (after-tax interest or dividends) divided by the change in the denominator (shares issued), for just the one item alone. Both the numerator and denominator reflect the number of months **before conversion** in the fiscal year.

5. **Identify the terms and conditions of convertible senior shares and debt outstanding during the year.** If there are various conversion alternatives at different dates, use the most dilutive alternative. **Calculate the individual effect** of the converted securities, using the if-converted method.

6. Compare the individual effects of the items identified in Steps 4 and 5. **Rank the items,** from most dilutive (lowest) to least dilutive (highest).

7. Return to the subtotal taken in Step 3. **Include the effects of actual and potential conversions** in cascading order, from most dilutive to least dilutive. Use the ranking from Step 6. **Calculate a subtotal** after each item is added. Exclude anti-dilutive items.

8. Use the **lowest calculation** as diluted EPS.

9. **Repeat the process,** beginning with basic EPS for net income. Use exactly the same adjustments to the numerator and the denominator as in the first calculation. (No second test for anti-dilution is allowed.)

In the first step in diluted EPS calculation (refer to Exhibit 19-2 for the list of steps), the basic EPS numbers are carried forward. There were no discontinued operations or extraordinary items, so the basic EPS based on net income is used for diluted.

No shares were issued under option contracts during the year. There were no actual conversions of senior securities during the period. Steps 2 and 4 can be skipped. (Later examples deal with these situations.)

EXHIBIT 19-3

FLOWCHART OF STEPS IN CALCULATING DILUTED EPS

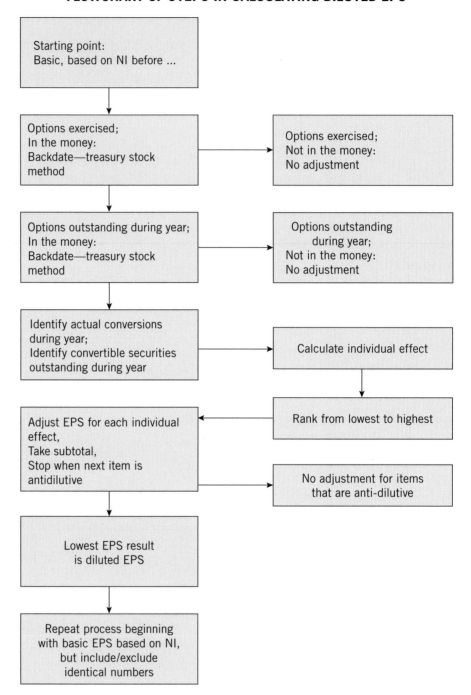

Outstanding options are the next thing to consider, in Step 3. There are options outstanding at the end of the year to issue 4,000 common shares at $50. These options are *in the money*, and therefore dilutive, because the $50 option price is less than the $125 average market price of shares during the period. They must be included when calculating diluted EPS.

If these shares had been issued at the beginning of the period, another 4,000 shares would have been outstanding for the whole period, and the denominator would be increased by 4,000 shares. A total of $200,000 (4,000 × $50) would have been raised by the company.

> ### EXHIBIT 19-4
>
> ## BASIC AND DILUTED EPS CALCULATIONS
>
> | | Earnings Available to Common Shares | Weighted-Average Number of Shares | Earnings per Share |
> |---|---|---|---|
> | **Basic EPS:** | | | |
> | **Earnings:** | | | |
> | Net income | $600,000 | | |
> | Less preferred dividends: | | | |
> | 1,000 shares × $150 | (150,000) | | |
> | Earnings available to common | 450,000 | | |
> | **Shares outstanding** | | 20,000 | |
> | **Basic EPS** | **$450,000** | **20,000** | **$22.50** |
> | | | | |
> | **Diluted EPS:** | | | |
> | Data from basic EPS, above | $450,000 | 20,000 | $22.50 |
> | Adjustments for assumed options exercise: | | | |
> | Shares issued | | 4,000 | |
> | Shares retired | | (1,600) | |
> | Subtotal | $450,000 | 22,400 | $20.09 |
> | Adjustments for debenture conversion: | | | |
> | Interest avoided (after-tax equivalent) | 72,000 | | |
> | Additional common shares issued | | 10,000 | |
> | Subtotal | $522,000 | 32,400 | $16.11 |
> | Adjustments for preferred share conversion: | | | |
> | Dividends avoided | 150,000 | | |
> | Additional common shares issued | | 10,000 | |
> | **Diluted EPS** | **$672,000** | **42,400** | **$15.85** |

In the diluted EPS calculation, using the treasury stock method, we assume that these proceeds would have been used to retire other common shares at the market price: 1,600 shares ($200,000 ÷ $125). The denominator increases by 2,400 shares (4,000 − 1,600) and the numerator doesn't change. It is also possible to make this 2,400 share calculation directly, as (4,000 − ($200,000 ÷ $125). A subtotal shows that the EPS amount has declined to $20.09.

In Step 5, the individual effects of assumed conversion of the two convertible securities are calculated. The numerator of the EPS fraction is adjusted by adjusting for dividends or after-tax interest that will be saved if the senior securities are converted. The effect to the denominator is the additional shares promised.

Note that the bond interest is deductible for income tax purposes, and since net income is an after-tax amount, the interest saved must be calculated on an after-tax basis. Assuming a tax rate of 40%, the interest saving is multiplied by the 60% after-tax equivalent: $120,000 × (1.0 − 0.4) = $72,000. Shares issued would be 10,000, and the individual effect of this convertible security is $7.20 ($72,000 ÷ 10,000). This is dilutive in relation to basic EPS of $22.50 (that is, $7.20 is lower than $22.50).

For preferred shares, $150,000 of dividends would be avoided if the preferred shares had been converted to common shares at the beginning of the period. Dividends are not tax deductible, and there is no need to adjust for tax. The shares may be converted at the rate of 5:1 until the end of 20X5, and then the conversion ratio changes to 10:1. The more dilutive 10:1 ratio must be used in these calculations. Thus, another 10,000 shares would be issued. This is an individual effect of $15, dilutive in relation to basic EPS, but less dilutive than the $7.20 bonds. This comparison is the Step 6 ranking.

Now for Step 7. The bonds are adjusted first, as they are more dilutive than the preferred shares. The subtotal is taken. Inclusion of the bonds reduces diluted EPS to $16.11, and the preferred shares, with an individual affect of $15, are still dilutive. They are then added in. Step 8 is the final determination of diluted EPS—$15.85.

Reporting Diluted EPS

Diluted EPS is reported on the face of the income statement, given equal prominence with basic EPS. Even if the two numbers are identical, they must both be disclosed. In the above example, the company would report:

Basic EPS	$22.50
Diluted EPS	$15.85

Diluted EPS Cascade

In Exhibit 19-4, we illustrated the diluted EPS calculation as a **cascade** of adjustments, going from the most dilutive to the least dilutive. Note that options that are in the money are always dilutive, because they involve no increase to the numerator. That's why they're *always done first* in diluted EPS calculations. Within option classes, the options with the lowest exercise price (largest differential between shares issued and share retired) will be the most dilutive.

After options, the convertible securities with the *lowest individual EPS effect* are the most dilutive, and are entered first. If inclusion of a later item causes EPS to *increase*, it is *anti-dilutive and excluded*. For instance, assume that basic EPS is $1, the result of dividing $100,000 income available to common shareholders by 100,000 weighted-average common shares. Two potentially dilutive securities are outstanding: Preferred shares, with a $45,000 dividend, and a 100,000 share entitlement ($0.45 individual effect), and bonds, with after-tax interest of $68,000, and a share entitlement of 75,000 shares ($0.91 individual effect). Preferred shares are the more dilutive but both elements look dilutive when compared to basic EPS of $1.

After the more dilutive element is included, diluted EPS is $0.73 ($100,000 + $45,000) ÷ (100,000 + 100,000). The second item, with an individual effect of $0.91, is *no longer dilutive*. If it were included, the EPS would *increase* to $0.77 ($100,000 + $45,000 + $68,000) ÷ (100,000 + 100,000 + 75,000). Diluted EPS is reported as $0.73, and the second security is omitted from the calculation. This is the cascade approach to diluted EPS calculations, and it results in diluted EPS being reported as the lowest possible number.

Actual Conversions During the Period

So far, we've illustrated diluted EPS giving effect to the year-end obligations to issue shares. Diluted EPS must also include calculations that reflect actual conversions, and actual options exercised, during the period. This adjustment is often called **backdating**: adjusting the actual issuance to pretend it took place at the beginning of the period. This backdating is done only if the result is dilutive. Backdating puts actual conversions on the same footing as potential conversions, which are effectively backdated to the beginning of the fiscal period. Steps 2 and 4 in Exhibit 19-2 deal with backdating.

The examples that follow demonstrate actual conversions of preferred shares, actual conversion of debt, and shares issued on the exercise of options.

backdating

in the context of EPS calculations, the assumption that a share transaction took place at an earlier date

Example 1—Converted Preferred Shares

Assume that a corporation has two classes of shares outstanding:

- Class A preferred shares, 600 shares issued and outstanding at the beginning of the year; annual dividend rate of $1,000 per share, cumulative, dividend paid at the end of each quarter; each share is convertible into 50 shares of Class B common.
- Class B common shares, 50,000 shares issued and outstanding at the beginning of the year.

Also assume that:

- There are no other senior securities.
- Net income for 20X1, the year of the conversion, is $2,175,000; there are no discontinued operations or extraordinary items.
- All 600 shares of Class A are converted into 30,000 Class B shares on 1 October 20X1; dividends for the first three quarters of the year were fully paid.
- Options are outstanding to issue 10,000 common shares to senior executives for $1 per share; the average share price during the year was $8. No options were exercised during the period. These options were outstanding during the whole year.

Basic earnings per share for 20X1 is $30, as calculated at the top of Exhibit 19-5. Diluted EPS begins with this figure, and then includes the effect of options. (Step 3 as listed in Exhibit 19-2). This reduces EPS to $26.04. Note that the options effect could be directly calculated as a reduction to the denominator of 8,750 shares [10,000 − (($10,000 × $1) ÷ $8)]. The result is the same.

In the year of conversion, 7,500 shares (600 shares × 50 common shares = 30,000, multiplied by the three months they were outstanding, or 3/12) were added to the *weighted-average* number of shares used in basic EPS. In future years, there will be 30,000 additional Class B shares outstanding *all year*. Diluted EPS backdates the conversion (Step 4). This is demonstrated in the second section of Exhibit 19-5. The essence of backdating is twofold:

- Income available to common shareholders, the numerator, is adjusted for the dividends on the converted Class A shares that would not have been paid if the shares had converted at the beginning of the period. This is $450,000 ($250 per quarter × 600 shares × 3 quarters).
- The weighted-average number of shares is adjusted to reflect the full volume of additional Class B shares issued for the conversion. That is, 30,000 shares × 9/12, or 22,500 shares.

The individual effect of this conversion is $20 ($450,000 ÷ 22,500), which is dilutive in relation to the diluted EPS subtotal of $26.04. The result of the calculation is diluted EPS of $24.51.

Example 2—Converted Debt

Assume that a corporation has one class of shares outstanding but also has convertible bonds that partially converted during the period:

- There are 50,000 common shares outstanding at the beginning of 20X1.
- Net income for 20X1, the year of the conversion, is $3,000,000; there are no discontinued operations or extraordinary items.
- The corporation has $40 million principal amount of 10-year, 9%, convertible debentures that were issued five years previously. The bonds are convertible at the investor's option. The full amount is outstanding at the beginning of 20X1. Interest is paid semiannually on 1 March and 1 September.
- The net proceeds from the bond issue amounted to $42 million. The present value of the liability cash flow at the date of issue was $40 million; the remaining $2 million was allocated to the conversion option. At the date of issuance, the market rate of interest for non-convertible bonds of similar risk was 9%. Each $1,000 face value of bonds is convertible into two shares of common stock.
- On 30 June 20X1, one-quarter of the bonds are converted.
- The corporation's income tax rate is 40%.

EXHIBIT 19-5

BASIC AND DILUTED EPS CALCULATIONS
ACTUAL CONVERSION OF PREFERRED SHARES

	Earnings Available to Common Shares	Weighted-Average Number of Shares	Earnings per Share
Basic EPS:			
Earnings:			
Net income	$2,175,000		
Less preferred dividends:			
600 shares × $250 per quarter for three quarters	(450,000)		
Earnings available to common	$1,725,000		
Shares outstanding			
50,000 × 9/12		37,500	
[50,000 + (600 Class A × 50 Class B)] × 3/12		20,000	
Basic EPS	**$1,725,000**	**57,500**	**$30.00**
Diluted EPS			
Data from basic EPS, above	$1,725,000	57,500	
Adjustments for assumed options exercise:			
Shares issued		10,000	
Shares retired (10,000 × $1) ÷ $8		(1,250)	
Subtotal	$1,725,000	66,250	$26.04
Adjustments for converted shares:			
Dividends on converted shares:			
600 shares × $250 for three quarters	450,000		
Adjust shares for preceding three quarters:			
(600 Class A × 50 Class B) × 9/12		22,500	
Diluted EPS	**$2,175,000**	**88,750**	**$24.51**

The conversion of $10,000,000 principal amount of bonds results in an additional 20,000 shares issued. In the basic EPS calculation, the additional shares are outstanding for the second half of the year and are weighted proportionately in the denominator. The EPS numerator includes, in net income, a deduction for interest expense on the $40,000,000 liability for the first half of the year and for the $30,000,000 liability for the second half of the year, following conversion. The calculation of basic EPS is shown at the top of Exhibit 19-6.

To calculate diluted EPS, the actual conversion must be backdated to the beginning of the year (Step 4). The effect of the remaining unconverted bonds must be included (Step 5). Both of these adjustments are made *only if dilutive*.

EXHIBIT 19-6

BASIC AND DILUTED EPS CALCULATIONS PARTIAL ACTUAL CONVERSION OF DEBT

	Earnings Available to Common Shares	Weighted-Average Number of Shares	Earnings per Share
Basic EPS:			
Earnings:			
Net income	$3,000,000		
Earnings available to common	$3,000,000		
Shares outstanding:			
50,000 shares × 6/12		25,000	
70,000 shares × 6/12		35,000	
Basic EPS	**$3,000,000**	**60,000**	**$50.00**
Diluted EPS:			
Data from basic EPS, above	$3,000,000	60,000	
Adjustments for converted debt:			
Remove after-tax interest on converted debt:			
$10,000,000 × 9% × (1.0 − 0.4) × 6/12	270,000		
Adjust shares for first six months:			
20,000 shares × 6/12		10,000	
Subtotal	$3,270,000	70,000	$46.71
Adjustment for remaining convertible debt			
Removed after-tax interest on remaining debt:			
$30,000,000 × 9% × (1.0 − 0.4)	1,620,000		
Shares:			
($30,000,000 ÷ $1,000) × 2 shares per bond		60,000	
Diluted EPS	**$4,890,000**	**130,000**	**$37.62**

The interest that must be adjusted in backdating is six months' interest on the $10,000,000 principal amount of converted bonds. (The bonds were outstanding for six months.) At 9% per annum and with a 40% income tax rate, the impact of interest on the converted bonds is:

$$\text{Interest expense} = \$10,000,000 \times 9\% \times 6/12 \times (1.0 - 0.4) = \$270,000$$

In general, the formula for computing the interest savings from conversion is:

Principal amount converted × interest rate × (1 − tax rate) × fraction of year *before* conversion.

For example, if the bonds had been retired after four months of the fiscal year, four months of interest would be added back.

The second section of Exhibit 19-6 shows the add-back of $270,000 after-tax interest expense, and the weighted-average number of shares is increased to reflect the full amount of shares issued on conversion. Shares are calculated as 20,000 shares × 6/12. The individual EPS effect is $27 ($270,000 ÷ 10,000), which is dilutive to basic EPS of $50. Next, the assumed conversion of the remaining dilutive convertible bonds, still outstanding at the end of the year, is considered. The impact of interest is:

$$\text{Interest expense} = \$30,000,000 \times 9\% \times (1.0 - 0.4) = \$1,620,000$$

Shares to be issued would be 60,000 [($30,000,000 ÷ $1,000) × 2], and the individual effect of the bonds is $27 ($1,620,000 ÷ 60,000). These bonds are dilutive. The adjustment is included in Exhibit 19-6, resulting in diluted EPS of $37.62. Note that the individual effect of the converted bonds and the unconverted bonds is identical; it does not matter which is done first in the cascade.

Example 3—Exercised Options

If options were exercised during the period, an adjustment would be made to backdate these shares to the beginning of the period *if they were dilutive*. Again, the treasury stock method would be applied and other common shares assumed retired for that portion of the year.

For example, assume that as a result of an options exercise, 10,000 shares were issued on 1 November for $50,000. The average share price for the first 10 months of the year was $18. These shares would be weight-averaged when calculating basic EPS. For diluted EPS, in Step (2), the shares are backdated. The denominator would be increased by 8,333 (10,000 × 10/12) for shares issued, and shares assumed retired for the 10 months, 2,315 (($50,000 ÷ $18) × 10/12), would be deducted. The adjustment is made only if dilutive. Note that the $18 average market price used was the average for the first 10 months of the year, which is more applicable to this calculation than the average for the entire year.

CONCEPT REVIEW

1. What is the purpose of calculating diluted EPS?

2. Explain the difference between dilutive and anti-dilutive.

3. What is added to the numerator of diluted EPS for convertible bonds? Preferred shares?

4. Assume basic EPS is $5. Two potentially dilutive elements exist, with an individual effect of $1 and $4.50, respectively. Under what circumstances would the $4.50 item be considered anti-dilutive?

5. How do actual conversions of senior securities affect the calculation of diluted EPS?

6. What assumption is made regarding the proceeds of option contracts when calculating diluted EPS? When are options dilutive?

COMPLICATING FACTORS

Convertible Securities and Options Issued During the Year

If convertible securities are issued during the year, the effect of a hypothetical conversion is backdated in the calculation of diluted EPS *only to the date of issue*. For example, suppose that DRV Corporation issued 8% convertible bonds payable on 1 November. When calculating net income, of course, only two months interest would have been recorded. In calculating diluted EPS, two month's interest (not 12 months!) is added to the numerator and two months of shares (not 12 months!) are added to the denominator. That is, the bond is assumed to be converted on the date of issuance *if it was issued during the period.* Next year, when the bonds have been outstanding for a full year, the adjustments revert to normal: a full year.

Similarly, if options are issued during the year, they are backdated *only to the date of issuance* in diluted EPS calculations. Employee stock options are often issued at the end of a fiscal period, which means that they do not affect diluted EPS in their first year.

Convertible Securities and Options Extinguished During the Year

What happens if a company has convertible securities or options during the year that are redeemed or settled in cash, or expire during the year? Potential common shares, *if dilutive,* are included in the calculation of diluted EPS up to the date of redemption, settlement, or expiry.

For example, assume that a convertible bond was repaid on 1 March, in cash. That is, the bond was extinguished but the conversion option was not exercised. If the conversion terms were dilutive, interest and shares would be included in diluted EPS calculations for the two months that the bond was outstanding.

Alternatively, assume that options were outstanding until 30 September, when they expired. The fact that they expired unexercised means that they were not in the money in the period leading up to the expiry date, but they may well have been in the money earlier in the fiscal year. The options would be factored into diluted EPS for the period before 30 September during which they were in the money. This is done by quarter or by month, as we will see.

Reference Point for Diluted EPS

Assume that basic EPS based on net income (e.g., $2.00) is lower than EPS based on income before discontinued operations (e.g., $2.50), because of a loss from discontinued operations. A potentially dilutive security has an individual effect (e.g., $2.25) that is anti-dilutive to EPS based on net income, but dilutive to EPS based on income before the discontinued operation. Should it be included or not? Accounting standards require that the yardstick used be *income before discontinued operations and extraordinary items.* All decisions are made with this as the starting point. So, if an item is included for income before discontinued operations and extraordinary items, it is *also always included* for EPS based on net income.

For example, assume that income before discontinued operations is $450,000, and there is an after-tax loss from discontinued operations of $200,000, so net income is $250,000. There are 10,000 common shares outstanding all year, and no preferred shares. Basic EPS is $45 based on income before the discontinued operation, and $25 based on net income. Convertible debt, with after-tax interest of $70,000 and a share entitlement of 2,500 shares, is outstanding.

The individual dilutive effect of the convertible debt is $28 ($70,000 ÷ 2,500). This is dilutive to EPS calculated on income before discontinued operations, but anti-dilutive to EPS calculated on net income. The item is included in diluted EPS for *both measures of diluted EPS.* Diluted EPS for income before discontinued operations is reported as $41.60 ($450,000 + $70,000) ÷ (10,000 + 2,500). Diluted EPS for the discontinued operation is ($16) ($200,000 ÷ 12,500), and diluted EPS for net income is $25.60 (($250,000 + $70,000) ÷ 12,500). Diluted EPS for net income, at $25.60, is higher than basic EPS of $25! But the bonds have to be included for both diluted EPS measures, since they were definitely dilutive for income before the discontinued operation.

Measuring Interest Expense

In the example shown in Exhibit 19-4, the bond was issued at 110, and the premium on issuance was entirely attributable to the conversion option. Thus, the convertible bonds' nominal interest rate could be used to measure interest expense. In this example, interest expense was measured (appropriately) at 9%.

There are many situations in which a bond is offered at a discount or premium. When that happens, interest *expense* will include discount or premium amortization and will not coincide with interest *paid*. In diluted EPS calculations, the adjustment to the numerator (i.e., earnings available to common shareholders) must be for interest *expense*. A simple adjustment based on the nominal rate of interest will not work—discount or premium amortization must also be taken into account.

For example, suppose that convertible, 10-year bonds with a stated interest rate of 9% payable semi-annually were issued for $40 million. The bonds have a par value of $40 million and are convertible at the investor's option. Some of the proceeds must be allocated to the conversion option, and therefore a discount on the bonds will arise. If the market rate of interest for non-convertible bonds of similar risk and maturity was 10% at the time of issuance, the allocation of $40 million proceeds would have been as follows:

Present value of liability:	
Interest = [($40,000,000 × 4.5%) × (P/A, 5%, 20)] =	$22,431,979
Principal = $40,000,000 × (P/F, 5%, 20) =	15,075,579
	$37,507,558
Common share conversion option (the residual)	2,492,442
Net proceeds	$40,000,000

The bond issuance would have been recorded as follows:

Cash	40,000,000	
Discount on bonds payable	2,492,442	
Bonds payable		40,000,000
Common share conversion rights		2,492,442

Each year, interest expense is recorded using the effective interest method. In the first period, interest expense is $1,875,378 ($37,507,558 × 5%); the discount is amortized, and the net carrying value of the bond is adjusted. This is not interest paid, which is $1,800,000 ($40,000,000 × 4.5%);

In EPS calculations, when making the adjustment to earnings available to common share-holders, the adjustment must be for interest expense, not interest paid. In the examples and problems in this chapter, it is often assumed that the nominal interest rate is the same as the market rate to simplify calculations. But be aware that if this simplifying assumption is not in place, the required adjustment is for *interest expense,* not interest payments.

Measuring the Dilutive Effect of Options

Options give the holder the right to acquire shares at a stated price. The price is stated in dollars per share acquired and may increase or decrease on a pre-determined schedule over time. In calculating diluted EPS, the *most dilutive price* is used; effectively, this means the lowest price.

So far, the examples have been based on the *yearly average* option price when calculating the number of common shares that would be bought back. This is a simplification. Options are dilutive at any time *during the year* that they are in the money. Consider the following quarterly data.

	Quarter			
	1	**2**	**3**	**4**
Average share price for the quarter	$16	$ 7	$ 5	$20
Option exercise price	$10	$10	$10	$10
Options outstanding	5,000	5,000	5,000	5,000

How should the calculations be done? One approach is based on the average price for the year. The options are dilutive with respect to the average share price for the year, taken as the simple average of the market values, $12 [($16 + $7 + $5 + $20) ÷ 4]. Five thousand shares would be issued at $10, and 4,167 shares retired [($10 × 5,000) ÷ $12]. However, in two quarters, the options were not dilutive (quarters 2 and 3) and in two quarters they were dilutive (quarters 1 and 4). Quarterly evaluation is more accurate.

Quarterly Evaluation Options should be evaluated according to the price behaviour *during the period*—this might mean weekly, monthly, or quarterly evaluation. Quarterly evaluation is the minimum expectation for the public companies, as specified in securities law. To demonstrate quarterly evaluation:

	Shares Issued	**Shares Retired**
Quarter 1—dilutive ($10 < $16)		
5,000 × 3/12	1,250	
((5,000 × $10) ÷ $16) × 3/12		781
Quarter 2—anti-dilutive ($10 > $7)	—	—
Quarter 3—anti-dilutive ($10 > $5)	—	—
Quarter 4—dilutive ($10 < $20)		
5,000 × 3/12	1,250	
((5,000 × $10) ÷ $20) × 3/12		625
Total	2,500	1,406

Notice the pro-ration of 3/12 for each calculation, to reflect the three months in each quarter. When calculating diluted EPS for the year, the denominator would be increased by 2,500 shares and reduced by 1,406 shares. This is a net increase of 1,094 shares.

Average Market Value In the prior examples in this chapter, we've assumed that the average market value for the year was steady, and that if the options were dilutive at the end of the year, they were also dilutive *at all times* during the year. We'll continue to make this unstated assumption in examples and problems, unless quarterly market values are presented. If quarterly data is provided, quarterly calculations are required. Otherwise, yearly evaluation is acceptable. Remember that quarterly or even monthly or weekly evaluation would be appropriate when share price has been volatile, and is commonplace in practice. We're not going to demonstrate monthly or weekly calculations, because we're sure you get the idea!

This brings up the question of how average share prices are supposed to be determined. The accounting standards state that a simple average of weekly or monthly prices is usually appropriate. When market prices are volatile, though, the average of the high and low prices during the period must be used.

Diluted EPS in a Loss Year

When a company has reported a loss, adding *anything* positive to the numerator, and/or increasing the number of common shares outstanding, will *reduce the loss per share* and be anti-dilutive. Thus, diluted EPS is generally equal to basic EPS in a loss year because all potentially dilutive items are classified as anti-dilutive.

For example, assume a company reports a $100,000 loss. It has 40,000 weighted-average common shares outstanding, and 10,000 cumulative preferred shares outstanding, with a total dividend entitlement of $5,000, convertible into 20,000 common shares. Basic *loss* per share is ($2.63) [($100,000 + $5,000) ÷ 40,000]. The preferred dividend increases the loss per share. If the preferred shares were assumed converted, diluted EPS would be ($1.67) ($105,000 − $5,000) ÷ (40,000 + 20,000). A smaller loss per share—*a better number*—results and demonstrates that the preferred shares are anti-dilutive. Diluted EPS would be reported as ($2.63).

What if this company reported a loss of $100,000 before discontinued operations, and a $500,000 gain from discontinued operations? Net income would be positive, at $400,000. The preferred shares *are still classified as anti-dilutive*, because the dilution test is performed with reference to income before discontinued operations and extraordinary items. If it is dilutive—or anti-dilutive—to the top line, it must be classified consistently thereafter.

Another twist relates to options. We saw in the discussion above that options can be measured on a quarterly basis. What if options are dilutive in a number of quarters during the year, but the company ends up with a loss overall? In this case, no weighted-average shares will be included for options.

For example, return to the previous options example, where quarterly calculations of the option status resulted in shares issued of 2,500, and shares retired of 1,406. Assume that basic EPS is negative, because of a loss year, say, ($5), the result of dividing a net loss of $450,000 by 90,000 weighted-average shares outstanding. If the options were included, the loss per share would *decrease* to ($4.94) [$450,000 ÷ (90,000 + 2,500 − 1,406)]. This is another example of the anti-dilutive effect of all share contracts in a loss year. The options would not be included, and diluted EPS would be the same as basic: ($5).

CONCEPT REVIEW

1. What is the reference point for the dilution test?
2. When there is a difference between interest expense and interest paid, which number is used for convertible bonds in diluted EPS?
3. Why is diluted EPS generally equal to basic EPS in a loss year?

COMPREHENSIVE ILLUSTRATION

Having discussed all of the pieces of basic and diluted EPS, we'll now turn to a comprehensive illustration. Exhibit 19-7 contains the basic information for this example, and Exhibit 19-8 works through the EPS calculations.

This example uses data from FRM Corporation, a public corporation. The company has a complex capital structure that includes three types of bonds and three classes of shares. Of the bond issues, only the 10% debentures are publicly traded. The mortgage bonds and the unsecured debentures were privately placed.

The Class A shares are publicly traded and are listed on the TSE. Each Class A share has one vote. The Class B common shares have 20 votes each. Class B shares are closely held by the company's founding family, as are the preferred shares. Although Class A and Class B have different voting rights, in all other respects the two classes of common shares are equal, including the rights to dividends and to assets upon dissolution.

As can be seen in Exhibit 19-7, two of the bond issues are convertible (into Class A), as are the preferred shares (into Class B). In addition, there are employee stock options outstanding that give the holder the right to acquire one Class A share for each option held.

EXHIBIT 19-7

FRM CORPORATION
DATA FOR COMPREHENSIVE EPS ILLUSTRATION

Year Ended 31 December 20X1

Capital structure, 31 December 20X1:

Long-term debt:

12% first mortgage bonds, due 1 July 20X9	$1,300,000
10% unsecured debentures, due 31 July 20X7, convertible into Class A common shares at $50 at any time prior to maturity	$ 960,000
8% unsecured debentures, due 15 April 20X20, convertible into 10,300 Class A common shares on or after 31 December 20X12	$1,500,000

Capital shares:

Preferred shares, dividend rate of $20 per share, cumulative and non-participating, convertible to Class B common shares at the rate of two shares of Class B for each share of preferred	5,000 shares
Class A common shares, one vote per share	104,800 shares
Class B common shares, 20 votes per share, sharing dividends equally with Class A common shares	10,000 shares

Options:

30,000 employee stock options issued on 31 December 20X0, each exchangeable for one Class A share as follows:

$30 per share prior to 1 January 20X4
$40 per share between 1 January 20X4 and 31 December 20X7
$55 per share between 1 January 20X8 and 31 December 20X10
The options expire at the close of business on 31 December 20X10

50,000 employee stock options, issued on 31 December 20X1, each exchangeable for one Class A share at a price of $35 per share prior to 31 December 20X11. The options expire at the close of business on 31 December 20X11.

Additional Information:

- Net income for year ended 31 December 20X1 was $1,200,000; there was a $200,000 gain from discontinued operations.
- The income tax rate was 40%.
- The average market value of common shares during the period was first quarter, $25; second quarter, $60; third quarter, $50; fourth quarter, $70.
- Dividends were paid quarterly on the preferred shares; there are no dividends in arrears.
- Dividends of $1 per quarter were declared on both Class A and Class B shares; the dividends were payable to shareholders of record at the end of each calendar quarter, and were paid five business days thereafter.
- On 1 October 20X1, 10% debentures with a principal amount of $240,000 were converted into 4,800 Class A shares (included in the outstanding shares listed above). At the beginning of the year, the total principal amount of the 10% debentures was $1,200,000.

Before beginning to work out earnings per share, it is important to take notice of any changes in the capital structure that occurred during the year. Exhibit 19-7 shows the capital structure at the *end* of the fiscal year, but the *additional information* states that there was a partial conversion of the 10% debentures on 1 October. That piece of information is important for two reasons:

1. Shares were outstanding for only *part* of the year, which means that the weighted-average number of shares outstanding must be calculated for basic EPS, *and*

2. If dilutive, the conversion must be backdated when calculating diluted EPS.

Of course, the existence of three convertible senior securities plus employee stock options indicates that diluted EPS must be calculated. Options calculations must be done by quarter, since quarterly averages are given.

The top section of Exhibit 19-8 presents the calculation of basic EPS. The starting point is income before discontinued operations. Income is reduced by the preferred dividends. Class A and Class B share *equally* in dividends, and therefore they are added together for the denominator without adjustment. The weighted-average number of shares reflects the new shares issued on 1 October. Basic EPS is $8.09 for income before discontinued operations. The EPS effect of the discontinued operation is $1.80 ($200,000 ÷ 111,200) and EPS for net income is $9.89 [($1,200,000 − $100,000) ÷ 111,200].

Diluted EPS must be calculated. The first item to evaluate is options, dilutive when the option price is less than market value. Refer back to the steps needed to calculate diluted EPS (see Exhibit 19-2). This is Step 3; Step 2 is not needed. Only the first group of options, for 30,000 shares, must be evaluated. The second set was issued on 31 December 20X1, and is eliminated because it must be backdated only to the day of issue (0/12). Returning to the first set of options, the lowest option price, $30, is used because it will be the most dilutive. The options allow the purchase of 30,000 shares. This will raise capital of $900,000 (30,000 × $30). Retirement is based on a quarter-by-quarter assessment:

	Shares Issued	Shares Retired
Quarter 1—anti-dilutive ($30 > $25)	—	—
Quarter 2—dilutive ($30 < $60)		
30,000 × 3/12	7,500	
($900,000 ÷ $60) × 3/12		3,750
Quarter 3—dilutive ($30 < $50)		
30,000 × 3/12	7,500	
($900,000 ÷ $50) × 3/12		4,500
Quarter 4—dilutive ($30 < $70)		
30,000 × 3/12	7,500	
($900,000 ÷ $70) × 3/12		3,214
Total	22,500	11,464

These numbers are included in the calculation of diluted EPS, reducing the subtotal to $7.36.

We now proceed to Steps 4, 5, and 6 (See Exhibit 19-2.). The second section of Exhibit 19-8 shows the calculation of individual effects for the preferred shares and convertible debt:

- *Preferred shares.* Each share of the convertible preferred has a dividend of $20. Each is convertible into two shares of Class B common. The individual effect is $20 ÷ 2 = $10. This is clearly anti-dilutive to basic EPS of $8.09. Preferred shares will be excluded from the diluted EPS calculation. (Note that the individual effect calculation can be

EXHIBIT 19-8

FRM CORPORATION
COMPREHENSIVE EPS ILLUSTRATION (BASED ON DATA IN EXHIBIT 19-7)

	Earnings Available to Common Shares	Weighted-Average Number of Shares	Earnings per Share
Basic EPS:			
Income before discontinued operations	$1,000,000		
Less preferred dividends: 5,000 shares × $20	(100,000)		
Shares outstanding:			
Class A			
100,000 × 9/12		75,000	
104,800 × 3/12		26,200	
Class B 10,000 × 12/12		10,000	
Basic EPS	**$ 900,000**	**111,200**	**$ 8.09**
Individual effect ratios:			
Preferred shares (per share)	$ 20	2	$10.00
Actual conversion of 10% debenture			
Interest saved: ($240,000 × 10%) ×			
(1 − 0.4) × 9/12	10,800		
Add'l weighted-average shares: 4,800 × 9/12		3,600	3.00
10% debentures (total; after tax)			
Interest saved: ($960,000 × 10%) × (1 − 0.4)	57,600		
Add'l shares: $960,000 ÷ $50		19,200	3.00
8% debentures (total; after tax)			
Interest saved: ($1,500,000 × 8%) × (1 − 0.4)	72,000		
Add'l shares: given		10,300	6.99
Diluted EPS:			
Data from basic	$ 900,000	111,200	
Adjustment for assumed options exercise:			
Shares issued		22,500	
Shares retired		(11,464)	
Subtotal	900,000	122,236	$ 7.36
Actual conversion of 10% debenture:			
Interest saved	10,800		
Add'l weighted average shares		3,600	
Subtotal	910,800	125,836	7.24
Adjustments for potential conversions:			
10% debenture:			
Interest avoided (after-tax equivalent)	57,600		
Additional common shares issued		19,200	
Subtotal	968,400	145,036	6.68
8% debenture:			
Anti-dilutive since $6.99 is higher than $6.68	—		
Adjustment for preferred shares			
Anti-dilutive since $10.00 is higher than $6.68		—	
Diluted EPS	**$ 968,400**	**145,036**	**$ 6.68**

based on the outstanding preferred share issue as a whole or on a per-share basis; the result is the same.)

- *10% debenture, actual conversion.* The conversion has to be backdated for 9/12 of the year, back from 1 October to 1 January. Both after-tax interest and shares are adjusted. Interest would be $24,000 ($240,000 × 10%) for a year, but is $10,800 after multiplied by (1 − tax rate) and 9/12 of the year. Shares issued were 4,800, as used in the basic calculation, but are backdated by multiplying by 9/12 of the year. The individual effect is $3.00.

- *10% debentures.* Interest on the $960,000 principal amount is $96,000. Since the interest is deductible for income tax purposes, the effect of the interest on net income is $57,600 ($96,000 × (1 − 0.4)). At a conversion price of $50, the $960,000 bonds can be converted into 19,200 ($960,000 ÷ $50) Class A common shares. The individual effect is $3.00.

- *8% debentures.* These debentures involve after-tax interest of $72,000 and are convertible into 10,300 Class A common shares. The individual effect is $6.99.

In Steps 7 and 8 (see Exhibit 19-2) the securities are included in diluted EPS in order of their dilutive effects: first the 10% debentures, both the actual conversion and the assumed conversion. Their order doesn't matter since their individual effects are the same. The subtotal is now $6.68. The 8% debentures, which looked dilutive with respect to basic EPS of $8.09, are anti-dilutive to the subtotal of $6.68. They are excluded. The preferred shares, with an individual effect of $10, are also anti-dilutive and excluded. The result is diluted EPS of $6.68 for income before discontinued operations.

Finally, the process is repeated because of the discontinued operations; this is Step 9 (see Exhibit 19-2). The diluted EPS effect of the discontinued operation is $1.38 ($200,000 ÷ 145,036) and diluted EPS for net income is $8.06 (($1,200,000 − $100,000 + $10,800 + $57,600) ÷ 145,036). Note that the same adjustments are made to the numerator with no dilution testing. Discontinued operations is disclosed as $1.80 ($200,000 ÷ 111,200 shares) and $1.38 ($200,000 ÷ 145,036 shares).

EPS disclosure on the income statement would be as follows:

Earnings per share:

	Basic	Diluted
Income before discontinued operations	$8.09	$6.68
Discontinued operations	1.80	1.38
Net income	$9.89	$8.06

The individual effect of the discontinued operations may, alternatively, be included in the disclosure notes.

RESTATEMENT OF EARNINGS PER SHARE INFORMATION

Once earnings are reported, they are restated (changed) only in limited circumstances. We'll take a close look at this in Chapter 20, and we'll see that changes in estimates, the most common classification of accounting change, affect only the current year and future years. Past earnings are changed only to correct an error, and to reflect the retrospective effect of a change in accounting principle. These retrospective changes are allowed to improve the integrity and the comparability of the financial statements. Reported EPS is also not often revised. EPS will be recalculated if:

- There has been a retrospective change in accounting principle or an error correction. Prior income will change and prior EPS also has to be revised.

- There has been a stock dividend or stock split during the fiscal year (or after the fiscal year but before the financial statements are issued). EPS data is retrospectively restated to reflect the different size of shares that are now outstanding—EPS numbers would halve after a two-for-one stock split, for instance.

Needless to say, the discontinuity is accompanied by extensive disclosure to ensure that financial statement users are adequately informed.

SUBSEQUENT EVENTS

Companies have special disclosures required for subsequent events—transactions or events that take place in the period between the end of the fiscal period and the date financial statements are released. If there have been common shares transactions in this period, then the effects of these share transactions must be disclosed. That is, if a subsequent event would significantly change the number of common shares or the potential common shares used in basic or diluted EPS, the transaction must be disclosed and described. Companies have a relatively short period after their fiscal year in which to report; you can see that they have added incentive to report quickly, to reduce the reporting burden by keeping this time period short.

Examples of transactions that would have to be disclosed include issuing common shares for cash, on the exercise of options, or for cash with the proceeds used to pay out other sources of financing. For example, if common shares were issued after the end of the fiscal year and the proceeds were used to retire preferred shares, disclosure would be required. Issuance of new options or convertible securities would introduce a new element into diluted EPS (potential shares) and also qualifies for disclosure.

TREASURY STOCK METHOD FOR DEBT COMPONENTS

The *if-converted method* is now used to reflect the impact of potential conversion of debt (and equity) elements—that is, the numerator is changed for avoided interest (or dividends), and the denominator is increased for shares issued. The *treasury stock method* is used for options, where the proceeds of options are assumed to be used to retire shares. Only the denominator is affected.

Under proposed international standards, the treasury stock method will be used for convertible elements recorded as debt. Assume, for instance, that a bond is convertible into 40,000 shares. Using the treasury stock method, the recorded value of the liability would be deemed to be used to redeem outstanding common shares, and then both the issued and retired shares would change the denominator of diluted EPS. There is no change to the numerator. If the common shares had a market value of $180, and the carrying value of the liability were $2,700,000, then 15,000 ($2,700,000 ÷ $180) shares would be retired. The denominator would change by 25,000 (+ 40,000 − 15,000) shares.

Canadian standards are expected to make this shift after the IASB has issued a final statement on the topic.

OTHER COMMITMENTS TO ISSUE SHARES

Bonds Convertible at the Issuer's Option Convertible bonds may be convertible at either the option of the investor or the issuer. The examples shown above have dealt with convertible bonds that are convertible at the option of the investor. If it is the company's option to issue shares or cash, there is one more factor to consider. If there is past experience or stated policy that gives *reasonable basis* to decide that cash will be paid rather than shares issued, then the bond is not considered in the calculation of diluted EPS *even if dilutive*. If shares are likely to be issued, or if the outcome is unknown, then the bond is considered in the calculation of diluted EPS like any other convertible bond.

For example, assume that a company has a bond outstanding that is redeemable in cash or convertible to common shares *at the company's option*. The conversion price is fixed, and thus the bond is recorded as partially interest liability and partially equity. However, company policy is to exercise the cash redemption clause, and this practice was followed is prior years for one other similar bond. In this case, the potential conversion of this bond should not be included in diluted EPS calculations.

Contingently Issuable Shares Sometimes, companies have contracts outstanding that require them to issue common shares contingent on another event happening. For example, additional shares might have to be issued to new investors based on net income or market value. There are usually no additional proceeds paid to the company for such shares. The standards require that such contingently issuable shares must be considered to be issued when calculating diluted EPS, and backdated to the beginning of the period if:

- The conditions for share issuance are met at the end of the period, or
- The conditions for share issuance have *not* been met, but the only unmet condition is that the *date of the contingency period* has not yet expired.

For example, say that a group of investors were promised 50,000 additional common shares if net income were above $10 million in each of 20X5, 20X6, and 20X7. It is now the end of 20X6, income targets have been met, and will likely be met in 20X7. The 50,000 shares would be included in diluted EPS.

REQUIRED DISCLOSURE

Accounting standards recommend that financial statements include the following:

1. Basic and diluted EPS must be disclosed on the face of the income statement for income before discontinued operations and extraordinary items, and for net income. The EPS effect of the extraordinary item and/or discontinued operation must also be disclosed, either on the income statement or in a disclosure note. Basic and diluted EPS must both be disclosed, regardless of the magnitude of the difference between the two. Materiality cannot be invoked to avoid disclosing diluted EPS! However, if basic and diluted EPS numbers are identical, dual presentation can be accomplished in one line on the income statement.

2. A disclosure note must include:

- A reconciliation of the numerator of basic and diluted EPS to the income numbers reported on the income statement, and a reconciliation of the denominators used to common shares outstanding. This includes an explanation of adjustments to the numerator of basic EPS for returns to senior securities.
- Details of securities excluded from the calculation of diluted EPS because they were anti-dilutive.
- Details of any stock dividends or stock splits, taking place after the fiscal year ended, that were included in the calculation of WACS.
- Details of share transactions, or the issuance of options or convertible securities, in the period after the end of the period but before the financial statements are issued.

The Thompson Corporation discloses basic and diluted EPS of $1.41 from continuing operations and $1.73 based on net income. This disclosure is on the face of the income statement. Thompson provides the following reconciliation of EPS numbers in the disclosure notes to the 2006 financial statements:

Earnings:		
(in millions)	**2006**	**2005**
Earnings from continuing operations	$919	$662
Dividends declared on preference shares	(5)	(4)
Earnings from continuing operations attributable to common shares	$914	$658

Weighted-average common shares:

	2006	2005
Weighted-average number of common shares outstanding	643,454,420	653,862,363
Vested deferred share units	677,104	574,385
Basic	644,131,524	654,436,748
Effect of stock and other incentive plans	1,894,821	531,283
Diluted	646,026,345	654,968,031

Source: www.sedar.com, The Thompson Corporation, Audited Annual Financial Statements, March 1, 2007.

This company has non-convertible preferred shares that affect the numerator of basic EPS, two classes of common shares (one called vested deferred share units), and two kinds of dilutive stock options that would reduce EPS if exercised.

Prohibited Disclosure EPS is the only per share statistic that can be presented in the audited financial statements. Companies are not permitted to disclose calculations such as **cash flow per share**, presumably because of the potential for confusing or misleading the investors. The only exception is for per-share amounts payable to owners, such as dividends payable. Of course, nothing prevents the company from including a wide variety of statistics elsewhere in the annual report or in other communication to shareholders.

cash flow per share

a calculation indicating the cash flow accruing to common shareholders; popular disclosure by some in the 1990s but now prohibited by accounting standards

USING EPS

EPS numbers can be used as follows:

- *Basic EPS.* This is an historical amount. It can be compared with basic EPS numbers from past years to see whether the company is earning more or less for its common shareholders. It is a common way to communicate earnings information to shareholders. Basic EPS may indicate a trend to assist in forecasting.

- *Diluted EPS.* Companies usually issue convertible securities with the hope and expectation that they will convert to common shares and become part of the permanent capital of the company. That is, if the company is successful in its financing strategy, the convertible senior securities will be converted rather than repaid. Therefore, diluted EPS gives an indication of the long-run impact that the likely conversions (and options exercises) will have on the earnings attributable to common shares.

One important aspect of EPS numbers is that they mean nothing by themselves. Like all economic indices, they are meaningful only as part of a series. Trend over time is important. The EPS trend may be easier to interpret than the trend in net income, because EPS is adjusted for changes in capital structure. This removes the normal earnings expansion effect that arises through additional share capital.

The absolute level of EPS is relatively meaningless. The fact that one company has EPS of $4 per share while another has EPS of $28 per share does not demonstrate that the company with the higher number is more profitable. It all depends on the number of shares outstanding. Therefore one company's EPS cannot be compared to another's. EPS numbers are meaningful only as part of the statistical series of the reporting company's historical and projected earnings per share.

Because it encapsulates a company's entire reported results for the year in a single number, EPS hides much more than it shows. Placing strong reliance on EPS as an indicator of a company's performance is accepting on faith the message put forth by management in its selection of accounting policies, its accounting estimates, and its measurement and reporting of unusual items. A knowledgeable user will use EPS only as a rough guide; it is no substitute for an informed analysis of the company's reporting practices.

ETHICAL ISSUES

EPS calculations are complex, and their meaning is sufficiently uncertain that many accountants believe the level of reliance on them is unwarranted. Using EPS as an important element in a company's goal structure can contribute to a short-term management attitude. For example, rather than investing cash in productive activities that enhance the company's earnings, management may engage in share buybacks in order to decrease the denominator of the EPS calculation. Such attitudes can lead to decisions that are detrimental to the long-term productivity and financial health of the company.

Nevertheless, EPS computations continue to be reported by companies and anticipated by shareholders, analysts, and management. Therefore, knowledge of how EPS amounts are calculated is essential if intelligent use is to be made of the resulting figures.

INTERNATIONAL PERSPECTIVE

In *IAS 33, Earnings per Share*, and *CICA Handbook* Section 3500, similar rules are established for calculating and presenting basic and diluted earnings per share. Canadian presentation and disclosure requirements are generally converged with *IAS 33*. Both standards use the treasury stock method for considering the effect of options in diluted EPS, a topic where there have been differences over the years.

IAS 33 is being amended to require use of the *treasury stock method* for debt elements that are convertible. The if-converted method is now used, as it is in Canada. This is a major change, which the IASB is undertaking to bring international standards in line with FASB requirements. Canadian standards are expected to follow the IASB lead, a change that will likely occur late in the decade.

In addition to this issue, there are other technical differences in existing standards, which may be of concern to individual companies in specific circumstances. For example, Canadian standards preclude disclosure of cash flow per share, and the international standard is silent on this issue.

Also, if a company has a financial instrument outstanding that *has* to be converted to common shares (mandatory conversion), *IAS 33* requires that the shares be considered to be outstanding from the date the contract is signed, which would be well in advance of the actual issuance of common shares. There are no similar Canadian requirements, although a changed Canadian standard may eliminate this and other differences.

There is also a difference in existing standards in the treatment of contracts that can be settled in shares or cash. In *IAS 33*, all such dilutive instruments are included in diluted calculations. In the Canadian standard, if past experience or stated policy provides a reasonable basis that the security will be repaid in cash rather than shares, the security may be excluded, even if it is dilutive.

For now, the status is that there are differences in the standards governing the calculation of EPS in the major jurisdictions, and changes are on the horizon to reduce those differences.

RELEVANT STANDARDS

CICA Handbook:
- Section 3500, Earnings per Share

IASB:
- *IAS 33*, Earnings per Share

SUMMARY OF KEY POINTS

1. Earnings per share is intended to indicate whether a company's earning performance has improved or deteriorated, compared to previous periods.

2. Because it is computed on a *per share* basis, EPS removes the effect on earnings of increases in net income due to larger invested capital obtained through new share issues.

3. Recommendations on earnings per share apply only to public companies. If other companies voluntarily disclose EPS, then must apply the recommendations of the accounting standards.

4. EPS figures are computed both before and after the impact of discontinued operations and extraordinary items. The EPS effect of discontinued operations and extraordinary items also must be disclosed, perhaps in the disclosure notes.

5. Basic EPS is calculated by dividing earnings available to common shareholders (e.g., earnings less preferred dividend claim) by the weighted-average number of shares outstanding.

6. Weighted-average common shares (WACS), used in the denominator of basic EPS, is calculated by weighting shares for the number of months they are outstanding. However, if there was a stock dividend or stock split during the reporting period, these additional common shares are not weight averaged, but treated as though they have always been outstanding.

7. If there are multiple classes of common shares with different dividend entitlements, separate basic EPS statistics must be calculated to reflect their claims.

8. When a company has dilutive senior securities or options, diluted EPS must be disclosed. The steps to calculate diluted EPS are shown in Exhibit 19-2.

9. Diluted EPS excludes the effects of any convertible securities or options contracts that are anti-dilutive. Anti-dilutive items have the effect of *increasing* EPS in relation to basic EPS before discontinued operations and extraordinary items.

10. For the purposes of calculating diluted EPS, elements are included at their most unfavourable (lowest) price.

11. Options are assumed issued at the beginning of the fiscal period (or date of issuance, if later), and proceeds used to retire shares at average market values. This is called the treasury stock method.

12. Convertible bonds and preferred shares are included in diluted EPS calculations using the if-converted method, whereby after-tax interest and preferred dividends are adjusted on the numerator, and common shares issued for the denominator. This reflects a hypothetical conversion to common shares at the beginning of the year (or date of issuance, if later).

13. Diluted EPS includes an adjustment that backdates actual conversions of senior securities (convertible debt and preferred shares) and shares issued under option contracts to the beginning of the fiscal period, if dilutive.

14. Securities and options issued during the period are backdated only to the date of issue. Dilutive conversion privileges and options that expired or were extinguished during the period are included for the period during which they were outstanding.

15. Potentially dilutive items are included in diluted EPS calculations in a cascade, beginning with the most dilutive. Diluted EPS is the lowest number obtainable.

16. Interest expense for convertible bonds is measured as the cash entitlement adjusted for discount or premium amortization, per the income statement.

17. The dilutive effect of options must be measured by quarter, or perhaps more frequently, if market price has been volatile during the period.

18. All potentially dilutive elements are anti-dilutive in a loss year because they would *decrease* a loss per share; this means that diluted EPS is equal to basic EPS in a loss year.

19. The treasury stock method has been adopted by FASB and the IASB, to account for the dilutive effect of a convertible element reported as debt. Only the denominator of EPS is affected. Shares issued increase the denominator, and the carrying value of debt is assumed to be used to retire common shares at market price, which is a reduction to the denominator.

20. A convertible bond that is convertible at the option of the issuer may be excluded from diluted EPS calculations if past experience or stated policy provides a reasonable basis to believe that the shares will not be issued. There are also specific rules covering contingently issuable shares, which must be included in diluted EPS if shares will likely be issued.

21. EPS is reported on the income statement. A disclosure note must include calculation details, including reconciliation of income and WACS data, and details of excluded anti-dilutive elements.

22. Comparative EPS figures for previous accounting periods are restated when there has been a share dividend or share split during the reporting period. Prior EPS figures are also restated if prior earnings are adjusted because of a retrospective change in accounting principle, or an error correction. These are the only cases in which EPS figures of prior years are restated.

23. Basic EPS is the basis for comparing the current period's earnings with that of prior periods, while diluted EPS gives an indication of the long-run impact that conversions and options could have on common earnings.

KEY TERMS

anti-dilutive element, 1143
backdating, 1148
basic earnings per share, 1136
cascade, 1148
cash flow per share, 1163
convertible senior securities, 1142
diluted earnings per share, 1136
dilutive, 1143
earnings dilution, 1142
if-converted method, 1143

in-the-money, 1143
individual effect, 1144
reverse split, 1138
senior shares, 1136
stock dividend, 1138
stock option, 1142
treasury stock method, 1143
weighted average common shares
   outstanding (WACS), 1137

REVIEW PROBLEM

Ice King Products Incorporated reported net income after tax of $6.5 million in 20X5. Its capital structure included the following as of 31 December 20X5, the *end* of the company's fiscal year:

Long-term debt:	
Bonds payable, due 20X11, 12%	$ 5,000,000
Bonds payable, due 20X15, 9%, convertible into common shares at the rate of two shares per $100	$10,000,000
Shareholders' equity:	
Preferred shares, $4.50, no-par, cumulative, convertible into common shares at the rate of two common shares for each preferred share, shares outstanding, 150,000	
Preferred shares, $2.50, no-par, cumulative, convertible into common shares at the rate of one common share for each preferred share, shares outstanding, 400,000	
Common shares, shares outstanding, 1,500,000	

Options to purchase common shares
(options have been outstanding all year):
Purchase price, $20; expire 20X11, 100,000 options
Purchase price, $52; expire 20X14, 200,000 options
Each option allows the purchase of one share.

Transactions during 20X5:
On 1 July, 400,000 common shares were issued on the conversion of 200,000 of the $4.50 preferred shares.
On 1 December, 100,000 common shares were issued for cash.

Other information:
Average common share price, stable during the year, $40
Tax rate, 25%
Quarterly dividends were declared on 31 March, 30 June, 30 September, and 31 December

Required:
Calculate basic and diluted earnings per share.

REVIEW PROBLEM—SOLUTION

	Earnings Available to Common Shares	Weighted-Average Number of Shares	Earnings per Share
Basic EPS:			
Net income	$6,500,000		
Less dividends on $4.50 preferred:			
($4.50 ÷ 4) × 350,000 shares × 2 quarters	(787,500)		
($4.50 ÷ 4) × 150,000 shares × 2 quarters	(337,500)		
Less dividends on $2.50 preferred:			
400,000 shares × $2.50	(1,000,000)		
WACS:			
1,000,000 shares × 6/12		500,000	
1,400,000 shares × 5/12		583,333	
1,500,000 shares × 1/12		125,000	
	$4,375,000	1,208,333	$3.62

Individual effect; dilution test

9% Bonds:			
Interest, ($10,000,000 × 9%) × (1.00 − .25)	$ 675,000		
Shares, ($10,000,000 ÷ $100) × 2		200,000	$3.38
$4.50 preferred actual conversion:			
Dividend adjustment:			
(4.50 ÷ 4) × 200,000 shares × 2 quarters	$ 450,000		
Add'l weighted-average shares: 400,000 × 6/12		200,000	$2.25
$4.50 preferred			
Dividends, $4.50 × 150,000 shares	$ 675,000		
Shares, 150,000 × 2 common shares		300,000	$2.25
$2.50 preferred			
Dividends, $2.50 × 400,000	$1,000,000		
Shares, 400,000 × 1 share		400,000	$2.50

Diluted EPS			
Basic EPS	$4,375,000	1,208,333	$3.62
$20 options—shares issued		100,000	
—shares retired (100,000 × $20) ÷ $40		(50,000)	
$52 options—excluded, $52 > $40			
Subtotal	$4,375,000	1,258,333	$3.48
$4.50 preferred actual conversion:			
Dividend adjustment:			
(4.50 ÷ 4) × 200,000 shares × 2 quarters	450,000		
Add'l weighted average shares 400,000 × 6/12		200,000	
$4.50 preferred:			
Dividends, $4.50 × 150,000 shares	675,000		
Shares, 150,000 preferred × 2 common shares		300,000	
Subtotal	5,500,000	1,758,333	3.13
$2.50 preferred shares: dividends,			
$2.50 × 400,000	1,000,000	400,000	
Subtotal	$6,500,000	2,158,333	3.01
9% Bonds			
Bonds, with an individual effect of $3.38, are anti-dilutive as their inclusion would increase diluted EPS above $3.01.	—	—	—
Diluted EPS	**$6,500,000**	**2,158,333**	**$3.01**

QUESTIONS

Q19-1 Why is the EPS statistic so important?

Q19-2 What kinds of companies are required to disclose EPS?

Q19-3 What is the formula for basic EPS? Describe the numerator and the denominator.

Q19-4 Explain why and when dividends on non-cumulative preferred shares must be subtracted from income to compute basic EPS.

Q19-5 What adjustments, in addition to preferred dividends, may be made to the numerator of basic EPS?

Q19-6 Why are weighted-average common shares used in EPS calculations?

Q19-7 A company split its common shares two-for-one on 30 June of its accounting year, which ends on 31 December. Before the split, 4,000 common shares were outstanding. How many weighted-average common shares should be used in computing EPS? How many shares should be used in computing a comparative EPS amount for the preceding year?

Q19-8 A company has 100,000 common shares outstanding on 1 January. On 1 June, 20,000 shares are redeemed and cancelled. On 1 October, there is a 20% stock dividend, and another 10,000 shares are issued for cash on 1 December. What is the weighted-average number of common shares outstanding during the period?

Q19-9 What is the required EPS disclosure if there are discontinued operations or extraordinary items on the income statement?

Q19-10 Assume that a company has two classes of shares that both have voting rights and are entitled to the proceeds of net assets on dissolution. One class is entitled to receive 10 times the dividends of the other class. How would the two classes be treated in calculating basic EPS?

Q19-11 What is the purpose of diluted EPS?

Q19-12 Define convertible senior securities.

Q19-13 A company had net income of $12.3 million. During the year, holders of $10 million of convertible preferred shares converted their investment into common shares. There was another $40 million of the convertible preferred shares still outstanding at the end of the year. Options for 40,000 common shares were outstanding all year. Assuming common share contracts are dilutive, review the steps to calculate diluted EPS.

Q19-14 What is the starting point in the calculation of diluted EPS?

Q19-15 Specify the numerator and/or denominator item(s) that would be used when calculating diluted EPS for (a) convertible preferred shares, (b) convertible debt, and (c) options.

Q19-16 Options are outstanding for 100,000 shares at $10. The average market price during the period is $25. What adjustment would be made to the denominator of diluted EPS?

Q19-17 What is the difference between a dilutive security and an anti-dilutive security? Why is the distinction important in EPS considerations?

Q19-18 MAC Corporation has basic EPS of $1.25, calculated as $1,250,000 ÷ 1,000,000. The capital structure of the company includes bonds payable, convertible into 400,000 common shares at the investor's option. Bond interest of $300,000 was paid but bond interest expense was $320,000. The tax rate is 40%. Calculate diluted EPS.

Q19-19 Assume that, in addition to the bonds mentioned in Question 19-18, MAC also has stock options outstanding for 100,000 common shares at $10 per share. The average market price of common shares during the period is $40. Calculate diluted EPS.

Q19-20 Xvest issued $5,000,000 of convertible preferred shares on 1 October this year. The 50,000 preferred shares have a $4 annual dividend, paid $1 at the end of each quarter. The $1 quarterly dividend was paid at the end of December this year. The shares are convertible into eight common shares each. They are dilutive. In calculating diluted EPS, what would be added to the numerator and the denominator?

Q19-21 CH Holdings has basic EPS of $14. The individual affect of convertible preferred shares is $12, and the individual effect of convertible bonds is $6. In which order should the convertible elements be included in diluted calculations? In what circumstances would the convertible preferred shares be anti-dilutive in sequence?

Q19-22 Wilson Limited reports basic EPS of $6 on income before discontinued operations, and $2 for net income. Convertible preferred shares with an individual effect of $4 are outstanding. Are the preferred shares dilutive? Explain.

Q19-23 ABC Company has a $14 million convertible bond outstanding that requires payment of $1.2 million in interest annually. Interest expense is $1.35 million. Why is interest expense different than the interest paid? For the purposes of diluted EPS, which interest figure is relevant?

Q19-24 Reston Limited has 40,000 options outstanding at a price of $10. Quarterly common share prices in 20X5 were $3, $16, $25, and $8. What adjustments to the denominator of diluted EPS are necessary?

Q19-25 What does it mean if options are said to be in the money? Are options dilutive when they are in the money? Explain.

Q19-26 Wilcorp Limited reported basic EPS of ($1.11), a loss of $1.11 per common share, calculated as ($610,500) ÷ 550,000. The company has stock options outstanding for 100,000 common shares at $10 per share. The average common share price was $25 during the period. Calculate diluted EPS.

Q19-27 What are the two cases that require EPS of prior years to be restated?

Q19-28 A company with a 31 December year-end issues shares for cash and retires non-convertible bonds with the proceeds. What disclosure is required? Why?

CASE 19-1

G SHOES LTD.

G Shoes Ltd. (GSL) is an integrated manufacturer and retailer of moderately priced high-fashion footwear, leather goods, and accessories. GSL is a public company listed on the Toronto Stock Exchange. GSL has stores in over 180 major Canadian shopping malls, and operates over 50 "boutiques" in larger retail stores. Until the current year, GSL had three retail stores in the United States. In general, operating results in 20X9 have been disappointing, with lower same-store sales trends and higher costs across the board.

Preliminary operating results for 20X9 are shown in Exhibit 1. Details of accounting issues that must be resolved before the financial statements can be finalized are in Exhibit 2. In particular, the company is discussing with the auditor whether the closure of the three U.S. retail stores, which occurred in March 20X9, can be accounted for as a discontinued operation. Company management has asked that any quantitative analysis reflect two alternatives—treating the closure as an unusual item, and then as a discontinued operation. Draft financial statements reflect the unusual item treatment. In addition, no accounting recognition has been given to stock options outstanding or granted during the year, as valuation estimates were not complete when the draft financial statements were prepared. This information has recently been provided. Finally, EPS calculations for 20X9 have not yet been made.

Required:

Analyze the accounting issues as identified, and prepare revised draft income statements, and EPS calculations.

EXHIBIT 1

G SHOES LIMITED
DRAFT INCOME STATEMENT

(in $ thousands)

For year ended 31 December	**20X9**
Revenue	
Sales	$166,200
Investment and other income	4,320
	170,520
Expenses	
Cost of sales, selling and administrative	142,860
Amortization	10,700
Closure costs, US operations	1,450
Interest, net	2,230
	157,240
Operating income, before tax	13,280
Income tax	5,180
Net income	$ 8,100

EXHIBIT 2

G SHOES LIMITED
ADDITIONAL INFORMATION

1. Outstanding share information:

	Number	Consideration (in thousands)
A. Multiple voting shares,		
31 December 20X8 and 20X9	1,580,000	Nominal
B. Subordinate voting shares		
Balance, 31 December 20X8	5,225,000	$23,890
Shares repurchased 20 March 20X9	(816,000)	(3,730)
Shares issued on exercise of stock options		
31 August 20X9	78,000	728
Balance, 31 December, 20X9	$4,487,000	$20,888

The multiple voting shares and subordinate voting shares have identical attributes except that the multiple voting shares entitle the holder to four votes per share and are entitled to four times the dividend, if declared, on the subordinate voting shares. The multiple voting shares are held by the company founder and his family. Only the subordinated voting shares are publicly traded.

2. On March 2, 20X9, the company received permission from the Toronto Stock Exchange for a Normal Course Issuer Bid that allows the company to repurchase up to 20% of its outstanding shares, or approximately 1,040,000 shares during the period from March 2, 2009 to March 2, 20X10. The share transaction in March of 20X9 was made pursuant to this Bid agreement.

EXHIBIT 2 *(cont'd)*

Consideration of $6,840 (thousand) was paid for the shares, with the excess over average paid in capital to date charged to retained earnings.

3. On 24 February, 20X6, GSL issued $40 million of convertible senior subordinated notes. The net proceeds after deducting offering expenses and underwriter's commissions were $37 million. The convertible debt was allocated between debt and equity elements, which are classified separately on the balance sheet. The debt element was based on the present value of the interest stream over the life of the note using an interest rate for a similar liability that did not have an associated conversion feature. The balance was recorded as equity.

   The notes are convertible at GSL's option at various dates between 20X14 and the maturity date of the note, 24 February 20X17. The conversion price is set at $15.00 per share until 20X15 and then changes to $10.00 per share. In 20X9, there is a charge for interest on the income statement amounting to $1,780 and a $590 after-tax reduction to retained earnings, representing accretion on the equity amount. When calculating basic EPS, the $590 must be deducted from the numerator.

4. GSL maintains a stock option plan for the benefit of directors, officers, and senior management. The granting of options and the related vesting period are at the discretion of the Board of Directors. The option price is set as the five-day average of the trading price of the subordinated voting shares prior to the effective date of the grant. Options granted vest 36 months after the date of issuance, and can be exercised from the vesting date until 10 years after the date of grant. Options are forfeit if the recipient leaves GSL before vesting. Options are granted on 31 December in the year of grant.

   Using the Black-Scholes option pricing model, the fair value of options granted was as follows:

Year of Grant	Per Share Value	Share Entitlements Originally Granted
Prior to 20X6	$3.075	404,000
20X6	5.807	210,000
20X7	6.473	176,000
20X8	5.540	206,000
20X9	7.180	25,000

A summary of the status of outstanding options:

	Shares under Option	Weighted Average Exercise Price
Outstanding at the beginning of the year	730,000	$11.21
Granted, 31 December, 20X9	25,000	10.53
Exercised	(78,000)	6.62
Forfeit (pre-20X6 options)	(35,000)	13.45
Outstanding at the end of the year	642,000	11.10
Options exercisable at the end of the year	405,800	10.90

   At the end of the year, the market price of subordinated voting shares was $11.25, and had been stable for most of the year. Any recorded compensation cost is a permanent difference for tax purposes and will not change recorded tax amounts.

5. In March 20X9, GSL announced that it would discontinue its U.S. retail operation, consisting of three retail stores. The stores had been a separate division of the company, reported separately with a dedicated retail manager. The stores were run using normal retail protocols established for other stores,

	EXHIBIT 2	*(cont'd)*

and relied on GSL infrastructure. However, fashion trends appeared to be unique in these locations, and GSL did not have adequate brand recognition to reach required sales targets. Two retail stores were closed at the end of March, with the third one closed at the end of April. Pre-tax information (in thousands) concerning these locations:

	20X9
Sales	$ 532
Operating loss	(467)
Writedown of capital assets	(1,045)
Lease and employee termination costs	(405)
Current assets	$ 23
Capital assets	—
Current liabilities	—

CASE 19-2

THURTECH LIMITED

ThurTech Limited (TTL) is a Canadian public company involved in network technology for mobility telecommunications. This network technology allows additional data services to be offered through a mobile platform, as a strategy to increase average revenue per user for the carriers. TTL's customers are mobility carriers throughout North America and internationally.

Through the first three quarters of 20X3, revenues were relatively flat, and profit forecasts, which promised growth of approximately 12% in EPS, were not achieved. An earnings growth rate of 8% was reported, largely generated through cost reduction. Internal projections indicated that this 8% growth in EPS would be reported for the annual results. At the beginning of the fourth quarter, senior management began to discuss ways to "close the gap" between the 12% target and the 8% actual EPS growth. (Projected annual 20X3 EPS figures, reflecting the 8% results from operations, are shown in Exhibit 1.) Mindful of the sluggish stock market share price, and with an eye on its own compensation and stock option packages, management has expressed interest in changes before the end of the 20X3 fiscal year.

TTL has 1.2 million common shares promised for future distribution under option contracts granted to senior management. Stock options are a material element of compensation. Additional options will be granted at the end of 20X3. The options granted will be at a price equal to the current share price and will vest immediately. They may be exercised in four years' time, as long as the manager is still with TTL. The quantity to be granted depends on corporate performance but could range from zero to 400,000 shares under option.

A number of situations and/or opportunities that would potentially affect EPS for the year have been discussed internally. For example, management has proposed that 850,000 common shares be repurchased and retired in the fourth quarter. The required funding for this, $16,150,000, would have to be borrowed. Management is permitted to borrow up to $2 billion without further Board of Directors' approval; at the end of the third quarter, outstanding debt amounted to $1.8 billion.

TTL has idle land on the books at an historical cost of $695,000. The market value of this land is $1,180,000; sale would therefore generate a before-tax profit of $485,000. The land is adjacent to one of the five current manufacturing facilities of TTL and has been held for future expansion. Management is confident that, when future expansion is necessary, land can be obtained at one or another of the existing locations for a reasonable sum. Therefore, sale of this idle land has been proposed in the fourth quarter of 20X3.

TTL reports one particular bond payable of $500 million on the books, at a fixed interest rate of 6%. Since the market interest rate is now in the range of 8%, the present value of this debt is $470 million. Management has suggested that this debt be recorded at its present value, recognizing the reduction in debt as a financing gain on the income statement.

TTL has several major orders for product that will be delivered in the first quarter of 20X4. Management is considering ways to expedite these orders to ensure that delivery is completed in the fourth quarter of 20X3. Management is confident that the company can complete production, although not installation at the customer site. In fact, one customer has indicated that installation will not be possible in 20X3, because of operational and technological issues. However, the customer is willing to accept delivery of the product on the condition that payment not be expected any earlier than if the regular delivery schedule were in force. TTL is willing to accept this condition and indeed will offer it to all customers with orders in 20X4 that will accept delivery in 20X3. If these orders are booked in 20X3, gross profit will increase in the range of $800,000 to $1.2 million.

TTL expects to conclude a transaction with an Indian company, Bombay Telecom Limited (BTL) in the fourth quarter of 20X3. In this transaction, TTL network technology will be exchanged for manufacturing equipment procured by BTL. This equipment will be used to produce a particular component for TTL that will help establish TTL's leading-edge product. Valuation of the transaction is problematic, however. TTL knows that the technology it is shipping to BTL would sell in the range of $1.5 million, but sales of this line are not common and the product was specifically produced for BTL at a cost of $600,000. The equipment acquired does not have a readily established market value, because it is unique. The product line that the equipment supports is projected to have a 10-year life, producing gross margins of 60%, but the eventual volume is highly speculative.

Required:

Analyze, for management, the EPS effect of the situations described above. Include a discussion of any concerns for management to consider. TTL has a 40% marginal tax rate.

EXHIBIT 1

PROJECTED EPS—20X3

Basic EPS: $\dfrac{\text{Net income} - \text{Preferred dividends}}{\text{Weighted-average common shares}} = \dfrac{\$50,621,900 - \$2,000,000}{19,765,500}$

$$= \dfrac{\$48,621,900}{19,765,500}$$

$$= \underline{\$2.46}\ (\$2.27 \text{ in 20X2})$$

Diluted EPS: $\dfrac{\text{Basic} + \text{preferred dividends}}{\text{Basic} + \text{common shares for preferred}} = \dfrac{(\$48,621,900 + \$2,000,000)}{(19,765,500 + 1,600,000)}$

$\qquad$ + shares under stock options $\qquad +1,200,000 - 160,000$
$\qquad$ − shares retired with
$\qquad\quad$ option proceeds

$$= \dfrac{\$50,621,900}{22,405,500}$$

$$= \underline{\$2.26}\ (\$2.10 \text{ in 20X2})$$

ASSIGNMENTS

★★ **A19-1 Basic EPS:** Crouse Co.'s 20X9 results include the following balances and amounts:

A. Bonds payable, 5%, non-convertible		$17,000,000
B. Preferred shares, no-par value, $0.65, non-convertible, non-cumulative, outstanding during year, 1,600,000 shares		8,000,000
C. Common shares, no-par value:		
Outstanding 1 Jan., 12,000,000 shares	$12,360,000	
Sold and issued 1 April, 240,000 shares	500,000	
Issued 10% stock dividend, 30 Sept., 1,224,000 shares	1,400,000	$14,260,000
D. Retained earnings (after effects of current preferred dividends declared during 20X9)		9,180,000
E. Income before discontinued operations		$ 5,640,000
Discontinued operations (net of tax)		(720,000)
Net income		$ 4,920,000

F. Preferred dividends declared, $920,000.
G. Average income tax rate, 40%.

Required:

1. Compute basic EPS.
2. Repeat requirement (1), assuming that the preferred shares are cumulative.

★ **A19-2 Basic EPS:** Nason Technologies Limited reported net income of $795,000 for the year ended 31 December 20X6, after a $67,000 gain on discontinued operations, net of tax. Nason declared but did not pay $120,000 of preferred dividends and $106,000 of common dividends. Preferred shares with an average issuance price of $649,500 were repurchased and retired for $659,700 during the year.

Nason Technologies ended the year with 1,485,000 common shares outstanding. Shares had been split three-for-one on 1 November. Forty thousand common shares with an average issuance price of $126,000 were retired for $195,000 on 1 June.

Nason Technologies has no stock options outstanding or convertible senior securities.

Required:

1. Compute basic EPS. Note that the 1,485,000 total for common shares is at the end of the year and the weighted average must work backward from this.
2. Show how basic EPS would be disclosed in the financial statements and indicate what additional information must be disclosed.

★ **A19-3 Weighted-Average Common Shares:** The following cases are independent:

Case A   Crow Limited had 4,920,000 common shares outstanding on 1 January 20X8. No shares were issued or retired during the year. On 15 January 20X9, before the audit report was issued, a four-for-one stock split was distributed.

Case B   Falcon Corp had 3,280,000 common shares outstanding on 1 January 20X8. On 1 March, 320,000 common shares were issued for cash. On 1 June, 200,000 common shares were repurchased and retired. On 1 November, 500,000 common shares were issued for cash.

Case C   Eagle Limited had 4,860,000 common shares outstanding on 1 January 20X8. On 1 March, 243,000 common shares were issued as a 5% stock dividend. On 1 June, 300,000 common shares were repurchased and retired. On 1 November, common shares were issued as a two-for-one stock split.

Required:

For each case, calculate the weighted-average number of common shares to use in the calculation of basic EPS in 20X8.

★ **A19-4 Weighted-Average Common Shares:** The following cases are independent.

Case A   Albion Company has 2,450,000 common shares outstanding on 1 January. 200,000 shares were issued for land and buildings on 27 February, and another 300,000 shares were issued for cash on 1 August. A two-for-one stock split was distributed on 30 August.

Case B   Bartle Corporation had 200,000 Series A shares and 400,000 Series B shares outstanding on January 1. Each non-voting Series A share has a $6 per share cumulative dividend and is convertible into two Series B shares. Series B shares are voting shares. During the year, 50,000 Series A shares and 40,000 Series B shares were issued for cash on 1 October. On 1 December 75,000 Series B shares were retired for cash.

Case C   Carrion Company began the year with 433,000 common shares. An additional 100,000 common shares were issued for cash on April 30. Forty thousand preferred shares were converted into common shares, at the rate of two-for-one, on 1 June. A 40% common stock dividend was declared and distributed on 1 November.

Required:

For each case, calculate the number of weighted-average common shares to use in the calculation of basic EPS.

★ **A19-5 Basic EPS for Three Years:** Ramca Corporation's accounting year ends on 31 December. During the three most recent years, its common shares outstanding changed as follows:

	20X7	20X6	20X5
Shares outstanding, 1 January	150,000	120,000	100,000
Shares sold, 1 April 20X5			20,000
25% stock dividend, 1 July 20X6		30,000	
2-for-1 stock split, 1 July 20X7	150,000		
Shares sold, 1 October 20X7	50,000		
Shares outstanding, 31 December	350,000	150,000	120,000
Net income	$375,000	$330,000	$299,000

Required:

1. For purposes of calculating EPS at the end of each year, for each year independently, determine the weighted-average number of shares outstanding.

2. For purposes of calculating EPS at the end of 20X7, when comparative statements are being prepared on a three-year basis, determine the weighted-average number of shares outstanding for each year.

3. Compute EPS for each year based on year computations in requirement (2). There were no preferred shares outstanding.

★ **A19-6 Basic EPS:** At the end of 20X6, the records of Security Systems Corporation showed the following:

eXcel

A.	Bonds payable, 7%, non-convertible	$ 320,000
B.	Preferred shares:	
	Class A, no-par, $0.60, non-convertible, non-cumulative, outstanding 60,000 shares	300,000
	Class B, no-par, $0.70, non-convertible, cumulative, outstanding 30,000 shares	600,000

C. Common shares, no-par, authorized unlimited shares:

Outstanding 1 January, 186,000 shares	$1,785,000	
Retired shares 1 May, 36,000 shares	(345,483)	
Issued a 300% stock dividend on 1 November, on outstanding shares (450,000 additional shares)	—	1,439,517

D. Retained earnings (no dividends declared)	1,710,000
E. Income before discontinued operations	$ 160,500
Discontinued operations, net of tax	10,000
Net income	$ 170,500

F. Average income tax rate, 40%

Required:
Compute basic EPS. Show computations.

★ **A19-7 Basic and Diluted EPS:** Toogle, a public company, is required to disclose earnings per share information in its financial statements for the year ended 31 December 20X6. The facts about Toogle's situation are as follows:

a. At the beginning of the year, 450,000 common shares, issued for $5.75 million, were outstanding. The authorized number of common shares is 1 million. On 1 January, 50,000, $5 cumulative preferred shares were also outstanding. They had been issued for $500,000.
b. On 30 September 20X6, Toogle issued 100,000 common shares for $1.5 million cash.
c. Toogle reported net income of $2.5 million for the year ended 31 December 20X6.
d. At 1 January 20X6, Toogle had outstanding $1 million (par value) of 8% convertible bonds ($1,000 face value), with interest payable on 30 June and 31 December of each year. Each $1,000 bond is convertible into 65 common shares, at the option of the holder, at any time before 31 December 20X11.
e. Toogle has options outstanding for 50,000 common shares at a price of $5 per share. The average market value of common shares during the period was $20.
f. Toogle has an effective tax rate of 40%.

Required:
Calculate the basic and diluted earnings per share figures for 20X6.

★ **A19-8 Multiple Common Share Classes:** Franklyn Corp. has two classes of voting shares. Type 1 shares have five votes per share, while Type 2 shares have one vote per share. Both participate in the distribution of net assets in the event of dissolution. There were 1,000,000 Type 1 shares outstanding in 20X5, and 3,000,000 Type 2 shares.

Type 1 shares are entitled to dividends as declared, in the amount of $1.50 per share, before the Type 2 shares receive any dividends. After the Type 1 dividend, Type 2 shares will receive dividends as declared up to $2 per share. If any dividends are declared above this amount, both types are to be allocated an identical per share dividend.

In 20X5, net income was $13,400,000, and dividends of $7,500,000 were declared and paid.

Required:

1. Determine basic EPS for each share class for 20X5.

2. Repeat requirement (1) assuming that excess dividends, if any, are split on a per-share basis between the two classes such that Type 1 shares each receive four times the Type 2 entitlement.

★ **A19-9 Multiple Common Share Classes:** Home Lake Mines Limited reported $984,000 of net income after tax in 20X8 and declared no dividends. At the end of 20X8, Home Lake Mines reported the following in the disclosure notes:

Share capital

Multiple Voting Shares, 400,000 shares are authorized but 60,000 shares were issued and outstanding all year. Multiple voting shares are voting shares with a residual interest in assets. Multiple voting shares are entitled to a base dividend of $3 per share. Dividends declared above the base level ($3 for multiple voting shares plus $0.60 for subordinated voting shares), are distributed between the two share classes. Multiple voting shares receive "extra" dividends at the rate of 15 times the "extra" dividend on subordinated voting shares. Multiple voting shares have six votes per share.

Subordinated voting shares, unlimited shares are authorized but 750,000 shares were issued and outstanding all year. Subordinated voting shares are voting shares with one vote each and a residual interest in assets. Subordinated voting shares are entitled to a base dividend of $0.60 per share. Dividends declared above the base level ($3 for multiple voting shares plus $0.60 for subordinated voting shares) are distributed between the two share classes as described above.

Required:

1. Calculate basic EPS for 20X8.

2. Repeat requirement (1) assuming that multiple voting shares are entitled to five times the dividend of subordinated shares, as declared, with no minima.

★ **A19-10 Diluted EPS, Actual Conversions:** Waves Sound Solutions (WSS) reports the following calculations for basic EPS, for the year ended 31 December 20X4:

Numerator: Net income, $18,600,000, less preferred dividends of $1,500,000
Denominator: Weighted-average common shares outstanding, 6,240,000
Basic EPS: $2.74 ($17,100,000 ÷ 6,240,000)

Case A Assume that WSS had 800,000 convertible preferred shares outstanding at the beginning of the year. Each share was entitled to a dividend of $2.00 per year, payable $.50 each quarter. After the third-quarter dividend was paid, 200,000 preferred shares converted, per the share agreement, to 600,000 common shares. The information above regarding dividends paid and the weighted-average common shares outstanding properly reflects the conversion for the purposes of calculating basic EPS.

Case B Assume instead that WSS had non-convertible preferred shares outstanding in 20X4, on which dividends of $1,500,000 were paid. Also assume that WSS had convertible bonds outstanding at the beginning of 20X4. On 1 November, the entire bond issue was converted to 2,400,000 common shares, per the bond agreement. The information above regarding net income properly reflects interest expense of $291,667 to 1 November. The weighted-average common share figure also reflects the appropriate common shares for the conversion. The tax rate is 30%.

WSS also had options outstanding at the end of the fiscal year, for 500,000 common shares at an option price of $15. The average common share price was $28 during the period.

Required:

Calculate diluted EPS for Case A and Case B, independently.

★ **A19-11 Basic and Diluted EPS:** At the end of 20X7, Info Solutions Limited's records reflected the following:

A. Bonds payable, 10%, $600,000 par value, issued
    1 January 20X0; entirely converted to common
    shares on 1 December 20X7; each $1,000 bond
    was convertible to 110 common shares $ 0

B. Preferred shares, 50 cents, convertible 2-for-1 into
    common shares, cumulative, non-participating; shares
    issued and outstanding during year, 30,000 shares   390,000

C. Common shares, no-par value, authorized unlimited shares;
    issued and outstanding throughout the period to
    1 July 20X7, 150,000 shares.
    300,000 shares were sold for cash on 1 July 20X7,
    additional shares were also issued on
    1 December when bondholders converted   2,820,000

D. Common stock conversion rights, related to
    10% bonds payable, above   0

E. Retained earnings (no dividends declared during year)   1,710,000

F. Net income (after $47,250 of interest expense to
    1 December on convertible bonds, above)   366,000

G. Average tax rate, 30%.

Required:

Compute the required EPS amounts. Show computations and round to two decimal places.

★ **A19-12 Basic and Diluted EPS:** Selected information regarding GRT Corporation at 31 December 20X4:

Bonds payable, 6 1/2%, par value $2,000,000, convertible
    into common shares at the rate of 90 shares for each
    $1,000 bond $ 2,000,000

Preferred shares, $3 dividend, cumulative, 100,000 shares
    outstanding. Redemption price $20 per share plus
    dividends in arrears, if any $ 1,600,000

Common shares, 900,000 shares outstanding at the end
    of the year after 300,000 shares were issued for cash on
    31 October $16,200,000

Common stock conversion rights re: convertible bond payable $ 154,000

Retained earnings, end of year $ 9,700,000

Dividends declared during the year (none in 20X3) $ 540,000

Net income in 20X4 $ 700,000

The income tax rate is 35%.

Required:

1. What dollar value of dividends declared was allocated to the common shares?

2. Calculate basic EPS.

3. Repeat requirements 1 and 2 if the preferred dividends were not cumulative and the dividend declared was $20,000.

4. Return to the originals facts. Will the bonds be dilutive or anti-dilutive with respect to diluted EPS? Show calculations.

5. Calculate diluted EPS.

★ **A19-13 Basic and Diluted EPS:** The following data relates to Gertron Ltd, a public company. Shares were outstanding for the entire year.

Case	Common Shares Outstanding	Preferred Shares Outstanding	Net Income	Pref. Share Dividend	Pref. Shares Convertible (2)	Pref. Shares Cumulative
A	350,000	50,000	$680,000 (1)	$2 per share; not declared	No	Yes
B	350,000	40,000	$750,000	$4 per share; declared	Yes	Yes
C	400,000	50,000	$675,000	$7 per share; declared	Yes	No
D	400,000	75,000	$540,000	$3 per share; not declared	Yes	No

(1) Includes $135,000 loss on discontinued operations in case A only
(2) If preferred shares are convertible, each preferred share is entitled to five common shares

Required:
For each case, calculate basic and diluted EPS, as appropriate.

★ **A19-14 Basic and Diluted EPS:** MacDonald Company has reported basic earnings per Class A common share of $2.61. MacDonald has a tax rate of 40%. The average share price during the year was $42. Review each of the following items:

A. Class B non-voting cumulative $1 shares, 75,000 shares outstanding all year, convertible into Class A shares at the rate of four class B shares for one Class A share. Dividends of $0.50 were declared this year and basic EPS properly reflects the dividend entitlement of these preferred shares.

B. Common stock options outstanding all year for 30,000 shares at a price of $65.

C. Common stock options outstanding all year for 30,000 shares at a price of $35.

D. Common stock options granted at the end of the fiscal year for 10,000 shares at $32 per share.

E. 12%, eight-year $5,000,000 convertible bonds outstanding all year, convertible into 18 Class A common shares for every $1,000 bond. A bond discount was recorded when the bond was originally issued and amortization of $43,750 was recorded on the discount this year. On issuance, $420,000 of common stock conversion rights were recorded in shareholders' equity.

F. 8%, 15-year, $9,000,000 convertible bonds outstanding all year, convertible into 24 Class A common shares for every $1,000 bond. A bond discount was recorded on issuance, and amortization of $19,200 was recorded on the discount this year. On issuance, $145,000 of common stock conversion rights were recorded in shareholders' equity.

G. 6%, 15-year, $9,000,000 convertible bonds outstanding at the beginning of the year, convertible into 20 Class A common shares for every $1,000 bond. A bond discount was recorded when the bond was originally issued, and amortization of $2,500 was recorded on the discount this year. On issuance, $145,000 of common stock conversion rights were recorded in shareholders' equity. The bonds converted into common stock on 1 April of the current year, and basic EPS properly reflects the common shares outstanding since 1 April.

Required:
Indicate whether each of the above times would be included or excluded in a calculation of diluted EPS, and why. The solution should include the individual effect of each item, as applicable. If the item is included, indicate the change to the numerator and denominator of diluted EPS.

★ **A19-15 Basic and Diluted EPS; Split:** Accounting staff at Linfei Corporation have gathered the following information:

- Common shares outstanding on 31 December 20X4, 300,000.
- A three-for-one stock split was distributed on 1 February 20X4.
- 280,000 common shares were sold for cash of $50 per share on 1 March 20X4.
- Linfei purchased and retired 40,000 common shares on 1 June 20X4.
- 50,000 Series II options were issued in 20X1, originally allowing the holder to buy one share at $25 for every option held beginning in 20X8. Terms of the options were adjusted for the split in February. (The shares were tripled and the price reduced to one-third.)
- Linfei has $4,000,000 par-value convertible bonds outstanding. There is $692,000 in a common stock conversion rights account with respect to the bonds. Each $1,000 bond was originally convertible into 30 common shares. Terms were adjusted for the split in February. Interest expense on the bond, including discount amortization of $48,000, was $420,000 in 20X4. The bonds are convertible at any time before their maturity date in 20X18.
- Net income in 20X4 was $860,000.
- The tax rate was 40% and the average common share price in 20X4, after being adjusted for the split, was $20.

Required:
Calculate all EPS disclosures for 20X4. Note that there were 300,000 common shares outstanding at the *end* of the fiscal period and calculations must work backward from this date.

★ **A19-16 EPS Computation:** On 1 January 20X6, NOW Limited had the following items in shareholders' equity:

Class A non-voting shares, 900,000 authorized, 660,000 issued and outstanding; $2 per share cumulative dividend, redeemable at the company's option at a price of $18 per share; each Class A share convertible to eight Class B shares; issued at stated value of $15 per share.

Class B voting shares, entitled to net assets on dissolution, 2,000,000 authorized, 970,000 issued and outstanding, issued at $4 per share.

Retained earnings: $3,445,000.

Due to a shortage of cash, no dividends had been declared on either class of shares for the past two years. However, in 20X6, all arrears were cleared up on the Class A shares and current dividends were paid—a total of $3,960,000 in dividends.

There was a stock option (Class B) outstanding to the president of the company: 600,000 shares at an exercise price of $6 per share. This was exercisable after 1 July 20X12. During the year, the following occurred:

a. Net income for the year was $2,714,000. The tax rate was 40%.
b. Class B shares sold for an average of $5 per share during the year.
c. On 1 April 20X6, the company sold 90,000 Class B shares for $17.50 per share. Another 75,000 Class B shares were issued on 1 December for $11.75 per share.
d. An additional stock option (Class B) of 250,000 shares at an exercise price of $3 per share was given to the president of the company on 1 April. This was exercisable after 1 July 20X18.

Required:
Prepare the earnings per share section of the income statement. Begin by deciding which share class constitutes "common shares."

(CGA-Canada, adapted)

★★ **A19-17 EPS Computation:** At the end of 20X6, the records of Learning Library Corporation showed the following:

Bonds payable, Series A, 7%, each $1,000 bond is convertible to 40 common shares after stock dividend (par value, $200,000), net of discount		$ 167,200
Bonds payable, Series B, 6%, each $1,000 bond is convertible to 90 common shares after stock dividend (par value, $1,000,000), net of discount		942,000
Preferred shares, no-par, $1, non-cumulative, non-convertible; issued and outstanding throughout the year, 40,000 shares		1,100,000
Common shares, no-par, authorized unlimited number of shares: outstanding, 1 January, 440,000 shares	$1,650,000	
Shares retired, 1 June, 2,200 shares at a cost of $15,000; book value	(8,250)	
Stock dividend issued, 1 November, 43,780 shares (10%; 1 additional share for each 10 shares outstanding)	394,020	2,035,770
Common share conversion rights		43,900
Retained earnings (no cash dividends declared during the year)		942,000
Income before discontinued operations		$ 426,000
Discontinued operations (net of tax)		50,000
Net income		$ 476,000

Net income includes interest expense of $17,200 on Series A bonds payable, and interest expense of $72,600 on Series B bonds. Average income tax rate for the year, 30%. Both bond series were issued prior to 1 January 20X6.

Required:
Prepare required EPS presentation with all supporting computations.

★★ **A19-18 EPS Computation:** Chowdhury Limited reported $12,200,000 of net income for the 20X6 fiscal year, after an after-tax loss from discontinued operations of $4,600,000. Income before discontinued operations was $16,800,000. Net income amounts are reported before preferred dividends. No dividends were declared in 20X6. The average common share price was $12 during the period, and the tax rate was 35%.

Chowdhury reported the following financial instruments as part of its capital structure at the end of 20X6:

1. 4,915,000 common shares outstanding. Of these, 2,500,000 had been issued for cash on 1 April 20X6.

2. 1,000,000 preferred shares, with a $3 per share cumulative dividend. There had been 1,500,000 shares outstanding at the beginning of 20X3. In January, 500,000 shares, with an average issuance price of $1,725,000, were retired for $1,865,000.

3. $10,000,000 of bonds payable, convertible into 120,000 common shares beginning in 20X12 at the option of the investor. The bonds are reported as a liability, with a discount, and as an element of equity. Interest paid this year was $600,000, and there was $150,800 of discount amortization recorded.

4. Options outstanding: 200,000 shares at an option price of $15, exercisable beginning in 20X7; 800,000 shares at an option price of $8, exercisable beginning in 20X12; 600,000 shares at an option price of $20, exercisable beginning in 20X13.

Required:
Calculate required EPS disclosures.

★★ **A19-19 EPS Computations, Financial Instruments:** On 31 December 20X3, the capital structure of Victor Varieties Limited was as follows:

- $4,500,000 face value of 12% debentures, due 1 April 20X10, convertible into eight common shares per $1,000. Interest on the 12% debentures is paid on 1 April and 1 October of each year. On 2 April 20X3, 12% debentures with a face value of $1,500,000 had been converted. Interest expense on these bonds was $48,000 in 20X3. Interest expense on all the 12% bonds amounted to $624,000, including the $48,000.
- $3,000,000 face value of 12.4% debentures, due 30 June 20X15, convertible into eight common shares per $1,000 after 30 June 20X7. Interest expense related to these bonds was $450,000 in 20X3. Interest is paid on 30 June and 31 December of each year.
- 30,000 cumulative preferred shares issued and outstanding, $8 per share dividend, callable at the shareholder's option at $100 per share. These preferred shares are classified as debt. Dividends are reported as a financing expense on the income statement.
- 100,000 options outstanding to senior management, exerciseable in 20X14. The options allow purchase of 100,000 at $25 per share. Average market price in 20X3 was $14.
- 60,000 common shares issued and outstanding.

Victor Varieties reported net income after tax of $600,000 for 20X3. The tax rate was 40%.

Required:
Compute the earnings per common share for 20X3.

★★ **A19-20 Basic and Diluted EPS:** Information for the 31 December 20X9 fiscal year of Crane Ltd:

Liabilities

Convertible bonds payable, 7% (each $1,000 bond is convertible to 160 Class 3 shares)		$2,250,000
Less: discount		102,000
		$2,148,000

Shareholders' Equity

Class 1 shares, no-par, non-voting, $0.60, cumulative, convertible (each share is convertible into .25 Class 3 shares); authorized, unlimited shares; outstanding during 20X9, 75,000 shares		$ 980,000
Class 2 shares, no-par, non-voting, $1, cumulative, authorized unlimited number of shares		
Outstanding 1 January, 300,000 shares	$ 800,000	
Sold and issued on 28 December, 75,000 shares	225,000	1,025,000
Class 3 shares, no-par, voting		
Outstanding 1 January, 885,000 shares	3,742,000	
Sold and issued 150,000 shares on 1 April	620,000	4,362,000
Class 3 share options outstanding (for 60,000 shares)		98,000
Common share conversion rights		363,500
Retained earnings, end of year		6,356,000

Additional data:
a. Stock options (above)—60,000 shares, option price, $4 per share; average market price of the Class 3 shares during the year, $6.
b. Convertible bonds—interest expense in 20X9, $171,000.
c. Average income tax rate, 30%.
d. Net income, 20X9, $1,950,000. No dividends were declared in the year.

Required:
Prepare the required EPS income statement presentation for 20X9. Show all computations.

★★ **A19-21 Diluted EPS:** In 20X4, Cuba Imports Incorporated (CII) had a net income of $1,800,000, and paid $450,000 in preferred dividends and $200,000 in common dividends. During 20X4, 450,000 common shares were outstanding on average. The following elements are part of CII's capital structure:

a. CII had 40,000 options outstanding at the end of 20X4 to purchase a total of 40,000 common shares at $25 for each option exercised. The average quarterly market value of common shares was $40, $15, $20, and $35.

b. CII had $5,000,000 (par value) of 11% bonds payable outstanding for the year. The bonds are convertible into common shares at the rate of 20 shares for each $1,000 bond. None of the bonds actually converted during the period. Bond interest expense was $562,000 this year.

c. CII had 300,000 preferred shares outstanding during the entire year. These cumulative preferred shares were entitled to a yearly dividend of $1.50 per share, paid quarterly, and were convertible into common shares at a rate of two for one for the next five years, and subsequently at a rate of one for one. No conversions took place during the year.

The tax rate is 40%.

Required:

1. Calculate the individual effect for each potentially dilutive element listed above. For options, calculate shares issued and shares retired, by quarter, where dilutive.

2. Compute basic and diluted EPS.

3. Repeat requirement (2) assuming that CII reported a net loss of $200,000.

★★ **A19-22 Diluted EPS, Cascade:** Bytol Corp had the following common share transactions and balances during 20X8:

    1 January—140,000 shares outstanding
    30 April—55,000 shares issued on conversion of $5,000,000 bonds payable
    30 September—25,000 shares issued on conversion of preferred shares
    1 December—three-for-one stock dividend

Bytol reported net income of $920,000 in the year. The bond that converted on 30 April had been a 6%, five-year $5,000,000 convertible bond. It converted at maturity. There had originally been a bond discount recorded, with a remaining balance of $8,333 at the beginning of the year. There was also a $216,000 common stock conversion option recorded in equity with respect to this bond. This was transferred to the common share account on bond conversion. There were preferred shares outstanding, $2.00 cumulative shares, convertible 5-for-1 prior to the split and 15-for-1 after the split. The preferred dividend was payable quarterly (that is, $0.50 per quarter) and 5,000 of the total 20,000 outstanding preferred shares converted after the dividend paid on 30 September. The tax rate was 40%.

Required:
Calculate basic and diluted EPS for 20X8.

★ **A19-23 Diluted EPS, Cascade:** The Birch Corporation has the following items in its capital structure at 31 December 20X7, the end of the fiscal year:

a. Options to purchase 400,000 common shares were outstanding for the entire period. The exercise price is $17.50 per share. The average common share price during the period was $40.

b. Preferred shares, $2, cumulative, no-par, convertible into common shares at the rate of five shares of common for each preferred share. Dividends were declared quarterly. Seven thousand shares were outstanding for the whole year.

c. $3 million par value of 9% debentures, outstanding for the entire year. Debentures are convertible into five common shares for each $100 bond. Interest expense of $285,000 was recognized during the year.

d. Preferred shares, $5, cumulative, no-par, convertible into common shares at the rate of three shares of common for each one preferred share. Four thousand shares were outstanding for the entire year. No dividends were declared in 20X7 on these shares.

e. $8 million par value of 11.5% debentures, outstanding for the entire year. Debentures are convertible into a total of 520,000 common shares. Interest expense of $660,000 was recognized during the year.

Required:

1. Calculate the individual effect for diluted EPS for each of the above items. The tax rate is 35%. For options, calculate shares issued and shares retired.

2. Assume Maple reported basic EPS before extraordinary items of $1.29 (($1,000,000 − $14,000 − $20,000) ÷ 750,000), an extraordinary gain of $1.00 ($750,000 ÷ 750,000) and EPS for net income of $2.29 (($1,750,000 − $14,000 − $20,000) ÷ 750,000). Calculate diluted EPS, and show how it would be presented on the income statement.

★ **A19-24 Diluted EPS, Cascade:** Ron Repo Limited (RRL) ended 20X6 with 900,000 common shares outstanding, after a two-for-one stock split on 1 November. There were no other common share transactions during the period. Net income was $2,100,000. The following elements are part of RRL's capital structure (shares and per share data quoted are post-split):

a. RRL had 100,000, $3 preferred shares outstanding. The shares were cumulative. No dividends were declared in 20X6. The shares were convertible into 500,000 common shares.

b. RRL had 160,000 options outstanding all during 20X6 to purchase 320,000 common shares for $10 per share. The average share price during the year was $25. The options were not exercisable until 20X10.

c. RRL had $10,000,000 (par value) of 10% bonds payable outstanding during the year. The bonds are convertible into 55 common shares for each $1,000 bond. Bond interest expense was $1,075,000 for the year.

d. RRL had $8,000,000 (par value) of 8% bonds payable outstanding during the year. The bonds are convertible into 80 common shares for each $1,000 bond. Bond interest expense was $672,000 for the year.

The tax rate is 35%.

Required:

Compute basic and diluted EPS for 20X6.

★★ **A19-25 EPS Computation, Bonds:** At the end of 20X6, the records of Ghazal Limited reflected the following:

Bonds payable, par value $900,000. Each $1,000 bond is convertible at the investor's option to 60 common shares after the stock split on 1 Feb. 20X6. At the beginning of the year, $1,200,000 of par value was outstanding but $300,000 par value bonds converted to common shares on 1 December. Bond is shown net of discount.	$861,000
Preferred shares, $0.75, cumulative, non-participating; shares issued and outstanding at the beginning of the year, 30,000 shares. Shares are convertible into common shares, 10-for-1 after the stock split, and all shares converted on 31 December after the dividend was declared.	0
Common share conversion rights re: convertible bonds	52,500
Common shares, no-par, authorized unlimited shares; issued and outstanding throughout the period to 1 Feb. 180,000 shares. A stock split was issued 1 Feb. that doubled outstanding shares. Shares were issued on the bond conversion on 1 December. Interest was paid to the conversion date. An additional 300,000 shares were issued on 31 December on conversion of preferred shares.	970,000

Retained earnings	570,000
Income before extraordinary items (after bond interest expense of $129,240, including $30,240 on the converted bonds)	$258,000
Extraordinary loss (net of tax)	(42,000)
Net income	$216,000
Average income tax rate, 30%.	

Required:

Compute the required EPS amounts and show how they would be presented on the income statement.

★ **A19-26 EPS Interpretation:** Selected information from Informus Limited, a Canadian public company:

	20X6	20X5	20X4
Earnings per share:			
Basic	$4.71	$3.94	$3.10
Diluted	4.24	3.76	3.08
(in thousands)			
Net income	$124,300	$146,900	$142,100
Income attributable to common shareholders—basic	116,900	139,500	132,800
Income attributable to common shareholders—diluted	134,200	141,100	135,600
Common shares outstanding at year-end	26,900	32,300	40,700
Weighted-average common shares outstanding—basic	24,820	35,407	42,839
Weighted-average common shares outstanding—diluted	31,651	37,527	44,026

Required:

1. Comment on the trends in basic and diluted EPS.

2. Why is net income not equal to income attributable to common shareholders—basic?

3. Why are weighted-average common shares—basic higher or lower than common shares outstanding at year-end? Compare 20X6 to 20X5 and 20X4.

4. Explain the types of adjustments needed to arrive at income and weighted-average share amounts for diluted EPS.

★★ **A19-27 EPS Interpretation:** Nixon Limited reported EPS as follows in the 31 December 20X6 financial statements:

	20X6	20X5	20X4
Basic			
Net income (loss)	1.06	$0.94	($1.64)
Diluted			
Net income (loss)	$0.95	$0.74	($1.64)

Other information (in thousands)

	20X6
Net income attributable to common shareholders—basic	$37,200
Dividends on preferred securities	1,100
After-tax interest on convertible bonds	705
Net income—diluted	$39,005
Weighted-average common shares—basic	35,093
$16 options for 500 shares; options issued 31 December 20X4; net effect	180
$30 options for 800 shares; options issued 31 December 20X5; excluded	—
$10 options for 500 shares; options issued 31 December 20X6; excluded	—
Assumed settlement of preferred securities	4,970
Assumed settlement of convertible bonds	700
	40,943

Required:

1. Why is basic EPS equal to diluted EPS in 20X4?

2. Comment on the trends in basic and diluted EPS.

3. Calculate the individual effects of the bonds and preferred shares.

4. Are the convertible bonds dilutive with respect to basic EPS? Were they dilutive in 20X5? Explain.

5. Why are the $30 options and $10 options likely excluded from diluted EPS calculations?

★ **A19-28 Loss per Share:** Brinkhurst Corporation's balance sheet at 31 December 20X6 reported the following:

Accrued interest payable	$ 12,000
Long-term notes payable, 10%, due in 20X9	1,000,000
Bonds payable, par value $9,000,000, 8%, each $1,000 of face value is convertible into 90 common shares; bonds mature in 20X13, net of discount	8,200,000
Preferred shares, no-par, $5, non-convertible, cumulative (75,000 shares outstanding at year-end)	3,500,000
Common shares, 2,700,000 shares outstanding	12,000,000
Common stock conversion rights	590,000

Additional data:

a. During 20X6, 15,000 preferred shares were issued at $50 on 1 July. Dividends are paid semi-annually, on 31 May and 30 November.

b. Common share rights are outstanding, entitling holders to acquire 700,000 common shares at $9 per share.

c. Interest expense on the convertible bonds was $825,000 in 20X6.

d. Income tax rate is 30%.

e. Common share price at the end of each quarter of the fiscal year was $5, $7, $2, and $10, respectively.

f. The net loss for 20X6 was $1,625,000.

Required:

Compute the EPS amount(s) that Brinkhurst should report on the income statement for 20X6.

★★   **A19-29 Basic and Diluted EPS:** MacDonald Corporation had the following securities outstanding at its fiscal year-end 31 December 20X7:

Long-term debt:	
Notes payable, 14%	$4,500,000
8% convertible debentures, par value $2,500,000, net of discount	2,410,000
9.5% convertible debentures, par value $2,500,000, net of discount	2,452,000
Equity preferred shares, $5 dividend, payable as $1.25 per quarter, no-par, cumulative convertible shares; authorized, 100,000 shares; issued, 30,000 shares	4,700,000
Common shares, no-par; authorized, 5,000,000 shares; issued, 600,000 shares	2,000,000
Common share conversion rights	189,000

Other information:
a. No dividends were declared in 20X7.
b. 20X7 net income was $790,000. Interest expense was $216,000 on the 8% debentures, and $250,000 on the 9.5% debentures.
c. Options were outstanding all year to purchase 200,000 common shares at $11 per share beginning in 20X15.
d. Options were issued on 1 May 20X7 to purchase 50,000 common shares at $27 per share in 20X9. The price per share becomes $25 in 20X10, and $20 in 20X11. The options expire at the end of 20X11.
e. The preferred shares are convertible into common shares at a rate of nine-for-one. They were issued on 1 October 20X7.
f. The 8% convertible debentures are convertible at the rate of seven shares for each $100 bond. The 9.5% convertible debentures are convertible at the rate of six shares for each $100 bond.
g. The tax rate is 40%; common shares sold for an average of $40 during the year.
h. No common shares were issued or retired during the year.

Required:
Calculate all EPS disclosures.

★   **A19-30 Basic and Diluted EPS:** Kwon Enterprises Incorporation needs to establish its EPS figures for its 20X7 reports. The following information is available:

a. Net income: $900,000; net income before tax, $1,500,000.
b. Class A common shares, voting with one vote per share, unlimited shares authorized, 140,000 shares outstanding 1 January.
c. Cumulative convertible preferred shares: 16,000 shares issued 1 August 20X2, and outstanding 1 January 20X7. Issued at $50 a share with a yearly $4 cumulative dividend paid semi-annually 30 June and 31 December. The shares are convertible on a share-for-share basis with Class A shares adjusted automatically for any stock dividends or splits.
d. 30 June: After the semi-annual dividend was paid, 15,000 of the preferred shares converted to common shares.
e. 1 April: Kwon declared a 20% stock dividend on Class A shares.
f. 31 October: Kwon purchased and retired 8,000 Class A shares for $54 per share.
g. All preferred dividends were paid on schedule. Common dividends of $3 per quarter were declared and paid.
h. Options were granted for 13,000 Class A shares on 31 December 20X7. The exercise price was $50, and the options expire in 20X16. The average share price during the period was $55.

Required:
Compute necessary EPS disclosures.

★★★ **A19-31 Complex EPS:** The shareholders' equity of Byrne Corporation as of 31 December 20X6, the end of the current fiscal year, is as follows:

$1 cumulative preferred shares, no-par, convertible at the rate of 4-for-1; 350,000 shares outstanding	$ 9,150,000
Common shares, no-par; 3,500,000 shares outstanding	15,000,000
Common stock conversion rights	231,000
Retained earnings	30,600,000

On 1 July 20X6, 150,000 preferred shares were converted to common shares at the rate of 4-for-1.

During 20X6, Byrne had 9% convertible subordinated debentures outstanding with a face value of $4,000,000. The debentures are due in 20X12, at which time they may be converted to common shares or repaid at the option of the holder. The conversion rate is 12 common shares for each $100 debenture. Interest expense of $175,000 was recorded in 20X6.

The convertible preferred shares had been issued in 20X0. Quarterly dividends, on 31 March, 30 June, 30 September, and 31 December, have been regularly declared. The company's 20X6 net income was $1,289,000, after tax at 48%. Common shares traded for quarterly average prices of $15, $12, $10, and $22.

Byrne had certain employee stock options outstanding all year. The options were to purchase 600,000 common shares at a price of $18 per share. The options become exercisable in 20X13.

Byrne had another 100,000 employee stock options outstanding on 1 January 20X6, at an exercise price of $16. They expired on 30 June 20X6.

Required:
Show the EPS presentation that Byrne would include on its 20X6 income statement.

★★★ **A19-32 Basic and Diluted EPS; Split:** At 31 December 20X6, Royal Limited had the following items on the balance sheet:

Preferred shares, Class A, non-voting, cumulative, par $10, $2 dividend per share, redeemable at par; 100,000 authorized, 60,000 issued	$ 500,000
Preferred shares, Class B, voting, cumulative, par $15, $3 dividend per share, redeemable at par plus 20%; convertible at the rate of one preferred share to two common shares; 200,000 authorized, 90,000 issued	$ 1,200,000
Common shares, voting; 1,000,000 authorized, 700,000 issued	$ 5,357,000
Retained earnings (deficit)	$(2,394,000)

The Class A preferred shares are redeemable in 20X11 at the investors' option and are classified as a liability.

At 31 December 20X6, there were two common share stock options outstanding:

a. $15 per share exercise price and 80,000 shares.
b. $15 per share exercise price and 150,000 shares, able to be exercised after 1 July 20X18 and expiring on 1 July 20X20.

During 20X7, the following occurred:

a. Net income was $1,900,000, before preferred dividends, including the Class A dividends.
b. Common shares were issued on 1 March 20X7 when the $15 options described above were fully exercised.
c. The tax rate was 40%.
d. The average common share price during the period was $16, after giving effect to the stock split described in (f). The average for January and February, before the split, was $40.
e. No dividends were declared or paid to any of the shareholders.

f. There was a three-for-one stock split of the common shares on 1 November. All outstanding shares, option contracts, and conversion terms were adjusted accordingly. (That is, the number of shares increased and the price per share decreased.)

Required:
Prepare the earnings per share section on the income statement for the year ended 31 December 20X7 in good form.

(CICA, adapted)

★★★ **A19-33 Complex EPS:** The following data relate to Freeman Incorporation:

Year Ended 31 December 20X6

From the Income Statement	
Net income	$18,000,000
From the Balance Sheet	
Long-term debt:	
10% convertible debentures, due 1 October 20X13	$ 9,000,000
Shareholders' equity (Note 1)	
Convertible, callable, voting preferred shares of no-par value, 20-cent cumulative dividend; authorized 600,000 shares; issued and outstanding 600,000 shares	10,600,000
Common shares, voting, no-par, authorized 5,000,000 shares; issued and outstanding, 3,320,000 shares	13,700,000
Common stock conversion rights	375,000

FROM THE DISCLOSURE NOTES
The 20-cent convertible preferred shares are callable by the company after 31 March 20X14, at $60 per share. Each share is convertible into one common share.
   Options to acquire 500,000 common shares at $53 per share were outstanding during 20X6.

Other information:
a. Cash dividends of 12.5 cents per common share were declared and paid each quarter.
b. The 10-year, 10% convertible debentures with a principal amount of $10,000,000 due 1 October 20X13, were issued 1 October 20X3. A discount was originally recorded, and discount amortization was $20,000 in the current year. Each $100 debenture is convertible into two shares of common. On 31 December 20X6, ten thousand $100 debentures with a total face value of $1,000,000 were converted to common shares. Interest was paid to the date of conversion, but the newly issued common shares did not qualify for the 31 December common dividend.
c. The 600,000 convertible preferred shares were issued for assets in a purchase transaction in 20X4. The dividend was declared and paid on 15 December 20X6. Each share is convertible into one common share.
d. Options to buy 500,000 common shares at $53 per share for a period of five years were issued along with the convertible preferred shares mentioned in (c).
e. At the end of 20X5, 3,300,000 common shares were outstanding. On 31 December 20X6, 20,000 shares were issued on the conversion of bonds.
f. A tax rate of 40% is assumed.
g. Common shares traded at an average market price of $75 during the year. Averages at the end of the four quarters were as follows: $100, $80, $50, $70.

Required:
Calculate all EPS disclosures.

★★★ **A19-34 Complex EPS:** Yee Lai Company (YLC), reported the following facts for the fiscal year ended 31 December 20X8:

a. 20X8 income from operations, after tax, of $1,050,000. The company also reported a before-tax gain from discontinued operations of $112,000.

b. The effective income tax rate was 40%. The average common share price in 20X8 was $45 and was fairly constant all year.

c. No dividends were declared in 20X8.

d. On 1 January 1 20X8, 470,400 common shares were outstanding. At that date, 10,000, $4.20 cumulative preferred shares were outstanding.

e. Options to purchase 20,000 common shares at $28 per share were outstanding all during 20X8. The options can be exercised beginning in 20X11.

f. On 1 September 20X8, YLC issued 30,000 additional common shares for cash.

g. YLC had $1,500,000 convertible bonds outstanding on 1 January 20X8 with interest payable on 1 June and 1 December and each $1,000 bond convertible into 30 common shares. $600,000 of the bonds were converted into common shares on 1 June 20X8. YLC reported interest expense of $78,200, which included $17,000 on the converted bonds.

h. Employee stock options (which can be exercised beginning in 20X15) to purchase 30,000 common shares at $50 per share were granted on 1 October 20X8.

Required:

1. Prepare EPS presentations for 20X8. Show all computations.

2. It is said that diluted EPS relates more to the future than to the past. Explain.

 A19-35 Complex EPS; Interpretation: Woo Corporation reported net income in 20X6 of $1,345,000, after an after-tax loss from discontinued operations of $677,800. Income before discontinued operations was $2,022,800. The tax rate was 30%.

Woo reports the following information regarding its securities:

a. 400,000 $2 no-par cumulative preferred shares, issued 1 July 20X6. The shares are convertible into Class A common shares 6-for-1 at the option of the investor. The dividend was paid on a quarterly basis.

b. There are 175,000 $1.20 no-par cumulative preferred shares outstanding during 20X6. These shares were convertible into Class A common shares 4-for-1 at the option of the investor. All preferred shares converted to Class A common shares on 31 December 20X6 after the preferred dividend was paid.

c. There are $3,000,000 of convertible bonds payable outstanding during 20X6, convertible into Class A shares at the rate of 30 shares per $1,000 bond, at the option of the investor. This bond was recorded as a hybrid financial instrument. During the year, interest expense of $281,000 was recorded.

Woo had 2,300,000 Class A common shares outstanding at the beginning of the year. On 1 February, the company repurchased and retired 750,000 Class A common shares on the open market for $18 per share. Woo sold 50,000 common shares for $22 per share on 1 December.

At the beginning of the year, 200,000 options were outstanding, allowing senior management to purchase 200,000 Class A shares for $5 per share. On 1 September, 60,000 of these options were exercised, when the market value of the common shares was $19 per share. The average market value for the first eight months of the year was $15 per share. The remaining options are still outstanding and will expire in 20X10.

All preferred dividends, plus common dividends of $1 per share, were paid on schedule in 20X6.

At the end of 20X6, another 400,000 options, for 400,000 Class A shares at a price of $24, were issued to management. These options have an expiry date of 20X15. The average common share price for the entire year was $22 per share.

Required:

1. Calculate required EPS disclosures.

2. Interpret the EPS calculations provided.

CHAPTER 20

Restatements

INTRODUCTION

Over a recent five-year period, 900 companies on the New York Stock Exchange issued restated financial statements; this is more than 10% of U.S. public companies. The list of restatements includes Enron, CMS Energy, Dynergy, Tyco, Reliant Resources, Computer Associates, Network Associates, Global Crossing, Trump, Xerox, Worldcom, and Lucent. Canadian examples include Livent, Nortel, Proprietary Industries, and Cinar. Areas of critical interest have been revenue and expense recognition, related party transactions, non-monetary transactions, accounting for foreign currency and business combinations, as well as a number of large-scale frauds perpetrated by management. The size and scope of restatements has resulted in increased public scrutiny of accounting policy choices, and an opportunity to improve the quality of financial reporting—or pay the price of decreased credibility.

Restatement involves changing previously reported results. Sometimes this is done to comply with new accounting standards, and annual financial statements are changed to reflect retrospective application of the new policy. In other cases, restatement is done in a crisis environment, because material errors in the published financial statements make them misleading. When this happens, restated, corrected financial statements are issued quickly, with accompanying description of the nature and extent of the changes. Clearly, the credibility of financial statements suffers when material restatements become common.

As we will see in this chapter, restatements may be the result of accounting policy changes or error corrections. In contrast, changes in the estimates that are so pervasive in financial reporting cause *prospective* changes to the financial statements. For all changes, required disclosure is critical, in order to help the financial statement user understand the nature and implications of the change.

TYPES OF ACCOUNTING CHANGES

There are three types of accounting changes:

1. Changes in accounting *policy*
   a. Mandatory, to comply with new GAAP recommendations
   b. Voluntary, at the option of management or at the request of a user

2. Changes in accounting *estimate*

3. Correction of an *error* in prior years' financial statements.

The general nature of each of these types of changes is discussed in the following sections. After discussing these three types, we then will explore the accounting methods that apply to each.

Changes in Policy

A change in accounting policy is a change in the way that a company accounts for a particular type of transaction or event, or for the resulting asset or liability. Accounting policy changes can be mandatory or voluntary:

- A change is **mandatory** when a primary source of GAAP requires a new accounting policy. Accounting standard-setters often issue new or revised recommendations. GAAP-constrained companies must alter their policies to conform to the new recommendations.
- A change is **voluntary** when management decides to make a change from one generally accepted method of accounting to another generally accepted method. This is allowed only if the new policy results in financial statement information that is both (1) reliable and (2) more relevant for the statement users.

A *change* in accounting policy must not be confused with adopting a *new accounting policy*. The following are *not* changes in accounting policy:

1. *Adopting an accounting policy for transactions or other events that differ in substance from those previously occurring.* An example would be a change in the method of generating revenue, such as introducing instalment sales in addition to sales that require full payment. There is a substantive difference in the way that revenue will be realized, and this change may call for applying a different accounting policy than the one previously used.

2. *Adopting a new accounting policy for transactions or other events that did not occur previously or were immaterial.* For example, a company may have been expensing all product development costs without applying the criteria for deferral because such costs were immaterial. If development costs become significant, the company then will begin applying deferral criteria. This is adoption of a new accounting policy, but is not a *change* of accounting policy because a material amount of development costs had not previously been incurred.

Mandatory Changes   Mandatory changes in accounting policy have been pervasive in recent years as new accounting standards have been introduced and existing standards altered. *Financial Reporting in Canada 2006* found that 150 of the 200 sample companies reported a change in accounting policy in the most recent year. Recently introduced or altered accounting standards have changed the methods of accounting for many types of transactions and measurements. Standards that have required most companies to change their accounting policies include those on inventories, asset retirement obligations, financial instruments, comprehensive income, discontinued operations, and asset impairments, among others.

Changes caused by application of new or revised standards are usually made **retrospectively**, which means that the new policy is applied as though it had always been in effect. **Prospective** treatment is sometimes allowed, which means the new policy is recognized only in the current and future periods, and not applied to earlier periods. Early adoption is also encouraged. We will discuss these different treatments a little later in the chapter.

Voluntary Changes Voluntary accounting policy changes are allowed only if the new policy results in information that is both (1) reliable and (2) more relevant.

Clearly, information has to be *reliable* in order to be included in the financial statements. However, the new policy has to be *more relevant* than the old policy in order to be adopted. Accounting standards do not provide guidance about judging the relevance of resulting information. Relevancy is subjective, so this will be difficult judgement in some circumstances.

Management may make a voluntary change in accounting policy in response to changes in the reporting enterprise's reporting circumstances, such as:

- A change in reporting objectives;
- A change in the way of doing business, for example, a shift to higher-risk business strategies that make the prediction of future outcomes more difficult and less reliable; or
- A desire to conform to common or emerging industry practice.

One of the most common reasons for changing one or more accounting policies is a change in reporting objectives. For example, when the ownership of a company changes, the priority of objectives often changes or new objectives that previously did not exist suddenly become important. Examples of changes in ownership include the following:

- A company that previously was privately held may decide to issue shares on the public market and will discontinue use of the differential reporting options.
- Control of the reporting enterprise may be acquired by another corporation in a business combination, and the acquired company may have to change its accounting policies to conform to those used by its new parent company.
- A new investor may purchase shares in a private company and have the power to specify that certain reporting objectives, such as cash flow prediction, are adopted.

Although information should be more relevant to the users, an underlying motivation may be management's desire to manage earnings. The following factors might be at play:

- Ratios specified in lending covenants
- Published expectations of financial analysts, feeding stock prices
- Stock options granted to management
- Tax minimization.

The constraint is that new policies be *more relevant* to financial statement users, thus establishing the need to evaluate all changes in an objective fashion.

Changes in Estimate

Changes in accounting estimates are very common. Accounting measurements are based extensively on future expectations. Many financial statement elements require estimates of future values or events, and estimates are frequently changed. Examples of significant accounting estimates include the following:

- Uncollectible accounts receivable
- Inventory obsolescence
- Fair values of financial assets
- Judgement concerning one or more of the criteria for capitalizing development costs

Changes in accounting estimates can occur for several reasons:

- New, reliable information is available.
- Experience has provided insights into such things as usage patterns or benefits.
- The company's economic environment has changed, requiring a re-evaluation of the assumptions underlying management's accounting estimates.
- Probabilities underlying accounting estimates have changed.
- There has been a shift in the nature of the company's business operations, so that past estimates may need adjustment to fit current business strategies.

Changes in accounting estimates are part of the accounting routine. They reflect the environmental changes that affect an organization on a continuing basis rather than reflecting substantive changes in the *way* that accounting is being done. Therefore, changes in accounting estimates are accounted for *prospectively*, by applying them only in the current and future periods.

Change in Policy or Estimate?

Accounting estimates are changed very often, sometimes annually, as a company accumulates new information and gains more experience. Normally, the financial statement effect is less dramatic with a change in estimate rather than a change in policy.

Also, the application method is usually different—policy changes are applied retrospectively while estimate changes are applied prospectively. Therefore, it is important to distinguish between estimates and policies. When it is difficult to decide whether a change is a change in policy or estimate, *the change should be treated as a change in estimate.*

Example—Changes in Amortization Method Companies occasionally change the amortization methods for tangible capital assets. Since this is an easy change to make, and the allocation of the cost of capital assets between periods is so arbitrary, there is often a hint that the primary reason for the change is to alter reported results—for example, to improve net income and net assets.

A change in estimated residual value or in the estimated useful life of a tangible capital asset can easily be seen as a change in estimate. On the other hand, a change from declining balance to straight line may appear to be a change in policy because the amortization *method* has changed, not just the estimates underlying application of the method. However, the choice of amortization method reflects management's estimate of the expected pattern of use. If the pattern of use is different than expected, then the change in method is a change of estimate, not policy.

Correction of a Prior-Period Error

Prior-period errors are omissions or mistakes that were made in the application of accounting principles in one or more earlier periods. Mistakes can be mathematical errors, oversights, misinterpretations of fact, or intentional fraud. Errors relate to information that:

1. Was available when the prior-period's financial statements were prepared; and

2. Could reasonably be expected to have been obtained and taken into account in the preparation and presentation of those financial statements.

An error correction is *not* an adjustment of an accounting estimate of a prior period. For example, suppose that, in 20X1, a company uses past experience with existing products to estimate a warranty liability for a new product. In 20X2, that estimate turns out to be seriously inadequate. In 20X2, the company will adjust its warranty liability and the related expense to recognize the new reality—a *change in accounting estimate*. However, if it turns out that the company's managers overlooked clear evidence that the liability would be significantly higher, and the evidence was available in 20X1, then the misstatement calls for an error correction.

Again, hindsight is not permitted to dictate error classification, but hindsight can be very illuminating when evaluating facts. Sometimes errors are quite clear cut:

- Management discovers that a portion of inventory at the beginning of the year was overlooked when the physical count was taken.
- The company sells through agents; the company failed to accrue commission liabilities that had not been paid at the end of the fiscal year.
- Routine repairs to equipment were capitalized instead of expensed.

However, errors are not always simple. For example, in 2005, Nortel Networks Corporation reduced its previously reported revenues by $261 million for 2003 and an additional $312 million for 2004. These corrections were part of an ongoing effort to correct its application of complex revenue recognition policies.

Events Not Reportable as Errors A vital aspect of errors is that they do not arise from a change in estimate or a change in policy. They are mistakes, whether accidental or intentional. Any item that is in error should have been recorded differently in the previous period given the accounting policies and accounting estimates at the time.

For example, a company may have followed a practice of deferring and amortizing development costs in earlier periods, only to discover later that the company would receive no future benefit from the expenditures. The policy to defer and amortize may have been completely rational and justifiable on the evidence at the time, but later evidence alters the situation. The company would write off the development costs when it became clear that no future benefit would be derived, but that is a *change in estimate*, not an error.

Another example of an event that is *not* accounted for as an error correction is an income tax audit. The income tax reported for a year is considered to be an estimate until confirmed by a CRA audit. If, in 20X5, an audit results in $100,000 of extra tax paid, specifically relating to 20X2 and 20X3, restatement is not appropriate. Instead, 20X5 income tax expense is increased by $100,000. This is prospective treatment.

Prior-Period Adjustments At one time, companies were permitted to make prior-period adjustments. A prior-period adjustment was a gain or a loss that was credited or charged directly to retained earnings instead of appearing in the income statement. Usually, these adjustments were retrospective adjustments to accounting estimates. Now, however, adjustments to prior-period estimates are not permitted; all estimates are accounted for prospectively. Nevertheless, the term "prior-period adjustment" appears to live on, especially in general international usage (although the term also does not exist in international accounting standards). It is now a general term sometimes used to refer to any restated prior-period results.

CONCEPT REVIEW

1. List the three types of accounting changes.

2. Suppose that a company discovers that it has more uncollectible accounts from the prior year than it had provided as expense (and as an allowance) in that year. Is this an error? Explain.

3. If a company is uncertain about whether an accounting change is a change in policy or a change in estimate, how should it treat the change?

REPORTING ACCOUNTING CHANGES

General Methodology

There are three ways of reporting accounting changes in the financial statements:

1. *Retrospective application with restatement of prior periods.* The new accounting policy or treatment is applied to events and transactions from the date of origin of each event or transaction. The financial statements for each prior period that are presented for comparative purposes are restated to reflect the new policy. Opening retained earnings for each comparative period is adjusted for the cumulative prior income effect. All summary financial information for earlier periods, such as net income, total assets, earnings per share, etc., is restated as well. All reported financial results after the change look as though the new policy had always been in effect.

2. *Retrospective application without restatement of prior periods.* The new accounting policy is applied to opening balances of the current year and a cumulative adjustment representing the effect of the change on prior years' income (net assets) is recorded in the period in which the change is made. Comparative information for prior periods is *not* restated. The summary impact of the change is stated as a one-line adjustment to opening retained earnings in the current period.

3. *Prospective application.* The changed treatment is applied only to events, transactions, and valuations beginning with the period in which the change is made. Previously reported results are *not* restated, and there is no cumulative catch-up adjustment.

Retrospective application of an accounting policy change has the advantage of making *current and future* financial information fully comparable with reported results for prior periods.[1] Earnings trends and other analytical data that are based on historical comparisons are not valid unless the same accounting policies are used throughout the time series. Restatement has the advantage of making all prior information fully compatible with current reported results. The qualitative criteria of *consistency* and *comparability* are enhanced by full restatement of comparative statements and of historical summary data.

If at all feasible, retrospective application should be used for (1) changes in accounting policy and (2) corrections of errors. Prospective application is permissible only when it is not practicable to determine the cumulative effect of the new accounting policy, or when a change in accounting standards specifically permits prospective application.

Changes in accounting estimate are always accounted for *prospectively*. This difference in treatment is the major reason that it is important to distinguish between changes in policies and changes in estimates.

Change in Accounting Policy

A change in accounting policy is applied retrospectively with restatement if it is feasible to determine the effect of the change on prior periods. The benefits of restatement are considerable, and every reasonable effort must be made to assemble the information needed for full retrospective restatement.

Restatement may require a great deal of very detailed information that is no longer available or available only at great cost. For example, a change in inventory method from average cost to FIFO requires the establishment of inventory layers at each balance sheet date. To fully restate prior years' net income, the details for each year's beginning and ending inventories must be determined in order to restate cost of goods sold. That data would not readily be available under the average cost method previously used. While it might theoretically be possible to reconstruct the necessary data by going back into archival purchase records, the benefit would almost certainly not be worth the cost.

If the effect on prior periods cannot be determined, then the policy should be applied *without restatement*. The company would adjust opening retained earnings for the cumulative effect of all prior periods but omit the restatement of comparative numbers. In order to accomplish this, it may be necessary to delay implementation of the new policy until the next period, to allow appropriate information to be collected.

Sometimes it is impracticable to measure the cumulative effect of a change at the beginning of the current period. In that case, a company may apply the new policy prospectively at the earliest practicable date, which usually is the next accounting period. Specific standards may also permit prospective treatment when the prior-year data would be excessively difficult to obtain.

For example, prospective treatment was allowed for the new financial instruments accounting policies introduced in 2006. The new policies were applied to existing balances but not to the comparative prior-year balances because it would not have been feasible to restate (or *remeasure*) financial assets retrospectively. Clearly, prospective treatment causes a loss of comparability. On the other hand, retrospective restatement was obviously judged to be not worth the additional reporting cost.

---

[1] The word "retrospective" was introduced into Canadian standards by the simultaneous issuance of *CICA Handbook* Section 1506 and revision of *IAS 8*. Previously, standards and companies used "retroactive." "Retrospective" and "retroactive" mean the same thing when used in accounting, a fact specifically stated in Section 1506. Many companies continue to use "retroactive."

Error Correction

The correction of an accounting error is accounted for retrospectively, with restatement. The error should not have happened, which means that the statements for one or more past periods were simply wrong. In many cases, the error will have reversed itself by the current period, requiring no adjustment to the current period's statements. In other cases, reversal is not complete and correction is needed.

For example, suppose that the inventory stored in a Cuban warehouse was accidentally not included in the ending inventory count for 20X1. The oversight will have understated ending inventory for 20X1, overstated cost of goods sold, and thereby understated net income for that year. The resulting understatement of beginning inventory in 20X2 will cause an understatement of cost of goods sold and an overstatement of net income for 20X2. If the ending inventory for 20X2 is correctly stated (that is, including the Cuban inventory), the cumulative error will wash out because the overstatement of 20X2 net income will offset the understatement of 20X1 net income; retained earnings at the end of 20X2 will be correct.

If the error is discovered in 20X3, no adjustment needs to be made *on the books* because there are no misstated accounts (either balance sheet or income statement) for 20X3. But an error that self-corrects over time still causes misstatements for the earlier periods that were affected. The comparative statements must be changed.

Changes in Estimate

Changes in an accounting estimate are relatively simple to account for. The new estimate should be accounted for prospectively, in the current and all affected future periods, as appropriate.

Although a change in an accounting estimate may *directly* affect the current period only, it most likely will implicitly affect the financial results of future periods as well. For example,

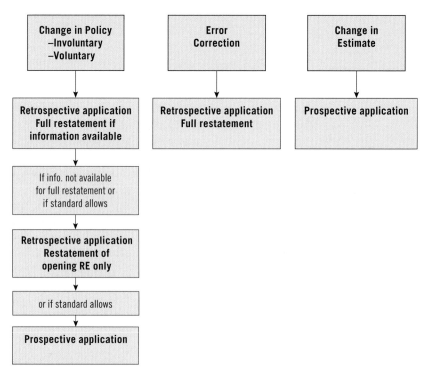

EXHIBIT 20-1

DECISION PROCESS FOR APPLYING ACCOUNTING CHANGES

Change in Policy −Involuntary −Voluntary	Error Correction	Change in Estimate
Retrospective application Full restatement if information available	Retrospective application Full restatement	Prospective application
If info. not available for full restatement or if standard allows		
Retrospective application Restatement of opening RE only		
or if standard allows		
Prospective application		

writing off an impaired asset will affect the net income directly only in the current period, but the absence of that asset will relieve future periods of amortization or loss recognition related to that asset. Past periods are never changed.

Income Tax Effect of Changes

Most changes are made only for accounting purposes and do not affect taxable income. In that case, future income tax must be adjusted, reflecting the temporary difference that is created or reduced in the change entry. On the other hand, if the change is also made for tax purposes, tax returns must be refiled, and tax payable or tax receivable is recognized.

Summary of Approaches

Exhibit 20-1 shows the decision process for applying the three kinds of accounting changes. Exhibit 20-2 summarizes the treatment of cumulative effects and prior-period restatements. It may be helpful to refer back to these two exhibits as you proceed through the following discussion of accounting approaches.

EXHIBIT 20-2

SUMMARY OF ACCOUNTING CHANGES AND REPORTING APPROACHES

Type of Accounting Change	Accounting Approach Recommended	Restatement Methodology	
		Cumulative Adjustment Identified With	Comparative Statements and Results of Prior Years
Accounting Policy			
a. Usual situation—prior-year restatement is practicable	Retrospective with restatement	Opening retained earnings retrospectively restated in all affected prior periods	Comparative prior years' results restated to new policy
b. Not feasible to restate prior years or, if permitted by a new accounting standard	Retrospective without restatement	Only the opening retained earnings of current period restated	Prior years' results remain unchanged
c. If (1) impracticable to determine cumulative effect at beginning of current period or (2) specifically permitted by a new accounting standard	Prospective	Cumulative adjustment not computed or reported	Prior years' results remain unchanged; new policy applied only to current and future events and transactions
Accounting Estimate	Prospective	Cumulative adjustment not computed or reported	Prior years' results remain unchanged. New estimates applied only to accounting for current and future periods.
Accounting Error	Retrospective with restatement	Opening retained earnings restated (if the error has not self-corrected)	Prior years' results restated to correct the error

1. Describe three different ways in which changes can be accounted for.

2. What is the preferred method of accounting for a change in accounting policy?

3. What method should be used for correcting errors that occurred in prior years?

RETROSPECTIVE APPROACH WITH RESTATEMENT

Guidelines The following guidelines apply to accounting policy changes that are accounted for by using retrospective application with restatement of prior years' financial data. The same approach is used for correction of prior years' accounting errors.

In the following list, notice that the first guideline refers to *recording* the impact of the change on the books of the company, while the next four guidelines refer to *reporting* in the financial statements and in disclosure notes.

1. The *cumulative* impact of the change on the *beginning* balances of the current year must be calculated. These changes are *recorded* in the accounts by means of a general journal entry. The cumulative impact of the accounting policy change on prior year's net income is recorded as an adjustment to the beginning balance of retained earnings.

2. The information necessary to make the change *in the current and prior periods* must be obtained from the underlying accounting records.

3. Account balances that affect the prior years' comparative financial statements must be recalculated using the new policy, including all affected balance sheet and income statement accounts. The comparative statements must be restated to reflect the changed amounts in the full financial statements.

4. Summary comparative information (e.g., earnings per share, total assets, shareholders' equity) that are presented publicly, such as in the annual report, must be recalculated using the new policy.

5. Opening retained earnings is restated to remove the effect of the accounting change from prior earnings. Opening retained earnings *as restated* is shown as a subtotal. This is done for all comparative years. The amount of the adjustment will change as the *number of prior years* declines.

Under the approach of retrospective restatement, all prior-period data are restated for financial reporting purposes, but the entry that is made on the books to record the change in accounting policy is made only for the current year. Prior years' books have been closed and any necessary adjustment is made to retained earnings.

Illustration Exhibit 20-3 presents the data for an illustration of the retrospective approach with restatement. In this example, we assume that Sunset Corporation has decided to change its method of accounting for inventories from average cost (AC) to first-in, first-out (FIFO), in the fiscal year ending 31 December 20X5. To make the change, Sunset must recalculate its inventory balances for the end of 20X4 in order to determine net income for 20X5, but also must recalculate its inventory balances for the beginning of 20X4 in order to restate the comparative results for 20X4.

The first step in restatement is to determine which balances will be affected by the change. For a change in inventory method, the following balances will be affected:

• Beginning inventory
• Ending inventory
• Cost of goods sold

- Income tax expense
- Future income tax (on the balance sheet)
- Retained earnings

The income statement, balance sheet, and retained earnings statement will require restatement for 20X4. A change in accounting policy does not affect cash flows, but a change in inventory method will affect the amounts reported in the operations section of the cash flow statement if the company uses the indirect method of presenting cash from operations, because:

- The policy change will alter both cost of goods sold and income tax expense, which affects net income, the starting point for determining cash flow from operations (using the indirect presentation approach); and
- The change in inventory and the change in future income tax are adjustments to convert net income to cash flow.

These two adjustments will net out, causing no change in the total reported cash from operations. Nevertheless, the changes must be made to maintain the articulation between the cash flow statement and the other two statements.

In our inventory example, the following impacts of the accounting change must be calculated:

1. The cumulative effect on balances up to 1 January 20X5 (the year of the change);

2. The cumulative effect on balances up to 1 January 20X4; and

3. The specific impact on the accounts for the year 20X4, for comparative restatement purposes.

EXHIBIT 20-3

SUNSET CORPORATION DATA FOR CHANGE IN ACCOUNTING POLICY CHANGE FROM AVERAGE COST (AC) TO FIFO FOR INVENTORY

1. During 20X5, Sunset Corporation decides to change its inventory cost method from average cost (AC) to first-in, first-out (FIFO) for accounting purposes, effective for fiscal year 20X5. AC will still be used for tax purposes. The reporting year ends on 31 December, and the company's income tax rate is 40%.
2. From its records, the company determines the following information relating to the change:

	20X5		20X4	
	FIFO	AC	FIFO	AC
a. Beginning inventory (from prior 31 December)	$ 60,000	$50,000	$47,000	$ 45,000
b. Ending inventory	80,000	65,000	60,000	50,000
c. Income before income tax	300,000*			270,000
d. Income tax expense	120,000			108,000
e. Retained earnings, beginning balance	174,000			92,000
f. Dividends declared and paid	88,000			80,000

*Reflects FIFO policy.

The new basis of accounting must then be used for the current year, 20X5. The calculations for Sunset Corporation are as follows, using the amounts presented in Exhibit 20-3.

Impact to 1 January 20X5

The journal entry to record the effects of the change in policy must be based on the cumulative effect at the beginning of 20X5. Opening inventory was $50,000 under AC and is $60,000 under FIFO, an increase of $10,000. After tax, the effect on retained earnings is $6,000. Assuming that the inventory method for income tax purposes is not changed retrospectively, the offset for the increase in income tax expense is the current future income tax account (or future tax liability account) on the balance sheet. The following entry will be made during 20X5, the year in which the inventory policy was changed:

Inventory	10,000	
Future income tax (40% tax rate)		4,000
Retained earnings, cumulative effect of policy change		6,000

This entry establishes the new accounting policy in the accounts; all future entries will be made on the basis of the new accounting policy. *This entry is always made effective 1 January of the year of the change, regardless of the date that the change was actually adopted.*

Since the change is made for accounting purposes but not for tax purposes, inventory becomes a source of temporary difference and future income tax is affected. If the change was also made for income tax purposes, income tax payable would be credited and tax returns adjusted appropriately.

Impact to 1 January 20X4

The change in beginning inventory for 20X4 reflects the cumulative impact of the change in policy on all previous years' cost of goods sold, which flows through to net income and thus to retained earnings, to that date:

$47,000 (FIFO) − $45,000 (Average Cost) = $2,000; income is higher.

After income tax, assuming a 40% tax rate, the impact on accumulated earnings is:

$2,000 × (1 − 40%) = $1,200; income is higher.

Effect on the Financial Statements of 20X4

Restatement of the 20X4 financial statements requires changing the beginning and ending inventory balance on the balance sheet and the cost of goods sold on the income statement. Changing the cost of goods sold has an impact on income tax expense, net income, and future income tax. The change in net income flows through to retained earnings and therefore to total shareholders' equity.

The ending 20X4 inventory under FIFO is $60,000, compared to the $50,000 originally reported in the 20X4 financial statements, as shown in Exhibit 20-3. Opening inventory is now $47,000, instead of $45,000. The effect on 20X4 net income is as follows:

- FIFO has a higher beginning inventory, increasing cost of goods sold and lowering pre-tax net income by $2,000.
- FIFO also has a higher ending inventory, lowering cost of the goods sold and increasing pre-tax net income by $10,000.
- The net effect of the changes in the beginning and ending inventories is to increase 20X4 income before tax by $8,000: $10,000 increase due to the impact on ending inventory minus the $2,000 decrease caused by the change in beginning inventory.
- The income tax rate is 40%; the increase in income tax expense from the change in policy is $3,200: $8,000 × 40%.

The changes to the 20X4 statements can be summarized as follows:

Income statement
Cost of goods sold decreases by $8,000 (credit).
Income tax expense increases by $3,200 (debit).
Net income increases by $4,800 (credit).

Balance sheet
Inventory (ending) increases by $10,000 (debit).
Current future income tax changes by $4,000 (credit).
Retained earnings increases by $6,000 (credit).

Notice that the changes in the income statement reflect the impact of the accounting policy change *only* for 20X4. The change in the balance sheet, however, reflects the *cumulative* impact of the changes up to the end of 20X4:

Impact on retained earnings prior to the beginning of 20X4, as calculated above	$1,200 credit
Impact on the net income and retained earnings for 20X4	4,800 credit
Total change in retained earnings	$6,000 credit

Restated Financial Statements Exhibit 20-4 shows the relevant amounts from the 20X5 and restated 20X4 comparative statements. The figures in the statements are based on the amounts shown in Exhibit 20-3, except that the 20X4 statement amounts have been restated for the change to FIFO, based on the analysis above. The comparative 20X4 balance sheet includes inventory at FIFO instead of average cost. The future income tax amounts are also restated.

The retained earnings statement shows an adjustment for *both* years, instead of just the single adjustment of $6,000 that was recorded. The reason is that the retained earnings statement for 20X5 must begin with the previously reported $174,000 retained earnings at 31 December 20X4, in order to preserve the continuity of the reported amounts. This balance must be adjusted for the entire cumulative adjustment of $6,000. The restated 20X4 statements must also start with $92,000 of retained earnings as previously reported, and show an adjustment in order for the restated retained earnings to agree with the restated inventory, net income, and tax amounts. Note that $6,000 was reported in 20X5. Of this amount, $4,800 was reported on the 20X4 income statement, and $1,200 relates to periods *before* 20X4.

EXHIBIT 20-4

SUNSET CORPORATION
SELECTED AMOUNTS FROM COMPARATIVE FINANCIAL STATEMENTS
CHANGE FROM AVERAGE COST TO FIFO FOR INVENTORY

	20X5 (FIFO Basis)	(Restated) 20X4 (FIFO Basis)
Balance sheet		
Inventory (FIFO)	$ 80,000	$ 60,000
Income statement		
Income before income tax	$300,000	$278,000[1]
Income tax expense	120,000	111,200[2]
Net income	$180,000	$166,800
Earnings per share (100,000 shares assumed)	$1.80	$1.67
Retained earnings statement		
Beginning balance, as previously reported	$173,000	$ 92,000
Add: Cumulative effect of inventory accounting policy change, net of tax of $4,000 in 20X5 (20X4—$800)	6,000	1,200
Beginning balance, restated	179,000	93,200
Add: Net income (from above)	180,000	166,800
Deduct: Dividends declared	(88,000)	(80,000)
Ending balance	$271,000	$180,000

(1) $278,000 = $270,000 + $8,000 (decrease in 20X4 CGS due to accounting change)

(2) $111,200 = $108,000 + $3,200 (future income tax due to accounting change)

Note to financial statements:
During 20X5, the Corporation changed its accounting policy for inventory from average cost to first in, first out. As a result, 20X4 net income was increased by $4,800 (4.8¢ per share). The change increased 20X5 net income by $3,000 (3.0¢ per share). The 20X4 statements have been restated to reflect the change in accounting policy.

The note discloses the impact of the change on each of 20X4 and 20X5. The 20X4 impact is apparent from the adjustments. The 20X5 impact, however, is derived from Exhibit 20-3. Under average cost, the increase in inventory for 20X5 would have been $15,000. Under FIFO, the increase is $20,000. Average cost causes an additional $5,000 of cost to flow into inventory rather than into cost of goods sold; the after-tax impact of that is $3,000 (i.e., $5,000 × 40%).

Reporting Example Vancouver-based Taseko Mines Limited, in Exhibit 20-5, provides an example of accounting policy change accounted for retrospectively with restatement. In fiscal year 2005, Taseko adopted the new standard on asset retirement obligations. This has reduced the accumulated deficit prior to 2005 by $5.9 million, prior to 2004 by $6.6 million, and prior to 2003 by $7.3 million.

An unusual aspect of Taseko's restatement is that the adjustment improved Taseko's financial position. The restatement *reduced* the accumulated deficit rather than increasing it.

EXHIBIT 20-5

TASEKO MINES LIMITED
CONSOLIDATED STATEMENTS OF DEFICIT

(in thousands)

Years ended September 30	2005	2004 (Restated)	2003 (Restated)
Deficit, beginning of year, as originally reported	$(202,712)	$(121,069)	$(116,670)
Adjustment for asset retirement obligation	5,903	6,627	7,254
As restated	(196,809)	(114,442)	(109,416)
Earnings (loss) for the year	24,365	(81,389)	(4,137)
Accretion expense on convertible debenture	(1,075)	(978)	(889)
Deficit, end of year	$(173,519)	$(196,809)	$(114,442)

Note: Emphasis added. Accompanying disclosure note has not been reproduced.

Source: www.sedar.com, Taseko Mines Limited, Audited Annual Financial Statements, December 30, 2005.

The reason is that Taseko had been providing an estimated reserve for future site closure and mine reclamation costs based upon the estimated costs to comply with existing reclamation standards. By discounting the estimated costs, in accordance with the then-new Canadian standard, the expense and liability were reduced.

Counterbalancing Changes

Most changes flow through retained earnings at some point in time. If and when the impact of the change has "washed through," no entry for the change is needed. For example, assume that an amortizable asset with a cost of $15,000 and a useful life of three years was expensed when it was purchased in early 20X1 instead of being capitalized and amortized over its three-year life. If the error is discovered in late 20X2, the following adjustment must be made, assuming there is no income tax:

Amortization expense [20X2 ($15,000 ÷ 3)]	5,000	
Capital assets	15,000	
Accumulated amortization		10,000
Retained earnings ($15,000 − $5,000 20X1 amortization)		10,000

However, if this error is discovered in 20X4, no entry is needed. The asset would have been fully amortized by the end of 20X3 and removed from the books. The $15,000 amortization that should have been recorded in 20X1, 20X2, and 20X3 is fully offset by the $15,000 expense erroneously recorded in 20X1. Both retained earnings and net assets are correct without any entries. The comparative figures do have to be adjusted, but such an adjustment does not require a book entry.

Example: Inventory Errors Counterbalancing takes place in the course of one year for errors that are made in valuing inventory, since closing inventory for one year is opening inventory for the next year. Consider the data in Exhibit 20-6. Look first at the original data, highlighted in **boldface**.

EXHIBIT 20-6

COUNTERBALANCING INVENTORY ERRORS

Income statement:	20X6—Original	20X6—Restated	20X5—Original	20X5—Restated
Sales	$6,000,000	$6,000,000	$5,500,000	$5,500,000
Opening inventory	450,000	**425,000**	325,000	325,000
Purchases	3,520,000	3,520,000	3,400,000	3,400,000
Closing inventory	345,000	345,000	450,000	**425,000**
Cost of goods sold	3,625,000	**3,600,000**	3,275,000	**3,300,000**
Gross profit	2,375,000	**$2,400,000**	2,225,000	**2,200,000**
Balance sheet				
Closing inventory	$ 345,000	$ 345,000	$ 450,000	**$ 425,000**
Retained earnings	$1,345,000	$1,345,000	$1,240,000	**$1,215,000**

What will change if the 20X5 closing inventory is found to be overstated by $25,000? That is, assume that the correct closing inventory for 20X5 is $425,000, not $450,000. Refer to the changes made in **boldface**, above. The error has made 20X5 income, assets, and retained earnings too high by $25,000, and they are corrected downward. However, 20X6 income was too low by $25,000, and it is corrected upward. By the end of 20X6, retained earnings and inventory are correctly stated. No entry is needed in 20X6 for this correction, although comparative financial results have to be changed.

CONCEPT REVIEW

1. A company changes from deferral to immediate recognition for certain promotion costs. What balance sheet accounts are affected?

2. Continue on with the information in question 1. The opening balance in deferred costs was $70,000 this year and $90,000 last year. The tax rate is 30%. What is the adjustment to opening retained earnings this year? Last year?

3. Refer to the data in question 2. How much would the previous year's net income change?

RETROSPECTIVE APPROACH WITHOUT RESTATEMENT

Sometimes, when a company has an accounting policy change, the company is not required to show full retrospective restatement, or is not able to restate its prior years' financial results due to a lack of sufficiently detailed information. In these circumstances, the effect of the change is reported as a single catch-up adjustment in the year of the change, but prior years' comparative statements and summary information are not restated.

Guidelines The following guidelines apply to accounting policy changes that are reported by using the retrospective approach without restatement:

1. The cumulative impact of the change on all of the relevant beginning balances for the current year is computed and *recorded*, including the change in retained earnings.

2. The cumulative impact of the change is *reported* as an adjustment to opening retained earnings for the current year.

3. Prior years' financial statements included for comparative purposes remain unchanged. All summary information reported for earlier years also remains unchanged.

4. The new policy is applied as of the beginning of the current year regardless of when, during the year, the decision was actually made. The current year's financial statements reflect the new policy; the prior year's comparative statements reflect the old policy.

Illustration Exhibit 20-7 presents information for a detailed example of retrospective application without restatement. This example illustrates a change in revenue recognition method for long-term contracts, from completed contract (CC) to percentage of completion (PC).

EXHIBIT 20-7

DATA FOR CHANGE IN ACCOUNTING POLICY
CHANGE FROM COMPLETED-CONTRACT TO PERCENTAGE-OF-COMPLETION
Sunrise Corporation

	20X5 Trial Balance Prior to Policy Change (Completed Contract)	As Reported in 20X4 (Completed Contract)
Balance sheet, 31 December		
Construction-in-progress inventory	$340,000	$140,000
All other assets (not detailed)	619,400	706,000
Total	$959,400	$846,000
Liabilities (including future income tax)	$282,920	$340,000
Common shares (100,000 shares outstanding)	300,000	300,000
Retained earnings	376,480	206,000
Total	$959,400	$846,000
Income statement, year ended 31 December		
Revenue	$770,000	$700,000
Gross profit from construction	—	—
Expenses (including 40% income tax)	(599,520)	(570,000)
Net income	$170,480	$130,000
Opening retained earnings	200,000	76,000
Closing retained earnings	$380,480	$206,000
Earnings per share (100,000 shares)	$1.70	$1.30

Contract information
Gross profits earned, percentage-of-completion method

Gross profit earned to 1 January 20X5	$ 40,000
Gross profit earned during 20X5	$ 70,000

No contracts were completed during 20X5.
Completed contract is used for tax purposes.

Analysis of the accounting change
1. This is a change in accounting policy; the change is reported retrospectively but without restatement because reconstruction of prior years' income figures is not feasible.

2. Computation of the catch-up adjustment:

Revenue relating to years prior to 20X5, PC method	$ 40,000
Catch-up adjustment, net of tax [$40,000 × (1 − 40%)]	$ 24,000

The financial statement information shown for both years in Exhibit 20-7 reflects the completed-contract method. The information that is necessary for making the change is shown following the completed-contract statements, as contract information.

In this example, the prior years' results are not restated because it is not possible to reconstruct the income effect on prior years' results. It simply is not feasible to go back and estimate, retrospectively, the cost to complete and the percentage of completion at each intervening year-end; these estimates must be made at the end of each period. The data for restatement often cannot be reconstructed when revenue recognition policies are changed.

Exhibit 20-7 discloses that the cumulative gross profit that was embodied in the beginning-of-year contracts in progress is $40,000, before tax. This amount also represents the difference in the construction-in-progress inventory balance between the two methods. If the PC method had been used during all previous years, the construction-in-progress inventory balance would be $180,000 (i.e., $140,000 + $40,000) at the end of 20X4. The following entry is made in 20X5 to record the accounting change:

Construction-in-progress inventory	40,000	
Future income tax ($40,000 × 40%)		16,000
Retained earnings—cumulative effect of policy change		24,000

This example assumes that the company continues to use the completed-contract method for tax purposes. Therefore, in this case, the tax impact of the prior years' earnings under percentage of completion is credited to the future income tax account.

Exhibit 20-7 shows that Sunrise earned gross profit of $70,000 *during* 20X5 on its construction in progress. No contracts were completed or closed out in 20X5, and therefore the full $70,000 represents gross profit that is recognized under percentage of completion but not under completed contract. Since percentage-of-completion profit is not reported for tax purposes (for contracts spanning no more than two years), the income tax relating to the $70,000 gross profit is also credited to future income tax. The entries to record the construction income for 20X5 will be:

Construction-in-progress inventory	70,000	
Gross profit from construction[2]		70,000
Income tax expense	28,000	
Future income tax		28,000

Exhibit 20-8 illustrates the comparative financial statements and the related note disclosure. The 20X4 statements use the old accounting method (completed contract) while the 20X5 statements use the new policy (percentage of completion). Notice that the retained earnings statement shows the cumulative effect only once, as an adjustment to 20X5 opening retained earnings. The ending construction-in-progress balance and gross profit from construction for 20X4 reflect completed contract, yet the corresponding 20X5 amounts reflect percentage of completion. This lack of consistency is mentioned in the note, which describes the nature of the change and the effect on 20X5 net income.

While the note points out the inconsistency, it does not really provide any information to help readers cope with the change since, by definition, the non-restatement approach is used when the available information cannot be obtained.

---

[2] Note that while, for simplicity, this illustration credits *gross profit from construction*, in the income statement the gross profit should be disaggregated into revenue less *costs of construction*, in compliance with the Canadian and international requirement that gross revenues be shown in the income statement. This reporting is explained in Chapter 6.

EXHIBIT 20-8

COMPARATIVE FINANCIAL STATEMENTS AFTER CHANGE IN ACCOUNTING POLICY
CHANGE FROM COMPLETED CONTRACT TO PERCENTAGE OF COMPLETION

Sunrise Corporation

	20X5 (Percentage of Completion)	20X4 (Completed Contract)
Balance sheet, 31 December		
Construction-in-progress inventory		
(20X5: $340,000 + $40,000 + $70,000)	$ 450,000	$140,000
All other assets (not detailed)	619,400	706,000
Total	$1,069,400	$846,000
Liabilities (20X5: $282,920 + $16,000 + $28,000)	$ 326,920	$340,000
Common shares (100,000 shares outstanding)	300,000	300,000
Retained earnings	442,480	206,000
Total	$1,069,400	$846,000
Income statement, years ending 31 December		
Revenues	$ 770,000	$700,000
Gross profit from construction	70,000	—
Expenses (20X5: $599,520 + $28,000 income tax)	(627,520)	(570,000)
Net income	$ 212,480	$130,000
Earnings per share	$2.12	$1.30
Retained earnings statement, years ending 31 December		
Beginning balance, as previously reported	$ 206,000	$ 76,000
Cumulative effect of change in accounting policy for		
long-term construction contracts, net of tax of $16,000	24,000	—
Opening retained earnings, restated for change in policy	230,000	76,000
Add: Net income	212,480	130,000
Ending balance	$ 442,480	$206,000

Note to financial statements:
During 20X5, the Corporation changed from the completed-contract method of accounting for long-term construction projects to the percentage-of-completion method. The effect of the change on 20X5 results is to increase gross profit from construction by $70,000 and net income by $42,000, or 42¢ per share. The change in accounting policy was applied retrospectively, but it was not practical to associate revenue with specific periods prior to 20X5.

Reporting Example An example of retrospective application without restatement is shown in Exhibit 20-9. Canadian standards began requiring companies to show the fair value of employee stock options on the income statement. Retrospective restatement would require companies to figure out what the fair values of options were over past years. This is a daunting task, especially for companies in technology fields that have been giving significant quantities of stock options for a long period of time.

CSI Wireless Inc. is an Alberta-based company that designs and manufactures innovative, cost-effective wireless and Global Positioning System (GPS) products for mobile and fixed applications in commercial and consumer markets. Exhibit 20-9 shows the brief lower portion of CSI's statement of operations and deficit. The change in accounting policy is applied only to the year of the change, 2004, with no restatement of prior years. The disclosure note then explains the reason for the change, including the treatment of stock options in prior years.

EXHIBIT 20-9

RETROSPECTIVE CHANGE WITHOUT RESTATEMENT

CSI Wireless Inc.

Years ended 31 December	2004	2003
Net earnings (loss)	$ 4,293,105	$ (552,609)
Deficit, beginning of year	(22,837,629)	(22,285,020)
Change in accounting policy (Note 2)	(398,134)	—
Deficit, end of year	$(18,942,658)	$(22,837,629)

Note 2. Change in accounting policies:
Prior to January 1, 2004, the Company applied the fair value based method of accounting prescribed by CICA Handbook Section 3870, *Stock-based Compensation and Other Stock-based Payments*, only to stock options granted to non-employees, and applied the intrinsic value method of accounting to employee stock options. Under the intrinsic value method, any consideration paid by employees on the exercise of stock options or purchase of stock was credited to share capital and no compensation expense was recognized.

The CICA Accounting Standards Board has amended CICA Handbook Section 3870—*Stock-based Compensation and Other Stock-based Payments*—to require entities to account for employee stock options using the fair value based method, beginning January 1, 2004. Under the fair value based method, compensation cost is measured at fair value at the date of grant and is expensed over the award's vesting period. In accordance with one of the transitional provisions permitted, the Company has retroactively applied the fair value based method to all employee stock options granted on or after January 1, 2002 and prior to January 1, 2004. The Company has not restated prior year's reported amounts, and accordingly, has adjusted 2004 opening retained earnings at January 1, 2004 by $398,134, and contributed surplus by the same amount. Options granted in 2004 are expensed in the current financial statements in accordance with the standard previously described.

Source: CSI Wireless Inc. 2004 Annual Report, pages 27 and 35.

CONCEPT REVIEW

1. A company changes from declining-balance to straight-line amortization, which results in a decrease to the accumulated amortization account. Will the future income tax account be debited or credited as a result? Explain.

2. A company changes from FIFO to weighted-average cost flow assumptions regarding inventory. At the beginning of the year, the FIFO inventory was $120,000, while weighted average was $105,000. If the tax rate is 30%, what is the amount of the cumulative adjustment to opening retained earnings?

3. Refer to the data in question 2. Does retained earnings increase or decrease?

PROSPECTIVE APPROACH

The prospective approach is used for all changes in accounting estimates. The prescriptive approach also is used for a change in accounting policy if allowed by a new accounting standard or if it is impracticable to restate prior periods.

When the prospective approach is used for changes in accounting policy, reporting requirements are reduced to the following disclosures:

1. The fact that the change has not been applied retrospectively;

2. The effect of the change on current and future financial statements; and

3. If it is not practicable to apply a new accounting policy retrospectively, the reasons that retrospective application cannot be done.

If the change is one of an accounting estimate, the new estimate is simply used for financial reporting in the current and future years (as appropriate).

Guidelines The following guidelines apply to changes in accounting estimates and to applying the prospective approach to changes in accounting policy:

1. Prior statements shown on a comparative basis are not restated or otherwise affected.

2. The new estimate is applied as of the beginning of the current period, generally based on the book value of the relevant balance sheet account remaining at that time. This is the amount to which the new estimates (e.g., bad debt estimates or residual values of capital assets) are applied for the current and future years.

3. No entry is made for prior-year effects; only the normal current year entry, which incorporates the new estimate, is made.

4. Future years continue to use the new estimate, if applicable, until the estimate is changed again in future periods.

Illustration Assume that equipment was purchased by LeMonde Limited for $160,000 on 2 January 20X1. At the time of purchase, management estimated that the equipment had a 10-year useful life and no residual value. On the basis of new information available during 20X5, management concludes that a 12-year total life seems more realistic. In addition, management now estimates that the equipment will have a residual value of $12,000 at the end of its useful life. LeMonde uses straight-line amortization.

The change is accounted for as of the beginning of the year of the change. That is, if this change were made in December 20X5, it would still be based on data as of 1 January 20X5. The book value of the equipment on 1 January 20X5 is $96,000:

Original cost	$160,000
Accumulated amortization at 31 December 20X4:	
[($160,000 ÷ 10) × 4 years]	64,000
Book value, 1 January 20X5	$ 96,000

The book value of $96,000 at the beginning of 20X5 is the basis on which amortization for 20X5 and future years will be based. The equipment is four years old at the beginning of 20X5, which leaves eight years (that is, $12 - 4$) of useful life remaining under the revised estimate. As well, the previous residual value of zero has now been changed to $12,000. Annual amortization beginning in 20X5 will be:

Annual amortization expense = ($96,000 − $12,000) ÷ 8 = $10,500

The entry on 31 December 20X5 to record amortization expense will be as follows:

Amortization expense	10,500	
Accumulated amortization		10,500

In its 20X5 comparative statements, LeMonde will include the following amounts related to the equipment:

	20X5	20X4
Income statement		
Amortization expense	$ 10,500	$ 16,000
Balance sheet		
Equipment	$160,000	$160,000
Accumulated amortization	74,500	64,000
Net book value	$ 85,500	$ 96,000

It is important to bear in mind, however, that unless this is the only equipment that LeMonde possesses, these amounts will be combined with those relating to other tangible capital assets and the change in amortization will not be visible.

Reporting Example Empire Company Limited provides an example of disclosure of a change in estimate:

During the year, the Company changed the estimated useful lives of its rental properties based on a review of its properties. This change in accounting estimate has been applied prospectively. Prior to 2001, estimated lives ranged from 20 to 50 years from the date of acquisition (now 20 to 40 years).

CONCEPT REVIEW

1. A company has accounts receivable of $200,000 and an allowance for doubtful accounts of $40,000. Bad debts have been estimated in the past at 25% of accounts receivable but now are estimated to be 15%. How much is bad debt expense (recovery) this year?

2. Capital assets with a cost of $500,000 have been amortized for three years assuming a useful life of five years and no residual value. This year, revised estimates are a total of eight years of useful life with no residual value. How much is amortization expense this year?

DISCLOSURE REQUIREMENTS

Accounting changes affect the consistency and comparability of financial statements, and therefore their reliability. When significant changes in accounting policies or measurements occur, readers should be warned about the changes and their impacts.

The general expectation for disclosure is that a company should disclose (1) *why* a change was made and (2) *how* it affects the financial statements for both the current period and all past periods used for comparison. These general types of disclosures apply to all types of accounting changes.

More specifically, changes in accounting policy should disclose:

- The reason for and nature of the change, specifically identifying:
  - for mandatory changes, the new or revised *CICA Handbook* section or *EIC Abstract* that necessitated the change, or
  - for voluntary changes, in what way the new policy provides reliable and more relevant information
- The general nature of the change
- The amount of the change, by financial statement line item, including cumulative prior-period adjustments
- If retrospective application is impracticable, the reasons therefore and the method used for the restatement.

Changes in accounting estimates normally are not disclosed unless they have a material effect on the current and/or future financial statements. When a change in estimate is material, such as a significant change in the estimated useful life of capital assets, both the nature of the change and its impact on current and/or future statements are disclosed.

For corrections of prior-period errors, a company should disclose (1) the nature of the error, (2) the impact on each affected financial statement item, including earnings per share, and (3) the amount of the correction at the start of the earliest comparative prior period.

These disclosure requirements apply only in the period in which the change was made. They do not need to be reported in subsequent years' financial statements.

CASH FLOW STATEMENT

Previous sections have shown that accounting changes affect the balance sheet, the retained earnings statement, and sometimes the income statement. It is not so obvious, however, that a new accounting policy may also affect the cash flow statement. A change in accounting policy will not usually affect the net change in cash—the "bottom line" of the cash flow statement. However, a new accounting policy may affect the classification of amounts in the cash flow statement.

For example, a change from expensing to capitalizing of start-up costs will move the annual start-up cost from the operations section to the investing section. Cash flow from operations will increase because the expense is no longer included, while the cash invested in long-term assets (i.e., capitalized start-up costs) will increase. In future years, the capitalized cost will be amortized, thereby reducing net income. Amortization is not a cash flow, however, and is added back under the indirect approach of presenting cash from operations (or ignored under the direct approach). The long-term effect on the cash flow statement, therefore, will be to shift the start-up costs from the *operating activities* section to the *investment activities* section of the cash flow statement. The shift will increase the apparent cash flow from operations, even though the overall cash flow is not affected.

Even if a change in accounting policy does not affect the classification of cash flows, retrospective restatement may require an adjustment to the prior cash flow statement. The operations section is changed if the indirect method of presentation is used, because the change may alter both net income and the addback. For example, a change in amortization policy from straight line to declining balance will increase amortization expense and decrease net income. Applying the change retrospectively, the comparative cash flow statement will be adjusted to show the lower net income, offset by the higher addback of amortization. The *net* cash flow from operations will be unaffected, but the amounts that are used to derive the net cash flow from operations will be altered as the result of the change in policy.

Similarly, the *correction of prior-period errors* may affect the amounts shown in prior periods' cash flow statements if the error affects the amounts previously reported.

Changes in accounting estimate will not affect the classification of cash flows. Changes in accounting estimate are applied prospectively, and therefore no restatement is necessary.

Also, changes in accounting estimates do not affect the method of reporting individual types of cash flows.

ETHICAL ISSUES

Accounting changes present something of an ethical minefield for the unwary professional accountant. Management is, quite properly, always concerned about the perceptions of outsiders who use the financial statements. Managers can often feel tempted to alter accounting policies to mollify the concerns of statement users. However, the current standards on policy changes do make it rather difficult for a company to make voluntary accounting policy changes, especially in a public company. Very few voluntary changes are observable in public companies. Private companies, however, have more opportunities to make policy changes because they are subject to less scrutiny and because they are less tightly constrained by a requirement for GAAP compliance.

Sometimes, an accounting policy is changed effectively, though not technically, by a change in assumptions and estimates. For example, Canadian software companies usually follow Canadian GAAP. Canadian GAAP requires companies to capitalize and amortize development costs if certain guidelines are satisfied. In doing so, however, the companies found themselves penalized in the U.S. stock market because they did not treat all development costs as expense, as required by U.S. GAAP. To make themselves more comparable to their U.S. competitors, many companies simply decided that the criteria for deferral were no longer being met, and therefore that the costs should be expensed immediately. This was not a change in accounting policy *per se*, but it had the same effect by means of a declared change in assumptions.

That particular example is fairly innocent in that the change had the effect of lowering reported earnings but improved investor perception of the transparency of financial reporting. The change did seem to provide more relevant information for the U.S. users, who felt that the Canadian standards were inadequate and therefore discounted the companies' share value.

In other instances, however, voluntary policy changes may be driven primarily by management's desire to maximize earnings or to maximize their own compensation rather than by any really demonstrable benefit to users. These changes lay a trap for the accountant who goes along with management's desires to manipulate earnings, and severe penalties may lie down the road.

Of course, we all are well aware of the subjectivity of accounting estimates. This subjectivity is unavoidable—it is the nature of estimates. But there is a fine line between reasonable estimates on one hand and earnings manipulation on the other hand. Manipulation leads to misstatement, and where the misstatement is deliberate, the accountant is guilty of fraud.

INTERNATIONAL PERSPECTIVE

The current Canadian standard on accounting changes came into effect at the beginning of 2007. At the same time, a revised IASB standard and a new FASB standard also became effective. The Canadian, U.S., and international standards were prepared as part of a harmonization project among the three jurisdictions. Therefore, Canadian, U.S., and international treatment of accounting changes will be uniform.

Nevertheless, there is one difference. Unlike the Canadian standard, the international standard permits optional treatments of prior-period errors: (1) retrospective application without restatement, or (2) prospective application. These alternatives are provided in the event that it is impracticable to determine either the period-specific effects or the cumulative effect of the error. The Canadian standard simply skips those paragraphs (and paragraph numbers). Presumably, the AcSB decided that if a company knows there is an error, management should be able to discern the extent and effect of the error; otherwise, it becomes impossible to correct.

RELEVANT STANDARDS

CICA Handbook:
- Section 1506, Accounting Changes

IASB:
- *IAS* 8, Accounting Policies, Changes in Accounting Estimates, and Errors

CONCEPT REVIEW

1. What additional disclosure does the *CICA Handbook* recommend for a voluntary change in accounting policy?

2. Since a retrospective change in accounting policy cannot affect prior years' cash flow, why might a change in accounting policy affect the cash flow from operations?

3. How is the cumulative effect of a change in accounting policy accounted for under U.S. rules?

SUMMARY OF KEY POINTS

1. Changes in accounting policy may be *mandatory*, caused by a new or revised accounting standard.

2. Changes in accounting policy may be *voluntary*, but only if the change results in information that is both reliable and more relevant.

3. Changes in accounting policy must be accounted for *retrospectively* (also known as *retroactively*), with restatement of prior periods if practicable.

4. If restatement of prior periods is not practicable, then application should be retrospective *without* restatement, but with opening retained earnings adjusted for the cumulative effect of the change.

5. If it is not feasible to measure the cumulative effect of the policy change, a mandatory change is applied *prospectively*. Prospective application may also, on rare occasion, be permitted by the transition provisions of a specific accounting standard.

6. Changes in accounting *estimate* may be caused by new information or by recent experience that changes previous predictions or perceptions. Changes in accounting estimates must always be applied prospectively.

7. If there is doubt as to whether a change is a change in estimate or a change in policy, it should be assumed to be a change in estimate.

8. On occasion, a company (or its auditors) discovers that there was an accounting error in a prior period. If the error was material, the error must be corrected in the comparative figures even if it has self-corrected over the long run.

9. Information must be disclosed to allow users to understand (1) why an accounting change has been made and (2) the effect of the accounting change.

10. Accounting changes do not typically affect underlying cash flows, but they can affect the amounts presented on prior years' cash flow statements, either by changing the section in which the cash flows are reported or by altering the amounts reported for reconciling net income to cash flow from operations.

KEY TERMS

changes in accounting estimate, 1194
mandatory changes in accounting
  policy, 1193
prior-period errors, 1195
prospective application, 1193

restatement, 1192
retrospective application, 1193
voluntary changes in accounting
  policy, 1193

REVIEW PROBLEM

Each of the following situations is independent:

1. *Change in estimated useful life and residual value.* Phelps Company purchases equipment on 1 January 20X6 for $36,000. The company uses the straight-line method of amortization, taking a full year's amortization in the year of acquisition. The equipment has an estimated residual value of $6,000 and an estimated useful life of three years. On 1 July 20X7, Phelps decides that the machine really had an original total life of four years and a residual value of $5,000.

Required:
What is the amortization expense for 20X7?

2. *Retrospective change in accounting policy.* Rhein Company changes its method of accounting for long-term construction contracts from the percentage-of-completion method (PC) to the completed-contract method (CC) in 20X7. The years affected by the change, and incomes under both methods, appear below (ignore income tax):

Year	PC	CC
20X5	$400	$200
20X6	300	150
20X7	500	800

Required:
If the financial statements for 20X6 and 20X7 are shown comparatively, what is the amount of the accounting policy adjustment to the 1 January balance of retained earnings for 20X6 and 20X7?

3. *Error correction and retrospective adjustment.* Helms Limited purchases a delivery truck for $14,000 on 1 January 20X6. Helms expects to use the truck for only two years and then sell it for $4,000. The accountant is instructed to use straight-line amortization but neglects to record any amortization in 20X6. Rather, the accountant charges the entire cost to delivery expense in 20X6. The company's controller discovers the error late in 20X7.

Required:
Provide the 20X7 entries to record amortization and the error correction, and indicate the amounts of the cumulative retrospective adjustment to opening retained earnings appearing in the 20X6 and 20X7 comparative retained earnings statements. Ignore income tax.

4. *Error correction, retrospective adjustment, and comparative statements.* On 1 July 20X7, a full year's insurance of $2,400, covering the period from 1 July 20X7 through 30 June 20X8, was paid and debited to insurance expense. Assume:

- The company uses a calendar fiscal year.
- Retained earnings at 1 January 20X7 is $20,000.
- No adjusting entry for insurance is made on 31 December 20X7.
- Reported net income for 20X7 (in error) is $22,800.
- Net income for 20X8 is $30,000 (assuming that the error has not been discovered).
- Net income for 20X9 is $40,000.
- There is no income tax.

Required:

a. List the effect of the error on relevant accounts, and net income, in 20X7 and 20X8.
b. Prepare the entry to record the error if it was discovered in 20X7.
c. Prepare the entry to record the error if it was discovered in 20X8, and prepare the 20X7 and 20X8 comparative retained earnings statements. The amount is deemed material.
d. Prepare the entry (if needed) to record the error if discovered in 20X9, and prepare the 20X8 and 20X9 comparative retained earnings statements.

REVIEW PROBLEM—SOLUTION

1. Book value, 1 January 20X7 = $36,000 − [($36,000 − $6,000) × 1/3] = $26,000

   Amortization for 20X7 = ($26,000 − $5,000) × 1/(4 − 1) = $7,000

2. The impact on the opening retained earnings is the cumulative difference in prior years' net income under the two methods:

   At 1 January 20X6: $200 dr. This is the $200 decline in 20X5 income from $400 under PC to $200 under CC.

   At 1 January 20X7: $350 dr. Also a decline in income, for 20X5 and 20X6: ($400 + $300) − ($200 + $150).

3. The purchase should have been debited to equipment, but instead was debited to delivery expense, which has since been closed to retained earnings. Therefore, retained earnings must be reduced (credited) by the difference between the (correct) amortization expense and the (incorrect) recorded delivery expense. The 20X7 entry to record the error correction is:

Equipment	14,000	
Retained earnings, error correction		9,000
Accumulated amortization—equipment		5,000
[20X6 amortization = ($14,000 − $4,000) × 1/2 = $5,000]		

   In 20X7, amortization expense is recorded for that year:

Amortization expense	5,000	
Accumulated amortization—equipment		5,000

   The opening retained earnings adjustment would be $9,000 for 20X7. There is none in 20X6, since the equipment did not exist prior to 20X6.

4. a. *Effect of error if not discovered* (− means understated; + means overstated)

Item	20X7	20X8
Insurance expense	+$1,200	−$1,200
Ending prepaid insurance	− 1,200	no effect
Net income	− 1,200	+ 1,200
Ending retained earnings	− 1,200	now correct

b. *If error discovered in 20X7*

Prepaid insurance	1,200	
Insurance expense		1,200

c. *If error discovered in 20X8*

Prepaid insurance	1,200	
Retained earnings, error correction		1,200

A second entry would be made to record 20X8 insurance expenses:

Insurance expense	1,200	
Prepaid insurance		1,200

Comparative retained earnings statement:

	20X8	20X7
Retained earnings, 1 January, as previously reported	$42,800*	$20,000
Error correction	1,200	0†
Retained earnings, 1 January, restated	44,000	20,000
Net income	28,800‡	24,000§
Retained earnings, 31 December	$72,800	$44,000

* This balance reflects erroneous 20X7 income: $42,800 = $20,000 + $22,800.

† No year prior to 20X7 was affected by the error.

‡ $30,000 erroneous income − $1,200 (20X8 income was overstated).

§ $22,800 + $1,200.

d. *If error discovered in 20X9*

No entry is needed because the error has counterbalanced.

QUESTIONS

Q20-1 A company has always used the allowance method to value accounts receivable and establish a bad debt expense on the income statement. In the current year, it changed from using the aging method to the percentage-of-sales method to determine the extent of the required allowance. How would you classify the change?

Q20-2 Explain the difference between a voluntary and involuntary change in accounting policy.

Q20-3 What criteria must be met for a voluntary accounting policy change to be allowed? What difficulty is there in justifying a voluntary change?

Q20-4 When is a change in amortization accounting policy considered a change in estimate? Why is this the case?

Q20-5 Why are changes in estimates so prevalent?

Q20-6 If there is doubt about whether a change is a change in policy or a change in estimate, how should it be treated? Why do you think accounting standards have this requirement?

Q20-7 What role do a company's reporting objectives play in changes in accounting policy?

Q20-8 Explain the difference between a change in estimate and an error correction.

Q20-9 Accounting changes involve (a) policies and (b) estimates. Using these letters and the letter (c) for error corrections, identify each of the following types of change:

a. A lessor discovers, while a long-term capital lease term is in progress, that an estimated material unguaranteed residual value of the leased property has probably become zero.

b. After five years of use, an asset originally estimated to have a 15-year total life is now to be depreciated on the basis of a 22-year total life.

c. Because of inability to estimate reliably, a contractor began business using the completed-contract method. Now that reliable estimates can be made, the percentage-of-completion method is adopted.

d. Office equipment purchased last year is discovered to have been debited to office expense when acquired. Appropriate accounting is to be applied at the discovery date.

e. A company that used 1% of sales to predict its bad debt expense discovers losses are running higher than expected and changes to 2%.

Q20-10 What are the three ways to account for the effects of accounting changes?

Q20-11 How is an accounting error accounted for?

Q20-12 How is a change in accounting estimate accounted for?

Q20-13 What is the preferred method of accounting for a change in accounting policy?

Q20-14 What are the advantages of retrospective restatement? Why is it not required for *all* changes in accounting policy?

Q20-15 A company changes from the straight-line to declining-balance method of amortizing capital assets, in a change that is to be applied retrospectively. The net book value at the beginning of the year was $357,000 under straight line, and $289,000 under declining balance. The tax rate is 40%. What will be the adjustment to this year's opening retained earnings to reflect the change?

Q20-16 Refer to Question 20-15. Assume that amortization for the year prior to the change had been $40,000 under straight-line, and $76,000 under declining balance. What would be the adjustment to opening retained earnings for this previous year? What amount of amortization would be reported on the income statement in the previous year?

Q20-17 A $100,000 asset is amortized for six years on the basis of a 10-year life and a $10,000 residual value. In year 7, the remaining life is changed to five years, with a $2,000 residual value. How much depreciation expense should be recorded in year 7?

Q20-18 What is the general disclosure requirement for all accounting changes?

Q20-19 Assume that a company had traditionally expensed development costs but now satisfies deferral criteria and thus has changed its policy. How will classification of development costs change on the cash flow statement?

CASE 20-1

LALANI COUTURE

Lalani Couture Limited (LCL) is a privately held company headquartered in Montreal. The company operates a chain of retail clothing stores in major cities across Canada, although the bulk of the company stores are in Ontario and Quebec. LCL manufactures most of its apparel in its facility in Montreal, although some manufacture is also contracted out to other manufacturers, principally in Quebec. The company prides itself on getting the latest fashions to its stores in a very short time, usually within a couple of weeks after a particular fashion trend has been detected. Because of the chain's quick response to the market, the company has been able to serve the youth market quite well despite offering no major "name brand" clothing. The primary emphasis is on clothing and fashion for young women, but about 20% of sales are of young men's clothing such as trendy jeans and pullovers.

Historically, the company has been quite successful. This success is largely due to employing a small group of young adults whose job it is to detect fashion trends among young people well before the major fashion houses do—finding out what's "cool" among youth. The local manufacturing then makes it relatively easy for LCL to quickly design and manufacture new styles of clothing, and to deliver the merchandise to the stores.

No merchandise stays in the stores very long. The store managers are told that as soon of sales of a product begin to decline, the product should go on sale at increasing discounts until it is all sold.

The founder-owners of the company no longer take an active part in running the day-to-day business. Operational activity is the responsibility of the professional managers. Financing has come mainly from retained earnings, although the balance sheet does show a moderate amount of long-term debt. That debt is in the form of debentures held by a municipal employees' pension fund investment trust, secured by LCL's tangible capital assets. Short-term financing is provided by a bank line of credit. The line of credit is secured by a proportion of accounts receivable and inventory. However, the accounts receivable are minimal, since the company's sales are mainly by cash and general credit card (i.e., Visa, MasterCard, and American Express). Therefore, inventory is the primary security. The balance sheet also shows a small amount of capital lease liability.

Recently, LCL has begun to have difficulty in achieving the profit levels to which the owners have been accustomed. While the company certainly is not in any financial distress, LCL managers decided in 20X9 to look more closely at certain aspects of the way LCL does business, as well as how the company reports the results of operations.

1. In 20X7, LCL purchased 100% of the shares of a small clothing manufacturer in Montreal, which then became a subsidiary of LCL. LCL was one of its customers, as were several other retailers. LCL paid $5,000,000 for that company, of which $2,000,000 was allocated to goodwill. Within a year of the purchase, many of the subsidiary's other customers left because they were concerned that LCL might steal their clothing designs. LCL managers had not expected those defections since LCL's designs were generally ahead of their competitors. As a result, the subsidiary has not been able to stay profitable. LCL has been in talks to possibly sell the subsidiary to a U.S.–based clothing chain.
2. LCL owns none of its stores because they are all located in shopping malls. LCL has preferred to use short-term leases (e.g., five years) in order to maintain flexibility. The company is now planning to renegotiate the leases for longer terms in order to spread the cost of store design (furniture and fixtures) over a longer time span.
3. The company has followed a practice of deferring and amortizing the start-up costs for new stores. However, a recent change in accounting standards has decreed that start-up costs cannot be deferred and amortized. LCL must present audited statements both to the provider of long-term debt and to many of the major shopping mall landlords.
4. LCL has large electronic billboards mounted on the fronts and roofs of some buildings, space that is leased from the building owners. The lease contracts require LCL to restore the facades and roofs to the owner's satisfaction at expiry. The LCL financial manager has discovered that LCL completely overlooked one significant lease and has not accounted for that restoration cost. As well, due to a decline in interest rates in 20X9, the auditor recommends that LCL remeasure all of LCL's asset retirement obligations.
5. The company has been following income tax allocation procedures. LCL's financial manager is concerned that future income tax expense unrealistically depresses LCL's earnings. Therefore, he has proposed that the company change to the taxes payable method beginning in the current year. The auditor does not object to the change.

6. In 20X8, the company's designers had made a rare error in anticipating a fashion trend that failed to develop. As a result, the company ended the previous year with a severe overstock of that line of clothing. In retrospect, the company should have written down that portion of the inventory. Instead, the merchandise was sold for about 20% of its manufacturing cost to a clearance house in San Francisco. The merchandise manager has recommended that the opening inventory for 20X9 be restated to recognize the loss in value of those items.

Required:

Assume that you are Chris Robins, an independent accounting consultant. The CFO of LCL has asked for a memo on the reporting implications for each of these issues. Write the memo.

CASE 20-2

REGIONAL AIRLINES

Regional Airlines (RA) is a wholly owned subsidiary of National Commercial Airlines (NCA). RA is reviewing the basis upon which it records amortization on certain aircraft. Up until the current year, RA had always amortized aircraft over 12 years, with a 52% residual value. In effect, this was an amortization charge of 4% of the cost of the aircraft per year. RA now recognizes that the aircraft will be used in operations for more than 12 years. Accordingly, the company will change the way it records amortization in the current year.

The proposal is to amortize the aircraft over 20 years, with a 20% residual value. The controller, Daniel Davison, complained:

> This still works out to amortization of 4% per year. We are just changing two estimates: useful life and residual value. Therefore, these changes should be treated prospectively. However, NCA's auditors are arguing that the changes should be accounted for retrospectively. How can that be? Four percent is four percent! Why should we have to change our opening retained earnings?

According to an international survey conducted by RA's auditors:

> Amortization is a prominent feature of the financial reporting in an industry that is as capital intensive as the airline industry. Estimated useful lives and residual values are subjective, and management scrutiny is essential due to the potential for technological change and development changes in the market for used aircraft and various fleet planning considerations.

This study established that the most common method of amortization used was straight-line (22 of 24 airlines). For a given aircraft classification, the estimates of useful lives ranged from 10 to 25 years and residual values ranged from zero to 40% of cost. Airlines typically review estimated useful life annually, and 10 of 24 airlines in the survey changed their estimates within the last three years. Finally, the survey noted that material profits were reported on a number of aircraft sales by airlines included in the survey. This implied that amortization rates generally were conservative and that book values were low when compared to market values.

Davison felt that the auditor's survey supported RA's position to amortize more of the cost of the aircraft. Some of RA's aircraft are now in their 11th year of use by the company. A 12-year life did not seem realistic, since the aircraft would not be retired or sold in the next (12th) fiscal year. A change in estimated useful life was deemed necessary.

Furthermore, RA's aircraft are declining in value at a very low rate. Market information suggests that these aircraft have held their market value extremely well. In addition, the standard industry price reference book, *Airline Pricing Guide*, included data that supported a 4% annual decline in market value and a residual value of 20%.

RA's position was that changes to estimates must be accounted for on a prospective basis, from the day of the change forward. The auditors, who issued unqualified audit reports in all prior years, argue that the changes are corrections of prior years' errors and, as such, should be adjusted retrospectively through retained earnings. According to the auditor's calculations, a retrospective adjustment would reduce amortization in prior years by about $5,000,000. Net income and retained earnings would increase.

Another difference of opinion is how to interpret a "20-year life." Some aircraft are purchased "used" by RA. RA has always amortized aircraft over the stated useful life from the date of purchase forward, as opposed to from the date of manufacture forward. The auditors argue that the estimated life of 20 years is *total life* and would include all years that the aircraft was used, whether by RA or prior owners. For example, if RA were to buy a six-year-old aircraft, the auditors suggest that RA would amortize it over 14 years. RA claims that 20 years would be appropriate.

The auditors have prepared a schedule calculating amortization under the assumption that useful life is calculated from the date of manufacture. These calculations suggest that cumulative amortization to the end of the current year is understated by $1 million. The auditors maintain that half of this amount applies to prior years and that opening retained earnings should be reduced. That is, prior amortization should be increased by $0.5 million. Current amortization expense should be increased by the remaining $0.5 million.

RA's position is that 20 years of useful life to RA is appropriate. Furthermore, all changes in the amortization amounts result from changes in estimates. Prospective treatment is logical in these circumstances. However, if the change from RA's useful life must be made, all of the $1 million charge should be recognized in the current year. Therefore, the entire $1 million, not just $0.5 million, should appear on this year's income statement.

"Besides," Davison stated, "We're having a bad year anyway. What's another half million dollars in expense? Our management incentives are based on income and the results this year—even before incorporating these changes—are terrible. It will be the first time that we will not receive a full bonus."

Davison would like you to provide him with a report to help him deal with the issues discussed and the arguments put forward by the auditors. You should provide a recommendation with respect to the $5 million suggested as an error correction and the $1 million adjustment related to "total life."

Required:
Prepare the report.

(Professor Judy Cumby, adapted)

CASE 20-3

MTC

Philip Roth is just finishing his first week as chief financial officer of MTC. He was recruited from Atkins Consulting to replace the former CFO who had been relieved of his duties when major errors and shortfalls in certain inventory and trading accounts were discovered.

MTC is the current corporate name of an enterprise once known as Midlands Telephone Corporation. Midlands had been providing telephone service to several mid-country provinces for most of the 20th century. The company had been reorganized in the early 1980s to separate its regulated telephone service from its more adventurous, non-regulated endeavours. The company had grown to a billion-dollar enterprise with investments in several fields, acquired largely through purchases of other going concerns. The core of MTC's earnings, however, remained in the telephone business.

Early this year, the company lost an appeal to the regulatory agency to protect its base market. The agency had ruled that MTC would no longer have a protected monopoly for local telephone service in its service region, but that other companies (including TV cable companies and wireless companies) could compete for local telephone service. MTC had an enormous asset base, built up over the years in order to generate the highest possible earnings. As is typical in regulated industries, the company had been permitted to set rates that would enable it to earn a set rate of return on its asset base—the larger the asset base, the higher the earnings. The company capitalized all betterments and replacements, and used the longest possible depreciation periods for its capital assets. With the advent of deregulation, the company would no longer be able to generate such an attractive rate of return on its assets, which raised questions in the financial press about the "overvaluation" of its capital asset base.

This regulatory ruling was only one blow that the company had suffered in recent months. A previous loss of protection in the long-distance telephone market had caused MTC's earnings to drop sharply, with the result that MTC had the first loss of its history in its telephone business last year. The loss was expected to be even larger in the current year.

To make matters worse, rumours began to circulate in the financial community that MTC was covering up huge losses in one of its non-telephone divisions, one that manufactured copper wire and electrical switching devices. Copper is a world-traded commodity that has a very volatile price, and most companies that use copper are engaged in hedging operations to protect themselves. MTC's Board of Directors hired Atkins Consulting to find out if there was any truth to the rumours, and, unfortunately, there was. Managers and traders in the division had been speculating heavily in copper, and had covered up massive trading losses over the past three years, some of which were hidden in fictitious inventory records. MTC's copper inventory (and other accounts) turned out to be overstated by over $100 million.

The company's employees were also becoming restive. In its latest labour negotiations, just completed last month for the telephone operations, the company had to promise redundancy protection for employees if the company was required to downsize its telephone operations. The company agreed not to lay off any employees with more than 15 years of service, although the company would have the right to place them in a "redundancy pool" to be redeployed anywhere else in the company that they might be useful. Employees who are laid off will be given a severance package amounting to two months' salary plus one month's additional salary for each year of service. The severance would not be given as a lump sum but would be paid to the individual over a one-year period following the departure. Furthermore, the new labour agreement provided that pension benefits for any laid-off employee would automatically vest, even if the employee hadn't reached the point at which the benefits would normally become vested. The remaining employees would benefit from a significant enhancement of their defined benefit pension plan; employees' benefits would increase by between 10% and 20%, depending on the length of service.

The company had just served notice to the first 1,200 of its employees that they would be laid off, but the Board of Directors expected that at least 5,000 employees would be laid off over the next two years.

Philip Roth was one of the consultants who uncovered the rogue copper trading. He had been hired as CFO of MTC to "clean up the mess" in the financial reporting and control areas. One of his first responsibilities was to recommend to the audit committee of the Board of Directors how the company should report the impacts of its recent changes in fortune in its financial statements for the current year. Although the company was only midway through the fiscal year, the Board and CEO would have to discuss financial projections in a public forum, and particularly with the investment analysts who closely followed the company's performance.

Required:

Assume that you are Philip Roth. Prepare a report to the audit committee.

ASSIGNMENTS

★ **A20-1 Overview—Types of Accounting Changes:** Analyze each case and choose a letter code under each category (type and approach) to indicate the preferable accounting for each case.

Type	Approach
P = Policy	RWR = Retrospective with restatement
E = Estimate	RNR = Retrospective, no restatement
AE = Accounting error	P = Prospective

1. New accounting policy required by GAAP.

2. Straight-line amortization for the past three years has been calculated with no deduction for residual value because of an oversight.

3. Straight-line amortization for the past three years has been calculated with no deduction for residual value because none was expected; management now believes a residual value of 10% of original cost is appropriate.

4. Math error in calculating closing inventory for 20X1; it is now 20X3.

5. Change in inventory valuation method from average cost to market value (net realizable value) for agricultural produce. Past market values cannot be determined.

6. Fair value of an available-for-sale investment was used in prior years but was incorrect. An estimate of fair value had to be made in the prior year because the security was not frequently traded.

7. Balance of deferred development costs is deemed worthless, and no further development costs will be deferred because of technological changes.

8. Adopted percentage of completion for long-term construction contract; all prior contracts were short term and used completed contract.

9. Changed from straight-line depreciation to units-of-production depreciation to conform to industry practice.

10. Changed from revenue recognition at cash collection to revenue recognition at point of delivery because of a marked improvement in the creditworthiness of the customer.

★ **A20-2 Overview—Types of Accounting Changes:** Analyze each case and choose a letter code under each category (type and approach) to indicate the preferable accounting for each case.

Type	Approach
P = Policy	RWR = Retrospective with restatement
E = Estimate	RNR = Retrospective, no restatement
AE = Accounting error	P = Prospective

1. Changed the expected useful lives of amortizable assets from 10 years to 25 years, backed up with engineering studies to justify the longer life.

2. Discovered that a $400,000 acquisition of machinery two years ago was debited to the land account.

3. Started using a new policy for calculating EPS because of a change in *CICA Handbook* standards.

4. Changed amortization method from declining balance to straight line because of information about how the assets were really used over the past three years.

5. Changed the percentage of bad debts accrued from 1% of credit sales to 3% of credit sales.

6. Recognized an impairment of $1.5 million in a capital asset group. An impairment of $1.0 million became apparent two years previously, but had not been recorded until this year.

7. Switched from FIFO to average cost to conform to parent company preferences. Only opening balances for the current year can be reconstructed.

8. Used the instalment sales method in the past five years when the facts clearly indicated that the cost recovery method should have been used.

9. Began capitalizing development costs because criteria for deferral were met this year for the first time; in the past, future markets had been too uncertain to justify capitalization.

10. Changed revenue recognition methods to report sales in a more appropriate manner.

★ **A20-3 Overview—Types of Accounting Changes:** Analyze each case and choose a letter code under each category (type and approach) to indicate the preferable accounting for each case.

Type	Approach
P = Policy	RWR = Retrospective with restatement
E = Estimate	RNR = Retrospective, no restatement
AE = Accounting error	P = Prospective

1. Recorded expense, $17,200; should be $71,200.

2. Changed useful life of a machine based on evidence of wear and tear over time.

3. Changed from FIFO to average cost for inventory to conform to industry practice. No prior balances can be reconstructed, not even opening balances.

4. Changed from straight-line to accelerated amortization to reflect the company's changing technological environment.

5. Change in residual value of an intangible operational asset based on changed economic circumstances.

6. Changed from cost to fair value basis for investments to conform to new accounting standard.

7. Changed from completed contract to percentage of completion for all contracts spanning more than two fiscal years. All prior balances can be reconstructed.

8. Changed from LIFO to FIFO for inventory to conform with new accounting standards. Only opening balances can be reconstructed.

9. Changed measurement method for asset retirement obligations to present value basis instead of undiscounted estimated costs.

10. Discovered that a capital asset with a 10-year life had been expensed when acquired five years ago.

★★ **A20-4 Analysis of Four Accounting Changes:** Four independent, unrelated situations relating to accounting changes are as follows:

a. The management of Axion Limited decided that the depreciable lives currently used for many of its tangible capital assets were too short, with the result that many assets remained in productive use long after they had been fully amortized. At the beginning of the current year, the company decided to significantly reduce its amortization rate on buildings and equipment.

b. On 31 December 20X6, Balken Corporation re-evaluated the estimated costs for fulfilling its asset retirement obligations. In response to rising interest rates, the company increased the discount rate being applied to these obligations.

c. In 20X6, the managers of Chalmers Inc. decided to expand revenue by selling its products to lower-income families on the instalment basis. Previously, the company had sold only by cash or general credit card. The company started using the instalment method of revenue recognition for all instalment sales.

d. Delilicious Ltd. had accumulated tax loss carryforwards amounting to $4.5 million at the end of 20X6. None of the future tax benefit of these carryforwards had previously been recognized. In January 20X7, however, company managers decided that, for preparing the 20X6 financial statements, it now was more likely than not that the benefits of $3.2 million would be realized within the carryforward period.

Required:

For each of these situations, write a memo that provides the information indicated below:

1. Type of accounting change.
2. Effect of the change on the financial statements, if any.
3. Manner of reporting the change, including a discussion of how amounts, if any, are computed.

(AICPA, adapted)

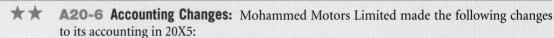

A20-5 Rationale for Accounting Changes: Arctic Charm Manufacturing Corporation is privately held. The company experienced poor operating results in the years 20X0 to 20X3, and, in 20X3, it reorganized and refinanced its operations. Creditors were asked to accept partial payment; shareholders invested additional capital. As part of the restructuring, ABC accepted restrictive debt covenants. Violation of these debt covenants would trigger a demand for immediate repayment of long-term debt and almost certainly mean that the company would be placed in receivership or bankruptcy. Debt covenants included minimum working capital and maximum debt-to-equity ratios.

The 20X4 operating results were acceptable. The company wishes to make the following accounting changes before the end of the 20X4 fiscal year:

a. Change depreciation policies from declining balance to straight-line. Capital assets are fairly new but have been depreciated for three to five years under declining-balance rates. The company would adjust all capital asset balances to the amounts that would have existed had straight-line amortization been always been used.
b. Invoke one of the permitted differential reporting options by changing to the taxes payable method instead of using comprehensive allocation.

Required:

Describe the impact of these changes on the financial statements and debt covenants. Consider the appropriateness of these changes in your response.

A20-6 Accounting Changes: Mohammed Motors Limited made the following changes to its accounting in 20X5:

a. Increased the interest rate used to discount its pension obligations from 6.0% to 6.5%.
b. Renewed a lease on a roof that the company has been using for a microwave transmission tower. The original lease had four years yet to run; the renewal is for an additional five years. The company is obligated to remove the tower and completely restore the roof when the lease expires.
c. Decided that it is more likely than not that the future benefits of tax loss carryforwards of $3.0 million will be realized. The company's tax rate is 30%.
d. Realized that a $10.0 million improvement in an automated production line had been charged as an expense in 20X3, rather than being recorded as a betterment of a capital asset. The production line should be amortized at 20% per year, declining balance, with a full year amortization in the year of acquisition.

Required:

Describe the impact of these changes on the financial statements. Whenever possible, determine the amount of financial statement impacts.

★★ **A20-7 Accounting Changes:** Ng Holdings Limited had its first audit in 20X4. Its preliminary income figure, before tax, was $786,000. The following items were discovered:

a. A truck was recorded at cost of $35,000 on 1 January 20X3. The truck was paid for in cash of $5,000, and a $30,000 no-interest loan. The loan is due in instalments, with $10,000 paid at the end of 20X3, $10,000 at the end of 20X4, and $10,000 at the end of 20X5. The 20X3 and 20X4 payments were made and journalized as reductions to the note payable, so there is now a $10,000 credit balance in this account. Market interest rates are in the range of 8%. The truck is amortized straight-line over six years with a $2,000 salvage value.

b. Ng issued a bond payable at the beginning of 20X1 and received par value for its $1,000,000 convertible bond. The bond is convertible at the option of the investor. A value of $84,000 should have been assigned to the conversion option and classified in shareholders' equity. Any discount on the bond should be amortized over its 15-year life, straight-line.

c. The company uses the aging method of estimating the required allowance for doubtful accounts. Analysis indicates that the allowance is understated at the end of 20X4 in the amount of $26,100.

d. In April 20X4, a building site was swapped for another, similar property. No cash changed hands. The land had a book value of $233,000; the transaction was recorded at the average appraised value of the properties, or $325,000.

Required:

1. Classify each of the changes described above and identify the correct accounting treatment.

2. Calculate revised 20X4 net income. The tax rate is 30%.

3. If a retrospective adjustment to retained earnings is needed, calculate the retrospective adjustment. The tax rate is 30%.

★ **A20-8 Change in Estimated Useful Life—Entries and Reporting:** Stacey Corporation has been amortizing equipment over a 10-year life on a straight-line basis. The equipment, which cost $24,000, was purchased on 1 January 20X1. It has an estimated residual value of $6,000. On the basis of experience since acquisition, management has decided in 20X5 to amortize it over a total life of 14 years instead of 10 years, with no change in the estimated residual value. The change is to be effective on 1 January 20X5. The annual financial statements are prepared on a comparative basis (20X4 and 20X5 presented); 20X4 and 20X5 incomes before amortization were $49,800 and $52,800, respectively. Disregard income tax considerations.

Required:

1. Identify the type of accounting change involved and analyze the effects of the change. Which approach should be used—prospective, retrospective with restatement, or retrospective without restatement? Explain.

2. Prepare the entry, or entries, to appropriately reflect the change (if any) and 20X5 amortization in the accounts for 20X5, the year of the change.

3. Illustrate how the change, the equipment, and the related amortization should be reported on the 20X5 financial statements, which include 20X4 results for comparative purposes.

★★ **A20-9 Change in Resource Exploration Costs—Entries and Reporting:** Gunnard Company was formed in 20X4 and has a 31 December year-end. Gunnard Company changed from successful efforts (SE) to full costing (FC) for its resource exploration costs in 20X5. SE is still used for tax purposes. The change was made to reflect changed corporate reporting objectives; more stable net income was deemed desirable to support a more stable stock market share price. Under FC, all exploration costs are deferred; under SE, only a portion are deferred. Under both approaches, the deferred cost balance is amortized yearly.

Had FC been used in 20X4, a total of $3,200,000 of costs originally written off under SE would have been capitalized. A total of $4,700,000 of such costs were incurred in 20X5. Gunnard discloses 20X4 and 20X5 results comparatively in its annual financial statements. The tax rate is 30% in both years.

Resource exploration costs represent a long-term asset, and amortization is charged directly to that account. Expense related to exploration costs for 20X4 and 20X5 under both methods was as follows:

	SE	FC
Amortization of resource development costs:		
20X4	$ 40,000	$240,000
20X5	200,000	850,000
Resource development costs expensed:		
20X4	$3,200,000	—
20X5	4,700,000	—

Additional information for Gunnard:

	20X5	20X4
Revenues	$7,100,000	$4,400,000
Expenses other than resource development costs, amortization, and income tax	2,050,000	720,000

Required:

1. Prepare a 20X5 comparative income statement using the old policy, successful efforts.

2. Prepare the 20X5 entry/entries for FC amortization, and the accounting change. Assume that no amortization has been recorded by Gunnard to date in 20X5.

3. Prepare the comparative income statements under FC, and include disclosures related to the accounting change.

4. Prepare the comparative retained earnings statement for 20X5, reflecting the change.

5. How will the classification of development costs on the CFS change as a result of the new policy?

★ **A20-10 Change in Policy and Useful Life—Amortization:** Lennox Corporation purchased a $360,000 machine for its assembly plant on 1 January 20X0. It was estimated that the machine would have a useful life of five years or 15,000 hours and a salvage value of $27,000. Lennox is eligible for a government grant of 5% on this equipment. It intends to claim the full amount of the grant in 20X0 and will account for the grant by netting it against the cost of the equipment.

Actual usage of the machine for the first four years was as follows:

Year	Hours Used
20X0	6,000
20X1	4,500
20X2	3,000
20X3	1,500

Lennox used the service-hours method for amortizing the machine for the first two years. It changed its accounting policy for amortization to the straight-line method for all capital assets on 1 January 20X2, based on experience regarding usage patterns. At that time, the original estimates of useful life and residual value were considered correct.

On 1 January 20X3, the company estimated that the machine had a remaining useful life of three years and a salvage value at that time of $36,000.

Required:

Compute amortization expense for the first four years of use of this machine.

(CGA-Canada, adapted)

★ **A20-11 Amortization Policy Change:** On 13 April 20X4, Flax Company acquired manufacturing equipment for $180,000. The equipment is expected to last for 10 years and have a residual value of $25,000. The company records a full year of amortization in the year of purchase.

The declining-balance method at a rate of 20% was used to amortize this equipment for 20X4 and 20X5. For 20X6, the company switched to the straight-line method for this equipment. Estimates are unchanged.

Required:

1. Explain the relationship, if any, between amortization and changes in the market value of the asset being amortized.

2. Explain the criterion to be used in determining whether the change from the declining-balance method to the straight-line method should be accounted for retrospectively or prospectively.

3. Suppose the change in method for this case is to be accounted for prospectively. Calculate amortization expense for the manufacturing equipment for 20X4, 20X5, and 20X6.

(CGA-Canada, adapted)

★★ **A20-12 Accounting Changes—Inventory and Revenue:** Late in 20X6, the management of Richter Minerals Inc. decided to change the company's inventory valuation method and, concurrently, its revenue recognition method. Historically, the company had used an average cost basis for all inventory and had recognized revenue when minerals were shipped to customers. Now, effective with the year beginning 1 January 20X7, Richter will recognize revenue when the minerals have been refined and are ready for sale, at which point the inventory will be adjusted to net realizable value at the end of each reporting period. Richter's minerals are easily sold at any time on the world market via electronic trading.

At the end of 20X6, Richter had inventory (at cost of production) totalling $70 million. Of that total, $20 million was of unrefined ore and $50 million was refined minerals. At NRV, Richter's refined minerals inventory was $72 million. The 20X6 opening inventory contained refined minerals of $44 million at cost; using market price indices, Richter's management was able to determine that the 20X6 opening inventory was worth $60 million at NRV. Richter's 20X6 sales revenue was $250 million.

During 20X7, Richter recognized revenue of $360 million, on the new reporting basis. Ending inventory of refined minerals amounted to $82 million; production cost was $55 million.

The income tax rate was 25% in both years.

Required:

1. How much will this change affect the previously reported net income for 20X6?

2. Can this change be applied retrospectively with restatement? Explain the difficulties that management might encounter when restating years prior to 20X6.

3. Prepare any journal entries that are necessary to record the change in accounting policies.

★ **A20-13 Change in Estimate:** Barker Company, which has a calendar fiscal year, purchased its only depreciable capital asset on 1 January 20X3. Information related to the asset:

Original cost	$560,000
Estimated residual value	16,000
Depreciation method	Declining balance
Depreciation rate	30%

In 20X5, Barker increased the estimated residual value to $48,000, and decreased the depreciation rate to 20%. Both changes are the result of experience with the asset and revised expectations about the pattern of usage.

Additional Information

	20X5	20X4
Revenue	$2,800,000	$2,240,000
Expenses other than depreciation and tax	1,680,000	1,534,400
Discontinued operations, loss, before tax	40,000	—
Tax rate	25%	25%

Required:

1. Provide the 20X5 entry/entries for depreciation and calculate the ending 20X5 accumulated depreciation balance.
2. Provide the comparative 20X4 and 20X5 income statements, including disclosures related to the accounting change.

★★ **A20-14 Accounting Changes—Depreciable Assets:** Tech Manufacturing Corporation reports the following situations in 20X6 with respect to its high-tech manufacturing equipment:

a. Machine 1 was acquired at a cost of $872,000 in 20X3. The machine was depreciated on a straight-line basis over its expected six-year life. At the end of 20X6, management decided that this machine should have been depreciated over a total useful life of eight years. Salvage value, expected to be negligible, has not changed.

b. Machine 2 was acquired at a cost of $448,500 in 20X5. It was being amortized on a declining-balance method using a rate of 40%. Salvage values were expected to be minimal. In 20X6, management decided that, based on the usage patterns seen to date, units of production would be a more appropriate method of depreciation. The machine is used sporadically and suffers from wear and tear only as used (that is, obsolescence is not much of a factor in the loss of utility). Estimated units of production total 350,000, of which 75,000 units were produced in 20X5 and 30,000 units in 20X6.

c. Machine 3 was acquired in 20X4 at a cost of $1,150,000. The estimated life was eight years, with no salvage value. Declining-balance depreciation was used, at a rate of 30%. At the end of 20X6, management decided it would be more appropriate to use a straight-line method, to reflect industry practice.

d. Machine 4 was acquired in 20X3 at a cost of $325,000. Management discovered in 20X6 that the machine was expensed in 20X3, despite the fact that it had a useful life of 10 years, with a 10% salvage value. Straight-line depreciation should have been used for this asset.

For all depreciation methods, the company follows a policy of recording a full year of depreciation charged in the first year, but no depreciation is charged in the year of sale.

Required:

1. Classify each of the changes described above and identify the correct accounting treatment.
2. For each machine, calculate 20X6 depreciation.
3. If a retrospective adjustment is needed, calculate the retrospective adjustment in 20X6. The tax rate is 30%.

★ **A20-15 Error Correction:** Shariff Ltd. signed an operating lease on 1 January 20X0. The lease was a 40-year term on a piece of land. The land reverts to the lessor at the end of the lease term. The lease requires annual payments, on each 1 January, of $45,000 for the first

10 years. Annual January 1 payments of $20,000 were required for the second 10 years, 1 January payments of $10,000 for the third 10 years, and 1 January payments of $2,000 for the final 10 years. The lease payments have all been made on schedule, but have all been expensed as paid. (That is, it is now the end of 20X3 and the 20X3 rent has been paid and expensed, but the 20X3 books are still open.) The lease should have been expensed evenly over the lease term, regardless of the payment scheme.

Required:

Provide the entry to correct the error.

★ **A20-16 Error Correction:** In 20X6, Cathode Company, a calendar fiscal-year company, discovered that depreciation expense was erroneously overstated $40,000 in both 20X4 and 20X5, for financial reporting purposes. Net income in 20X6 is correct. The tax rate is 35%. Tax depreciation, CCA, had been recorded correctly. The error was made only for financial reporting, affecting depreciation and future income tax accounts.

Additional Information:

	20X6	20X5
Beginning retained earnings	$265,000	$180,000
Net income (includes error in 20X5)	125,000	145,000
Dividends declared	80,000	60,000

Required:

1. Record the entry in 20X6 to correct the error.
2. Provide the comparative retained earnings statement for 20X6, including any required note disclosure.

★★ **A20-17 Error Correction**—Excerpts from the 31 December financial statements of Simpson Limited, before any corrections.

	20X7	20X6	20X5
Income statement			
Cost of goods sold	$790,000	$705,200	$676,800
Balance sheet			
Inventory	$ 34,500	$ 30,900	$ 16,100
Retained earning statement			
Opening retained earnings	$331,000	$260,800	$211,500
Net income	104,700	91,200	70,300
Dividends	(21,000)	(21,000)	(21,000)
Closing retained earnings	$414,700	$331,000	$260,800

After these financial statements were prepared, but before they were issued, a routine review revealed a major mathematical error in calculating 20X5 closing inventory. Instead of $16,100, closing inventory should have been $19,700.

There is no income tax.

Required:

1. What entry is needed to correct the error in 20X7? Explain.
2. Restate all the above information, as appropriate, to retrospectively correct the error.
3. What disclosure of the error is needed?

★★ **A20-18 Error Correction:** Trelarkin Forpas Limited (TFL) reported the following in its 31 December financial statements:

	20X9	20X8	20X7
Income statement			
Depreciation expense (all assets)	$ 100,400	$ 91,600	$ 92,400
Balance sheet			
Capital assets (net)	$1,216,200	$1,147,600	$1,005,400
Retained earnings statement			
Opening retained earnings	$ 879,200	$ 905,800	$ 655,800
Net income (loss)	(135,700)	41,200	317,800
Dividends	(67,800)	(67,800)	(67,800)
Closing retained earnings	$ 675,700	$ 879,200	$ 905,800

After the draft 20X9 financial statements were prepared but before they were issued, TFL discovered that a capital asset was incorrectly accounted for in 20X5. A $160,000 capital asset was purchased early in 20X5, and it should have been amortized straight line over 10 years with a $20,000 residual value. Instead, it was written off to expense.

The error was made on the books, but the capital asset was accounted for correctly for tax purposes. The tax rate was 40%.

Required:

1. What entry is needed to correct the error in 20X9?
2. Restate all the above information, as appropriate, to retrospectively correct the error.
3. What disclosure of the error is needed?

★★ **A20-19 Change in Expense Method:** CT Corporation has always deferred product promotion costs and amortized the asset balance on a straight-line basis over the expected life of the related product. The company decided to change to a policy of immediately expensing such costs to more closely conform to industry practice. The change was adopted at the beginning of 20X7. Costs incurred:

Year	Amount	Life Span
20X3	$102,000	10 years
20X4	60,000	4 years
20X5	30,000	5 years
20X6	78,000	10 years
20X7	67,500	9 years

Required:

1. Identify the type of accounting change involved. Which approach should be used—prospective, retrospective with restatement, or retrospective without restatement? Explain.
2. Prepare the entry/entries to appropriately reflect the change in 20X7, the year of the change, and the entry to record 20X7 expenditures. Disregard income tax.
3. Explain how the change should be reported on the 20X7 financial statements, which include the 20X6 results for comparative purposes.
4. Prepare the entries to reflect the change in the accounts in 20X7, including the 20X7 expenditures, if only the opening 20X7 balance can be reconstructed. What would change in financial statement presentation?
5. Explain how classification of the costs on the cash flow statement would change as a result of the new accounting policy.

★★ **A20-20 Accounting Change—Bad Debts:** Betteroff Company was incorporated on 1 January 20X3. In the past, it has not provided an allowance for doubtful accounts. Instead, uncollectible accounts were expensed when written off and recoveries were credited to bad debt expense when collected. Accounts were written off if they were outstanding for more than four months.

In December 20X5, the company decided to change its accounting policy to account for bad debts as a percentage of credit sales, as this is the industry norm and the company wants its financial statements to be comparable to those of its competitors. Statistics for the past three years are summarized as follows:

		Accounts Written off and Year of Sale			Recoveries and Year of Sale	
Year	Credit Sales	20X3	20X4	20X5	20X3	20X4
20X3	$100,000	$550	—	—	$10	—
20X4	150,000	650	$750	—	30	$20
20X5	225,000	—	900	$950	—	40

Accounts receivable at 31 December 20X5 were $50,000 after write-offs but before any allowance for doubtful accounts.

Required:

1. How should the change in accounting policy be accounted for?
2. Prepare the journal entry to reflect the change in accounting policy and to adjust 20X5 bad debt expense. State your assumptions and show your supporting calculations, in arriving at a percentage rate for bad debts. Disregard income tax.

(CGA-Canada, adapted)

★★ **A20-21 Change from AC to FIFO—Entries and Reporting:** On 1 January 20X5, Baker Company decided to change the inventory costing method used from average cost (AC) to FIFO to conform to industry practice. The annual reporting period ends on 31 December. The average income tax rate is 30%. The following related data were developed:

	AC Basis	FIFO Basis
Beginning inventory, 20X4	$ 30,000	$30,000
Ending inventory		
20X4	40,000	70,000
20X5	44,000	76,000
Net income		
20X4: AC basis	80,000	
20X5: FIFO basis		82,000
Retained earnings		
20X4 beginning balance	120,000	
Dividends declared and paid		
20X4	64,000	
20X5		70,000
Common shares outstanding, 10,000		

Required:

1. Identify the type of accounting change involved. Which approach should be used— prospective, retrospective without restatement, or retrospective with restatement? Explain.
2. Give the entry to record the effect of the change, assuming the change was made only for accounting purposes, not for income tax purposes.

3. Complete the following schedule:

	FIFO Basis	
	20X5	**20X4**
Comparative balance sheet		
Inventory	$	$
Retained earnings		
Comparative income statement		
Net income		
Earnings per share		
Comparative retained earnings statement		
Beginning balance, as previously reported		
Cumulative effect of accounting change		
Beginning balance restated		
Net income		
Dividends declared and paid		
Ending balance		

 A20-22 Retrospective Policy Changes: Linfei Limited has a 31 December year-end, and a tax rate of 35%. Management has asked you to respond to the following situations:

1. The company has always used the FIFO method of determining inventory costs; starting in 20X7, it will now use weighted-average cost. Opening and closing inventories for 20X7 under FIFO are $3,300,000 and $2,655,000, respectively. Opening and closing inventories under weighted average are $2,600,000 and $2,100,000, respectively. Provide the journal entry to record the change.

2. Return to situation 1. This year, 20X7, opening retained earnings was $4,365,000. Net income, before any adjustment from situation 1, was $1,600,000. Dividends were $235,000. Last year, in 20X6, opening retained earnings was $4,010,000, net income was $565,000, and dividends were $210,000. For 20X6, opening inventory was 2,600,000 under FIFO and $2,200,000 under weighted average. Prepare a comparative retained earnings statement giving full retrospective effect to the change in accounting policy.

3. Return to your retained earnings statement in situation 2. Prepare a comparative retained earnings statement assuming that comparative balances could not be restated; that is, the only information you have to work with, in addition to the income, retained earnings, and dividend information, is that provided about opening and closing inventory balances in situation 1.

4. An asset, with an original cost of $400,000 and an original salvage value of $40,000, was amortized using the declining-balance method, using a rate of 20%, in 20X4, 20X5, and 20X6. On 1 October of this year, 20X7, management decides to change amortization methods and will now use the straight-line method. This change is made on the basis of usage information that indicates that the asset is used about the same amount in each year of life. The new estimates are a *total* life of 12 years and a salvage value of $25,000. Amortization expense has not yet been recorded for 20X7. Provide the appropriate journal entry/entries.

 A20-23 Retrospective Policy Changes: Kate Limited has asked you to prepare appropriate journal entries for the following unrelated situations. There is no income tax.

Case A An investment with an original cost of $400,000 was accounted for using the cost method in 20X0, 20X1, and 20X2. This year, 20X3, the company must conform to new accounting standards and classified the investment as available for sale. Fair values were $390,000, $410,000, and $450,000 at the end of 20X0, 20X1, and 20X2, respectively. The investment had a fair value of $466,000 at the end of 20X3. The change is to be accounted for retrospectively with no restatement. Provide the entry to record the retrospective change in 20X3, and to adjust the investment account to fair value at the end of 20X3. *Note*: the retrospective impact affects the shareholders' equity account, *accumulated other comprehensive income*, instead of retained earnings.

Case B The company has always recognized revenue on delivery but, because of a change in reporting objectives, will now recognize revenue according to the industry norm, which is on cash collection. Opening and closing accounts receivable are $1,600,000 and $2,355,000, respectively. The gross profit margin is 60%. (*Note*: accounts receivable are recorded but no unearned revenue is on the books.)

 A20-24 Retrospective Policy Change: From 20X0 through 20X8, Hughes Company used declining-balance depreciation for external reporting. Early in 20X9, management decided to switch to straight-line depreciation. Accordingly, for 20X9 and subsequent years, the straight-line method was used for determining the net income. An analysis revealed the following:

Year	Pre-Tax Excess of Declining-Balance over Straight-Line Depreciation	After-Tax Net Income Previously Reported	Dividends Declared
20X0 through 20X6*	$320,000	$1,020,000	$255,000
20X7	60,000	760,000	190,000
20X8	40,000	1,104,000	276,000

*20X0 was the company's first year of operations.

Hughes Company reported net income of $750,000 for 20X9, using the straight-line method. The company declared dividends of $187,500 in 20X9.

Required:

1. Under what circumstances would this change in policy be accounted for retrospectively?
2. Assume retrospective application is appropriate. Give the entry to reflect the accounting change in 20X9, the year of the change. The tax rate was 30%.
3. Prepare the restated 20X9 retained earnings statement in good form, including the 20X8 comparative figures.
4. What note disclosure would be required? (Do not prepare the note, just describe its contents.)

 A20-25 Retrospective Policy Change: Armstrong Limited has used the average cost (AC) method to determine inventory values since first formed in 20X3. In 20X7, the company decided to switch to the FIFO method, to conform to industry practice. Armstrong will still use average cost for tax purposes. The tax rate is 30%. The following data has been assembled:

	20X3	20X4	20X5	20X6	20X7
Net income, as reported, after tax	$56,000*	$65,000*	$216,000*	$255,000*	$125,000**
Closing inventory, AC	35,000	45,000	56,000	91,000	116,000
Closing inventory, FIFO	41,000	57,000	52,000	84,000	130,000
Dividends	5,000	7,000	7,000	10,000	14,000

*Using the old policy, average cost
**Using the new policy, FIFO.

Required:

Present the comparative retained earnings statement for 20X7, giving effect to the change in accounting policy.

★★ **A20-26 Change from Completed Contract to Percentage of Completion—Entries and Reporting:** Ring Unlimited manages real estate properties and sometimes engages in building construction. In 20X4, Ring Unlimited contracted to build an office building. The construction began on 1 July 20X4 and was completed in 20X6. The company had a fixed price contract of $240 million. The following data (in $ millions) relate to the construction contract:

	20X4	20X5	20X6
Costs to date (cumulative)	$ 70	$170	$205
Estimated cost to complete	120	30	0
Progress billings to date	58	160	240
Cash collected to date (cumulative)	40	164	240

Selected information (in $ millions) from the company's records for its first three years of business is presented below:

	20X4	20X5	20X6
Net income	$30	$32	$45
Dividends paid	4	6	8
Retained earnings (ending)	26	52	89

Until now, the company has used (and the above data reflect) the completed-contract method to account for its long-term construction contracts. When preparing the 20X6 financial statements, the company decided to change to the percentage-of-completion method, a change to be accounted for retrospectively with restatement.

Required:

1. Prepare the journal entry at 31 December 20X6, to record the change to the percentage-of-completion method. The company will use a construction-in-progress account in conjunction with its construction activities. Ignore income tax.

2. Assuming that the company changed to the percentage-of-completion method, prepare, in good form, a statement of retained earnings for Ring Unlimited for the year ended 31 December 20X6, with comparative amounts for 20X5. Ignore income tax.

3. In what circumstances would it *not* be appropriate to account for a change in accounting policy retrospectively? Explain.

(CGA-Canada, adapted)

★★ **A20-27 Change Regarding Construction Contracts:** KLB Corporation has used the completed-contract method to account for its long-term construction contracts since its inception in 20X3. On 1 January 20X7, management decided to change to the percentage-of-completion method to better reflect operating activities and conform to industry norms. Completed contract was used for income tax purposes and will continue to be used for income tax purposes in the future. The income tax rate is 40%. The following information has been assembled:

Year ended 31 December	20X3	20X4	20X5	20X6	20X7
Net income, as reported	$100,000	$120,000	$150,000	$140,000	160,000*
CC income, included in above	0	60,000	0	120,000	0
PC income, as calculated	40,000	65,000	50,000	40,000	75,000
Opening retained earnings	0	90,000	190,000	320,000	440,000
Dividends	10,000	20,000	20,000	20,000	20,000
Closing retained earnings	90,000	190,000	320,000	440,000	580,000

*Includes PC income, not CC income, in earnings.

Required:

1. Identify the type of accounting change involved. Which approach should be used—current, retrospective with restatement, or retrospective without restatement? Explain.

2. Give the entry to appropriately reflect the accounting change in 20X7, the year of the change.

3. Restate the 20X7 retained earnings statement, including the 20X6 comparative figures.

4. Assume that only the opening balance in 20X7 can be restated and that the cumulative effect cannot be allocated to individual years. Recast the 20X7 comparative retained earnings statement accordingly.

5. Assume that no balances can be restated. Can the change be made in 20X7? Explain.

★ **A20-28 Two Assets—Useful Life and Residual Value Changed; Entries and Reporting:** Medbio Company owns a patent that cost $255,000 when it was acquired on 15 January 20X5. It was being amortized over its legal life of 20 years (no residual value). On 1 January 20X8, the patent was estimated to have a *total* useful life of only 13 years (no residual value).

On 5 March 20X1, the company had purchased a machine that cost $590,000. The estimated useful life was 15 years with an estimated residual value of $60,000. Starting on 1 January 20X8, the company revised its estimates to 4 years of *remaining* useful life and $50,000 residual value.

The company uses the straight-line method for both of these assets, taking a full year's amortization in the year of acquisition. The annual reporting period ends 31 December. Disregard income tax considerations.

Required:

1. What kinds of accounting changes are involved? How should each change be accounted for—retrospective with restatement, retrospective without restatement, or prospective? Explain.

2. Give all entries required in 20X7 and 20X8 related to these assets.

★★ **A20-29 Change in Policy, Error:** TXL Corporation has tentatively computed income before tax as $660,000 for 20X4. Retained earnings at the beginning of 20X4 had a balance of $3,600,000. Dividends of $270,000 were paid during 20X4. There were dividends payable of $60,000 at the end of 20X3 and $90,000 at the end of 20X4. The following information has been provided:

1. The company used FIFO for costing inventory in deriving net income of $660,000. It wishes to change to average cost to be comparable with other companies in the industry. Accordingly, the change in policy should be applied retrospectively. The comparable figures for ending inventory under the two methods are as follows:

	FIFO	Average
December 20X1	$420,000	$408,000
December 20X2	450,000	435,000
December 20X3	480,000	462,000
December 20X4	510,000	486,000

2. In January 20X3, the company acquired some equipment for $2,100,000. At that time, it estimated the equipment would have an estimated useful life of 12 years and a salvage value of $150,000. In 20X3, the company received a government grant of $300,000, which assisted in purchasing the equipment. The grant was credited to income in error. The company has been amortizing the equipment on the straight-line basis and has already provided for amortization for 20X4 based upon the $2,100,000 cost. Management realizes that the company must account for the government grant by crediting it directly to the equipment account.

The income tax rate for the company is 30%. Assume that all of the stated items are fully taxable or deductible for income tax purposes.

Required:

1. Prepare a schedule to show the calculation of the correct net income for 20X4 in accordance with generally accepted accounting principles.

2. Prepare, in good form, a retained earnings statement for the year ended 31 December 20X4. Comparative figures need not be provided.

(CGA-Canada, adapted)

 A20-30 Change in Accounting for Natural Resources: In 20X6, Black Oil Company changed its method of accounting for oil exploration costs from the successful efforts method (SE) to full costing (FC) for financial reporting because of a change in corporate reporting objectives. Black Oil has been in the oil exploration business since January 20X3; prior to that, the company was active in oil transportation.

Pre-tax income under each method is as follows:

	SE	FC
20X3	$ 15,000	$ 45,000
20X4	66,000	75,000
20X5	75,000	105,000
20X6	120,000	180,000

Black Oil reports the result of years 20X4 through 20X6 in its 20X6 annual report and has a calendar fiscal year. The tax rate is 30%. The change is made for accounting purposes but not for tax purposes. Thus, the future income tax account is changed.

Additional Information:

	20X3	20X4	20X5	20X6
Ending retained earnings (SE basis)	$54,000	$69,000	$93,000	n/a
Dividends declared	27,000	31,200	28,500	$36,000

Required:

1. Prepare the entry in 20X6 to record the accounting change. Use "natural resources" as the depletable asset account.

2. Prepare the comparative retained earnings statement. Include 20X6, 20X5, and 20X4.

3. Describe how the accounting policy change would affect the cash flow statement.

 A20-31 Analysis of Three Accounting Changes: During 20X4, Sugarland Corporation completed an analysis of its operating assets with the purpose of updating its accounting procedures used for inventory costing and amortization. The annual reporting period ends 31 December. Decisions have been made concerning three different assets listed below (designated Cases A, B, and C). The indicated accounting changes are to be implemented starting 1 January 20X5, the fifth year of operations for this company. Disregard income tax considerations.

Case A Machine A, acquired on 1 January 20X1, at a cost of $60,000, is being amortized straight-line over an estimated 10-year useful life; residual value is $5,000. On 1 January 20X5, the company will start using 20% declining balance (with no other changes). The change was based on information gathered concerning the expected pattern of benefit.

Required:

1. Explain the type of accounting change and the approach that should be used— retrospective with restatement, retrospective without restatement, or prospective.

2. Give the following entries:
   a. Amortization adjusting entry at the end of 20X4.
   b. The 20X5 entry to record the accounting change in 20X5, if any. Explain.
   c. Depreciation adjusting entry at the end of 20X5.

3. Explain how the 20X4 financial statement amounts are reported in the 20X5 comparative statements.

Case B On 1 January 20X5, the company changed from LIFO to FIFO for inventory costing purposes to conform to revised accounting standards. The ending inventory for 20X4: LIFO basis, $12,000; FIFO basis, $17,000. Ending inventory for 20X5, FIFO basis, was $19,000. No other balances could be reconstructed.

Required:

1. Explain the type of accounting change and the approach that should be used—retrospective with restatement, retrospective without restatement, or prospective.

2. Give the entry to record the accounting change in 20X5.

3. Explain:
   a. How the effect of the change, recorded in requirement (2), is reported in the 20X5 comparative financial statements.
   b. How the 20X4 income statement amounts are reported on the 20X5 comparative statements.

Case C A patent, purchased for $17,000 on 1 January 20X1, is being amortized (straight-line) over its legal life of 20 years; there is no residual value. On 1 January 20X5, the company decided to change to a more realistic total useful life of 12 years.

Required:

1. Explain the type of accounting change and the approach that should be used—retrospective with restatement, retrospective without restatement, or prospective.

2. Give the following entries:
   a. Amortization adjusting entry at the end of 20X4.
   b. The 20X5 entry to record the accounting change in 20X5, if any. Explain.
   c. Amortization adjusting entry at the end of 20X5.

3. Explain how the 20X4 financial statement amounts are reported in the 20X5 comparative statements.

 A20-32 Accounting Changes, Comprehensive: EC Construction Limited (EC) has 100,000 common shares outstanding. The balance of retained earnings at the beginning of 20X7 was $2,400,000. On 15 December 20X7 EC declared dividends of $3 per share payable on 5 January 20X8. Income before income tax was $600,000 based on the records of the company's accountant.

Additional information on selected transactions/events is provided below:

a. At the beginning of 20X6, EC purchased some equipment for $230,000 (salvage value of $30,000) that had a useful life of five years. The accountant used a 40% declining-balance method of amortization, but mistakenly deducted the salvage value in calculating amortization expense in 20X6 and 20X7.

b. As a result of an income tax audit of 20X5 taxable income, $74,000 of expenses claimed as deductible expenses for tax purposes was disallowed by the CRA. This error cost the company $29,600 in additional tax. This amount was paid in 20X7 but has been debited to a prepaid expense account.

EC contracted to build an office building for RD Corporation. The construction began in 20X6 and will be completed in 20X8. The contract has a price of $30 million. The following data (in millions of dollars) relates to the construction period to date:

	20X6	20X7
Costs incurred to date	$ 8	$13
Estimated costs to complete	12	7
Progress billings during the year	6	10
Cash collected on billings during the year	5	8

The accountant has been using the completed-contract method in accounting for this contract. You determine that the percentage-of-completion method should be used.

d. On 1 January 20X7, EC purchased, as a long-term investment, 19% of the common shares of One Limited for $50,000. On that date, the fair value of identifiable assets of One Limited was $220,000 and was equal to the book value of identifiable assets. Goodwill has not been impaired. No investment income has been recorded. One paid no dividends, but reported income of $25,000 in the year. EC has significant influence over One.

e. EC has an effective tax rate of 40%.

Required:

1. Calculate 20X7 net income for EC.

2. Prepare the 20X7 retained earnings statement in good form. Comparative numbers need not be shown.

 A20-33 Multiple Accounting Changes: You are reviewing the accounting records for Hungary Limited for the year ended 31 December 20X8, the 30th year of business for the company. In the past, the company has used the declining-balance method to record amortization on tangible assets and LIFO for inventory. Management now believes that certain changes in accounting policies should be made to improve the financial information being presented to the shareholders.

The changes being proposed are identified below. Because of antiquated accounting records, you are able to obtain information related to these changes only for the past three years.

a. Management has decided to change the method of amortization from the declining-balance method (20% rate) to the straight-line method. The only capital asset now owned is a machine, which was purchased in January 20X6 at a cost of $150,000. The machine has an estimated useful life of 10 years and a residual value of $9,000.

b. Management wants to change the method of accounting for inventory from LIFO to FIFO in accordance with new accounting standards. The value of ending inventory under these two methods at the end of each year for the past two years was as follows:

	Value of Ending Inventory under	
	FIFO	**LIFO**
20X7	110,000	92,000
20X8	118,000	95,000

c. A trademark was purchased in January 20X6 for $51,000 and was being amortized over its initial registration period of 15 years. Although management believes that the correct useful life was used for amortization in 20X6 and 20X7, it now believes that the economic benefits of the trademark would likely last only for a total of eight years from the date of acquisition. The company uses the straight-line method of amortization for the trademark.

Income before tax for 20X6, 20X7, and 20X8 was $900,000, $1,125,000, and $1,275,000, respectively. These income figures were based on the old accounting policies, that is, declining-balance amortization for equipment, LIFO for inventory, and a useful life of 15 years for the trademark. The tax rate is 40%.

Required:

1. Should the changes be accounted for retrospectively or prospectively? Explain.

2. Assume that the change in amortization method is to be applied retrospectively. Other changes affect only 20X8. Calculate the revised income before tax for 20X6, 20X7, and 20X8. Show your calculations.

3. Prepare the retained earnings statement to reflect the accounting changes. Opening retained earnings was $4,750,000 in 20X7, with dividends of $200,000. Opening retained earnings was $5,225,000 in 20X8, with dividends of $225,000.

 A20-34 Multiple Accounting Changes: Zealand Company made several financial accounting changes in 20X6:

First, the company changed the total useful life from 20 years to 14 years on a $350,000 asset purchased 1 January 20X2. The asset was originally expected to be sold for $50,000 at the end of its useful life, but that amount was also changed in 20X6, to $200,000. Zealand applies the straight-line method of amortization to this asset. Amortization has not yet been recorded in 20X6.

Second, the company changed inventory costing from FIFO to weighted average (WA) but is unable to recreate WA inventory layers. The FIFO 20X6 beginning and ending inventories are $30,000 and $45,000. Under WA, the 20X6 ending inventory is $35,000. The company expects WA to render income numbers more useful for prediction, given inflation.

Third, the company changed its policy for accounting for certain staff training costs. Previously, the costs were capitalized and amortized straight-line over three years, starting with the year of the expenditure. The new policy is to expense training costs as incurred, in compliance with revised accounting standards for intangible assets. A total of $100,000 was expended in 20X3, $0 in 20X4, $60,000 in 20X5, and $45,000 in 20X6.

Fourth, an error in amortizing patents was discovered in 20X6. Patents costing $510,000 on 1 January 20X4 have been amortized over their legal life (20 years). The accountant neglected to obtain an estimate of the patents' economic life, which totalled only five years.

Zealand is a calendar fiscal-year company and is subject to a 30% tax rate.

Other information:

	20X6	20X5
Beginning retained earnings	$489,000	$319,000
Income before extraordinary items, after tax	325,000*	220,000
Extraordinary gain, net of tax	10,000	
Dividends declared	70,000	50,000

*This is the correct reported amount and includes the appropriate amounts related to all the expenses affected by the accounting changes. However, it includes FIFO cost of goods sold. WA costs would be $17,000 higher.

Required:

1. Record the 20X6 entries necessary to make the accounting changes. If the change cannot be made, explain why.

2. Prepare the 20X5 and 20X6 comparative retained earnings statement and note disclosures for the accounting changes.

CHAPTER 21

Financial Statement Analysis

INTRODUCTION

WestJet Airlines Ltd. reported net earnings of $24 million in 2005, as compared to a loss of $17 million in 2004 and profits of $97 million, $83 million, and $58 million in 2003, 2002, and 2001 respectively. Between 2001 and 2005, earnings improved by 65%, yet EPS declined by 53%, from $0.36 to $0.19 per share. The company had (in 2005) assets of $2.2 billion, and liabilities of $1.5 billion (plus lease commitments of over $0.8 billion). The company's revenues are mainly in Canadian dollars, but its aircraft lease payments and fuel costs are in U.S. dollars. If you were an investor in WestJet, or a major lender, how would you go about analyzing the company's asset and liability structure, its earnings performance, its return on assets and equity, and its ability to service its large debt load?

Entire books (and whole university courses) are devoted to financial statement analysis. There is a professional designation, Chartered Financial Analyst (CFA) that requires significant study. Thus, financial statement analysis is a broad and complex field. In this book, we can touch only on the major aspects of financial analysis.

Company analysis must always be a forward-looking process. In this chapter, the focus will be on analysis of the statements themselves. But the statements of individual companies must be interpreted within the context of the general economic environment, the economic and competitive climate of the country or region in which the company operates, and the structure and outlook of the industry in which the company competes. For investors, the company's financial outlook must be evaluated in relationship to the market price of its shares. For lenders, the company's future must be evaluated as its ability to service its debt without binding its current operations and its competitiveness.

This chapter describes several different techniques for analysis, but most space is devoted to traditional ratio analysis. It is possible to compute dozens of financial statement ratios, but an analyst should decide first what he or she needs to find out and then select just a few ratios to look at.

Ratios are useless unless they can be compared to something else, such as historical trends or "average" ratios of other companies or benchmark ratios of companies in the same industry. To be comparable, the companies used for comparison must have similar accounting policies (and estimates). Ratio analysis can be useful, but can also be very misleading if inappropriate comparisons are made.

OVERVIEW OF STATEMENT ANALYSIS

Clarify the Decision Focus

The starting point is to be clear about what decision is to be made as a result of the financial statement analysis. Possible decisions include:

1. Equity investment decisions

2. Lending decisions

3. Contractual decisions, such as accepting employment, negotiating collective agreements, or entering into a joint venture

4. Regulatory decisions, including the need for rate or price increases, or the impact of past regulatory decisions

Each of these decisions will require a somewhat different approach to the analysis and a different set of priorities. For example, a prospective investor in common shares will be concerned with the long-term profitability of the company (along with other contributing aspects, such as solvency and stability), while a trade creditor will be primarily interested in the short-run liquidity (while still being interested in the long-term survival possibilities of the company). This difference in emphasis is illustrated by the fact that many creditors will continue to extend credit to a company with declining profitability in which no investor in her or his right mind would buy shares.

There also is a difference between looking at a company (1) as a new, prospective stakeholder and (2) as an existing stakeholder who needs to decide whether to continue the relationship or to bail out. A new stakeholder (e.g., an investor, creditor, or contractor) is concerned about the future safety and profitability of a contemplated investment or contract. In contrast, an existing stakeholder will be concerned about the financial and/or operational ramifications of terminating an existing investment or contract.

Therefore, it is crucial to know the nature of the decision in question.

Examine the Auditor's Report

A public company must have a clean opinion in order to be traded on major stock exchanges, but a private company may use one or more non-GAAP accounting policies. In such cases, the auditor will qualify the opinion. A qualification in an **auditor's report** should not *necessarily* be cause for concern. A company may choose to use accounting policies that are more in accordance with the interests of the primary stakeholders than GAAP would be. A privately held company, for example, may:

- Report its pension expense on the basis of its funding in order to achieve closer correspondence between reported earnings and cash flow from operations, or
- Report its capital assets at a restated value that reflects the value against which its lenders have extended loans.

Normally, an auditor will attempt to quantify the impact (i.e., on net income) of a deviation from GAAP and will either report the impact in the auditor's report or refer the reader to a financial statement note that discusses the deviation.

If a private company does not have an audit, an auditor may nevertheless be retained for a **review engagement**, in which a full audit is not performed but the auditor does review the financial statements for general consistency with GAAP (or with a disclosed basis of accounting) and for reasonableness of presentation. Banks often rely on auditor's statements in review engagements as assurance that the company's accounting practices are reasonable and that the financial statements are plausible. However, a review engagement provides no assurance that the company's internal control policies and procedures are operating properly, or that there is external evidence to support the amounts presented on the financial statements. Investors and lenders use unaudited statements at their own risk!

review engagement

examination of the financial statements by an independent accountant, for general consistency with specified standards and reasonableness of presentation; generally does not require the reviewer to seek external, third-party corroborating evidence

Examine Accounting Policies

We have stressed throughout this book that managers' accounting policy choices are governed by the objectives of financial reporting in the particular circumstance.

The financial reporting objectives adopted by a company may not correspond with a specific user's preferred objectives. Therefore, the first task of an analyst is to determine the reporting objectives that are implicit in the financial statements. If the implicit objectives do not correspond to the user's objectives, then adjustments to the financial statements will probably be needed before they are of maximum use. Discerning the implicit objectives often is easier said than done.

Notes to Financial Statements To the extent that they exist, most of the clues to the implicit reporting objectives can be found in the notes to the financial statements. The first note to financial statements is (or should be) the accounting policy note, in which the company describes its accounting policy choices. In practice, the information revealed is often not very helpful. Three problems arise:

1. The disclosure is too vague to be of any use to an analyst without additional inside information.

2. The disclosure is specific, but the numerical data needed to make sense of possible alternatives is not disclosed.

3. There is no disclosure at all of crucial policies, such as revenue recognition.

Often, the accounting policy note gives only the broadest possible explanation of an accounting policy, but more information can be found in the other notes. For example, details on depreciation methods may be more complete in the plant and equipment note than in the policy note, and the policy on financial instruments may be more fully explained in the long-term debt note.

Lack of detail is also a problem. The note on inventories may say simply that "some of the inventory has been valued on a lower-of-cost-or-market basis," or "inventories are valued on a variety of bases, predominantly at average cost" without suggesting how average cost is determined.

Focus of the Analyst

An analyst looks in the notes mainly for revenue and expense recognition policies. For example:

- If a company is using policies that tend to recognize revenue early in the earnings cycle but that defer many costs to later periods (i.e., capitalize and amortize), then the company seems to be applying a profit maximization strategy.

- If both revenue and expense tend to be deferred and amortized, then a smoothing strategy may be paramount.

- If revenue recognition is deferred but all operating costs are expensed as incurred, income minimization may be the objective for income tax or political reasons.

Other accounting (and operating) policies relate to the balance sheet, and the analyst must examine those as well. Is the company keeping its capital assets at a minimum by using operating leases to acquire the use of assets that are crucial to its operations? Such a practice suggests that the company has both off-balance-sheet assets and liabilities. Off-balance-sheet assets will increase the apparent return on assets, while off-balance-sheet financing will improve the apparent debt-to-equity ratio. But the use of operating leases may be significantly more expensive than simply buying assets or entering into long-term capital leases, as we discussed in Chapter 17.

A further clue may be gleaned from the cash flow statement. If earnings (with amortization added back) are significantly and repeatedly larger than cash flow from operations, the company may be maximizing net income. If cash flow is significantly larger than earnings, the company may be very conservative in its accounting practices, reporting minimum net earnings (for example, by anticipating future expenditures through current provisions) or may be trying to minimize its current tax bill.

As well, the analyst will look at the cash flow statement to see if cash flow from operations excludes important operating expenses (such as development costs) that management has capitalized and thereby shifted from the operating section to the investing section. Many analysts reclassify such expenses for cash flow analysis purposes (and sometimes for recomputing net income), and may also reclassify to operations the necessary continuing reinvestment in equipment.

For example, a computer training company must continually upgrade its computers in order to be able to provide currently relevant courses to its clients. Since the computers are amortized over three to five years, they are reported as an investing activity. However, the expenditure is crucial to the successful operation of the company, and therefore some analysts (including some bankers) will reclassify the purchase of new computers as part of operating (or "free") cash flow. In such a situation, it is important to try to distinguish between replacements needed to maintain current operations and those that represent expansion of operations.

For a public company, the MD&A (Management's Discussion and Analysis) may help distinguish between replacements and new investment. For a private company, the analyst usually has no choice but to ask management. Management makes itself open to questions from major external users such as bankers, but may not respond to information requests from relatively minor users.

Finally, the income statement must be examined for non-recurring items. Companies have a tendency to include non-recurring gains along with operating revenues while showing non-recurring losses as unusual items. Of course, given the extreme brevity of most published income statements, significant non-recurring gains and losses may easily be included with operating items and not be separately disclosed.

Recast the Financial Statements

It is often necessary for users to recast the financial statements to suit their needs before applying other analytical approaches. The restatement is an approximation because the user never has full information. Situations that suggest a needed restatement include the following examples:

- The income statement is revised to remove non-recurring gains and losses.
- The income statement and balance sheet are revised to remove the effects of future income tax liabilities and assets.
- The income statement and balance sheet are revised to reflect a different policy on capitalization of certain costs:
  - capitalized costs are shifted to the income statement in the year they occurred, and amortization is removed, or
  - expenditures charged directly to the income statement are removed, capitalized, and amortization is added.
- Necessary recurring reinvestments are reclassified on the cash flow statement from investing activities to operating activities.
- Interest expense and taxes are removed from net income to yield a measure commonly referred to as EBIT (earnings before interest and taxes). Depreciation and amortization may also be removed, yielding EBITDA, which is often used as a rough measure of cash flow from operations. These measures are known as non-GAAP earnings measurements, but they can be quite useful.
- Loans to and from shareholders are reclassified as owners' equity.
- Retractable preferred shares are reclassified as long-term debt.
- The estimated value of assets under continuing operating leases is added to capital assets and to liabilities.

In recasting the statement to reflect different accounting policies, it is important to remember to adjust for both sides of transactions. For example, deleting future income tax expense must be accompanied by adding the balance of the future income tax liability to retained earnings and not by simply *ignoring* the balance.

An illustration of recasting financial statements is presented in the Appendix to this chapter.

Seek Comparative Information

Data are useless unless there is some basis for comparison. Sometimes the comparison is with a mental database accumulated by the analyst over years of experience in analyzing similar companies. For less experienced analysts, empirical comparisons are necessary. There are two bases for comparison: (1) cross-sectional and (2) longitudinal.

Cross-sectional comparison analyzes a company in relation to other companies in the same year. Comparisons of this type frequently appear in the business press in articles that compare the recent performance of one company with its competitors. Cross-sectional comparison is very useful, but caution must be exercised that similar measurements have been used. If the comparison companies used significantly different accounting policies, then no comparison can be valid unless the companies have all been adjusted to reflect similar accounting policies. Comparison of the return on assets for a company that owns all of its capital assets with one that uses operating leases for its capital assets will be invalid.

Longitudinal comparisons look at a company over time, comparing this year's performance with earlier years. A comparison is often made to other companies or to general economic returns during the same time span.

Some databases facilitate both types of comparison on an industry basis. These industry comparisons can be helpful but must be used with a great deal of caution. Industry statistics are constructed without attention to underlying reporting differences or accounting policy differences, and therefore it seldom is clear whether the comparisons are truly valid. In addition, it is tempting to decide that one company is a good investment (for example) because its profitability ratios are better than its competitors. It may well be, however, that the entire industry is sick, and that the company being analyzed is just less sick.

Apply Analytical Techniques

Once the statements have been adjusted to suit the needs of the analyst (that is, to facilitate making the decision at hand), the statements may be subject to numerical analysis or "number crunching." The basic tool of numerical analysis is ratios. A ratio is simply one number divided by another. Given the number of numbers in a set of financial statements, especially over a series of years, an incredible number of ratios could be computed. The trick to avoiding overwork (and total confusion) is to identify which ratios have meaning for the analyst's purpose, and then focus just on those few instead of computing every ratio in sight.

Certain types of ratios have been given generic names. Two commonly cited types of ratio are:

1. *Vertical analysis* or *common-size analysis*, in which the components of one year's individual financial statements are computed as a percentage of a base amount, using (for example) total assets as the base (= 100) for the balance sheet and net sales as the base for the income statement.

2. *Horizontal analysis* or *trend analysis*, in which longitudinal ratios for a single financial statement component (e.g., sales) are computed with a base year's amount set at 100 and other years' amounts recomputed relative to the base amount.

Both vertical analysis and horizontal analysis are really just the construction of index numbers within a year (vertical) or between years (horizontal). All index numbers must have a *base*, and the base amount is set at 100%.

Vertical Analysis Vertical analysis is useful for seeing the relative composition of the balance sheet or income statement. Analysts sometimes use these numbers for comparisons with industry norms. For example, an analyst may want to compare the *gross margin* of one company with another by comparing the relative proportion of sales that is consumed by cost of goods sold (when cost of goods sold is disclosed). Similarly, an analyst may look at common-size numbers to see if a company's inventory is too large, relative to others in the industry. Vertical analysis is the simplest of a broader set of techniques known as *decomposition analysis*; the more complex approaches to decomposition analysis will not be discussed in this text.

Managers sometimes are sensitive to the uses that analysts make of vertical analysis and adopt accounting policies accordingly. For example, managers who are aware that analysts look closely at the relative proportion of cost of goods sold may elect accounting policies that treat most overhead costs as period costs rather than as inventory costs. By reducing inventory costs, the gross margin percentage appears to be higher (i.e., cost of goods sold is lower relative to sales because fewer costs are inventoried), and the relative proportion of inventory in the total asset mix is also reduced.

Horizontal Analysis **Horizontal analysis** is used to determine the relative change in amounts between years. Obvious calculations include the trend of sales over time and the trend of net income over time. Analysts may construct special measures, such as EBIT (earnings before interest and taxes) or EBITDA (earnings before interest, taxes, depreciation, and amortization), and perform trend analysis on those measures. If the trend of sales is stronger than the trend of earnings, then the company is experiencing declining earnings relative to sales, even though earnings are increasing in absolute terms. That may be either good or bad (as will be explained in the following section), depending on other factors in the analysis.

Illustration

We will illustrate the use of vertical and horizontal analysis by examining the financial statements of CAE Inc. CAE designs and provides aircraft and marine simulation equipment and services. CAE also develops integrated training solutions for the military, commercial airlines, business aircraft operations, aircraft manufacturers, and marine vessel operators.

The basic data for the analysis is shown in Exhibit 21-1. Two years of balance sheet data and three years of income statement data are provided. These data are in the format and level of detail shown by the company in its annual financial statements and annual report. Note that CAE Inc. provides a discontinuous income statement. Revenues are disclosed, as are operating profits by major segments. However, no individual expenses are disclosed, other than those that must be disclosed to comply with GAAP standards.

The vertical analysis is shown in Exhibit 21-2. On the balance sheet, total assets is set equal to 100%, and all other numbers are computed as a percentage of total assets.[1] For example, property, plant, and equipment was 49.0% of assets in 20X2 but is 52.7% of assets in 20X3.

In the income statement, the base (= 100%) is sales revenue. All other amounts are calculated as a proportion of sales. In Exhibit 21-2, we can see that cost of sales declined slightly from 20X1 to 20X2, then rose significantly to 64.1% of revenue) in 20X3. The increase in cost of sales largely accounted for the dip in net earnings in 20X3 (10.5%) from 20X2 (13.3%).

The horizontal analysis is presented in Exhibit 21-3. In this example, the earliest year (20X1 or 20X2) is set as the base year (that is, equal to 100%) and all other years' amounts are calculated as a percentage of the base year. The base year doesn't have to be the earliest year—it could just as well be the most recent year.

Horizontal analysis is best used when the nature of the company's operations is relatively stable, with few changes in lines of business and without significant business combinations. Otherwise, it is difficult, if not impossible, to discern whether significant changes in balance

---

[1] The calculations for vertical and horizontal analysis are easy to do in a computer spreadsheet, since in each case the process is simply one of dividing all cells by a constant. The tedious part is entering the data in the worksheet in the first place.

EXHIBIT 21-1

DATA FOR VERTICAL AND HORIZONTAL ANALYSIS

Balance Sheet, 31 December (in millions)

	20X3	20X2
Assets		
Current assets:		
Cash and cash equivalents	$ 17.1	$ 88.8
Short term investments	45.8	75.9
Accounts receivable	373.1	378.2
Inventories	136.3	130.9
	572.3	673.8
Property, plant, and equipment	1,245.7	1,165.7
Intangible assets	171.7	163.4
Goodwill	366.8	375.5
	$2,356.5	$2,378.4
Liabilities and shareholders' equity		
Current liabilities:		
Accounts payable and accrued liabilities	$ 514.5	$ 609.6
Long-term debt due within one year	55.8	87.9
	570.3	697.5
Long-term debt	937.6	962.7
Future income taxes	98.4	106.1
	1,606.3	1,766.3
Shareholders' equity		
Capital stock	190.5	186.8
Retained earnings	559.7	425.3
	750.2	612.1
	$2,356.5	$2,378.4

Income Statement, Years ended 31 December (in millions)

	20X3	20X2	20X1
Revenue	$1,116.7	$1,127.6	$893.8
Cost of sales	718.0	690.7	556.3
Other operating expenses	190.9	194.8	185.5
	908.9	885.5	741.8
Earnings from continuing operations	207.8	242.1	152.0
Interest expense (recovery)	30.4	22.7	(6.3)
Income tax	60.2	69.9	52.2
Net earnings	$ 117.2	$ 149.5	$106.1

sheet and income statement amounts are the result of continuing business or of entering and leaving new lines of business. This is particularly a problem with conglomerate companies that buy many other companies during a year.

For this example, horizontal analysis emphasizes the decrease in cash and short-term investments (19% and 40% of the base year); and the 7% increase in property, plant, and

EXHIBIT 21-2

VERTICAL ANALYSIS*

Consolidated Balance Sheet, 31 December

	20X3	20X2
Assets		
Current assets:		
Cash and cash equivalents	0.7	3.7
Short-term investments	1.9	3.2
Accounts receivable	15.8	15.9
Inventories	5.8	5.5
	24.2	28.3
Property, plant and equipment	52.9	49.0
Intangible assets	7.3	6.9
Goodwill	15.6	15.8
	100.0%	100.0%
Liabilities and shareholders' equity		
Current liabilities:		
Accounts payable and accrued liabilities	21.8	25.6
Long-term debt due within one year	2.4	3.7
	24.2	29.3
Long-term debt	39.8	40.5
Future income taxes	4.2	4.5
	68.2	74.3
Shareholders' equity		
Capital stock	8.1	7.8
Retained earnings	23.8	17.9
	31.8	25.7
	100.0%	100.0%

Consolidated Income Statement, Year Ended 31 December

	20X3	20X2	20X1
Revenue	100.0%	100.0%	100.0%
Cost of sales	64.3	61.3	62.2
Other operating expenses	17.1	17.3	20.8
Total operating expenses	81.4	78.5	83.0
Earnings from continuing operations	18.6	21.5	17.0
Interest expense	2.7	2.0	(0.7)
Income tax	5.4	6.2	5.8
Net earnings	10.5%	13.3%	11.9%

equipment. There has been a significant decrease (to 82%) in current liabilities and retained earnings has grown to 132% of the base.

On the income statement, revenue grew by 31% since 20X1, while profit jumped by 41% in 20X2, only to drop back to an overall increase of only 15% over the two years. Obviously, revenue is growing faster than profit. What about interest expense—did it really go down by almost 500%? Well, hardly! The percentages not only were on a small base, but also the base was a negative expense. One must be very wary of large percentage changes like this. They almost always are the result of small base numbers and the percentages usually have little significance.

One thing to notice about horizontal analysis—you cannot add up the percentages in a given year to derive any totals. That is why there are no underscores in Exhibit 21-3.

EXHIBIT 21-3

HORIZONTAL ANALYSIS
Balance Sheet, 31 December

	20X3	20X2
Assets		
Current assets:		
Cash and cash equivalents	19%	100%
Short-term investments	60	100
Accounts receivable	99	100
Inventories	104	100
	85	100
Property, plant, and equipment	107	100
Intangible assets	105	100
Goodwill	98	100
	99%	100%
Liabilities and shareholders' equity		
Current liabilities:		
Accounts payable and accrued liabilities	84%	100%
Long-term debt due within one year	65	100
	82	100
Long-term debt	97	100
Future income taxes	93	100
	91	100
Shareholders' equity		
Capital stock	102	100
Retained earnings	132	100
	123	100
	99%	100%

Income Statement, Years ended 31 December

	20X3	20X2	20X1
Revenue	131%	126%	100%
Cost of sales	129	124	100
Other operating expenses	103	105	100
Total operating expenses	123	119	100
Earnings from continuing operations	137	159	100
Interest expense	(483)	(360)	100
Income tax	115	134	100
Net earnings	111%	141%	100%

CONCEPT REVIEW

1. Why is it crucial to approach financial statement analysis with a clear understanding of the decision focus?

2. How can an analyst find out what accounting policies a company is using?

3. Why would a financial analyst want to recast a company's financial statements before performing ratio analysis or other analytical techniques?

4. What is the difference between vertical analysis and horizontal analysis of financial statement components?

RATIO ANALYSIS

Common-size (vertical) and trend (horizontal) analysis are systematic computations of index ratios, but the term **ratio analysis** is most commonly applied to a large family of ratios that compare the proportional *relationship* between two different accounts amounts in a single year's financial statements. Common-size ratios are strictly within single financial statements, but other ratio analyses can be either between amounts within a single statement or between amounts in two statements. However, there are some potential drawbacks to using ratios:

- Ratios are meaningful only if there is a clear understanding of the purpose of each relationship.
- Ratios are only as valid as the data from which they are derived.
- Ratios require a basis for comparison.
- Ratios are a clue to areas needing investigation—they rarely, if ever, supply answers.

Throughout this book, we have emphasized that different accounting policy decisions and different accounting estimates can yield dramatically different reported results. If the basic financial data are subject to variability, then ratios calculated from that data are unreliable.

Indeed, managers may deliberately select accounting policies and estimates with the intent of affecting certain ratios; we have repeatedly referred to this motivation throughout the book. For example, the decision to lease major operating assets through an operating lease rather than a capital lease often is motivated by management's desire to keep the implicit debt off the balance sheet. In using ratios, therefore, the rule most certainly must be: *analyst be wary!*

There are literally dozens of ratios that can be computed from a single year's financial statements. The important task for an analyst is to focus on the ratios that have primary meaning for the decision at hand. There are many ways of grouping ratios, but those that will be discussed in the following pages are grouped as follows:

- Profitability ratios
- Efficiency ratios
- Solvency ratios
- Liquidity ratios

Profitability Ratios

It is common for the press and individual investors to talk about the return on sales that a company is earning, such as "WestJet had earnings of $24 million on revenues of $1,395 million, a return of less than 2%."

Statements like this suggest that the most important profit relationship is between profit and revenue. However, the driving force in capitalistic enterprise is to earn a return *on invested capital.* If you are going to put money into a savings account, you normally will want to put it in the bank or trust company that will give you the largest interest rate. You want to know how much you will make on your investment, *in percentage terms.* You will compare *rates* of interest, not absolute amounts, because the amount that you have in your savings account will probably vary over time.

The same principle is true for all investments. An enterprise's profitability is measured by the rate of return that it can earn on its invested capital, and not by the absolute dollar profit that it generates. It is common in the newspapers and other popular press to cite huge profit figures, such as the multi-billion dollar profits for the large Canadian banks. There is always a strong undertow of suspicion that these amounts are "excessive" because they are so large.

A billion dollars in profit is high if it was earned on an investment of only $2 or $3 billion. But if it was the return on a $50 billion investment, then the investment is yielding very poor returns indeed.

Similarly, companies may proudly cite sharply increased profit figures, perhaps up 40% or 50% over the preceding year or maybe even doubled, as evidence of the managers' fiscal and business acumen. But if a 50% increase in profit was accompanied by a 100% increase in invested capital, then the return on investment has gone down, not up.

Sometimes an increase in absolute profit is due to a takeover of another company; the current year's earnings are a reflection of *both* companies' performance, whereas the previous year's results included only the parent company. The return on the current combined company has to be compared to the return on the sum of both companies in the previous year in order to get any meaningful comparison.

The basic point is that profitability must always be assessed as some form of *return on investment.* By its very nature, a return on investment figure will consist of a numerator from the income statement and a denominator from the balance sheet. Therefore, **profitability ratios** always cross statements. Assessments of profitability that focus only on the income statement will always be inadequate. The ratio of net income to sales is of limited use because it says nothing about the amount of investment that was employed to generate that level of sales and net income.

A return on investment figure will always reflect the impact of the accounting policy choices made by the company (as will all ratios), and often it is necessary to recast the statements before computing the ratios. There is no truer context for the old GIGO adage (garbage in, garbage out); ratios are only as useful as the measurements underlying the numerator and denominator.

Some Types of Profitability Ratios When profitability is assessed, the analyst has to view *investment* from the appropriate standpoint for the decision at hand. A common shareholder will be interested primarily in **return on equity;** a preferred shareholder will be interested in the return on total shareholders' equity; and a bond holder will be interested in the return on long-term capital (i.e., shareholders' equity plus long-term debt, often called **total capitalization**). All analysts will be interested in the underlying **return on total assets**. These are some of the possible denominators for a profitability ratio.

The numerator of any profitability ratio will reflect a return *over time* because it is derived from the income statement. In contrast, the denominator will reflect balance sheet values at a *point in time.* In order to make the numerator and denominator consistent, the denominator should be calculated as the *average* over the year. Ideally, the denominator should be based on an average of monthly or quarterly investment, but a simpler and more common approach is to average the balance sheet numbers at the beginning and end of the year being analyzed. However, if there were major changes in investment during the year (such as the acquisition of another company in the first quarter of the year), then a weighted average should be estimated.

The numerator of any ratio must be consistent with its denominator in substance as well as on the time dimension. The return to common shareholders is measured not by net income, but by *earnings available to common shareholders* (which basically is net income less preferred share dividends, as explained in Chapter 19).

Similarly, the **return on long-term capital** must be calculated by dividing total capitalization into a profit measure that removes the effects of financing. Since interest expense is included in net income, and since interest also affects income tax, the numerator must have the effects of interest on long-term debt removed and must adjust income tax, either (1) by

profitability ratios

ratios designed to assess profitability of operations

removing tax completely (to get EBIT, a pre-tax return on investment) or (2) by adding back the after-tax interest expense by multiplying interest by $1 - t$, where t = average tax rate for the corporation.

Return ratios are as follows:

Return on long-term capital, before tax:

$$\frac{\text{Net income} + \text{Interest expense on long-term} + \text{Income tax expense (EBIT)}}{\text{Average long-term debt} + \text{Average total owners' equity}}$$

Return on long-term capital, after tax:

$$\frac{\text{Net income} + [\text{Interest expense on long-term debt} \times (1 - t)]}{\text{Average long-term debt} + \text{Average total owners' equity}}$$

Return on *total assets* can be measured by dividing total assets into EBIT, where the interest addback is for total interest, on both long-term and short-term debt. This will yield a pre-tax return:

Return on total assets, before tax:

$$\frac{\text{Net income} + \text{Total interest expense} + \text{Income tax expense}}{\text{Average total assets}}$$

An after-tax rate of return can easily be found by adjusting the interest expense to an after-tax amount by multiplying it by $(1 - t)$:

Return on total assets, after tax:

$$\frac{\text{Net income} + [\text{Total interest expense} \times (1 - t)]}{\text{Average total assets}}$$

Whatever profitability ratio(s) is (are) used, the effects of accounting policies (and of operating policies, where these create off-balance-sheet assets and liabilities) must be considered. Even when assets are reflected on the balance sheet, their values are hard to assess. Asset carrying values are normally at historical cost, which means that the equity values also implicitly reflect historical costs. If the assets are old and the profitability is compared to a company that has newer assets, the company with the older assets should appear to be more profitable because its asset base reflects pre-inflationary dollars and is more fully depreciated. The net income figure will reflect lower relative depreciation expenses, due to the relatively lower cost of older assets. The apparent profitability in such a company can be quite misleading; if new investment were made, the same return would probably not be earned.

Some analysts attempt to adjust for differing relative accumulated depreciation by basing the measurement on EBITDA, earnings before interest, taxes, depreciation, and amortization.[2]

---

[2] In the airline industry, aircraft rental payments usually are also added back, so the measure becomes EBITADAR: earnings before interest, tax, amortization, depreciation, and aircraft rental.

Return on gross assets, before tax:

$$\frac{\text{Net income + Depreciation and amortization expense + Total interest expense + Income tax expense}}{\text{Average total assets + Average accumulated depreciation and amortization}}$$

Return on common shareholders' equity:

$$\frac{\text{Net income − Preferred dividends}}{\text{Average shareholders' equity}}$$

This ratio measures the return that the company has been able to earn on the shareholders' equity after all other prior claims on the company's earnings have been subtracted. Net income already includes interest expense (and its tax benefit), and thus it is necessary only to deduct the dividends on any preferred shares that are outstanding. The preferred dividends are deducted *whether or not they have been paid*, as long as they are cumulative.

It is very useful to compare this ratio with the return on assets. If financial leverage is positive, the return on shareholder's equity will be higher than the return on assets. However, if after-tax interest on debt is higher than the return on assets, this ratio will be lower than the return on assets and may be negative.

Operating margin:

$$\frac{\text{Net income + Interest + Income taxes (EBIT)}}{\text{Total revenue}}$$

In the financial press, this is the most commonly used ratio. It tells us how much the company earns on each dollar (or euro, yuan, yen, peso, etc.) of revenue. Since the numerator is EBIT, it removes the effect of financing and makes it easier to compare profitability between companies that use different proportions of debt versus equity.

However, this is an incomplete ratio. It gives no indication of the return on *investment* that the company is achieving. Operating margin must be used in conjunction with asset turnover, a ratio that we discuss in the next section (and illustrated in Exhibit 21-5).

Lessons to Remember When Evaluating Profitability:

The moral of this tale is:

- Profitability ratios must have a measure of investment in the denominator (based on the balance sheet) and a measure of profitability in the numerator (based on the income statement).
- The denominator and the numerator must be logically consistent.
- Both the denominator and the numerator are the product of many accounting policy choices and even more accounting estimates by management.
- Both components of the ratio may need adjustment both for accounting policies and for off-balance-sheet financing and investment.

Profitability ratios are summarized in Exhibit 21-4.

EXHIBIT 21-4

SUMMARY OF PROFITABILITY RATIOS

Ratio Name	Computation	Significance and Difficulties
Return on long-term capital, before tax	$$\frac{\text{Net income} + \text{Interest expense on long-term debt} + \text{Income tax}}{\text{Average long-term debt} + \text{Average owners' equity}}$$	Indicates the return on invested capital, before considering the form of financing. Useful for comparing to interest rates to test for leverage effect.
Return on long-term capital, after tax	$$\frac{\text{Net income} + [\text{Interest expense on long-term debt} \times (1-t)]}{\text{Average long-term debt} + \text{Average owners' equity}}$$	Measures the return on long-term capital investment, excluding current liabilities.
Return on total assets, before tax	$$\frac{\text{Net income} + \text{Total interest expense} + \text{Income tax expense}^*}{\text{Average total assets}}$$	Indicates the overall return that the company is earning on its asset investment. Old, depreciated assets will tend to increase the apparent rate of return.
Return on total assets, after tax	$$\frac{\text{Net income} + [\text{Total interest expense} \times (1-t)]}{\text{Average total assets}}$$	Similar to the above, but after taxes.

*usually called EBIT: **E**arnings **B**efore **I**nterest and **T**axes

Return on common shareholders' equity	$$\frac{\text{Net income} - \text{Preferred dividends}}{\text{Average total shareholders' equity} - \text{Average preferred share equity}}$$	Shows the historical after-tax return to shareholders for the period. Uses *earnings available to common shareholders*, which is after interest and dividends for all senior securities.
Return on gross assets, before tax	$$\frac{(\text{EBIT} + \text{Depreciation})^*}{\text{Average total assets} + \text{Average accumulated depreciation}}$$	Indicates the return on invested capital without including return of capital (that is, depreciation or amortization).

*called EBITDA: **E**arnings **B**efore **I**nterest, **T**axes, **D**epreciation and **A**mortization

Operating margin	$$\frac{\text{Net income} + \text{Interest} + \text{Income tax}^*}{\text{Total revenue}}$$	Indicates the profit margin (before taxes) earned on each dollar of sales. Should be used in conjunction with *asset turnover*.

*EBIT (see Exhibit 21-5).

Profitability ratios do have one clear advantage over other measures of profitability (such as earnings per share or total net income). The advantage is that since profitability is expressed as a *percentage* of investment, it is possible to separate true increased profitability from normal growth. Most profitable companies pay out only a portion of their earnings as dividends. Some companies pay no dividends at all. The earnings retained by the company are reinvested in operations; since shareholders' equity increases, so must the net assets of the company. Since there is more invested capital, the company will have to generate a larger net income in order to maintain the same return on invested capital. This is normal growth.

The proper test of managerial competence is not whether management has been able to increase EPS or net income; in a profitable industry and good economic times, managers have to be truly incompetent *not* to enjoy increased profits. The proper test is whether management has been able to maintain or, preferably, increase the rate of return on the increasing investment base.

Components of Profitability Ratios The previous section discussed several overall measures of profitability. A key to profitability analysis, however, involves breaking profitability down to its basic components. For example, any company's return on total assets can be dissected into two components: asset turnover and operating margin. Recall that return on assets is calculated as follows:

Earnings before interest and taxes (EBIT) ÷ Average total assets = **Return on assets**

This can be disaggregated into two other ratios:

1. EBIT ÷ Total revenue = **Operating margin**
2. Total revenue ÷ Average total assets = **Asset turnover**

Operating margin multiplied by asset turnover equals return on assets:

$$\frac{EBIT}{Revenue} \times \frac{Revenue}{Assets} = \frac{EBIT}{Assets}$$

Earlier, we pointed out that earnings as a proportion of revenues (i.e., **operating margin**), by itself, is not a useful measure of profitability because it ignores the amount of investment that was employed to generate that level of sales and income. Unfortunately, the financial press is full of articles that talk about companies' profit margins without giving the other half of the picture. A valid and often successful strategy for a company is to increase its sales volume (i.e., its *asset turnover*) by cutting its profit margin. Although the profit margin goes down, the return on assets will rise if the increase in sales volume is enough to make up for the reduced profit margin. If profitability is assessed only by means of operating margin, then the analyst is ignoring the increase in sales that results from the decreased profit margin per dollar of sales.

Other companies may use a strategy of increasing the operating margin, even at the risk of a possible loss of sales volume. If the operating margin is very small, such as 4%, only a 2% increase in price will increase the operating margin by 50% (that is, from 4% of sales to 6% of sales). The company will be better off unless sales volume drops by 33%; that will depend on the price elasticity of demand. In a highly competitive market, a small increase in price could easily cost the company more through a drop in sales volume than it gains in margin.

The point is that *judging profitability by using only the operating margin is always wrong*. Operating margin does not reflect the level of investment, and profitability can be judged only in relation to investment.

Efficiency Ratios

The objective of **efficiency ratios** is to analyze certain aspects of operational efficiency. Efficiency ratios are also known as **turnover ratios** because the two most commonly cited efficiency ratios are *accounts receivable turnover* and *inventory turnover*.

Accounts Receivable Turnover This ratio is intended to measure the average length of time that it takes to collect accounts receivable. The turnover ratio is determined by dividing sales revenue by average accounts receivable.

Accounts receivable turnover = Sales revenue ÷ Average accounts receivable

If the ratio is 4:1, for example, it supposedly indicates that, on average, the accounts receivable "turns over" four times a year, which implies that the average collection period is one fourth of a year, or three months.

This ratio is translated into a parallel ratio called the **average collection period of accounts receivable** by dividing the accounts receivable turnover into 365 days; a turnover of four yields an apparent collection period of 91 days.

The numerator should include only sales on account, but an external analyst of a retail enterprise will have no way of knowing how much of the sales revenue was on account. In some industries, however, it is rare to have cash sales and therefore the total sales can safely be assumed to be sales on account.

The **accounts receivable turnover ratio** is difficult to interpret. Presumably, a short period is better than a long one because it indicates that the company is able to realize cash from its sales in a short period of time. It also implies that there are very few long-outstanding accounts that may prove to be uncollectible. This might be true for companies in industries where there is a widespread customer base and essentially equal terms given by each company to its customers.

However, one is quite likely to encounter companies that have special relationships with major customers. The major customers may effectively dictate payment terms. For example, a company that derives most of its revenue from government contracts may show a very slow turnover, and yet the collectibility of the accounts is assured despite the "age" of the accounts.

Another problem for an external analyst is that the accounts receivable shown on the balance sheet may not be typical throughout the year. The fiscal year of a business may be established on the basis of the *natural business year* and the balance sheet date may be the lowest period of activity in a seasonal business. The accounts receivable may be at their lowest level of the whole year. Bankers and other analysts who use the turnover ratio may insist on monthly data. However, an even more likely scenario for such analysts is to request an **accounts receivable aging schedule**, in which the receivables are categorized by the length of time they have been outstanding (e.g., less than 30 days, 31–60 days, 61–90 days, and more than 90 days). Any special payment terms (such as extra-long payments for related companies) are specifically indicated.[3]

In summary, the accounts receivable turnover ratio can be used by an external analyst only as a very rough indication of collection period. It is difficult to interpret, but it can be used as the basis of inquiries to the company's management. Because of the problems cited above, an analyst may be more interested in the *trend* of the ratio, as an indicator of whether the collection period is stable or is getting longer or shorter. If the ratio is changing, it will not be easy for an external analyst to determine the cause of the change and whether the change is good or bad.

For detailed analysis of the creditworthiness of the accounts receivable, an aging schedule is much more useful but is unavailable to most external analysts.

Inventory Turnover The **inventory turnover ratio** indicates the relationship between the cost of goods sold and the average inventory balance:

Inventory turnover = Cost of goods sold ÷ Average inventory

average collection period of accounts receivable

the number of days required by a company to collect sales made on credit; the accounts receivable turnover stated in days

accounts receivable aging schedule

a schedule categorizing accounts receivable by the length of time they have been outstanding

---

[3] Some companies give different payment terms to different customers. In that case, aging schedules are usually based on the due date of payment and reflect the number of days past due.

A high turnover ratio is often presumed to be better than a low ratio because a high ratio suggests that less investment in inventory is needed to generate sales. A low ratio, on the other hand, suggests that there may be excessive quantities of inventory on hand or that there are a lot of slow-moving or unsaleable items in inventory.

The objective of inventory management is to maintain *optimum* inventory levels rather than *minimum* inventory levels. Maintaining too low an inventory may result in items not being available for sale when the customer requests them, and therefore sales are less than they should be. Furthermore, with the advent of just-in-time inventory systems in many businesses, suppliers are sometimes left with the burden of maintaining inventories. This means that a supplier's inventory may be higher than in former years, and yet the sale ability of that inventory may be virtually guaranteed through the supplier arrangements. Therefore, a low inventory turnover may not necessarily be bad, and a high turnover may not necessarily be ideal.

In a manufacturing enterprise, the inventories include raw materials, work in process, and finished goods. If the total inventory figure is used in computed inventory turnover, the ratio will yield an estimate of the number of times that the full production cycle is completed during the year. If the ratio is based only on finished goods, the ratio will indicate the number of times that the finished goods inventory turns over during the year. Dividing the finished goods inventory turnover into 365 will yield the average number of days that finished inventory is held before being sold.

Asset Turnover   As we have seen, **asset turnover** is a major component of return on assets. It measures the sales dollars generated by assets. The higher this ratio, the more efficient the company is at using its assets in its sales effort.

The principal efficiency ratios are summarized in Exhibit 21-5.

Solvency Ratios

The basic objective of **solvency ratios** is to assess the ability of the company to make both the interest and principal payments on its long-term obligations. These ratios stress the long-term financial and operating structure of the company. They can be further classified as follows:

- **Leverage ratios**, which measure the relative amount of the company's financing that was obtained through debt; and

- **Debt service ratios**, which test the ability of the company to generate sufficient cash flow from operations to pay the debt interest or the debt interest plus principal payments.

Solvency ratios interact with profitability ratios, because a company's long-run solvency is in doubt if the company cannot generate enough profit not only to service the debt but also to earn an adequate return for shareholders.

Leverage Ratios   Leverage is the extent to which a company uses fixed-term obligations to finance its assets. In public companies, the focus is on long-term debt (plus retractable preferred shares, if any). For analysis of a private company, the focus is on interest-bearing debt, primarily bank debt, both short term and long term; loans from shareholders are not included but are reclassified as owners' equity.[4]

The concept of leverage is that if a company can earn a rate of return on its assets that is higher than the rate it has to pay on debt, the shareholders will benefit because the surplus return (i.e., above the rate of interest) will flow through to benefit the shareholders in the form of higher earnings per share. Of course, if a company earns *less* on its investment than

---

[4] The concept of leverage is discussed more extensively in financial management texts. For example, see *Fundamentals of Corporate Finance, 3rd Canadian Edition* by Richard Brealey, Elizabeth Maynes, et al. (McGraw-Hill Ryerson, 2006).

EXHIBIT 21-5

SUMMARY OF EFFICIENCY RATIOS

Ratio Name	Computation	Significance and Difficulties
Accounts receivable turnover	$$\frac{\text{Sales revenue (on account)}}{\text{Average trade accounts receivable}}$$	Indicates efficiency of trade accounts receivable collection but is difficult to interpret without knowledge of the customer base. Average year-end accounts receivable balances may not be representative of seasonal variation.
Average collection period of accounts receivable	$$\frac{\text{365 (days)}}{\text{Accounts receivable turnover}}$$	Converts the accounts receivable turnover into the average collection period, in days. Has the same measurement problems as does the turnover ratio.
Inventory turnover	$$\frac{\text{Cost of goods sold}}{\text{Average inventory}}$$	Yields the number of times that the inventory "turns over" during a year. A low ratio may indicate possible overstocking, if valid comparative information is available. Year-end average inventory balances may not be representative of seasonal variation.
Asset turnover	$$\frac{\text{Total revenue}}{\text{Average total assets}}$$	Shows the level of sales that are being generated per dollar of investment in assets. This is one component of return on assets, and should be used in conjunction with *operating margin* (see Exhibit 21-4).

negative leverage

whereby a company earns a lower rate on equity than the rate of return on assets because the company uses debt financing that has a cost in excess of the return on assets

the rate of interest, the shareholders' interests will suffer; this is known as **negative leverage**. Therefore, leverage plays an important role in the assessment of profitability because it affects the distribution of the earnings to the different providers of capital. Leverage also is a measure of solvency, because it is one measure of risk.

If a company has a large amount of debt relative to its owners' equity, the company is said to be *highly levered* (or *highly leveraged*). Leverage increases the volatility of the residual earnings to the shareholders, because fluctuations in earnings will be amplified when the constant of interest expense is deducted.

Some companies try to lessen this risk by entering into variable-rate loans instead of fixed-rate loans. If the company's earnings are responsive to the general economy, and if interest rates tend to decrease when the economy slows, then a decrease in earnings might be at least partially matched by a decrease in interest rates. Some companies that have substantial fixed-rate obligations effectively convert these to variable-rate obligations by entering into interest rate swaps.

The most basic measure of leverage is the **debt-to-equity ratio**. The denominator is the total owners' equity (excluding retractable preferred shares, which should be classified as debt, but including shareholders' loans). The numerator of the ratio can be defined in a number of ways, depending on the nature of the company and the objectives of the analyst. At a minimum, the numerator would include all long-term fixed-term obligations and any retractable preferred shares that may exist. Many analysts also reclassify the future income tax liability as equity. Included in the numerator can be the following:

- Retractable preferred shares
- Capital lease obligations shown on the balance sheet
- Estimated present value of operating lease obligations on assets essential to operations
- Current portion of long-term debt
- Short-term bank loans
- All other monetary obligations, including trade accounts payable

When the ratio is computed for assessing solvency (and risk of insolvency), all monetary obligations are normally included (excluding future income taxes, unearned revenues, and other miscellaneous deferred credits). The return on total assets (EBIT ÷ total assets) can be directly compared to the average interest rate on debt to see if leverage is positive or negative. The margin by which the return on assets exceeds the average interest rate is the **margin of safety**; the closer they get, the greater the risk of negative leverage.

Variants to the basic debt-to-equity ratio use some measure of *invested capital* as the denominator, which includes both debt and equity. These can be defined as follows:

Debt-to-total capitalization = Long-term debt ÷ (Long-term debt + Owners' equity)

Debt-to-capital employed = (Long-term debt + Current liabilities) ÷ (Long-term debt + Current liabilities − Current assets (or liquid current assets) + Owners' equity)

Debt-to-total assets = (Long-term debt + Current liabilities) ÷ Total assets

Instead of computing debt relative to owners' equity, these variants calculate debt as a portion of a broader definition of investment.

As is the case with the basic debt-to-equity ratio, the numerator and denominator may vary somewhat depending on the point of view of the analyst. These ratios answer the question: how much of the company's invested capital has been obtained through debt? The components of these alternative ratios are the same as for the basic debt-to-equity ratio, except that the numerator is also included in the denominator. Therefore, the value for a debt-to-equity ratio will be higher than for a debt-to-total-assets ratio. A debt-to-equity ratio of 1:1 will be a debt-to-total capitalization ratio of 1:2. This arithmetic may seem obvious, but since all of these types of ratios are commonly referred to as debt-to-equity ratios, it is important to be clear when discussing a debt-to-equity ratio that all parties to the discussion are in agreement on the definition of the ratio.

The debt-to-equity ratio (and its variants) is a measure of *financial risk*. Because leverage increases the volatility of earnings, the increase in return to shareholders is offset by an increase in risk. A high debt-to-equity ratio is safest when a company has a high and steady level of earnings, particularly when the company can control its return on assets. High levels of financial risk can be most safely used in companies that have low levels of *operating risk*. Operating risk is the responsiveness of a company's earnings to fluctuations in its level of revenue. The more volatile operating earnings are, the less a company should rely on financial leverage.

For example, leverage is high in the financial services sector and in regulated public utilities. In financial institutions, the interest being paid on debt and the interest charged to borrowers are both responsive to money market conditions. As long as the debt portfolio is matched (in maturities) to the asset portfolio, net earnings can be relatively stable. In public utilities, rates are set in order to achieve a rate of return on assets that has been approved by the regulators; the permitted rate of return on assets is too low to attract share equity, but by levering up the earnings through lower-rate debt, utilities can provide an adequate return to attract share capital.

Debt-Service Ratios A traditional ratio used in solvency analysis is the **times-interest-earned ratio**, which is the ratio of interest expense to earnings before interest and taxes (EBIT). This is believed to indicate the relative amount by which earnings can decrease before there is not enough net income to pay the interest. In reality, the interest would be paid, since failure to do so would risk throwing the company into receivership and possibly bankruptcy.

Since interest expense is tax deductible, the numerator of the ratio normally is EBIT. Again, it may be appropriate to use earnings adjusted for accounting policies, as described in earlier sections. Also, the numerator should include interest on all indebtedness, long term and short term, plus interest on capital leases. Default on any component of interest can have dire consequences.

If a times-interest-earned ratio is approaching 1:1, the company already is suffering negative financial leverage. It is possible to estimate the number of times by which EBIT must exceed interest expense in order to avoid negative leverage. To avoid negative leverage, a company must earn an overall rate on its total capitalization that is at least equal to the interest being charged on the debt. Therefore, if the amount of owners' equity is three times the amount of debt, EBIT should be at least four times the total interest expense (that is, the earnings on one part debt *plus* three parts owners' equity).

A broader debt-service ratio is **times debt service earned**. This ratio goes well beyond the times-interest-earned ratio to look not only at the amount of interest that must be paid, but also at the amount of principal payments that must be made. The times-interest-earned ratio implicitly assumes that debt can be refinanced, which may be a valid assumption in prosperous times. But if the company's fortunes decline or interest rates soar, it may be difficult to obtain new financing to "roll over" the debt. The debt-service ratio therefore attempts to look at the ability of a company to *service* its debt load.

The numerator of this ratio is *cash*, not earnings. The starting point is the cash flow from operations as reported on the cash flow statement. This amount should be adjusted by adding back interest paid. Interest is tax deductible, and therefore the current income tax paid should also be added back to the cash flow from operations.

The denominator should include not only interest paid, but also the cash outflows for principal repayments and capital lease payments. Of interest are not only the flows in the current period but also the flows disclosed for future periods. The numerator is not always easy to measure and requires a careful reading of the notes. The cash flows relating to debt and capital leases for the next five years should be disclosed in the notes to the financial statements.

Taxes raise a particular problem, because interest is deductible for tax purposes while principal payments are not. Since principal payments have to be paid in after-tax dollars, it takes a higher pre-tax cash flow from operations to generate enough cash to repay principal. On the other hand, capital lease payments usually are deductible in full, including both the capital portion and the implicit interest expense, thereby adding an additional complication. The easiest way around this problem is to divide the non-tax-deductible cash flows by 1 minus the company's average tax rate: $1 - t$. This converts the principal payments to pre-tax equivalents and then all amounts in the ratio are comparable.

Major solvency ratios are summarized in Exhibit 21-6.

Liquidity Ratios

The general objective of **liquidity ratios** is to test the company's ability to meet its short-term financial obligations. Therefore, the focus is on the composition of current assets and current liabilities.

Current Ratio The grandparent of all ratios is the **current ratio**. Use of this ratio has been traced back almost 100 years. It is a simple ratio to calculate:

$$\text{Current ratio} = \text{Current assets} \div \text{Current liabilities}$$

The current assets are the "reservoir" of assets from which the current liabilities will be paid. Therefore, this ratio suggests the margin of safety for creditors. A common rule of thumb is that current assets should be twice the current liabilities; the ratio should be 2:1.

EXHIBIT 21-6

SUMMARY OF SOLVENCY RATIOS

Ratio Name	Computation	Significance and Difficulties
Debt to equity	$$\frac{\text{Total long-term debt}}{\text{Total owners' equity}}$$ or	Indicates the relative proportions by which "permanent" investment is financed through debt versus owners' equity. Retractable preferred shares and loans from shareholders should be classified in accordance with their substance. Some analysts also reclassify the future income tax liability as equity.
	$$\frac{\text{Total liabilities, current + long term}}{\text{Total owners' equity}}$$	Similar indication as above, but includes *all* liabilities. May vary if the level of current liabilities changes year by year. Reclassifications may be necessary, as indicated above.
Debt to total capitalization	$$\frac{\text{Long-term debt}}{\text{Long-term debt + Owners' equity}}$$	Indicates the proportion of long-term capital that is financed through debt.
Debt to capital employed	$$\frac{\text{Long-term debt + Current liabilities}}{\text{Long-term debt + Current liabilities} - \text{Current assets + Owners' equity}}$$	Shows the total debt burden of the company when current assets are netted out. Future income tax is often excluded, and only liquid current assets may be netted against current liabilities.
Debt to total assets	$$\frac{\text{Long-term + Current liabilities}}{\text{Total assets}}$$	Indicates the proportion by which assets are financed through debt.
Times interest earned	$$\frac{\text{Net income + Interest expense + Tax}}{\text{Interest expense}}$$	Indicates the ability of the company to withstand a downturn in earnings and still be able to earn enough to pay interest (and avoid default). Reflects accounting earnings rather than cash flow.
Times debt service earned	$$\frac{\text{Cash flow from operations + Interest + Tax}}{\text{Interest + [(Projected annual principal payments and capital lease payments)} \div (1 - t)]}$$	Indicates the ability of the company to service its debt, including leases, from its pre-tax operating cash flow. Operating cash flow must include changes in current monetary items.

But like all rules of thumb, a ratio of 2:1 may not be appropriate for a particular company. If cash flows are steady and reliable, then there is no need for such a high ratio. On the other hand, a volatile cash inflow may require a higher average ratio in order to provide a margin of safety so that the company can continue to pay its payroll and other immediate cash expenses.

If the current ratio is used as a measure of liquidity, then the components of current assets must be "liquid" or realizable in the short run. Current assets include inventory and prepaid expenses. Prepaid expenses obviously are not convertible into cash, but they do indicate expenses that have already been paid and that therefore will not require an additional cash outflow in the next period.

Inventories are a bigger problem. If the inventories are readily saleable, then it is appropriate to include them as a liquid asset. But there is no way for an external analyst to tell whether the inventories are saleable or not; there is no disclosure that can help. In fact, inventories that are not very saleable will accumulate, increasing the current assets and increasing the current ratio. If inventories are an important component of current assets, increasing inventory levels can be a danger sign.

Current liabilities may include unearned revenue. As with prepaid expenses, unearned revenue represents past cash flow. It does not represent a cash obligation of the company in the same way that accounts and notes payable do.

Quick Ratio The **quick ratio** is also called the **acid-test ratio.** It is intended to overcome the deficiencies of the current ratio by excluding inventories and other non-monetary current assets. To be consistent, non-monetary current liabilities (e.g., unearned revenue and other deferred credits) should also be excluded. Therefore, the ratio is determined as follows:

$$\text{Quick ratio} = \text{Monetary current assets} \div \text{Monetary current liabilities}$$

A ratio of less than 1:1 is generally considered to be undesirable. However, a low ratio is no cause for concern if the company's operating cash flow is steady and reliable. As with solvency ratios, liquidity ratios can be effectively interpreted only in reference to the *operating risk* and *financial risk* of the company. If cash inflows are stable, a low liquidity ratio should not be cause for concern. But if cash flows are very volatile, even a high liquidity ratio should not make the analyst complacent. Cash can vanish from a high-risk operation very quickly.

Defensive-Interval Ratio The current ratio and the quick ratio are static ratios, in that they look only at the ability of the company to pay its short-term obligations with the short-term assets that exist at the balance sheet date. Both ratios are flawed because they do not consider the rate at which expenditures are incurred. An alternative ratio is one that tests the number of days that the company could operate if the cash inflow were cut off, such as by a strike or by an emergency shutdown. While many expenses are eliminated in a shutdown, others continue. In order for a company to survive a shutdown, it has to be able to pay its continuing operating costs. The intent of the **defensive-interval ratio** is to see how many days the company could pay its continuing expenses in the absence of an inflow of cash from operating revenue. The basic form of the ratio is as follows:

$$\frac{\text{Monetary current assets}}{\text{Annual operating expenditures} \div 365}$$

The difficulty with this ratio is in deciding what should be in the numerator and what should be in the denominator. The numerator clearly should be restricted to monetary assets (e.g., cash, accounts receivable, and temporary investments), but the numerator should be reduced by any short-term monetary liabilities that could not be deferred if the company faced a shutdown.

The denominator would include only those cash expenses that will continue in the event of a shutdown. Many labour costs would be eliminated in a shutdown, as would acquisitions of new inventories and supplies. The problem for the external analyst, however, is that the financial statements seldom give enough detail to permit this analysis. Therefore, external analysts usually use short-term monetary assets (without deduction for monetary liabilities) as the numerator and operating expenses less non-cash charges (e.g., depreciation and amortization) in the denominator. The name of the ratio, by the way, comes from the concept of the short-term monetary assets as being *defensive assets.*

The major liquidity ratios are summarized in Exhibit 21-7.

Consolidated Statements

Most Canadian corporations, whether incorporated federally or provincially, operate through a series of subsidiaries. This is true even of some quite small companies. One small chain of three restaurants, for example, has each restaurant set up as a separate corporation. A company that operates in more than one province almost certainly will have at least one subsidiary in each province. Therefore, the analyst must be aware of just what he or she is analyzing: an individual corporation or a corporate group?

Canadian GAAP requires that the primary set of statements for a company with subsidiaries is the *consolidated* financial statements, wherein all of the assets, liabilities, revenues, and expenses of all of the companies in the group are combined. When the company under analysis is a public company, *only* the consolidated statements will be publicly available. The statements will give no clue as to which items belong to which legal corporate entity. But if the company is a private corporation, there may be no consolidated statements because a private company can opt out of preparing consolidated statements under differential accounting.

An investor who is considering purchasing the shares of a corporation usually will want to see statements that show the full resources under control of the corporation, including those held by subsidiaries. The prospective investor is investing in the *economic entity*, and the consolidated statements are the appropriate basis of analysis.

A creditor or lender is in a different position, however. A creditor or lender holds an obligation only of the *separate legal entity*, not of the corporate group. Therefore, creditors or lenders must be careful to analyze the separate-entity statements of the specific corporation to which they are extending credit or granting loans. The consolidated statements can give a very misleading view; lenders have been burnt in the past by lending money to a parent company on the basis of consolidated statements only to discover later that all of the cash flow is in the operating subsidiaries. Lenders may demand cross-company guarantees of debt, but trade creditors usually cannot demand such a guarantee. Cross-company guarantees may not be very effective anyway, since they are usually subordinated and there may be legal impediments to their enforcement when they cross borders, especially national borders.

EXHIBIT 21-7

SUMMARY OF LIQUIDITY RATIOS

Ratio Name	Computation	Significance and Difficulties
Current	$\dfrac{\text{Current assets}}{\text{Current liabilities}}$	Indicates ability to pay liabilities with current assets; but includes inventories, deferred charges, and deferred credits.
Quick (acid-test)	$\dfrac{\text{Monetary current assets}}{\text{Monetary current liabilities}}$	A more refined test than the current ratio because it excludes non-monetary assets and liabilities.
Defensive interval	$\dfrac{\text{Monetary current assets}}{\text{Projected daily operating expenditures}}$	Indicates the approximate number of days that the company can continue to operate with the currently available liquid assets. Denominator is very difficult to estimate by an external analyst.

Therefore, financial statement analysis must be performed on the statements that are appropriate for the decision being made. Generally speaking, equity investors will use consolidated statements while creditors and lenders should use unconsolidated statements for their primary analysis.

Multi-Industry Corporations

Many corporations engage in several lines of business. These corporations may be either public or private. Because they have a broad spectrum of activities, they cannot be classified as being in a specific industry. Since industry comparisons are a common aspect of financial statement analysis (and particularly of ratio analysis), the inability to slot many corporations into a specific industry classification may appear to create a problem for the analyst. However, the inability to classify a corporation by industry should not, in itself, be of concern.

At the level of profitability analysis, the rate of return *on investment* should not vary by industry. The competition for capital is economy-wide and worldwide, so an investor should expect the same return on investment *at a given level of risk* no matter what industry or industries a company is in.

Risk Assessment is also a function of risk and return: While companies in a certain industry often have similar capital structures because of an underlying commonality of operating risk, there also are significant differences between companies in an industry. Industry classification is not an adequate definition of risk. For example, there is a relatively low risk level inherent in the operations of established cable companies as contrasted to the high risk borne by new entrants to the market.

The key is *risk*; the analyst must be able to evaluate the risks to the company and its ability to survive downturns and benefit from upturns in its fortunes. Industry analysis is useful because the general *market risk* is broadly similar to all of the players in that market. When a company's participation in several different markets is summarized in annual financial statements, it is impossible to tell just what the company's exposure to different risks is in different markets. Therefore, public companies are required to provide **segment reporting** as supplementary information in their annual financial statements. The volume of activity is reported both by industry and by geographic region.

Segment reporting gives the analyst a better idea of the exposure of the company to the risks inherent in different industries and in different parts of the world. However, it is not feasible to perform ratio analysis at the same level of detail as for the company as a whole, because the numbers included in the segment data are distinctly "fuzzy"; the revenues include revenues between segments at transfer prices, the costs include allocated amounts with no useful disclosure of the nature of the allocations, and the operating profits therefore are the net result of two approximations. Segment disclosures certainly are better than no disclosures at all, but they do need to be taken with a grain of salt.

Conclusion

The following are some concluding observations on ratio analysis:

- The apparent simplicity of ratio analysis is deceptive; ratios are only as good as the underlying data.
- The analyst must take care to analyze the correct set of financial statements: consolidated or separate legal entity.
- Financial statements often have to be adjusted to suit the analyst's needs before meaningful ratio analysis can be performed.
- Industry comparisons can be helpful, but there is no assurance that the industry averages (or quartiles) are "right" or are based on similar accounting policies and measurements.
- Assessments of profitability, solvency, and liquidity are not really industry-dependent, but they do depend to some extent on an analysis of risk for each line of business.

- There is no point in computing masses of ratios; it is more important to identify one or two key ratios in each category that are relevant to the analyst's decision needs and concentrate on those.
- Given the many estimates and approximations underlying both the numerator and denominator of *all* ratios, it is absurd to calculate them to more than two significant digits; computing to three or more digits gives ratios an appearance of precision that is wholly unwarranted.

CONCEPT REVIEW

1. What is the essential relationship between the numerator and denominator of any profitability ratio?

2. Is it necessarily a good thing for efficiency ratios to be very high?

3. Why do some analysts prefer to use debt-service ratios such as times debt service earned rather than the more common times interest earned?

4. Why should creditors and lenders be wary of basing their analyses on consolidated financial statements?

OTHER ANALYTICAL TECHNIQUES

In addition to basic ratio analysis, other more sophisticated analytical techniques can be applied to the amounts in the financial statements or to the ratios themselves. These techniques include the following:

- *Time-series analysis.* The purpose of time-series analysis is to predict the future values of the ratios. Time-series analysis can be applied to cross-sectional ratios themselves or to the underlying financial data. The data can be used "raw," or can be subjected to transformations such as logarithmic transformation.
- *Residual analysis.* This is a time-series analysis based on the differences between computed ratios and industry (or economy) averages. The intent is to identify the extent to which changes in a company's ratios are common to the industry (or economy) as a whole. Such an analysis may help to discover when a company is performing better or worse than other companies over a period of time.
- *Statistical multivariate ratio analysis.* In this approach, ratios are not analyzed one by one but fitted into a statistical model in an attempt to predict some type of outcome, such as impending bankruptcy.

An implicit assumption of these approaches is that the underlying *economic processes* that generate the numbers and ratios are stable. Furthermore, there is an implicit assumption that the underlying *measurement methods* (i.e., accounting policies and accounting estimates) also are stable and remain unchanged over the period of analysis and into the period being predicted. Neither assumption should automatically be taken as correct in a rapidly changing economic environment. This book will not delve further into these sophisticated statistical approaches.

SUMMARY OF KEY POINTS

1. Before analyzing the financial statements of a company, it is essential to clearly understand the objective of the analysis.

2. The auditor's report should be reviewed with an eye to qualifications and to comments regarding accounting policies, if any. The auditor's report serves only as an assurance that accounting policies are within GAAP.

3. The essential first step in statement analysis is to fully understand the financial statements. The statements cannot be meaningfully analyzed unless they are viewed within the framework of management's reporting objectives and accounting policies.

4. Clues to the accounting policies being used by management may be found in the notes to the financial statements. The policy note may give only sketchy information, but the notes relating to individual financial statement components may provide more useful information.

5. The accounting policies used by management may not be the most suitable for the purpose of the analyst's decision needs. The analyst may find it useful to recast the financial statements using different policies, such as by removing the effects of non-recurring gains and losses from net income, or by treating as expense certain expenditures that the company has capitalized.

6. When the analyst recasts a company's financial statements, there may not be adequate information provided in the notes for an accurate restatement. Approximations often are necessary.

7. *Vertical analysis* (or *common-size analysis*) involves calculating financial statement components as a percentage of the total, such as balance sheet amounts as a percentage of total assets.

8. Vertical analysis is useful for removing the effects of absolute changes in amounts; changes in the relative composition of balance sheet and income statement components may become more readily apparent.

9. *Horizontal analysis* (or *trend analysis*) involves calculating individual financial statement components over several years as an index number, with a base year set at 100. Horizontal analysis is used to determine the relative change in amounts between years.

10. *Ratio analysis* compares the proportional relationship between different items within a single year's financial statements. Often, it is necessary to adjust the numerator and denominator of a ratio by excluding or reclassifying certain components.

11. *Profitability ratios* are those that compare a measure of earnings (the numerator) to a measure of investment (the denominator). It is essential that the numerator and denominator be logically consistent.

12. *Efficiency ratios* attempt to measure selected aspects of the company's operations, such as inventory turnover or the accounts receivable collection period. Efficiency ratios must be used with great caution by an external analyst because the balance sheet amounts may not be typical of the balances throughout the period.

13. *Solvency ratios* reflect the ability of the company to meet its long-term obligations. Static solvency ratios include various forms of the debt-to-equity ratio; flow ratios examine the ability of the company to meet its debt financing obligations through its cash flows from operations.

14. *Liquidity ratios* test the company's ability to cover its short-term obligations with its existing monetary assets.

15. All ratios are based on accounting numbers that are the result of the company's accounting policies and that include the effects of many estimates made by management. Despite the fact that ratios can be computed to many decimals, they really are very approximate measures that must be interpreted with extreme caution.

KEY TERMS

accounts receivable aging schedule, 1257
accounts receivable turnover ratio, 1257
acid-test ratio, 1263
asset turnover ratio, 1258
auditor's report, 1243
average collection period of accounts
    receivable, 1257
cross-sectional comparison, 1246
current ratio, 1261
debt service ratios, 1258
debt-to-capital employed ratio, 1260
debt-to-equity ratio, 1259
debt-to-total assets ratio, 1260
debt-to-total-capitalization ratio, 1260
defensive-interval ratio, 1263
efficiency ratios, 1256
horizontal (trend) analysis, 1247
inventory turnover ratio, 1257
leverage ratios, 1258

liquidity ratios, 1261
longitudinal comparisons, 1246
margin of safety, 1260
negative leverage, 1259
operating margin ratio, 1256
profitability ratios, 1252
quick ratio, 1263
ratio analysis, 1251
return on equity ratio, 1252
return on long-term capital ratio, 1252
return on total assets ratio, 1252
review engagement, 1243
segment reporting, 1265
solvency ratios, 1258
times-debt-service-earned ratio, 1261
times-interest-earned ratio, 1260
total capitalization, 1252
turnover ratios, 1256
vertical (common size) analysis, 1246

APPENDIX

RECASTING FINANCIAL STATEMENTS— DEMONSTRATION CASE

Introduction

This chapter has emphasized that it may be necessary for an analyst to recast a company's financial statements before any ratio analysis is undertaken. To illustrate the task of restatement, we have chosen the financial statements of a Canadian company, QDO Limited (not the real name). We will restate these financial statements to reflect different accounting policy choices. After the restatement, we will compare the results of ratio analysis before and after restatement.

The Company

QDO is a large software development company. Its primary line of business is the design and development of large-scale custom software for specific large clients. Clients include several of the provinces, one of the largest Canadian banks, and two large international insurance companies. Between 20X5 and 20X8, gross revenue tripled and net income increased from $262,725 to over $2 million. Operating margin, based on the published (and audited) financial statements, increased from 0.26% in 20X5 to 7% in 20X8. The company's statements of operations for the most recent four years are shown in Exhibit 21A-1; the balance sheets are

EXHIBIT 21A-1

QDO LIMITED CONSOLIDATED STATEMENTS OF INCOME AND RETAINED EARNINGS
[IN $ THOUSANDS]

Years ended 31 December	20X8	20X7	20X6	20X5
Gross revenue	$29,276	$19,305	$14,317	$10,231
Investment income (interest on cash deposits)	1,265	—	—	—
	30,541	19,305	14,317	10,231
Less cost of hardware sold	4,497	2,519	1,519	1,407
Operating revenue	26,044	16,786	12,798	8,824
Expenses				
Operating and administrative*	22,762	15,108	11,718	8,323
Depreciation and amortization				
Fixed assets	203	49	22	6
Capital leases	143	85	23	1
Software development costs	141	67	—	—
Interest	164	224	238	95
	23,413	15,533	12,001	8,425
Income before income tax	2,631	1,253	797	399
Income tax	569	(199)	(3)	137
Net income	$ 2,062	$ 1,452	$ 800	$ 262
Retained earnings, beginning of year	1,952	1,056	475	252
Dividends declared	(14)	(295)	(176)	(33)
Cost of share issue net of income tax	(1,185)	(202)		
Premium on shares purchased for cancellation		(59)	(43)	(6)
Loss on sale of repurchased common shares	(46)			
Retained earnings, end of year	$ 2,769	$ 1,952	$ 1,056	$ 475
Net income per common share	$ 0.19	$ 0.16	$ 0.09	$ 0.03

*Includes $372 of amortization of other development costs in 20X8

shown in Exhibit 21A-2; the cash flow statements are shown in Exhibit 21A-3. The terminology used in these exhibits is that used by the company.

In 20X7, the company's managers decided to develop some of its large-scale custom software designs into off-the-shelf turn-key proprietary products that would be adaptable to any prospective user. In addition, the company launched an ambitious sales expansion plan,

---

EXHIBIT 21A-2

QDO LIMITED CONSOLIDATED BALANCE SHEETS [IN $ THOUSANDS]

Years ended 31 December	20X8	20X7	20X6	20X5
ASSETS				
Current assets				
Short-term deposits	$ 8,716	$ —	$ —	$ —
Accounts receivable	6,459	4,658	5,112	2,370
Work in progress	7,451	2,780	—	—
Hardware inventory	569	—	—	—
Prepaid expenses and supplies inventory	1,151	470	126	123
	24,346	7,908	5,238	2,493
Fixed assets				
Leasehold improvements	852	317	278	16
Furniture, fixtures and computer equipment	624	121	138	16
Assets under capital lease	1,374	817	359	156
	2,850	1,255	775	188
Less accumulated amortization	(293)	(90)	(38)	(11)
	2,557	1,165	737	177
Other assets				
Software development costs	13,037	5,157	1,580	112
Other development costs	2,196	—	—	—
Future income tax	—	355	409	409
	15,233	5,512	1,989	521
Total assets	$42,136	$14,585	$7,964	$3,191
LIABILITIES AND SHAREHOLDERS' EQUITY				
Current liabilities				
Bank and other loans	$ 2,806	$ 3,371	$2,653	$ 900
Accounts payable and accrued liabilities	7,054	3,550	2,131	918
Current portion of non-current liabilities	281	161	85	23
Deferred revenue	530	461	183	140
Future income tax	—	—	104	104
	10,671	7,543	5,156	2,085
Non-current liabilities				
Capital lease obligations	1,488	1,101	662	134
Future income tax	214	—	—	—
Total liabilities	12,373	8,644	5,818	2,219
Shareholders' equity				
Share capital	29,892	3,989	1,090	497
Retained earnings	2,769	1,952	1,056	475
Less: treasury shares	(2,898)	—	—	—
	29,763	5,941	2,146	972
	$42,136	$14,585	$7,964	$3,191

EXHIBIT 21A-3

CONSOLIDATED STATEMENTS OF CASH FLOWS [IN $ THOUSANDS]

Years ended 31 December	20X8	20X7	20X6	20X5
Operations				
Net income for the year	$ 2,062	$ 1,452	$ 799	$ 263
Add non-cash items				
Future (deferred) income tax	569	(50)	—	50
Depreciation and amortization	859	200	45	7
Deferred lease rent credits	—	82	142	—
	3,490	1,684	986	320
Net change in working capital items	(3,846)	(724)	(1,427)	(294)
	(356)	960	(441)	26
Investment				
Investment in software products	(8,020)	(3,645)	(1,469)	(110)
Other development costs	(2,568)	—	—	—
Purchase of fixed assets	(1,034)	(36)	(162)	(89)
Proceeds from disposal of fixed assets	—	—	—	160
	(11,622)	(3,681)	(1,631)	(39)
Financing				
Current maturities of lease obligations	(325)	(161)	(55)	(24)
Issue of shares	21,858	2,525	2,138	244
Loss on sale of repurchased shares	(46)	—	—	—
Dividends declared	(14)	(295)	(176)	(33)
Shares purchased and cancelled	(214)	(66)	(1,588)	(9)
	21,259	2,003	319	178
Increase (decrease) in cash during year	$ 9,281	$ (718)	$(1,753)	$ 165
Cash and short-term investments, beginning of year, net of current borrowings	(3,371)	(2,653)	(900)	(1,065)
Cash and short-term investments, end of year, net of current borrowings	$ 5,910	$(3,371)	$(2,653)	$ (900)
Changes in cash and cash equivalents				
Increase (decrease) in cash and short-term investments	$ 8,716	—	—	—
Decrease (increase) in current borrowings	565	$ (718)	$(1,753)	$ 165
Net change in cash and cash equivalents	$ 9,281	$ (718)	$(1,753)	$ 165

establishing 11 offices in Canadian cities and 10 in U.S. cities, plus one in Singapore. To help finance the expansion, the company raised approximately $30 million through a public issue of common shares early in 20X8. The company also increased its line of credit with its bank, the Royal Dominion Bank, to $5 million.

The product development expenditures for the proprietary products were accounted for in accordance with the requirements of Section 3450 of the *CICA Handbook*. Since, in management's judgement, all of the criteria for capitalization were satisfied, it was acceptable to capitalize the development expenditures. Also, the costs of establishing the international sales offices were deferred as "other development costs" on the balance sheet.

It is now 20X9. Over the first three months of the year, the company has completely used the cash and short-term deposits that are shown on the year-end 20X8 balance sheet, and has begun to near the limit of its line of credit. The company's CEO has approached the Royal Dominion Bank with a proposal to further extend the company's line of credit to enable the company to continue development of its proprietary software and to support the costs of the new sales offices until the offices become self-supporting.

Task

You are an analyst for the Royal Dominion Bank. The bank's Credit Committee is interested in the sustainable operating cash flow of QDO. Investment in software development is considered by the bank to be an ongoing operating activity, crucial to the success of the company. Therefore, the chair of the credit committee has asked you to recast QDO's 20X7 and 20X8 financial statements to show all development costs as a current expense. The bank's policy is to reverse out any future income tax amounts. Therefore, any future income tax amounts that exist in the statements should be eliminated in your recast statements.

Once the statements have been restated, the Credit Committee would like you to calculate a few ratios that relate to the company's ability to sustain increased borrowing. Specifically, the requested ratios are:

1. Return on total assets, before tax

2. Total liabilities to shareholders' equity

3. Times interest earned.

Non-recurring items of revenue or expense should be eliminated before calculating any ratios based on net income. The ratios should be calculated both on the original financial statements and on the restated amounts.

Additional Information

The following information is extracted from QDO's disclosure notes:

1. **Summary of significant accounting policies**

    (c) *Software product costs*

    Costs, including an allocation of interest and overhead, which relate to the development and acquisition of computer-based systems, where the systems are expected to be sold in substantially the same form in the future, are capitalized. It is the Company's policy to charge these costs to income, commencing in the year of development completion, based on projected unit sales over a period of not longer than three years or when it is determined that the costs will not be recovered from related future revenues.

    (d) *Other development costs*

    During 20X8 the Company adopted the policy of capitalizing certain start-up costs related to the establishment of proprietary software products operations and the major expansion of its professional services branch network. These capitalized costs are being charged to earnings over the subsequent four quarters.

5. **Software product costs**

    The following is an analysis of software product costs:

	20X8	20X7
Balance, beginning of year	$ 5,157,271	$1,579,174
Additions during the year	8,020,181	3,644,763
	13,177,452	5,223,937
Less: amortization	(140,753)	(66,666)
Balance, end of year	$13,036,699	$5,157,271

6. Other development costs

Other development costs at 31 August 20X8 include:

Sales network development costs	$ 543,944
Branch pre-opening start-up losses	1,428,506
Hiring and relocation costs	595,587
	2,568,037
Less amounts charged to income in 20X8	(371,958)
	$2,196,079

Demonstration Case—Solution

Approach

The assignment from the Credit Committee is to recast the statements by making two changes:

- The accounting policy for development costs should be changed from capitalization to immediate expensing.
- The effects of income tax allocation are to be removed, so that the statements reflect only the current income tax due.

To make these changes, we need to take the following steps:

1. *Income statement*

- Add expenditures on development costs to expenses.
- Remove amortization expense from expenses (to avoid double-counting).
- Remove future income tax expense, if any.
- Adjust retained earnings balances for the restated net income.

2. *Balance sheet*

- Remove development costs from assets.
- Reclassify future income tax balances—move from other assets, current liabilities, and non-current liabilities to retained earnings.
- Restate retained earnings.

3. *Cash flow statement*

- Reclassify development expenditures—move from investing activities to operations.
- Remove development cost amortization addbacks.
- Remove future income tax addbacks.

Income Statement

The income statement shows "software development costs" of $141 for 20X8 and $67 for 20X7. These numbers tie in to Note 5, which shows the same amounts as amortization. Therefore, these amounts must be removed from the income statement. As well, Note 6 shows amortization of other development costs of $372, which must be removed from operating and administrative expenses. Expenditures on development costs are shown in Notes 5 and 6. These must be added to expenses in the recast income statements.

Since the bank wants to see the effects of using a "flow-through" approach for income tax, the future income tax expense must be removed. The 20X7 balance sheet shows a debit balance for future income taxes of $355. In 20X8, the balance is a credit of $214. The net change, therefore, is a credit of $569 on the balance sheet. To balance, the company must have charged $569 in future income tax to the income statement. This amount can be verified by referring to the cash flow statement, which shows a non-cash addback of $569 for future income taxes. This is also the total amount of income tax expense shown in the income statement. The company had no current taxes due in 20X8.

For 20X7, the cash flow statement shows a *negative* addback for future income tax of $50. This indicates that the amount was a *credit* to income. This can be verified by looking at the change in the net balance of future income taxes on the balance sheet. At the end of 20X6, there were two future income tax balances, a current credit for $104 and a non-current debit of $409, for a net debit balance of $305. In 20X7, the company recorded a net future income tax credit to income of $50. The net change can be reconciled in the form of a general journal entry:

Change in Future Tax Amounts, Year-End 20X6 To Year-End 20X7

Future income tax, current ($104 − $0)	104	
Future income tax, non-current		54
Income tax expense, future ($409 − $355)		50

The balance sheet effect of this change is to eliminate the current credit balance of $104 and reduce the non-current debit balance from $409 to $355.

In summary, the adjustments to net income for 20X8 and 20X7 are as follows:

	20X8	20X7
Net income, as reported	$ 2,062	$ 1,452
Plus amortization of software development costs	141	67
Plus amortization of other development costs	372	
Less expenditures on software development costs	(8,020)	(3,645)
Less expenditures on other development costs	(2,568)	
Plus (less) future income tax expense (credit)	569	(50)
Restated net income (loss)	$(7,444)	$(2,176)

These adjustments obviously will change retained earnings for both year-ends. However, there are two other adjustments that must be made to the 20X7 *beginning* balance of retained earnings:

1. The balance sheet at year-end 20X6 shows software development costs as an asset of $1,580. Using the bank's preferred policy of expensing development costs, these costs would have been charged to operations when incurred. Reclassifying this amount means removing it as an asset and charging it against year-end 20X6 retained earnings.

2. The change to flow-through reporting of income tax expense requires that the balances of both the current and non-current future tax balances at the beginning of 20X7 (i.e., at year-end 20X6) be eliminated. The net balance at the end of 20X6 is $409 debit (non-current) minus $104 credit (current), for a further net reduction in retained earnings of $305.

Therefore, the 20X7 beginning retained earnings on the statement of income and retained earnings must be restated to a deficit of $829:

	20X6
Ending retained earnings, as reported	$1,056
Adjustment to reclassify capitalized software development costs	(1,580)
Adjustment to eliminate future tax balances	(305)
Restated retained earnings (deficit), 31 December 20X6	$ (829)

The adjustments shown above for 20X6 retained earnings and for 20X7 and 20X8 net income can be used to restate the statements of income and retained earnings for the two years. The restated income statements are shown in Exhibit 21A-4.

EXHIBIT 21A-4

QDO LIMITED CONSOLIDATED STATEMENTS OF INCOME AND RETAINED EARNINGS—RESTATED
[IN $ THOUSANDS]

	As Reported		Restated	
Years ended 31 December	20X8	20X7	20X8	20X7
Gross revenue	$29,276	$19,305	$ 29,276	$19,305
Investment income	1,265	—	1,265	—
	30,541	19,305	30,541	19,305
Less cost of hardware sold	4,497	2,519	4,497	2,519
Operating revenue	26,044	16,786	26,044	16,786
Expenses				
Operating and administrative	22,762	15,108	22,390	15,108
Depreciation and amortization				
Fixed assets	203	49	203	49
Capital leases	143	85	143	85
Software development costs	141	67	8,020	3,645
Other development costs			2,568	
Interest	164	224	164	224
	23,413	15,533	33,488	19,111
Income before income tax	2,631	1,253	(7,444)	(2,325)
Income tax	569	(199)	—	(149)
Net income	$ 2,062	$ 1,452	$ (7,444)	$ (2,176)
Retained earnings, beginning of year	1,952	1,056	(3,561)	(829)
Dividends declared	(14)	(295)	(14)	(295)
Cost of share issue net of income taxes	(1,185)	(202)	(1,185)	(202)
Premium on shares purchased for cancellation		(59)		(59)
Loss on sale of repurchased common shares	(46)		(46)	
Retained earnings, end of year	$ 2,769	$ 1,952	$(12,250)	$ (3,561)

Balance Sheet

The restated retained earnings amounts that are shown in Exhibit 21A-4 are used in the restated balance sheet. Other adjustments are:

- The asset amounts shown for software development costs and other development costs in the original balance sheets are both removed.
- The future (deferred) income tax balances are removed.
- The restated balance sheets are shown in Exhibit 21A-5.

Cash Flow Statement

On the cash flow statement, the operations section begins with the restated net income for each year. The two amounts of amortization must be adjusted by the amounts of amortization included in the original statements but now eliminated in the restatement. Also, the addback for future income taxes is eliminated.

In the investment section, investment in software products and other development costs must be eliminated. The total cash flows for each year do not change, of course, but the subtotals for operating and investment change considerably. The restated cash flow statements are shown in Exhibit 21A-6.

> EXHIBIT 21A-5

QDO LIMITED CONSOLIDATED BALANCE SHEETS—RESTATED [IN $ THOUSANDS]

	As Reported		Restated	
Years ended 31 December	20X8	20X7	20X8	20X7
ASSETS				
Current assets				
Short-term deposits	$ 8,716	$ —	$ 8,716	$ —
Accounts receivable	6,459	4,658	6,459	4,658
Work in progress	7,451	2,780	7,451	2,780
Hardware inventory	569	—	569	—
Prepaid expenses and supplies inventory	1,151	470	1,151	470
	24,346	7,908	24,346	7,908
Fixed assets				
Leasehold improvements	852	317	852	317
Furniture, fixtures and computer equipment	624	121	624	121
Assets under capital lease	1,374	817	1,374	817
	2,850	1,255	2,850	1,255
Less accumulated amortization	(293)	(90)	(293)	(90)
	2,557	1,165	2,557	1,165
Other assets				
Software development costs	13,037	5,157		
Other development costs	2,196	—		
Future income tax	—	355		
	15,233	5,512		
Total assets	$42,136	$14,585	$26,903	$9,073
LIABILITIES AND SHAREHOLDERS' EQUITY				
Current liabilities				
Bank and other loans	$ 2,806	$ 3,371	$ 2,806	$3,371
Accounts payable and accrued liabilities	7,054	3,550	7,054	3,550
Current portion of non-current liabilities	281	161	281	161
Deferred revenue	530	461	530	461
Future (deferred) income tax	—	—	—	—
	10,671	7,543	10,671	7,543
Non-current liabilities				
Capital lease obligations	1,488	1,101	1,488	1,101
Future income tax	214	—	—	—
Total liabilities	12,373	8,644	12,159	8,644
Shareholders' equity				
Share capital	29,892	3,989	29,892	3,989
Retained earnings	2,769	1,952	(12,250)	(3,561)
Less treasury shares	(2,898)	—	(2,898)	—
	29,763	5,941	14,744	428
	$42,136	$14,585	$26,903	$9,073

EXHIBIT 21A-6

CONSOLIDATED STATEMENTS OF CASH FLOWS—RESTATED [IN $ THOUSANDS]

Years ended 31 December	As Reported		Restated	
	20X8	**20X7**	**20X8**	**20X7**
Operations				
Net income for the year	$ 2,062	$ 1,452	$ (7,444)	$(2,176)
Add items not involving working capital				
Future income tax	569	(50)	—	—
Depreciation and amortization	859	200	346	133
Deferred lease rent credits	—	82	—	82
	3,490	1,684	(7,098)	(1,961)
Net change in working capital items	(3,846)	(724)	(3,846)	(724)
	(356)	960	(10,944)	(2,685)
Investment				
Investment in software products	(8,020)	(3,645)		
Other development costs	(2,568)	—		
Purchase of fixed assets	(1,034)	(36)	(1,034)	(36)
Proceeds from disposal of fixed assets	—	—	—	—
	(11,622)	(3,681)	(1,034)	(36)
Financing				
Current maturities of lease obligations	(325)	(161)	(325)	(161)
Issue of shares	21,858	2,525	21,858	2,525
Loss on sale of repurchased shares	(46)	—	(46)	—
Dividends declared	(14)	(295)	(14)	(295)
Shares purchased and cancelled	(214)	(66)	(214)	(66)
	21,259	2,003	21,259	2,003
Increase (decrease) in cash during year	$ 9,281	$ (718)	$ 9,281	$ (718)
Cash and short-term investments, end of year, net of current borrowings	(3,371)	(2,653)	(3,371)	(2,653)
Cash and short-term investments, end of year, Net of current borrowings	$ 5,910	$(3,371)	$ 5,910	$(3,371)
Changes in cash and cash equivalents				
Increase (decrease) in cash and short-term investments	$ 8,716	—	$ 8,716	—
Decrease (increase) in current borrowings	565	$ (718)	565	$ (718)
Net change in cash and cash equivalents	$ 9,281	$ (718)	$ 9,281	$ (718)

Ratios

It is obvious that changing the development cost accounting has a major impact on QDO's financial statements. Instead of showing a profit, the restated amounts indicate a substantial loss. Assets are significantly reduced and retained earnings goes into a deficit position.

The operating loss situation in 20X8 is actually even worse than stated, when non-recurring items are considered, as requested. Net income for the most recent year includes investment income of $1,265,000. This investment income is the result of temporary investment of the proceeds of the common share issue. The case states that all of the cash and short-term investments were used in operations (and development) early in 20X9. Since there are no investments, there will be no investment income in 20X9. Removing the non-recurring income increases the 20X8 loss:

	As Reported	Restated
Net income (loss)	$2,062	$(7,444)
Less: non-recurring investment income	(1,265)	(1,265)
Income (loss) on continuing operations	$ 797	$(8,709)

The ratios requested, before and after restatement, are as follows:

1. Return on total assets, before tax, 20X8

$$\frac{\text{Net income} + \text{interest expense} + \text{income tax expense}}{\text{Total assets (average)}}$$

Before restatement:
($2,062 + $164 + $569) ÷ [($14,585 + $42,136) ÷ 2] = $2,795 ÷ $28,361
   = **9.9%**

After restatement:
(−$8,709 + $164) ÷ [($9,073 + $26,903) ÷ 2] = − $8,545 ÷ $17,988
   = **−47.5%**

2. Total liabilities to shareholders' equity

$$\frac{\text{Total liabilities}}{\text{Shareholders' equity}}$$

Before restatement: $12,373 ÷ $29,763 = **42%**
After restatement: $12,159 ÷ $14,744 = **82%**

Times interest earned

$$\frac{\text{Net income} + \text{Interest expense} + \text{Income tax expense}}{\text{Interest expense}}$$

Before restatement: ($2,062 + $164 + $569) ÷ $164 = $2,795 ÷ $164
   = **17.0**
After restatement: (−$8,709 + $164) ÷ $164 = −$8,545 ÷ $164 = **−52.1**

Conclusion

This case demonstrates not only the process that must be followed for restatements, but also the importance of ensuring that the financial statements reflect accounting policies that are consistent with the decision to be made. If the bank looked at the financial condition of the company only as shown in the published statements, it would receive a much different picture of the financial health and profitability of the company than is presented in the recast statements. Changing the underlying reporting objective to cash flow prediction results in using accounting policies that give a much more negative view of the company.

The moral of this story? It is foolish to undertake any ratio analysis without first examining the appropriateness of the underlying financial accounting policies of the company!

QUESTIONS

Q21-1   List three financial statement users and a decision for each that may rest on financial statement analysis.

Q21-2 Why is a potential investor's perspective different than an existing investor's perspective?

Q21-3 Explain why financial analysts and others, in analyzing financial statements, examine the summary of accounting policies.

Q21-4 Explain why the actual disclosure of accounting policies in financial statements might not be as helpful as analysts and other financial statement users might wish.

Q21-5 What conclusions might an analyst reach if the following are observed about a set of financial statements:

a. Cash flow from operations is consistently higher than net income.

b. The balance sheet contains significant deferred costs.

c. Revenue recognition is deferred, as are expenses.

d. Revenue recognition is deferred, but expenses are recognized very close to the time they are incurred.

Treat each case separately.

Q21-6 What does it mean to "recast" the financial statements? Why are financial statements recast?

Q21-7 Distinguish between vertical and horizontal analysis. Briefly explain the use of each.

Q21-8 Describe the primary ratios used for profitability analysis.

Q21-9 Explain the two ratios that combine to form return on assets. What strategies can a company use to maximize return on assets?

Q21-10 Explain the return-on-assets ratio. Why is it a fundamental measure of profitability?

Q21-11 Explain the primary ratios used to evaluate efficiency.

Q21-12 Moller Company's average collection period for accounts receivable is 24 days. Interpret this figure. What is the accounts receivable turnover ratio? What does it reveal?

Q21-13 Maddox Steel Company has an inventory turnover of 9; interpret this figure.

Q21-14 Explain the primary ratios used to evaluate solvency.

Q21-15 Explain and illustrate the effect of financial leverage.

Q21-16 Explain the circumstances where a company has debt financing and the leverage factor is (a) positive, (b) negative, and (c) zero.

Q21-17 Explain the primary ratios used to evaluate liquidity.

Q21-18 Current assets and current liabilities for two companies with the same amount of working capital are summarized below. Evaluate their relative liquidity positions.

	Co. X	Co. Y
Current assets	$300,000	$900,000
Current liabilities	100,000	700,000
Working capital	$200,000	$200,000

Q21-19 What is the purpose of a consolidated financial statement? Segment reporting disclosure?

Q21-20 Describe some of the limitations of ratio analysis.

CASE 21-1

FOREST INDUSTRY

You are evaluating two companies in the forest industry. Both companies are public, and are integrated companies that own or lease timber properties, harvest trees, and make building supplies and paper products. This industry is very volatile.

Their profiles, from published annual reports:

Company #1

A North American–based producer of building materials including oriented strand board, medium-density fibreboard, hardwood plywood, lumber, I-joists, specialty papers, and pulp. The company is also the United Kingdom's largest producer of wood-based panels, including particleboard and value-added products. The company employs over 2,600 people in North America and 1,000 in the United Kingdom.

Company #2

The company is a leading Canadian integrated forest products company. The company employs approximately 6,800 people. The company has extensive woodlands operations and manufacturing facilities in British Columbia and Alberta, and a lumber remanufacturing plant in the United States. The company is a major producer and supplier of lumber and bleached kraft pulp. It also produces semi-bleached and unbleached kraft pulp, bleached and unbleached kraft paper, plywood, remanufactured lumber products, hardboard panelling and a range of specialized wood products, including baled fibre and fibremat. Products are sold in global markets.

You have limited industry norms, which relate to years prior to those presented for the two companies; industry norms are difficult to establish for the current years.

Select set of ratios for the forest industry in Canada

	20X3	20X2	20X1
Debt to equity (%)	81	68	72
Operating profit margin	15.8	13.4	7.7
Return on assets	7.6	6	0.7
Return on equity	17.4	12.5	1.5
Current ratio	2.1	2.1	1.9

Summarized financial data for each company is shown in Exhibit 1. A standard financial statement analysis form is included.

The companies both have unqualified audit reports and have similar accounting policies except for the following:

1. Company #1 uses FIFO while Company #2 uses weighted-average cost for inventory.
2. Both companies use a combination of straight-line and units-of-production amortization methods for capital assets, but Company #1 uses useful lives that are approximately 25% longer than those used by Company #2.

Required:

Provide an analysis that compares Company #1 and Company #2 from the perspective of:

1. a potential short-term creditor
2. a potential common stock investor

Assume a tax rate of 40% for both companies.

EXHIBIT 1

COMPARATIVE FINANCIAL STATEMENTS (IN MILLIONS)

Balance Sheet

	Company 1		Company 2	
	20X6	20X5	20X6	20X5
Assets				
Cash and cash equivalents	$ 20	$ 67	$ 208	$ 17
Temporary investments	—	—	24	—
Accounts receivable	267	242	304	321
Inventory	492	500	312	353
Future income tax	23	30	13	28
Total current assets	802	839	861	719
Property, plant, & equipment	1,984	1,903	1,469	1,518
Other assets	27	22	230	190
Total assets	$2,813	$2,764	$2,560	$2,427
Liabilities				
Current liabilities				
Bank debt				
Accounts payable	$ 323	$ 316	$ 480	$ 364
Current portion of long-term debt	4	15	53	49
Total current liabilities	327	331	533	413
Long-term debt	1,077	921	556	384
Other liabilities	96	97	170	65
Future income tax	38	112	147	363
	1,211	1,130	873	812
Total liabilities	1,538	1,461	1,406	1,225
Shareholders' equity				
Preferred shares	60	60	—	—
Common shares	889	880	657	657
Retained earnings	326	363	497	545
	1,275	1,303	1,154	1,202
Total liabilities and equity	$2,813	$2,764	$2,560	$2,427

Income statement

	Company 1		Company 2	
	20X6	20X5	20X6	20X5
Net sales	$2,066	$2,134	$1,986	$2,265
Costs and expenses				
Manufacturing/product costs	1,793	1,722	1,759	1,622
Amortization and depletion	148	144	106	113
Selling and administration	90	90	58	67
	2,031	1,956	1,923	1,802
Operating income	**35**	**178**	**63**	**463**
Interest expense	52	40	64	60
Other (income) expense	(62)	25	(9)	(6)
Income before income tax	45	113	8	409
Income tax expense (recovery)	26	(34)	(18)	84
Net income	$ 19	$ 147	$ 26	$ 325

| | | | EXHIBIT 1 | | *(cont'd)* |

	Company 1		Company 2	
	20X6	**20X5**	**20X6**	**20X5**
Dividends				
Preferred	$ 2	$ 2	—	—
Common	$ 54	$ 50	$ 74	$ 25

Financial Statement Analysis

	Company 1		Company 2	
	20X6	**20X5**	**20X6**	**20X5**
Profitability—base denominator on year-end figures				
Return on long-term capital, after tax*				
Return on total assets, after tax				
Return on common shareholders' equity				
Operating margin				

*Include all long-term credit elements as long-term debt

	Company 1		Company 2	
Efficiency—base denominator on year-end balances				
Asset turnover				
Accounts receivable turnover*				
Inventory turnover				

*assume all sales on account

	Company 1		Company 2	
Solvency				
Long-term debt to equity*				
Long-term debt to total capitalization				
Debt to total assets				
Times interest earned				

*Include all long-term credit elements as long-term debt

	Company 1		Company 2	
Liquidity				
Current ratio				
Quick ratio				

Cash Flow from Operations 20X6

Cash flow from operations	Company 1	Company 2
Net income		
Plus/less: non-cash charges		
Changes in working capital		
Accounts receivable		
Inventory		
Future income tax—current		
Accounts payable and accrued liabilities		
Future income tax—non-current		
Cash flow from operations		

(CGA-Canada, adapted)

PETERSON PRODUCTS LIMITED

You have just returned from a meeting with a friend who is considering an opportunity to invest in non-voting shares in Peterson Products Limited (PPL). Your classmate was very enthusiastic about the company, pointing out the company's unusually high return on assets, its low debt-to-equity ratio, and its high operating margin, as compared to other companies of a similar nature. Your classmate is also impressed with the company's high positive cash flow, which has exceeded $1 million in each of the past two years.

PPL is a product development company. It contracts with other companies to develop product ideas to a state where they can be readily produced and marketed. The services offered by PPL range from lining up suppliers to provide the raw product, to packaging and distribution of a rather simple product at the most modest level of service, to full development and design work, manufacturing design, pilot plant construction, and product testing for complex industrial products.

The development of specific products is done under contract. The standard contract provides for PPL to be reimbursed for all direct costs plus a fixed percentage of direct costs to cover overhead and provide a profit. Most contracts contain an upper limit on costs that PPL cannot exceed without approval of the contracting party.

Some of the work on contracts is carried out directly by engineering and other product staff who are employed directly by PPL. Frequently, however, segments of contracts are subcontracted to specialist companies. The subcontracts usually are fixed-fee contracts, and since any cost overruns will have to be absorbed by the subcontractor, it is the practice of PPL to recognize all of PPL's profit on the subcontracted portion of the contract as soon as the subcontract is signed. About 60% of PPL's contracts have been fulfilled by subcontractors in the past two years, and the new president intends to increase that proportion in order to "reduce the overhead" of PPL.

Although specific product development is done under contract, PPL also engages in development work of its own in order to have a storehouse of development knowledge and expertise that it can apply to future contracts. The amortization of these development costs is included in the overhead component of contracts.

While the company has been in existence for over 25 years, it has become much more aggressive in the last two years since Dale Peterson assumed the positions of president and CEO. Dale is the daughter of Ian Peterson, the founder of the company. She completed an MBA at Concordia University and took over management of the company when her father decided to retire to Australia.

The new president and CEO has altered the way in which PPL acquired its equipment. In the old days, PPL purchased the equipment and other fixed assets that it needed. Now the company owns only minor furniture, etc. The bulk of assets are leased on a month-to-month basis from Imaginative Rental Services Corporation (IRS). IRS purchases any equipment that PPL needs and rents it to PPL. The vast majority (90%) of the equipment that PPL owned three years ago has since been sold, much of it to IRS, at fair market values. IRS finances purchase of the assets through loans from the bank. IRS is owned by Dale Peterson. Dale and other shareholders have personally guaranteed the IRS bank loans, but PPL is not a guarantor.

PPL is a private corporation. The shares at present are owned equally by Ian, Dale, and Christopher, Dale's brother. Christopher does not participate in the management of the company or take any active interest in its affairs aside from welcoming the dividends that he receives.

Dale has proposed issuing 100 shares of a new class of non-voting shares to a limited number of new investors for $10,000 per share. The new shares would receive dividends equally with the voting common shares and would have the same rights as voting shares if the company is liquidated. The non-voting shareholders would be able to sell their shares back to the company at any year-end at the net book value per share.

Your friend has left with you, for your perusal, the audited financial statements that follow. He also left some information that shows the following comparative ratios for product development companies:

Debt to equity   40:60
Operating margin   6%
Return on assets   10%

Required:

Analyze the financial statements of Peterson Products Limited and advise your friend as to the wisdom of investing in PPL non-voting shares.

BALANCE SHEET

31 March	20X7	20X6
Current assets		
Cash	$ 75	$ 58
Contract billings receivable	520	413
Unbilled contract receivables	417	110
Work in progress	541	736
	1,553	1,317
Equipment, furniture, and fixtures—net (Note 2)	350	1,750
Deferred development costs	1,512	917
Total assets	$3,415	$3,984
Current liabilities		
Accounts payable and accrued expenses	$ 487	$ 441
Bank overdraft (Note 4)	—	1,000
	487	1,441
Future income tax (Note 3)	915	615
Shareholders' equity		
Common shares (Note 5)	600	600
Retained earnings	1,413	1,328
	2,013	1,928
Total liabilities and shareholders' equity	$3,415	$3,984

INCOME STATEMENT

Years ended 31 March	20X7	20X6
Revenue		
Contract revenue	$5,250	$4,640
Gain on disposal of fixed assets	340	104
	5,590	4,744
Expenses		
Contract costs	3,870	3,169
General selling and administrative expenses	805	670
Interest expense	70	175
Income tax expense	410	355
	5,155	4,369
Net income	$ 435	$ 375

RETAINED EARNINGS STATEMENT

Years ended 31 March	20X7	20X6
Balance, 1 April	$1,328	$1,403
Net income	435	375
Dividends	(350)	(450)
Balance, 31 March	$1,413	$1,328

CASH FLOW STATEMENT

Years ended 31 March	20X7	20X6
Operating activities:		
Net income	$ 435	$ 375
Depreciation	123	263
Amortization of development costs	183	121
Future income tax	300	230
Gain on sale of fixed assets	(340)	(104)
	701	885
Decrease (increase) in working capital balances	(173)	(244)
Cash provided by operations	528	641
Financing activities:		
Dividends paid	(350)	(450)
Investing activities:		
Investment in development costs	(778)	(432)
Proceeds from disposal of fixed assets	1,617	1,472
Increase (decrease) in cash and cash equivalents	$1,017	$1,231

NOTES TO FINANCIAL STATEMENTS

31 March 20X7

1. *Accounting policies*
   a. *Revenue.* Revenue from contracts is recognized on a percentage-of-cost-completion basis as work is performed. The component of revenue relating to work subcontracted is recognized upon signing of the subcontract.
   b. *Work in progress.* Work-in-progress inventory is reported at cost, net of billed and unbilled revenue that has been recognized in earnings.
   c. *Fixed assets.* Equipment and other fixed assets are reported at cost less accumulated depreciation. Fixed assets are depreciated on a straight-line basis over an average of 10 years.
   d. *Development costs.* Development costs are deferred and amortized on a straight-line basis over five years. Amortization commences in the year following incurrence of the costs.
   e. *Income tax.* Income tax is reported on a comprehensive allocation basis, wherein the tax effects of items of revenue and expense are reported in the income statement in the year of accounting recognition rather than in the year in which the tax impact actually occurs.
2. *Equipment, furniture, and fixtures* are reported net of related accumulated depreciation of $235,000 in 20X7 and $1,132,000 in 20X6.
3. *Future income tax* arises from differences between tax and accounting treatment of depreciation, development costs, and subcontract revenue. The primary difference is that related to development costs, which are deductible in the year of incurrence for income tax purposes.

4. *Bank overdraft* is backed by an operating line of credit extended by the Canadian Bank at a floating rate of prime plus 3%. The loan is secured by a fixed and floating charge on all the company's receivables and tangible assets and an assignment of contracts supported by performance bonds.

5. *Common shares* consist of 300 shares issued and outstanding.

6. *Lease commitments.* The company rents the bulk of its operating equipment and furniture on a monthly basis. The rental agreements are cancellable upon 60 days' notice by the company. At year-end 20X7, aggregate commitments under these rental agreements amount to $29,500 per month (20X6: $17,700). The rental costs are included in contract costs.

7. *Contingency.* The company is contingently liable to remedy any deficiencies or nonperformance by subcontractors. To the extent that revenues from uncompleted subcontracts have been included in revenues, the company's contingent liability is $580,000 (20X6: $179,000).

8. *Related party transactions.* The company entered into agreements with Imaginative Rental Services Corporation (IRS), a company owned and controlled by the president of the company, whereby Imaginative acquired furniture and equipment for the company. Such transactions aggregated $1,433,000 in 20X7 (20X6: $1,385,000). IRS also purchased assets from the company, as disclosed on the cash flow statement. The company subsequently entered into monthly rental agreements with Imaginative for these and other items, as disclosed in Note 6.

AUDITOR'S REPORT

To the Shareholders of Peterson Products Limited:

We have audited the balance sheet of Peterson Products Limited as at 31 March 20X7 and 31 March 20X6 and the statements of income, retained earnings, and cash flow for the years ended 31 March 20X7 and 20X6. These financial statements are the responsibility of the company's management. Our responsibility is to express an opinion on these financial statements based on our audit.

We conducted our audit in accordance with generally accepted auditing standards. Those standards require that we plan and perform an audit to obtain reasonable assurance whether the financial statements are free of material misstatement. An audit includes examining, on a test basis, evidence supporting the amounts and disclosures in the financial statements. An audit also includes assessing the accounting principles used and significant estimates made by management, as well as evaluating the overall financial statement presentation.

In our opinion, these financial statements present fairly, in all material respects, the financial position of Peterson Products Limited as at 31 March 20X7 and 20X6 and the results of its operations and changes in its financial position for the years then ended in accordance with generally accepted accounting principles.

Able and Waller
Chartered Accountants
29 May 20X7

ASSIGNMENTS

A21-1 Horizontal and Vertical Analysis—Income Statement: Simard Trading Company's income statements (condensed) for two years are shown below:

eXcel

31 December	20X4	20X5
Gross sales	$550,000	$606,000
Sales returns	(10,000)	(6,000)
	540,000	600,000
Cost of goods sold	(270,000)	(360,000)
Gross margin	270,000	240,000
Expenses		
Selling	(135,000)	(138,000)
Administrative (including income tax)	(75,600)	(66,000)
Interest (net of interest revenue)	(5,400)	6,000
Net income before extraordinary items	54,000	42,000
Extraordinary gain (loss), net of tax	10,800	(6,000)
Net income	$ 64,800	$ 36,000

Required:

1. Prepare vertical percentage analysis of the income statement. Round to the nearest percent.
2. Prepare a horizontal percentage analysis of the income statement. Use a single-step format. Round to the nearest percent.

A21-2 Horizontal and Vertical Analysis—Balance Sheet: Bryant Company's balance sheet (condensed and unclassified) for two years is shown below:

31 December	20X4	20X5
Cash	$ 60,000	$ 80,000
Accounts receivable (net)	120,000	116,000
Inventory (FIFO, LCM)	144,000	192,000
Prepaid expenses	8,000	4,000
Funds and investments (at cost)	60,000	88,000
Capital assets	560,000	664,000
Accumulated depreciation	(104,000)	(196,000)
Intangible assets	12,000	60,000
Total	$860,000	$1,008,000
Accounts payable	$160,000	$ 100,000
Other current liabilities	40,000	40,000
Long-term mortgage payable	200,000	172,000
Common shares, no par	340,000	520,000
Retained earnings	120,000	176,000
Total	$860,000	$1,008,000

Required:

1. Prepare a comparative balance sheet in good form, including vertical percentage analysis. Round to the nearest percent.
2. Prepare a horizontal percentage analysis of the comparative balance sheet. Round to the nearest percent.

★★   **A21-3 Vertical and Horizontal Analysis:** The balance sheet for Heresy Limited is as follows:

Balance Sheet	31 December		
	20X5	**20X4**	**20X3**
Cash	$ 516,000	$ 330,000	$ 295,000
Receivables, net	450,000	510,000	550,000
Marketable securities	420,000	570,000	630,000
Inventory	1,725,000	1,494,000	1,234,000
Capital assets	7,644,000	5,439,000	4,039,000
Less accumulated depreciation	(1,951,200)	(1,461,000)	(976,000)
Goodwill	378,000	405,000	50,000
	$9,181,800	$7,287,000	$5,822,000
Current liabilities	$ 279,000	$ 258,000	$ 679,000
Debentures payable	1,978,500	2,022,000	500,000
Common shares	3,450,000	2,100,000	2,100,000
Retained earnings	3,474,300	2,907,000	2,543,000
	$9,181,800	$7,287,000	$5,822,000

Required:

1. Prepare a comparative vertical percentage analysis. Round to the nearest percent.
2. Prepare a horizontal percentage analysis of the comparative balance sheet. Round to the nearest percent.
3. What conclusions can you reach about the changes in the company's asset and liability structure between 20X3 and 20X5?

★★   **A21-4 Vertical and Horizontal Analysis:** Four-year comparative income statements and balance sheets for Forest Products Incorporated (FPI) are shown below. FPI has been undergoing an extensive restructuring in which the company has discontinued or sold several divisions in order to concentrate on its core business. As a result, the size of the company has decreased considerably.

Income Statement

Years ended 31 December	20X8	20X7	20X6	20X5
Net sales	$ 284.1	$ 949.6	$1,388.8	$2,153.9
Cost of products sold	369.2	793.5	1,045.9	1,649.0
Depreciation, depletion, and amortization	38.4	94.8	88.7	146.9
Selling and administrative	46.4	49.0	53.4	82.7
Operating earnings (loss)	(169.9)	12.3	200.8	275.3
Interest expense	(1.7)	(14.8)	(16.2)	(40.5)
Other income (expense)	32.6	(0.5)	(5.3)	34.8
Earnings (loss) before income tax and non-controlling interest	(139.0)	(3.0)	179.3	269.6
Income tax (recovery)	(46.9)	(2.6)	79.7	115.4
Earnings (loss) before non-controlling interest	(92.1)	(0.4)	99.6	154.2
Non-controlling interest	—	—	—	(34.1)
Earnings (loss) from discontinued operations	390.7	119.9	54.8	—
Net earnings (loss)	$ 298.6	$ 119.5	$ 154.4	$ 120.1

Condensed Balance Sheets

31 December	20X8	20X7	20X6	20X5
Assets				
Working capital	$ 957.7	$ 407.6	$ 126.2	$ 197.7
Investments and other	90.6	36.3	65.8	97.8
Fixed assets	1,289.2	1,286.5	1,318.2	2,200.3
Assets of discontinued operations	—	647.4	1,262.9	—
Net assets	$2,337.5	$2,377.8	$2,773.1	$2,495.8
Liabilities and shareholders' equity				
Long-term debt	$ —	$ —	$ 75.0	$ 227.6
Future (deferred) income taxes	161.8	202.8	136.7	190.0
Liabilities of discontinued operations	—	174.5	438.3	—
Preferred shares issued by subsidiaries	—	—	—	34.3
Non-controlling interest	—	—	176.2	174.5
Shareholders' equity	2,175.7	2,000.5	1,946.9	1,869.4
Total capitalization	$2,337.5	$2,377.8	$2,773.1	$2,495.8

Required:

1. Prepare a vertical analysis of both the income statement and the balance sheet.
2. Prepare a horizontal analysis of the income statement and balance sheet. Use 20X5 as the base year.

 A21-5 Ratio Interpretation: Wilcox Limited has total assets of $35,000,000, and manufactures fine hand tools. Selected financial ratios for Wilcox and industry averages are as follows:

	Wilcox			Industry
	20X5	20X4	20X3	Average
Current ratio	2.41	2.12	2.04	2.28
Quick ratio	1.11	1.10	1.05	1.22
Inventory turnover	2.62	2.78	2.90	3.50
Return on equity	0.16	0.14	0.15	0.11
Debt-to-equity ratio	1.44	1.37	1.41	0.95
Return on assets	.12	.11	.11	.10
Asset turnover	3.14	3.01	3.00	3.70
Operating margin	.06	.05	.05	.05
Basic EPS	.48	.45	.43	1.43
Diluted EPS	.31	.30	.29	1.41

Required:

Referring to the information presented above:

1. Identify two financial ratios of particular interest to:
   a. A financial institution that provides an operating line of credit for daily cash management needs. The line of credit is secured with a charge on inventory.
   b. A supplier, about to decide whether to sell to Wilcox on credit.
   c. An investment banker, consulting with Wilcox on a potential public offering of common shares.

2. Explain why diluted EPS is lower than EPS.

3. Discuss what these financial ratios reveal about Wilcox.

★ **A21-6 Ratio Interpretation:** Presented below are selected ratios for four firms:

	Mining Co.	Software Co.	Tobacco Co.	Wholesale Co.
Liquidity ratio				
Current ratio	1.60	.64	1.32	2.78
Solvency ratio				
Long-term debt to equity	0.47	0.11	0.89	0.61
Efficiency ratios				
Average collection period	62.0	46.3	43.0	113.0
Asset turnover	0.71	1.98	1.80	1.36
Profitability ratios				
Operating margin	2.6	5.6	14.2	3.2
Return on assets	2.9	7.4	9.9	6.1
Return on equity	4.6	29.8	24.5	11.4

Required:

1. Which company manages its accounts receivable the most effectively? On what did you base your answer?

2. What impact would the choice of FIFO versus average cost have on the current ratio?

3. Why are there significant differences among the current ratios of the firms?

4. Explain why return on assets is lower than return on equity in the ratios above.

5. What impact would the choice of straight-line versus declining-balance amortization have on total asset turnover?

★ **A21-7 Ratio Interpretation:** The following ratios are available for a three-year period for Woolfrey Limited.

	20X6	20X7	20X8
Current ratio	1.70	1.79	1.86
Quick ratio	1.14	0.89	0.97
Average collection period of accounts receivable	51 days	57 days	66 days
Inventory turnover	4.51	4.02	3.32
Debt to total assets	51.0%	46.0%	41.0%
Long-term debt to shareholders' equity	52.0%	57.0%	62.0%
Sales as a percentage of 20X6 sales	100.0%	103.0%	107.0%
Gross profit percentage	36.0%	35.1%	34.6%
Operating margin	6.9%	7.0%	7.2%
Return on total assets	7.7%	7.7%	7.8%
Return on shareholders' equity	13.6%	13.1%	12.7%

Required:

1. Explain why the current ratio is increasing while the quick ratio is decreasing.

2. Comment on the company's use of financial leverage.

★ **A21-8 Compute and Explain Profitability Ratios:** The 20X5 comparative financial statements for Thompson Corporation reported the following information:

	20X3	20X4	20X5
Sales revenue	$18,000,000	$19,500,000	$20,250,000
Net income	150,000	180,000	142,500
Interest expense, long-term debt	15,000	18,000	27,000
Income tax expense	60,000	90,000	90,000
Long-term debt	1,200,000	1,500,000	1,650,000
Shareholders' equity, common			
and preferred*	2,100,000	2,175,000	2,190,000
Total assets	5,250,000	5,250,000	5,700,000
Preferred share dividends	9,000	15,000	18,000
Income tax rate	30%	35%	40%

*Preferred shares, $150,000 in all years.

Required:

1. Based on the above financial data, compute the following ratios for 20X4 and 20X5:
   a. return on total assets, before tax
   b. return on total assets, after tax
   c. return on long-term capital, before tax
   d. return on long-term capital, after tax
   e. return on common shareholders' equity
   f. operating margin
   g. asset turnover

2. As an investor in the common shares of Thompson, which ratio would you prefer as a primary measure of profitability? Why?

3. Explain any significant trends that appear to be developing.

★★ **A21-9 Ratios to Measure Profitability—Evaluate Implications:** The following annual data were taken from the records of McKeon Trading Corporation:

	20X2	20X3	20X4	20X5	20X6
Sales revenue	$600,000	$620,000	$650,000	$640,000	$690,000
Pre-tax income	40,000	43,000	62,000	21,000	80,000
Net income	25,000	26,000	40,000	15,000	50,000
Total assets	300,000	340,000	330,000	340,000	350,000
Accumulated					
amortization	36,000	31,000	28,000	22,000	19,000
Long-term debt	100,000	110,000	90,000	125,000	90,000
Owners' equity	150,000*	160,000	170,000	165,000	190,000
Shares outstanding	4,000	4,000	4,000	3,900	3,800
Interest expense,					
long-term debt	10,000	11,000	11,200	12,000	10,500
Amortization					
expense	5,000	5,000	5,000	5,000	5,000
Income tax					
expense (tax					
rate, 40%)	15,000	17,000	22,000	6,000	30,000

Required:

Compute ratios to measure profitability for the years 20X3, 20X4, 20X5, and 20X6. Calculate return on assets and long-term capital on an after-tax basis only. Immediately following each ratio, evaluate and comment on the results (e.g., trends, problems, and favourable/unfavourable implications).

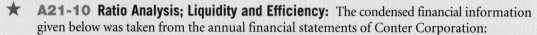

★ **A21-10 Ratio Analysis; Liquidity and Efficiency:** The condensed financial information given below was taken from the annual financial statements of Conter Corporation:

	20X3	20X4	20X5
Current assets (including inventory)	$ 840,000	$1,008,000	$1,176,000
Current liabilities	630,000	672,000	588,000
Cash sales	3,360,000	3,276,000	3,444,000
Credit sales	840,000	1,176,000	1,050,000
Cost of goods sold	2,352,000	2,457,000	2,520,000
Inventory (ending)	504,000	588,000	420,000
Accounts receivable	252,000	268,800	256,200
Total assets (net)	4,200,000	5,040,000	5,880,000
Projected daily operating expenditures	12,600	13,020	12,180

Required:

1. Based on the above data, calculate the following ratios for 20X4 and 20X5. Briefly explain the significance of each ratio listed. Use the following format:

Ratio	20X4	20X5	Significance
Current			
Quick			
Defensive interval			
Asset turnover			
Accounts receivable turnover			
Average collection period of accounts receivable			
Inventory turnover			

2. Evaluate the overall results of the ratios, including trends.

★★ **A21-11 Compute and Summarize Significance of Ratios:** Fader Corporation's 20X4 and 20X5 balance sheets and 20X5 income statement are as follows (in $ millions, except per share amounts):

Balance sheet

31 December	20X4		20X5	
Cash	$ 11		$ 20	
Investments (short term)	3		4	
Accounts receivable (net of allowance)	23		19	
Inventory (FIFO, LCM)	31		37	
Prepaid expenses	4		3	
Funds and investments, long term	31		31	
Capital assets (net of accumulated amortization of $29 (20X4), $37 (20X5)	81		72	
Accounts payable		$ 22		$ 10
Accrued liabilities		2		2
Notes payable, long term		41		45
Common shares, no par (60,000 shares outstanding)		76		76
Retained earnings (including 20X4 and 20X5 income)		43		53
Totals	$184	$184	$186	$186

Income statement, 20X5

Sales revenue (1/3 were credit sales)	$153
Investment revenue	4
Cost of goods sold	(70)
Distribution expense	(20)
Administrative expense (includes $8 of amortization)	(15)
Interest expense	(4)
Income tax expense (the tax rate is 40%)	(20)
Net income	$ 28

Other information
Cash flow from operations	$ 22

Required:
Compute the 20X5 ratios that measure:

a. profitability (after tax only)
b. efficiency
c. solvency
d. liquidity

For each category, use a format similar to the following (example given):

Ratio	Formula	Computation	Significance
Current ratio	Current assets / Current liabilities	$83 ÷ $12 = 6.9	Short-term liquidity; adequacy of working capital

---

★ **A21-12 Selected Ratios:** The 20X9 condensed income statement and the 20X9 and 20X8 condensed balance sheets for Farouk Limited are shown below.

Required:
Compute the following ratios for 20X9:

a. inventory turnover
b. average collection period of accounts payable
c. asset turnover
d. operating margin
e. return on shareholders' equity

Condensed Income Statement

Year ended 31 December 20X9
Sales revenue (all on credit)	$20,000
Cost of goods sold	8,750
Gross profit	11,250
Operating expenses	8,107
Operating income	3,143
Interest expense	1,000
Income before income taxes	2,143
Income tax expense	643
Net income	$ 1,500

Condensed Balance Sheet

31 December	20X9	20X8
Cash	$ 2,750	$ 3,750
Accounts receivable (net)	6,625	7,125
Inventory	4,100	3,100
Plant and equipment	20,250	20,000
Accumulated amortization	(4,000)	(5,000)
Land	20,275	10,025
Total	$50,000	$39,000
Accounts payable	$ 2,900	$ 3,000
Interest payable	350	—
Long-term notes payable	6,500	5,000
Common shares	34,000	25,000
Retained earnings	6,250	6,000
Total	$50,000	$39,000

(CGA-Canada, adapted)

★★ **A21-13 Selected Ratios:** Frenette Limited's 20X5 financial statements are as follows:

Balance Sheet

31 December	20X5	20X4
Cash	$ 516,000	$ 330,000
Receivables, net	450,000	510,000
Marketable securities	420,000	570,000
Inventory	1,725,000	1,494,000
Capital assets	7,644,000	5,439,000
Less accumulated depreciation	(1,951,200)	(1,461,000)
Goodwill	378,000	405,000
	$9,181,800	$7,287,000
Current liabilities	$ 279,000	$ 258,000
Bonds payable	1,500,000	1,500,000
Premium on bonds payable	478,500	522,000
Common shares	3,450,000	2,100,000
Retained earnings	3,474,300	2,907,000
	$9,181,800	$7,287,000

Income Statement

Year ended 31 December 20X5		
Sales (on credit)	$4,296,000	
Cost of goods sold	2,268,000	
Gross profit	2,028,000	
Depreciation	1,003,200	
Other expenses, including interest of $90,000	729,300	
Net income before income taxes	295,500	
Income taxes (40%)	118,200	
Net income	$ 177,300	

Required:

Compute the 20X5 ratios as follows:

1. Profitability
   a. return on assets, after tax
   b. return on common shareholders' equity, after tax
   c. operating margin
2. Efficiency
   a. asset turnover
   b. accounts receivable turnover (all sales on credit)
   c. inventory turnover
3. Solvency
   a. debt to equity (total liabilities)
   b. debt to total assets (total liabilities)
4. Liquidity
   a. current
   b. quick

(CGA-Canada, adapted)

★ **A21-14 Profitability and Solvency Ratios, Competing Companies** Abacus Limited and Zandi Corporation are competing businesses. Abacus owns all of its operating assets, financed largely by secured loans. Zandi rents its operating assets from a major industrial leasing company. The 20X2 income statements and balance sheets for the two companies are shown below.

Income Statements

Year ended 31 December 20X2	Abacus	Zandi
Sales revenue	$ 540,000	$270,000
Direct costs of providing services	300,000	150,000
Amortization	100,000	10,000
Other expenses	60,000	87,000
Total operating expenses	460,000	247,000
Net operating earnings	80,000	23,000
Interest expense	24,000	—
Earnings before income taxes	56,000	23,000
Provision for income taxes	17,000	7,000
Net earnings	$ 39,000	$ 16,000

Balance Sheets

31 December 20X2	Abacus	Zandi
Current assets	$ 260,000	$130,000
Tangible capital assets	1,000,000	50,000
Accumulated amortization	(600,000)	(30,000)
Total assets	$ 660,000	$150,000
Current liabilities	$ 120,000	$ 60,000
Long-term liabilities	360,000	—
Common shares	100,000	50,000
Retained earnings	80,000	40,000
Total liabilities and shareholders' equity	$ 660,000	$150,000

Required:

1. Compute the following ratios for both companies (for convenience, use 20X2 year-end balance sheet amounts instead of averages):
   a. operating margin
   b. asset turnover
   c. return on assets
   d. return on share equity
   e. total debt-to-shareholder's equity

2. Evaluate the two companies, based on the ratios you have calculated. Which company do you think is more profitable?

★ **A21-15 Competing Companies, Continuation:** Refer to the information in A21-14; Zandi's financial statements contain the following note disclosure:

Commitments:

The Company has commitments for operating lease payments for the next five years as follows:

20X3	$53,000
20X4	49,000
20X5	45,000
20X6	40,000
20X7	35,000

Required:
Determine how this additional information would affect the ratios for Zandi that are required in A21-14. Assume that the disclosed lease payments are due at the end of each year and that Zandi's incremental borrowing rate is 8%. Ignore any income tax impact.

★★ **A21-16 Recasting, Selected Ratios:** A loan officer for the Dominion Bank of Alberta wishes to recast her client's financial statements so that they reflect income tax expense on a taxes payable basis. The tax rate is 30%. One of her clients is Frobisher Bay Corporation (FBC). FBC's condensed year-end 20X4 statements are shown in Exhibit 1.

Required:

1. Recast FBC's statements.

2. Compute the following ratios, both before and after recasting the statements:
   a. operating margin
   b. return on total assets (after tax)
   c. total liabilities to shareholders' equity

Earnings Statement

Year ended 31 December 20X4

Sales revenue	$660,000
Cost of goods sold	360,000
Amortization expense	72,000
Interest expense	12,000
Other expenses	96,000
	540,000
Earnings before income tax	120,000
Income tax:	
—current	14,400
—future	21,600
	36,000
Net earnings	$ 84,000

Balance Sheet

31 December 20X4

Current assets	$144,000
Capital assets:	
—Tangible (net)	624,000
—Identifiable intangible	168,000
Total assets	$936,000
Current liabilities:	
Accounts payable and accrued liabilities	96,000
Future income tax	24,000
	120,000
Long-term debt	384,000
Future income tax, non-current	192,000
Total liabilities	696,000
Common shares	60,000
Retained earnings	180,000
Total shareholders' equity	240,000
Total liabilities and shareholders' equity	$936,000

★★ **A21-17 Compute and Evaluate Ratios:** Data from the financial statements of LMR Manufacturing Company for a three-year period follow:

	20X4	20X5	20X6
Total assets	$2,400,000	$2,440,000	$2,340,000
Total current assets	468,000	550,000	580,000
Monetary current assets	165,000	110,000	105,000
Total current liabilities	330,000	250,000	250,000
Operational assets (net)	1,548,000	1,557,600	1,560,000
Total liabilities (of which $1,000,000 is long term each year)	1,490,000	1,510,000	1,300,000
Common shares, no par (10,000 shares, 11,000 in 20X6)	600,000	600,000	700,000
Retained earnings	310,000	330,000	340,000
Sales revenue (net)	6,600,000	7,000,000	7,100,000
Net income (after tax)	50,000	70,000	40,000
Interest expense (pre tax)	34,000	38,000	30,000
Income tax (marginal rate, 20%)	16,000	23,000	12,000

Required:

1. Based on the above data, compute the following ratios to measure liquidity position for each year:
   a. current ratio
   b. quick ratio

   Evaluate the current position. What additional information do you need to adequately evaluate the current position? Explain.

2. Based on the above data, compute the following ratios to measure solvency:
   a. debt to equity (total liabilities)
   b. debt to total assets (total liabilities)
   c. times interest earned

   Evaluate solvency. What additional information do you need to adequately evaluate solvency? Explain.

3. Based on the above data, compute the following ratios to measure profitability and leverage:
   a. operating margin
   b. return on assets (after tax)
   c. return on common shareholders' equity
   Evaluate profitability and financial leverage.

 A21-18 Leverage—Sell Share Capital versus Debt, Analysis: Bui Limited is considering building a second plant at a cost of $4,800,000. Management has two alternatives to obtain the funds: (a) sell additional common shares or (b) issue $4,800,000, five-year bonds payable at 10% interest. Management believes that the bonds can be sold at par for $4,800,000 and the shares at $80 per share. The balance sheet (before the new financing) reflected the following:

Long-term liabilities	$ 600,000
Common shares, no par (40,000 shares)	2,000,000
Retained earnings	800,000
Average income for past several years (net of tax)	250,000

The average income tax rate is 30%. Dividends per share have been $4.00 per share per year. Expected increase in pre-tax income (excluding interest expense) from the new plant is $800,000 per year.

Required:

1. Prepare an analysis to show, for each financing alternative,
   a. Expected total net income after the addition;
   b. After-tax cash flows from the company to prospective owners of the new capital; and
   c. The (leverage) advantage or disadvantage to the present shareholders of issuing the bonds to obtain the financing, as represented by comparing return on assets to return on equity.
2. What are the principal arguments for and against issuing the bonds, as opposed to selling the common shares?

 A21-19 Comparative Analysis: Frank Smythe, the owner of Cuppola Limited, has asked you to compare the operations and financial position of his company with those of Ling Limited, a large company in the same business and a company that Frank Smythe considers representative of the industry.

Balance Sheet

	Cuppola Limited		Ling Limited	
	20X1	20X0	20X1	20X0
Balance Sheet				
Assets				
Cash	$ 100,000	$ 20,000	$ 100,000	$ 125,000
Accounts receivable	70,000	60,000	800,000	750,000
Inventories	230,000	190,000	2,400,000	1,825,000
	$ 400,000	$ 270,000	$3,300,000	$2,700,000
Capital assets	$ 500,000	$ 500,000	$5,300,000	$5,000,000
Accumulated amortization	(300,000)	(270,000)	(2,600,000)	(2,300,000)
Goodwill	—	—	500,000	500,000
	$ 200,000	$ 230,000	$3,200,000	$3,200,000
	$ 600,000	$ 500,000	$6,500,000	$5,900,000

	Cuppola Limited		Ling Limited	
	20X1	**20X0**	**20X1**	**20X0**
Liabilities and shareholders' equity				
Bank indebtedness	$ 40,000	$ 30,000	$ 500,000	$ 300,000
Trade accounts payable	135,000	100,000	1,300,000	650,000
Current portion of long-term debt	20,000	20,000	300,000	300,000
	$ 195,000	$ 150,000	$2,100,000	$1,250,000
Long-term debt	30,000	50,000	1,400,000	1,700,000
	$ 225,000	$ 200,000	$3,500,000	$2,950,000
Capital stock				
—preferred	—	—	$ 500,000	$ 500,000
—common	$ 50,000	$ 50,000	1,500,000	1,500,000
Retained earnings	325,000	250,000	1,000,000	950,000
	$ 375,000	$ 300,000	$3,000,000	$2,950,000
	$ 600,000	$ 500,000	$6,500,000	$5,900,000
Income statement				
Sales	$1,300,000	$1,000,000	$9,000,000	$7,500,000
Cost of sales	(936,000)	(700,000)	(6,120,000)	(5,250,000)
Expenses, including income tax	(266,500)	(250,000)	(2,100,000)	(1,800,000)
Net income	$ 97,500	$ 50,000	$ 780,000	$ 450,000

Required:

Compare the operations and financial positions of the two companies, supporting your comments with useful ratios and percentages.

★★ **A21-20 Investment Analysis:** Sandy Panchaud has come to you for some independent financial advice. He is considering investing some of his money in an operating company and he wants to know which of the two alternatives he has identified is the better investment. They are both in the same industry, and Mr. Panchaud feels he could buy either for book value. Your reply to Mr. Panchaud should include a selection of ratios and a common-size (vertical analysis) income statement.

	Company A	Company B
Income statement		
Sales	$2,797,000	$2,454,000
Cost of goods sold	1,790,000	1,594,000
Gross margin	1,007,000	860,000
Operating expenses	807,000	663,000
Operating income	200,000	197,000
Interest expense	70,000	43,000
Income before income tax	130,000	154,000
Income tax expense	52,000	62,000
Net income	$ 78,000	$ 92,000

	Company A	Company B
Balance sheet		
Cash	$ 66,000	$ 27,000
Accounts receivable (net)	241,000	262,000
Merchandise inventory	87,000	110,000
Prepaid expenses	12,000	7,000
Plant and equipment (net)	792,000	704,000
	$1,198,000	$1,110,000
Accounts payable and accrued liabilities	$ 191,000	$ 173,000
Long-term debt	635,000	310,000
Common shares	50,000	200,000
Retained earnings	322,000	427,000
	$1,198,000	$1,110,000

★★ **A21-21 Reconstruction:** The following ratios are available concerning the balance sheet and income statements of BVR Limited.

Current ratio	1.75 to 1
Acid-test ratio	1.27 to 1
Working capital	$33,000
Capital assets to shareholders' equity ratio	.625 to 1
Inventory turnover (based on cost of closing inventory)	4 times
Gross profit percentage	40%
Earnings per share	50¢
Average collection period for outstanding accounts receivable (based on calendar year of 365 days)	73 days
Share capital outstanding	20,000 shares
Earnings for year as a percentage of share capital	25%
Working capital to total assets	.25

The company had no prepaid expenses, deferred charges, intangible assets, or long-term liabilities.

Required:

Reconstruct an income statement and balance sheet in as much detail as possible from this information.

★★ **A21-22 Reconstruction:** Frank Argo, the president of Argo Sales Corporation, has accumulated some data about his major competitor, Xeta Sales Corporation. He has consulted you in the hope that you can reconstruct Xeta's 20X1 financial statements.

Mr. Argo has reason to believe that Xeta maintains the following relationships among the data on its financial statements:

Gross profit rate on net sales	40%
Net profit rate on net sales	10%
Rate of selling expenses to net sales	20%
Accounts receivable turnover	8 per year
Inventory turnover	6 per year
Quick ratio	2 to 1
Current ratio	3 to 1
Quick-asset composition: 8% cash, 32% marketable securities, 60% accounts receivable	
Asset turnover	2 per year
Ratio of total assets to intangible assets	20 to 1
Ratio of accumulated depreciation to cost of capital assets	1 to 3
Ratio of accounts receivable to accounts payable	1.5 to 1
Ratio of working capital to shareholders' equity	1 to 1.6
Ratio of total liabilities to shareholders' equity	1 to 2

Frank also tells you the following:

- Xeta's 20X1 net income was $120,000 and earnings per share, $5.20.
- Share capital authorized, issued, and outstanding: common shares issued at $11; preferred shares issued at $110 per share.
- Preferred dividends paid in 20X1, $3,000.
- Number of times interest earned in 20X1, 21.
- The amounts of the following were the same at 31 December 20X1 and at 1 January 20X1: inventory, accounts receivable, 8% bonds payable (due 20X3), and total shareholders' equity.
- All purchases and sales were "on account."
- There is no income tax.

Required:
Frank has specifically asked for a condensed balance sheet and condensed income statement, and has also asked you to calculate the rate of return on common shareholders' equity.

(AICPA, adapted)

A21-23 Integrative Problem, Chapters 17–21: The following information is available for Davison Limited for the year ended 31 December 20X6:

Balance Sheet	($ thousands)	
As at 31 December	**20X6**	**20X5**
Cash	$ 1,720	$1,110
Receivables, net	1,150	1,170
Marketable securities	450	550
Inventory	2,575	2,110
Capital assets	3,984	3,396
Less: accumulated amortization	(1,650)	(1,487)
Goodwill	135	135
Deferred development costs	555	417
	$ 8,919	$7,401
Current liabilities	$ 2,190	$1,900
Convertible bond payable	833	834
Future income tax	619	585
Preferred shares	500	500
Common stock conversion rights	166	166
Common shares	2,150	1,700
Retained earnings	2,461	1,716
	$ 8,919	$7,401

Income Statement

for the year ended 31 December	**20X6**
Sales (on account)	$10,450
Cost of goods sold	7,619
	2,831
Operating expenses	1,548
Income tax	513
Net income	770
Less: dividends	(25)
Increase in retained earnings	745
Opening retained earnings	1,716
Closing retained earnings	$ 2,461

Other information:

- There is a $1,000,000, 10% bond outstanding. Each $1,000 bond is convertible into 50 common shares at the investor's option. The bond proceeds were split between the debt and equity when the bond was issued. In 20X6, interest expense of $98 was recognized.
- The tax rate is 40%.
- In 20X6, there were stock options outstanding to key employees allowing them to buy 40,000 common shares for $16 per share at any time after 1 January 20X18. The average common share price during the year was $20.
- There were 420,000 common shares outstanding on 31 December 20X6; 40,000 shares had been issued for cash on 1 February 20X6.
- Preferred shares are cumulative, and have a dividend of $4 per share; 10,000 shares are outstanding. Each share can be converted into four common shares at any time.

Required:

1. Calculate the following ratios for 20X6 based on the financial statements above and before making any adjustments for requirements (2) to (4).
   a. basic EPS
   b. diluted EPS
   c. debt to equity (total debt)
   d. inventory turnover
   e. quick ratio
   f. return on assets (after tax)
   g. return on common shareholders' equity
   h. accounts receivable turnover (all sales are on account)
   i. asset turnover
   j. return on long-term capital, after tax
   k. operating margin

2. As the year-end adjustments were being finalized, accounting staff realized that a pension covering factory workers, first adopted in 20X4, had been accounted for incorrectly. Pension payments had been expensed, rather than an appropriate pension expense calculated. Information is as follows:

	20X6	20X5	20X4
Pension payments			
Current service			
(paid each 31 December)	$41,000	$46,000	$45,000
Past service*			
(paid each 31 December)	73,800	73,800	73,800
Expected rate of return and interest rate	6%	6%	6%
Benefits paid to employees	0	0	0
Actual return	15,000	7,000	0
EPFE and ARSP (all employees)	28	24	29

*Past service liability was calculated as of January 20X4, but the first payment was due, and was paid, on 31 December 20X4. Past service cost is funded over 20 years.

   a. Calculate the plan assets and pension obligation for each year, 20X4 to 20X6.
   b. Calculate the appropriate pension expense for each year. No actuarial revaluations were conducted over the period. The ARSP and EPFE at the inception of the plan for employees earning past service was 25 years. Expected earnings are used in the calculation of pension expense.

3. Prepare the entry to correct the accounts for the pension expense as calculated in requirement (2), and prepare the lower section of the 20X6 income and retained earnings statement, beginning with net income.

4. Accounting staff also realized that a lease has not yet been properly reflected in the financial statements. The lease was signed, and the first lease payment was due, on 31 December 20X6. The lease payment was paid and expensed. Details of the lease follow:

- The lease term begins on 31 December 20X6 and runs for three years. Payments of $41,400 include insurance costs of $2,000.

- At the end of the initial lease term, the lease may be renewed at Davison's option for a further three years at an annual rate of $6,000 per year. This does not include any insurance, which would become Davison's responsibility.

- The expected residual value of the asset is $29,000 at the end of the first lease term, and $500 at the end of the second. The lessor may choose to leave the asset with Davison if the value is low.

Provide the appropriate journal entry to capitalize the lease. Davison does not know the interest rate implicit in the lease but has an incremental borrowing rate of 10%.

Complex Cash Flow Statement Illustration

APPENDIX

The cash flow statement (CFS) was the subject of Chapter 5 of Volume 1 of this text. Subsequent chapters have reviewed the impact of various transactions and accounting policies on the CFS, as topics were covered. This appendix summarizes that material and reviews a comprehensive example of a CFS.

The CFS has three main sections—operating, investing, and financing activities. The operating activities section deals with cash generated, or used, from the primary operating activities of the enterprise. The operating activities section has two formats, the indirect method, which involves a reconciliation of net income to cash flow, and the less common direct method, which shows cash inflows from customers, and cash outflows to suppliers, employees, and so on. When the indirect method of presentation is used, the adjustments for non-cash items are presented first, with a subtotal, and then the changes in working capital, providing a two-step method of presentation. The investing activities section deals with cash flows related to capital assets, investments, and other assets, both purchase and sale. The financing activities section includes cash flow from or for borrowing, repayment of debt, and transactions with shareholders, including dividends paid.

The major points to remember about the CFS are summarized in Exhibit A-1.

Comprehensive Example

The data for a comprehensive example is found in Exhibit A-2, and includes an income statement, balance sheet, and additional information concerning critical transactions. To analyze the data, the changes in the transactions will be translated into journal entries, then entered on a worksheet that backs up the CFS. The information may also be analyzed through journal entries alone or T-accounts. All analysis alternatives will produce the same CFS.

CASH FLOW STATEMENT

Cash	• Cash is defined as cash plus cash-equivalent temporary investments (e.g., money market certificates; maximum of three-month term) less bank overdrafts.
Extraordinary items and discontinued operations	• Begin CFS with net income before extraordinary items and discontinued operations. • Show cash flow impact of extraordinary item or discontinued operation separately in appropriate section.
Working capital items	• Adjust net income for the change in working capital items that relate to income statement items. • If working capital item does not relate to net income (e.g., investments, dividends payable), adjust for the change in the appropriate section (e.g., investing, financing).
Investments	• Purchase price is an outflow under investing activities; proceeds of sale are an inflow. • Changes in fair value that are unrealized are non-cash and are adjusted to net income (on the CFS) or to shareholder's equity. • Gains and losses on sale are adjusted in operating activities. • Equity-based net income is backed out of net income; dividends received are included in operating activities.
Capital assets	• Purchase price (if cash) is an outflow under investing activities; proceeds of sale are an inflow. • Swaps are non-cash transactions and excluded. • Depreciation and amortization are added back in operating activities. • Gains and losses on retirement are adjusted in operating activities. • Impairment writedowns are added back in operating activities.
Deferred costs	• Purchase price (if cash) is an outflow under investing activities; proceeds of sale are an inflow. • Amortization is added back in operating activities. • Impairment writedowns are added back as a non-cash charge in operating activities.
Goodwill	• Purchase price (if cash) is an outflow under investing activities; proceeds of sale are an inflow. • Amortization is added back in operating activities. • Impairment writedowns are added back in operating activities.
Liabilities	• Amount borrowed is an inflow under financing activities; repayments are outflows. • Netting new and old loans is not permitted. • Amortization of discount is adjusted in operating activities. • Amortization of premium is considered principal repayment and is classified as financing. • Gains and losses on retirement are adjusted in operating activities.
Equity	• Cash investment by shareholders is an inflow under financing activities. • Amount paid to retire shares is an outflow under financing activities. • The difference between the amount paid to retire shares and the average issuance price changes equity accounts.
Dividends	• Dividends paid are an outflow in financing activities. • Stock dividends and splits are not cash flows and do not appear on the CFS.

continued on next page

CASH FLOW STATEMENT

Complex financial instruments	• Amount borrowed/invested is an inflow under financing activities; repayments are outflows.
	• If a hybrid instrument is issued, only one cash inflow is recorded on the CFS for both elements.
	• Amortization of discount is adjusted in operating activities.
	• Amortization of premium is considered principal repayment and is classified as financing.
	• Conversion of a financial instrument into common shares is a non-cash transaction and is excluded from the CFS.
	• Gains and losses on retirement are adjusted in operating activities.
Stock options	• Expense is adjusted in operating activities; added back as a non-cash transaction.
	• Cash received for shares issued under options, if any, is recorded as an inflow in financing activities. The value of options recorded in common shares upon exercise is a non-cash transaction and is not recorded on the CFS.
	• If options are recorded on the receipt of non-cash assets, the transaction is a non-cash transaction and is excluded from the CFS.
Income tax	• Income tax is an operating activities item.
	• Change in future income tax is adjusted in operating activities.
Leases	• Increase in assets and liabilities because of a new capital lease for the lessee is a non-cash transaction and excluded from the CFS.
	• Reduction in lease liability is an outflow under financing activities.
	• Depreciation and amortization are added back in operating activities.
Pensions	• Change in pension obligation is adjusted in operating activities.

HEPTOP LIMITED

The records of Heptop Limited show the following:

Income statement, for the year ended 31 December, 20X8:

Sales	$1,402,300
Cost of goods sold	631,100
Gross profit	771,200
Amortization expense	43,200
Selling expenses	107,900
Administrative expenses	119,900
Interest expense	35,300
Other expenses	43,200
Investment revenue	(1,400)
Loss on sale of machinery	16,000
Gain on sale of available-for-sale investments	(16,100)
Income before income tax	423,200
Income tax expense	174,000
Net income	$ 249,200

EXHIBIT A-2   *(cont'd)*

HEPTOP LIMITED

December 31	20X8	20X7
Balance sheet, year ended		
Assets:		
Cash	$ 40,000	$ 29,200
Available-for-sale investments	226,300	70,700
Accounts receivable (net)	112,500	147,200
Inventory	179,100	187,300
Prepaid rent	4,700	—
Land	276,000	204,000
Machinery	1,899,000	1,743,900
Accumulated amortization	(801,600)	(839,000)
Goodwill	890,400	890,400
Total	$2,826,400	$2,433,700
Liabilities and shareholders' equity:		
Accounts payable	$ 139,000	$ 215,200
Salaries payable	46,100	45,500
Taxes payable	21,000	29,000
Bonds payable; 6%	—	652,200
Bonds payable; 7.2%	600,000	—
Discount on bonds payable	(11,200)	—
Future income tax	198,900	214,800
Deferred pension obligation	14,900	16,700
Common shares, no par	1,500,000	930,000
Common stock conversion rights	—	83,300
Contributed capital: stock options	70,000	60,000
Retained earnings	184,200	165,000
Accumulated other comprehensive income:		
unrealized holding gains	63,500	22,000
Total	$2,826,400	$2,433,700

Analysis of selected accounts and transactions:

1. Issued additional 7.2% bonds payable for cash, $588,000.
2. Cash dividends were declared and paid.
3. Available-for-sale investments with an original cost of $47,200 were sold in 20X8. The investments had a carrying value of $50,000 at the beginning of 20X8. Investments with a cost of $161,300 were acquired during the year.
4. There is a stock option plan for senior administrative staff, accounted for using the fair value method. Stock options with a book value of $14,000 were exchanged, along with $37,400 cash, for common shares in 20X8. The remaining increase in the stock options account is explained by additional compensation expense recorded, using the fair value method.
5. The 6% bond payable was converted into common shares at the beginning of the fiscal year.
6. Land was acquired for cash.
7. Machinery with an original cost of $106,000 and a net book value of $25,400 was sold for a loss of $16,000. Additional machinery for other activities was acquired for common shares.
8. Common shares with an average original issue price of $478,000 were retired for $699,200.

The entries that follow *re-create* the transactions for the year, reflecting (in summary) the company's entries for the year. The entries must be sufficient to change the opening balance to the closing balance, per the financial statements provided. In the re-creation of entries, the CFS amounts are represented by cash or income statement items in an entry.

As a first step, the net income is entered as an increase to retained earnings and the first item in the operating activities sections:

a. CFS-Operating—NI	249,200	
Retained earnings		249,200

Next, the changes in all non-cash working capital accounts that relate to income statement items are adjusted to the operating activities section:

b. CFS-Operating—decrease in accounts receivable	34,700	
Accounts receivable		34,700
c. CFS-Operating—decrease in inventory	8,200	
Inventory		8,200
d. Prepaid rent	4,700	
CFS-Operating—increase in prepaid rent		4,700
e. Accounts payable	76,200	
CFS-Operating—decrease in accounts payable		76,200
f. CFS-Operating—increase in salaries payable	600	
Salaries payable		600
g. Taxes payable	8,000	
CFS-Operating—decrease in taxes payable		8,000

The obvious non-cash expenses are adjusted:

h. CFS-Operating—add back amortization	43,200	
Accumulated amortization		43,200
i. Future income tax	15,900	
CFS-Operating—decrease in future income tax		15,900
j. Deferred pension obligation	1,800	
CFS-Operating—decrease in deferred pension obligation		1,800
k. CFS-Operating—add back discount amortization	800	
Discount on bonds payable ($12,000 − $11,200)		800

The original discount on the bond was $12,000 ($600,000 − $588,000). The discount appears as $11,200 in the closing trial balance, implying discount amortization of $800 during the period.

Remaining non-cash items, and gains and losses on various transactions will be adjusted as other accounts are analyzed.

Available-for-sale investments were purchased during the period:

l. Available for sale investments	161,300	
CFS Investing—purchased available for sale investments		161,300

Other available-for-sale investments were sold. The cash proceeds are calculated as the original cost plus the gain on sale from the income statement. The investment has a carrying value of $50,000 at the beginning of the year. They had been written up from their cost of $47,200 through the recognition of an unrealized holding gain in accumulated other comprehensive income. This unrealized holding gain is reversed when an actual sale takes place.

m. CFS-Investing—sale of investments		
($47,200 + $16,100)	63,300	
Accumulated other comprehensive income:		
unrealized holding gains ($50,000 −		
$47,200)	2,800	
CFS-Operating—gain on sale of investments		
(per IS)		16,100
Available-for-sale investments		50,000

The remaining change in the investments account and accumulated other comprehensive income is explained by the revaluation of available-for-sale investments to fair value at year-end. There is no effect on the CFS.

n. Available for sale investments ($70,700 − $50,000		
+ $161,300 = $182,000 vs. $226,300)	44,300	
Accumulated other comprehensive income:		
unrealized holding gains ($22,000 −		
$2,800 = $19,200 vs. $63,500)		44,300

Land was purchased during the period:

o. Land ($204,000 − $276,000)	72,000	
CFS-Investing—purchase of land		72,000

Machinery was sold:

p. CFS-Investing—sale of machinery		
($25,400 − $16,000)	9,400	
Accumulated amortization ($106,000 − $25,400)	80,600	
CFS-Operating—loss on sale on machinery (per IS)	16,000	
Machinery		106,000

The accumulated amortization account has been increased by current-year amortization expense, and decreased by the accumulated amortization on the machinery sold. These two entries completely explain the change in the accumulated amortization account.

Machinery was acquired for common shares. This transaction is assumed to explain the remaining change in the machinery account. The acquisition is a non-cash transaction that is not reflected on the CFS:

q. Machinery ($1,899,000 −		
($1,743,900 − $106,000)	261,100	
Common shares		261,100

Bonds were converted into common shares, which explains the decrease in the 6% bond and the common stock conversion rights account. Again, this is a non-cash transaction that does not appear on the CFS.

r. Bonds payable, 6%	652,200	
Common stock conversion rights	83,300	
Common shares		735,500

Bonds were also issued in 20X8:

s. CFS-Financing—issuance of bond	588,000	
Discount on bonds payable	12,000	
Bonds payable		600,000

The original discount was $12,000; it has already been amortized by $800, and thus the closing balance of $11,200 is fully explained in the entries.

Common shares were retired, at a price higher than average issuance price. The difference is a direct debit to retained earnings:

t. Common shares	478,000	
Retained earnings	221,200	
CFS-Financing—retirement of common shares		699,200

Common shares were issued under the terms of stock options, which results in a cash inflow to the company:

u. CFS-Financing—issued common shares	37,400	
Contributed capital: stock options	14,000	
Common stock		51,400

The common stock account has had many changes, but the entries now explain all the changes. The opening balance was $930,000, decreased by $478,000 because of the retirement, and increased by common shares issued for machinery, $261,100; common shares issued on bond conversion, $735,500; and shares issued under option terms, $51,400. This equals the closing balance of $1,500,000.

Stock options were also recorded as compensation expense, which is a non-cash expense:

v. CFS-Operating—non-cash compensation expense	24,000	
Contributed capital: stock options		
($60,000 − $14,000 = $46,000 vs. $70,000)		24,000

Finally, there were cash dividends:

w. Retained earning ($165,000 + 249, 200 −		
221,200 = $193,000 − $184,200)	8,800	
CFS-Financing—dividends		8,800

To complete the CFS, the change in cash is recorded:

x. Cash	10,800	
CFS—Increase in cash		10,800

These entries retrace the effects of all transactions, isolating their impact on the CFS. The next step is to post them to the worksheet (Exhibit A-3), and then prepare the CFS itself (Exhibit A-4).

EXHIBIT A-3

HEPTOP LIMITED
ADJUSTMENTS LEADING TO CASH FLOW STATEMENT
YEAR ENDED 31 DECEMBER 20X8

Item	Beginning Balance	Debits		Credits		Ending Balance
Assets						
Cash	29,200	v.	10,800			40,000
Available-for-sale investments	70,700	l.	161,300	m.	50,000	226,300
		n.	44,300			
Accounts receivable (net)	147,200			b.	34,700	112,500
Inventory	187,300			c.	8,200	179,100
Prepaid rent	—	d.	4,700			4,700
Land	204,000	o.	72,000			276,000
Machinery	1,743,900	q.	261,100	p.	106,000	1,899,000
Accumulated amortization	(839,000)	p.	80,600	h.	43,200	(801,600)
Goodwill	890,400					890,400
Total assets	2,433,700					2,826,400
Liabilities and shareholders' equity						
Accounts payable	215,200	e.	76,200			139,000
Salaries payable	45,500			f.	600	46,100
Taxes payable	29,000	g.	8,000			21,000
Bonds payable, 6%	652,200	r.	652,200			—
Bonds payable, 7.2%	—			s.	600,000	600,000
Discount on bonds payable	—	s.	12,000	k.	800	(11,200)
Future income tax	214,800	i.	15,900			198,900
Deferred pension obligation	16,700	j.	1,800			14,900
Common shares, no par	930,000	t.	478,000	q.	261,100	1,500,000
				r.	735,500	
				u.	51,400	
Common stock conversion rights	83,300	r.	83,300			—
Contributed capital: stock options	60,000	u.	14,000	v.	24,000	70,000
Retained earnings	165,000	t.	221,200	a.	249,200	184,200
		w.	8,800			
Accumulated other comprehensive income	22,000	m.	2,800	n.	44,300	63,500
Total	2,433,700		2,209,000		2,209,000	2,826,400

continued on next page

EXHIBIT A-3 *(cont'd)*

HEPTOP LIMITED
ADJUSTMENTS LEADING TO CASH FLOW STATEMENT
YEAR ENDED 31 DECEMBER 20X8

Adjustments for CFS		Debits		Credits
Operating activities (indirect method)				
Net income	a.	249,200		
Items not involving cash:				
Amortization	h.	43,200		
Future income tax			i.	15,900
Deferred pension obligation			j.	1,800
Compensation expense	v.	24,000		
Amortization of discount	k.	800		
Gain on sale of investments			m.	16,100
Loss on sale of machinery	p.	16,000		
Non-cash working capital accounts:				
Accounts receivable	b.	34,700		
Inventory	c.	8,200		
Prepaid rent			d.	4,700
Accounts payable			e.	76,200
Salaries payable	f.	600		
Taxes payable			g.	8,000
Financing activities				
Bonds issued	s.	588,000		
Common shares retired			t.	699,200
Common shares issued	u.	37,400		
Dividends paid			w.	8,800
Investing activities				
Investments purchased			l.	1,61,300
Sale of investments	m.	63,300		
Sale of machinery	p.	9,400		
Land purchased			o.	72,000
		1,074,800		1,064,000
Change in cash for the year		—	x.	10,800
		1,074,800		1,074,800

Direct Method for Operating Activities The operating activities section for Heptop has been restated, using the direct method of presentation, in Exhibit A-5. The operating activities section now reflects cash received from customers, and cash paid for various income statement items. If an income statement line item does not involve cash (amortization), or does not reflect the actual cash flow (gains and losses on sale) it is excluded from the operating activities section.

To prepare the direct method disclosure, begin with the income statement item. For example, revenues imply an inflow of $1,402,300 in this example, which is the sales figure on the income statement. Next, any adjustment from the indirect method reconciliation is included. In our case, this is a decrease in accounts receivable, increasing cash collected,

EXHIBIT A-4

HEPTOP LIMITED
CASH FLOW STATEMENT
YEAR ENDED 31 DECEMBER 20X8

Cash provided by (used in) operating activities

Net income	$249,200	
Add (deduct) items not involving cash:		
Amortization	43,200	
Decrease in future income tax	(15,900)	
Decrease in deferred pension obligation	(1,800)	
Compensation expense re: stock options	24,000	
Amortization of discount on long-term debt	800	
Gain on sale of investments	(16,100)	
Loss on sale of machinery	16,000	
	299,400	
Changes in non-cash working capital accounts:		
Accounts receivable decrease	34,700	
Inventory decrease	8,200	
Prepaid rent increase	(4,700)	
Accounts payable decrease	(76,200)	
Salaries payable increase	600	
Taxes payable decrease	(8,000)	
		$254,000
Cash provided by (used in) financing activities		
Bonds issued	588,000	
Common shares retired	(699,200)	
Common shares issued	37,400	
Cash dividend paid	(8,800)	
		(82,600)
Cash provided by (used in) investing activities		
Investments purchased	(161,300)	
Sale of investments	63,300	
Sale of machinery	9,400	
Land purchased	(72,000)	
		(160,600)
Increase in cash and cash equivalents		10,800
Cash and cash equivalents at beginning of year		29,200
Cash and cash equivalents at end of year		$ 40,000

by $34,700, so the cash collected is $1,437,000. For the expenses, the beginning point is an outflow, per the income statement. For example, interest expense was $35,300, implying a ($35,300) outflow of this amount. The indirect method included an add-back (positive amount) of amortization of the discount of $800. When the negative and positive are combined, the outflow for interest is ($34,500). All adjustments used with the indirect method must be incorporated for the direct method, and will eliminate the non-cash income statement lines.

EXHIBIT A-5

HEPTOP LIMITED
CASH FLOW STATEMENT
DIRECT PRESENTATION OF OPERATING ACTIVITIES
YEAR ENDED 31 DECEMBER 20X8

Operating Activities—Direct Method

Cash from customers ($1,402,300 + $34,700)	$1,437,000
Cash from investment revenue ($1,400)	1,400
Cash paid to suppliers (− $631,100 + $8,200 − $76,200)	(699,100)
Cash paid for salaries and other expenses (−$107,900 − $119,900 − $43,200 − $1,800 + $24,000 − $4,700 − $600)	(252,900)
Cash paid for interest (− $35,300 + $800)	(34,500)
Cash paid for income taxes (− $174,000 − $8,000 − $15,900)	(197,900)
	$ 254,000

Note: Other sections of the CFS are identical.

ASSIGNMENTS

A-1 Cash Flow Statement: The following financial information is available for Crane Incorporated for the 20X3 fiscal year:

Balance Sheet

As at 31 December	20X3	20X2
Cash	$ 5,000	$ 20,000
Receivables	220,000	180,000
Marketable securities	190,000	230,000
Inventory	731,000	632,000
Land	330,000	410,000
Building	1,040,000	1,120,000
Accumulated amortization, building	(470,000)	(380,000)
Machinery	1,080,000	875,000
Accumulated amortization, machinery	(219,000)	(212,000)
Goodwill	100,000	110,000
	$3,007,000	$2,985,000
Current liabilities	$ 76,000	$ 146,000
Bonds payable	810,000	810,000
Premium on bonds	180,000	185,000
Preferred shares	1,048,000	843,000
Common stock conversion rights	190,000	190,000
Common shares	565,000	500,000
Retained earnings	138,000	311,000
	$3,007,000	$2,985,000

Income Statement

For the year ended 31 December 20X3

Sales	$1,684,000
Cost of goods sold	1,103,000
Gross profit	581,000
Amortization	
Building	110,000
Machinery	75,000
Goodwill	10,000
Interest	115,000
Other expenses	361,000
Loss on writedown of marketable securities	40,000
Gain on sale of land	(22,000)
Loss on sale of machine	27,000
	716,000
Net income (loss) before income tax	(135,000)
Income tax	54,000
Net income (loss)	$ (81,000)

Additional information:

1. No marketable securities were purchased or sold. The marketable securities are not cash equivalents.

2. A partially amortized building was sold for an amount equal to its net book value.

3. Cash of $40,000 was received on the sale of a machine.

4. Preferred shares were issued for cash on 1 March 20X3. Preferred shares are voting and entitled to a share of net assets on company dissolution. Dividends of $50,000 were paid on the non-cumulative preferred shares. Each preferred share was convertible to seven common shares, and there were 97,000 preferred shares outstanding at the end of the year. Preferred shares are considered to be akin to common shares for analysis purposes.

5. On 1 September 20X3, 25,000 common shares were purchased and retired. The shares had an average issuance price of $55,000 and were purchased for $57,000. On 1 November 20X3, 65,000 common shares were issued in exchange for machinery. This brought the total common shares issued to 476,000 at 31 December 20X3.

6. Because of its loss, the company received a refund of taxes paid in prior years of $54,000.

7. Bonds payable, with a 10% coupon rate of interest, have a face value of $810,000. The bonds are convertible to common shares at the rate of 17 common shares per $1,000 bond after 1 July 20X5 at the investor's option. A portion of the proceeds was allocated to the conversion option when the bonds were first issued.

8. A total of 80% of sales were made on credit.

The company has a 31 December year-end.

Required:

Prepare a cash flow statement, in good form. Use the direct method for cash flows from operations.

★★★ **A-2 Cash Flow Statement and Ratios:** Presented below are comparative balance sheets of Alfa Company as of 31 December 20X4, and the income statement for the year ending 31 December 20X4.

Balance Sheet

As at 31 December	20X4	20X3
Assets		
Cash	$ 5,200	$ 44,000
Marketable securities (not a cash equivalent)	8,000	16,000
Accounts receivable (net)	230,400	192,000
Inventories	360,400	316,000
Long-term investments	27,000	64,000
Land, plant, and equipment (net)	274,000	264,000
Total assets	$905,000	$ 896,000
Liabilities and shareholders' equity		
Bank overdraft	$ 86,000	$ 70,000
Accounts payable	90,000	90,000
Wages payable	26,000	24,000
Income tax payable	30,000	—
Cash dividends payable	6,000	—
Bonds payable, 10%	200,000	240,000
Convertible bonds payable	19,000	30,000
Common share conversion rights	1,900	3,000
Common shares (no par)	279,100	277,000
Retained earnings	167,000	162,000
Total liabilities and equities	$905,000	$ 896,000

Income Statement

Year ended 31 December 20X4		
Sales (all on account)		$1,260,000
Interest and dividends		5,600
Total revenues		$1,265,600
Cost of sales	$948,000	
Wages expense	124,000	
Interest expense, long term	16,600	
Amortization expense	28,000	
Other expenses	75,000	
Loss on sale of investments	5,000	1,196,600
Income before income tax		$ 69,000
Income tax—all current; marginal rate, 50%		30,000
Net income		$ 39,000

The following additional data has been provided:

- Marketable securities were sold at their recorded cost of $8,000. In addition, Alfa sold its interest in Bravo Products for $32,000.

- Equipment costing $43,000 was purchased during 20X4, and used equipment was sold at its book value of $5,000.

- The 10% bonds are being retired at the rate of $40,000 per year, and were retired at par value. A portion of the convertible bonds was exchanged for common shares during 20X4.

- The company spent $17,000 to reacquire and retire its own common shares. These shares had an average issue price of $10,000.

- Alfa declared cash dividends of $27,000 during 20X4.

Required:

1. Prepare a cash flow statement in good form. Use the indirect method to present the operating activities section.
2. Compute the 20X4 ratios to evaluate profitability, efficiency, solvency, and liquidity, as far as possible with the above information.
3. Provide an assessment of the company based on requirements (1) and (2).

(CGA-Canada, adapted)

 A-3 Cash Flow Statement and Ratios: Presented below are the financial statements of Maple Leaf Company for the year ending 31 December 20X3:

Balance Sheet

31 December	20X3	20X2
Assets		
Cash	$ 50,000	$ 45,000
Accounts receivable (net)	105,000	70,000
Inventories	130,000	110,000
Land	162,500	100,000
Plant and equipment (net)	245,000	266,500
Patents	15,000	16,500
	$707,500	$608,000
Liabilities and Equities		
Accounts payable	$130,000	$100,000
Wages payable	100,000	105,000
Future income tax liability	70,000	50,000
Bonds payable	65,000	90,000
Common shares (no par)	241,500	190,000
Retained earnings	101,000	73,000
	$707,500	$608,000

Income Statement

Year ended 31 December 20X3		
Sales		$500,000
Cost of sales		280,000
Gross margin		220,000
Expenses		
Wages expense	$ 95,000	
Amortization expense	10,000	
Amortization of patents	1,500	
Interest expense	8,000	
Gain on retirement of bonds	(10,000)	
Miscellaneous expense	3,500	
Loss on sale of equipment	2,000	110,000
Income before income tax		110,000
Income taxes—current	29,500	
—future	20,000	49,500
Net income		$ 60,500

Additional information:

- On 3 March 20X3, Maple Leaf issued a 10% stock dividend to shareholders of record on 16 February 20X3. The market price per share of the common stock was $7.50 on 3 March 20X3.
- On 2 April 20X3, Maple Leaf issued 3,800 shares of common stock for land. The common stock and land had current market values of approximately $20,000 on 2 April 20X3.
- On 16 May 20X3, Maple Leaf retired bonds with a face value of $25,000.
- On 31 July 20X3, Maple Leaf sold equipment costing $26,500, with a book value of $11,500, for $9,500 cash.
- On 31 October 20X3, Maple Leaf declared and paid a $0.02 per share cash dividend to shareholders of record on 2 September 20X3.
- On 10 November 20X3, Maple Leaf purchased land for $42,500 cash.
- The future income tax liability represents temporary differences relating to the use of CCA for income tax reporting and straight-line amortization for financial statement reporting.
- Bonds payable mature 31 December 20X5.
- Common shares issued and outstanding at 31 December 20X2 were 42,000.

Required:

1. Prepare a cash flow statement in good form. Use the indirect method to present the operating activities section.
2. Compute the 20X3 ratios to evaluate solvency and liquidity, as far as possible with the above information.
3. Provide an assessment of the company's solvency and liquidity based on requirements (1) and (2).

(CGA-Canada, adapted)

★★ **A-4 Cash Flow Statement; Financing Activities:** Information for CFS Limited follows.

	31 Dec 20X5	31 Dec 20X4
10% bonds payable	$ —	$2,000,000
Plus: Premium	—	45,600
	—	2,045,600
Convertible bonds payable	3,000,000	—
Less: discount	(57,000)	—
	2,943,000	—
Preferred shares	520,000	400,000
Common shares (500,000 shares as of 1 January 20X5)	8,678,000	6,800,000
Common share conversion rights	210,000	—
Contributed capital on common share retirement	—	52,000
Stock options outstanding	80,000	—
Warrants outstanding	400,000	605,000
Retained earnings	9,754,000	8,950,000

Other information:

1. The 10% bonds payable were redeemed for cash during the year at a redemption price of 102. Premium amortization of $3,000 was recorded in the year prior to the redemption.
2. Convertible bonds were issued during the period. Discount amortization of $3,000 was recorded in 2003 after issuance.

3. On 1 January 20X5, 20,000 common shares were retired for $410,000.

4. Stock options, for 10,000 common shares at $3.00 each, were issued for land on 1 October 20X5.

5. Net income for the period was $1,450,000.

6. A portion of the warrants, outstanding at the beginning of the year, was exercised. This resulted in the issuance of 100,000 common shares at $11.50 each.

7. Additional common shares were issued for cash.

Required:

Prepare the financing activities section of the cash flow statement, in good form, for the year ended 31 December 20X5. The change in accounts is explained by the "other information" and/or by a logical transaction.

★★ **A-5 Cash Flow Statement:** The following data is provided regarding Tema Corporation:

Income Statement

For the year ended 31 December 20X8

Revenues		
Sales	$ 760,000	
Interest and dividends	30,500	
Gain on sale of long-term investments	7,000	
		$ 797,500
Expenses and losses		
Cost of goods sold	$ 350,000	
Selling expenses	40,200	
Depreciation expense	19,600	
Interest expense	8,300	
Loss on sale of capital assets	2,100	
Income tax expense	113,200	533,400
Net income		$ 264,100

Balance Sheet

As at 31 December 20X8	20X8	20X7
Assets		
Cash	$ 67,200	$ 49,100
Short term investments (cash equivalents)	16,000	4,000
Accounts receivable	209,000	240,000
Inventory	182,100	175,000
Investments	—	8,900
Property plant and equipment (net)	814,200	695,000
	$1,288,500	$1,172,000
Liabilities and shareholders' equity		
Accounts payable	$ 89,900	$ 104,300
Tax payable	75,700	47,100
Cash dividends payable	16,000	—
Bonds payable	200,000	—
Less: unamortized discount	(14,000)	—
Preferred shares	90,000	50,000
Common shares	395,000	350,000
Retained earnings	435,900	620,600
	$1,288,500	$1,172,000

Other information:

1. Capital assets with an original cost of $45,200 were sold for $17,100.
2. A stock dividend valued at $25,000 was issued in June of 20X8.
3. Capital assets valued at $40,000 were acquired for preferred shares during the year.
4. Bonds were issued for cash in January of 20X8.
5. The bond discount was amortized by $4,000 during the year.
6. Assume other changes to balance sheet accounts represented normal events.

Required:

Prepare a CFS for the year ended 31 December 20X8. Use the indirect method for operations.

TABLE I-1: Present value of 1: (P/F, *i*, *n*)

$$P/F = \frac{1}{(1 + i)^n}$$

n	2%	2.5%	3%	4%	5%	6%	7%	8%	9%	10%	11%	12%	14%	15%
1	0.98039	0.97561	0.97087	0.96154	0.95238	0.94340	0.93458	0.92593	0.91743	0.90909	0.90090	0.89286	0.87719	0.86957
2	0.96117	0.95181	0.94260	0.92456	0.90703	0.89000	0.87344	0.85734	0.84168	0.82645	0.81162	0.79719	0.76947	0.75614
3	0.94232	0.92860	0.91514	0.88900	0.86384	0.83962	0.81630	0.79383	0.77218	0.75131	0.73119	0.71178	0.67497	0.65752
4	0.92385	0.90595	0.88849	0.85480	0.82270	0.79209	0.76290	0.73503	0.70843	0.68301	0.65873	0.63552	0.59208	0.57175
5	0.90573	0.88385	0.86261	0.82193	0.78353	0.74726	0.71299	0.68058	0.64993	0.62092	0.59345	0.56743	0.51937	0.49718
6	0.88797	0.86230	0.83748	0.79031	0.74622	0.70496	0.66634	0.63017	0.59627	0.56447	0.53464	0.50663	0.45559	0.43233
7	0.87056	0.84127	0.81309	0.75992	0.71068	0.66506	0.62275	0.58349	0.54703	0.51316	0.48166	0.45235	0.39964	0.37594
8	0.85349	0.82075	0.78941	0.73069	0.67684	0.62741	0.58201	0.54027	0.50187	0.46651	0.43393	0.40388	0.35056	0.32690
9	0.83676	0.80073	0.76642	0.70259	0.64461	0.59190	0.54393	0.50025	0.46043	0.42410	0.39092	0.36061	0.30751	0.28426
10	0.82035	0.78120	0.74409	0.67556	0.61391	0.55839	0.50835	0.46319	0.42241	0.38554	0.35218	0.32197	0.26974	0.24718
11	0.80426	0.76214	0.72242	0.64958	0.58468	0.52679	0.47509	0.42888	0.38753	0.35049	0.31728	0.28748	0.23662	0.21494
12	0.78849	0.74356	0.70138	0.62460	0.55684	0.49697	0.44401	0.39711	0.35553	0.31863	0.28584	0.25668	0.20756	0.18691
13	0.77303	0.72542	0.68095	0.60057	0.53032	0.46884	0.41496	0.36770	0.32618	0.28966	0.25751	0.22917	0.18207	0.16253
14	0.75788	0.70773	0.66112	0.57748	0.50507	0.44230	0.38782	0.34046	0.29925	0.26333	0.23199	0.20462	0.15971	0.14133
15	0.74301	0.69047	0.64186	0.55526	0.48102	0.41727	0.36245	0.31524	0.27454	0.23939	0.20900	0.18270	0.14010	0.12289
16	0.72845	0.67362	0.62317	0.53391	0.45811	0.39365	0.33873	0.29189	0.25187	0.21763	0.18829	0.16312	0.12289	0.10686
17	0.71416	0.65720	0.60502	0.51337	0.43630	0.37136	0.31657	0.27027	0.23107	0.19784	0.16963	0.14564	0.10780	0.09293
18	0.70016	0.64117	0.58739	0.49363	0.41552	0.35034	0.29586	0.25025	0.21199	0.17986	0.15282	0.13004	0.09456	0.08081
19	0.68643	0.62553	0.57029	0.47464	0.39573	0.33051	0.27651	0.23171	0.19449	0.16351	0.13768	0.11611	0.08295	0.07027
20	0.67297	0.61027	0.55368	0.45639	0.37689	0.31180	0.25842	0.21455	0.17843	0.14864	0.12403	0.10367	0.07276	0.06110
21	0.65978	0.59539	0.53755	0.43883	0.35894	0.29416	0.24151	0.19866	0.16370	0.13513	0.11174	0.09256	0.06383	0.05313
22	0.64684	0.58086	0.52189	0.42196	0.34185	0.27751	0.22571	0.18394	0.15018	0.12285	0.10067	0.08264	0.05599	0.04620
23	0.63416	0.56670	0.50669	0.40573	0.32557	0.26180	0.21095	0.17032	0.13778	0.11168	0.09069	0.07379	0.04911	0.04017
24	0.62172	0.55288	0.49193	0.39012	0.31007	0.24698	0.19715	0.15770	0.12640	0.10153	0.08170	0.06588	0.04308	0.03493
25	0.60953	0.53939	0.47761	0.37512	0.29530	0.23300	0.18425	0.14602	0.11597	0.09230	0.07361	0.05882	0.03779	0.03038
26	0.59758	0.52623	0.46369	0.36069	0.28124	0.21981	0.17220	0.13520	0.10639	0.08391	0.06631	0.05252	0.03315	0.02642
27	0.58586	0.51340	0.45019	0.34682	0.26785	0.20737	0.16093	0.12519	0.09761	0.07628	0.05974	0.04689	0.02908	0.02297
28	0.57437	0.50088	0.43708	0.33348	0.25509	0.19563	0.15040	0.11591	0.08955	0.06934	0.05382	0.04187	0.02551	0.01997
29	0.56311	0.48866	0.42435	0.32065	0.24295	0.18456	0.14056	0.10733	0.08215	0.06304	0.04849	0.03738	0.02237	0.01737
30	0.55207	0.47674	0.41199	0.30832	0.23138	0.17411	0.13137	0.09938	0.07537	0.05731	0.04368	0.03338	0.01963	0.01510
31	0.54125	0.46511	0.39999	0.29646	0.22036	0.16425	0.12277	0.09202	0.06915	0.05210	0.03935	0.02980	0.01722	0.01313
32	0.53063	0.45377	0.38834	0.28506	0.20987	0.15496	0.11474	0.08520	0.06344	0.04736	0.03545	0.02661	0.01510	0.01142
33	0.52023	0.44270	0.37703	0.27409	0.19987	0.14619	0.10723	0.07889	0.05820	0.04306	0.03194	0.02376	0.01325	0.00993
34	0.51003	0.43191	0.36604	0.26355	0.19035	0.13791	0.10022	0.07305	0.05339	0.03914	0.02878	0.02121	0.01162	0.00864
35	0.50003	0.42137	0.35538	0.25342	0.18129	0.13011	0.09366	0.06763	0.04899	0.03558	0.02592	0.01894	0.01019	0.00751
36	0.49022	0.41109	0.34503	0.24367	0.17266	0.12274	0.08754	0.06262	0.04494	0.03235	0.02335	0.01691	0.00894	0.00653
37	0.48061	0.40107	0.33498	0.23430	0.16444	0.11579	0.08181	0.05799	0.04123	0.02941	0.02104	0.01510	0.00784	0.00568
38	0.47119	0.39128	0.32523	0.22529	0.15661	0.10924	0.07646	0.05369	0.03783	0.02673	0.01896	0.01348	0.00688	0.00494
39	0.46195	0.38174	0.31575	0.21662	0.14915	0.10306	0.07146	0.04971	0.03470	0.02430	0.01708	0.01204	0.00604	0.00429
40	0.45289	0.37243	0.30656	0.20829	0.14205	0.09722	0.06678	0.04603	0.03184	0.02209	0.01538	0.01075	0.00529	0.00373
45	0.41020	0.32917	0.26444	0.17120	0.11130	0.07265	0.04761	0.03133	0.02069	0.01372	0.00913	0.00610	0.00275	0.00186
50	0.37153	0.29094	0.22811	0.14071	0.08720	0.05429	0.03395	0.02132	0.01345	0.00852	0.00542	0.00346	0.00143	0.00092

TABLE I-2: Present value of an ordinary annuity of *n* payments of 1: (P/A, *i*, *n*)

$$P/A = \frac{1 - \dfrac{1}{(1 + i)^n}}{i}$$

n	2%	2.5%	3%	4%	5%	6%	7%	8%	9%	10%	11%	12%	14%	15%
1	0.98039	0.97561	0.97087	0.96154	0.95238	0.94340	0.93458	0.92593	0.91743	0.90909	0.90090	0.89286	0.87719	0.86957
2	1.94156	1.92742	1.91347	1.88609	1.85941	1.83339	1.80802	1.78326	1.75911	1.73554	1.71252	1.69005	1.64666	1.62571
3	2.88388	2.85602	2.82861	2.77509	2.72325	2.67301	2.62432	2.57710	2.53129	2.48685	2.44371	2.40183	2.32163	2.28323
4	3.80773	3.76197	3.71710	3.62990	3.54595	3.46511	3.38721	3.31213	3.23972	3.16987	3.10245	3.03735	2.91371	2.85498
5	4.71346	4.64583	4.57971	4.45182	4.32948	4.21236	4.10020	3.99271	3.88965	3.79079	3.69590	3.60478	3.43308	3.35216
6	5.60143	5.50813	5.41719	5.24214	5.07569	4.91732	4.76654	4.62288	4.48592	4.35526	4.23054	4.11141	3.88867	3.78448
7	6.47199	6.34939	6.23028	6.00205	5.78637	5.58238	5.38929	5.20637	5.03295	4.86842	4.71220	4.56376	4.28830	4.16042
8	7.32548	7.17014	7.01969	6.73274	6.46321	6.20979	5.97130	5.74664	5.53482	5.33493	5.14612	4.96764	4.63886	4.48732
9	8.16224	7.97087	7.78611	7.43533	7.10782	6.80169	6.51523	6.24689	5.99525	5.75902	5.53705	5.32825	4.94637	4.77158
10	8.98259	8.75206	8.53020	8.11090	7.72173	7.36009	7.02358	6.71008	6.41766	6.14457	5.88923	5.65022	5.21612	5.01877
11	9.78685	9.51421	9.25262	8.76048	8.30641	7.88687	7.49867	7.13896	6.80519	6.49506	6.20652	5.93770	5.45273	5.23371
12	10.57534	10.25776	9.95400	9.38507	8.86325	8.38384	7.94269	7.53608	7.16073	6.81369	6.49236	6.19437	5.66029	5.42062
13	11.34837	10.98318	10.63496	9.98565	9.39357	8.85268	8.35765	7.90378	7.48690	7.10336	6.74987	6.42355	5.84236	5.58315
14	12.10625	11.69091	11.29607	10.56312	9.89864	9.29498	8.74547	8.24424	7.78615	7.36669	6.98187	6.62817	6.00207	5.72448
15	12.84926	12.38138	11.93794	11.11839	10.37966	9.71225	9.10791	8.55948	8.06069	7.60608	7.19087	6.81086	6.14217	5.84737
16	13.57771	13.05500	12.56110	11.65230	10.83777	10.10590	9.44665	8.85137	8.31256	7.82371	7.37916	6.97399	6.26506	5.95423
17	14.29187	13.71220	13.16612	12.16567	11.27407	10.47726	9.76322	9.12164	8.54363	8.02155	7.54879	7.11963	6.37286	6.04716
18	14.99203	14.35336	13.75351	12.65930	11.68959	10.82760	10.05909	9.37189	8.75563	8.20141	7.70162	7.24967	6.46742	6.12797
19	15.67846	14.97889	14.32380	13.13394	12.08532	11.15812	10.33560	9.60360	8.95011	8.36492	7.83929	7.36578	6.55037	6.19823
20	16.35143	15.58916	14.87747	13.59033	12.46221	11.46992	10.59401	9.81815	9.12855	8.51356	7.96333	7.46944	6.62313	6.25933
21	17.01121	16.18455	15.41502	14.02916	12.82115	11.76408	10.83553	10.01680	9.29224	8.64869	8.07507	7.56200	6.68696	6.31246
22	17.65805	16.76541	15.93692	14.45112	13.16300	12.04158	11.06124	10.20074	9.44243	8.77154	8.17574	7.64465	6.74294	6.35866
23	18.29220	17.33211	16.44361	14.85684	13.48857	12.30338	11.27219	10.37106	9.58021	8.88322	8.26643	7.71843	6.79206	6.39884
24	18.91393	17.88499	16.93554	15.24696	13.79864	12.55036	11.46933	10.52876	9.70661	8.98474	8.34814	7.78432	6.83514	6.43377
25	19.52346	18.42438	17.41315	15.62208	14.09394	12.78336	11.65358	10.67478	9.82258	9.07704	8.42174	7.84314	6.87293	6.46415
26	20.12104	18.95061	17.87684	15.98277	14.37519	13.00317	11.82578	10.80998	9.92897	9.16095	8.48806	7.89566	6.90608	6.49056
27	20.70690	19.46401	18.32703	16.32959	14.64303	13.21053	11.98671	10.93516	10.02658	9.23722	8.54780	7.94255	6.93515	6.51353
28	21.28127	19.96489	18.76411	16.66306	14.89813	13.40616	12.13711	11.05108	10.11613	9.30657	8.60162	7.98442	6.96066	6.53351
29	21.84438	20.45355	19.18845	16.98371	15.14107	13.59072	12.27767	11.15841	10.19828	9.36961	8.65011	8.02181	6.98304	6.55088
30	22.39646	20.93029	19.60044	17.29203	15.37245	13.76483	12.40904	11.25778	10.27365	9.42691	8.69379	8.05518	7.00266	6.56598
31	22.93770	21.39541	20.00043	17.58849	15.59281	13.92909	12.53181	11.34980	10.34280	9.47901	8.73315	8.08499	7.01988	6.57911
32	23.46833	21.84918	20.38877	17.87355	15.80268	14.08404	12.64656	11.43500	10.40624	9.52638	8.76860	8.11159	7.03498	6.59053
33	23.98856	22.29188	20.76579	18.14765	16.00255	14.23023	12.75379	11.51389	10.46444	9.56943	8.80054	8.13535	7.04823	6.60046
34	24.49859	22.72379	21.13184	18.41120	16.19290	14.36814	12.85401	11.58693	10.51784	9.60857	8.82932	8.15656	7.05985	6.60910
35	24.99862	23.14516	21.48722	18.66461	16.37419	14.49825	12.94767	11.65457	10.56682	9.64416	8.85524	8.17550	7.07005	6.61661
36	25.48884	23.55625	21.83225	18.90828	16.54685	14.62099	13.03521	11.71719	10.61176	9.67651	8.87859	8.19241	7.07899	6.62314
37	25.96945	23.95732	22.16724	19.14258	16.71129	14.73678	13.11702	11.77518	10.65299	9.70592	8.89963	8.20751	7.08683	6.62881
38	26.44064	24.34860	22.49246	19.36786	16.86789	14.84602	13.19347	11.82887	10.69082	9.73265	8.91859	8.22099	7.09371	6.63375
39	26.90259	24.73034	22.80822	19.58448	17.01704	14.94907	13.26493	11.87858	10.72552	9.75696	8.93567	8.23303	7.09975	6.63805
40	27.35548	25.10278	23.11477	19.79277	17.15909	15.04630	13.33171	11.92461	10.75736	9.77905	8.95105	8.24378	7.10504	6.64178
45	29.49016	26.83302	24.51871	20.72004	17.77407	15.45583	13.60552	12.10840	10.88120	9.86281	9.00791	8.28252	7.12322	6.65429
50	31.42361	28.36231	25.72976	21.48218	18.25593	15.76186	13.80075	12.23348	10.96168	9.91481	9.04165	8.30450	7.13266	6.66051

TABLE I-3: Present value of an annuity due of n payments of 1: (P/AD, i, n)

$$P/AD = \left[\frac{1 - \dfrac{1}{(1 + i)^n}}{i} \right] \times (1 + i)$$

n	2%	2.5%	3%	4%	5%	6%	7%	8%	9%	10%	11%	12%	14%	15%
1	1.00000	1.00000	1.00000	1.00000	1.00000	1.00000	1.00000	1.00000	1.00000	1.00000	1.00000	1.00000	1.00000	1.00000
2	1.98039	1.97561	1.97087	1.96154	1.95238	1.94340	1.93458	1.92593	1.91743	1.90909	1.90090	1.89286	1.87719	1.86957
3	2.94156	2.92742	2.91347	2.88609	2.85941	2.83339	2.80802	2.78326	2.75911	2.73554	2.71252	2.69005	2.64666	2.62571
4	3.88388	3.85602	3.82861	3.77509	3.72325	3.67301	3.62432	3.57710	3.53129	3.48685	3.44371	3.40183	3.32163	3.28323
5	4.80773	4.76197	4.71710	4.62990	4.54595	4.46511	4.38721	4.31213	4.23972	4.16987	4.10245	4.03735	3.91371	3.85498
6	5.71346	5.64583	5.57971	5.45182	5.32948	5.21236	5.10020	4.99271	4.88965	4.79079	4.69590	4.60478	4.43308	4.35216
7	6.60143	6.50813	6.41719	6.24214	6.07569	5.91732	5.76654	5.62288	5.48592	5.35526	5.23054	5.11141	4.88867	4.78448
8	7.47199	7.34939	7.23028	7.00205	6.78637	6.58238	6.38929	6.20637	6.03295	5.86842	5.71220	5.56376	5.28830	5.16042
9	8.32548	8.17014	8.01969	7.73274	7.46321	7.20979	6.97130	6.74664	6.53482	6.33493	6.14612	5.96764	5.63886	5.48732
10	9.16224	8.97087	8.78611	8.43533	8.10782	7.80169	7.51523	7.24689	6.99525	6.75902	6.53705	6.32825	5.94637	5.77158
11	9.98259	9.75206	9.53020	9.11090	8.72173	8.36009	8.02358	7.71008	7.41766	7.14457	6.88923	6.65022	6.21612	6.01877
12	10.78685	10.51421	10.25262	9.76048	9.30641	8.88687	8.49867	8.13896	7.80519	7.49506	7.20652	6.93770	6.45273	6.23371
13	11.57534	11.25776	10.95400	10.38507	9.86325	9.38384	8.94269	8.53608	8.16073	7.81369	7.49236	7.19437	6.66029	6.42062
14	12.34837	11.98318	11.63496	10.98565	10.39357	9.85268	9.35765	8.90378	8.48690	8.10336	7.74987	7.42355	6.84236	6.58315
15	13.10625	12.69091	12.29607	11.56312	10.89864	10.29498	9.74547	9.24424	8.78615	8.36669	7.98187	7.62817	7.00207	6.72448
16	13.84926	13.38138	12.93794	12.11839	11.37966	10.71225	10.10791	9.55948	9.06069	8.60608	8.19087	7.81086	7.14217	6.84737
17	14.57771	14.05500	13.56110	12.65230	11.83777	11.10590	10.44665	9.85137	9.31256	8.82371	8.37916	7.97399	7.26506	6.95423
18	15.29187	14.71220	14.16612	13.16567	12.27407	11.47726	10.76322	10.12164	9.54363	9.02155	8.54879	8.11963	7.37286	7.04716
19	15.99203	15.35336	14.75351	13.65930	12.68959	11.82760	11.05909	10.37189	9.75563	9.20141	8.70162	8.24967	7.46742	7.12797
20	16.67846	15.97889	15.32380	14.13394	13.08532	12.15812	11.33560	10.60360	9.95011	9.36492	8.83929	8.36578	7.55037	7.19823
21	17.35143	16.58916	15.87747	14.59033	13.46221	12.46992	11.59401	10.81815	10.12855	9.51356	8.96333	8.46944	7.62313	7.25933
22	18.01121	17.18455	16.41502	15.02916	13.82115	12.76408	11.83553	11.01680	10.29224	9.64869	9.07507	8.56200	7.68696	7.31246
23	18.65805	17.76541	16.93692	15.45112	14.16300	13.04158	12.06124	11.20074	10.44243	9.77154	9.17574	8.64465	7.74294	7.35866
24	19.29220	18.33211	17.44361	15.85684	14.48857	13.30338	12.27219	11.37106	10.58021	9.88322	9.26643	8.71843	7.79206	7.39884
25	19.91393	18.88499	17.93554	16.24696	14.79864	13.55036	12.46933	11.52876	10.70661	9.98474	9.34814	8.78432	7.83514	7.43377
26	20.52346	19.42438	18.41315	16.62208	15.09394	13.78336	12.65358	11.67478	10.82258	10.07704	9.42174	8.84314	7.87293	7.46415
27	21.12104	19.95061	18.87684	16.98277	15.37519	14.00317	12.82578	11.80998	10.92897	10.16095	9.48806	8.89566	7.90608	7.49056
28	21.70690	20.46401	19.32703	17.32959	15.64303	14.21053	12.98671	11.93516	11.02658	10.23722	9.54780	8.94255	7.93515	7.51353
29	22.28127	20.96489	19.76411	17.66306	15.89813	14.40616	13.13711	12.05108	11.11613	10.30657	9.60162	8.98442	7.96066	7.53351
30	22.84438	21.45355	20.18845	17.98371	16.14107	14.59072	13.27767	12.15841	11.19828	10.36961	9.65011	9.02181	7.98304	7.55088
31	23.39646	21.93029	20.60044	18.29203	16.37245	14.76483	13.40904	12.25778	11.27365	10.42691	9.69379	9.05518	8.00266	7.56598
32	23.93770	22.39541	21.00043	18.58849	16.59281	14.92909	13.53181	12.34980	11.34280	10.47901	9.73315	9.08499	8.01988	7.57911
33	24.46833	22.84918	21.38877	18.87355	16.80268	15.08404	13.64656	12.43500	11.40624	10.52638	9.76860	9.11159	8.03498	7.59053
34	24.98856	23.29188	21.76579	19.14765	17.00255	15.23023	13.75379	12.51389	11.46444	10.56943	9.80054	9.13535	8.04823	7.60046
35	25.49859	23.72379	22.13184	19.41120	17.19290	15.36814	13.85401	12.58693	11.51784	10.60857	9.82932	9.15656	8.05985	7.60910
36	25.99862	24.14516	22.48722	19.66461	17.37419	15.49825	13.94767	12.65457	11.56682	10.64416	9.85524	9.17550	8.07005	7.61661
37	26.48884	24.55625	22.83225	19.90828	17.54685	15.62099	14.03521	12.71719	11.61176	10.67651	9.87859	9.19241	8.07899	7.62314
38	26.96945	24.95732	23.16724	20.14258	17.71129	15.73678	14.11702	12.77518	11.65299	10.70592	9.89963	9.20751	8.08683	7.62881
39	27.44064	25.34860	23.49246	20.36786	17.86789	15.84602	14.19347	12.82887	11.69082	10.73265	9.91859	9.22099	8.09371	7.63375
40	27.90259	25.73034	23.80822	20.58448	18.01704	15.94907	14.26493	12.87858	11.72552	10.75696	9.93567	9.23303	8.09975	7.63805
45	30.07996	27.50385	25.25427	21.54884	18.66277	16.38318	14.55791	13.07707	11.86051	10.84909	9.99878	9.27642	8.12047	7.65244
50	32.05208	29.07137	26.50166	22.34147	19.16872	16.70757	14.76680	13.21216	11.94823	10.90630	10.03624	9.30104	8.13123	7.65959

Index

Charity

Lesley Pearse was born in Rochester, Kent, but was brought up in South London. She has three daughters and a grandson. Her novels have sold over ten million copies worldwide. Lesley now lives in Bristol and writes full-time.